Czech & Slovak Republics

Neal Bedford, Jane Rawson, Matt Warren

Contents

NORTH BOHEMIA p166

PRAGUE p79

EAST BOHEMIA p247

WEST BOHEMIA p182

CENTRAL BOHEMIA p152

NORTH MORAVIA p269

SOUTH BOHEMIA p210

SOUTH MORAVIA p286

HIGH TATRAS p387

EAST SLOVAKIA p399

CENTRAL SLOVAKIA p362

WEST SLOVAKIA p346

BRATISLAVA p329

Destination: Czech & Slovak Republics

If you're looking for the heart of Europe, then look no further. The Czech and Slovak Republics, two Slavic countries lying side by side in the middle of Europe's diverse continent, are both its physical and emotional centre. These are lands of real spirit; where folk traditions have survived the domination of foreign rulers, where a plethora of castles and chateaux pay testament to untold wars and civil conflicts, where societies have purposefully shaken off the smothering cloak of communism and are now forging into the 21st century.

And what is there to see? Well, everyone's heard of Prague, the Golden City, Mother of Cities, undisputed Champ, but how about the glorious alpine peaks of the High Tatras? The pristine gorges and forest-clad valleys of Slovenský raj? The architectural gems within the confines of Český Krumlov and Levoča? The strongholds of the once powerful and mighty at Orava and Karlštejn? The perfectly preserved folk village of Čičmany, with its painted houses? The heavenly cathedral at Kutná Hora or the humble, yet equally impressive, wooden churches of East Slovakia? The list goes on.

But it's not just about sights, sounds and splendour. It's also about people, and it's about connection. Strike up a conversation at a bar (over a pint of the best beer in the world) and you'll find an intelligent, engaging and friendly person at the other end. Quite often that person will humbly accept your compliments about their home country, will make you laugh and will make you welcome.

All of these things and more are here, waiting for you. But be careful, you may just become a Czech and Slovakophile.

RICHARD NEBESKY

SANDSTONE ROCKS OF LABE (p178)
Superb hiking trails through prehistoric canyons and past striking rock formations

PRAGUE (p79)
The Golden City: breathtaking architecture, romantic settings and pumping nightlife

ADRŠPACH-TEPLICE ROCKS (p262)
Bizarre landscapes of forest-fringed, sandstone pinnacles and gorges, criss-crossed with fascinating hiking trails

KARLŠTEJN (p73)
14th-century castle perfect for castle lovers, in the heart of Bohemia

ČESKÝ KRUMLOV (p219)
Achingly beautiful medieval town dominated by a picture-perfect chateau

OLOMOUC (p272)
Laid-back university town with fascinating architecture and a vibrant pub scene

BRATISLAVA (p329)
Slovakia's capital, with a lively café and bar scene and a rejuvenated old town

ELEVATION

1500m
1200m
900m
600m
300m
0

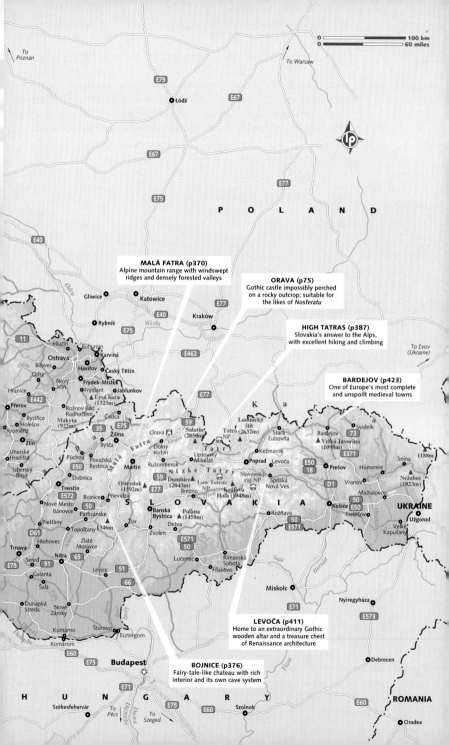

MALÁ FATRA (p370)
Alpine mountain range with windswept ridges and densely forested valleys

ORAVA (p75)
Gothic castle impossibly perched on a rocky outcrop; suitable for the likes of *Nosferatu*

HIGH TATRAS (p387)
Slovakia's answer to the Alps, with excellent hiking and climbing

BARDEJOV (p423)
One of Europe's most complete and unspoilt medieval towns

LEVOČA (p411)
Home to an extraordinary Gothic wooden altar and a treasure chest of Renaissance architecture

BOJNICE (p376)
Fairy-tale-like chateau with rich interior and its own cave system

Gothic, Renaissance, baroque: whatever your choice of architectural styles, there's something for everyone. Wander the tourist-free streets of **Olomouc** (p272), with all the dazzle of Prague, but none of the hustle. Discover what the fuss is all about in Unesco-listed **Bardejov** (p423) and **Český Krumlov** (p219).

Explore Levoča (p411), a treasure chest of Renaissance architecture

MARTIN MOOS

RICHARD NEBESKY

Wine and dine in the bustling, renovated old town of Bratislava (p329)

Lose yourself in the breathtaking beauty of Prague's Old Town (p97)

JONATHAN SM

The Czech and Slovak Republics are castle country; it's hard to find a better place to explore the mighty fortresses of the once rich and powerful. Join the crowds at **Karlštejn** (p73), Bohemia's blueprint *hrad* (castle). Climb to dizzying heights at Gothic **Orava** (p75) and explore the richness of fairytale **Bojnice** (p71).

Size up Prague Castle (p88), the largest ancient castle in the world

Roam the crumbling ruins of Spiš (p75), Slovakia's largest castle

Take in the elegant interiors and imposing exteriors of Krumlov Chateau (p74), the Czech Republic's second-biggest castle

Once you've had enough of man-made wonders, it's time to escape to the hills and revel in the republics' natural beauty. Explore the unspoilt **Malá Fatra** range (p370), and if you're happier on water, float on down the **Vltava river** (p221) past romantic vistas and run the gentle rapids of the Dunajec river in **Pieniny National Park** (p417).

Hike in the Slovenský raj (p408), a paradise of rugged ravines and narrow gorges

RICHARD NEBESKÝ

RICHARD NEBESKÝ

Ramble along the superb trails of the Sandstone Rocks of Labe (p178) to Pravčická Gate

Climb the dominating High Tatras (p387), with some 25 peaks over 2500m

MARK DAFF

Getting Started

In many ways the Czech and Slovak Republics are a traveller's dream destination. Jaw-dropping beauty – both natural and artificial – abounds, and tourist trails are well trodden and easy to follow, but it's also just as simple to escape the crowds and create your own tailor-made itinerary. Distances aren't massive so it's not as though you'll spend too much of your hard-earned holiday with your bum on a seat. And to top it all off, it will suit all budgets; whether your tastes are top-quality hotels and fine dining, or dorms beds and a baguette on the run, it's here to be had.

Both republics require a minimum of planning, but a few nights mulling over what you'd like to see doesn't do any harm and will allow your travels to become all that more fluid once you hit the road. But the best piece of advice we can give is book your first night's accommodation, pack a pair of comfortable shoes and sturdy hiking boots, and jump on a plane, train, bus or car.

WHEN TO GO

For the majority of visitors to the Czech and Slovak Republics, the best time to go is May, June and September. For starters, a large percentage of museums, galleries, castles and the like have seasonal opening times and are at their most accessible between the months of May and September. Plus, many festivals are held between the end of spring and the beginning of autumn so it's a perfect time to attend festivities. April and October are chillier but you'll benefit from smaller crowds and cheaper rooms. Winter is low season; everything pretty much shuts up shop, except the ski resorts, but you'll get to see it all under a blanket of snow, and who doesn't love that?

Most Czechs and Slovaks, like the rest of Europe, take their holidays in July and August, and then again over the Easter and Christmas-New Year holiday period. It's the height of the tourist season and can often be the worst time to visit: accommodation facilities and tourist sights are usually packed; crowds, particularly in Prague and the mountain resort areas, can be unbearable; and prices are high (by Czech and Slovak standards). The supply of bottom-end accommodation, however, increases in large towns during this time, as student accommodation is thrown open to visitors.

See Climate Charts (p434) for average temperatures and precipitation.

Seasons are distinct. Summer, which lasts from June till August, receives the highest temperatures and also the heaviest rainfall. The cold, bitter winter months of December, January and February often have temperatures reaching as low as -5°C in the cities and -10°C to -15°C (-30°C

DON'T LEAVE HOME WITHOUT...

- Double checking the visa situation (p447) and your passport expiry date
- Organising a good health-insurance policy (p441)
- A spattering of the language (p435), or a phrase book – a little goes a long way
- A healthy liver and a thirst for arguably the best beer in the world
- A good sense of humour and a large helping of patience – waiters can at times be a little infuriating
- Ear plugs if you plan to stay in Prague's Old Town
- A wistful longing for '80s fashion and music; you'll see and hear it everywhere

at higher altitudes) in the mountainous areas. They are tailor-made for skiing and other winter pursuits; the mountains receive about 130 days of snow a year. Spring and autumn bring with them changeable weather, but can be the most pleasant time to visit. Autumn, for instance, can experience daily temperatures as high as 20°C.

COSTS & MONEY

By European standards, the Czech and Slovak Republics are cheap. Food, transport and sights are still a bargain; accommodation will far and away be the most expensive item on your budget. Consumer goods remain relatively inexpensive, but a few, such as clothing and CDs, are generally on a par with Western prices. Surprise costs in both countries include parking fees at most attractions and having to fork out to take a camera or video into museums, castles and caves.

How much you spend will depend on how you travel. If you're a budget backpacker who likes to stretch your koruna as far as it will go, 600Kč/700Sk will get you from one place to another, a bed in a dorm, entry into a museum or castle, two cheap meals a day and three or four beers a night. Those who like a little more luxury can expect to pay around 2000Kč/2000Sk per day for a *pension* or hotel, train trip between cities, lunch and dinner at a decent restaurant including coffee and/or wine and entry to a couple of big-ticket attractions. If money is no object, 5500Kč/5500Sk is sufficient to cover all your needs, including a night in a top hotel and car hire for the day.

Prague, however, is another story; whack on another third to the prices above.

TRAVEL LITERATURE

Considering how long the Czech and Slovak Republics have played host to a multitude of travellers, travel literature about either country is pretty thin on the ground. There are, however, a couple of gems worth dipping into before heading off on your own travels.

A fine start is Patrick Leigh Fermor's *A Time For Gifts* (1970), which details his walk from Holland to Hungary in the pre-WWII 1930s and includes rich descriptions of a Czechoslovakia never to come again.

While not exactly travel literature per se, Timothy Garton Ash's *We the People: the Revolutions of 1989* (1990) is well worth reading for its gripping first-hand account of the revolutions that swept away the region's old guard.

Czech and Slovak Touches: Recipes, History, Travel, Folk Arts (1999) by Pat Martin touches on a multitude of subjects, including travel excursions to some of the more popular destinations in both the Czech and Slovak Republics.

INTERNET RESOURCES

Czech Tourist Authority (www.czechtourism.com) Its tourist information is the perfect starting point for travellers looking for a general low-down on the Czech Republic; in a multitude of languages.
Lonely Planet (www.lonelyplanet.com) Supposedly a fantastic site for travellers, but we're a bit dubious.
Ministry of Foreign Affairs (www.mzv.cz; www.foreign.gov.sk) Official websites for both countries, with up-to-date visa and embassy information.
Slovak Tourism Board (www.slovakiatourism.sk) Gateway to Slovakia, also in number of languages.
Slovakia Document Store (http://slovakia.eunet.sk) Loads of general information and links to more specific sites.
Tourist Server of the Czech Republic (www.czecot.com) Snapshot of attractions in the Czech Republic, online maps and a plethora of useful links to Czech sites.

HOW MUCH?

Night in hostel
350Kč/300Sk

Double room in *pension*
900Kč/900Sk

Goulash
100Kč/100Sk

Shot of Slivovice
35Kč/45Sk

Postcard home
9Kč/16Sk

LONELY PLANET INDEX

Litre of petrol
25Kč/35Sk

Litre of bottled water
30Kč/40Sk

Beer – glass of Budvar
30Kč/30Sk

Souvenir T-shirt
300Kč/250Sk

Street snack – ice cream
8Kč/6Sk

TOP 10s
MUST SEE FILMS

One of the best and most relaxing ways to do a bit of pre-departure planning and dreaming is to curl up on a comfy sofa with a bowl of popcorn and press play on your remote. Head down to your local video store to pick up these flicks, from the best known Czech and Slovak films to the cheesiest. See the Culture chapter (p46-9) for reviews.

- *Kolya* (1996)
  Director: Jan Svěrák

- *Sedím na konári a je mi dobre*
  (I'm Sitting on a Branch and I'm Fine; 1989)
  Director: Juraj Jakubisko

- *Samotáři* (2000) Director: David Ondříček

- *Černý Petr* (1963) Director: Miloš Forman

- *Kruté Radosti* (2003) Director: Juraj Nvota

- *Divided we Fall* (2000) Director: Jan Hrebejk

- *Ruzové sny* (1977)
  Directors: Dušan Hanák & Dušan Dušek

- *Pásla kone na betóne* (1983)
  Director: Štefan Uher

- *Obchod na korze* (1965)
  Directors: Ján Kadár & Elmar Klos

- *Swimming Pool* (2001)
  Director: Boris von Sychowski

TOP READS

Immersing yourself in a good book is the perfect way to learn about contemporary issues and culture and grasp a sense of people and place. The following page-turners have won critical acclaim in the Czech and Slovak Republics and abroad. See the Culture chapter (p43-6) for reviews.

- *Utz*
  Bruce Chatwin

- *The Amazing Adventures of Kavalier & Clay*
  Michael Chabon

- *Closely Watched Trains*
  Bohumil Hrabal

- *The Unbearable Lightness of Being*
  Milan Kundera

- *Year of the Frog*
  Martin Šimečka

- *Bringing up Girls in Bohemia*
  Michal Viewegh

- *Babička*
  Božena Němcová

- *The Book of Laughter & Forgetting*
  Milan Kundera

- *The Taste of Power*
  Ladislav Mňačko

- *Metamorphosis*
  Franz Kafka

OUR FAVOURITE FESTIVALS & EVENTS

The Czechs and Slovaks really know how to let their hair down, and you can always count on some kind of celebration going on. The following list is our Top 10, but other festivals and events are listed on p439 and throughout this book.

- Prague Spring (Prague),
  May (p125)

- International Festival of Spirits and Ghosts
  (Bojnice), May (p71)

- Ride of the Kings Festival (Vlčnov),
  May (p319)

- International Folk Festival (Strážnice),
  June (p317)

- Východna Folk Festival (Východná),
  June/July (p383)

- Bratislava Cultural Summer Festival
  (Bratislava), June to September (p339)

- Karlovy Vary Film Festival (Karlovy Vary),
  July (p197)

- Open-air Cinema Festival (Prague),
  July/August (p125)

- International Music Festival (Český Krumlov),
  August (p222)

- Salamander Festival (Banská Štiavnica),
  September (p369)

Itineraries

CLASSIC ROUTES

THE CZECH LIST

Up to one month

This 1500km, one-month route circumnavigates the Czech Republic, from Prague to Olomouc, then through the gentle hills of South Moravia, before hightailing it to West Bohemia's spa towns.

Spend three days in **Prague** (p79) followed by day trips to **Kutná Hora's** (p160) diverse cathedrals, photogenic **Karlštejn Castle** (p156), medieval-come-neo-Gothic **Konopiště Castle** (p155) and/or evocative **Terezín** (p169). Pursue the outdoors in the **Český ráj** (p257) and the **Adršpach-Teplice Rocks** (p262) then peek at **Hradec Králové's** (p249) architectural mix and **Pardubice's** (p253) Renaissance façades. Soak up **Olomouc's** (p272) atmosphere and visit **Bouzov Castle's** (p276) pointed turrets. See **Rožnov pod Radhoštěm's** (p282) superb open-air museum, before heading to elegant **Brno** (p289). Tour the caves of the **Moravian Karst** (p299) then carry on to the pickled gherkins of **Znojmo** (p310), **Vranov Castle's** (p313) impossibly built walls, picture-perfect **Telč** (p306) and **Jindřichův Hradec's** (p243) eclectic architecture. Head south to **České Budějovice** (p213), home of Budvar beer, before drowning in **Český Krumlov's** (p219) aching beauty. Take a break from city life in the **Šumava hills** (p226) and the spa towns of **Mariánské Lázně** (p189) and **Karlovy Vary** (p193) before trekking back to Prague. If you only have a week try Prague, Kutná Hora, České Budějovice and Český Krumlov. For two weeks add Karlštejn and Konopiště Castles, Terezín, Olomouc, Brno, Telč, Jindřichův Hradec, Šumava hills, Mariánské Lázně and Karlovy Vary.

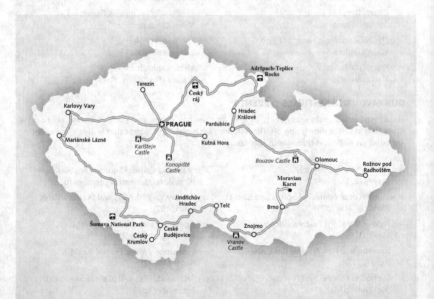

SLOVAKIAN SOJOURNS

Up to one month / Bratislava to Košice

The obvious starting point is **Bratislava** (p329); spend a couple of days wandering the old town and sampling its museums, restaurants and bars before taking rewarding day trips to **Devín Castle** and **Danubiana Museum** (p344). Once you've had your fill head for Poprad, breaking the journey at bustling **Žilina** (p373) for a side trip to the **Vratná Valley** (p377), hidden among the peaks of the **Malá Fatra** (p376), or the painted houses of **Čičmany** (p376) and romantic **Bojnice Chateau** (p376). Also include a detour to imposing **Orava Castle** (p380). **Poprad** (p392) is the gateway to the **High Tatras** (p387) and the **Slovenský raj** (p408). Hike along alpine mountain trails or through steep, water-sprayed gorges, rejuvenating the soul, and take a day trip to baroque **Levoča** (p411) or ruined **Spiš Castle** (p413). From Poprad you can also head north to **Pieniny National Park** (p417) for a gentle boat trip down the Dunajec river. After Poprad, continue onto **Bardejov** (p423) and its architecturally-uniform square and medieval battlements, then to **Košice** (p402), a thriving city and a traditional melting pot of Slovak, Hungarian and Roma (Gypsy) culture. Using Košice as a base, envelop yourself in the Eastern Borderlands and its **wooden churches** (p427), before exploring the underworld caves of the **Slovenský kras** (p419).

For a one-week visit to Slovakia, we suggest two days in Bratislava before heading directly to Poprad to access the High Tatras and the Slovenský raj. Squeeze in a day trip to Levoča or Spiš Castle.

If your time frame is closer to two weeks, spend two days in Bratislava before heading to Poprad via Žilina as for the one-month itinerary, skipping the detour to Orava Castle. Hike in the High Tatras and the Slovenský raj, visit Levoča or Spiš Castle then continue to Bardejov and Košice.

This month-long, one-way, 1330km route goes from Bratislava through the Malá Fatra ranges to the High Tatras, then north to the Pieniny National Park before continuing east to Bardejov, then south to Košice and the remote east.

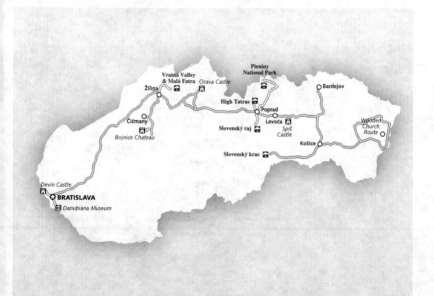

ROADS LESS TRAVELLED

EAST MEETS WEST
Two weeks / Ostrava to Trenčín

Avoid the grandiose and the touristy and mix in with the locals for a spell in little-visited Moravia and West Slovakia.

Start at **Ostrava** (p278), a working city with a kicking nightlife. **Olomouc** (p272), with its old-world architecture and new-world energy, is the next port of call, after which a stop at **Kroměříž** (p324) and its lavish chateau is called for. From here, the **Moravské Slovácko** (p317), a region with an uncountable wealth of folk tradition, is within sight. This is also wine country, so be prepared to clear the palate between glasses of Bacchus' best. Confess your sins at **Velehrad's Cistercian Monastery** (p321) before accumulating them all over again in **Brno** (p289). Afterwards, head down to **Moravský Krumlov** (p303) and Mucha's sublime *Slav Epic* – a collection of 20 huge paintings.

If your timing is immaculate, you'll catch the biggest folk festival in the Czech Republic at **Strážnice** (p318) before crossing the border into West Slovakia, first stopping for a brisk walk in the **Lesser Carpathian mountains** (p353) and then calling in at **Modra** (p353) to savour some of Slovakia's best whites and reds. Head onto compact **Trnava** (p354), Slovakia's oldest town, and **Nitra** (p348), further east, site of Slovakia's first Christian church. Your trail then veers north to the spa town of **Piešťany** (p357) and a well-deserved thermal dip, after which a tour of **Trenčín's** (p359) mighty castle awaits.

Starting in the northeast of the Czech Republic, this two-week, 660km trail takes in rolling countryside and bustling cities before crossing the Lesser Carpathian mountains into the flatlands of West Slovakia and finishing in Trenčín.

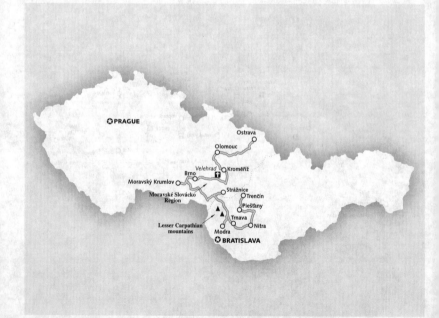

TAILORED TRIPS

WORLD HERITAGE SITES

The Czech and Slovak Republics have 17 sites on the illustrious Unesco World Heritage list and of these, we've picked our 'must sees'.

Prague (p79), who's historical centre simply defies words, must be on everyone's list. The Cathedral of St Barbara, in the old mining town of **Kutná Hora** (p160), is probably the finest Gothic cathedral in Europe, and nearby Cathedral of Our Lady at **Sedlec** (p164) is not so much appealing as gruesome. **Český Krumlov's** (p219) labyrinth of lanes and eye-catching chateau will delight and stun, while a stroll through **Telč's** (p306) Renaissance heart will have you gushing terrible poetry. The Holy Trinity Column in **Olomouc** (p272) is a baroque medley of gold and grey in a town full of surprises, and the contemporary Tugendhat Villa in **Brno** (p289) was one of the first open-plan homes to be built.

The folk village of **Vlkolínec** (p384) in Central Slovakia is remarkable for its uniformity, while the Renaissance mining town of **Banská Štiavnica** (p368) blends in perfectly with the surrounding countryside. **Spiš** (p75) is the epitome of the proud medieval castle, and **Bardejov** (p423) is a supreme example of a fortified medieval town.

Those that missed out in our top selection are the Pilgrimage Church of St John of Nepomuk (p306); the Lednice-Valtice Cultural Landscape (p315); Holašovice Historical Village Reservation (p218); the gardens and castle at Kroměříž (p324); Litomyšl Castle; the Jewish Quarter and St Procopius' Basilica (p309) and the Caves of Slovak Karst (p418).

NATURAL DELIGHTS

If the 'call of the wild' is strong in your heart and loud in your ears, then it's time to head for the hills. Wander past cool alpine lakes and heavenly peaks in Slovakia's **High Tatras** (p387), and meander through peaceful **Slovenský raj** (p408), home to bears and wolves. Traverse the windswept ridges of the **Malá Fatra National Park** (p376) or its close neighbour **Veľká Fatra** (p373). Take time to float down the **Dunajec gorge** (p417), and to hike or cycle in the shadow of its 500m-tall cliffs. Go east, to the remote trails of **Poloniny National Park** (p426), an area of untouched, virgin forest. Climb the weird rock formations of the small but stunning **Súľov Highlands** (p375), dotted with crumbling castles.

Lose yourself (not literally) in the Czech Republic's highest peaks, the rounded, rolling giants of **Krkonoše** (p265) and be inspired by the wooded hills, gentle farmland and striking rock formations of nearby **Český ráj** (p257). Find adventure and fun, and a climber's paradise, among the rugged and dramatic rock formations of **Adršpach-Teplice** (p262) and discover the source of the mighty Vltava and a peaceful retreat in the mountains of **Šumava** (p226).

The Authors

NEAL BEDFORD

Having extensively travelled Hungary, explored pockets of the Czech Republic and woken up every morning to the vista of the Lesser Carpathian mountains (on a very clear day and with a bit of imagination) from his Viennese flat, it was only a matter of time before Neal ventured into the lands of Slovakia. Around half a dozen trips later his interest in the country is nowhere near sated; in fact, it has only begun. With friends he made on his travels constantly SMSing him, inviting him on hiking trips, to festivals or simply to help them move house, he can see himself spending an ever-increasing amount of time in the forgotten gem of Europe.

My Favourite Trip

Start in bustling Prague (p79), and include a day trip to Sedlec Cathedral (p164), before escaping to Adršpach-Teplice Rocks (p262) for some rock climbing. Head south to Český Krumlov (p219) to soak up the atmosphere before moving onto Olomouc (p272) to sample the multitude of Czech beers. As a hangover cure I'd spend a couple of days hiking in the Slovenský raj (p408), stopping at Orava Castle (p75) on the way. Košice (p402) is the next port of call, which would include a couple of days poking around the wooden churches of the Eastern Borderlands (p427). I'd finish it all up with a sedate beer in Bratislava's old town (p329).

JANE RAWSON

Once upon a time Jane wanted to be a Bohemian, thinking it had something to do with strong coffee, existentialism and black cashmere pullovers. Now that she knows it means bread dumplings with cabbage, Gothic cathedrals in the rain, tripping over (repeatedly) on cobblestones, plurals ending in 'y', beer-stand smažený sýr (fried cheese with potatoes and tartare sauce) at 3am, men in newspaper hats presenting cartoons on TV, absurdist sculpture and spala jsem jako když mě do vody hodí (when people say they slept 'as if thrown under water'), she wants it even more. Be warned: Prague sneaks up on you.

MATT WARREN

Matt first travelled through Eastern Europe as the Iron Curtain was lifting in the early 1990s, hitching the route from Turkey to the frozen Baltic and taking a long breather in the Andel district of Prague. It was the Czech Republic's untamed, rustic side (coupled with absinthe) that captured his imagination, however, and he has more recently used a spate of stag nights in Prague as an excuse to delve deeper into the countryside. His latest visit, as part of an overland motorcycle journey from Edinburgh to Istanbul, compounded the love affair and he now dreams of settling down in a smallholding near Slavonice.

Snapshot

The topic on everyone's lips is the start of a new political era, that of the EU. As of 1 May 2004, the Czech and Slovak Republics will become part of the EU, and, it would seem, they're rapturous about it; 77% of Czechs and 92% of Slovaks voted in favour of the union in 2003's deciding referendums.

While it is seen as a step towards higher living standards and a brighter future for subsequent generations, many are still sceptical, fearing even greater price hikes than they've witnessed over the past 15 years, and a slow but sure death to the republics' unique folk culture and lifestyle. Both countries are a mix of Western capitalism and Eastern socialism; with the introduction of the EU, some feel that Europe will become another USA and the diversity between countries will slowly blur until the cultures and lifestyles become 'Westernised' – and lose their uniqueness.

Concerns have also been raised over the possibility of foreigners taking advantage of low prices and buying up property. It hasn't happened in the republics yet, but it's happened in other EU countries; take Portugal or parts of Spain for instance, where large amounts of low-priced land have been purchased by foreigners. Or Sweden, where many Germans have purchased holiday homes because prices are much cheaper than in Germany.

Compounding the problem is a lack of information; in the lead up to the referendums voters complained that the governments did not tell them about the true effects it would bring. Voters were only told that the EU would benefit them but not precisely how. The governments did not – and have not at the time of writing – inform the populace on how EU membership would affect the legal system, the monetary system, government spending, minimum wages, foreign policy, whether prices would actually rise etc. While a high percentage of Czechs and Slovaks voted in favour of the union – so at face value the populace is almost unanimous – there was a low voter turnout (only 55% of eligible voters turned up to voice their opinion in the Czech Republic, 52% in Slovakia), indicating that not everyone is happy about joining.

Apart from the immediate effect EU membership will have on the average person, its political ramifications could also prove far-reaching. In recent international events, both countries have backed the US (sending military personnel to Iraq) – possibly for political positioning on the world stage and their desire to show that they've moved on from the 'Eastern bloc' – which could tip the balance of power in favour of the UK/Spanish/Portuguese stance against that of the Franco-German wing.

Politically, both countries appear as two unsteady ships in rough seas. Vladimir Spidla, the Czech Republic's prime minister, started his parliamentary term with a resounding 72% public support, which, by the end of 2003, had shrunk to a mere 27%. In the first 15 months in power, his coalition government almost collapsed three times under external, and internal, pressure. He and his political buddies have managed to survive though, due to a lack of a clear alternative. Mikulaš Dzurinda, Spidla's Slovak counterpart, rules over an increasingly divided coalition of four diverse political parties. Its members regularly vote against their own party's reforms, and political scandals and internal bickering are rife. Not surprisingly, a recent poll indicated that one third of Slovak citizens do not trust any politician. And to top it all off, former Prime Minister Vladimír Mečiar (see p28) could feasibly become the next president; polls rank him as a close runner-up in the popularity stakes.

FAST FACTS

Population Czech Republic/Slovakia: 10,249,000/5,379,000

GDP growth: 1.5%/4%

Inflation: 0.6%/3.3%

Unemployment: 9.8%/17.2%

Average monthly wage: €450/€325

Total combined railway system: 13,130km

Slovakia makes more ice-pucks than any country in the world

Of the OECD countries, only Ireland and Denmark consume more alcohol per capita than the Czech Republic

Semtex, a Czech-made plastic explosive, has become a recent bone of international contention. Both the US and NATO are putting pressure on the republic to improve security at army depots amid fears that terrorists are laying their hands on vast quantities of the stuff. It is reported that poorly paid Czech soldiers are selling it to middlemen who then pass it on to terrorist organisations. A reputed 60 tonnes of unmarked Semtex is stored in army depots (just 250g is enough to blow up an airliner). The whole sordid story is nothing new though; in the 1970s as much as 700 tonnes was sold to Libya. Enough, as Václav Havel (see p26) put it, to 'support terrorism throughout the world for 150 years'.

Financial indicators suggest the economies of both republics are going from strength to strength. In the '90s Slovakia severely lagged behind the Czech Republic in pro-market reforms (the Mečiar years basically stalled the economy) but change is in the air; privatisation is in full swing, a flat tax rate of 19% was introduced in 2003 and foreign direct investment is estimated at US$10 billion. These factors, along with a well-educated and stable workforce, wage rates only 15% of the EU average, and around 350 million people within a day's drive of its borders, could see Slovakia become the next Hong Kong or Ireland. The Czech Republic has seen a massive US$26 billion investment since the Velvet Divorce (see p26), and this is only set to increase. Major car manufacturers, such as Volkswagen, Peugeot, Citroën and Toyota, are investing heavily in the country, taking advantage of skilled workers who earn 75% less than their German counterparts and a well-developed industrial infrastructure. While it looks as though everything's coming up roses, not everyone is reaping the rewards. Many Czechs and Slovaks have witnessed skyrocketing prices since the early '90s (due mainly to the influx of Western goods at Western prices) while wages have only crept forward, and though there are goods in the shops, there's no money to buy them with. The Czech National Bank, which has expressed concern that debts are rising faster than people's incomes, reported that 25% of Czech households are on average US$1500 in debt and loans have increased sixfold since the beginning of the '90s.

Racism and discrimination against Roma (Gypsies) has caused the republics major headaches in the lead up to EU entry (see p34). Both have a poor record when dealing with minorities and Roma are no exception. Three-quarters of Roma children are forced to attend schools for the disadvantaged, and unemployment among Roma is around 30% to 40%, and even as high as 100% in some communities. Living standards in Roma ghettos are quite often appalling; some have no power, heating or clean sanitary facilities. The governments and Non-Government Organisations (NGOs) are attempting to turn this tide of disadvantage by funding support programmes to promote Roma language, culture, education, housing and social welfare, but some international observers feel that not enough is being done. Officially 31,000 Roma live in the Czech Republic and approximately 90,000 in Slovakia, but realistically the figure could be as high as 200,000 and 500,000, respectively. Many are more than ready to try their luck elsewhere once the republics become EU members, and it's safe to say quite a few Czechs and Slovaks won't be sorry to see them go.

History

Czech and Slovak history is in large part the story of a people doing whatever they could to survive occupation, and they themselves are far more interested in the history of their rebels and heretics than they are of the royal families who oppressed them.

Slap-bang in the middle of Europe, the Czechs have been invaded by the Habsburgs, the Nazis, the Soviets, and tour groups; some see membership of the EU as just another occupation. At the same time, the Czechs' location has meant that none of their local upheavals has remained local for long: their rejection of Roman Catholicism in 1418 resulted in the Hussite Wars; the revolt against Habsburg rule in 1618 set off the disastrous Thirty Years' War; the annexation of the Sudetenland in 1938 was the first stuttering step towards WWII; the liberal reforms of the 1968 Prague Spring led to a rolling of tanks from all over the Eastern bloc; and the peaceful overthrow of the government during the Velvet Revolution stands as a model for freedom-seekers everywhere.

Invasion is a common theme for Slovakia too; exchange tour groups with Magyars (they go by the alias 'Hungarians' these days) and Turks, and you'll have the short list of Slovak oppressors through the centuries. And although many of its struggles were localised, rather than played out on the international stage the Czechs seemed destined to occupy, their effect on the Slovak nation was no less traumatic, or inspirational.

A SIGN OF THINGS TO COME

Slav tribes started heading into the area from Eastern Europe during the late 5th and early 6th centuries, but – setting the scene for the next 1500 years – were soon conquered by the Avars, a nomadic tribe of whom not much else was heard. Present-day Moravia became the centre of the aptly named Great Moravian Empire, which lasted from 830 to 906, taking in Bohemia, Silesia and parts of Germany, Slovakia, Poland and Hungary. Rastislav, the second Moravian emperor, decided the empire needed to embrace one of the major world religions. Of the emissaries who visited

Visit http://archiv.radio.cz/history/ for Czech kids' drawings of great moments in national history.

At www.radio.cz/en/archive/witness Czech people tell their stories of living through history.

See www.adc.sk/english/slovakia/ for a step-by-step online history of Slovakia.

WHAT'S IN A NAME?

Which is correct, the Czech Republic or Czechia? Slovakia or the Slovak Republic? Not only are we confused, and our PC spellchecker confused, but also some of the locals are confused.

Most English-speakers still call the Czech Republic by that name, but some (including one of our authors, but we won't name names will we Jane), particularly in Europe, use 'Czechia'. There is no precedent for the use of Czechia in English, and this book does not use it. Surprisingly, not even in Czech is there a single word that describes the joint Czech and Moravian lands. Debates on a name went back and forth until a final conclusion for Česká republika was made.

The situation in Slovakia is, thankfully, different. Both 'Slovak Republic' (Slovenská republika) and 'Slovakia' (Slovensko) are used, virtually interchangeably, both in that country and abroad. We predominantly use Slovakia throughout this book, simply because it rolls off the tongue more easily, and saves on printing space.

TIMELINE **870** **907**

| Founding of the Přemysl dynasty and Prague Castle. | Defeat of the Great Moravian Empire by the Magyars. |

him, he was most taken by the Orthodox Christians (later saints) Cyril and Metoděj (Methodius), who showed up in 864 with a Bible written in the Cyrillic alphabet. When the Bible was translated into Slavic, the Slavs acquired a written language.

Czech tribes displaced the Moravians early in the 10th century. The first Czech dynasty, the Přemysls, threw up a couple of huts on a hill in what was to become Prague around 870 and called it Pražský hrad; their regal aspirations were cut short in 950, when German King Otto I conquered Bohemia and made it part of the Holy Roman Empire. The Přemysls – including Václav, or Good 'King' Wenceslas – ruled as princes on behalf of the Germans until 1212, when the pope decided they'd been very well behaved and allowed them to start calling themselves kings. Otakar II did the kingly thing, expanding the empire into Austria and Slovenia and declaring himself Holy Roman Emperor. Rudolf Habsburg begged to disagree and knocked off Otakar in 1278, the first step towards Habsburg domination of the Czech people. While the kings were squabbling, the Czechs were doing quite nicely: Germans were flooding in, bringing a new wave of farming and artisan technology; large deposits of gold and silver were discovered and in the 1350s central Europe's first gold coin, the Czech florin, was issued.

When Václav III was mysteriously murdered in 1306, the Přemysl throne was left heirless. But a bit of marital manoeuvring by the royal family of Luxemburg allowed them to step into the gap, and eventually produced Holy Roman Emperor Karel (Charles) IV, who made Prague centre of the Holy Roman Empire and did a nice renovation job on the city. Karel's son, the mercurial Václav IV, gave Bohemia its patron saint when he tortured Jan of Nepomuk to death over a bureaucratic dispute with Jan's boss, the archbishop – but during Václav's rule the Czech Lands remained relatively prosperous.

In Slovakia, things pretty much went the same way, although it wasn't Slovak tribes that displaced the Moravians in 907, but the Hungarians. They seemed to like the look of the place, and decided to stick around for the next 1000 years. The only part of Slovakia not under Hungarian rule until 1918 (not allowing for a couple of short time-outs) was the Spiš region, which belonged to Poland from 1412 to 1772.

To begin with, the Hungarians were fair and just rulers, as central European rulers go. Industry blossomed, especially mining (silver, copper and gold) and trade (gold, amber and fur), and Slovaks were allowed to hold onto their language and culture, and also purchase land. The invasion of the Tatars from the east, the first of which took place in 1237 and then again four years later, shattered the region's developing economy, and forced the Hungarians to invite settlers, mainly Saxon German artisans, into the area to help rebuild the mercantile base. Their legacy can still be found in the mining towns in Central and Eastern Slovakia.

THE RULE OF THE CHALICE

A century before Martin Luther nailed his demands to a church door, the Czechs were agitating for church reform. Jan Hus (1372–1415), a fan of English theologian John Wycliffe, led a movement which espoused – among other things – services given in Czech rather than Latin,

Prague in Black & Gold by Peter Demetz is an excellent, readable history of the major Czech city, taking in events that affected the whole country.

1415	1419
Church reformer Jan Hus burned at the stake.	Catholic councillors are thrown from the Town Hall window by Hussites intent on taking Prague.

letting the congregation taste the sacramental wine as well as the host (the Hussites' symbol was the chalice) and an end to the selling of indulgences (and church wealth in general). When he was burned for heresy, Hus' martyrdom sparked a religious, nationalist and class-based rebellion in Bohemia, led by the preacher Jan Želivský and operating mainly out of Tábor, Plzeň and Prague's Nové Město.

The Hussites moved swiftly from rhetoric to warfare: on 30 July 1419 Želivský preached a blood-stirring sermon at St Mary of the Snows in Prague, then led the congregation to the New Town Hall to confront the Catholic burghers. Militant Hussite Jan Žižka led a charge up the stairs and the councillors were thrown out the windows and beaten to death by the mob. After four months of church burning and street battles, the Hussites held Prague and Emperor Sigismund had retreated to Moravia.

The pope told Sigismund to take Prague back, but the Catholic attack in 1420 was defeated by the forces of ferocious, flail-wielding commander Žižka (Vitkov Hill, where the battle took place, is now called Žižkov Hill and is topped by a massive equestrian statue of the general). Eventually moderate Hussites let Sigismund back into town and joined forces with him to defeat radical Hussites at the Battle of Lipany, near Kolín. Jiří z Poděbrad (1458–71) was elected Hussite king, and though he had a few radical ideas, such as a European council to solve international problems by diplomacy rather than war, the rest of Europe was unconvinced by the Hussite regime. After Jiří's death, despite a few Polish kings holding the throne, real power in Bohemia continued to lie with the Protestant Utraquist nobles, the so-called Bohemian Estates.

While all this upheaval was going on across the border, Slovaks were having a relatively easy time of it with the Hungarians. Not everyone, however, was happy with the status quo. For a decade or two in the early 14th century a powerful warlord named Matúš Čák ruled much of what is now Slovakia from Trenčín (in West Slovakia). The Hussites also managed to dislodge the ruling Hungarians for a time and ruled much of Slovakia until their defeat at the Battle of Lipany. Juraj Dáža was not so successful. His rebellion in the early 16th century with an army of 50,000 peasants was ruthlessly crushed.

UNDER THE AUSTRIAN & HUNGARIAN THUMB

In 1526 the Czech kingdom again came under the control of the Catholic Habsburgs. In the latter half of the century Prague became the seat of their empire, lifting the country's fortunes. On 23 May 1618, the Bohemian Estates, angry that the Habsburgs had failed to deliver on promised religious tolerance, threw two Habsburg councillors from a Prague Castle window (they survived with minor injuries). The squabble escalated into the Catholic–Protestant Thirty Years' War, which was to devastate much of central Europe and shatter Bohemia's economy. The war had barely begun when the Bohemian Estates were thrashed at the Battle of Bílá Hora (White Mountain) on 8 November 1620: the 27 nobles who had started the revolt were executed and the war moved on to the rest of Europe.

The Czechs lost their rights and property, and almost their national identity, through forced Catholicisation and Germanisation. Saxons occupied Prague and much of Bohemia in 1631 and 1632; Swedes also

DID YOU KNOW?

Hussite general Jan Žižka is widely regarded by military historians as one of the greatest strategists of all time.

DID YOU KNOW?

Hussite King Jiří z Poděbrad proposed a European union about 550 years before Czechs voted to join the current EU.

DID YOU KNOW?

The Central Slovakian mining firm Fugger-Turzo operated eight-hour working shifts, paid its workers sickness and old-age insurance and organised pensions for their widows – in the 15th century.

1526	1683
Defeat of Hungarians by the Turks at the Battle of Mohács; Hungarian royalty move house to Slovakia.	Turks sent packing by the Habsburgs, ending their excursions into Slovakia.

seized large parts of the kingdom. By 1648 the population of the Czech Lands had been reduced by up to 40% in many areas.

With power in the hands of mainly non-Czech Catholic nobles, the country suffered economically as well. The Habsburgs moved their throne back to Vienna, and Prague was reduced to a provincial town for over a century. With the passing of time, the Habsburg line softened; serfdom was abolished between 1781 and 1785, and religious freedom was allowed, but Czech dissatisfaction with the foreign rulers continued.

By the 19th century, the Czechs were fired up with nationalistic sentiments. Thanks to educational reforms by Empress Maria Theresa, even the poor had access to schooling; a vocal middle class was emerging with the Industrial Revolution; and economic and industrial reforms were forcing Czech labourers into the bigger towns, where they soon overwhelmed the German minorities. Political activity was banned under the Habsburgs, so the movement was linguistic: Josef Jungmann, Josef Dobrovský and František Palacký, the author of the *History of the Czech Nation*, all worked on regenerating the Czech language.

For the Slovaks the year 1526 was also important; Hungary suffered a major defeat by Ottoman Turks at Mohács, which started a chain of events that almost destroyed the Hungarian kingdom and forced its nobility to move all and sundry to Slovakia. The Austrian Habsburgs, already Holy Roman emperors and rulers of the Czech Lands, assumed the Hungarian crown and moved the Hungarian capital to Bratislava. In 1683, with the help of the Polish King Ján Sobieski, the Habsburgs defeated the Turks, practically at the gates of Vienna. The Turks were driven out of central Europe for good, leaving behind a legacy of war, economic ruin and bags of coffee beans. Bratislava's spell as the Hungarian capital then came to an end.

Economically, this was not a profitable time for Slovakia. Constant war with the Turks cut trade routes to the east, and the Spanish, Portuguese, French and British plunder of the Americas for its minerals – Slovakia's main source of income – caused its mines to deteriorate. The country remained little more than a backwater, part of Habsburg Hungary, though in the second half of the 18th century Empress Maria Theresa and Emperor Joseph II made life easier for Slovaks with educational and labour reforms, including basic schooling for all children. Later, in the 19th century, serfdom was abolished in Slovakia, and economic development, including the appearance of a garment industry, began to gather pace. New mines and foundries were established and older ones re-established, accounting in 1860 for some 75% of Hungary's production in these industries.

The late 18th century brought about a national cultural awakening in Slovakia, much of it a reaction against Hungarian domination, in step with a similar struggle by Czechs against their Germanic overlords. One of its early leaders was a Catholic priest named Anton Bernolák, who founded the Slovak Learned Society (Slovenské učené tovarišstvo) in Modra, Western Slovakia, in 1792.

Early on the movement gained momentum with Slovak intellectuals who saw a chance to subvert the Austro-Hungarian aristocracy. Yet the movement fell on deaf ears within the Slovak lower classes until the 1840s, when Ľudovít Štúr, a major figure in the Slovak cultural renaissance, developed

1781

the first grammar rules for Slovak, based on the Central Slovak dialect of the time. His inspirational efforts created a Slovak literary language that would make nationalist ideas more accessible to the mass of Slovak people.

By 1848 revolutions were widespread in Europe, and Slovakia was ripe for change. Hungary revolted against the Austrians, and Slovak nationalists reasoned it was the perfect time to take up arms against their rulers and declare Slovakia as an independent state. Due to Russian intervention, however, the Habsburgs were able to reassert authoritarian control and the rebellions of 1848 were swiftly crushed. They annulled the Hungarian constitution and made German the main language, even in Hungary. Things, however, were not completely hunky-dory within the Austrian Empire, and after losing a war with Prussia in 1867, it was forced to join with the Hungarians in a 'dual monarchy'. Under the new Austro-Hungarian Empire, the Hungarians took out their frustrations on the Slovaks and subjected them to a brutal programme of 'Hungarisation' – only Hungarian was taught in Slovak schools, and large swathes of land were confiscated for Hungarian settlers, causing poverty and famine throughout Slovakia. It is estimated that during this time, up to a third of the population emigrated rather than suffer under such a totalitarian rule.

Nonetheless, throughout this time, the gradual awakening of a Slovak national consciousness continued, and 1863 saw the founding of the cultural and educational foundation known as Matica slovenská. This was a major milestone in the Slovak National Revival, confronting Hungarisation head-on.

INDEPENDENCE, THEN WAR

During WWI, Czechs and Slovaks had no interest in fighting for the empire, and a large number defected to fight against the Germans and Austrians. Meanwhile, politicians of both nationalities began to argue the case for independence; US President Wilson, keen to establish stronger ties with Europe, was all for it. Eventually, Czechs and Slovaks agreed to form a single federal state of two equal republics. The Pittsburgh Agreement was signed by representatives of Czech and Slovak organisations in America proposing the creation of a Czechoslovak State. On 28 October 1918 the new Czechoslovak Republic was declared, with Prague as its capital and Tomáš Garrigue Masaryk its first president. Industry boomed in the Czech Lands and the new republic set about industrialising Slovakia, a traditionally agrarian-based country.

Czechs were happy, Slovaks mildly content, Germans downright miserable. By the mid-1930s, many of Bohemia's three million German-speakers wanted to be part of a greater Germany. Germans in the Sudetenland, along the border, had been discriminated against by Czechs and wanted out, so when Hitler demanded the Sudetenland in 1938, the Czechs prepared for war. The British and French governments pressed the Czechoslovak president, Beneš, to give up these lands for the sake of European peace and, in October 1938, under the infamous Munich Agreement between the Germans, French, British and Italians (the Czechs were notably absent), the Nazis occupied the Sudetenland. The Poles took part of Silesia in Northern Moravia and the Hungarians seized Ruthenia and southern areas of Slovakia (some 22% of the Slovak territory). On 15

Slovakia: Escape from Invisibility by Karen Henderson is loaded with facts and plenty of gusto; a book that spells out Slovakia's struggle for independence over the centuries.

In the book *Good Soldier Švejk*, Jaroslav Hašek's iconic satire reveals the Czech state of mind during WWI.

1792	1848
Founding of the Slovak Learned Society.	Slovak nationalists rebel against ruling Hungarians.

Hangmen also Die is
director Fritz Lang's
melodramatic
interpretation of the
Czech Resistance's
assassination of Bohemia's
Nazi governor.

*Are You Here in This Hell
Too?* by Elizabeth Sommer-
Lefkovits is a harrowing
tale of the Holocaust
through the eyes of a
Jewish pharmacist in
Prešov up until 1944.

The film *Obecná Skola
(The Elementary School)*,
directed by Jan Sverák,
shows life in a Czech
village during WWII,
quirkily seen through the
eyes of its children.

March 1939 Germany occupied all of Bohemia and Moravia, declaring the whole region a 'protectorate'.

The rapid occupation meant the country's buildings suffered little damage. However, most of the Czech intelligentsia and 80,000 Jews died at the hands of the Nazis. When Czech paratroopers assassinated the Nazi governor in 1942, the entire town of Lidice was wiped out in revenge.

On 5 May 1945 Prague rose against the German forces as the Red Army approached from the east. US troops had reached Plzeň, but held back in deference to their Soviet allies. The Czechs, assisted by Russian renegades, granted the Germans free passage out of Prague provided they left the city intact; they began pulling out on 8 May. Most of Prague was thus liberated before Soviet forces arrived the following day.

While all this was going on on the western front, things started to sour on the eastern front. Slow development, an influx of Czech bureaucrats, and the breaking of the promise of a Slovak federal state (as stipulated in the Pittsburgh Agreement) generated calls for Slovak autonomy. Unemployment in Slovakia approached an unprecedented 50% during the 1930s Depression, and the federal government in Prague was demonised for its inability to offer relief. In the 1935 elections, more than 60% of the Slovak vote went to the Communists and right-wing nationalist groups that were agitating for an independent Slovak state.

When Hitler took the Sudetenland, Czechoslovakia began to unravel. Slovaks declared their urgent wish for autonomy and although the Czech government attempted to halt Slovak independence by sacking the Slovak government and declaring martial law on 9 March 1939, it was all a foregone conclusion. On 14 March, the day before Hitler declared that Bohemia and Moravia were to be a German 'protectorate', the separate state of Slovakia was announced.

The government of the new state was headed by Jozef Tiso, leader of the nationalist Hlinka Slovak National People's Party (Hlinkova slovenská ľudová strana, or HSĽS), which had been seeking autonomy from the Czechs. Tiso immediately banned all opposition political parties and instituted censorship along Nazi lines. In 1941 the HSĽS promulgated its own 'Jewish Code', and drew up its own list of Jewish targets (during the war 73,500 Jews were deported from Slovakia to the Nazi extermination camps). Jews, however, were not the only victims of ethnic cleansing; Roma (Gypsies) were also targets of the Nazi regime, but the number of deaths during the war is not known.

Not all Slovaks supported this Nazi puppet state. In August 1944, units of the Slovak army and thousands of poorly armed partisans rose up against Tiso's government and began the Slovak National Uprising (Slovenské národné povstanie, or SNP). It was quashed after two months by 35,000 German troops, apparently invited by Tiso. This short, ill-fated uprising is today remembered in monuments and street names all over Slovakia.

COMMUNISM, LESS COMMUNISM, THEN MORE COMMUNISM

After the war, the Czechoslovak government expelled 2.5 million Sudeten German speakers – including antifascists who had fought the Nazis – from the Czech borderlands, confiscating their property. During the forced marches out of Czechoslovakia many were beaten, robbed, raped

1867	28 October 1918
Austro-Hungarian Empire formed; 'Hungarisation' of Slovakia begins.	Czechoslovakian Republic declared.

or murdered. Others were interned in concentration camps. It is estimated that tens of thousands of German speakers died. In 1997 Czech Prime Minister Václav Klaus and German chancellor Helmut Kohl signed a declaration of mutual apology.

Also after the war, some 75,000 Hungarians were deported in exchange for Slovakians living in Hungary, changing the ethnic makeup of the country. In the first Czechoslovak state, Slovaks ranked third, after Czechs and Germans; in the new, Czechs formed the majority of the population and Slovaks were the largest minority by far, outnumbering the nearest, Hungarians, by nine to one.

In the 1946 elections the Communists became the largest party, forming a coalition government. In February 1948 the Communists staged a coup d'état with the backing of the Soviet Union. A new constitution established the Communist Party's dominance, and government was organised along Soviet lines. Thousands of noncommunists fled the country. And while the Communists represented both Czech and Slovak communities, the party was based in Prague and dominated by Czechs. Slovak interests, and representation, were largely forgotten in the halls of power right up until the fall of communism.

The 1950s was an era of harsh repression and decline as communist economic policies nearly bankrupted the country. Many people were imprisoned, and hundreds were executed or died in labour camps, often for little more than a belief in democracy. The only woman to be officially executed was Milada Horáková, a former member of parliament and the National Socialist Party. Later, a series of Stalinist purges was organised by the Communist Party, during which many people, including top members of the party itself, were executed. The most notorious was the Slánský Process in 1951–52, where Jewish deputy premier Rudolf Slánský, who had ordered Horáková's death, was himself executed on trumped up charges as a leader of an antigovernment conspiracy.

As the 1960s rolled along and the rest of the world was all about peace and love, the Czechoslovak Communist Party also started to let its hair down. Under reformist general secretary Alexander Dubček, who took over in January 1968, the party started talking democracy and an end to censorship, or 'socialism with a human face'. The party's April 1968 'Action Program' of reform filled Czech hearts with hope, and there was an outpouring of literature, art and political expression known as the 'Prague Spring'.

Soviet leaders, unable to face the thought of a democratic society within the Soviet bloc, invaded their Czech and Slovak 'friends' on the night of 20 August 1968. More than 200,000 Soviet and Warsaw Pact troops rolled into Prague, killing 58 people. Dubček was replaced by the orthodox Dr Gustav Husák and exiled to Krasňany, a village close to Bratislava, to work as a mechanic. Around 14,000 Communist Party functionaries and 500,000 members who refused to renounce their belief in reform were expelled from the party. Many educated professionals – including teachers and doctors – were forbidden to work in their field. Totalitarian rule was re-established, and dissidents were routinely imprisoned.

In 1977 the trial of a rock group, the Plastic People of the Universe, inspired a group of 243 writers, artists and intellectuals, including Václav

Too Loud a Solitude by Bohumil Hrabl is a tiny, perfect look at life under communism through the eyes of one factory worker.

A classic film of the Prague Spring, *Vsichni dobrí rodáci (All My Good Countrymen)* directed by Vojtech Jasny tells the story of a small Czech village coming to terms with communism.

The Unbearable Lightness of Being by Milan Kundera has sections on the Prague Spring that are an easy-to-read, emotive look at this turbulent time.

1938	1939
The Sudetenland handed to Hitler at Munich agreement.	Slovakia becomes an independent state.

See
www.slovakradio.sk/rsi
/index.html
for the Slovak take on
the Prague Spring and
its demise; includes
sound bites.

Bizarre Czech director Jan
Svankmajer interprets
his country's history
post-1948 in the short
animated film *The Death
of Stalinism in Bohemia*.

Havel, to sign a public demand for basic human rights known as the Charter '77 (Charta '77). This became a focus for opponents of the regime.

THE VELVET REVOLUTION & DIVORCE

Even when the Berlin Wall fell in 1989 and Soviet Premier Gorbachov embraced *perestroika* and *glasnost*, the Czechoslovak Communist Party refused to bend. But on 17 November 1989 things changed. Prague's communist youth movement organised an officially sanctioned demonstration in memory of nine students executed by the Nazis in 1939. A peaceful crowd of 50,000 was cornered in Národní třída in Prague, some 500 were beaten by the police and about 100 were arrested – some now say the whole thing was precipitated by reformist party members to trigger a revolution.

The following days saw constant demonstrations by students, artists and writers, and finally by most of the populace. Though news of the uprising was kept from many Czechoslovaks, demonstrations spread throughout the country. They culminated in a rally of 750,000 people on Letná Hill in

VÁCLAV HAVEL

The Czech Republic's first president, Václav Havel, was a rarity in the world of politics – a playwright, a poet and former dissident.

Born on 5 October 1936 in Prague, Havel was supposed to be a laboratory technician, but couldn't resist the stage, taking jobs as a stage technician and eventually becoming an assistant director. In 1963 his first play, *The Garden Celebration* (Zahradní slavnost), premiered at divadlo na Zábradlí. Its theme was the oppressive political system in Czechoslovakia.

This and other plays of his were banned from public performance after the Soviet invasion of 1968; constantly hounded by the Communists, Havel helped found an opposition group, Charta '77, which became one of the main targets of the police system. Despite four spells in jail, he kept writing, his works being published by underground *(samizdat)* presses and in the West. Two of his better-known works are *Letters to Olga* (Dopisy Olze, 1983), a compilation of 144 letters he sent to his former wife from prison, and the play *Largo desolato* (1984).

In the Velvet Revolution, Havel led the artists who joined students to bring down the fall of the Communist regime through constant street demonstrations, and helped form Civic Forum, the main reform party. His refusal to give in to the Communist regime had brought him a lot of respect, and his role in the revolution only added to that: on 29 December 1989 he was elected president of Czechoslovakia. However, the obligations of the presidential office took him away from both writing and Civic Forum, and only in 1991 did he manage to publish *Summer Meditations* (Letní přemítání), his outline of the problems Czechoslovakia faced and how he would like to solve them. When Czechoslovakia split, he was elected president of the Czech Republic. His wife died of cancer in 1996, and in the same year he had one of his lungs removed. Havel remarried in 1997 and was also re-elected as president in 1998.

Comparisons have been made between Havel and another former president, TG Masaryk. Both men, within the same century, freed Czechoslovakia from foreign ideological domination; both found themselves caught up in the problem of reconciling the differing aims of Czechs and Slovaks. Havel also remained, just as Masaryk did, profoundly democratic and committed to individual rights. Since retiring from office in 2003, Havel has suffered recurrent bouts of pneumonia and some tarnishing of his saintly reputation – even a poet can't run a country without getting his hands dirty occasionally – but it seems likely that Havel's presidency will always be remembered as a shining moment in international politics and a proud time for the Czech people.

1944	1948
Slovak National Uprising against the Nazis.	Communist coup.

Prague. Leading dissidents, with Havel at the forefront, formed the anti-Communist Civic Forum that negotiated the government's resignation on 3 December. A 'Government of National Understanding' was formed, with the Communists as minority members. Havel was elected president of the republic by the federal assembly on 29 December, and Alexander Dubček was elected speaker of the national assembly.

The days after the 17 November demonstration became known as the 'Velvet Revolution' (Sametová revoluce), because there were no casualties. The downside of this nonviolent transformation is that ex-Communists who killed and oppressed their fellows still walk free, while many who fought the Communists and were sentenced by them have not been pardoned.

With the strong central authority provided by the Communists gone, old antagonisms between Slovakia and Prague re-emerged. A resurgence of Slovak nationalism and agitation for Slovak autonomy resulted in the Slovak parliament rejecting a treaty that would have perpetuated a federal Czechoslovakia, and would eventually culminate in the creation of two nations.

Meanwhile the Civic Forum had split into factions over differences on economic policy, creating the right-of-centre Civic Democratic Party (Občanská demokratická strana, ODS) led by Václav Klaus, and the left-of-centre Civic Forum. As finance minister, Klaus forced through some tough economic policies, the success of which gave the ODS a slim victory in the Czech Republic in the June 1992 elections.

The elections only deepened the rift between the two countries, and brought to power the left-leaning nationalist Movement for a Democratic Slovakia (HZDS), headed by the controversial Vladimír Mečiar, a firm believer in Slovak independence and slow economic reform. In 1991 Mečiar had been dismissed by the Slovak National Council from his post as prime minister because of both his autocratic temperament and revelations of involvement with the former secret police.

In July, goaded by Mečiar's fiery rhetoric, the Slovak parliament voted to declare sovereignty. Mečiar held negotiations with Klaus, as neither could form a stable government. Despite numerous efforts the two leaders could not reach a compromise. The incompatibility of Klaus and Slovak leader Mečiar became apparent and they decided (or Klaus persuaded Mečiar) that splitting the country was the best solution. Many people, including President Havel, called for a referendum (Havel actually proposed two), but even a petition signed by a million Czechoslovaks was not enough for the federal parliament to agree on how to arrange it. On 1 January 1993 Czechoslovakia ceased to exist for the second time in the 20th century. Prague became capital of the new Czech Republic, and Havel was elected its first president.

The Czech Republic is an independent state and a parliamentary democracy headed by the president, who is elected for a five-year term. The president is the head of state, but it's the prime minister (chosen by the president), with the *vláda* (cabinet), who wields the most power.

Thanks to Klaus' economic policies, booming tourism and a solid industrial base, the Czech Republic started strongly. Unemployment was negligible, shops were full and many cities were getting face-lifts: by 2003 Prague had the highest standard of living in Eastern Europe. However, capitalism also meant a shortage of affordable housing, rising crime and a deteriorating health system.

Hope Dies Last; The Autobiography of Alexander Dubček are the memoirs of probably the most famous Slovak in contemporary history; it's just a pity that the text is dry, tedious and unfeeling.

Summer Meditations by Václav Havel is the former president's take on where the Czech Republic has been and where it's going.

A History of Slovakia – The Struggle for Survival by Stanislav J Kirschbaum is a highly readable account of the suppressed Slovak nation up until its final split with the Czech Republic in 1993.

1968	**17 November 1989**
Prague Spring crushed by Soviet invasion.	Velvet Revolution.

In 2003, after two terms as president, Havel was replaced by former prime minister Klaus – it took three elections for Czechs to settle on a new president, and the uncharismatic Klaus is far from the popular leader Havel was. While Klaus stands for free-market economy and ever-increasing privatisation, the current prime minister, Vladimír Špidla, is much more left-leaning.

THE FALL & RISE OF VLADKO

Vladimír Mečiar – Slovakia's prime minister from 1993 to 1998 and leader of the Movement for a Democratic Slovakia (HZDS) – is a politician of the old guard: power hungry, uncompromising and seemingly willing to explore all avenues to hang onto power. And he is both the most popular and the most reviled politician in Slovakia.

His opponents believe that the autocratic and authoritarian Mečiar – known as Vladko to his supporters – mismanaged the economy during his spell as prime minister and almost ruined Slovakia's international image. In 1994 President Michal Kováč – Mečiar's former ally – asked parliament for a vote of no confidence in the government. Mečiar was duly ousted and many Slovaks breathed a collective sigh of relief.

But Mečiar is an ex-amateur boxer, a tough-talking man with an insatiable desire for power, and when he promised to get even with Kováč, few people took him seriously – until the 1994 elections, when Mečiar's party won 34.9% of the popular vote and 61 of the parliament's 150 seats. Despite the mediocre results, Mečiar formed a coalition with the ultra-nationalist Slovak National Party (SNS) and the socialist Association of Slovak Workers (ZRS), giving him 83 seats and control of the government.

And then things got weird. In August 1995 the son of President Kováč, Michal Jr, was kidnapped. According to *Time* magazine, 'armed men halted his car just outside Bratislava, forced him into another vehicle, blindfolded and beat him, and applied electric shocks to his genitals. They poured a bottle and a half of whisky down his throat, drove him across the border to Austria and dumped him, unconscious, outside a police station'.

The subsequent investigation uncovered some curious facts – mainly that members of the SIS, Slovakia's secret police, carried out the kidnapping on orders from 'the highest levels of government'. Shortly afterwards, two detectives on the case were suddenly sacked, and a crucial witness was killed in a mysterious car explosion.

The investigation faded into obscurity, but resurfaced spectacularly in April 2000 when masked commandos arrested Mečiar in a dramatic dawn raid. He was charged with paying illegal bonuses to ministers during his period in office and was questioned in relation to the Kováč kidnapping before being released on bail. But he typically turned events into a publicity coup by claiming he had been betrayed and arrested in the week before Easter 'just like Jesus Christ'.

Despite setbacks, Vladko's pulling power is still strong. He stood in the presidential elections in 1999, and lost only narrowly to Rudolf Schuster. In July 2000 he delivered a petition with 700,000 signatures to President Schuster calling for a referendum on whether to hold an early general election. During the 2002 elections, his HZDS party won 36 seats – the most of any political party – but failed to form a coalition government. Since then, 11 of those elected politicians have walked out to form an independent party.

Most recently, it seems as though Vladko has mellowed with age. His criticism of the current government is less damning and he has even supported EU-related laws and Slovakia's entry into NATO. However, most ruling coalition politicians distrust Mečiar's political turnaround – and wisely so. Considering his dubious past and resilient qualities, who knows what the man will pull out of the hat next.

1 January 1993	February 1995
Czechoslovakia splits into the Czech and Slovak Republics.	First edition of Lonely Planet's *Czech & Slovak Republics* published.

The Czech Republic became a member of NATO in 1999 and in a 2003 referendum voted to join the EU in May 2004 (it will take on the Euro in 2007).

Slovakia's transition from communism to capitalism was not so smooth. The early days of Slovak independence were taken up by dividing the remaining federal assets between the two republics. Within 15 months Mečiar's dictatorial rule – and his reluctance to embark on privatisation when Slovakia needed it most – reduced a government with a comfortable majority to one in minority. The minority government had little chance to stay in power. Mečiar even managed to alienate his ally, President Michal Kováč, by accusing him of 'corrupt, immoral and destabilising acts'.

The turmoil resulted in a vote of no confidence in the prime minister. A broad coalition of parties was formed, and an interim government was put in place until the 1994 elections. Under the fear of Mečiar's return, it seems, the second stage of the privatisation scheme (initiated in 1992) was hurriedly passed.

Parliamentary fears were indeed founded. In September 1994, Mečiar's party won 34.9% of the vote in the general election, and formed a new coalition government with an extreme left-wing and a right-wing party. Most Slovaks voting for Mečiar were pensioners, workers and people living in rural villages; students and city dwellers tended to vote for leftish parties like the Democratic Union of Slovakia (DU).

Immediately after the elections, Mečiar upped his heavy-handed style of politics and cancelled the sale of state-owned enterprises, halted Slovakia's privatisation scheme and threatened independent radio stations and newspapers with legal action if they dared criticise the government.

It's estimated that between 1994 and 1998 some 4000 civil servants were fired for their liberal (ie anti-Mečiar) political beliefs. A law passed in 1995 recognised Slovak as the only official language, meaning that, officially, the large Hungarian minority could not use their mother tongue in public places (this was later repealed). A separate law passed in 1995 to protect the Slovak Republic allowed the arrest of anyone criticising the government.

Not surprisingly, many Slovaks started to lose patience with Mečiar. The passing of antidemocratic laws also brought criticism from various human-rights organisations, European leaders and the USA. The elections of October 1998 finally saw Mečiar ousted by the reform-minded Mikuláš Dzurinda, leader of the right-leaning Slovak Democratic Coalition (SDK). The 1999 vote for president saw Rudolf Schuster taking up the post.

Elections in 2002 saw Dzurinda win again, but only just. The ruling coalition consists of four quite different political parties with only a slim majority in parliament, which, at the time of writing, it was about to lose due to defections within its ranks.

The poor economic performance and high unemployment rate that have dogged Slovakia over the last 10 years seem to be easing ever so slightly. However, ethnic tensions with the country's Hungarian and Roma minorities are still causing major problems, although the government is attempting to rectify the problem (some would say only superficially).

Along with the Czech Republic, Slovakia will join the EU in May 2004, and also become a member of NATO.

August 2002	May 2004
Prague suffers devastating floods.	Czech & Slovak Republics join EU.

The Culture

THE NATIONAL PSYCHE

Like many former Soviet-bloc countries, the Czechs have a reputation for surliness and immovability. Praguers also carry the burden of bohemianism: brooding melancholy, profound intelligence and a talent for literature. Those who lived the majority of their life under communism may well be a little reserved and unfriendly, but young Czechs have embraced their new culture and are eager to talk about life in the Czech Republic, international politics, beer, jokes and just about anything else you can come up with. Most Czechs are deeply patriotic and love to talk about national history, the end of communism, where Czechs are heading next, and what the EU means for Czech culture. Laid-back on the surface, easy to get along with, but many Czechs have strongly held views – some of which you may disagree with – that they tend to keep to themselves unless pushed.

Slovaks are similar in many ways. The older generation can be rather rude and a little distant at first, the younger genuinely friendly, open (as Eastern European societies go), funny, and able to hold an engaging conversation on a plethora of topics. It has to be said though; tolerance of the minorities of this world is low and sensitive subjects are best left untouched. Like many peoples from small nations with relatively few visitors, the Slovaks are both modest and proud of their country, and somewhat surprised to see you. Compliment the natural beauty of the country or simply mention you're having a great time, and more often than not they'll turn a bright shade of pink.

LIFESTYLE

The Czech Republic is still a society in flux. Years of careful silence, of restricted rights and of having little reason to try at anything have all left their mark. Overall, however, the Czech Republic is not that dissimilar to Western Europe or the United States. Most apparent is the Czechs' slight aversion to anyone different to themselves; while intolerance is rarely overtly expressed, many Czechs are afraid of, uncomfortable with or just flat-out don't like gays, foreigners or people who think differently to themselves. However, this is almost entirely unreflected in social policy (the real exception is the attitude to the Roma, see p34; jail sentences for white Czechs who assault Roma are still notoriously lax).

While things are moving towards a more American model of work, Czechs still prefer to take it easy whenever possible. They do get up horrendously early for work (many jobs start by 7am), but on the whole they expect a decent lunch break, no overtime and as much vacation time as possible. Spending time with family and friends (preferably with beer involved) and getting out of town every weekend are still much more important than career success. The average Czech earns around €500 a month; state employees get a little more. Most Czechs are supportive of the welfare state.

The Czech Republic is predominantly atheist, and this is reflected in social policies that are generally live and let live. Divorce, abortion and childbirth outside marriage are all fairly uncontentious issues, and while many Czechs are uncomfortable with homosexuality, Czech law does not discriminate against gays. However, fear of crime has risen since the end of communism, and risen at a greater rate than crime itself, so it's possible Czech law may become more uptight about drugs, vagrancy and minorities, always popular scapegoats for rising crime.

DID YOU KNOW?

It's acceptable for Czech men to walk around in public wearing Speedos.

THE 'OTHER' TOURIST INDUSTRY

Since the Velvet Revolution, sex clubs and streetwalkers have proliferated along the roads heading into Germany and Austria, with the heaviest concentration along the E55 Highway between Dubi and Cinovec.

The huge demand for sex workers in border towns, and the apparent lack of willing women have caused organised crime gangs to kidnap locals, who are then shipped out to Germany and Italy. Others come from – or are brought against their will from – Russia, Eastern Europe and the Balkans; some are underage. Customers are mainly truck drivers and German men.

Child prostitution is such a big problem that the German government has warned its citizens they will be prosecuted if they commit an act of paedophilia outside the country.

The councils of many larger and tourist-frequented towns in the border regions have kept out the sex clubs, but Cheb is an exception. The streets were cleaned up in the late 1990s, but prostitution is now back in force. Prague also has its red-light district, mostly around the Mustek metro station; it's not a dangerous place, as it's also one of the main shopping strips and tourist hang-outs.

Czechs are well educated, with a 98% literacy rate and a very good grasp of what's going on elsewhere in the world and at home. Education is fully funded by the state and the republic has three universities; sciences, technology and mathematics produce the most graduates.

Slovaks regard religion as integral part of society and its importance in the community is on the increase; over the past 10 years, the percentage of religiously affiliated persons rose by 11% to 84%. This has equated to a relatively conservative community, one which is distrustful of anything differing from the norm, in particular homosexuals and Roma (Gypsies), but it seems to have no qualms about sex; Slovakia has the fourth highest teenage birth rate of Organization for Economic Co-operation and Development (OECD) countries.

Find your Name Day at www.slovakian.info /cgi-bin/calendar.pl and then make sure your friends throw you a party!

Like the Czechs, Slovaks make the most of their time off and will often take a weekend trip to the countryside with friends and relatives. Work ethic varies from place to place; people in Bratislava are prepared to put in long hours to get ahead, in smaller towns and rural communities they are more inclined to avoid overtime.

Many young Slovaks live at home until they either marry or move in with their partner. This has partly to do with conservative nature of society but also due to low wages.

Slovakia has a high proportion of educated citizens (66% of the population complete secondary school), and a 99% literacy rate. Nearly all schools are government-run, and students must complete year nine (around 15 years of age). There are a number of university institutions in the country, the largest of which are in Bratislava and Košice.

POPULATION

The Czech Republic is a homogenous place: of the around 10.3 million people who live here, just over 95% identify themselves as ethnic Czechs (like Russians and Slovaks, Czechs are Slavs). Of the rest, 3% are Slovaks, 0.6% Polish, 0.5% German, 0.3% Roma and 0.2% Hungarian. About a third of those living in Moravia identify as Moravians rather than Czechs; historically, they believe, Moravians are a different nationality than their Bohemian neighbours, and some talk about becoming their own country (though it seems an unlikely prospect). Population density is 130 people per sq km, similar to the UK but more than twice that of the USA. The average life span is 70.5 years for men, 77.5 years for women. A little over a quarter of the population lives in the major cities, more than a tenth in Prague.

Almost 86% of Slovakia's 5.4 million people class themselves as ethnic Slovaks; the largest minority, the Hungarians, make up around 10% of the population and live mostly in southern and eastern Slovakia. Roma come in third with 1.7%, which equates to 90,000 people, the vast majority of which live in East Slovakia. Czechs only count for 0.8% of the population. Population density is 111 people per sq km; Bratislava and West Slovakia are the most densely populated areas, Central Slovakia the least. There is a current exodus from larger cities to smaller towns and rural communities. The average life span for men is 70.2 years, and for women 78.4 years.

SPORT

The Czechs may not care much for physical exercise, but they love their spectator sport. Far and away the most popular sports are football (soccer) in the summer and ice hockey in the winter; everything else is very much an also-ran.

Slovaks love the outdoors – the geography of the country demands it – but are generally so-so about sport. Like the Czech Republic, football is the most popular sport by far, although ice hockey has given it a run for its money in the popularity stakes since the national team won the World Cup in 2002.

Football

No-one but the most ardent patriot would consider the Czech Republic a force in European football. While they regularly make it to European championships (and usually have a league team in the Champions League), and while they generally acquit themselves quite well, Czech footballers are more loved at a local than an international level. Most years the top teams are from Prague: SK Slavia Praha, based in Vršovice and dressed in red and white, and AC Sparta Praha, based in Holešovice and wearing crimson, are always contenders (see p144 for information about watching matches in Prague). Bohemia, another Prague team, is notable for having a kangaroo as its mascot.

Visit
http://czechfootbal
.czweb.org/history.htm
for links to everything
about Czech football.

The soccer season runs September to December and March to June. Games are usually on Sunday afternoon, and are televised. Watching football with a pub full of Czech partisans is a real experience.

There is also a women's league, but attendance figures are abysmal – the women's teams are lucky to get 100 people showing up for a game.

For the official site of the
Czech football league,
mostly in Czech, see
www.fotbal.cz.

The Slovak national team has yet to make its mark on the international stage, but it does have a long tradition of local league teams. SK Slovan Bratislava is the country's most famous and successful team, having won the Czechoslovak league eight times and knocked off the Cup-Winners Cup in 1969, the only Slovak team to do so. The Union of European Football Associations (UEFA) Cup normally sports two or three Slovak teams each year. Unfortunately football in Slovakia has been dogged by violent clashes between hooligans and police in the last couple of years. Organised fights between local-team supporters have been reported by Slovak media, and the Slovakia Football Association was heavily fined for verbal attacks against visiting English players in 2002.

Visit the CzechPoint, a
personal site about Czech
hockey, at
http://user.tninet.se
/~gwa036b/.

Ice Hockey

The Czech ice hockey team is a world-beater and its stars pepper the North American leagues. At the 1998 Winter Olympics in Nagano, the Czechs upset the undisputed favourite, Canada, in the semifinals, then went on to beat Russia and win the gold (last time they beat them was in an emotionally loaded final at the 1969 world championships). Since then, the team has won two more world titles.

Dominik Hasek, the 'Dominator', was once regarded as the world's best goaltender; after winning a Stanley Cup with the Red Wings in 2001, he retired to play roller hockey in the Czech Republic, but later came out of retirement to rejoin Detroit. Jaromir Jagr is perhaps even better known. This forward, one of the National Hockey League's (NHL) leading scorers, won Stanley Cups with Pittsburgh in 1991 and '92, and now plays for Washington. Young players to keep an eye on include Marion Gaborik and Marion Hossa.

As with football, women's hockey attracts very little interest in the Czech Republic.

Ice hockey in Slovakia has a long history; the first puck was placed on Slovak ice just after WWI. The Czechoslovak team always included a handful of Slovak nationals, and many have made it into Canadian and US league teams. On an international level, Slovakia hit the big time in 2000 by becoming runners-up to the Czechs in the world championships, but in 2002 they went one better by beating the Russians in the final to take the world title. In 2003 they took their third medal in four years by defeating their arch-rivals, the Czech Republic, to take bronze.

There are rinks all over both republics where local games can be seen (see p144 and p343 for information about games in Prague and Bratislava). The season runs from September to April.

Tennis

Before achieving gold in ice hockey at the 1998 Winter Olympics in Nagano, the sport where Czechs did best was tennis. The country has had a disproportionate number of great stars, including Ivan Lendl, Martina Navrátilová and Jana Novotná. However, within the country tennis has nothing like the following of hockey or football.

Tennis doesn't have much standing in Slovakia, but it has produced the occasional top player. Martina Hingis spent her formative years in Košice before moving to Switzerland, while the country's current favourite, Daniela Hantuchova, has ranked as high as fifth in the world.

Other Sports

In recent years the Czech Republic, and Prague in particular, has become a magnet for alternative sport championships. In 2003 both international skateboarding and international footbag (hacky sack) championships were held in Prague. The footbag competition was a particular coup for the Czech Republic, whose 16-year-old star Vasek Klouda blitzed the finals and defeated, for the second time running, the favourite and American champion.

Canoeing and kayaking have been gaining in popularity over the past few years in Slovakia, due mainly to recent international success that has included golds at the Olympics, world champs and European champs. Martina Moravcová, a household name in Slovakia, is the country's top swimmer, having broken an amazing 192 records in her career and collecting two silver medals at the Sydney 2000 Olympics.

MULTICULTURALISM

Almost 95% of the Republic's population define themselves as ethnically Czech – this country is no melting pot, and Czechs tend to be a bit suspicious of outsiders. Roma, or Gypsies *(romové* or *cikáni)* are one of the

DID YOU KNOW?

Czechoslovak runner Emil Zátopek won three gold medals in the 1952 Olympics.

For the history of Slovakia's triumphs in the sporting arena see www.sportslovakia.sk.

DID YOU KNOW?

Czech jokes about misers are generally aimed at the Dutch.

most conspicuous minorities. Their numbers here have increased sharply since the 1950s, both from births and from immigration for work. Most Czechs dislike Roma, to varying degrees, and talk about them committing crimes, refusing to send their kids to school or destroying homes given to them by the government. Czechs are also sensitive about other countries' opinions of how they treat the Roma – this is definitely not a subject for polite dinner-table conversation. Whether or not their bad reputation is deserved, the Roma have not been warmly embraced by Czech society, and these days many Czechs talk hopefully of how opened borders under the EU might affect the Roma population: that is, they're looking forward to them resuming an itinerant lifestyle.

There is a small Vietnamese minority, originally brought as guest workers when Czechoslovakia and Vietnam were 'brother countries' – communist nations had a policy of sharing labour forces where necessary. They have also faced racism, and claim to be underpaid. Their future is uncertain; the government would like to see most of them return to their homeland.

ROMA & RACISM

Racist attacks on Roma are nothing new in the Czech and Slovak Republics but what was different about the appalling murder of Anastázia Balážová in Žilina, Slovakia, in August 2000, was the widespread condemnation from politicians and press. The 50-year-old Roma mother of eight died after being struck on the head while defending her daughters from three men who broke into her house wielding baseball bats and shouting racist abuse. Cynics claimed that the driving force behind these displays of compassion was Slovakia's up-and-coming entry into the EU.

Roma, a tribe of people that migrated to Europe from India in the 10th century, have never been made welcome. Prejudice, harassment and religious exile have doggedly followed Roma throughout the centuries; a reputed 6 million Roma now live in the Czech and Slovak Republics. Their nomadic lifestyle, inability to mix in with other communities and steadfast reluctance to give up their traditional way of life have only added fuel to the fire of racial resentment; these days the majority of Czechs and Slovaks hold a low opinion of Roma, and politicians have not been afraid of making outrageous racist remarks in parliament, on television or in front of journalists. They are often labelled as lazy, filthy, uneducated, and a lower class full of criminals.

The emergence of far-right political parties and neo-Nazi groups since 1989 has seen an increase in overt hostility and racial violence directed towards the Roma, culminating in several brutal murders in Slovakia over the past years:

- **1995** Skinheads doused Roma youth Mário Goral with petrol and burnt him to death.
- **1996** Skinheads in northwest Slovakia set a Roma house on fire, killing one occupant and leaving two with severe burns.
- **1996** Roma youth Gustav Baláž was stabbed to death by skinheads; in retaliation, a skinhead was stabbed and killed by a Roma.
- **1999** In Poprad, a Roma man suspected of stealing a bicycle was shot dead by police.
- **2000** Anastázia Balážová was beaten to death in Žilina.
- **2001** Karol Sendrei died in police custody after being seriously assaulted by a local mayor.

Both governments are theoretically trying to curb this flow, but figures indicate that things are only getting worse. Slovakia's racially motivated crimes trebled from 2001 to 2002, and the Czech Republic's doubled over the same period. Only 10 police staff in Slovakia have the job of monitoring and acting against extremists, while neighbouring Czech Republic has 160. Regular criticism is aimed at the governments for their failure to consistently punish racially motivated crimes.

Activists are hoping that continuing pressure from the EU will bring tolerance, better treatment and improved opportunities for the Roma, but no-one is holding their breath.

Slovakia is similar in its racial make-up to the Czech Republic. The population is solidly Slovakian, and other nationalities hardly get a look-in (you'll be hard-pressed to see even a handful of Africans on your travels). Hungarians and Roma are the largest minorities, while Rusin are a small but important minority in the east (see the boxed text on p427 for more details). Racial attitudes are even worse than in the Czech Republic – not only is the general populace often quite happy to degrade Roma, politicians have been known to drop racial slurs into their parliamentary speeches. If you are dark-skinned you may encounter low-level discrimination yourself, though overt hostility towards visitors is very rare.

The majority of Slovakia's Hungarian population is concentrated along the southern border and its influence is plain to see; the cuisine is decidedly Hungarian, menus and signs are in both languages, and quite often you'll be greeted with *jó napot* rather than *dobrý deň*. Roma towns can be seen the length and breadth of Slovakia, but the further east you go the more you'll come across.

MEDIA

New media outlets – particularly radio stations – are popping up all the time in the Czech Republic as different corporations jostle for a piece of the pie, post State-ownership. Over 80% of Czech media is foreign-owned, mostly by Swiss and German companies. Printing and distribution companies are also largely owned by Germans. Two of the biggest papers, *Mlada Fronta* and *Lidove Noviny*, have the same owner. *Impuls* is currently the only wholly Czech-owned paper, but it's quite likely it will have gone out of business by the time you read this.

The majority of media emanates from Prague and has a decided slant towards news from the capital, but regional papers do still make up about a quarter of the market.

Public radio has about a third of the market. Czech TV has one public station, two big commercial stations and a host of smaller channels. TV Nova, the biggest station, was the first commercial channel in the former Soviet bloc.

The years of Vladimír Mečiar rule were a disaster for press freedom in Slovakia, but since his political demise things have been looking up. The media is still not 100% unbiased towards politicians (but then again, where are they?) but journalists won't get fired for criticising the current government's failures. In saying that, a third of Slovaks think that local media is politically biased, driven by the interests of various politicians, and that story choice is influenced by media owners.

Slovakia's largest publishing house, Petit Press, which publishes *SME*, *The Slovak Spectator* and *Práca* to name a few, is majority owned by a joint venture between the Slovak VMV (a Bratislava-based publishing house) and German firm Verlagsgruppe Passau. The country's most popular TV station, *Markíza*, is privately owned by Pavol Rusko, a Berlusconi-type media magnate in miniature. The leader of the National Citizen's Alliance (ANO), one of the political parties forming the current coalition government, he also owns interests in *Národna Obroda*, a prominent Slovakian newspaper.

RELIGION

Despite the Czech Republic's religious history (see p19) the country is these days phenomenally uninterested in God; a 2003 *Prague Post* article cites the republic as having Eastern Europe's lowest involvement in organised religion.

DID YOU KNOW?

During the 1960s, *Tom & Jerry* was made in Prague.

DID YOU KNOW?

George W. Bush's reply to a Slovak journalist: 'The only thing I know about Slovakia is what I learned first-hand from your foreign minister, who came to Texas'. He'd met the leader of Slovenia.

THE CONCEALED CHURCH

While the Communists were in power, priesthood and church attendance were greatly discouraged. Priests were hounded by the secret service (StB) and people who attended services were also persecuted. To avoid potential problems priests were ordained in secret and performed religious rites behind closed doors for small groups or individuals: this was known as the Concealed Church (skrytá církev).

There is still no officially documented historical work about the Concealed Church or any factual information about the number of people involved. The StB knew of its activities, but only managed to infiltrate some of the Concealed Church's cells. We know little about its workings because of its secretive nature; the many independently run cells had limited contact with each other or the émigré circles outside the country. Even the secret service files don't reveal much.

A number of the priests have tried to become part of the official church since 1989 but their requests are regularly declined by the Roman Catholic Church.

The largest church is the Roman Catholic Church, with 40% of Czechs calling themselves Catholics. The next largest church is the Hussite Church, with 4% of the population, and there are numerous other Protestant denominations, the largest being the Evangelical Church of Czech Brethren, claiming about 2% of the population as members. Officially the country is 40% atheist.

The first Christian church in Slovakia was founded at Nitra way back in 833, and since then religion has never looked back. The last census reported that 84.1% of the population has a religious affiliation, and this can be seen in practice right across the country; people often stop at church on the way home from work, and fill the churches to overflowing on Sunday. The Pope has visited the country three times.

There are 15 registered churches in Slovakia. The Roman Catholic Church is by far the largest group, with about 3.7 million members. Next comes the Evangelical Church of the Augsburg Confession, with 373,000 members, followed by Greek-Catholic, with 220,000 members.

Jews have been in the Czech Republic since before the 11th century – they were among Prague's first inhabitants – and in Slovakia since the 13th century. When Czechoslovakia was founded in 1918, Jews comprised about 4% of the population (around 137,000 people). During WWII around 70% of the Jewish population was killed. Today about 3000 Jews remain in Slovakia, while in the Czech Republic numbers are unclear as many – for obvious reasons – are reluctant to register their religion (see the boxed text on p100 for more information).

ARTS
Visual Arts
CZECH REPUBLIC

Romanesque, illuminated manuscripts and church frescoes (such as at Znojmo's rotunda, see p311) are the earliest examples of graphic art in the region. Byzantine influences start to appear in the late 13th century, and Gothic in the early 14th (such as in Strakonice Monastery). It wasn't long before the Czechs took the Gothic template and gave it their own Bohemian twist; medieval art from this region seems brighter, more humorous and more personal than much of the dour work produced in Italy, France and Germany. For example, the vibrantly coloured *Brno Law Book* and Bibles made for Arnošt z Pardubic in the Brno Municipal Museum, and the trio of late-14th-century altar panels by the anonymous Master of the Třeboň Altar in the Convent of St Agnes in Prague (see p107), or the Master Theodoric panels in Karlštejn castle; see p73 (the originals can be seen at St Agnes Convent). In sculpture, the 14th century Jihlava Crucifix, in the Strahov Gallery in Prague (see p93), is a striking piece, while Gothic realism in the latter 15th century culminated in the work of the Master of Sorrows from Žebrák, also at St Agnes.

During the Renaissance, Czechs painters dedicated themselves to book illumination. The baroque Counter-Reformation brought a wave of religious sculpture to the country, including hundreds of Marian columns, carved to give thanks to the Virgin for protection against the plague. Towards the end of the period, Ignác František Platzer was commissioned to produce statues all over Prague. While the Counter-Reformation produced vast quantities of sculpture and architecture, it also supported a few dark, pensive religious painters, including Petr Brandl, Karel Škréta (whose work can be seen in the Malá Strana St Nicholas in Prague; see p95) and Václav Reiner.

In the late 18th and early 19th centuries the Czech National Revival spurred an interest in Czech themes and representation of everyday life. The biggest name from this period is Josef Mánes; some of his work can be seen in the Centre for Modern and Contemporary Art in Prague (see p117), which is an excellent place for all kinds of post-18th-century Czech painting. Mikuláš Aleš is regarded as one of the best artists of folk and national themes – there's a museum dedicated to him at the Star Palace outside Prague (see p122). The National Revival was a godsend for sculptors, who created monuments to historic Czech figures. Prague has some of the most striking examples: Josef Myslbek's late-19th-century Romantic sculptures immortalise legendary Czechs in the sculpture garden at Vyšehrad (p115). One of Myslbek's students, Stanislav Sucharda, produced the Palacký Monument in Nové Město (p113), while Ladislav Šaloun sculpted the epic monument to Jan Hus in Prague's Old Town Square (p102). Bohumil Kafka's muscular 1941 statue of Jan Žižka – again, found in Prague (see p121) – was at the tail end of this Czech-pride movement. Meanwhile, František Bílek was sculpting tortured monuments to his metaphysical religious beliefs, much to the dismay of the church: his work is on display at the Bílkova Villa in Prague (p122).

Think Art Nouveau and you're probably thinking Alfons Mucha. Though he predominantly lived in Paris and is associated with the French Art Nouveau movement, Mucha's heart remained at home in Bohemia, and much of his work visits and revisits themes of Slavic suffering, courage and cross-nation brotherhood. The most outstanding of his works is a series of 20 large canvasses called the *Slav Epic*, which are presently in Moravský Krumlov (see p303), and his interior decoration in the Municipal House (Obecní dům) in Prague (see p106), but his design and print work can be seen all over the Czech Republic. Czech landscape art developed in the works of Anton Kosárek and Julius Mařák, and was followed by a wave of impressionism and symbolism under artists like Antonín Slavíček and Max Švabinský.

In the early 20th century, Prague became a major European centre for avant-garde art, centred on a group of artists who called themselves Osma (the Eight). Leading cubist painters included Josef Čapek and Emil Filla. Between the two world wars functionalism evolved and flourished in a group called Devětsil, led by Karel Teige, who worked in all kinds of media. Surrealists included Zdeněk Rykr, Josef Šíma and Jindřich Štýrský; one of the leading lights was a woman who went by the pseudonym Toyen. Graphic arts were also booming at this time, with book and text designers František Kysela and Josef Váchal producing some stunning work – you can see a lot of it at the Museum of Decorative Arts in Prague (see p101).

'hundreds of Marian columns, carved to give thanks to the Virgin for protection against the plague'

FOLK ART

The Czech and Slovak Republics may be modern, forward thinking nations galloping into the 21st century on the back of the EU and NATO, but they are also countries rich in folk culture. The excessive use of the 'happy peasant' as a communist propaganda tool probably put many city people right off the idea of folk culture, but the Communists unwittingly helped many traditions to survive in places where folk culture was alive and well by overlooking these areas when it came to economic development.

Folk art first received serious scrutiny in the course of the mid-19th-century national revival. In fact, little of the physical evidence for folk traditions reaches much further back than this, because of the perishability of traditional materials (one major exception being pottery) and the ravages of the Thirty Years' War.

Today folk art is kept alive through two very different routes of preservation. The first is how it's always been done; passing knowledge and customs down from one generation to the next within the family sphere. The second is a public transmission through museums and festivals. The festivals, held in summer or autumn, are incredibly popular and bring neighbours together for an old-fashioned knees-up, enlivened by music and dancing troupes (plus a few shots of Becherovka, a herbal spirit), and brightened with traditional dress.

The Moravské Slovácko region (p317), in the Czech Republic's southeast, contains by far the country's most fascinating pockets of traditional culture. The more modernised regions of Chodsko (p208), in southwestern Bohemia around Domažlice, and Walachia (Valašsko; see p281), in north-eastern Moravia, are also top places to catch a glimpse of life from yesteryear. Slovakia is even more folk-orientated; a dense area of the country, to the east and northeast and encompassing Spiš (p407), Bardejov (p423), Svidník (p429) and Humenné (p428) has a rich vein of folk culture running through it. Throughout these areas you'll find older women (but only a few men) wearing traditional clothing, mainly on Sunday and holidays.

In addition to clothing, even everyday tools, utensils, musical instruments, linen, furniture and entire buildings may be decorated with elaborate folk designs. Besides a unique architectural style, buildings may also be adorned with carved or moulded plaster, or intricately painted. The Slovak villages of Čičmany (p376) and Vlkolínec (p384) are prime examples of this, and should not be missed. In some areas, like Kostice in South Moravia, villagers draw designs on windows with soap or on the ground with fine sand at times of religious festivals. Local artists may show off their skills by painting Easter eggs, glass bottles and pots. Even food may be decorated or shaped. Stronger influences on the survival of folk culture are its songs, stories, music and dance.

Skansens

Both countries are dotted with fine open-air museums of traditional architecture and furnishings called *skansens* (derived from the Swedish word for the first one that opened in Stockholm in 1891). Within the confines of a *skansen* you'll find an array of houses, barns, churches and other buildings. Quite often it's an eclectic collection of architectural styles transported from around a whole region. The better ones, however, make an attempt to show whole communities. Inside the buildings you'll find typical furniture, linen, clothing, utensils, tools and decorations.

Photographers such as Jaroslav Rössler (who worked largely in montage), Jindrich Styrský (who was recording Prague life during the 1930s), Josef Koudelka and Josef Sudek all made a splash on the international scene.

Communism pushed most visual arts, apart from social realism, underground, but some of this work is now resurfacing. Jiří Kolář was an outstanding graphic artist as well as a poet, while Milena Dopitová and František Skála used junk and everyday items to express their social statements. Sculptor David Černý spent a lot of the late-communist era trying to get himself arrested, performing stunts such as painting the tank monument to the liberating Soviet army pink. More recent Černý works include the *Miminka* sculpture: giant babies clambering all over the TV

There are 15 *skansens* in the Czech and Slovak Republics. It's hard to say which is the best, although the first one to open, in 1895, in Přerov nad Labem (p160) is excellent it is overshadowed by the much larger and exceptional Rožnov pod Radhoštěm (p282). The *skansens* at Svidník (p429) and Pribylina (p383) are arguably Slovakia's best.

Music

The basic, traditional musical instruments were flutes (or pipes), drums and *cymbalum* (a copper-stringed dulcimer of Middle Eastern origin, which stands on four legs and is played by striking the strings with two mallets). Other traditional Slovak folk instruments include the *fujara* (a 2m-long flute) and the *konkovka* (a strident shepherd's flute). Bagpipes *(dudy/gajdy)* were also popular, and though you don't hear them often, a core of musicians is trying to keep this instrument and its music alive.

Most music played today is polka-like, with fiddle, bass, clarinet, and sometimes dulcimer, trumpet, or accordion. There are almost always dances, which involve a lot of skirt-twirling and foot-stamping, to go with the music, and in some regions unaccompanied songs as well.

Folk songs helped preserve the Czech and Slovak languages during Austro-Hungarian rule, and in southeastern Moravia and East Slovakia ancient folk traditions are still a living part of village life. Song themes are quite similar to today's pop music with plenty of heart-wrenching lament and sickly sweet love. In Moravian Slovácko the whirling couples dance the *vrtěná*, while the *hošije* and *verbuňk* are vigorous male solo dances. Don't be surprised if you hear a high-pitched squeal intermittently throughout a song; it's not one dancer treading on another, but a sign of joy and enthusiasm.

Folk Dress

Eastern Europe is renowned for its colourful and elaborate folk dress, and the Czech and Slovak Republics are no exception. The highly decorative and festive garments you see today evolved from simple peasant outfits used in everyday life. The most striking feature is usually detailed embroidery in bright colours and abstract or pictorial designs. They often vary according to the season, the age of the wearer or whether they are potential marriage material.

In the more traditional corners of the region you'll still see villagers (mainly women) on weekends and holidays dressed to the nines in embroidered skirts, shawls, jackets, fur coats, colourful belts and shoes. But it's less and less common because, like everywhere, the younger generation is more interested in the latest high-street fashion labels.

The big regional variations in traditional dress can be categorised in any number of ways: west (Bohemia and central Moravia) versus east (the Carpathians and the rest of Moravia); or north (Polish and western Ukrainian) versus south (Austrian, Hungarian, South Slav and Romanian). The western Czech Republic has few actual folk dresses to be seen, but specific styles of headgear, shawls, belts and shoes abound. The eastern Czech Republic and Slovakia contain the most attractive, with hand-sewn shirts, skirts, aprons, jackets, fur coats, pants, shawls and scarves for both men and women. The Moravské Slovácko region of southeastern Moravia shows the most pronounced variations in dress between villages.

tower in Žižkov, Prague. Zdeněk Palcr (1927–96) was perhaps one of the best Czech sculptors of the 20th century with his unique use of geometric lines, rather than true shapes of the human body, to portray people.

Interesting names in the early 21st century include sculptor Pavel Opočenský, a member of Charter '77 (a group that strove for artistic freedom during the communist era) and friend of Václav Havel, perhaps known as much for his passion for underage girls as for his abstract, geometric works; and designer Maxim Velcovský, who mostly works with household accessories but is also renowned for his modern crucifix, *Design for Messiah*, which lives in the Gočár-designed Protestant church in Hradec Králové (see p252).

SLOVAKIA

Among the earliest examples of painting to be found in Slovakia are the remains of 12th-century Romanesque frescoes in the church at Dechtice, and in the Chapel of the Twelve Apostles at Bíňa. Gothic influences soon took hold and spread throughout the country. The most notable frescoes still to be seen today include the magnificent, 15th-century panel paintings that adorn the Church of St James in Levoča (see p412) and the Cathedral of St Elizabeth in Košice (see p404). Some of the most striking Gothic paintings, however, can be found within the plain walls of wooden churches of Eastern Slovakia (see p425); the Church of St Francis of Assisi in Hervartov, near Bardejov, contains a particular iconical gem.

It was a long time between famous Slovak sculptors. The first of any significance after the chap who carved the *Venus of Moravany* 25,000 years ago was an outstanding Gothic craftsman-sculptor called Master Pavol of Levoča. His moving, painted-wood figures are the highlights of the Church of St James in Levoča and the Church of Our Lady in Banská Bystrica (see p365). Fine stone sculptures were also the handiwork of Master Štefan of Košice, and can be seen in the Cathedral of St Elizabeth in Košice.

Among notable baroque painters were Ján Kupecký and Jakub Bogdan, though the most decorative baroque works in Slovakia are the frescoes by Jan Kracker in the closed Jasov Chateau, near Košice, and the rococo frescoes of Antonín Maulpertsch in the chapel of Trenčianske Bohuslavice. Two of the most treasured art pieces from the time can be found in simple wooden churches in the east. The lower iconostasis (screen with doors and icons set in tiers), by Andrej Gajecký in the Orthodox Church of SS Cosmas & Damian in Lukov, near Bardejov, and a 1780 rococo iconostasis in the Greek-Catholic church in Jedlinka, are works of wonder (for more information see p425).

Sculpture of the baroque era is best exemplified by the Austrian Georg Raphael Donner, who worked in Bratislava in the early 18th century. Some of his finest pieces are in the St Johann Capistran Chapel in Bratislava; his masterpiece, an *Equestrian Statue of St Martin* and the beggar, is on show in Bratislava's St Martin Cathedral (p335).

The Slovak National Revival in the 19th century brought a crop of painters eager to do justice to the new movement, including the portraitist Petr Bohúň, Ladislav Medňanský, known for his vivid landscapes, and Dominik Skutecký, who drew scenes of daily life in the area around Banská Bystrica.

While Slovak art took its major influences from Hungary before WWI, it looked to Bohemia after the birth of Czechoslovakia. Prominent, 20th-century artists who painted Slovakia's landscapes and the spirit and essence of rural Slovakian life were Martin Benka, Ľudovít Fulla and Miloš Bazovský. Mikuláš Galanda was a big name from the early avant-garde movements of the 1930s, and during WWII Peter Matejka managed to capture sensualism and surrealism on canvas. The paintings of Koloman Sokol, with their expressive forms and dark emotions, are probably more famous in America. Under communism, Július Bártfay sculpted numerous WWII monuments and contributed, though less successfully (due to the popularity of the monument), to the Red Army memorial outside Bratislava.

In recent years political art has been competing for attention against older influences. This trend has seen the emergence of Stano Filko from banishment under communism; his art is known for its use of military objects. The younger artists Klára Bočkayová and Martin Knut draw on naive folk art to depict a more autobiographical vision. The perfect place to view contemporary Slovak artists, alongside international names, is the Danubiana Museum near Bratislava (see p345).

'Some of the most striking Gothic paintings can be found within the plain walls of wooden churches'

Architecture

CZECH REPUBLIC

Most early Czech architecture, made of wood, has rotted to dust; of the buildings and urban layouts that still exist, 13th-century Gothic is the oldest you're likely to see; look for town centres comprising a square surrounded by arcaded houses. In the 14th century, King Karel (Charles) IV sponsored a massive Gothic (13th–16th centuries; look for stained glass, pointed arches and external flying buttresses) building boom in Prague, under the guidance of his chief architect, Peter Parler: extant works include the Charles Bridge (p101) and St Vitus Cathedral (p89). The diamond vaulting you'll see in ceilings all over Prague and the rest of the country is also a product of this era.

Italian architects seconded to Bohemia in the early 16th century brought Renaissance (16th century; look for symmetry, elaborate gables and exterior walls covered in sgraffito, a mural technique in which the top layer of plaster is scraped away or incised to reveal the layer underneath) styles in chateaux, summer palaces and merchants' houses. The Summer Palace at Prague Castle (p89) was one of the earliest examples: it took the city by storm, spawning a host of imitators. A unique 'Czech Renaissance' style evolved, with ornamental stucco decorations that often featured legendary or historical scenes.

> 'a portion of the money spent on every building must be devoted to decorating its exterior'

When the Catholics thrashed the Hussites at the 1620 Battle of the White Mountain (following a couple of hundred years of sporadic street battles that demolished large parts of the capital), the Jesuits sponsored lavish, baroque (17th–18th centuries; look for domes, gilding and elaborate, emotional sculpture) rebuilding throughout Prague. Germanic landowners took a fancy to the style, and it spread to the rest of the country. The best-known practitioners of baroque architecture were the unstoppable Bavarian father-and-son team Kristof and Kilian Ignatz Dientzenhofer, whose obsession with gold-plating can be seen all over Prague.

With the 19th century came numerous 'revivalist' (late 18th and early 19th century; look for pediments, columns and huge, square buildings) movements – neoclassical, neo-Gothic, neo-Renaissance – which in their later stages coincided with the Czech National Revival movement. The Habsburgs did their bit to encourage innovation by decreeing that a portion of the money spent on every building must be devoted to decorating its exterior; you can see the results on a brief wander through any big Czech city, where apartment buildings are adorned with busts, frescoes and mosaics.

In the early 20th century the Czechs went nuts for Art Nouveau, a design movement based on recurrent elements, often taken from nature, and known as *secese* in Bohemia. Prague's extraordinary Municipal House (Obecní dům; p106) is a showcase of Art Nouveau design; some of the buildings at Prague's fairground (p117) are also gorgeous, as are the façades of apartment and business buildings throughout the city. Under the influence of Jan Kotěra, some of Art Nouveau's more fanciful tendencies gave way to a functionalist approach, as embodied in Gahura's work at Zlín (South Moravia; p321) for the Baťa shoe company. One of the finest examples of the rigorously clean constructivist style is the Villa Tugendhat in Brno (see p296) by Ludwig Mies van der Rohe; see also Slovenian Josef Plečnik's 1932 church in Prague's náměstí Jiřího z Poděbrad (p121).

Prague is one of the few cities in the world where you can see cubist architecture. A simple, nonconfrontational style that's extremely functional, cubist works include houses built by Josef Chochol and Josef Gočár, and Gočár's chart-topping House of the Black Madonna (dům U černé Matky Boží) on Celetná (p105).

The communist era was, architecturally, a wasteland. The 1960s saw vast, well-built and badly needed housing estates spring up all over the country, but there was little to speak of in decorative terms.

Restoration is the biggest architectural movement these days; nothing particularly interesting is being done with new buildings. One exception is Prague's most idiosyncratic and appealing example of new architecture, Vlado Milunć and Frank Gehry's Dancing Building (Tančící dům; p113), an exercise in fluid unconventionality.

SLOVAKIA

'The communist era basically dotted the landscape and cities with eyesores'

The earliest form of architecture on show in Slovakia dates from 1002: the Romanesque remains of a Benedictine monastery at Diakovce, southeast of Trnava. Of more interest is the tiny 11th-century Romanesque chapel, an offshoot of Nitra's St Emeram Cathedral (p349), which is said to incorporate the remains of the first Christian church in the Czech and Slovak Republics, which was founded here in 833. Slovakia's grandest and most photogenic fortress, Spiš Castle (Spišský hrad; p75), dates from 1209.

Hungarian and Slovak nobles fell heavily for the elaborate façades of the Gothic period and built some grandiose cathedrals. First prize is divided between the colourful Cathedral of St Elizabeth in Košice (see p404) and the majestic Church of St James in Levoča (see p412), with the Basilica of Egídius in Bardejov (see p423) coming in a close runner-up. Among Slovakia's finest late-Gothic works is the small mausoleum chapel of Spišský Štvrtok (p411).

Renaissance is also well represented throughout Slovakia, the best of which can be seen in Bardejov, a town of uniform beauty; its town hall is a sublime construction (see p423). Other examples include the church and nearby houses in Fričovce (East Slovakia) and the restored castle at Bratislava (see p334).

The baroque style, with a Viennese twist, was appreciated by wealthy Slovak aristocrats and merchants of the 17th century. A fine example of early works is the 1637-built University Church of St John the Baptist in Trnava (see p356), with beautiful stucco decorations and a grand high altar.

In the 18th century the ruling Habsburgs declared that only Roman Catholics could build stone churches, which left the Orthodox followers, quite literally, out in the cold. Instead, they built wooden churches, many of which are still standing. Their simple but evocative structures are scattered throughout East Slovakia (see p425).

Art Nouveau arrived in Slovakia from Vienna and Budapest. One of the style's more prominent structures is the strikingly blue Church of St Elizabeth, in Bratislava (see p338), designed by Hungarian architect János Ödön Lechner. The lesser-known of the two Slovak architects with the name Dušan Jurkovič designed a quaint, peasant house in Skalica, West Slovakia. His more famous namesake worked mainly in the Czech Republic, where all his most notable works are, including the bathhouse at Luhačovice (p323).

The communist era basically dotted the landscape and cities with eyesores, but also left some monumental structures such as the New Bridge (Nový most), see photo between pp344-5, and the colossal council estate of Petržalka in Bratislava. The last 10 or so years has seen a massive push to restore and renovate the architectural history of the country, which can be seen in Bratislava's historical centre (p335) and in the likes of Bardejov (p423) and Levoča (p411).

Music
CLASSICAL
Early Czech folk music has largely disappeared, and only a handful of Hussite-era hymns remain (you can hear snatches of them in German Protestant music). The real flowering of Czech music took place in the mid-19th century. Bedřich Smetana, the first great Czech composer and an icon of Czech pride, created a national style by incorporating folk songs and dances into his classical compositions. His best-known pieces are the operas *Prodaná Nevěsta* (The Bartered Bride) and *Dalibor a Libuše*, and the symphonic-poem cycle *Má vlast* (My Country). The Prague Spring (see p125), the country's biggest festival, is dedicated to Smetana, and begins with a parade from his grave to the Smetana Hall, where *Má vlast* is performed.

Antonín Dvořák is perhaps everyone's favourite Czech composer. Among his best-known works are his symphony *From the New World* (composed in the USA while lecturing there for four years), his *Slavonic Dances* of 1878 and 1881, the operas *The Devil & Kate* and *Rusalka*, and his religious masterpiece, *Stabat Mater*.

Well-known, early-20th-century composers such as Zdeněk Fibich, Josef Suk and Bohuslav Martinů also became famous outside their country. Some of the most recent composers are Jan Novák with his best-known work, the sonata *Chorea Vernales*, or Svatopluk Havelka whose first symphony *Pěna* (1965) is still his most notable.

One of the earliest Slovak pieces of classical music, the *Bratislava Missal*, dates from the mid-14th century. Unfortunately little else has survived from this era. In the 17th century, German and Italian music became popular and influential. Two important local composers of the time were Kašpar Plotze and Jan Schimbraczký.

During the 18th century the likes of Haydn, Mozart, Schubert and Beethoven graced the courts of the nobility. Of Slovak composers, the most prominent at this time were Juraj Jozef Zlatník, and Anton Zimmermann, a cathedral organist who composed cantatas, symphonies, concertos and chamber music. Another contemporary was Georg Druschetzky, known for his solo, orchestral and chamber pieces.

Slovaks began to redefine their folk song heritage in the 19th century, and Slovak composers of the time often used traditional folk motifs in their classical compositions. Only Ján Levoslav Bella and Mikulás Schneider-Trnavský, however, achieved any substantial fame. Among Bella's best works are the opera *Kovář Wieland* and the symphonic poem *Fate & Dreams*.

More recently the symphonies of Alexander Moyzes have become established as probably the best Slovak compositions of the mid-20th century. One of Moyzes' students, Dezider Kardoš, has written the country's most innovative post-WWII music, especially his second symphony, *Hero's Ballad* and *Concerto for Orchestra*.

JAZZ
Jazz has been popular with amateurs and professionals since the mid-1930s, though mostly as an accompaniment to dancing. A pioneer of dance jazz was pianist, composer, singer, publisher and eventually bandleader RA Dvorský. Other star bands have included EF Burian's Červené sedmy, the Ježkův Orchestr, Gramoklub and the Karla Vlacha Orchestr.

After WWII Czech musicians were at the forefront of European jazz, but this came to an end with the 1948 communist putsch. Restrictions were gradually lifted in the 1960s. One of the top bands was the SH Quintet,

The Unbearable Lightness of Being is Kundera's most popular work, with a faithful following from Goa to Khao San Road to Berkeley. The book explores unfaithfulness, truth and the impossibility of ever knowing if we've lived a worthwhile life while never getting bogged down in unreadable sophistry.

The Taste of Power by Ladislav Mňačko is a powerful novel delving into the depths of corruption, particularly of ideals, after the communist takeover of Czechoslovakia.

though it only played for three years at Prague's Reduta Club (p143), the first Czech professional jazz club. Another group was the Junior Trio, with Jan Hamr and the brothers Miroslav and Allan Vitouš, who all escaped to the USA after 1968. Jan Hamr (keyboards) became prominent in 1970s American jazz-rock as Jan Hammer, and even received a Grammy for the *Hawaii Five-O* theme. Miroslav Vitouš (bass) also rose to fame in several American jazz-rock groups.

One of the most outstanding musicians in today's jazz scene is Jiří Stivín who in the 1970s produced two excellent albums with the band System Tandem and is regarded as the most original European jazz musician. Another is Milan Svoboda, who, despite being a good pianist, is best known for his conducting abilities. Jazz is a mainstay of the tourist entertainment scene in Prague, and while a lot of it is easy listening dross, there are some real diamonds among the gravel – keep an ear out.

The popularity of jazz in Slovakia comes nowhere near to that of its larger neighbour. It's development began later, in the 1950s, though the only outstanding band to emerge at this time was Traditional Jazz Studio, led by P Smetáček. Its boom was short-lived, as rock and roll took over as popular entertainment. Some good jazz bands did appear in the 1960s, among them the Traditional Club Bratislava, Combo 4, the Bratislava Jazz Quartet and Medik Quintet. You'll see plenty of 'Jazz Cafes' throughout the country but quite often the only connection they'll have to jazz is their name.

ROCK & POP

Rock was banned by the communist authorities because of its Western 'corrupting influence'. Pop music was allowed, but mainly harmless local clones of Western groups like ABBA. Rock found fans among political dissidents like Václav Havel, but remained an underground movement with a handful of bands playing to small audiences in obscure pubs and country houses. Raids and arrests were common. The Plastic People of the Universe gained international fame by being imprisoned after a 1970s show trial intended to discourage underground music. The tactic was successful only temporarily and by the mid-1980s there was a lively underground scene.

Today, some of these bands, such as The Plastic People, Psí vojáci and Tony Ducháček & Garage, have re-formed and are worth seeing live as their music is very Czech. The largest communist-era punk and underground music scene was in Teplice, in northern Bohemia; the grim, heavily polluted, industrial north seemed a perfect setting for such music.

An unavoidable part of the modern Czech music scene is a strong nostalgia for the 1980s and '90s (and not necessarily the hits of those decades). Popular radio stations play a syrupy mix of Bryan Adams, early Kylie Minogue, Racy and Roxette, and many local artists have been caught up in the insanity: while it seems impossible that anyone would want to make a Czech-language cover of the Pointer Sisters' 'I'm so Excited' or Sheena Easton's 'Morning Train', they did; what's more, people bought these singles by the truckload.

When the hilarious kitsch value of the pop scene wears thin, there are plenty of quality local acts to turn to. Veterans of the scene Support Lesbiens were once a hard-rock outfit but these days are producing catchy dance-pop; diva Lucie Bílá is another mainstay. Rockers Lucie (no relation) are a little Faith No More, Chinaski and MIG21 are performing fun, sometimes pretty, post-punk pop, three-piece Jolly Jester and the Plastic Beatles of the Universe pump out irresistible rap-funk-metal hybrids and

Metamorphosis by Franz Kafka is the story of a young Prague man who awakes to find he's become an insect. This one of Kafka's best-loved (if loved is the right word) novels. The brevity of this book makes it a good introduction to his work – you might make it to the end without wanting to kill yourself.

Ordinary people brace themselves for small acts that add up to heroism in the face of horror in *Closely Watched Trains* by Bohumil Hrabal, a beautifully told story of Czech partisans in WWII.

Božena Němcová is loved as much for her ground-breaking views on women's rights as her literature. Němcová's main work *Babička* is an impressionistic study of Czech folk tradition and the importance of knowing your roots.

Monkey Business are all funk (and worth seeing live). Czechs are also churning out quality dance music and metal.

The Slovak modern music scene is small but slowly coming of age; the biggest problems facing musicians these days is the lack of performance venues and a desire to churn out tacky '80s covers. One of the longest-established pop artists is Singer Paľo Habera, who gained popularity with his former band Team. Elán is another well-known pop band that's been around for years. Bands to look out for from the 21st century include creatively named No Name, Peha and female vocalist Jana Kirschner.

Drum 'n' bass has made significant inroads into Slovakia's dance scene, and the country has produced a couple of world-class DJs. Galagha & Gabanna were the first on the decks back in 1995 and are still going strong. Newcomer Larry+ is another name to look out for.

Literature

The giants of Czech literature – that is, the only Czech authors you're likely to have heard of – are Franz Kafka, whose bleakly paranoid works were made just before WWII, and Milan Kundera, an expat Czech living in Paris who hit the big time in the 1980s with *The Unbearable Lightness of Being*. With icons like these, it's no wonder most people think of Czech writers as dark, mystical, otherworldly, philosophical and obsessed with sex. Since the collapse of communism, however, a new breed of Czech writers has been flexing their wings – oppression and the legacy of history are still major themes, but these days you'll be reading more about SMSing and less about the labyrinths of bureaucracy. But don't worry: there's still plenty of sex.

A solid Czech literature didn't really get underway until the 14th century, when the *Legendy sv Kateřiny* (Legends of St Catherine) were written. Later Hussitism introduced a new kind of literature, starting with religious tracts such as Jan Hus' *De orthographia Bohemica* (The Bohemian Orthography) and continuing along revolutionary lines with anti-Catholic hymns, poems and chronicles.

Prose in the 16th and 17th centuries took up themes of humanism, morality, chronicles, daily life, travel and poetry. Two good pieces of the times are the *Kosmografie* of Zikmund z Půchova, and the Hussite *Kralická bible* (Kralice Bible). After 1620 the Czech language pretty much died as a written art form. The best-known author-in-exile was Jan Ámos Komenský (known in the West as Comenius), who wrote in Czech and Latin on education and theology.

The frustration of Czech scholars unearthing their own history in an alien tongue, usually German, was one factor in reviving the Czech language: Josef Dobrovský and Josef Jungmann separately developed a Czech literary language closer to the vernacular, while František Palacký wrote a seminal history of Bohemia and Moravia in Czech.

Possibly the greatest of all Czech poets, Karel Hynek Mácha was a leading romanticist of the early 19th century; his most famous work, *Máj* (May), came to symbolise the spring of the new movement, though when it was published it was derided as 'un-Czech' and nihilist.

Romantic views of traditional Slav life took hold in the mid-19th century with some outstanding pieces on country life: Božena Němcová's *Babička* and Karel Erben's *Kytice*.

Czech history was a great source of inspiration for world-renowned poet Jan Neruda, as well as for Alois Jirásek at the end of the 19th century. Nationalist Jirásek reinterpreted Czech legends from the arrival of Czechs in Bohemia to the Middle Ages, and wrote nationalist historical novels, his best being *Temno* (Darkness).

Bringing up Girls in Bohemia by Michal Viewegh is a snapshot of modern Prague and the joys and trials of capitalism – the mafia, sex, millionaires and expats in one very funny package.

The Book of Laughter & Forgetting by Milan Kundera is one of the author's better books, mingling bites of philosophy with sex and humour into a very entertaining and thought-provoking package.

The slender novel *Utz* by Bruce Chatwin looks back on the life of a Prague ceramics collector, recently dead, and is a sharp and charming insight into Czech life.

Though he wrote in German, one of Bohemia's greatest writers – and certainly the best-known and most-marketed today – was Franz Kafka who, with a circle of other German-speaking Jewish writers in Prague, played a major role in the literary scene at the beginning of the 20th century.

After WWI, Jaroslav Hašek devoted himself to taking the piss out of the Hapsburg empire and its minions – itinerant and impoverished, he wrote *The Good Soldier Švejk*, a rambling, hysterical study of one Czech soldier during WWI (this book is a great read and we highly recommend it – it's laugh-out-loud-in-public-places stuff). In the years between the two world wars, Karel Čapek was probably the best-known author; his science fiction works included *Rossum's Universal Robots* (from which the word 'robot' entered the English language). Poets of the time included Jaroslav Seifert (awarded the Nobel Prize for Literature in 1984) and Vítěslav Nezval.

The 1960s liberalisation of socialism encouraged a resurgence in Czech literature. Writers like Josef Škvorecký, Milan Kundera, Bohumil Hrabal, Ivan Klíma, Věra Linhartová, Zdena Salivarová and many others drafted their first masterpieces during the years of liberalisation (before 1968). After the Warsaw Pact invasion of that year some left, while others stayed and wrote for the underground *(samizdat)* press, or had their manuscripts smuggled to the West.

Škvorecký and Kundera, writing mainly about communist oppression in Czechoslovakia, became widely known in translation. Kundera is commercially the best-known writer with one of his novels, *The Unbearable Lightness of Being*, having been made into a film. Other figures were the philosopher Jan Patočka, the poet Jiří Kolář, and, of course, the playwright Václav Havel. Since the end of communism, young writers like Iva Pekarkova and Michal Viewegh have been writing about modern life in the Czech Republic.

Slovaks had no literary language until 1790, when Anton Bernolák published his *Slovak Grammar*, followed in 1827 by a Slovak dictionary; early landmarks in the gathering Slovak National Revival. Two writers quick on the uptake were Jozef Bajza, whose novel *René* was the first published in the new language, and Ján Holý, who wrote several epics about national heroes, as well as lyrics and poems.

The 19th-century nationalist and linguist Ľudovít Štúr took Bernolák's work one step further in 1845 by creating a grammar based on central Slovak dialects, and it is not surprising that writers of this era produced romantic fiction with a 'folk' flavour. One of the first works from the 'Štúr generation' was the stylish *Marína*, by Andrej Sládkovič, but the towering figure of the time was the Pan-Slavic poet and hero of the 1848 revolution Janko Kráľ, who barely escaped execution by the Hungarians.

The Austro-Hungarian monarchy continued to oppress the Slovaks through the elimination of Slovak-language secondary education, and it was through literature that Slovaks fought back for political and national rights. Poetry was their strongest suit. Slovakia's best-loved poet at the turn of the 20th century was Pavol O Hviezdoslav, whose works have been translated into several foreign languages. Other outstanding poets of the era were Svetozár H Vajanský, who was preoccupied with the links between the Slovak and Russian nations, and Ivan Krasko, whose *Verše* (Verses) is regarded as one of the masterpieces of Slovak literature.

Post-WWI, Slovak literary giants include Petr Jilemnický, whose immense leftist, and visionary *Kronika* (Chronicle), describes the Slovak National Uprising (SNP), and Dominik Tatrka, who wrote in surrealist prose, the only Slovak writer to do so.

While Michael Chabon is not a Czech, his recent story of a Prague Jew who leaves his home and family at the beginning of WWII in *The Amazing Adventures of Kavalier & Clay* has some gorgeous evocations of Prague's Jewish Quarter, with grim insights into the psychological damage of the Holocaust.

Year of the Frog by Martin Šimečka is the story of a young intellectual living in Bratislava during the communist era, who can only work menial jobs because he is barred from college due to his family's antigovernment attitudes.

Kruté Radosti (2003) by Juraj Nvota is a comedy of unwanted family reunions and love set in small-town Slovakia in 1993.

Cinema

Czech cinematography began in the 1850s, when JE Purkyněv cobbled together some basic animated films. The first internationally popular film was *Stavitel chrámů* (The Cathedral Builder, 1919), directed by Karel Degl and Antonín Novotný. In 1921 an American-Czechoslovak co-production of *Jánošík*, about the legendary, 17th-century Slovak 'Robin Hood', produced two versions: a domestic version showing his execution, and an American one with the hero escaping and living happily ever after.

In the 1930s many films were produced at the newly built Barrandov studios in Prague; these studios are still running. The first film ever to show full frontal nudity, *Extaze* (Ecstasy), was directed by Gustaf Machatý in 1932. A hit (and a scandal) at the 1934 Venice Festival, even the pope objected to its screening in Venice. Revealing all was one Hedvige Kiesler, who went on to Hollywood fame as Hedy Lamarr. Another Czech, Hugo Haas, directed an excellent adaptation of Karel Čapek's anti-Nazi, science-fiction novel *Bílá smrt* (White Death, 1937) before finding fame in Hollywood. Two stars of Czech comedy between the two world wars, Voskovec and Werich, also produced some well-known films.

Three outstanding films were made in the second half of the 1940s. *Předtucha* (Premonition, 1947) and *Krakatit* (1948), both by Otakar Vávra, and Alfréd Radok's *Daleká cesta* (The Long Journey, 1949), which used radically new lighting and camera work. The latter dealt with the deportation of Jews to concentration camps.

The 'New Wave' of Czech cinema began in 1963, but ended five short years later with the Soviet-led invasion. It was from the early 1960s onwards that Czech films began to win international awards. The young directors of the time escaped censorship because they were among the first graduates of the Academy of Film under communist rule, and therefore assumed to be ideologically 'clean'.

Among the earliest and best were *Černý Petr* (Black Peter, 1963; the American version was called Peter & Paula) and *Lásky jedné plavovlásky* (Loves of a Blonde, 1965) by Miloš Forman, who fled following the Soviet invasion, later to become a successful Hollywood director with films like *One Flew Over the Cuckoo's Nest*, *Amadeus* (filmed in Prague) and *The People vs Larry Flint*.

Films critical of the post-invasion regime were made during 1969 and 1970, but were promptly banned from public screening. The most outstanding of these were the morbid *Spalovač mrtvol* (The Cremator of Corpses) by Juraj Herz, *Žert* (The Joke) by Jaromil Jireš, the gloomy *Ucho* (The Ear) by Karel Kachyňa and *Nahota* (Nakedness) by Václav Matějka. Probably the best among the films of the next two communist decades was the comedy *Vesničko má středisková* (My Sweet Little Village, 1985) by Jiří Menzel, a subtle look at the workings and failings of socialism in a village cooperative.

One of the greatest Czech exports is the animated work of Jan Švankmajer: his creepy *Alice* (1988) is a masterpiece. You can also watch *The Cabinet of Jan Švankmajer* (1984), a tribute to the filmmaker made by underground American animators, the Quay Brothers.

Director Jan Svěrák and his screenwriting brother Zdeněk are among the biggest names of modern Czech cinema: their 1994 hit *Akumulátor* was the most expensive Czech film produced at the time. In 1996 it was surpassed at the box office by the internationally acclaimed *Kolja* ('Kolya' in English), another of Svěráks' works, which managed to score the two big film prizes of 1997: the best foreign film award at the Cannes Film Festival and at the US Academy Awards. Věra Chytilová also continues

A big hit in the Czech Republic, *Samotáři* (2000) by David Ondříček quirkily tells the story of young Czechs looking for love and money.

Obchod na korze (1965) by Ján Kadár & Elmar Klos is a moving film depicting the life of Jews in Slovakia under Nazi occupation.

German-made *Swimming Pool* (2001) by Boris von Sychowski is an unintentionally funny teen-slasher flick, in the *Scream* genre, set at a party at Prague's biggest swimming pool.

Pásla kone na betóne (1983) by Štefan Uher is a warm-hearted and amusing tale of the trials and tribulations of single motherhood in an East Slovak village.

to produce good films and win prizes at film festivals. *Samotáři* (released in 2000) by the director David Ondříček centres on a group of people trying to find love in the 1990s.

Prague itself has become a major star in big-budget Hollywood films: *Amadeus* was shot here, as were Stephen Soderbergh's *Kafka*, Barbara Streisand's *Yentl*, as well as *Mission Impossible* and the Jackie Chan vehicle, *Shanghai Knights*, where Prague stood in for Victorian London.

The Czech film industry is by no means a powerhouse, and only a handful of Czech-language movies are box office successes in their home country. There is almost no funding for cinema in the Czech Republic, and most directors make their money from commercials, using that to fund their films. Average budgets are under $1 million and few movies make a profit. Most Czech cinemas screen Hollywood movies in English with Czech subtitles; Czech TV reflects the same ethos, with American shows dubbed into Czech rating alongside locally made products. Successful Czech films tend to be arty, romantic pieces, and are often historic or nationalistic. Some of the best Czech television is made for children: the hugely successful *Krtek* (Little Mole) is a cartoon following the peaceful adventures of, you guessed it, a little mole (Czech cartoons like to emphasise cooperation and innovation rather than violence). Cartoons are presented every night on TV (and have been since 1968) by one of Czech television's most charming characters, the animated storyteller *Večerníček*, drawn by Radek Pilar.

Dušan Hanák and Dušan Dušek directed *Ruzové sny* (1977), a love story of a Roma girl and Slovak boy, and the unmovable differences separating their communities.

One of the earliest Slovak films made was a cops and robbers flick entitled *Siciliána*, directed by Imrich Darányi. Few Slovak films were made before WWII, but cinematography saw a real evolution after the war, typified by the light-hearted and ever-popular *Cathy* (1949), by Ján Kádar. In 1953 Koliba, Slovakia's first film studio, opened in Bratislava, creating a backbone for Slovak cinema for years to come.

The 1960s heralded a Slovak film movement known as 'New Wave'. Director Ján Kádar forged ahead with *Smrt si říká Engelchen* (Death Calls Itself Engelchen, 1963) and teamed up with Elmar Klos to produce *Obchod na korze* (The Shop on Main Street, 1965), which won an Oscar. Martin Holly was another renowned director who won international acclaim with his expressive *Ballad of Seven Hanged Men* (1969).

The '70s introduced Dušan Hanák and Dušan Dušek and their stark, gritty, and powerful documentaries and films to Slovak cinema. Quite often their films were banned during the communist years, but their popularity remained strong. Slovakia's best loved director is Juraj Jakubisko, whose films reflect and comment on life in Slovakia. His *Sedím na konári a je mi dobre* (I'm Sitting on a Branch and I'm Fine, 1989), *Tisicrôčna včela* (Millennial Bee, 1983) and *Vtáckovia, siroty a blázni* (Little Birds, Orphans and Fools, 1969) are timeless classics.

The film *Divided we Fall* (2000) by Jan Hrebejk is a compelling tale of a Czech couple trying to ignore WWII, who end up hiding a Jewish friend for three years.

Recent years have seen success and failure in Slovak cinema, with six feature films premiering in 2002, the most since the Velvet Divorce, and Koliba studios closing its doors for the last time amid dubious privatisation deals and asset stripping. Funding is at a minimum, and many films are made outside Slovakia. Hollywood is, however, once again discovering Slovakia's potential as a filming location; spooky Orava Castle (p75) appeared in the seminal vampire chiller *Nosferatu* way back in 1922, and recent films *Dragonheart* (1996), *Ravenous* (1999) and *Behind Enemy Lines* (2001) used Slovakia's natural beauty as a backdrop.

Theatre

Czech-language theatre did not develop fully until the 16th century. Themes, mostly biblical, were used to make comparisons between contemporary and biblical times. At Prague's Charles University, drama was performed in Latin and also used as a form of teaching. The best plays, known as *schola ludus* (school games), were written in the 17th century by the expat educator Comenius, who fled Bohemia after the Battle of White Mountain (see p21).

In 1785 Czech reappeared at the Nostické (now Stavoské or Estates) Theatre, and Prague became a centre for Czech-language theatre. Major 19th-century playwrights included Josef Kajetán Tyl and Ján Kolár. Drama, historical plays and fairy tales contributed to the Czech National Revival, with the first professional companies appearing in Prague and Brno.

Nonetheless, no venues specifically for independent Czech-language theatre existed until 1862, when the Prozatimní divadlo (Temporary Theatre) opened in Prague, closely followed by imitators. The first permanent Czech theatre was opened in 1883 in Prague.

In the early years of the First Republic the leading lights among playwrights were the novelist Karel Čapek and the brilliant František Langer. The comedy duo of Voskovec & Werich (or V&W, as they were known), at the Osvobozené divadlo (Liberated Theatre) in Prague, produced some of the best theatre during the 1930s – you can still rent their films today if you speak Czech. Actor and playwright EF Burian was known for experimental drama.

During the communist years, classical theatre was of a high quality, but the modern scene was stifled. Exceptions included the excellent mime/puppetry/multimedia of the Black Theatre (Černé divadlo), and the pioneering *Laterna Magika* by Alfréd Radok; these are now mainstays of tourist Prague, and you can barely move in the Golden City without stumbling over a Black Light Theatre.

Some excellent plays, including those by Václav Havel, went unperformed locally because of their antigovernment viewpoint, but appeared in the West. In the mid-1960s, free expression was explored in Prague's divadlo na Zábradlí (Theatre on the Balustrade), with works by Ladislav Fialka, Havel, and Milan Uhde, and by the comedy duo of Jiří Suchý and Jiří Šlitr. Suchý is still performing today and has a successful show.

MARIONETTE & PUPPET THEATRE

Marionette plays have been popular since the 16th century, and puppet plays since before that. This form peaked in the 17th and early 18th centuries. A legendary figure was Matěj Kopecký (1775–1847), who performed original pieces. The composer Bedřich Smetana also wrote plays for marionettes.

Marionette theatre for adults was revived in the 20th century, when theatres opened in Prague and Plzeň. Plzeň's Feriálních osad Theatre was the home of Josef Skupa's legendary puppets Špejbl & Hurvínek, who still perform in Prague; replicas of the little chaps can be seen in tourist shops all over the country. Even under communism, puppet and marionette theatre was officially approved of and popular, and Czech performances ranked among the best in the world.

Sedím na koňári a je mi dobre (I'm Sitting on a Branch and I'm Fine; 1989) by Juraj Jakubisko is an excellent but bizarre tale of life in Slovakia after the WWII, involving stolen gold, murder, bad luck and tree climbing.

The film *Černý Petr* (1963) by Miloš Forman shows a funny day in the life of Czech teenager trying to hold down a job and deal with his family.

Kolya (1996) by Jan Svěrák is the winner of an Academy Award. It is a slightly sugary story about a confirmed Czech bachelor saddled with a small Russian child on the eve of the Velvet Revolution.

Environment

THE LAND

The 78,864 sq km of the Czech Republic, squeezed between Germany, Austria, Slovakia and Poland, is made up of Bohemia in the west and Moravia in the east.

Roughly speaking, Bohemia is a 500m-high plateau surrounded by low mountains, forming a basin drained by the Labe (upper Elbe) river and its tributary, the Vltava (Moldau), the republic's longest river at 430km. Encircling Bohemia is a natural barrier of mountains. Along the German border are the Šumava in the southwest, the Český les (Bohemian Forest) in the west and the Krušné hory (Ore Mountains) in the northwest. At the Polish border rise the impressive Krkonoše (Giant Mountains), which contain the republic's highest peak, Sněžka (1602m). South Bohemia's most unusual landscape is the Třeboňsko, a region of broad fields that consists of a network of hundreds of linked fish-ponds and artificial lakes. The biggest dam in the republic, the 4870-hectare Lipno, is also in South Bohemia. East Bohemia is home to the striking 'rock towns' of Český ráj and Adršpach-Teplice Rocks.

Moravia is mostly lowlands, drained by the river Morava flowing south to the Danube, and by the Odra (Oder), which rounds the eastern end of the Sudeten Range into Poland. While Moravia is generally flat, it does have a few mountains, namely Bílé Karpaty (White Carpathians) and Javorníky in the east, and Beskydy and Jeseníky in the north. The 120-sq-km Moravian Karst north of Brno features limestone caves and subterranean lakes.

Almost 80% of Slovakia's 49,035 sq km is over 750m above sea level. Bordered by Austria, Hungary, the Ukraine, Poland and the Czech Republic, it sits on the western end of the great Carpathian mountain chain that arcs up through Romania and the western Ukraine.

Much of Slovakia is steep, forested mountains, and these are probably its most endearing feature. Best known are two parallel branches of the western Carpathians: the High Tatras (Vysoké Tatry), rising to about 2500m and spilling over into Poland, and the Low Tatras (Nízke Tatry), reaching about 2000m in Central (and bits of Eastern) Slovakia. The republic's highest peak, the 2654m Gerlachovský štít, is in the High Tatras. Outdoor enthusiasts also frequent two subsidiary ranges of the Tatras, the Malá Fatra and Veľká Fatra. Slovakia faces the Czech Republic across mountains as well: the modest White Carpathians (Bílé Karpaty) and Javorníky.

At the eastern end of the Low Tatras is the Slovenský raj (Slovak Paradise), a karst (limestone) region popular with hikers. South of the Low Tatras is a third Carpathian branch, the lesser known Slovenské rudohorie (Slovak Ore Mountains). Several thousand limestone caves dot much of Central Slovakia, of which only a handful are open to the public.

The main exception to all this high relief is the southwestern lowland region, which is also Slovakia's main agricultural area. The Danube (Dunaj) and two tributaries form much of the area's boundary with Hungary, and the Váh, Slovakia's longest river at 433km, joins the Danube here. Slovakia's largest natural lake is the 217.9-hectare Velké Hincovo in the High Tatras. Its biggest dam is the 3501-hectare Orava, west of the High Tatras near the Polish border.

The Czech Republic probably developed an industrial base due to its general flatness, while Slovakia's hilly landscape was more suited to farming. The Czech Republic's population is evenly distributed (outside

DID YOU KNOW?

The Czech Republic is a landlocked country about one-third the size of the UK. Slovakia is approximately half the size of Portugal.

DID YOU KNOW?

The largest meteor to hit Europe landed near the small town of Zboj in East Slovakia in 1866; its flight could be seen from the High Tatras, about 200km away.

DID YOU KNOW?

The Ochinská Aragonite Cave in East Slovakia is one of only three such caves in the world containing aragonite formations. Aragonite formations are hollow – normally stalactites and stalagmites are solid.

the crowd-puller Prague of course) while Slovakia's population is concentrated on its flat lands, such as Bratislava, West Slovakia, and Košice and the surrounding area in East Slovakia.

WILDLIFE

Even though there is a plethora of plant and animal life in the Czech and Slovak Republics, wildlife-watching is not a huge tourist drawcard. This is due mainly to the republics' natural features; steep alpine mountains don't make life easy for amateur animal spotters and densely forested hills provide perfect cover for many species. The flood plains of the Danube river in West Slovakia, however, are an excellent region for bird-watching, particularly during the migration periods of spring and autumn.

As for animal dangers, there's not much to speak of; Slovakia witnesses the occasional bear attack, but that's about it. Bears, wolves and lynxes freely roam the bigger national parks and protected areas in Slovakia, but a pile of excrement is the closest you'll come to them and, quite frankly, that's as close as you'd want to.

The Slovak Wildlife Society is a nonprofit organisation supporting and promoting the long-term survival of endangered species. Find out more at www.slovakwildlife.org.uk.

Animals

The most common types of wildlife in the Czech mountains are marmots (giant ground squirrels), otters, martens (weasel-like carnivores) and mink. In the woods and fields there are pheasants, partridges, deer, ducks and wild geese. Rarer are lynxes, eagles, vultures, osprey (large, long-winged hawks), storks, bustards and grouse. Very occasionally, wolves and brown bears wander across the Carpathian mountains into eastern Moravia.

Slovakia's most diverse wildlife area – home to brown bears, wolves, lynxes and other wild cats, marmots, otters, golden eagles and mink – is the High Tatras, and most of these animals are protected from hunting within the Tatra National Park. One animal protected even outside national parks is the chamois, a mountain antelope, which was for a time near extinction but is now making a comeback. Deer, pheasants, partridges, ducks, wild geese, storks, grouse, eagles and vultures can be seen throughout the countryside. Europe's largest bird – the dropie – makes its home on the Danube flood plains.

Plants

Despite centuries of clear-felling for cultivation, forests – mainly oak, beech and spruce – still cover about one-third of the Czech Republic. Dwarf pine is common near the tree line (1400m). Above it there is little but grasses, shrubs and lichens.

Most remaining virgin forest is in inaccessible mountain areas. Over half of the high-altitude forest in Northern Bohemia – especially in the Krušné hory, Jizerské hory and Krkonoše mountains – has been killed or blighted by acid rain from unregulated industrial development.

Forests still cover 40% of Slovakia despite centuries of deforestation and the effects of acid rain. Low-lying areas (up to 800m) are populated by oak and beech, mid-range (700–1500m) with fir and spruce, and upper alpine (above 1500m) dotted with dwarf pine.

www.nature.cz is the website of the Agency for Nature Conservation and Landscape Protection, listing its offices around the Czech Republic.

NATIONAL PARKS

Though national and local authorities have set aside numerous national parks and protected landscape areas, the emphasis is on visitor use as well as species protection.

National parks and protected areas make up approximately 15% of the Czech Republic and 20% of Slovakia. Their diverse landscapes and

CZECH REPUBLIC NATIONAL PARKS & NOTABLE PROTECTED LANDSCAPES

Park	Features	Activities	Best time to visit	Page
Šumava National Park (685 sq km)	gentle rolling hills & pristine forest: lynxes, deer, grouse	hiking, cycling, skiing	year-round	(p226)
Krkonoše National Park (363 sq km)	rounded, alpine mountains: boar, deer, badgers, foxes, martens, buzzards, hawks, eagles	hiking, skiing	year-round	(p265)
Czech Switzerland National Park	sandstone rocks & rich forest	hiking, cycling, rock climbing	May-Sep	(p178)
Podyjí National Park (63 sq km)	river valleys and gentle pastures: otters, bats, fire salamanders, buzzards, eagle-owls	hiking, cycling	May-Sep	
Bohemian Paradise Protected Landscape (92 sq km)	sandstone rock formations & wetlands	hiking, rock climbing	May-Sep	(p257)
Adršpach-Teplice Rocks Protected Landscape (20 sq km)	mesmerising sandstone pinnacles & caves	hiking, rock climbing	May-Sep	(p262)

SLOVAKIA NATIONAL PARKS & NOTABLE PROTECTED LANDSCAPES

Park	Features	Activities	Best time to visit	Page
Tatra National Park (795 sq km)	pristine mountains: deer, boar, foxes, lynxes, otters, golden eagles	hiking, cycling, skiing, rock climbing	year-round	(p389)
Pieniny National Park (21 sq km)	steep gorge & gentle river: lynxes, otters, black storks, owls, woodpeckers	hiking, cycling, rafting	May-Sep	(p417)
Low Tatras National Park (810 sq km)	dense forest & alpine meadows: brown bears, wolves, deer, foxes, golden eagles	hiking, cycling, skiing, rock climbing	year-round	(p382)
Slovak Paradise National Park (197 sq km)	waterfalls & stunning gorges: brown bears, wolves, lynxes, martens, golden eagles, deer, chamois	hiking, cycling, caving	May-Sep	(p408)
Malá Fatra National Park (226 sq km)	steep alpine pastures: golden eagles, deer, bears	hiking, cycling, skiing	year-round	(p376)
Poloniny National Park (668 sq km)	dense forest, rugged hills & mountain meadows: wolves, lynxes, wild cats, golden eagles	hiking, cycling	May-Sep	(p426)
Veľká Fatra Protected Area (403 sq km)	subalpine meadows & grassy uplands: brown bears, lynxes, boar, deer, golden eagles	hiking, cycling, skiing	year-round	(p373)
Slovak Karst Protected Landscape Region (440 sq km)	gentle hills & a plethora of caves: brown bears, wolves, lynxes, deer, otters, bats, common vipers	hiking, cycling, caving	May-Sep	(p418)
Muránska Plain National Park (219 sq km)	dense woodlands, deep chasms & unexplored caves: brown bears, wolves, lynxes, deer, hucul mountain horses	hiking, cycling	May-Sep	

easy accessibility make them popular with both locals and tourists. Out of the four national parks in the Czech Republic, Šumava and Krkonoše win the popularity race hands down; both are well-known winter ski resorts and summer hiking areas. Of the seven national parks in Slovakia, the High Tatras and the Slovak Paradise are the most frequented; the former has the highest hiking trails of the republics while the latter is crisscrossed by gentler, flatter paths, suitable for families and weekend outings.

ENVIRONMENTAL ISSUES

While much of the Czech Republic consists of gentle rolling hills dotted with picturesque towns and villages, parts of it rank among the most polluted in Europe. Problems started with the Industrial Revolution, but it was the single-minded, industrial-development policies of successive communist governments that really screwed things up.

Forests have suffered under constant acid rainfalls, particularly in North Bohemia. In parts of the eastern Krušné hory, most trees are dead or totally defoliated, and conifers in the Krkonoše mountains are stricken by airborne pollutants blown in from Polish Silesia. The country is also littered with hundreds of brownfields – polluted or abandoned industrial or military sites – which the government and private investors are reluctant to clean up, opting instead to develop new sites and expand the urban sprawl. The floods of 2002 caused major damage to towns and cities as well; Greenpeace believes that all kinds of toxins from Prague, which was severely hit, were washed into the Vltava.

Temelín, one of two nuclear plants in the Czech Republic, commenced operations in 2000 but things have not exactly gone to plan. The year 2002 saw a swathe of shutdowns due to faulty valves and sensors, and a pipe being welded on incorrectly (it was out by 180 degrees). While radiation leaks have yet to be reported, environmental agencies think it is only a matter of time. Dukovany, the nation's second plant, is situated in South Moravia and has been in operation since 1985.

Most power, however, comes from coal-burning power plants. In the early 1990s, Czechs experimented with alternative energy sources such as solar and wind power, but due to a lack of government initiative only 12 wind farms survived. The Czech Society for Wind Energy believes the country could sustain up to 1100 such farms.

Things are improving though. Currently industry emits some 1,400,000 tonnes of sulphur annually, mainly from the burning of low-grade brown coal, but is now mostly controlled by filtered chimneys. In many cities the burning of coal for household heating has been replaced by natural gas, thus pollution levels have decreased significantly. Labe river, where in the past there were no fish and nobody dared to swim, now has a replenished fish stock, and beavers and people are once again fighting for water space.

Compared to the Czech Republic, Slovakia is less industrialised and consequently has not been as badly damaged by pollution; overall, its rivers and forests are in far better shape than the Czech Republic's. That said, Slovakia's larger towns suffer from air pollution, Bratislava and Košice especially, but also Banská Bystrica, Žilina and Trenčín.

Slovakia's first nuclear power station was built in the 1970s at Jaslovské Bohunice, near Trnava, and is scheduled for decommissioning in 2006–08. A controversial second plant at Mochovce, east of Nitra, currently operates three of its four reactors and like Temelín has experienced a spat of shutdowns due to malfunctioning equipment. The government is in

The Regional Environmental Centre for Central and Eastern Europe website www.rec.org has a mountain of environmental information on the Czech and Slovak Republics, including Non-Government Organisations (NGOs) and environmental agency contact details.

DID YOU KNOW?

A worker in the Czech Republic in the 1980s received a labour medal for saving electricity. His secret? He figured that since no-one sees factory smoke at night, the trick was to operate the plant's smokestack filters only during the day. *Not* very environmentally friendly.

the throes of selling up to 50% of the state-owned power assets, which could mean both nuclear power plants may end up in private hands.

Slovakia has been slow in tapping into its renewable energy resources. The first wind farm opened in 2003, but only with the help of EU funding, and solar panels are still a thing of the future. The Gabčíkovo hydroelectric project, on the Danube west of Komárno, became very controversial after Hungary backed out of the joint project in 1989 because of environmental considerations. Even today the dam causes debate; experts still can't decide whether it helped or hindered the amount of damage suffered during the disastrous floods of 2002. Gabčíkovo produces enough electricity to cover the needs of every home in Slovakia and its canal allows the largest river vessels to reach Bratislava year-round.

For information on environmental projects throughout Slovakia, visit the Slovak Environmental Agency at www.sazp.sk

Outdoor Activities

The republics, with their undulating landscapes and central European climate, are perfect for outdoor activities year-round. As soon as the snow melts, people are ploughing along mountain trails, traversing steep gorges, zipping along cycle paths, rolling over river rapids and floating peacefully on lakes. And just as the last of the autumn rays dip below the horizon, skiers and snowboarders are out carving up the slopes.

HIKING

With a network of some 48,000km of well-marked and very well-connected hiking trails, the Czech and Slovak Republics are brilliantly equipped for walking or tramping *(trampování/trampovanie* or *turistika)*. The way-marked, colour-coded trails – the first established near Banská Štiavnica in 1874 – are maintained by the volunteers of the **Czech Hiking Club** (Klub českých turistů; ☎ 235 514 529; kct@klubturistu.cz; Archeologická 2256, Prague 5) and **Slovak Hiking Club** (Klub slovenských turistov; ☎ 02-49 24 92 23; kst@kst.sk; Junácka 6, Bratislava) and are clearly marked on a range of great hiking maps (see p57). There are hikes to suit every taste, from one or two hours to one or two months.

Many trailheads link up with train stations and bus stops, making access to starting and finishing points straightforward. Camp sites, *chaty* (mountain huts) and *horský hotely* (mountain hotels) are conveniently situated along the main trails. Note that camping is restricted to designated camp sites and open fires are prohibited everywhere.

Walks

Slovakia has more rugged and unspoilt scenery than its neighbour, the highlight of which is the High Tatras (Vysoké Tatry; p387). Here you'll find the tallest peaks out of both countries and plenty of alpine hiking, including the Tatranská magistrála (65km), a four-day trek along the southern flank of the High Tatras between Podbanske and Tatranská Lomnica. Its southern neighbour, the Low Tatras (Nízke Tatry; p382), is no less impressive; its 80km ridge cuts through forested slopes and bare mountain passes. Some may prefer the Malá Fatra (p370), a range of mountains with great access and more greenery. The Slovak Paradise (Slovenský raj; p408) may not have alpine hiking but its trails cut through pristine gorges and dense forest, while the remote Vihorlatské Highlands (Vihorlatské vrchy) and Poloniny National Park (p426) contain meandering trails and a chance to escape the crowds.

The main long-distance route across Slovakia is the Cesta hrdinov SNP (Path of the Heroes of the Slovak National Uprising; 762km; four weeks), stretching from Devín, west of Bratislava, to Dukla, on the Polish border, and taking in the Malé Karpaty, the Nízke Tatry and the Slovenský raj.

The Czech Republic's landscapes may not be as dramatic as Slovakia's, but they're no less appealing. The gentle hills of Šumava (p226) offer the best and longest hikes; it's possible to trek the length of the range from Nová Pec, at the northern tip of Lake Lipno, up to Nýrsko, southwest of Klatovy (about 120km). The thinly forested Krkonoše mountains (p265) contain the country's highest peaks and the Czech-Polish Friendship Trail (Cesta česko-polského přátelství), a path following a border ridge. The Bohemian Paradise (Český ráj; p257) and the Sandstone Rocks of Labe (Labské pískovce; p178) are a maze of low, wooded hills and 'rock towns' while the Adršpach-Teplice Rocks (Adršpašsko-Teplické skály; p262) has rugged rock formations and dense pine forest. The Jeseníky Mountains (p277) and Beskydy hills (p281) have few foreign tourists and a plethora of trails.

Several long-distance European footpaths pass through the Czech and Slovak Republics. Route E8 runs along the southern border of the Czech Republic and on to Bratislava, then follows the Cesta hrdinov SNP to Prešov before turning south through Košice and into Hungary. Route E3 roughly follows the northern borders of the two republics, and E10 traverses the Czech Republic from north to south.

The more popular walks are detailed in the destination chapters.

Equipment

Backpacks, hiking boots and other camping gear are easy to find in shops, but campers who are particular about certain high-quality brands should

CONSIDERATIONS FOR RESPONSIBLE HIKING

The popularity of hiking is placing great pressure on wilderness areas. Please consider the following tips when hiking and help preserve the ecology and beauty of the Czech and Slovak Republics.

Rubbish

Carry out all your rubbish. If you've carried it in you can carry it out. Don't overlook those easily forgotten items, such as silver paper, orange peel, cigarette butts and plastic wrappers. Empty packaging weighs very little anyway and should be stored in a dedicated rubbish bag. Make an effort to carry out rubbish left by others.

Never bury your rubbish: digging disturbs soil and ground cover and encourages erosion. Buried rubbish will more than likely be dug up by animals, who may be injured or poisoned by it. If animals don't get to the rubbish it will probably take years to decompose, especially at high altitudes.

Minimise the waste you must carry out by taking minimal packaging and taking no more than you will need. Take reusable containers or stuff sacks (sacks or bags that you can stuff a lot of gear into).

Don't rely on bought water in plastic bottles. Disposal of these bottles is creating a major problem, particularly in developing countries. Use iodine drops or purification tablets instead.

Human Waste Disposal

Many think our ability to rationalise separates us from the animal kingdom – we beg to differ. It's our ability to use a toilet; where there is one, please use it.

Contamination of water sources by human faeces can lead to the transmission of hepatitis, typhoid and intestinal parasites, such as *Giardia*, amoebae and round worms. It can cause severe health risks not only to members of your party, but also to local residents and wildlife.

If there is no toilet, bury your waste. Dig a small hole 15cm deep and at least 100m from any watercourse. Consider carrying a lightweight trowel for this purpose. Cover the waste with soil and a rock. Use toilet paper sparingly and bury it with the waste. In snow, dig down to the soil otherwise your waste will be exposed when the snow melts.

Ensure that these guidelines are applied to a portable toilet tent if one is being used by a large hiking party. Encourage all party members to use the site.

Washing

Don't use detergents or toothpaste in or near watercourses, even if they are biodegradable. For personal washing, use biodegradable soap and a water container (or even a lightweight, portable basin) at least 50m away from the watercourse. Widely disperse the waste-water to allow the soil to filter it fully before it finally makes it back to the watercourse.

Wash cooking utensils 50m from watercourses using a scourer, sand or snow instead of detergent.

bring gear with them. Mountain weather is incredibly changeable here – even in summer freak snowstorms are possible – and warm, water-resistant clothing is essential.

Information

The best hiking maps are VKÚ's *edice Klub Českých turistů* series (1:50,000) and Kartografie Praha's *soubor turistických map* series (usually at 1:100,000) for the Czech Republic; and VKÚ's *turistická mapa* series (1:25,000 or 1:50,000) and Slovenská Kartografia's *edícia turistických map* (1:100,000) series for Slovakia. Knapsacked produces a series of detailed hiking books, in English and German, on the popular walking areas in Slovakia.

Both maps and books are generally available in bookshops throughout the republics.

Erosion

Hillsides and mountain slopes, especially at high altitudes, are prone to erosion. It is important to stick to existing tracks and avoid short cuts that bypass a switchback. If you blaze a new trail straight down a slope it will turn into a watercourse with the next heavy rainfall and eventually cause soil loss and deep scarring.

If a well-used track passes through a mud patch, walk through the mud: walking around the edge will increase the size of the patch.

Avoid removing the plant life that keeps topsoils in place.

Fires & Low Impact Cooking

Don't depend on open fires for cooking. The cutting of wood for fires in popular hiking areas can cause rapid deforestation. Cook on a light-weight kerosene, alcohol or Shellite (white gas) stove and avoid those powered by disposable butane gas canisters.

Fires may be acceptable below the tree line in areas that get very few visitors. If you light a fire, use an existing fireplace rather than create a new one. Don't surround fires with rocks as this creates a visual scar. Use only dead, fallen wood. Remember the adage 'the bigger the fool, the bigger the fire'. Use minimal wood, just what you need for cooking. In huts leave wood for the next person.

Ensure that you fully extinguish a fire after use. Spread the embers and douse them with water. A fire is only truly safe to leave when you can comfortably place your hand in it.

Wildlife Conservation

Do not engage in or encourage hunting. It is illegal in all parks and reserves.

Don't buy items made from endangered species.

Don't assume animals in huts to be introduced vermin and attempt to exterminate them. In wild places they are likely to be protected native animals.

Don't encourage the presence of wildlife by leaving food scraps behind you. Place gear out of reach of animals and tie packs to rafters or trees.

Do not feed the wildlife as this can lead to animals becoming dependent on trekker hand-outs, to unbalanced populations and to diseases such as 'lumpy jaw' (a fungal disease).

Camping & Walking on Private Property

Seek permission to camp from landowners. They will usually be happy if asked, but confrontational if not.

Park Regulations

Take note of and observe any rules and regulations particular to the national or state reserve that you are visiting.

CYCLING

One of the best ways to enjoy the Czech and Slovak Republics is from the saddle of a bike. There are over 60 clearly marked cycle paths (*cyklotrasy*) across the length and breadth of both republics, maintained by the **Slovak Cycling Club** (Slovenský Cykloklub; ☎ 033-774 05 48; sck@nextra.sk; Námestie Slobody 6; Piešťany) and the **Czech Cycling Club** (Cykloclub; info@cykloclub.cz; PO Box 83, Vizovice).

Many of Slovakia's mountainous areas are great for cycling – if you have the energy and the willpower. The Slovak Paradise (p408), High Tatras (p387), Low Tatras (p382) and Malá Fatra area (p370) all have fine, if strenuous, trails. The popular Danube cycle way (200km) may suit some cyclists better; it follows the banks of the Danube through gently undulating countryside from Bratislava to Komárno. Another well-marked trail leads from Piešťany to Žilina (250km) along the Váh river.

Some of the finest regions for riding in the Czech Republic are the foothills of the Šumava mountains (p226) in South Bohemia, Bohemian Paradise (p257), the Moravian Karst and around Znojmo, Břeclav, Hodonín and Uherské Hradiště in South Moravia (p310). The Greenways Prague–Vienna trail (456km) that passes through Jindřichův Hradec and Znojmo is excellent and if you have the time, and the stamina, it's possible to circumnavigate the entire Czech Republic by bicycle, a distance of some 1780km.

Cycle paths also link up with the Europe-wide network of trails, Euro Velo (www.eurovelo.org). Three pass through the Czech Republic: route N4 runs west–east via Prague and Brno, N7 north–south through Prague and onto Berlin, and N9 north–south via Olomouc and Brno to either Vienna or Poland. Slovakia has two trails: the N6 hugs the Danube banks on its way to the Black Sea, and N11 dissects Košice before traveling onto Warsaw to the north or Belgrade to the south.

Equipment

A mountain bike or touring bike with at least 18 gears are a good choice, since both republics are hilly. There are cycle shops and repair centres in large towns, but for rural riding you should carry all essential spare parts. Security – a lock and chain for the frame and both wheels – is essential, as bikes are popular targets for theft. Children up to 15 years of age are required to wear helmets. See p455 for information on renting and buying bikes.

Information

For online maps, in Czech mind you, try www.cykloatlas.cz.

Cycle paths are marked on hiking maps. Regional cycling maps (*cykloturistická mapa*; 1:75,000 to 1:100,000), published by SHOCart and VKÚ, are available in many bookstores; these often come with a handy booklet in English and German. The Czech Tourist Authority also publishes a special cycling brochure entitled *Cycling – Free and Easy*, in English and German, that gives details of long-distance and regional cycle routes.

Getting Around

Away from cycle tracks, stick to minor roads where possible. Motorists tend to give cyclists a wide berth, though narrow country roads are still potentially dangerous, especially at night. Like everywhere else, cycling in big cities is more of an adrenaline rush than fun.

You can take your bike on the train quite safely. The charge is usually 60% of your own fare; present your ticket at the railway luggage office and fill out a tag, to be attached to the bike, with your name, address, departure station and destination. If time is short, take it directly to the freight carriage and the conductor will load it for a small fee.

Bicycles can be transported on buses at the discretion of the driver.

ROCK CLIMBING & MOUNTAINEERING

The majority of climbing options in the Czech Republic are concentrated in North and East Bohemia. The most famous are the Sandstone Rocks of the Labe in North Bohemia, and the Adršpach-Teplice Rocks (p262) in East Bohemia. Climbing at the latter has a long history; the first route was ascended in 1914. The rock in both places is a fairly soft sandstone, which has eroded into a spectacular profusion of pinnacles, towers, walls and arêtes (a sharp ridge separating two valleys), with many routes of a very high standard. The more modest Bohemian Paradise also attracts wanna-be spidermen and women, as does the Moravian Karst in South Moravia.

The High Tatras (p387) of Central Slovakia offer summer mountaineering routes on a near-alpine scale (the main summits rise to 2600m), and serious winter climbing. Other popular areas for rock climbing include the weird rock formations in the Súľov Highlands (p375), near the town of Žilina, and the Demänova Valley (p384) in the Low Tatras.

Tourist offices in these regions have details of mountaineering clubs, otherwise contact the **Czech Mountaineering Union** (Český horolezecký svaz; ☎ 233 017 347; Atletická 100/2, Praha-Strahov) or the **Slovak Mountaineering Union** (Slovenský horolezecký spolok; ☎ 02-49 24 92 11; office@james.sk; Junácka 6, Bratislava).

There is little detailed information available in English. The climbing guide *Böhmischer Sandstein* (Bohemian Sandstein) by P Weredermann is in German, but the route topos are easily understood.

SKIING & SNOWBOARDING

The Alps it ain't, but skiing and snowboarding in the Czech and Slovak Republics is plentiful, popular and cheap; a ski pass at the top resorts will cost at most €17 per day or €95 per week, the less-frequented ski resorts can be half that price. The downhill ski areas are small, however, and during school holidays you'll be jostling with other snow-lovers for a spot on the slopes and a place in the ski-lift queues. Rental equipment is decent, but skiers who are particular about certain brands should bring their own. The season lasts from late December to early April.

The best ski area is at Jasná (p385) in Slovakia's Low Tatras where there are a dozen linked runs and chairlifts. Other good spots in Slovakia include the Štrbské Pleso and Skalnaté Pleso resorts of the High Tatras (p387) and the Vratná Valley (p377) in the Malá Fatra mountains. In the Czech Republic, the Krkonoše mountains (p265) have the best downhill skiing, at the resorts of Pec pod Sněžkou, Špindlerův Mlýn and Harrachov.

Ranges with lower peaks, gentler terrain and fine scenery are better suited to cross-country skiing and ski touring. These include the Šumava (p226) in West and South Bohemia, the Beskydy and Jeseníky (p277) of North Moravia, and the Veľká Fatra (p373) and Slovenský raj (p408) in Slovakia. VKÚ (see p57) publishes ski-touring maps *(lyžiarska a turistická mapa)* that mark cross-country trails, downhill runs, chair lifts and areas of avalanche danger. Their blue covers distinguish them from the green hiking maps.

Accommodation is available in hotels, chalets, cabins or *chaty* (mountain huts). For more information contact the local tourist office.

WATER SPORTS

Both flat-water and white-water canoeing and kayaking are very popular in the Czech and Slovak Republics, which have produced several world and Olympic champion paddlers.

The top canoe-touring rivers in the Czech Republic include the scenic, but rather polluted, Sázava, which stretches from West Moravia into Central Bohemia; the equally popular upper reaches of the Vltava (p221); and Otava

The website www.jamesak.sk /sprskalk.htm is an online guide to all the rock-climbing areas in Slovakia. It's mostly in Slovak (with a bit of German) but the topos are easy to read.

For a zillion links to clubs, climbers and mountaineering regions check the International Mountaineering and Climbing Federation's website www.uiaa.ch.

For online information, including a full list of resorts and snow reports, check out www.ski.sk and www.holidayinfo.cz; both are in English and German.

in South Bohemia and Berounka in Central and West Bohemia. In Slovakia there's the upper Váh, the swift Hornád, which stretches the narrow gorges of the Slovenský raj (permission is needed from park authorities to use it), and a 16km section of the Dunajec on the Polish border (see p417).

White-water canoeing is popular on the Labe river below Špindlerův Mlýn in the Krkonoše, and on the Vltava river below the Lipno dam in South Bohemia, where there is a famous spot known as the Devil's Currents (Čertovy proudy). The artificial slalom course *(slalomový kanál)* at the Troja weir, on the Vltava just north of Prague, is a regular venue for world championship white-water competitions, as is the Čunovo artificial channel, created by the Gabinčíkovo dam in West Slovakia.

For those in pursuit of more tranquil waters, the Czech Republic and Slovakia offer plenty of opportunities to sail, windsurf or simply splash about. Dammed sections of the Vltava river, in particular at Lipno (p231) in South Bohemia and Slapy in Central Bohemia, are perfect lakes to try your hand at windsurfing and sailing. Close to Cheb in West Bohemia are two more lakes with boat-hire facilities, Skalka and Jesenice.

Popular swimming, sailing and windsurfing spots in Slovakia include Orava Lake (p381) just west of the High Tatras, Zemplínska šírava (p426) in the Eastern Borderlands and Liptovská Mara at Liptovský Mikuláš (p382).

CAVING

For comprehensive online information on river conditions, accessibility and boat rental throughout the Czech and Slovak Republics consult Super Frog Max and his bilingual website www.raft.cz.

Both republics are honeycombed with dramatic caves, the best of which are in the Moravian Karst area (p299), north of Brno, and the Slovak Karst (p418), in East Slovakia (which includes one of the largest caves in central Europe). Another fine cave system is beneath the Demänova Valley (p384) in Central Slovakia.

In general, caving is not about climbing into a boiler suit, donning a hard hat mounted with a torch, and scrambling around in a dark place on your hands and knees getting extremely wet or dirty. It's about a gentle, albeit cold, stroll through underground caverns on a tour guide's leash. The Krásnohorská cave in the Slovak Karst, which was about to open at the time of writing, is the only cave in either republic that comes close to proper spelunking (exploration), and contains the tallest stalagmite in the world (32.6m). Otherwise try your luck with the **Speological Guide Service** (☎ 058-734 34 26; stankov@ke.psg.sk; Slovak Karst, Roznava); they may be willing to take you on an underground excursion.

FISHING

Committed boaties may be interested to hear that Czech railways organise boat transportation services during the summer months; see www.cdrail.cz for more information.

Fishing is governed by considerable restrictions, with limited seasons, trout and nontrout fishing grounds, and day, week, month and year-long licenses. Contact the **Czech Angling Union** (Český rybářský svaz; ☎ 274 811 751; www.rybsvaz.cz; Nad Olšinami 31, Prague) or the **Slovak Fishing Union** (Slovenský rybársky zväz; ☎ 041-562 31 93; ekonom@srzrada.sk; Kmeťa 20, Žilina) for conditions and regulations.

OTHER ACTIVITIES

If you'd prefer a bird's-eye view of the republics, there are a couple of options open to you. The Tatras in Slovakia and the Krkonoše in the Czech Republic are centres for paragliding and scenic flights; contact the **Amateur Aviatic Association of the Czech Republic** (Letecká amatérská asociace ČR; ☎ 271 085 270; laacr@laacr.cz; Ke Kablu 289, Prague) or check the sport and leisure section of the Slovak Tourist Board's website (www.slovakiatourism.sk).

Exploring the countryside can often be more fun on four legs than two. Horse riding centres are scattered throughout the republics; look in the Yellow Pages or ask at the local tourist offices for more information.

Food & Drink

On the surface of it, Czech food seems very similar to German or Polish food: lots of meat served with dumplings and cabbage. The little differences are what make the food here special – eat a forkful of *svíčková* (roast beef served with a sour cream sauce and spices) sopped up with fluffy bread dumpling and you'll be wondering why you haven't heard more about this cuisine.

Slovak food, with its peasant-culture roots, generally runs along the same lines: hearty, heavy dishes based mainly on pork with generous helpings of cabbage and cheese. But it also comes with a spicy twist, a gift from the former Hungarian rulers.

Note: two names separated by a slash (/) in this chapter are the Czech and Slovak terms; those without a slash are the same in both languages.

STAPLES & SPECIALITIES

The Czechs and Slovaks are proud of their food and it holds a fond place in their heart. Most of their traditional dishes are everyday meals, constantly linking them to the history of their cuisine. International cooking has made very few inroads into average, everyday life.

Traditionally, a big feed of meat and dumplings is taken at lunch time, although the meal is eaten quickly and there's no time for a nap afterwards. However, if you ask a Czech what they had for lunch yesterday, they're just as likely to say 'a sandwich' or 'nothing, I had a meeting'. In Prague, particularly, the Western way of life is catching on, and most people are too busy to take an hour out for lunch. Czechs who eat breakfast *(snídaně/raňajky)* at home generally have bread with butter, cheese, eggs, ham or sausage, jam or yoghurt. Commuters gobble down soup and frankfurters at a *bufet* (self-service, cafeteria-style place).

The solid heart of Czech cooking is roast pork with dumplings and sauerkraut *(vepřové s knedlíky a kyselé zelí)*: the meal really isn't complete unless it's washed down with beer *(pivo)*. The pork is roasted with salt and caraway seeds; good roast pork should fall apart at the touch of a fork. While it's usually served with sauerkraut *(zelí/kyslá kapusta*, cabbage pickled in vinegar) it can be accompanied by cabbage steamed with onions, apple, salt and caraway – it should be crunchy, not like English boiled cabbage. The dumplings are what Czech food is really all about. Fluffy, light and soft, bread dumplings *(houskové knedlíky)* are made from flour, yeast, egg yolks and milk, with cubes of baguette added to the mix. They are raised like bread dough, then boiled in hot water and sliced.

Some dishes are served with potato dumplings *(bramborové knedlíky)*. Much heavier than the bread version, they are made from shredded, boiled potato mixed with flour and egg yolk.

It's hard to mess up roasted and marinated beef *(svíčková na smetaně)*: however tough the beef is, when you marinade it for hours in vinegar, herbs and vegetables, then stew it for another few hours, it's always deliciously tender. The beef is served in a sour cream sauce, garnished with lemon and tart cranberries.

Goulash *(guláš)* is a staple of every menu and usually the cheapest meal available; most pubs have their own special recipe. Cubes of beef or pork are mixed with an equal quantity of sliced onions and fried with paprika, then stewed with stock and tomatoes. The best goulash is three days old (though EU regulations now prohibit serving warm, cooked

The Littlest Czech Cookbook by Milada Williams is pocket-sized and quirkily written, and has easy-to-follow instructions for all your favourites.

Cherished Czech Recipes by Czech-American Pat Martin has around 100 recipes and includes some great baked treats.

food that's been standing more than three hours, so you'll have to visit a Czech home to try it) and each fresh batch should be seasoned with a spoonful of the last batch.

Potato salad *(bramborový salát)* is served as a side dish and used as the base spread for most Czech open sandwiches *(chlebíčky)*. As any Czech will tell you, the most important step when making potato salad is to leave it to sit for a day – apparently it just keeps getting better, right up until the time when it gives you food poisoning. Boiled potatoes are mixed with carrots, onions, celeriac, mayonnaise, yoghurt, pickles, ham, salami, eggs, cheese and parsley.

The classic *Czechoslovak Cookbook* by Joza Brizova is the Czech version of *The Joy of Cooking*, now translated into English.

Most pubs have a 'with your beer' section of the menu, devoted to snacky treats. These include spicy pork or beef sausages *(klobásy)*, fried or boiled, served with mustard on rye bread or a roll; frankfurters *(párky)*; a Hungarian snack of fried pastry coated with garlic, cheese, butter or jam *(langoše)*; a patty made from strips of raw potato and garlic *(bramborák)*; and chips or French fries *(hranolky)* or fried sliced potatoes *(brambůrky)*. Beer cheese – cheese marinated in garlic, spices and oil – is a great accompaniment for a couple of cold lagers. Look for the word *syr* (cheese) in the 'with your beer' section of the menu.

The traditional local dessert is fruit dumplings *(ovocné knedlíky)*. Bad fruit dumplings are almost inedibly heavy, so this is one dish it's worth ordering at a decent restaurant. Yeast or potato dumplings are filled with plums *(švestkové knedlíky)* or strawberries *(jahodové knedlíky)*. They are served with sugar and cottage cheese, or with yoghurt, poppy seeds or melted butter.

Despite spicy Hungarian influences, Slovak food is on the whole quite similar to Czech cuisine, though dumplings are not as common. Eating habits are also on par with its bigger cousin. Most restaurants have big menus, but in the end you will come across the same dishes again and again. There is a vast difference between restaurant and home-cooking, so if you have a chance to eat in a local's home don't pass it up.

Slovaks love sheep's cheese and fried bacon and pile it on national dishes such as *bryndzové halušky* – is a must for anyone on a culinary tour. It consists of small potato dumplings, similar in looks and texture to the Italian gnocchi, topped with sheep's cheese and a sprinkling of fried bacon bits. A sheep's whey, called *žinčica*, is traditionally drunk with it, but you are only likely to find it served at homes in remote villages. Another variation on the sheep's cheese/fried bacon story is *pirohy*, a potato pastry stuffed with (more) sheep's cheese, topped with (more) fried bacon and served with sour cream.

TRAVEL YOUR TASTEBUDS

Many dishes bear names that don't offer a clue as to what's in them, but certain words will give you hints: *šavle* (sabre), something on a skewer; *tajemství* (secret), cheese inside rolled meat; *překvapení* (surprise), meat, capsicum and tomato paste rolled into a potato pancake; *kapsa* (pocket), a filling inside rolled meat; and *bašta* (bastion), meat in spicy sauce with a potato pancake.

Two dishes that all Czechs know are *Španělský ptáčky* (Spanish birds), veal rolled up with sausage, gherkin and egg, served with rice and sauce; and *Moravský vrabec* (Moravian sparrow), a fist-sized piece of roast pork. But even Czechs may have to ask about the following: *Meč krále Jiřího* (the sword of King George), beef and pork roasted on a skewer; *tajemství Petra Voka* (Peter Voka's mystery), carp with sauce; *Šíp Malínských lovců* (the Malín hunter's arrow), beef, sausage, fish and vegetables on a skewer; and *Dech kopáče Ondřeje* (Digger Ondřej's breath), fillet of pork filled with an Olomouc cheese stick.

Goulash is popular in Slovakia too, but varies in consistency; it can be ordered as a stew served with potatoes or dumplings, or as a watery soup *(gulášová polievka)*.

To finish a meal off, don't pass up the chance to sample the traditional dessert, *palačinky*. Basically crepes, they are best served smothered in rich chocolate sauce with a dash of whipped cream on the side; they also come with jam and, believe it or not, farmers cheese.

DRINKS
Nonalcoholic Drinks

Most Czechs don't like the taste of their tap water so bottled water is cheap and easy to get. Fizzy Mattoni is from the springs of Karlovy Vary. The Czech Republic's own 'energy drink' goes by the attention-grabbing name of Semtex. Yes, it's named after the plastic explosive.

In Slovakia, the popular brands of mineral water are Salvator or Baldovska, bottled in the Prešov and Levoča areas respectively. But the nonalcoholic drink that wins the popularity race hands-down is Vinea, a fizzy grape-juice produced by wine maker Vinarsky Zavod Pezinok. Ask any young Slovak about the drink, and they'll drift off into happy, wistful remembrances from their childhood; Vinea was basically the only fizzy soft drink available during the communist years.

COFFEE & TEA

Basic coffee *(káva* or *kafe)* is Turkish-style: hot water poured over ground beans that end up as sludge at the bottom of your cup. Espresso – a lot of it pretty good – is available everywhere in Prague and in most other big cities, so you needn't forego your cappuccino.

Most tea *(čaj)* is weak, and served with a slice of lemon; if you want it with milk, ask for *čaj s mlékem*. Prague is in the grip of teahouse *(čajovna)* fever, which means there are any number of cellar locales where you can while away hours lounging on kilims, smoking a hookah and drinking tea from pretty much anywhere in the world.

Alcoholic Drinks
WINE

Wine *(víno)* in the Czech Republic is only big in Moravia, though it's available in most restaurants, taverns *(hostinců)* and wine bars *(vinárny/ vinárně)*. White wines are markedly better than reds. The best reds are Vavřinec, Rulandské červené and Frankovka; good dry whites are Tramín and Rulandské bílé. Czechs tend to prefer sweetish whites.

Southeast Moravia produces the best Czech wines. People still gather at *vinné sklípky*, semi-underground, family-run wine cellars, for a tipple and a song. Bohemia's main wine area is around Mělník; the white wines are reasonable.

A popular summer cooler is *vinný střik*, which is half white wine and half soda, with ice. A popular winter drink is hot wine *(svařené víno/ varené víno)*. At the end of summer, when the grape harvest begins, shops and bars all over the republic start selling *burčak*, the fermented juice of the first grapes. It tastes deceptively unalcoholic, but rapidly produces giggling and a severe need to sit down.

Slovaks produce and consume more wine per capita than Czechs. Their wine history dates back to the 7th century BC, when Celtic tribes, under the watchful Romans, planted grapevines in the hills north of Bratislava. The communists, however, heralded a change of attitude: focus was on quantity and the majority of production was mediocre, to say the least.

We believe that *The Best of Slovak Cooking* by New Hippocrene is the only English-language book devoted solely to Slovak cuisine – which is a pity as it's thin on recipes and the title is not exactly telling the truth.

Czech & Slovak Kolache Recipes & Sweet Treats by the Guild National Czech & Slovak Library & Museum is for those out there with a sweet tooth; recipes for pastries, cakes and the like.

PIVO

No matter how many times you tell yourself, 'today is an alcohol-free day', Czech beer *(pivo)* will be your undoing. Light, clear, refreshing and cheaper than water, Czech beer is recognised as one of the world's best – the Czechs claim it's so pure it's impossible to get a hangover from drinking it (scientific tests conducted by Lonely Planet authors have found this to be not entirely true). Brewing traditions go back to the 13th century.

The Czechs get through an ocean of beer. In 1999 Czechs averaged 159.6 litres of beer per person per year (as compared to 83 litres per person in the USA and 95 in Australia); 56% of alcohol drunk in the Czech Republic is beer. Liver disease and alcoholism are on the decline, peaking with beer consumption in the early '90s.

Most Czech beers are lager style – this is where pilsner was invented – and are filtered for clarity. As in neighbouring Germany, there are no chemicals in the beer. The whole process uses only natural ingredients – water, hops and barley for the fermentation process – which is why you can drink quite a lot without too many ill effects. Beer is served at cellar temperature with a (some may say overly) large head on it. Draught beer normally comes as a *malé pivo* ('small beer', 300mL) or as *pivo* or *velké pivo* ('large beer', 500mL); dark beers are *černý*. Beer is generally *dvanáctka* (12-degree) or *desítka* (10-degree); this local indicator of its 'gravity', which takes into account its texture and malt content, doesn't correspond to alcohol percentage, but normally the higher the degree, the higher the alcohol content. Most beers are between 3% and 6% alcohol; watch out for Velvet, a British-style ale that packs a bit more of a punch.

The strong beer culture here is centuries old and is one of the few traditions to survive the communist era relatively intact; though spirit-drinking rose during this time, it has dropped off again since 1989.

There are over 60 breweries in the Czech Republic. The Belgian brewery Interbrew owns Prague Breweries, made up of Staropramen, Braník, Měšťan, Kelt, Ostravar, Vratislav and Velvet. SABMiller, a South African company that owns American beer Miller, controls 45% of the Czech market with the well-known breweries Plzeňský prazdroj (Pilsner Urquell, Gambrinus and Primus labels; all from Plzeň in West Bohemia), Radegast (Novošice, North Moravia) and Velkopopovický Kozel (Velké Popovice, Central Bohemia).

One of the oldest brands is Krušovice (owned by the German Binding Brauerei), established in 1581. This brewery is now one of the largest in the Czech Republic – its Mušketýr is excellent. The small, privately owned microbrewery Bernard (established in 1597) in Humpolec, East Bohemia, won five gold awards during Pivex beer fairs in the late 1990s, and is still managing to make a profit.

The largest Czech beer exporter, Budvar, is also known by the German name Budweiser. It is not connected in any way to the American brewery Anheuser-Busch (except by an ongoing trademark dispute) and its Budweiser label, whose beer pales in comparison to the far superior, stronger and slightly bitter Czech Budvar. The US brewery has tried to buy the small Czech company, but national pride and government intervention halted the near-disastrous sale. Anheuser Busch has since attempted to aggressively acquire the majority of the world market share. Anheuser-Busch's Michelob was also, originally, a Czech label.

Most glass bottles can be returned to the point of purchase for a three-crown refund; in other words: for every four empties you return, you can buy a full.

Slovak beer, essentially Pilsens, is also top-quality stuff. It is, however, nowhere near as famous as its neighbour's brew, and hardly recognised, or available, outside its borders. As many as two dozen varieties of Slovak beer line supermarket shelves, but like the Czech Republic, its largest breweries are foreign owned.

Well knowns include Zlatý Bažant (Golden Pheasant), Šariš, Corgoň, Steiger, Topvar, Martiner, Stein, Gemer and Tatran. Dark *(tmavé)* beer, a richer, thicker, and often more appealing choice than its lighter *(svelté)* brother, is commonplace throughout the republic. You'd be a fool not to sample a bottle (or five) of the smooth, malty and altogether charming liquid. Most breweries produce one dark beer alongside their light beer variety.

These days though, things are looking healthier. Vineyards, concentrated around the southern region of Tokaj, along the Hungarian border, and in the Small Carpathian mountains running north from Bratislava, are once again starting to produce some fine drops. Tokaj wines are predominately sweet white wines, similar to its famous Hungarian counterpart Tokay; look for the labels of producers such as Galafruit and J Ostrožovič. Wine production in the Small Carpathians is concentrated around the villages of Modra and Pezinok; bottles from wine makers such as Masaryk, Matyšák, Borik and Karpatská perla are well worth seeking out.

SPIRITS

Slivovice is a fiery, potent plum brandy said to have originated in Moravia, where the best brands, like Jelínek, still come from. If you have a sweet tooth, try cherry liqueur *(griotka)*. *Meruňkovice* is made from apricots, *borovička* from juniper berries.

Czechs love the unique herbal spirit Becherovka, from the spa town of Karlovy Vary – it tastes cinnamony, and is supposed to aid the digestion. Another popular bitter spirit is Fernet – the 'stock' version tastes like medicine, but try the citrus version with tonic water. Locally made vodka and rum (which is really vodka with rum flavouring) are sold by the (incredibly cheap) shot from all kinds of outlets, including bakeries and sausage stands. Warming grog is rum, hot water and lemon.

Absinthe is another popular spirit. Traditionally absinthe was hallucinogenic, but the version you get these days is just incredibly alcoholic (75%). Absinthe got its hallucinogenic properties from wormwood, and though wormwood is no longer included, wormwood flavouring is (note that there is no such thing as wormwood-flavoured ice cream. That's because wormwood tastes terrible). The correct way to drink it is to soak a cube of sugar in a glass of absinthe, and then light the cube. When the sugar has melted, stir it into the glass and add a little water. The most popular way to drink it is as part of a B52 shooter with Kahlua and Baileys.

Slovenská Rodinná Kuchárká (Slovakian Family Cookbook) by Cesty is the mother-of-all cookbooks; over 500 pages of the best Slovak recipes from throughout the country, but unfortunately only in Slovakian.

WHERE TO EAT & DRINK

Apart from a few outstanding exceptions (see the Author's Choice box on p133 for more information), food in most restaurants is the same no matter the price. Your pork and dumplings will taste the same in a *hospoda* (pub) for 50Kč/80Sk as in a four-star hotel restaurant for 150Kč/200Sk, because the chefs have all been trained in the same school. In Prague, a little extra money may buy you a better cut of meat, but in most cases prices are higher because the restaurant is somewhere people will pay higher prices (the difference between many cheap and expensive places is the atmosphere and décor).

A *bufet* or *samoobsluha* is a self-service, cafeteria-style place with open sandwiches *(chlebíčky)*, tasty salads, spicy sausages *(klobásy)*, mild pork sausages *(špekačky)*, frankfurters *(párky/párok)*, goulash *(guláš)* and of course dumplings. Some of these places are tucked to the side of food shops *(potraviny)*. *Bageteria* are simpler establishments, with made-to-order sandwiches and baguettes.

A *pivnice/pivnica* is a pub without food. *Hospoda* or *hostinec* is a pub or beer hall that serves basic meals. A *vinárna/vináreň* or wine bar may have anything from snacks to a full-blown menu. The occasional coffee shop *(kavárna)* has a full menu but most serve only snacks and desserts. A *restaurace/reštaurácia* is any restaurant. *Koliba* are Slovak-style, rustic, country restaurants found across both republics that specialise in barbecued chicken and sometimes other lunch-time items. The Slovak *salaš* is a basic, usually rural, place, originally a shepherd's summer hut, serving standard Slovak fare.

If you have small kids, you may prefer a *restaurace*, as pubs are pretty smoky; if you're eating alone, you won't be alone (so to speak) in the average *hospoda*, where diners just pull up a chair at the nearest communal table. Women by themselves may feel uncomfortable in the male-dominated *hospodas* and *hostinecs*, but once the ice is broken, they're generally fine places to be. If you'd rather skip it, try a *restaurace*, *kavárna* or *vinárna*.

Restaurants start serving as early as 11am and carry on till midnight; some take a break between lunch and dinner. Main dishes may stop being served well before the advertised closing time, with only snacks and drinks after that.

Most restaurants are honest, though of course it pays to watch out for mistakes. Prague is a different matter; see the boxed text on p135 for ways to cope with restaurants there. Expect a couvert (cover charge), in the pricier restaurants everywhere. Even in the best restaurants waiters tend to remove your plate as soon as you finish your meal, even if everyone at your table is still eating.

DID YOU KNOW?

The world record for eating plum dumplings is 191, held by Kamil Hamersky of Central Bohemia.

Quick Eats
Bufets or *bageteria* are the usual place to grab a quick meal. Bakeries also sell savoury and sweet pastries that are good for a quick snack. In bigger towns (and, happily, along hiking trails in areas where people have their weekend cottages), beer stands can often provide you with a sausage, fries or fried cheese *(smažený syr)* served on a roll with mayonnaise; hygiene is generally pretty good. Supermarket delis have good spreads, meats and bread rolls.

VEGETARIANS & VEGANS
Outside of Prague, vegetarians will have a very hard, and dull, time of it. Vegans will find life next to impossible. There are a few standard meatless dishes *(bezmasá jídla/bezma/bezmäsité jedlá)* served by most restaurants: the most common are *smažený sýr/vysmážaný syr* (fried cheese) and vegetables cooked with cheese sauce. Vegan dishes are almost nonexistent. While there are many vegetarian side dishes, lots of pubs and restaurants in Prague won't let you order a side unless you also order a main. Outside Prague, it's generally quite easy to combine side dishes to create a meal.

DID YOU KNOW?

One of the most popular crisp flavours in the Czech Republic is bacon with horseradish.

If something appears to be vegetarian, ask what's gone into it – it often doesn't occur to restaurants that you won't want your vegetable soup made with beef stock. In most cases, your best bet is to make dishes yourself; fresh fruit and vegetables, grains, margarine and other ingredients are easy to obtain at most *potraviny*, fruit and vegetable stores and supermarkets.

WHINING & DINING
Children are generally very welcome in eating establishments throughout both republics. If you have small kids, you may prefer a *restaurace* as menus regularly offer half-price meals for the littl'uns and pubs are often pretty smoky.

See p466 for more information on travelling with children within the republics.

HABITS & CUSTOMS
There's very little in the eating and drinking habits of Czechs and Slovaks that you'll find unusual. Czechs do tend to eat fast. If you're invited to someone's house for a meal, bring some flowers or a bottle of wine, and

---

PUB ETIQUETTE

Always ask if a chair is free before sitting down (*Je tu volno?*). Service is normally quick, but if it's slow, chasing the waiter is a sure way to guarantee that you'll be ignored. Your tab is run on a slip of paper left at your table. Tipping is the same as in a restaurant, ie 5% to 10%, and the bill is usually rounded up to the next 5Kč or 10Kč to make it 5%.

---

when you get there ask if you should take your shoes off (most Czechs and Slovaks switch to slippers inside the house).

Come Christmas, while the rest of the world is scoffing chicken, turkey or goose, Czechs and Slovaks prefer to dine on carp. Slovaks will often start with the humble cabbage soup; a perfect warmer on a cold winter day. Christmas dinner is eaten on Christmas Eve.

Whether you're drinking in a bar or with a meal, you should always toast with the first drink of the evening – it's terrible manners to start drinking without a toast. The standard toast involves clinking together first the tops, then the bottoms of glasses, then touching the glass to the table; most people say '*Na zdraví*' (your health).

EAT YOUR WORDS

For more information on how to pronounce Czech and Slovak words, see the Language chapter (p468).

Useful Phrases

Table for ..., please.	*Stůl pro ... osob, prosím./Stôl pre ... osôb, prosím.*
We've booked a table.	*Zamluvili jsme si místo./Objednali sme si miestoli.*
May I have the menu please?	*Jídelní lístek, prosím?/Jedálny lístok prosím?*
What is today's special?	*Jaká je specialita dne?/Aká je dnešná špecialita?*
Does it cost extra?	*Platí se zato zvlášť./Platí zato zvlášť?*
Bon appétit.	*Dobrou chuť./Dobrú chuť.*
Cheers!	*Nazdraví!/Nazdravie!*
The bill, please.	*Účet, prosím.*
I'm a vegetarian.	*Jsem vegetarián/ka (m/f)./Som vegetarián/ka (m/f).*
I don't eat ...	*Nejím .../Nejem ...*
meat	*maso/mäso*
chicken	*kuře/kura*
fish	*rybu*
ham	*šunku*
Some more ..., please.	*Ještě ..., prosím./Ešte ..., prosím.*
drinking water	*pitná voda*
boiled water	*vařící voda/vriaca voda*

Menu Decoder

SOUPS (POLÉVKA/POLIEVKA)
bramborová/zemiaková – potato
bujón – broth with egg
dršťková/držková – sliced tripe
guláš – thick, spicy beef and potato soup
houbová/hríbová – mushroom
hovězí/hovädzia – beef in broth
hrachová – thick pea soup with bacon
kapustnica – cabbage
rajská/rajčinová – tomato and rice
zeleninová – vegetables

COLD STARTERS (STUDENÉ PŘEDKRMY/STUDENÉ PREDJEDLÁ)
chlebíčky – open sandwiches on French bread, with cold meat, eggs, cheese, or mayonnaise salads like lobster, fish, potato or ham and peas
Pražská šunka s okurkou (uhorkou) – Prague ham with gherkins
ruská vejce/ruské vajcia – hard-boiled egg, potato and salami, with mayonnaise
sýrový nářez/syrový tanier – cheeseboard
tlačenka s octem a cibulí/tlačenka s octom a cibulou – jellied meat loaf with vinegar and onion
uherský salám s okurkou/maďarský salám s uhorkou – Hungarian salami with gherkin
utopeneci – literally 'the drowned one' – sliced pickled pork sausage
zavináče – pickled herring fillets

DID YOU KNOW?

According to a 2003 British study, drinking beer does not give you a beer gut.

WARM STARTERS (TEPLÉ PŘEDKRMY/TEPLÉ PREDJEDLÁ)
ďábelská topinka/hrianka – a piquant toast with meat and cheese
míchaná vejce s klobásou/miešané vajcia s klobásou – scrambled eggs with spicy sausage
pečená šunka s vejci/šunka pečená s vajcem – fried ham with egg

MAIN DISHES (HLAVNÍ JÍDLA/HLAVNÉ JEDLÁ)
This category is usually subdivided as ready-to-serve dishes (*hotová jídla/hotová jedlá*) and dishes prepared as they're ordered (*jídla na objedna/jedlá na objednávku*).
dušená roštěnka/dusené hovädzie – braised beef slices in sauce
hovězí guláš/hovädzí guláš – beef chunks in brown sauce
karbanátky/karbonátky – hamburger with breadcrumbs, egg, a sliced roll and onion
kuře na paprice/kurací paprikáš – chicken boiled in spicy paprika cream sauce
plněná paprika/plnená paprika – capsicum stuffed with minced meat and rice, served with tomato sauce
přírodní řízek/prírodný rezeň – pork or veal schnitzel without breadcrumbs
rizoto – a mixture of pork, onion, peas and rice
segedínský guláš/koložárska kapusta – goulash with beef, pork, lamb and sauerkraut in a cream sauce
svíčková na smetaně/sviečková na smotane – roast beef with a sour cream sauce and spices
tatarský biftek – raw steak
telecí pečeně/teľacie pečené – roast veal
vepřová játra/bravčové pečeň – pork liver fried with onion
vepřová pečeně/bravčové pečené – roast pork with caraway seeds
zajíc na smetaně/zajac na smotane – hare in cream sauce
znojemská pečeně/znojemská roštenka – sliced roast beef in gherkin sauce

MEATLESS DISHES (BEZMASÁ JÍDLA/BEZMÄSITÉ JEDLÁ)
knedlíky s vejci/knedle s vajcem – fried dumplings with egg
omeleta se sýrem a bramborem – cheese and potato omelette
smažené žampiony/vysmažené šampióny – fried mushrooms with potatoes
smažený květák/smažený karfiol – fried cauliflower with egg and onion
smažený sýr/vysmážaný syr – fried cheese with potatoes and tartare sauce

SIDE DISHES (PŘÍLOHY/PRÍLOHA)
bramborový salát/zemiakový šalát – potato salad
dušené fazole/dušená fazuľa – steamed beans
dušená mrkev/dušená mrkva – steamed carrots
krokety – deep fried mashed potato
okurka/kyslá uhorka – dill pickle
opékané brambory – fried potatoes
smažené žampiony – fried mushrooms
špenát – finely chopped spinach, cooked with onion, garlic and cream
tatarská omáčka – a creamy tartar sauce

SALADS (SALÁT/ŠALÁTKY)
hlávkový – lettuce
míchaný/miešaný – mixed
okurkový/uhorkový – cucumber
rajský/rajčinový – tomato and onion
šopský/balkánský – lettuce, tomato, onion and cheese

DESSERTS (MOUČNÍK/MÚČNIKY)
jablečný závin or **štrúdl/jablková štrudľa** – apple strudel
makový koláč – poppy seed cake
ovocné knedlíky/ovocné knedle or guíky – fruit dumplings
palačinky – pancakes
rakvičky – literally 'coffin'; meringues topped with whipped cream
zmrzlina – ice cream

English-Czech/Slovak Glossary
MEAT & FISH
Maso uzeniny/mäso refers to meat, smoked meat and sausages.

beef	*hovězí (maso)/ hovädzie (mäso)*
beef steak	*biftek*
boar	*kanec/divá sviňa*
carp	*kapr/kapor*
chicken	*kuře/kura*
cutlet, chop	*kotleta/rebierko (karé)*
duck	*kachna/kačica*
fish	*ryba*
goose	*husa/hus*
ham	*šunka*
hamburger	*karbanátek/karbonátka*
hare	*zajíc/zajac*
liver	*játra/pečeň*
pheasant	*bažant*
rabbit	*králík*
sirloin	*svíčkova/sviečková*
trout	*pstruh*
turkey	*krůta/morka*
veal	*telecí (maso)/teľacie mäso*
venison	*jelení/jelenina*

FRUIT & VEGETABLES
apricot	*meruňka/marhuľa*
beans	*fazolové lusky/fazuľová*
capsicum	*paprika*
carrot	*mrkev/mrkva*
cauliflower	*květák/karfiol*
cucumber or pickle	*okurka/uhorka*
fruit	*ovoce/ovocie*
garlic	*česnek/cesnak*
horseradish	*křen/chren*
lemon	*citrón*
mushrooms	*houby/hríby*
onion	*cibule/cibuľa*
pear	*hruška*
peas	*hrášek/hrášok*
pickled cabbage	*sterelizované zelí/sterelizovaná kapusta*

Visit
www.budvar.cz/jsp
/index_en.jsp?menuid=1
for a cranky rundown on
the Budvar/Anheuser-
Busch dispute.

Eleanor's mother is Czech,
her father Slovak, her
recipes delicious. Check
them out at
e.schrabal.home.att.net/.

pineapple	*ananas/ananás*
plum	*švestka/slivka*
potato	*brambory/zemiak*
raspberries	*maliny*
sauerkraut	*zeli/kyslá kapusta*
spinach	*špenát*
strawberries	*jahody*
tomato	*rajče/rajčina*
vegetables	*zelenina*

OTHER ITEMS

black pepper	*pepř/čierne korenie*
bread	*chléb/chlieb*
butter	*máslo/maslo*
caraway	*kmín/rasca*
cheese	*syr*
chips, French fries	*hranolky*
chocolate	*čokoládová/čokoláda*
coffee	*kávová/káva*
cottage cheese	*tvaroh*
cream	*smetana/smotana*
dumplings	*knedlíky/knedle*
eggs	*vejce/vajcia*
honey	*med*
jam	*džem*
mustard	*hořčice/horčica*
nut	*oříšková/orech*
omelette	*omeleta*
pasta	*těstoviny/cestoviny*
rice	*rýže/ryža*
salt	*sůl/soľ*
sugar	*cukr/cukor*
vanilla	*vanilová/vanilka*

COOKING TERMS

boiled	*vařený/varený*
broiled	*roštěná (na roštu)/roštěnka (na ražni)*
fresh	*čerstvý*
fried	*smažený/vypražený*
grilled or on the spit	*grilovaný/na rošte*
home-made	*domácí/domáci*
roasted or baked	*pečený*
smoked	*uzený/údené*
steamed	*dušený/dusený*
sweet	*sladký*

UTENSILS

ashtray	*popelník/popolník*
cup	*šálek/šálka*
fork	*vidlička*
glass	*sklenice/pohár*
knife	*nůž/nôž*
plate	*talíř/tanier*
spoon	*lžíce/lyžica*
toothpick	*párátko/špárátko*

Martin Mihal collects Czech chocolate wrappers. See them at mujweb.cz/www /chocolate/Csr/Diana /diana1.htm.

At www.slovakheritage.org /Recipes/recipes _home.htm there are over 20 recipes to try before you buy the real thing in Slovakia.

Castles & Chateaux

If there's one concrete benefit the Czech and Slovak Republics gained from raiding tribes, conquering empires and untold wars, it's a plethora of castles and chateaux. They're famed for it – everywhere you look there seems to be a spectacular castle, romantic chateau, or crumbling ruin dominating a town or resting peacefully on a lonely hilltop. The range on offer is simply awe-inspiring; you'll see everything from grim Gothic ruins clinging to a dizzy pinnacle of rock to majestic, baroque mansions filled with the finest furniture that Europe's artisans could provide.

Upon visiting a castle or chateau, you'll quite often be forced to join a Czech- or Slovak-language tour, but don't despair; many supply you with an English-language text but if not, ask the tour guide very, very sweetly and they may just do a bit of translating for you. More annoying is the parking charge, which sometimes exceeds the entrance fee.

Since you'd need a month of Sundays to visit half of the 600 or so castles or chateaux in the Czech Republic and Slovakia, we've selected some of the best, and most popular, there are to see. One glaring omission here is Prague Castle, which is extensively covered in the Prague chapter (p88).

BOJNICE (CENTRAL SLOVAKIA)

Bojnice Chateau (☎ 543 06 33; www.bojnicecastle.sk; adult/child 130/70Sk; ☽ 9am-5pm Tue-Sun May-Sep (also Mon Jul & Aug), 10am-3pm Tue-Sun Oct-Apr) looks like something straight out of a fairy tale, which should be the first clue that it is not the original 12th-century Gothic version, but an early 20th-century reconstruction modelled on French romantic castles. It belonged to the Pálffy family from 1643 until 1945, when the state took over. Nevertheless, a few remains of the original Gothic and Renaissance parts of the castle survive within the present structure.

The castle has the usual exhibits of furniture, paintings, statues, weapons, glass and porcelain in lavishly decorated rooms. Highlights include the **Bojnice Altar**, the only surviving complete work of Nardo di Cione, the **Golden Hall**, with its gilded ceiling and a small **cave system**, some 26m below the courtyard, complete with its own well. Rumours that the castle is haunted are kept alive by the **International Festival of Spirits and Ghosts** (adult/child 180/90Sk) held on the first two weekends in May. There's also spooky **night tours** (admission 150Sk; ☽ 9pm Fri & Sat Jul & Aug) if you're up to it.

This is the most visited castle in Slovakia and the queues get very long on weekends and holidays, so get there early. See p376 for information about getting to Bojnice.

BOUZOV (NORTH MORAVIA)

The impressive pile of **Bouzov Castle** (☽ 9am-4pm Tue-Sun May-Sep, 9am-3pm Sat & Sun Apr & Oct) was the seat of the Grand Masters of the Order of Teutonic Knights from 1799 to 1939. The oldest parts date from the 14th century, but it was renovated in neo-Gothic style between 1895 and 1910. The order was abolished in 1939 and the castle occupied and looted by the Nazis during WWII.

The restored apartments include the **Grand Master's Bedroom** and office, the **Hunter's Hall** and huge basement kitchens kitted out with the latest labour-saving devices of the early 20th century. The magnificent **Knights' Hall** has elaborate woodcarvings and a barrel-vaulted wooden ceiling decorated with the sun and the stars. The sculptures of St George and a jousting knight symbolise the spiritual and material aspects of the order.

There's a choice of guided tours through the castle lasting from 20 minutes to two hours: the **'classic' tour** (adult/concession 60/30Kč, or in a foreign language 100/50Kč) takes in the main sights.

See p276 for information about getting to Bouzov.

HLUBOKÁ (SOUTH BOHEMIA)

A crow pecking the eyes from a Turk's head, the grisly crest of the Swarzenberg family, may be the recurrent motif of **Hluboká's** (☎ 387 967 045; fax 387 965 526; ☯ 9am-6pm daily Jul & Aug, 9am-6pm Tue-Sun May-Jun, 9am-5.30pm Apr, Sep & Oct) décor but it is hard to imagine an image more at odds with the chateau's overtly romantic theme. Originally thrown up by the Přemysl rulers in the latter half of the 13th century, Hluboká was taken from the Protestant Malovec family in 1662 for supporting an anti-Habsburg rebellion, and sold to the Bavarian Schwarzenbergs. Two centuries later, they gave the chateau the English-Tudor, Gothic-style face it wears today, purportedly modelling its exterior on Britain's Windsor Castle. Crowned with wedding-cake crenellations and surrounded by a daintily tended garden, Hluboká's chocolate box looks are rather too sickly for some, but this remains the second-most visited chateau in Bohemia after Karlštejn, and for good reason.

There are four tours through the chateau: the **main tour** (adult/concession 80/40Kč, or in a foreign language 150/80Kč) passes through the Schwarzenberg's ceremonial chambers, including the Private Apartments of Duchess Leonora, some extraordinarily ornate reception rooms and the grandiose Large Dining Room, which would once have seated 72 guests. **Tour B** (adult/concession 50/25Kč, or in a foreign language 110/60Kč) takes in the armoury, the second largest in Bohemia, after Konopiště; **Tour C** (adult/concession 90/50Kč, or in a foreign language 200/120Kč) covers the same ground as the main tour, plus the chapel; and **Tour D** (adult/concession 90/50Kč, or in a foreign language 200/100Kč) delves into the chateau's unique kitchen, where the families' favourite recipes are still on show.

Unless the chateau is extremely crowded, tours do not run from 12.30pm to 1pm (lunch time) and the last tour commences an hour before closing time. The chateau grounds are open year-round, free of charge. See p219 for information about getting to Hluboká.

The Gothic-Tudor Hluboká Chateau, built in the 13th century

RICHARD NEBESKY

JINDŘICHŮV HRADEC (SOUTH BOHEMIA)

It's a bit off the beaten track, but this is the Czech Republic's third-largest **chateau** (☎ 331 321 279; zamekjindrichuvhradec@elsynet.cz; ⊙ 9.30am-4.15pm Tue-Sun Jun-Aug, 10am-noon & 1-4.15pm May & Sep, 10am- 3.15pm Apr & Oct), covering 3.5 hectares and boasting a hotchpotch of treasures – architectural and otherwise. A lavish 16th-century monument to the Renaissance at first glance, the chateau is in fact a medley of architectural styles, spanning the ages from its foundation at the hands of Jindřich Vitek in the early 13th century, right through to the present day.

The jewel of the Renaissance chateau is the **Rondel**, an unusual Italianate garden pavilion decorated with gilded stucco and colourful frescoes, designed in 1591 by Baldassare Maggi. The highlight of the older, Gothic part of the castle is the **Ceremonial Hall**, where original, 14th-century frescoes illustrate scenes from the life of St George.

There are three **routes** (1 route adult/concession 65/35Kč, or in a foreign language 140/70Kč, 3 routes 170/80Kč, or in a foreign language 400/180Kč) through the castle; you can choose to do one or all three. **Route A** takes in Adam's Building, the Renaissance interiors, Napoleon's bed from Vienna and the piano played by Mozart; **Route B** covers the medieval, Gothic interiors; and **Route C** explores the 18th- and 19th-century interiors as well as the Rondel. See p245 for information about getting to Jindřichův Hradec.

KARLŠTEJN (CENTRAL BOHEMIA)

The true star in the constellation of castles and chateaux that pepper the region of Central Bohemia, **Karlštejn** (☎ 274 008 154-5; rezervace@stc.npu.cz; ⊙ 9am-6pm Tue-Sun Jul & Aug, 9am-5pm May, Jun & Sep, 9am-4pm Apr & Oct, 9am-3pm Jan, Mar, Nov & Dec, closed Feb) will fulfil even the wildest expectations as to what Middle Europe's most stately structures should look like. Perched high on a crag that overlooks the Berounka river, and sporting a spotless new paint job, this cluster of turrets, high walls and looming towers is as immaculately maintained as it is powerfully evocative. Rightly one of the top attractions of the Czech Republic, the only drawback of Karlštejn is its overwhelming popularity: in the summer months it is literally mobbed with visitors, ice-cream vendors and souvenir stalls – book ahead.

Karlštejn was born of a grand pedigree, starting life in 1348, as a hideaway for the crown jewels and treasury of the Holy Roman Emperor, Charles IV. Run by an appointed Burgrave, the castle was surrounded by a network of landowning knight vassals, who came to the castle's aid whenever enemies moved against it.

Karlštejn again sheltered both the Bohemian and Imperial crown jewels during the Hussite wars, but fell into disrepair as its defences became outmoded. Considerable restoration work, not least by Josef Mocker in the late 19th century, has enabled Karlštejn to return to its former glory.

There are two tours through the castle: **Tour I** (adult/concession 200/100Kč) passes through the Knight's Hall, still daubed with the coats-of-arms and names of the knight vassals, Charles IV's Bedchamber, the Audience Hall and the Jewel House, which includes treasures from the Chapel of the Holy Cross and a replica of the St Wenceslas Crown.

Tour II (adult/concession 300/100Kč) *must* be booked in advance and takes in the Great Tower, the highest point of the castle, which includes a museum on Mocker's restoration work, the Marian Tower and the exquisite Chapel of the Holy Cross, with its decorative ceiling.

See p156 for information about getting to Karlštejn.

KONOPIŠTĚ (CENTRAL BOHEMIA)

Archduke Franz Ferdinand d'Este, heir to the Austro-Hungarian throne, is best known for being assassinated – his June 1914 murder triggered WWI. But he was also Konopiště's last owner, transforming this medieval stronghold into a handsome, neo-Gothic **chateau** (☎ 274 008 154-5; rezervace@stc.npu.cz; ☼ 9am-5pm Tue-Sun May-Aug, 9am-4pm Sep, 9am-3pm Apr & Oct) in the 1890s. Stately and elegant, Konopiště's façade is relatively understated these days – not so the interior.

Statue in the garden of the Konopiště Chateau, Central Bohemia

RICHARD NEBESKÝ

The archduke was an obsessive hunter and much of the chateau is crammed with a grotesque and frankly immodest collection of trophies, ranging from birds and badgers to tigers and antelope. In 25 years he dispatched around 300,000 creatures (and kept an obsessive tally of every one). All guided tours take in the archduke's trophies, a veritable necropolis of mounted heads, antlers and teeth.

There are three tours through the chateau: **Tour I** (adult/concession 95/45Kč, or in a foreign language 145/75Kč) looks at the stately apartments with their Italian cabinets, Dürer graphics and Meissen porcelain, including bedrooms used by Kaiser Wilhelm II and Admiral Alfred von Tirpitz; **Tour II** (adult/concession 95/45Kč, or in a foreign language 145/75Kč) takes in the renowned Este Armoury, the chapel and a plush men's room attached to the so-called Harem; **Tour III** (adult/concession 140Kč, or in a foreign language 250Kč), limited to groups of eight, is the most interesting and explores the archduke's living quarters and Princess Sophie's salon.

If that's not enough, go around the back to witness another of the archduke's fetishes – St George. Here he collected scores of renderings of the mythical dragon-slayer (this is only some 10% of the hoard) in a purpose-built gallery.

The English-style wooded grounds – dotted with lakes – are a much-appreciated antidote to the heavily visited chateau.

See p155 for information about getting to Konopiště.

KRUMLOV (SOUTH BOHEMIA)

Krumlov Chateau (☎ 380 704 721; ☼ 9am-noon & 1-6pm Tue-Sun Jun-Aug, 9am-5pm Apr, May, Sep & Oct), capped with its enigmatic, proto-psychedelic Round Tower, is one of the most evocative, and certainly the most photographed, sights in South Bohemia. And in a town like Český Krumlov, that's really saying something.

The first documented mention of Český Krumlov was in 1253, when the Vítkovec barons, who ruled the region, built their castle here. In 1302 it came into the hands of the Rožmberks (see p224), and in the late 16th century Vilém Rožmberk rebuilt the castle in Renaissance style. The lords of Rožmberk, who were seated here, possessed the largest estate in Bohemia; when their line died out it was given to the Eggenbergs in 1622, and in 1719 to the Schwarzenbergs, who owned the castle until 1945.

Approaching from the south, you cross the wooden **Lazebnický Bridge** (Lazebnický most) and climb to the courtyard via the **Chateau Steps** (Zámecké schody). A more traditional approach is from the north via the **Budějovická Gate** (Budějovická brána; 1598); pass the post office and go through the Red Gate (Červená brána) into the chateau's first courtyard.

Below the entrance bridge are two brown – and, frankly, unhappy – bears, traditional residents since the 16th century. Through a passageway is the second courtyard, with the ticket office, and here you can climb the multicoloured **Round Tower** (válcová věž; adult/concession 30/20Kč; ☼ 9am-5.30pm Tue-Sun Jun-Aug, 9am-4.30pm Apr & Oct, 9.30am-3.30pm Apr & Oct), painted in 1590 by Bartholomew Beránek. Another passageway leads into courtyards three and four, their walls covered in trompe l'oeil painting.

There are three tours of the chateau: **Tour I** (adult/concession 90/45Kč, or in a foreign language 150/75Kč) runs through the opulent Renaissance rooms, including the chapel, Baroque Suite, Picture Gallery and Masquerade Hall, while **Tour II** (adult/concession 70/40Kč, or in a foreign language 140/70Kč) covers the Schwarzenberg Portrait Gallery and more sedate 19th-century interiors.

Just across the bridge behind the chateau is the rococo Chateau Theatre (Zámecké divadlo), which can only be seen on **Tour III** (adult/concession 100/50Kč, or in a foreign language170/90Kč; ☼ 10-11am & 1-4pm Tue-Sun May-Oct). This amazing theatre is one of the only two left in the world that still has all its original decorated stage set and working wooden machinery. Behind the theatre, a ramp to the right leads up to the former Riding School (Zámecká jízdárna). Above the school are the serene chateau **gardens** (☼ 8am-7pm Jun-Aug, 8am-6pm May & Sep, 8am-5pm Apr & Oct).

See p219 for information about getting to Český Krumlov and its chateau.

ORAVA (CENTRAL SLOVAKIA)

This massive Gothic **castle** (☎ 582 03 90; adult/child 100/60Sk; ☼ 8.30am-5pm Jun, 8.30am-5.30pm Jul & Aug, 8.30am-4pm May, Sep & Oct; by appointment only Nov-Apr), perched high above the river overlooking the village of Oravský Podzámok, was for centuries the seat of regional power. Its oldest parts date from at least 1267, with later additions by many royal and aristocratic owners. The present fairy-tale look is mainly the result of reconstruction after a fire in 1800.

The castle, whose pointed towers rise Disneyland-style from an impossibly narrow blade of rock, featured in the classic 1922 vampire film *Nosferatu*. The most spectacular views are from the north and east.

The compulsory guided tour is a little bit on the long side but it's the only way you'll see one of the most complete castles in Slovakia. Once inside, there are rooms full of weapons, paintings, tapestries and period furniture and you'll be treated to unintelligible, but entertaining, theatrical period performances. Highlights include the **Rococo Chapel**, the castle **Galleries** and at its highest level, the **Citadel**, where the sheer drop from its windows brings on vertigo.

The castle hosts the occasional night tour; times and dates are quite random so call ahead. See p380 for information about getting to Orava.

SPIŠ (EAST SLOVAKIA)

Two kilometres southeast of Spišské Podhradie, standing out like a beacon, are the spectacular and photogenic ruins of **Spiš Castle** (☎ 454 13 36; adult/child 60/30Sk; ☼ 8.30am-6pm), one of the biggest castles in Central Europe and a Unesco site since 1993. You may think you're experiencing déjà vu the first time you catch a glimpse of its crumbling walls; the castle appears on many Slovakian promotional posters and brochures. The ridge-top fortress, founded by Hungarian kings in 1209, burned down in 1780 and has been deserted ever since. These days only a small part of the castle's interior is restored, where you'll find displays of torture instruments, medieval weapons and artefacts. It has to be said though, there isn't a lot to see up close – the best views are definitely from afar. However, it's well worth climbing the claustrophobic stairwell of the castle's **Gothic Tower** for impressive 360-degree views of the surrounding countryside.

Throughout the summer months the castle hosts medieval festivals, which consist mainly of concerts and mock battles.

See p414 for information about getting to Spiš Castle.

VRANOV (SOUTH MORAVIA)

Vranov Chateau (☎ 515 296 215; vranov@pambr.cz; 🕒 9am-noon & 1-6pm Tue-Sun Jul & Aug, 9am-5pm May, Jun & Sep, 9am-4pm Sat & Sun Apr & Oct) enjoys one of the most dramatic sites of any castle in Bohemia, atop a high crag thrusting out over the valley of the Dyje river. The chateau's Gothic core dates from the 14th century, but when it came into the possession of the Althan family in 1680 it was rebuilt in baroque style. Most of the chateau, including its chapel, is the work of the renowned baroque architect, Fischer von Erlach.

The most impressive part of the castle, perched right on the edge of the cliff, is the oval **Hall of the Ancestors** (Sál předků), decorated with famous frescoes by Johann Michael Rottmayr depicting the Apotheosis (glorification) of the Althan family, and statues representing the Althan ancestors.

The guided **tour** (adult/concession 60/30Kč, or in a foreign language 120/90Kč) of the castle takes you through many ornate apartments, from the time when the 18th-century Spanish princess Maria Anna Pignatelli lived here. There is a royal bath that looks like a modern hot tub, and two elegant ceramic stoves in the Pignatelli bedroom. One of the rooms was used for Freemasonry – a very fashionable pursuit for 18th-century aristocrats – and is decorated with masonic symbols, including the set square and compasses, the pyramid and the Star of David.

See p313 for information about getting to Vranov Chateau.

Czech Republic

RICHARD NEBESKY

CZECH REPUBLIC

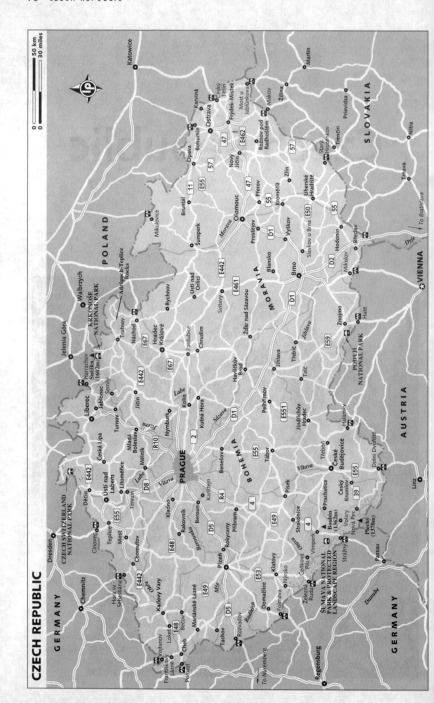

Prague

There's no denying Prague's gorgeousness, the overwhelming, relentless charm of its winding lanes, stone bridges, baroque domes, Renaissance palaces, Gothic cathedrals and Art Nouveau façades. There's also no denying that the charm is often entirely obscured by tourists, traffic and tacky commercialism. More than a decade after the end of communism, Prague is fizzing with energy. It has abandoned brooding Bohemianism – it's so last century – and is churning out dance music, visual arts, hard rock and cutting-edge fashion, and attracting some of Europe's best music and alternative sport festivals. It's also doing its level best to squeeze every crown out of its new-found popularity.

Don't be angry with yourself if Prague leaves you a bit cold. Packed in among thousands of other visitors, trying like crazy to see the city in three days, worrying about getting ripped off; it's no wonder you think the city is overrated. Relax. It takes some searching and some time to find quiet moments when Prague reveals its full beauty, but they are there: the Charles Bridge at dawn; the castle on a stormy night; the view from Letná as the sun sets behind shifting clouds and a cold beer chills your hand; finding yourself entirely alone on the glistening, rain-washed cobblestones of a back-street alley; midnight seagulls wheeling over the murky Vltava; six old women singing hymns in a tiny, ancient church… And when you stumble across one of those moments, there is nowhere more heartbreakingly glorious in the world than Prague.

HIGHLIGHTS

- Wander through the courtyard fronting **St Vitus Cathedral** (p89) at Prague Castle in the early morning, just before the crowds arrive
- Gasp at the overblown magnificence of the **Church of St Nicholas** (p95) in Malá Strana
- Admire the glowing medieval paintings at the **Convent of St Agnes** (p107) in the Old Town
- Giggle at David Černý's endlessly amusing *Miminka*, on the Žižkov **TV Tower** (p121)
- Sip your first cold *pivo* (p139) after a long day of cobblestone-pounding sightseeing

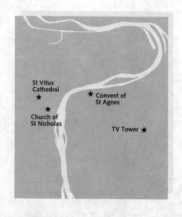

- POPULATION: 1,193,000

HISTORY

According to legend, Prague was founded in the 7th century by Libuše, the mother of the Přemysl line (see Vyšehrad p114); according to archaeologists, the first permanent communities settled here in 4000BC.

King Karel (Charles) IV sponsored a building boom in the mid-14th century, throwing up Charles University, Charles Bridge and St Vitus Cathedral. Adding the New Town to the freshly Gothicised city made Prague one of the biggest cities on the continent.

The Hussite rebellion turned Prague into a Protestant-run city in the 15th century. The Hussite Wars began when fiery preacher Jan Želivský had several Catholic councillors tossed out a window of the New Town Hall in 1419 (see Charles Square p113). A year later, Hussite forces led by General Jan Žižka successfully defended the city against an anti-Hussite, Catholic crusade.

The Catholic Habsburgs took over again in 1526, and later that century Prague became the seat of the Habsburg Empire and, under Emperor Rudolf II, a focal point for European art and science. But in 1618 religious squabbling began anew when representatives of the city's Protestant nobles threw two Habsburg councillors out a Prague Castle window, sparking Europe's Thirty Years' War. Prague's Protestants lost early on in the piece: in 1620 the Habsburgs routed them at the Battle of Bílá Hora (White Mountain), just west of the city, and they sat out the rest of the war they'd started until 1648, when Swedish troops seized Hradčany and Malá Strana. Prague's population shrank from 60,000 in 1620 to 24,600 in 1648.

Eventually, the Habsburgs moved back to Vienna, reducing Prague to a provincial town. A devastating fire in 1689 led to a baroque rebuilding, and in 1784 the four towns of Prague – Staré and Nové Město, Malá Strana and Hradčany – officially became one city.

As Czechs struggled to define themselves independently of the Habsburgs and Germany in the 19th century, Prague architects built several proud Czech monuments, including the National Theatre (p112) and the National Museum (p109). Czechoslovakia, with Prague – historically the most important city in the region – as its capital, declared its independence towards the end of WWI. Several days after the announcement, the country's new government had to ask Prague's citizens to please stop partying and do a little work, or the fresh-minted country's economy would collapse. On 1 January 1922, Greater Prague absorbed several surrounding towns and became a city of 677,000. By 1938 the population had grown to one million.

After Britain handed the Sudetenland to Hitler in the Munich Agreement of March 1939 (see p23), Germany marched into Prague without a fight and the city's buildings consequently suffered little damage.' However, its people – particularly the Jewish community – suffered a great deal. The Nazi Governor (Reichsprotektor) of Czechoslovakia, Reinhard Heydrich, was assassinated by British-backed Czech paratroopers in the city in June 1942; in a lather of revenge the Nazis executed a large number of Prague's intellectuals, pretty much wiping out the Czech resistance (see the Church of SS Cyril and Methodius p113). On 8 May 1945 Prague rose up against its occupiers, negotiating the Nazis – who were already militarily on the back foot – out one day before the Soviets marched in.

After the communist coup in February 1948, economic and social policies almost bankrupted the country and crushed all dissent, sending Prague into a slow decline.

In 1968, under the leadership of Alexander Dubček, the party introduced reforms to decrease censorship and increase democracy. The resultant flowering of artistic and intellectual activity was known as the Prague Spring. The Soviet Union, unimpressed by the direction Czechoslovakia was taking, sent in the tanks (supported by Warsaw Pact troops) on the night of 20–21 August. Fifty-eight Praguers died.

The extraordinary 'Velvet Revolution' was set in motion on 17 November 1989, when marchers in Prague commemorating the execution of nine students by the Nazis 50 years earlier were beaten by the police. The communist government was brought down within a fortnight. On 1 January 1993, by agreement between the elected Czech and Slovak leaders, Czechoslovakia ceased to exist and Prague became the capital of the new Czech Republic.

PRAGUE

GREATER PRAGUE

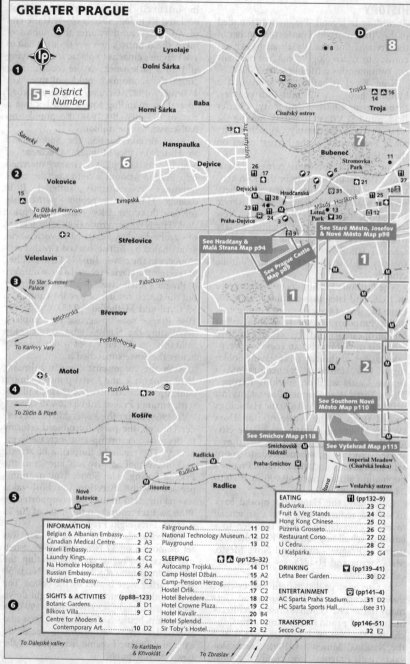

5 = District Number

INFORMATION
Belgian & Albanian Embassy........1 D2
Canadian Medical Centre..............2 A3
Israeli Embassy..............................3 C2
Laundry Kings................................4 C2
Na Homolce Hospital.....................5 A4
Russian Embassy............................6 D2
Ukrainian Embassy.........................7 C2

SIGHTS & ACTIVITIES   (pp88–123)
Botanic Gardens.............................8 D1
Bílkova Villa...................................9 C3
Centre for Modern &
   Contemporary Art.....................10 D2

Fairgrounds..................................11 D2
National Technology Museum......12 D2
Playground...................................13 D2

SLEEPING   (pp125–32)
Autocamp Trojská........................14 D1
Camp Hostel Džbán......................15 A2
Camp-Pension Herzog..................16 D1
Hostel Orlík.................................17 C2
Hotel Belvedere...........................18 D2
Hotel Crowne Plaza......................19 C2
Hotel Kavalír................................20 B4
Hotel Splendid.............................21 D2
Sir Toby's Hostel..........................22 E2

EATING   (pp132–9)
Budvarka......................................23 C2
Fruit & Veg Stands.......................24 C2
Hong Kong Chinese.....................25 D2
Pizzeria Grosseto.........................26 C2
Restaurant Corso.........................27 C2
U Cedru.......................................28 C2
U Kašpárka...................................29 G4

DRINKING   (pp139–41)
Letna Beer Garden.......................30 D2

ENTERTAINMENT   (pp141–4)
AC Sparta Praha Stadium.............31 D2
HC Sparta Sports Hall..............(see 31)

TRANSPORT   (pp146–51)
Secco Car.....................................32 E2

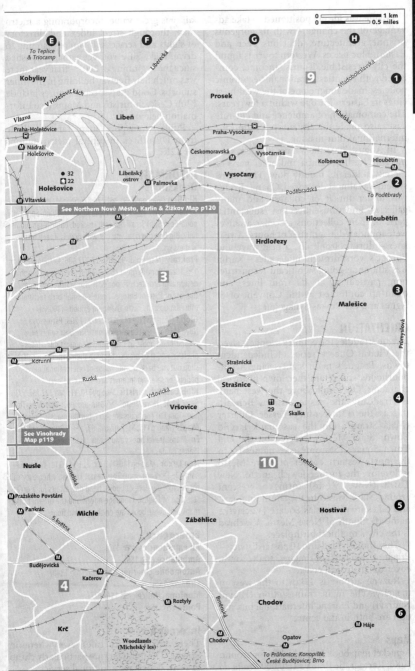

Prague was ideally positioned to take advantage of the change – with its gorgeous pristine architecture, delicious beer and Eastern bloc prices, Western tourists found the city irresistible. Tourist income, combined with relentlessly rationalist economic policies, made Prague one of the wealthiest cities in Eastern Europe within a few years. The combination of ambience and cut-rate costs also made the city a top location for international film-making.

In August 2002 the Vltava flooded, submerging Karlín, Kampa and other parts of the city under its muddy flow. The metro system was almost destroyed, Charles Bridge was under threat of collapse and many galleries and museums lost substantial parts of their collections as cellar archives were inundated in a matter of hours. A year later – during, ironically, a heat wave and Europe's worst drought in decades – Karlín was still undergoing significant reconstruction, particularly of its tram lines, and clean-up continued at the Convent of St Agnes and the Pinkas Synagogue.

ORIENTATION

Prague straddles the country's longest river, the Vltava. Once a series of independent towns, Prague's main sight-seeing neighbourhoods still retain their own historical character. On a hill above the west bank is Hradčany, the castle district. Beneath this is the 13th-century Lesser Quarter (Malá Strana). On the east bank is Old Town (Staré Město), centred on the Old Town Square (Staroměstské náměstí). In the northwestern corner of Staré Město is Josefov, the former Jewish ghetto. New Town (Nové Město) forms a crescent around Staré Město to the south and east, and takes in Wenceslas Square (Václavské náměstí). South of Nové Město, Vyšehrad is the city's mythical birthplace.

The city is divided into 10 postal districts – Prague 1, and parts of Prague 2 to the south, cover the historical centre.

Ruzyně airport is 17km to the west of the city. The main train station (Hlavní Nádraží) and Florenc international bus station are both in the centre.

Maps

A pocket map book is invaluable: for around 70Kč, Kartografie Praha's 1:20,000 *Praha do kapsy* is great value, incorporating a metro map, thorough street index and directory of sights and services. If you're planning to drive, make sure you get a map published since the beginning of 2003 – that year there was much new freeway building in the inner suburbs. Good map specialist stores include Klub Českých turistů and Mapis (see Information below).

Public transport maps are available from DP offices in central metro stations for 12Kč.

INFORMATION
Bookshops

Big Ben (Map pp98-9; ☎ 224 826 565; Malá Štupartská 5, Staré Město; ☼ 9am-6.30pm Mon-Fri, 10am-5pm Sat, noon-5pm Sun) Small but well stocked, English-language only, Big Ben can help you out with novels, Czech history and essays.

Fraktaly (Map pp98-9; ☎ 222 222 186; Betlémské nám; ☼ 10am-9pm) A great collection of Czech photography, design and architecture books; it also features art from the rest of Eastern Europe. There's a small architecture museum upstairs, with changing exhibits (100Kč).

Globe (Map pp110-11; ☎ 224 934 203; Pštrossova 6, Nové Město; ☼ 10am-midnight) The best selection of second-hand books in town, and a comfortable atmosphere in which to browse through them. There's a coffee shop out the back, a wide range of international newspapers for sale and Internet access (see below).

Klub Českých turistů (Map pp110-11; ☎ 222 232 593; Řeznická 15, Nové Město; ☼ 8am-noon & 1-4pm Mon-Thu, 8am-1pm Fri) The hours are short, but the maps are plentiful.

Mapis (Map p118; Štefanikova 63; ☼ 9.30am-6pm Mon-Fri) Maps, travel books and a very good range of Lonely Planet guides.

Neo Luxor (Map pp110-11; ☎ 221 111 311; Václavské nám 41; ☼ 8am-8pm) They're not kidding when they call themselves a palace of books. Head downstairs for a great selection of English-language novels and the Internet café; maps and guide books are on the ground floor.

Emergency

All emergencies (☎ 112)
Ambulance (☎ 155)
Automobile Emergencies (ABA; ☎ 1240)
Fire (☎ 150)
Municipal Police (☎ 156)
Police (☎ 158)

Internet Access

There are Internet cafés everywhere in Prague. The following are particularly cheap or central, or have additional services.

PRAGUE IN...

Two days

Walk across **Charles Bridge** in the early morning light and head up to the **castle** before the crowds arrive. Take the tram to Nové Mešto and have a traditional Czech lunch at **U Pinkasů**, then look around the **Museum of the City of Prague**. Take in an evening show of classical music at Malá Strana's **St Nicholas Church**, then have dinner and a drink on the roof garden at **Bazaar**.

Start your second morning with a tour of the **Municipal House**, then head over to Josefov for a day at the **Jewish Museum**. Taste the new Prague at hip restaurant **Dynamo**, then wander through **Old Town Square** after dark to one of Staré Mešto's many bars – try **Chateau** or **U zlatého tygra**.

Four days

Follow the two-day itinerary, then spend a relaxed day at **Vyšehrad**. Head back to the river and rent a **pedal-boat** to watch the sunset, then treat yourself to a fancy dinner at **Vinárna v zátiši**.

On day four, spend the morning at the **Museum of Decorative Arts** and the Convent of St Agnes' exhibition of **Medieval Bohemian art**; after lunch take in the **Museum of Communism**. Have dinner at **Kampa Park**, with its awesome views of the river and the Charles Bridge.

One week

You clever person, you. Spread the four-day itinerary out over five days and give yourself time to sit around in some parks: **Kampa Park**, the **Wallenstein Gardens** and **Ledeburská Gardens** all have their charms.

On day six, head out to Žižkov to take a look at the graves of **Jan Palach** and **Franz Kafka**, the **TV Tower** and the tiny, uncrowded **Jewish Cemetery** below it. Beer break! Stop off at Riegrovy Sady's **Park Café** for a sausage and a cleansing pilsner, then hike up Žižkov Hill to see the **Jan Žižka statue**. Spend the evening at **Futurum's** '80s and '90s party or get some jazz at **Železná**. Grab a fried cheese and a beer in Wenceslas Square on your way home.

By day seven you should be exhausted. Take the funicular railway up to **Petřín**. Revisit anything you really need to see again, and top it off with a few shots of slivovice at **Palírna Igor Sevčík**.

Bohemia Bagel (Map pp98-9; ☎ 224 812 560; www.bohemiabagel.cz; Masná 2, Staré Mĕsto; per min 1.50Kč; ☺ 7am-midnight Mon-Fri, 8am-midnight Sat & Sun) There's another outlet in Malá Strana at Újezd 18, open the same hours.

Globe (Map pp110-11; ☎ 224 934 203; www.globe bookstore.cz; Pštrossova 6, Nové Mĕsto; per min 1.50Kč; ☺ 10am-midnight) One of the first Internet cafés in Prague. Laptop connections available, same price.

Grial Internet Café (Map p115; ☎ 224 910 193; www.grial.cz; Vratislavova 12, Vyšehrad; per min 0.50Kč; ☺ 9am-11pm Mon-Fri, 11am-9pm Sat, 11am-11pm Sun) Out of the way, but among the cheapest in town and with very fast access. Purists will enjoy the absence of Microsoft products. Also services computers.

Pl@neta (Map pp120-1; ☎ 267 311 182; www.planeta .cz in Czech; Vinohradská 102, Žižkov; per min from 0.30Kč; ☺ 8am-11pm) Good luck finding cheaper Internet access. Pl@neta also has computers loaded with Microsoft Office – if you need to work on your CV or use Outlook – or you can connect your own laptop.

Internet Resources

Badpoint (www.badpoint.com) Up-to-date club listings and reviews; Prague information for the young and alternative.

CzechSite (www.czechsite.com) Good for pre-arrival planning.

DP Information (www.dp-praha.cz) Prague's public transport system.

Lonely Planet Online (www.lonelyplanet.com) Pre-planning info, travel literature, links and the Thorn Tree travellers' bulletin board.

Ministry of Foreign Affairs (www.czech.cz) Official information on being a foreigner in Prague; includes employment regulations.

Prague Post (www.praguepost.com) News and current affairs, also has reviews and listings.

Prague TV (www.prague.tv) Probably the most useful site once you're in Prague: entertainment and eating listings, news, reviews and apartments, all with an alternative bent.

Radio Prague (www.radio.cz) News and current affairs.

Laundry

Laundry Kings (Map pp82-3; ☎ 603 713 855; Dejvická 16, Dejvice; per load wash & dry approx 100Kč; ☼ 6am-10pm Mon-Fri, 1am-10pm Sat & Sun) Prague's original expat self-service laundry. Good bulletin board, snacks and newspapers, Internet and a drop-off service. From metro station Hradčanská, take the 'Praha Dejvice' exit, turn left into Dejvická.

Laundryland (☎ 777 333 466 for delivery; www .laundryland.cz for pick-up locations; per load wash & dry approx 120Kč) Nové Město (Map pp110-11; 1st fl, Černá růže shopping mall, off Na příkopě; ☼ 9am-8pm Mon-Fri, 9am-7pm Sat, 11am-7pm Sun, closed 1.15-2pm); Žižkov (Map pp120-1; down steps beside Táboritská 3; ☼ 8am-10pm, closed 1.15-2pm); Vinohrady (Map p119; Londýnská 71; ☼ 8am-10pm, closed 1.15-2pm) The bar downstairs opens at 4pm.

Prague Cyber Laundromat (Map p119; ☎ 222 510 180; Korunní 14, Vinohrady; per load wash & dry approx 130Kč; ☼ 8am-8pm, until 9pm in summer) Internet café, graffiti wall and children's play area.

Left Luggage

There are left luggage services at Hlavní nádraží (main train station) and Florenc bus station: see Getting There and Away (p147) for more information.

Media

The weekly English-language *Prague Post* (50Kč) is fairly meagre reading, but its 'Night & Day' lift-out is an invaluable entertainment and dining resource. The monthly *Prague Tribune* covers expat business matters in the Czech Republic.

The BBC World Service broadcasts in English and Czech on 101.1FM. The city's most popular commercial station is Radio Impuls, at 96.6FM – it's an eye-opener.

Czech-language TV runs plenty of American sitcoms and films in the evening, but they're all dubbed: surrealists may get a kick out of watching *Friends* and *Baywatch* in Czech. If you have satellite TV, your choices in English include Discovery, Euronews and CNN.

Medical Services

Canadian Medical Centre (Map pp82-3; ☎ 235 360 133, after hrs ☎ 724 300 301; Veleslavínská 1, Veleslavín; ☼ 8am-6pm Mon, Wed & Fri, 8am-8pm Tue & Thu) English-speaking doctors, 24-hour medical aid, physiotherapist and a pharmacy. A first visit will cost 1700Kč. It's the seventh stop – Nádraží Veleslavia – on tram No 20 or 26 from Dejvická metro.

European Dental Service (Map pp110-11; ☎ 224 228 984; Wenceslas Sq 33, Nové Město)

Lékárna U sv Ludmily (Map p119; ☎ 222 513 396; Belgická 37, Vinohrady; ☼ 24hr) This pharmacy is right by náměstí Míru metro.

Na Homolce Hospital (Map pp82-3; ☎ 257 271 111, after hrs ☎ 257 272 527; Na Homolce 724, Motel) The best hospital in Prague, with English, French, German and Spanish spoken. Take bus No 167 from Anděl metro station. The foreigners' polyclinic and emergency entrance are on the northern side, 2nd level. There's a separate **children's clinic** (☎ 257 274 547, after hrs ☎ 257 272 225) and a dental service.

Policlinic (Map pp98-9; ☎ 222 075 119, after hrs ☎ 606 461 628; www.poliklinika.narodni.cz; Národní 9, Staré Město; ☼ 8.30am-5pm Mon-Fri) A district clinic with after-hours emergency services (call the after-hours number if you need these), English-speaking staff and dental services.

Prague 1 clinic (Map pp110-11; ☎ 224 946 986; Palackého 5, Nové Město) Off Jungmannova, this is another district clinic that has medical and after-hours dental and pharmaceutical services.

Money

Avoid changing money at small exchange offices, which advertise 0% commission but charge from 4% to 10% 'admin fees' or give terrible rates. The main foreign-exchange banks – Československá obchodní banka (ČSOB), Komerční banka (KB) and Česke Spořitlena – have branches all over town and are generally open from 8am to 5pm Monday to Friday. If you need to change money out of hours, there are 24-hour bureaux de change on Wenceslas Square, with awful rates. Using your debit card in the city's ubiquitous ATMs will get you the best rate of all.

American Express Nové Město (Map pp110-11; ☎ 222 800 237; Wenceslas Sq 56; ☼ 9am-7.30pm); Staré Město (Map pp98-9; Staroměstské náměstí 5)

Thomas Cook (Map pp110-11; ☎ 221 105 371; Národní 28, Nové Město; ☼ 9am-9pm Mon-Fri, 9am-6pm Sat, 10am-6pm Sun)

Post

Most of the city's post offices are open 8am to 6pm Monday to Friday, and until noon Saturday.

At the **main office** (Map pp110-11; Jindřišská 14, Nové Město; ☼ 2am-midnight), take a ticket from one of the machines in the entrance corridors – press button No 1 for single-item stamps, letters and parcels or No 4 for Express Mail Service – and when your ticket number is displayed go to the desk number shown. Pick up poste-restante mail *(výdej listovních zásilek)* in the main post office at desks Nos 1 and 2 (at the far left) 7am to 8pm weekdays, and to noon Saturday. Mail should be addressed to Poste Restante, Hlavní pošta, Jindřišská 14, 110 00 Praha 1, Czech Republic. You must present your passport to claim mail (check under your first name, too). Mail is held for one month.

Holders of American Express and Thomas Cook cards and travellers cheques can have letters sent to the Prague offices (see Money opposite).

Telephone

Prague has coin-phones and lots of cardphones. Telephone cards *(telekarty)* are sold in post offices, newsagents and in the telephone bureau in the main post office in 175Kč and 320Kč sizes. Bohemia Bagel (see Internet Access p84) has phones for making international calls (5Kč per minute).

The Czech Republic has 10 million people and eight million mobile phones. Eurotel, Oskar and T-Mobile all have outlets throughout the city. If you have your own phone, a Czech SIM card costs about 700Kč and comes with credit. A second-hand phone costs about 2000Kč. You can rent a phone and card at steeper rates – Eurotel and T-Mobile both have booths in the arrivals area at the airport. Recharge cards are available at phone stores, *tabacs* and small grocery and snack shops, or you can replenish your credit at KB and ČSOB ATMs.

Toilets

There are public toilets in every metro station, though they are open shorter hours than the metro itself. Each has an attendant, who charges 3Kč. Coin-operated street toilet booths can be pretty nasty. Men's toilets are marked *muži* or *páni*; women's are *ženy* or *dámy*.

Tourist Information

Prague Information Service (Pražská informační služba, PIS; Map pp110-11; ☎ 124 44; www.prague-info .cz; Na příkopě 20, Nové Město; ☻ 9am-7pm Mon-Fri, to 6pm in winter, 9am-5pm Sat & Sun) A municipal agency that has Prague well covered, with good maps and detailed brochures (including accommodation, historical monuments and monthly entertainment), all free. All offices have Ticketpro's concert tickets and AVE's accommodation

services. There are other branches at **Old Town Hall** (Map pp98-9; Staroměstské nám, Staré Město), also the office of Pragotur city tours; **Main Train Station** (Map pp120-1; Hlavní nádraží, Nové Město) and **Malá Strana Bridge Tower** (Map pp94-5; Křižovnické nám, Malá Strana; ☻ summer only).

Czech Tourist Authority (Česká centrála cestovního ruchu, ČCCR; Map pp98-9; ☎ 224 826 984; www.czechtourism.com; Staroměstské nám 6, Staré Město; ☻ 9am-6pm, closed Sat & Sun in winter) Information about sights, museums and festivals for the whole of the Czech Republic.

Travel Agencies

Bohemiatour (Map pp110-11; ☎ 224 947 707; www.bohemiatour.cz in Czech; Jungmannova 4, Nové Město; ☻ 9am-6pm Mon-Fri, 9am-noon Sat) Low overheads, books international bus tickets and package tours.

Čedok (Czech Transport Office, Česká dopravní kancelář; Map pp98-9; ☎ 224 197 777, 800 112 112; www.cedok.cz; Na příkopě 18, Nové Město; ☻ 9am-7pm Mon-Fri, 9am-1pm Sat) Tour operator and travel agency. Main office also does accommodation bookings, excursions, concert and theatre tickets, car rental and money exchange. There are other offices in Nové Město (Map pp110-11; ☎ 221 965 243; Václavské nám 53) and Ruzyně airport (☎ 224 223 479).

CKM Travel (Map pp120-1; ☎ 222 721 595; ckmprg@ login.cz; Mánesova 77, Vinohrady; ☻ 10am-6pm Mon-Thu, 10am-4pm Fri) Bus tickets, cheap air tickets, budget accommodation and student cards.

GTS International (Map pp110-11; ☎ 222 211 204; gts.smecky@gtsint.cz; Ve Smečkách 33, Nové Město; ☻ 8am-7pm Mon-Fri, 11am-3pm Sat) Student cards, bus, train and air tickets.

DANGERS & ANNOYANCES

Prague is still among the safest cities in Europe, though locals talk about how crime has risen since the revolution.

Pickpockets work the crowds wherever tourists congregate. Keep an eye on your things if someone starts pushing a map under your nose or a baby into your face. Don't hand over money or passports to anyone stopping you on the street and claiming to be a plain-clothes police officer – insist on going back to the police station.

The area around Můstek metro is the home of Prague's sex industry. If one of these women starts patting your butt, make sure they're not taking your wallet at the same time. Male prostitution is centred on Hlavní Nádraží, the main train station – in 2003 several tourists were robbed and at least one murdered by boys they picked up off the street. On the whole, the park in front of Hlavní Nádraží is the least savoury place in central Prague – unpleasant during the day, it can be downright dangerous at night.

Thanks to Prague's cheap beer and easyJet's cheap fares, summer weekends see rowdy, loudly sexist and sometimes violent stag parties flying in from the UK. Police seem reluctant to do anything about this source of tourist dollars, and most of the city appears to be silently praying they'll find somewhere new to go in the near future. If seeing a T-shirt that says 'Dead women don't struggle' annoys you, avoid the Old Town and Wenceslas Square on Saturday nights.

If you take a taxi on the street, it's almost inevitable they'll rip you off. Public transport here is excellent, even at 3am, but if you must catch a taxi, call one of the companies listed in Getting Around (p148) rather than flagging a cab.

Unless you have Czech friends who can help, if you need to see the police go to either the police van in Old Town Square during the day, or the **Nové Město police station** (Jungmannovo nám 9), the only station that can organise an interpreter (police do not generally speak English); the interpreter will then take you to the station in the district where the crime occurred. Making a police report can take several hours, so be patient. You may be better off going to your embassy first.

SIGHTS

For visitors from outside Europe, walking the ancient, winding streets of central Prague is incredible enough to count as a

sight in its own right. Budget some time to just get lost and wander (let's face it, it'll happen to you whether you plan it or not) – if you spend all your time with your nose buried in a map, you'll miss some of the best spontaneous moments the city has to offer.

The most popular sights are in Staré Město (Old Town), Hradčany (the castle district) and Malá Strana (the Lesser Quarter). Nové Město (the New Town) is also packed with interesting things, including the city's best Art Nouveau architecture. Try to get outside the centre for at least half a day. Quiet Vyšehrad, the birthplace of Prague, is worth a visit, while the inner suburbs of working-class Holešovice and Smíchov, genteel Vinohrady or grungy, youthful Žižkov will give you an insight into what regular Praguers get up to while the rest of us are watching the Astronomical Clock.

Prague Castle   Map p89

Prague Castle (Pražský hrad), simply called *hrad* by the Czechs, is the most popular sight in Prague; if you don't like crowds, come early in the day (by 10am in summer the place is packed). According to the *Guinness Book of Records*, the *hrad* is the largest ancient castle in the world – 570m long, an average of 128m wide and occupying 7.28 hectares. The surrounding complex of churches and former ecclesiastical buildings covers an additional 38 hectares.

The castle's history goes back to the 9th century, when Prince Bořivoj built a few houses here and put a wall around them. It grew as rulers made their own additions, which is why it's a jumble of architectural styles. Prince Soběslav did a Romanesque makeover in the 12th century, and Empress Maria Theresa gave the place a classical facelift in the 18th century. In the 1920s, President Masaryk contracted a Slovenian, Josef Plečnik, to renovate the castle. For centuries this was the home of Bohemia's kings; since 1918 it's been used by Czech presidents.

FIRST COURTYARD

On either side of the main gate at the west end are the **Battling Titans** by Ignác Platzer (1767–70). The castle guards below them are known to crack smiles now and then, and their heads definitely turn when a nice-looking girl goes by. Havel hired the costume designer for the film *Amadeus* to

---

PRAGUE CARD

If you're only in Prague for a few days and have a lot of energy, the Prague Card is great value. Valid for three days, it costs 560Kč and gives entry to over 2000Kč-worth of sights (including the castle) and unlimited rides on public transport (worth 200Kč). If you think you can manage about five sights in three days you'll get your money's worth. The card is available at American Express, Čedok, GTS and Holešovice and Muzeum metro stations.

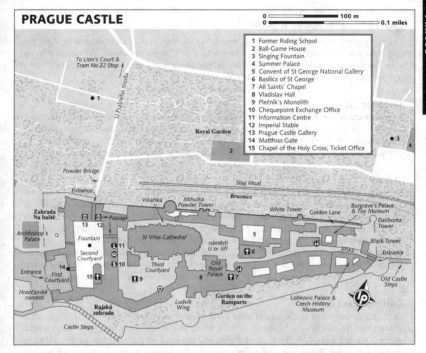

PRAGUE CASTLE

0 ——— 100 m
0 ——— 0.1 miles

1 Former Riding School
2 Ball-Game House
3 Singing Fountain
4 Summer Palace
5 Convent of St George National Gallery
6 Basilica of St George
7 All Saints' Chapel
8 Vladislav Hall
9 Plečnik's Monolith
10 Chequepoint Exchange Office
11 Information Centre
12 Imperial Stable
13 Prague Castle Gallery
14 Matthias Gate
15 Chapel of the Holy Cross; Ticket Office

replace their communist-era khaki uniforms with the present ones. The guard is changed every hour from 5am to 11pm; the best display is at noon.

The pointy flagpoles are among Plečnik's controversial 1920s' additions.

SECOND COURTYARD

The second courtyard is entered through the baroque **Matthias Gate** (1614). The **Chapel of the Holy Cross** (kaple sv Kříže), on the right, was built in 1763 and was once the treasury of St Vitus Cathedral; now it's the ticket office and castle information centre. In the middle of the courtyard are a baroque fountain and a 17th-century well with Renaissance lattice work.

The **Prague Castle Gallery** (admission 50Kč; 10am-6pm Apr-Oct, 10am-5pm Nov-Mar) features 17th- and 18th-century European and Czech art. Opposite is the **Imperial Stable** (Císařská konírna), which hosts temporary art exhibits. Past the gallery, the 1540 **Powder Bridge** (Prašný most) crosses the **Stag Moat** (Jelení příkop), used to raise deer for the royal table.

ROYAL GARDEN

Ferdinand I built this **Renaissance garden** (Královská zahrada; 10am-6pm Apr-Oct) in 1534, with money raised from taxing the Jewish population. To the left of the entrance is the **Lion's Court**, once Prague's first private zoo. The Habsburgs played an early version of badminton in the **Ball-Game House**, built by Bonifác Wohlmut in 1569; it's only open for exhibitions.

This well-kept park was Europe's first tulip garden. At the far end is the **Singing Fountain** (Zpívající fontána) and the **Summer Palace** (Letohrádek). The palace, built by Ferdinand I for his wife Anna between 1538 and 1564, was one of the first Renaissance buildings in the city, built in authentic Italian style. West of the Royal Garden is the 1695 **Riding School**, now a venue for temporary modern art exhibitions.

THIRD COURTYARD

The most visible part of the castle, and its synecdochal silhouette, is **St Vitus Cathedral** (katedrála sv Víta); entering from the second courtyard brings you straight to its main

CASTLE TICKETS, HOURS & ENTRY

The castle grounds are open from 5am to midnight daily from April to October; and to 11pm the rest of the year. Most sights are open from 9am to 5pm daily (to 4pm in winter), although the hours vary. The gardens – except the Garden on the Bastion, which is open the same hours as the castle – are open only in summer, from 10am to 6pm.

Information

An **information centre** (☎ 224 373 368; ☯ 9am-5pm, until 4pm in winter) is in the third courtyard and there is a smaller office in the second courtyard's Chapel of the Holy Cross. The post office is in the third courtyard, opposite the main entrance to St Vitus Cathedral. The Chequepoint exchange office, by the post office, charges a 10% commission and is open during regular castle hours.

Tickets

Entrance to the castle grounds and most of St Vitus is free. There are three kinds of ticket for the rest: ticket A lets you see the lot (St Vitus crypts, choir and tower, the Old Royal Palace, St George Basilica, Powder Tower and the Golden Lane) and will cost 220/180Kč per adult/child; ticket B covers St Vitus, the Old Royal Palace and the Golden Lane and costs 110/90Kč; ticket C, covering Golden Lane only, costs 40Kč. The mid-range ticket is probably the best value; buy the Golden-Lane-only ticket if you want to pay for the privilege of being crammed into a souvenir-shop arcade. The tickets are valid only for one day (despite what it says on all the castle's literature). Guided tours can be organised for an extra 400Kč per person, or you can rent an audio tour.

Getting There & Away

Most approaches to the castle require some walking uphill. The usual ones are from the tram stop in Malostranské náměstí, up Nerudova and Ke Hradu to the main gate; and from Malostranská metro station, up the Old Castle Steps – probably the least pleasant option, as the stairs are packed with other visitors and watercolour hawkers. The approach with the least walking, and all of it on the flat, is along U Prašného mostu from the Pražský hrad stop on tram No 22 or 23, which you can pick up at Malostranská or Národní Třida metro stations. This option reaches the castle at the Royal Garden.

entrance. Originally a Romanesque rotunda built by Duke Václav in 929, it's now the largest church in the country with a whopping 97m steeple.

The doorways are richly decorated with carvings of historical and biblical scenes – take a look at the *Mosaic of Last Judgment* (1370–71) on the southern doorway. Gargoyles on every promontory of the roof act as guttering, and it's worth coming up here during a rainstorm to see them in action.

The stained-glass windows in the nave are modern – that's Alfons Mucha's history of SS Cyril and Methodius over the New Archbishop's chapel. The ornate **Chapel of St Wenceslas** (kaple sv Václava) was built in the 14th century by Peter Parler and is full of frescoes and more than 1300 semiprecious stones. On the southern side of this chapel, a small door – secured with seven locks – hides the Czech crown jewels.

To get into the choir, crypt and tower you'll need an A or B ticket (see boxed text above). The choir includes the Royal Mausoleum with images of Ferdinand I, his wife, Anna Jagellonská, and son, Maxmilián II, and a silver monument to St Jan of Nepomuk. In the royal crypt are the remains of Karel IV, Václav IV, Jiří z Poděbrad and Rudolf II. The Great Tower is closed if the weather is bad, but on a clear day the views are great.

In the courtyard facing the cathedral's southern entrance is Plečnik's 16m granite **monolith** (1928), dedicated to the victims of WWI. At the southeastern end of the courtyard, a gate leads to the Garden on the Ramparts (Zahrada na Valech), an elegant, manicured space with fine views over the city. The grass areas are considered sacred here and if you bend even one blade, you risk a verbal ear-bashing in Czech on the virtues of STAYING OFF THE GRASS.

The 1135 **Old Royal Palace** (Starý Královský palác), for which you'll need an A or B ticket, is one of the oldest parts of the castle. At its heart is the Vladislav Hall (Vladislavský sál). With its rough wooden floors and vast, rustic spaces it feels more medieval than anywhere else in the castle, and may make you want to pull out a tankard and gnaw on a hapless animal's roasted limb. It was used for banquets, councils and coronations and, during bad weather, jousting: hence the sloping Riders' Staircase leading in from the northern side. In one corner of the hall is the entrance to the Ludvík Wing where, on 23 May 1618, Bohemian nobles threw two Catholic councillors from the window, triggering the Thirty Years' War. There are no reports on whether the Hussites sued for copyright infringement.

Across the hall from the Ludvík Wing is the New Land Rolls Room, a repository for land titles, with walls covered with coats of arms of the clerks who looked after them. Downstairs, the Gothic Floor – dim and damp-smelling – includes a giant fireplace from the medieval kitchen and models of older incarnations of the hrad.

The WC in the Old Royal Palace has much shorter lines than those outside, so if you're about to 'do a Tycho' (see Church of Our Lady before Týn p103), pull out that A or B ticket.

ST GEORGE SQUARE (NÁMĚSTÍ U SV JIŘÍ)

This is the plaza behind the cathedral, and the heart of Prague Castle. The very plain-looking **Convent of St George** (klášter sv Jiří; ☎ 257 535 832; adult/child 100/50Kč; ❧ 10am-6pm Tue-Sun) was Bohemia's first convent, established in 973 by Boleslav II. It's now a branch of the National Gallery, with an excellent collection of Czech Renaissance and baroque art.

The **Basilica of St George** (bazilika sv Jiří) is the striking red church adjoining the convent, established in the 10th century; you'll need an A ticket to enter. It's the best-preserved Romanesque structure in the Czech Republic, though most of what you see is from an 1887–1908 reconstruction. The Přemysl princes are buried here. On the left wall is a hole that enabled the nuns from the convent next door to communicate with the rest of the world.

MIHULKA POWDER TOWER

The 20m **Mihulka Powder Tower** (Prašná věž), an A-ticket attraction on the northern side of St Vitus, was built at the end of the 15th century as part of the castle's defences. Later it was used as a workshop; the bells of St Vitus were cast here. Alchemists employed by Rudolf II worked here, kicking off Prague's reputation for mystery and magic. The tower got its name in the 19th century from the *mihule* (lamprey eels) bred in the area. Today it's a museum of alchemy, bell and cannon forging, and Renaissance life in Prague Castle – all labels are in Czech.

JIŘSKÁ ULICE

Off Jiřská, along the northern wall of the castle, is **Golden Lane** (Zlatá ulička), also known as Goldsmiths' Lane (Zlatnická ulička) – all tickets are valid. Its tiny, colourful cottages were built in the 16th century for the sharpshooters of the castle guard, and later used by goldsmiths. In the 18th and 19th centuries they were occupied by squatters, and later by artists like Kafka (who stayed at No 22 in 1916–17) and the Nobel-laureate poet Jaroslav Seifert. These days, the houses are souvenir shops and the street is crammed with tour groups trying to get into them.

At the western end of the lane is the **White Tower** (Bílá věž), touted as a prison where failed Irish alchemist Edward Kelley was locked up by Rudolf II – in reality, Kelley's prison sentences, for killing someone in a duel, were served outside the capital. At the eastern end is the **Daliborka Tower**, which got its name from the knight Dalibor of Kozojed, who played the violin when he was imprisoned here in 1498: Smetana based his opera *Dalibor* (1868) on the tale.

Just inside the eastern gate, with its Black Tower (Černá věž), is the Lobkovic Palace (Lobkovický palác), built in the 1570s. It has a good **Czech History Museum** (adult/child 40/20Kč; ❧ 9am-4.30pm Tue-Sun), covering the period from the arrival of the Slavs until 1848. Exhibits include the sword of Prague's executioner Jan Mydlář (who lopped off the heads of 27 rebellious Protestant nobles in Old Town Square in 1621) and some of the country's oldest marionettes. Opposite Lobkovic Palace is the Burgrave's Palace (Purkrabství) and its **Toy Museum** (adult/child 50/30Kč; ❧ 9.30am-5.30pm), allegedly the world's second largest, with tons of Barbies and toys going back to Greek antiquity. The exhibits are very static, and kids may quickly get bored.

Hradčany

The lanes and stairways of Hradčany are an ideal place to wander – most of this area around the west gate of Prague Castle is residential, with just a few strips of shops, pubs and restaurants. Before it became a borough of Prague in 1598, Hradčany was almost levelled by Hussites and fire – in the 17th-century palaces were built on the ruins. Today Hradčany reaches as far as Pohořelec and the Strahov Monastery.

CASTLE SQUARE
(HRADČANSKÉ NÁMĚSTÍ)   Map pp94–5

Hradčanské náměstí has kept its shape since the Middle Ages. At its centre is a **plague column** by Ferdinand Brokoff (1726).

On the square is the imposing **Schwarzenberg Palace** (Švarcenberský palác) sporting a dramatic sgraffito façade as startling as a Hawaiian shirt. The Schwarzenbergs acquired the palace in 1719; it's currently being refitted by the National Gallery and will host its old masters collection from 2007.

Opposite is the rococo **Archbishop's Palace** (Arcibiskupský palác), bought and remodelled by Archbishop Antonín Bruse of Mohelnic in 1562, and the seat of archbishops ever since. Its wonderful interior is only open on the day before Good Friday; chances are you won't have time to wait around that long.

Diagonally behind it is the 1707 baroque **Sternberk Palace** (Šternberský palác), home to the **National Gallery** (☎ 220 514 599; adult/child 150/70Kč; ☷ 10am-6pm Tue-Sun) and its splendid collection of 14th- to 18th-century European art. Fans of medieval altarpieces will be in heaven; there's also a number of Rubens, a Dürer, some Rembrandt and Breughel, and a large collection of Bohemian miniatures. It's worth a trip to the back of the first floor to see van Heemskerck's *The Tearful Bride*, who seems to have stepped right out of a travesty show.

Along Úvoz, between Hradčanské náměstí and the Loreta, the **Josef Sudek Gallery** (☎ 224 811 241; Úvoz 24; adult/child 10/5Kč; ☷ 11am-5pm Wed-Sun Oct-Mar, 11am-7pm Wed-Sun Apr-Sep) was once the home of this Prague photographer.

These days it shows the work of its namesake, between-the-wars Czech photography and photos of Prague.

LORETA SQUARE
(LORETÁNSKÉ NÁMĚSTÍ)   Map pp94–5

From Hradčanské náměstí it's a short walk to Loretánské náměstí, created early in the 18th century when the **Černín Palace** (Černínský palác) was built. This palace today houses the foreign ministry, but during the Nazi occupation it was SS Headquarters and in 1948 the foreign minister Jan Masaryk, son of the founding president of Czechoslovakia, fell to his death from his bathroom window here (no-one knows if he jumped or was pushed by the communist secret servicemen interrogating him).

At the northern end of the square is a **Capuchin Monastery**, unfortunately closed to the public. Built from 1600 to 1602, it is the oldest operating monastery in Bohemia.

The square's main attraction is the **Loreta** (☎ 224 510 789; Loretánské náměstí 7; adult/child 80/60Kč; ☷ 9am-12.15pm & 1-4.30pm), an extraordinary baroque place of pilgrimage founded by Benigna Kateřina Lobkovic in 1626. The centrepiece of the Loreta is a replica of the Virgin's house, the **Santa Casa**. Its interior has a naive charm, despite the opulence of its silver altar.

Across from it is the decidedly unnaive **Church of the Nativity of Our Lord** (kostel Narození Páně), built in 1737 by Kristof Dientzenhofer. This church features two skeletons, of Spanish saints Felicissima and Marcia, dressed in nobles' clothing with wax masks over their skulls. The **Chapel of Our Lady of Sorrows** (kaple Panny Marie Bolestné) features a crucified bearded lady, St Starosta. She was the daughter of a Portuguese king who promised her to the king of Sicily against her wishes. After a night of tearful prayers she awoke with a beard, the wedding was called off, and her loving father had her crucified. She was later made patron saint of the needy and godforsaken.

The Loreta's most eye-popping sight is the treasury on the 1st floor. Though its treasures have been looted at least four times over the centuries, there's still plenty of sumptuousness. Most valuable is the diamond-studded **Prague Sun** (Pražské slunce) monstrance: try not to get confused when you see the boxes asking for donations.

Above the Loreta's entrance are 27 bells, made in Amsterdam in the 17th century, which play *We Greet Thee a Thousand Times*.

STRAHOV MONASTERY   Map pp94–5
At the back of Hradčany, the **Strahov Monastery** (Strahovský klášter; www.strahovmonastery.cz) is an enclosed oasis, a quiet escape from the castle-going crowds. Founded in 1140 by Vladislav II for the Premonstratensians, what you see today is mostly from the 17th and 18th centuries. The monastery functioned until the communist government closed it and imprisoned most of the monks – these days you'll see robed figures striding across courtyards and slipping into cloisters once more.

At the western end of the compound, the 1612 **Church of St Roch** (kostel sv Rocha) is home to the **Miro Gallery** (☎ 233 354 066; admission 100Kč; ⏲ 10am-5pm), with regularly changing exhibits by contemporary artists.

The centrepiece of the courtyard is the stocky **Church of the Assumption of Our Lady** (kostel Nanebevzetí Panny Marie), whose green domes you can see from everywhere else in Prague. Built in 1143, the church is filled with baroque gilt; Mozart allegedly played the organ here on one visit.

But what the tour groups come here to see is the **Strahov Library** (Strahovská knihovna; adult/child 60/40Kč; ⏲ 9am-noon & 1-5pm), the largest monastic library in the Czech Republic. Line up to take a peek at the two-storey Philosophy Hall (Filozofický sál), with its carved floor-to-ceiling shelves lined with beautiful old tomes and ceiling fresco by Franz Maulbertsch. Down the hallway, you can peer between the other visitors at the Theology Hall, with a ceiling fresco by Siard Nosecký (if you want a close-up view, Nosecký's studies for this fresco are in the Strahov Gallery). Unfortunately, there's not a lot of context given, and you might get more out of a visit to the Baroque Library (p104).

In the small entrance hall is a tiny exhibit of miniature books and other replica manuscripts. There's also a 'cabinet of curiosities' display of inexplicable dried undersea creatures and, um, apples.

Tucked behind the library and largely ignored, the **Strahov Gallery** (Strahovská obrazárna; adult/child 40/20Kč; ⏲ 9am-noon & 1-5pm, closed Mon) contains a fabulous collection of Bohemian Gothic, baroque, rococo and Romantic works. Some of the medieval works are extraordinary – don't miss the very modern-looking 14th-century Jihlava Crucifix. The cloisters here are placid and peaceful.

The 'write your name on a grain of rice' movement may have undermined the respectability of miniature artists, but Siberian technician Anatoly Konyenko will restore your faith with his **Miniature Museum** (Muzeum Miniatur; ☎ 233 352 371; www.muzeumminiatur.cz; Strahovské Nádvoří 11; adult/child 50/30Kč; ⏲ 10am-5pm). Konyenko used to manufacture tools for eye microsurgery, but these days he'd rather spend seven-and-a-half years crafting a pair of gold horseshoes for a flea. See those, plus the world's smallest book and strangely beautiful silhouettes of cars on the leg of a mosquito.

Malá Strana
Malá Strana (the Lesser Quarter) clusters at the foot of Prague Castle. Most tourists only see the Royal Way, climbing along Mostecká and Nerudova on their way to the castle. Slip off into the narrow back streets and you'll find the quarter is surprisingly quiet. This historical reserve is now a favourite movie set and commercial centre.

Malá Strana started life in the 8th or 9th century as a market settlement and was nearly destroyed twice – during the Hussite War in 1419, and in the Great Fire of 1541. In the 17th and 18th centuries the baroque churches and palaces that stud Malá Strana were constructed.

NERUDA WAY
(NERUDOVA ULICE)   Map pp94–5
Nerudova, part of the Royal Way, is an architectural delight. Most of its Renaissance façades have been 'baroquefied'; many still have their original shutter-like doors, while others are adorned with emblems of some kind. No 47 is the **House of Two Suns** (dům U dvou slunců), an early baroque building where the Czech poet Jan Neruda lived from 1845 to 1891.

On the corner with Janský vršek is **Bretfeld Palace**, which Josef of Bretfeld made a centre for social gatherings starting in 1765; among his guests were Mozart and Casanova. At No 24 is the baroque **Church of Our Lady of Unceasing Succour** (kostel Paní Marie ústavičné pomoci).

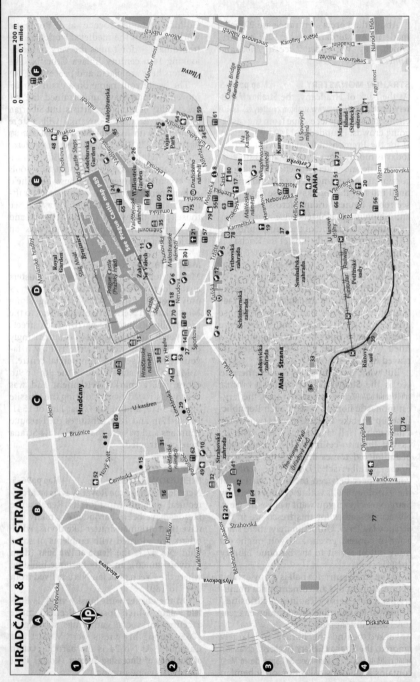

HRADČANY & MALÁ STRANA

MALÁ STRANA SQUARE (MALOSTRANSKÉ NÁMĚSTÍ)   Map pp94-5

This is really two squares, with the Church of St Nicholas – Malá Strana's primary landmark – between them. It has been the hub of Malá Strana since the 10th century.

Malostranská beseda, at No 21, was once the **Old Town Hall**, where in 1575 the non-Catholic nobles wrote the 'Czech Confession' (České konfese), a pioneering demand for religious tolerance eventually passed into law by Rudolf II in 1609. In practice the demands were not fully met, and the nobles eventually got angry enough to fling two Habsburg councillors out of a castle window (see History p81).

In a city of butt-kicking churches, the **Church of St Nicholas** (kostel Sv Mikuláše; ☎ 257 534 215; www.psalterium.cz; admission 50Kč; ☺ 9am-6pm, to 4pm in winter & on concert days) has to be the best of all. Baroque star designer Kryštof Dientzenhofer pulled out all the stops on this one (not to be confused with the Hussite St Nicholas on Old Town Square) and when he died (perhaps from a surfeit of gold-plating), his son Kilián Ignác picked up where he left off. The huge green dome is a true Prague landmark, and the reason this is considered one of central Europe's finest baroque buildings.

No matter how many baroque churches you've peered into over the last few days, this one will take your breath away. The ceiling fresco (1770) by Johann Kracker is the largest in Europe. Take the stairs up to the gallery to see Škréta's gloomy 17th-century Passion Cycle paintings and the scratchings of bored 1820s tourists and wannabe Franz Kafkas.

BELOW THE CASTLE TO KLÁROV   Map pp94-5

The **Castle Steps** (Zámecké schody) were originally the main route to the castle; the houses around them were built later. The steps merge at the top into Thunovská. Around the corner at Sněmovní is the **Parliament House** (Sněmovna) in the Thun Palace; today it is the seat of the lower house of parliament, but historically it was also the seat of the national assembly, which on 14 November 1918 deposed the Habsburgs from the Czech throne.

On Valdštejnské náměstí is the first of the monumental baroque structures built by Albrecht of Wallenstein, general of the Habsburg armies and astrology fan. The **Wallenstein Palace** (Valdštejnský Palác), built between 1623 and 1629, displaced 23 houses, a brickworks and three gardens. It's now occupied by the Senate of the Czech Republic.

Beside the palace is the huge, geometrically designed **Wallenstein Garden** (Valdštejnská zahrada; ☉ 10am-6pm Apr-Nov), a mannerist folly of ponds and hedges. The 'dripstone' wall here is one of Prague's more bizarre sights. At the eastern end of the garden, the **Wallenstein Riding School** (Valdštejnská jízdárna; admission fee depends on what's showing; ☉ 10am-6pm Tue-Sun) is home to changing exhibitions of modern art.

OTHER PARKS & GARDENS   Map pp94–5
From Valdštejnská, the immaculately kept terraces of the **Ledeburská Garden** (Ledeburská Zahrada; ☎ 257 010 401; Valdštejnksé nám 3; adult/child 95/40Kč; ☉ 10am-6pm) rise steeply north to the castle. This beautiful formal garden has espaliered vines, soft patches of lawn, fruit orchards, herb gardens, flowers and statuary and a lot of steep stairs.

Established in 1248, the quiet and sprawling **Vojan Park** (Vojanovy sady), entered from U lužického semináře, is Prague's oldest – although you're supposed to keep off the grass, the rules seem to be regularly flouted.

SOUTH OF NERUDOVA TO
KAMPA   Map pp94–5
In Karmelitská is the unimposing 1613 **Church of Our Lady Victorious** (kostel Panny Marie Vítězné). On one of its altars is a waxwork figure of the baby Jesus dressed in an embroidered coat, brought from Spain in 1628. The so-called **Infant of Prague** (Pražské jezulátko) is alleged to have worked numerous miracles – including saving Prague from the plague and from the destruction of the Thirty Years' War. It's still visited by a steady stream of pilgrims from around the world. The infant's wardrobe consists of 60 costumes donated from all over the world – see some in the upstairs museum.

The little Maltézské náměstí got its name from the Maltese Knights, Czech crusaders who established a monastery beside the **Church of Our Lady Below the Chain** (kostel Panny Marie pod řetězem) in 1169. All that remains today are sections of the church, but tourists are forbidden to enter. A short way east is Velkopřevorské náměstí and, opposite the French embassy, the **John**

Lennon Wall. After his death, Lennon became a pacifist hero among young Czechs – Western pop music was banned – and the wall served as a monument to him and his ideas: the secret police never managed to keep it clean. Today it's home to lightweight graffiti of the 'Wendy & Michele wuz 'ere' variety, plus the odd incitement to give peace a chance. Graffiti is encouraged here. Why not bring some paint and lift the tone a bit?

On Říční is one of the oldest Gothic buildings in Malá Strana, the **Church of St John at the Laundry** (kostel sv Jana Na prádle), built in 1142 but converted to a laundry in 1784 (hence the name), then reconsecrated in 1935.

Lying off the Malá Strana bank, with Charles Bridge passing over one end, **Kampa** is the most picturesque of Prague's islands. In the 13th century the town's first mill, the Sovovský mlýn, was built on Devil's Stream (Čertovka) separating Kampa from the mainland, and other mills followed. You can now drink beer in one of them (see Tato Kojkej in Drinking p140).

The **Museum of Decorative Arts' Jewellery Collection** (☎ 221 451 333; Cihelná 2b; adult/child 60/50Kč) has its own little museum just north of Kampa. Everything here is gorgeous, of course, including some Fabergé eggs and a selection of jewels designed by Tiffany, of *Breakfast at* fame. The gift shop here is a great place to pick up some very pricey, but unique, jewellery designs.

The southern part of Kampa is a park, ideal for summertime naps, frisbee and picnics – local hippies love the place.

Across Legii most, **Marksmen's Island** (Střelecký ostrov) has a small sandy beach at its northern end. Lounge about with a beer from Letní Bar (see p140) or take a paddle in the Vltava if you dare.

PETŘÍN   Map pp94–5
One of the largest green spaces in Prague, 318m Petřín is great for cool, quiet walks and outstanding views of the city. Once upon a time there were also vineyards, and a quarry from which most of Prague's Romanesque and Gothic buildings were assembled.

Petřín is easily accessible from Hradčany and Strahov, or you can ride the funicular railway from Újezd (at U lanové dráhy). It runs from 9.15am to 11.30pm, for the same price as a bus ride (and you can use city transit tickets).

Just south of the funicular railway terminus is a rose garden and the **Štefánik Observatory & Planetarium** (Štefánikova hvězdárna; ☎ 257 320 540; www.observatory.cz - Czech only; Petřín 5; ⏱ 2-7pm & 9-11pm Tue-Fri, 10am-noon, 2-7pm & 9-11pm Sat & Sun Apr-Sep, 6-8pm Tue-Fri, 10am-noon & 2-8pm Sat & Sun Oct-Mar).

North of the terminus on the summit is the **Petřín Tower** (Petřínská rozhledna; adult/child 50/40Kč; ⏱ 10am-10pm Apr-Oct, 10am-5pm Sat & Sun Nov-Mar), a 60m Eiffel Tower lookalike built in 1891 for the Prague Exposition. Those who don't think climbing 299 steps is an act of lunacy will enjoy the best views of Prague and surrounds from the top. On the way to the tower you pass through the **Hunger Wall** (Hladová zeď), built by the poor in the 1360s in return for food – another of Karel IV's bright ideas. Stations of the Cross – small markers depicting the stages of Jesus' journey from conviction to crucifixion – run along the wall, part of the way down to Malá Strana.

Below the tower is the **mirror maze** (admission 40Kč; ⏱ 10am-10pm Apr-Oct, 10am-5pm Sat & Sun Nov-Mar), also built for the 1891 Exposition and later moved here. It's a damn fine laugh.

Staré Město & Josefov

A settlement and marketplace existed on the eastern bank of the Vltava by the 10th century. In the 12th century this was linked to the castle district by the Judith Bridge, since replaced by Charles Bridge (p101). Old Town (Staré Město) has been Prague's working heart ever since, and the city you see now still largely follows the medieval layout.

Many of Staré Město's buildings have Gothic insides and Romanesque basements. To ease the devastation of frequent flooding by the Vltava, the level of the town was gradually raised, beginning in the 13th century, with new construction simply building on top of older foundations.

The slice of Staré Město within Kaprova, Dlouhá and Kozí streets contains the remains of the once-thriving mini-town of Josefov, Prague's former Jewish ghetto: half a dozen old synagogues, the town hall, a ceremonial hall and the cluttered and picturesque Old Jewish Cemetery. In an act of hubris that brilliantly backfired, the Nazis spared these to be a 'museum of an extinct race' – instead, they have survived as a memorial to seven centuries of oppression, and a celebration of a still-flourishing way of life.

As well as being a repository of ancient Jewish buildings, modern Josefov – particularly along Pařížská, Kozí and V kolkovně – is a neighbourhood of très hip sidewalk cafés, international designer boutiques, and drop-dead-cool cocktail bars. Parisian Ave (Pařížská třída), built at the time the ghetto was cleared, is lined with courtly four- and five-storey residential French Art Noveau buildings adorned with stained glass and sculptural flourishes – just off the strip, Maiselova 21 is particularly stunning.

JEWISH MUSEUM   Map pp98–9

The **Jewish Museum** (☎ 222 317 191; www.jewish museum.cz; U Starého hřbitova 3a; adult/child 450/300Kč; ⏱ 9am-4.30pm Nov-Mar, 9am-6pm Apr-Oct), as the area's attractions are known, takes in the cemetery, ceremonial hall, Gallery Roberta Guttmanna, and Spanish, Maisel, Pinkas, Klaus and Old-New Synagogues. The Old-New Synagogue is still used for religious services; the others have been converted to exhibition halls holding what is probably the world's biggest collection of sacred Jewish artefacts, many of them saved from demolished Bohemian and Moravian synagogues.

You have the choice of paying to see all of them (adult/child 450/300Kč) or splitting the museum in two – the Old-New Synagogue alone (200/140Kč), and everything else (250/160Kč). All tickets include the gallery. (At the time of writing, the Pinkas Synagogue was closed due to flood damage, and prices reflect this: if it's reopened, tickets that include that synagogue may now be 500/340Kč and 300/200Kč.) Czechs get a significant discount on all tickets. Tickets are sold at Klaus Synagogue (p99), Pinkas Synagogue (p100), the Spanish Synagogue (p101), and at **Starožisnosti Antik** (Maiselova 15; ☎ 9am-5.30pm, closed 1-1.30pm), where the lines are frequently shorter.

The price for the Old-New Synagogue is high, but the other attractions can easily keep you occupied for a whole day if become really absorbed. If you don't think you'll make it around the lot, start with the cemetery, follow it up with the excellent exhibition at the Maisel and then see the exhibition's continuation in the gorgeous Spanish Synagogue.

PRAGUE

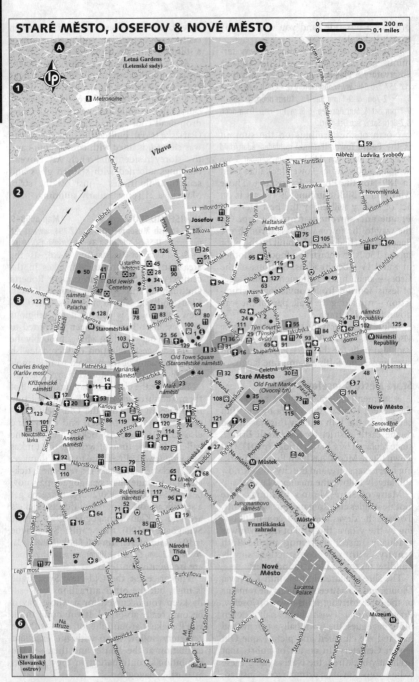

STARÉ MĚSTO, JOSEFOV & NOVÉ MĚSTO

0 ——— 200 m
0 ——— 0.1 miles

Old-New Synagogue

Completed about 1270, the **Old-New Synagogue** (Staronová Synagóga; Červená 1) is one of Prague's earliest Gothic buildings and Europe's oldest 'working' synagogue – it hosts weekly Orthodox ceremonies. The oxymoronic name caught on because this is one of two synagogues built in the 13th century, at a time when Prague already had one old synagogue – of the two new ones, this one is slightly older. Around the central chamber are an entry hall, a winter prayer hall and the room from which women watch the men-only services (it's at the back, through the vents in the wall). The interior, with a pulpit surrounded by a 15th-century, wrought-iron grille, looks much as it would have 500 years ago. The 17th-century scriptures on the walls were recovered from beneath a later 'restoration'. On the eastern wall is the Holy Ark that holds the Torah scrolls, hidden by a wall hanging. Rumour has it the steep roof hides the slumbering golem automaton (see the boxed text next page). The synagogue keeps museum hours, except on Friday, when it's open from 9.30am to 5pm.

Other Jewish Museum Sights

Opposite the Old-New Synagogue is the elegant, 16th-century **High Synagogue** (Vysoká Synagóga; Židovská Radnice) and the **Jewish Town Hall** (Židovská Radnice; ☎ 776 355 841), both closed to the public.

By the cemetery exit, the **Klaus Synagogue** (Klausová Synagóga; U Starého hřbitova 1), a 1694 baroque building, holds the museum's exhibits related to Jewish ceremonies for

THE JEWS OF PRAGUE

Among Prague's earliest inhabitants, Jews first started seeing serious trouble from the Christian community when, in 1096, marauding Crusaders passed through town on the way to the Holy Land, encouraging the locals to put to the sword any Jews who wouldn't convert. Prague's Jewish community was first moved into a walled ghetto in about the 13th century, when the Pope decreed Jews and Christians should live separately. A pogrom in 1389 wiped out a sizable number of the Jewish population, and Ferdinand I forbade Jews any commercial activity other than moneylending.

The reign of Rudolf II saw honour bestowed on Prague's Jews, a flowering of Jewish intellectual life and prosperity in the ghetto. Mordechai Maisel (or Maisl), mayor of the ghetto, Rudolf's finance minister and Prague's wealthiest citizen, bankrolled some lavish redevelopment. Another major figure was Judah Löw ben Bezalel, or Rabbi Löw, a prominent theologian, chief rabbi, student of the mystical teachings of the cabbala, and nowadays best known as the creator of the mythical golem – a giant Jewish superhero made of mud from the Vltava and brought to life by supernatural means.

When they helped repel the Swedes on the Charles Bridge in 1648, Prague's Jews won the favour of Ferdinand III, who had the ghetto enlarged: for 150 years from the beginning of the 17th century this was the most populated Jewish centre in Christian Europe. But in 1744 Empress Maria Theresa expelled all Jews from the country – she said they'd been disloyal in recent wars. They were grudgingly allowed back three years later when Praguers realised they needed their business. In the 1780s Emperor Joseph II outlawed many forms of discrimination, and in 1848 the ghetto walls were torn down and the Jewish quarter was made a borough of Prague, named Josefov in honour of the emperor.

The demise of the Jewish quarter (which had slid into squalor as its Jewish population moved elsewhere) came between 1893 and 1910 when it was cleared, ostensibly for public health reasons, slashed through the middle by Pařížská and lined with new Art Nouveau housing.

The 1867 Constitution granted Jews equality, and Jews tried to assimilate, abandoning German and making an effort to speak Czech. German occupation wasn't the first time Jews were forced to wear a defining mark – in 1551 Ferdinand introduced a yellow circular badge; in the 17th century they were wearing yellow ruffs. However, the 1939 invasion marked a new low point for Prague's Jewish community. Most were shipped to Terezín, a freshly built ghetto outside town that was a way-station to Auschwitz and other concentration camps. At the beginning of the war there were 118,310 Jews in Prague – many had fled there from Sudetenland and rural parts of Bohemia and Moravia. By the end of the war 80,000 of them were dead. Around 1800 of the survivors are currently paid DM1800-3000 (approximately €920 to €1534) a year by the German government as restitution. The communist regime slowly strangled what was left of Jewish cultural life, and thousands emigrated. Ironically, communist Czechoslovakia was very supportive of the new state of Israel, hoping it would become the Middle East's first communist country. Today a few thousand Jews live in Prague – the numbers are unclear, as many are not willing to be registered.

birth, worship and special holy days. In the **Ceremonial Hall** (Obřadní Síň; U Starého hřibitova 3), built in 1906 on the other side of the cemetery exit, you'll see exhibits on Jewish rituals for illness and death – if you're particularly interested in the importance of the cemetery, you may choose to visit this exhibition first.

The handsome **Pinkas Synagogue** (Pinkasova Synagóga; Široká 3) was built in 1535 and used for worship until 1941. After WWII it was converted into a powerful memorial,

with the names, birth dates and dates of disappearance of the 77,297 Bohemian and Moravian victims of the Nazis inscribed across wall after wall (at one point the communist regime removed them, but they've since been reinscribed). It also has a collection of paintings and drawings by children held in the Terezín concentration camp (p169) during WWII.

The neo-Gothic **Maisel Synagogue** (Maiselova Synagóga; Maiselova 10) hosts the pre-1780 part of the museum's exhibit on the history of

Jews in Bohemia and Moravia. The quantity and quality of artefacts is astounding, and the text accompanying them is excellent. The exhibition continues up to the present day (taking in the Nazi occupation) at the **Spanish Synagogue** (Španělská Synagóga; Vežeňská 1), though your eyes may be drawn away from the exhibits to the building's intensely beautiful Moorish interior.

Gallery Roberta Guttmanna (☎ 224 819 456; U Staré Skoly 1; adult/child 30/15Kč; ☯ 9am-6pm Sun-Fri Apr-Oct, 9am-4.30pm Sun-Fri Nov-Mar), behind the Spanish Synagogue, hosts rotating exhibits of Jewish artists – the ticket price is included in your Jewish Museum ticket, or you can visit individually.

Founded in the early 15th century, the **Old Jewish Cemetery** (Starý Židovský Hřbitov) is Europe's oldest surviving Jewish cemetery (it was closed in 1787). Some 12,000 toppling, faded stones lean up against one another, but beneath them are perhaps 100,000 graves, piled in layers. The oldest standing stone (now replaced by a replica) dates from 1439. The most prominent graves, marked by pairs of marble tablets with a 'roof' between them, are near the main gate. They include those of Mordechai Maisel and Rabbi Löw. You'll see pebbles and notes (prayers) balanced on many of the stones along the edges of the path – these are left as a mark of respect. There's also a Braille trail around the cemetery. Since the cemetery was closed, burials have taken place at the Jewish Cemetery in Žižkov.

The ancient cemetery is certainly picturesque and can be quite eerie; although it was closed long before the Nazis arrived in Prague, it's hard not to feel the weight of the 80,000 Jewish deaths the invaders caused. However, this is also one of the most popular sights in Prague, and if you're hoping to have a moment of quiet contemplation you'll probably be disappointed (try either of the Žižkov cemeteries for a more solitary, and cheaper, experience).

MUSEUM OF DECORATIVE ARTS   Map pp98–9
One of those museums where every little item is just begging to be stroked, the **Museum of Decorative Arts** (☎ 224 811 241; 17 listopadu 2; permanent exhibition adult/child 80/40Kč, child under 10 free; ☯ 10am-6pm, closed Mon) collects jewellery, furniture, knick-knacks, ceramics, glass,

textiles and graphic arts. There are glass cases full of 1940s frocks, walls of Art Noveau poster art, beautifully illuminated ancient religious texts, pocket watches in the shape of leering skulls and the rococo grandfather of all grandfather clocks. Even the museum's quarters, built in 1898, are gorgeous.

One of Prague's highlights, this wonderful museum of European and Czech 'applied art' arose as part of a European movement to encourage a return to aesthetic values sacrificed to the Industrial Revolution. The collection on display is only a fraction of what the museum owns; other bits appear now and then in single-theme exhibitions (60/30Kč, or 120/60Kč for entry to permanent and temporary exhibitions).

The little gift shop here has some sublime pieces of ceramic, glass and jewellery design.

RUDOLFINUM   Map pp98–9
Presiding over Jan Palach square (náměstí Jana Palacha) is the **Rudolfinum**, home of the Czech Philharmonic (see Entertainment p142). This and the National Theatre, both designed by the architects Josef Schulz and Josef Zítek, are considered Prague's finest neo-Renaissance buildings. Completed in 1884, the Rudolfinum served between the wars as the seat of the Czechoslovak parliament. Across the road, on the philosophy faculty building where student martyr Jan Palach was a student (see boxed text p112), is a memorial sculpture incorporating his death mask.

CHARLES BRIDGE   Map pp98–9
Part of Karel IV's Gothic building frenzy, **Charles Bridge** (Karlův most) was constructed to replace the earlier Judith Bridge (Juditín most; named after Vladislav I's queen), which had been irreparably damaged by ice. Designed by Peter Parler, it was completed in about 1400, though it was called the Prague Bridge until the 19th century. Despite occasional flood damage, it withstood wheeled traffic for 600 years without a shudder – thanks, legend says, to eggs mixed into the mortar – until it was made pedestrian-only after WWII. During the floods of 2002, cranes stood watch over the bridge, pulling large pieces of detritus out of the water so the pillars would not be damaged.

Many of the statues were later additions, put up to promote their particular ecclesiastical orders. These days the most popular is that of the country's patron saint, Jan of Nepomuk, tortured to death by Václav IV. It's said that if you rub the plaque at the statue's base, you'll one day return to Prague – a more reliable method is to buy a return plane ticket. Most of the statues are copies – the originals are preserved in Vyšehrad (p114) and at the Fairgrounds Lapidárium (p116).

Strolling across the bridge is everybody's favourite Prague activity. If you come in the early morning you might have the place to yourself, but by 11am you might as well be in the front row of a Linkin Park concert for all the room you'll have to yourself. On a warm evening, even with the throng, it's a pretty romantic place.

In summer you can climb up into the old **defensive towers** (adult/child 40/30Kč, child under 10 free; 🕐 10am-10pm) for an even better view.

Gangs of pickpockets work the bridge day and night, so watch your valuables.

OLD TOWN SQUARE
(STAROMĚSTSKÉ NÁMĚSTÍ)   Map pp98–9
The huge, 1.7-hectare Old Town Square (also called Staromák) has been Prague's heart since the 10th century, and was its main marketplace until the beginning of the 20th century. These days it's a seething mass of humanity, as tourists nudge one another for space in front of the Astronomical Clock, peer bemusedly at maps or try to find a place to sit down for a minute without forking over half their budget. Regular Praguers also use the square as the site for art and sporting events, and on days when something's going on here you can't move for people. Despite all this, it remains an awesome conglomeration of architecture and history – late at night, in particular, it's incredibly atmospheric. Stand still for a moment, take a deep breath, and really look around you.

Ladislav Šaloun's brooding, melting Art Nouveau sculpture of **Jan Hus** dominates the square. It was unveiled on 6 July 1915, the 500th anniversary of the death of Hus' at the stake.

OLD TOWN HALL   Map pp98–9
Founded in 1338, Staré Město's ancient **town hall** (Staroměstská Radnice) looks like a row of private buildings with a tower at the end because that's what it is – the skint medieval town council bought it from previous owners one house at a time whenever funds were available.

The sgraffito-covered building at the corner, called **Dům U minuty**, was one of Franz Kafka's childhood homes. A Gothic chapel and a neo-Gothic north wing were destroyed by the retreating Nazis in 1945, on the day before the Soviet army marched into Prague. The chapel has been laboriously reconstructed.

A plaque on the tower's eastern face contains a roll-call of the 27 Czech Protestant nobles beheaded in 1621 after the Battle of Bílá Hora (White Mountain); crosses on the ground mark the spot where the deed was done.

It's *de rigueur* to wait for the hourly show by the hall's slightly overrated **Astronomical Clock** or *orloj* (see boxed text opposite) – you can't really see what's going on if you're standing at an angle, but to get a spot in front you'll need to arrive half an hour early. You can visit selected rooms of the town hall, the Gothic chapel and the clock's Apostles for 50Kč. The 60m **tower** (admission 40Kč; 🕐 11am-5pm Mon, 9am-6pm Tue-Sun) is the only one in Prague with a lift all the way to the top – perhaps more interesting than watching the clock is nipping up here to watch the people watching the clock.

ST NICHOLAS CHURCH   Map pp98–9
The baroque wedding cake in the northwestern corner of the square is **St Nicholas Church** (Kostel Sv Mikuláše; 🕐 noon-4pm Mon, 10am-4pm Tue-Sat, noon-3pm Sun), built in the 1730s by Kilian Dientzenhofer. This is now a Hussite church, though its Protestant inhabitants have held onto the gilt extravagances and phenomenal chandelier.

Franz Kafka was born next door, though the building was later demolished. The building that replaced it is now a privately run and pretty uninteresting **Franz Kafka Exhibition** (U Radnice 5; admission 40Kč; 🕐 10am-6pm Tue-Fri, 10am-5pm Sat).

KINSKÝ PALACE   Map pp98–9
Fronting the late-baroque Kinský or Goltz-Kinský Palace (Palác Kinských; ☎ 224 301 003; 12 Staroměstské náměstí; adult/child 100/50Kč; 🕐 10am-5.30pm) is probably the city's finest rococo

ASTRONOMICAL!

The mechanical marvel you see on Old Town Hall tower was made in 1490 by clockmaker Master Hanuš. Legend has it he was afterwards blinded so he could not duplicate the work elsewhere, and for revenge crawled up into the clock and disabled it. (Documents from the time suggest that he carried on as clock master for years, unblinded, although the clock apparently didn't work properly until it was repaired in about 1570.)

Four figures beside the clock represent 15th-century Praguers' deepest civic anxieties: Vanity, Greed (originally a Jewish money-lender, cosmetically altered after WWII), Death and Pagan Invasion (represented by a Turk). The four figures below these are the Chronicler, Angel, Astronomer and Philosopher.

On the hour, Death rings a bell and inverts his hourglass, and a parade of Apostles passes two windows, nodding to the crowd. At the end a cock crows and the hour is rung: the whole show takes about a minute.

On the upper face, the disk in the middle of the fixed part depicts the world known at the time – with Prague at the centre, of course. The gold sun traces a circle through the blue zone of day, the brown zone of dusk in the west, the black disk of night, and dawn in the east. From this the hours of sunrise and sunset can be read. The curved lines with black Arabic numerals are part of an astrological 'star clock'.

When looking at the face of the clock you can see that there are two rings. The sun-arm points to the hour (adjusted for daylight-saving time) on the inner, Roman-numeral ring; the top XII is noon and the bottom XII is midnight. The outer ring, with Gothic numerals, reads traditional 24-hour Bohemian time, counted from sunset; the number 24 is always opposite the sunset hour on the fixed (inner) face.

The moon, with its phases shown, also traces a path through the zones of day and night, riding on the offset moving ring. On the ring you can also read which houses of the zodiac the sun and moon are in. The hand with a little star at the end of it indicates stellar time.

The calendar-wheel beneath all this astronomical wizardry, with 12 seasonal scenes in praise of rural Bohemian life, is a duplicate of one painted in 1866 by the Czech Revivalist Josef Mánes. You can have a close look at the beautiful original in the Museum of the City of Prague (see p108).

façade, completed in 1765 by the very productive Kilian Dientzenhofer. In 1948 Klement Gottwald proclaimed communist rule in Czechoslovakia from the building's balcony. These days it's a branch of the **National Gallery**, showing temporary exhibitions.

HOUSE OF THE STONE BELL   Map pp98–9

The 14th-century Gothic **House of the Stone Bell** (Dům U Kamenného Zvonu), named after the house sign at the corner of the building, houses two restored Gothic chapels. It is a branch of the **Prague City Gallery** (13 Staroměstské náměstí; adult/child 60/30Kč; 🕙 10am-6pm Tue-Sun), with changing modern art exhibits.

CHURCH OF OUR LADY
BEFORE TÝN   Map pp98–9

The spiky-topped 'Týn church' (Kostel Panny Marie Před Týnem) is early Gothic, though it takes some imagination to visualise the original in its entirety because it's strangely hidden behind the contemporaneous four-storey Týn School. Inside it's smothered in heavy baroque, but you'll be lucky to get a decent look – the glassed-in vestibule at the church's entrance is always crammed full of visitors. The church actually looks best from a distance – in our opinion, the best view is from Letná beer garden (p117).

The Danish astronomer Tycho Brahe, one of Rudolf II's most illustrious 'consultants' (who died in 1601 of a burst bladder – he was too polite to leave the table during a royal function), is buried near the chancel.

TÝN COURT   Map pp98–9

The Týn church's name comes from a medieval courtyard for foreign merchants, the Týn Court (Týnský dvůr), behind it on Štupartská. This atmospheric renovated courtyard and the tiny lanes around it now house shops and restaurants.

On another corner, in the restored Renaissance House at the Golden Ring (Dům

U zlatého prstenu), is a branch of the **Prague City Gallery** (☎ 224 828 245; Týnská 6/630; adult/child 60/40Kč; ☺ 10am-6pm Tue-Sun), with a fine collection of 20th-century Czech art.

ST JAMES CHURCH   Map pp98–9
The long, tall Gothic **St James Church** (Kostel sv Jakuba), behind the Týnský dvůr on Malá Štupartská, began in the 14th century as a Minorite monastery church. It had a beautiful baroque face-lift in the early 18th century. Pride of place goes to the over-the-top tomb of Count Jan Vratislav of Mitrovice, an 18th-century lord chancellor of Bohemia, on the northern aisle.

Hanging to the left of the main door is a shrivelled human arm. In about 1400 a thief apparently tried to steal the jewels off the statue of the Virgin. Legend says the Virgin grabbed his wrist in such an iron grip that his arm had to be lopped off. (The truth may not be far behind: the church was a favourite of the guild of butchers, who may have administered their own justice.)

It's well worth a visit to enjoy St James' splendid pipe organ and famous acoustics – check the notice board outside.

KLEMENTINUM   Map pp98–9
After the Protestants took a beating at the Protestant–Catholic Battle of White Mountain (see History p81), Jesuits flooded into Prague and began building. Selecting one of the city's choicest bits of real estate, they set to work in 1578 on Prague's flagship of the Counter-Reformation, the Church of the Holy Saviour on what is now Karlova.

After gradually buying up most of the adjacent neighbourhood, the Jesuits started building their college, the Klementinum, in 1653 – by the time of its completion a century later, it was the second-largest building in the city. When the Jesuits fell foul of the pope in 1773 and lost most of their property, it became part of Charles University.

The western façade of the **Church of the Holy Saviour** (kostel Nejsvětějšího Spasitele/Salvátora) faces Charles Bridge, its sooty stone saints glaring down at the crowds of snap-happy tourists and sailor-suited touts. Follow Karlova ulice and you'll see it takes a bend at the little round **Assumption Chapel** (Vlašská kaple Nanebevzetí Panny Marie), completed in 1600 for the Italian artisans who worked on the Klementinum.

Eastwards on Karlova you can look inside **St Clement Church** (kostel sv Klimenta), lavishly rehabilitated in baroque style from 1711 to 1715 and with a *trompe l'oeil* altar that really does fool the eye. It's now Greek Orthodox, with services on Sunday at 8.30am and 10am, to which conservatively dressed visitors are welcome. It's worth going to hear the angelic acoustics of the choir.

The three churches form most of the southern wall of the Klementinum, a vast complex of beautiful, rococo halls. Though most of the buildings are closed to the public, from gates on Křižovnická, Karlova and Seminářská you can detour through several courtyards. In a courtyard at the centre of the complex is an 18th-century **astronomical tower** (☎ 603 231 241; admission 100Kč; ☺ noon-7pm Mon-Fri, 10am-7pm Sat & Sun). Guided tours run on the hour and are the only way to see the tower. As well as the impressive collection of 1750s astronomical instruments and the 360° views from the top of the tower, the tour takes in the stunning **Baroque Library**, with manuscripts from 1520 to the late 17th century: the old-book smell is overwhelming and the commentary fascinating. Much of the rest of the complex is occupied by the **Czech National Library**, largely closed to the public. You can enter the **Chapel of Mirrors** (Zrcadlová kaple) during concerts (see the notices posted outside). One architectural handbook casts aspersions on what the Jesuits were up to in here (with mirrors on the ceiling).

NEAR THE KLEMENTINUM   Map pp98–9
Beside the Old Town tower of Charles Bridge is the 17th-century **Church of St Francis Seraphinus** (kostel sv Františka Serafinského), its dome decorated on the inside with a fresco of the Last Judgment. The church belongs to the Order of Knights of the Cross, the only Bohemian order of Crusaders still in existence.

Just south of the bridge, at the site of the former Old Town mill, is Novotného lávka, a pedestrian lane full of sunny, overpriced *vinárny* (wine bars) with smashing views. At the river end, the **Bedřich Smetana museum** (☎ 222 220 082; Novotného lávka; adult/child 50/20Kč; ☺ 10am-5pm, closed Tue) isn't that interesting for nonfans, and only has limited English labels. There's a good exhibit on pop culture's feverish response to *The Bartered Bride* – it seems Smetana was the Britney Spears of his day.

Prague restaurant with views of St Vitus Cathedral (p89) in the distance

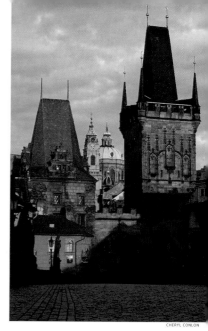

RICHARD NEBESKY

Bridge Tower and the Church of St Nicholas (p95), Prague

CHERYL CONLON

St Vitus Cathedral and Plečnik's monolith (p90), Prague

RICHARD NEBESKY

RICHARD NEBESKY

The Dancing Building (p113), Prague

RICHARD NEBESKÝ

The Žižkov TV Tower (p121),
Prague

MŮSTEK

RICHARD NEBE

Můstek Metro Station, Nové Město, Prague

JONATHAN SMITH

Old Town Hall Astronomical Clock (p103),
Prague

Old Town Square (p102), Prague

RICHARD NEBESKÝ

At the corner of Karlova and Husova, the **Czech Museum of Fine Arts** (České muzeum výtvarních umění; ☎ 222 220 218; Husova 19-21; admission 50Kč; ⏰ 10am-6pm Tue-Sun) has revolving exhibits of local contemporary art.

LITTLE SQUARE
(MALÉ NÁMĚSTÍ)   Map pp98–9
Little Square is surrounded by several fine, baroque and neo-Renaissance exteriors decorating some of Staré Město's oldest structures. Have a gander at the **VJ Rott Building** at No 3, a perfect example of the Art Nouveau impulse to never leave well-

enough alone. This square is a good place to stand at five minutes to the hour, when you can watch panicked tourists sprint through on their way to catch the Astronomical Clock show.

CELETNÁ ULICE   Map pp98–9
This largely pedestrianised lane from Old Town Square to the Powder Tower is an open-air museum of well-groomed, pastel-painted, baroque façades over Gothic frames. But the most interesting façade dates from 1912: Josef Gočár's unique Cubist front (Prague's first), on the **House of the**

A DAY IN THE LIFE OF KAFKA

Prague seemingly can't get enough of its favourite literary son, and luckily for tourist operators, the itinerant Kafka lived in a multitude of different houses and worked in buildings all over the city. Get a feeling for what it was like being Franz by wandering around some of the spots he favoured in 1913, the year he turned 30.

In that year, Franz was living with his mother and father and his youngest sister, Ottla, aged 21, in a top floor flat in the **Oppelt building** (Map pp98-9) at the northern end of Old Town Square, across Pařížská from St Nicholas Church. All three of Franz's sisters died in the ghettos or camps in WWII. Franz's domineering father was a wholesale haberdasher with a store on the ground floor of the **Kinský Palace** (p102).

Since 1908 Franz had been working at the Workers Accident Insurance for the Kingdom of Bohemia at Na poříčí 7, Nové Město; the cream building now houses a hotel, the Mercure. It's rumoured that while working this job, Franz came up with the bright idea that on sites where workers might get hit on the head, they should wear hard hats.

At this time he wrote in his diary, 'From 8 until 2 or 2.30 office, until 3 or 3.30 dinner, after that sleep in bed…until 7.30, then 10 minutes exercise, naked, with open window, then an hour taking a walk…then evening meal with the family…then at 10.30 sit down to write and remain there as long as strength, desire, and happiness permit until 1, 2, 3 o'clock, once even until 6 in the morning'.

The writing at this time would have included letters to Felice Bauer, the first of five women he fell in love with, wrote copious letters to, and never married. His *Meditations*, a collection of some early short stories, had just been published, and he was working on *amerika*.

When he wasn't writing, Franz wasn't above a little idle fun. In his diary he wrote, 'Went to the cinema. Wept. Matchless entertainment': the cinema would probably have been in the **Estates Theatre** (p107).

On Tuesday evenings the radical chic of Prague met at the salon of Berta Fanta at her apartment on the first floor at the **House of the Unicorn** (Map pp98-9; Staroměstské náměstí 17). There is now a plaque on the wall, commemorating Einstein playing his violin at these salons. Franz and his friend and biographer Max Brod also went to fortnightly meetings at **Cafe Louvre** (Map pp110-11; ☎ 224 930 949; Národní Trida 20, Nové Město; ⏰ 8am-11pm) to debate philosophy and to read from their work. At the **Cafe Savoy** (Map p118; ☎ 251 510 433; Vítezná 5, Malá Strana; closed for refurbishing at time of writing) Franz met and became friends with the Yiddish theatre troupe actor, Isaac Lowy, sparking a hitherto dormant interest in his own Jewishness.

In this café society Franz revealed himself, to Brod at least, as 'one of the most amusing men' who 'liked a good hearty laugh, and knew how to make his friends laugh too'. Whether Franz, a vegetarian who drank no alcohol, became addicted to coffee is not known.

If you fancy a full Kafka pilgrimage, see Marilyn Bender's paper 'Franz Kafka's Prague: a literary walking tour' (www.nysoclib.org/travels/kafka.html).

Black Madonna (dům U černé Matky Boží), at No 34, at the corner of the **Old Fruit Market** (Ovocný trh). By the time you read this, a **Museum of Czech Cubism** should have opened here.

POWDER TOWER   Map pp98–9

The gloomy 65m-tall **Powder Tower** (Prašná Brána; adult/child 30/40Kč; ✆ 10am-10pm) was begun in 1475 during the reign of King Vladislav II Jagiello but never finished. Used to store gunpowder in the 18th century, it was refurbished in the 19th century and the steeple and decorations were added. You can climb the tight spiral staircase to the first floor for free, or pay the admission to go higher for great views and some exhibits on the history of the tower.

MUNICIPAL HOUSE   Map pp98–9

Don't even consider missing the **Municipal House** (Obecní Dům; ☎ 222 002 101; www.obecni-dum .cz; náměstí Republiky 5; admission free; ✆ 10am-6pm), Prague's most sensually beautiful building, with an unrivalled Art Nouveau interior and a façade that looks like a Victorian Easter egg. Bring your smelling salts – the sheer relentlessness of the decoration may make you woozy.

The house was built between 1906 and 1912 in an attempt to one-up German architectural developments. Thirty of the leading artists of the day worked together to make this the architectural climax of the Czech National Revival.

The mosaic above the entrance, *Homage to Prague*, is set between sculptures representing the oppression and rebirth of the Czech people. You pass beneath a wrought-iron and stained-glass canopy into an interior that is Art Nouveau down to the doorknobs. To go upstairs, you have to join a **guided tour** (admission 150Kč; ✆ 10.15am & noon) – it's entirely worth it. You'll see half a dozen over-the-top salons, including the incredible Lord Mayor's Hall, done up entirely by Art Nouveau superstar Alfons Mucha, who didn't let a single fitting escape his attention. Also here is **Smetana Hall**, Prague's biggest concert hall, and a **gallery** (admission 100Kč) with temporary art exhibits.

Symbolic moments here include the proclamation of an independent Czechoslovak Republic on 28 October 1918, and meetings between Civic Forum and the Jakeš regime in November 1989. The Prague Spring music festival always opens on 12 May, the anniversary of Smetana's death, with a procession from Vyšehrad to Municipal House, and a gala performance of his symphonic cycle *Má vlast* (My Country) in Smetana Hall.

ON THE MOAT (NA PŘÍKOPĚ)   Map pp98–9

Na příkopě means 'on the moat'; with Národní, 28.října and Revoluční this street marks the moat (filled in at the end of the 18th century) by the old Staré Město walls.

This was the haunt of Prague's German café society in the 19th century. Today it is (along with Národní) the main upmarket shopping precinct, lined with banks, bookshops, tourist cafés and shopping malls.

Na příkopě continues southwest across the foot of Wenceslas Square as 28.října (28 October; Czechoslovak Independence Day). Here Na můstku (On the Little Bridge) runs northwest where a footbridge once crossed the moat – you can see an arch of it, on the left just past the ticket machines in the underground entrance to Můstek metro station.

ST GALL'S MARKET AREA   Map pp98–9

In about 1230 a new market quarter, Havelské Město or St Gall's Town was laid out. Modern-day Rytířská and Havelská were at that time a single plaza, surrounded by arcaded merchants' houses. Specialist markets included those for coal (Uhelný trh) at the western end – now a hang-out for Left-Bank-style painters and the homeless – and for fruit (Ovocný trh) at the eastern end – now a spick-and-span square of tourist cafés. In the 15th century an island of stalls was built down the middle.

All that remains of St Gall's market today is the souvenir, flower, fruit and vegetable **Havelská Market** on Havelská ulice. Full of poorly made tourist junk, it's no match for the original, but it's still Prague's most central open-air market.

At the eastern end of Havelská is the 13th-century **Church of St Gall** (Kostel sv Havla), where Jan Hus and his predecessors preached church reform. The Carmelites took possession of it in 1627, and in 1723 added its present, shapely baroque face. At the western end of Havelská is the plain, 12th-century **Church of St Martin in the Wall** (Kostel sv Martina ve zdi), a parish church enlarged and 'Gothicised' in the 14th century. The name comes from its having had the Old Town wall built right around it. In 1414 the church was the site of the first-ever communion service *(sub utraque specie)*, with both bread and wine.

KAROLINUM   Map pp98–9
Charles University – central Europe's oldest university, founded by Karel IV in 1348 – originally set up shop at Železná 9. With Protestantism and Czech nationalism on the rise, the reform preacher Jan Hus became rector in 1402. On 18 January 1409, in an effort to increase his voting bloc in manoeuvrings to regain the crown of Holy Roman Emperor, Václav IV slashed the voting rights of the university's German students and lecturers. The 'Decree of Kutná Hora', as it was known, meant thousands of Germans left Bohemia in disgust, and the previously world-beating university became considerably more parochial.

Charles University now has faculties all over Prague, and the Karolinum is used only for some medical faculty offices, the University Club and occasional academic ceremonies. Its finest room is the high-ceilinged assembly hall upstairs.

Among pre-university Gothic traces is the **Chapel of SS Cosmas & Damian**, with its extraordinary oriel protruding from the southern wall. Built around 1370, it was renovated in 1881 by Josef Mocker.

ESTATES THEATRE   Map pp98–9
Beside the Karolinum is the **Estates Theatre** (Stavovské Divadlo; Železná 11), Prague's oldest theatre and its finest neoclassical building. Opened in 1783 as the Nostitz Theatre (after its founder, Count Anton von Nostitz-Rieneck), it was patronised by upper-class German Praguers. It was later named after the local nobility, known as the Estates. During summer it hosts performances of Mozart's *Don Giovanni*, which premiered here.

CONVENT OF ST AGNES   Map pp98–9
In the northeastern corner of Staré Město are the surviving buildings of the former **Convent of St Agnes** (Klášter sv Anežky; U milosrdných 17), Prague's oldest standing Gothic structures. Although they were finely restored in the last few decades, the ground floor was quite badly damaged by the 2002 floods; at the time of writing all of the convent apart from the gallery was closed for renovation.

In 1234 the Franciscan Order of the Poor Clares was founded by the Přemysl king Václav I, who made his sister Anežka (Agnes) its first abbess; since 1989 she's been St Anežka.

The complex consists of the cloister, a sanctuary and a church in French Gothic style. In the **Chapel of the Virgin Mary** (kaple Panny Marie), within the Sanctuary of the Holy Saviour (svatyně sv Salvatora), are the graves of St Anežka and Václav I's queen Cunegund. Alongside is the smaller **Church of St Francis** (Kostel sv Františka), where Václav I is buried in the chancel.

The 1st floor of the cloister now holds the **National Gallery's Medieval Bohemian Art Collection** (☎ 224 810 628; adult/child 100/50Kč; ☽ 10am-6pm Sun-Tue). It's a brilliantly curated exhibition of extraordinary, glowing works, including some of Master Theodoricus' paintings from Karlštejn Castle (p73), the beautiful three-piece Třeboň altarpiece and the terrifically ungloomy work of the Master of Sorrows from Žebrák.

The winding lanes around St Agnes and Haštalské náměstí feel like something out of the Middle Ages. Only furious lobbying by residents and Prague intellectuals saved the area from the same clearance that ravaged Josefov at the turn of the 20th century. This area was flooded in 2002 and many buildings are abandoned – it's quite an eerie part of town.

BETHLEHEM CHAPEL   Map pp98–9
The square and simple **Bethlehem Church** (Betlémská Kaple; Betlémské náměstí; admission 35Kč; ☽ 9am-6.30pm Tue-Sun) is one of Prague's most important, the real birthplace of Hussitism (though what you see is largely a reconstruction).

Reformist Praguers won permission to build a chapel where services could be held in Czech instead of Latin, and in 1391 began constructing the biggest chapel Bohemia had ever seen, for some 3000 worshippers. Architecturally it was a radical departure, with a simple square hall focused on the pulpit rather than the altar. Jan Hus preached here from 1402 to 1412, taking church reform out of the university (where he had been rector) and on to the streets.

In the 19th century the chapel was torn down. Remnants were discovered around 1920 and – because Hussitism, a working-class movement, had official blessing as an antecedent of communism – the whole thing was painstakingly reconstructed from 1948 to 1954 in its original form. It's now a National Cultural Monument.

Only the street-facing wall is brand new. You can still see some original bits in the eastern wall: the pulpit door, several windows and the door to the original preacher's quarters. Once used by Hus, they now house exhibits on his life and times. The wall paintings are modern, based on old Hussite tracts. Every year on the night of 5 July, the eve of Hus's burning at the stake in 1415, a commemorative celebration is held here.

ST GILES CHURCH Map pp98–9

It's worth dropping by **St Giles Church** (Kostel Sv Jiljí; cnr Zlatá & Husova) after you've visited Bethlehem Chapel: the contrast is striking. With Romanesque columns, Gothic windows and baroque interior (even the paintings are wearing gold crowns), this is a good place to appreciate the religious dimension to Prague's past architectural fortunes. The church was founded in 1371. The proto-Hussite reformer Jan Milíč of Kroměříž preached here before the Bethlehem Chapel was built. The Dominicans gained possession during the Counter-Reformation, built a cloister next door and 'baroquefied' it in the 1730s. Václav Reiner, the Czech painter who did the ceiling frescoes a few years before his death, is buried here.

CHAPEL OF THE HOLY CROSS Map pp98–9

The **Chapel of the Holy Cross** (Kaple Sv Kříže; Konviktská; mass 5pm Sun, 6pm Tue) is a tiny Romanesque rotunda and one of Prague's oldest buildings. It started out as a parish church in about 1100. Saved from demolition and restored in the 1860s by a collective of Czech artists, it still has the remnants of some 600-year-old wall frescoes, though you may have to attend Mass to see them.

POLICE & SECRET POLICE Map pp98–9

Staré Město's charm goes a bit cold along Bartolomějská. Before November 1989, the block was occupied by the StB (Státní bezpečnost, or State Security), the hated secret police.

An old convent and the 18th-century **St Bartholomew Church** (Kostel sv Bartoloměje), for a time part of the StB complex but now returned to the Franciscans, backs onto Bartolomějská. The enterprising Pension Unitas has rented some of the space from the nuns, and guests can now spend the night in refurbished StB prison cells, including the one where Václav Havel spent a night (see Sleeping p128).

Nové Město

Although it's called New Town, this part of Prague isn't particularly: a crescent of land east and south of Staré Město, it was founded in 1348 by Karel IV. The New Town's first buildings were constructed on the corner of Wenceslas Square and Jindřišská. Its outer fortifications were knocked down in 1875. The layout has been essentially preserved, although most surviving buildings are from the 19th and early 20th centuries. Many blocks are honeycombed with pedestrian-only passages, some lined with shops, cafés and theatres – if you see a doorway marked *pasáž*, go on in.

Nové Město extends eastward from Revoluční and Na příkopě to Wilsonova and the main railway line, and south from Národní almost to Vyšehrad. Its focus is Wenceslas Square (Václavské náměstí), a broad, 750m-long boulevard lined with late-19th-century and early-20th-century buildings almost completely obscured by modern shops, sloping down from the National Museum towards Staré Město.

MUSEUM OF THE CITY OF PRAGUE Map pp120–1

Tucked in a bit of wasteland near the Florenc metro station, this excellent **museum** (Muzeum Hlavního města Prahy; ☎ 24 81 67 72; www.muzeumprahy.cz - Czech only; Na poříčí 52; admission 40Kč; 9am-6pm Tue-Sun) displays the rich pickings of Prague's florid pre-19th century history. Brutal Hussite 'beating weapons' (what good Protestant doesn't need one?), elaborate ancient door furniture and some choice medieval and Renaissance carvings are excellent appetisers for the main attraction, Antonín Langweil's incredible scale model of Prague circa 1830: the poor hobbyist (who died without the recognition he so richly deserved) even included teeny tiny frescoes and broken windows. Don't miss the ceilings of the museum's upstairs galleries (one gallery hosts rotating contemporary exhibitions).

AROUND JINDŘIŠSKÁ ULICE   Map pp110–11

Squarely at the end of Jindřišská is the **Jindřišská Tower** (Jindřišská věž), a former watchtower or bell tower built in the 15th century, now home to a fancy restaurant.

Around the corner is the 1906 **Jubilee Synagogue** (Jubilejní synagóga; Jeruzalémská 7; admission 30Kč; ☉ 1-5pm Sun-Fri, closed Jewish holidays), also called the Great (Velká) Synagogue. Note the names of donors on the colourful, stained-glass windows, and the grand organ above the entrance.

Mucha Museum (☎ 221 451 333; www.mucha.cz; Panská 7; adult/child 120/60Kč; ☉ 10am-6pm) features the sensuous Art Nouveau works of Alfons Mucha as well as sketches, photographs and other memorabilia. Because the exhibit focuses on his prints without much consideration of his work in object design, it gets a bit samey. There's also an interesting video on his life (available in English or Czech) and a substantial gift shop.

NATIONAL MUSEUM   Map pp110–11

Taxidermophiles rejoice! The **National Museum** (☎ 224 497 111; www.nm.cz; Václavské náměstí 68; adult/child 80/40Kč; free 1st Mon of month; ☉ 10am-6pm May-Sep, 9am-5pm Oct-Apr, closed 1st Tue of month) scoffs at multimedia and modern theories of materials interpretation. The museum does the classics – rocks, dead animals, bones – and does them well. Among the more interesting of the exhibits (very few have English labels, but a multi-language audio tour is available for 200Kč) is a large collection of stuffed anteaters, pangolins and aardvarks, the corpse of an extinct Thylacine, a cross-section of a domestic cat and – for those who don't care for roadkill – a display of Czech printed works.

Looming above Wenceslas Square, the neo-Renaissance building was designed in the 1880s by Josef Schulz as an architectural symbol of the Czech National Revival. The interior of the museum is quite overwhelming, with its grand stairwell and pantheon gallery. The upstairs murals feature a boys' own interpretation of Czech legends and history by František Ženíšek and Václav Brožík, and pink-bottomed cherubs by Vojtěch Hynais.

Across the road to the east is the former National Assembly building (1973), which retains within its walls the former Stock Exchange (1936–38) and today houses **Radio Free Europe**. The security cordon went up around the station, which broadcasts to Central Asia and the Middle East, after 11 September 2001. The next building beyond it is the Smetana Theatre or **Prague State Opera House** (Statní opera).

MUSEUM OF COMMUNISM   Map pp98–9

Ironically located inside a casino next to a McDonald's, the **Museum of Communism** (☎ 224 212 966; www.museumofcommunism.com; Na příkopě 10; admission 180Kč; ☎ 9am-9pm) devotes itself to presenting the corruption, empty shops, oppression, fear and double-speak of life in socialist Czechoslovakia. It's a bit one-sided, and more than a little text-heavy, but definitely worth a visit. Make sure to watch the video about protests leading up to the Velvet Revolution: you'll never think of it as a pushover again.

WENCESLAS SQUARE
(VÁCLAVSKÉ NÁMĚSTÍ)   Map pp110–11

A horse market in medieval times, Wenceslas Square (also called Václavák) got its present name during the nationalist upheavals of the mid-19th century, and since then it's been the favourite spot for anyone trying to make their mark on Czech history. In 1918 the creation of the new Czechoslovak Republic was celebrated here. In January 1969, in protest against the Warsaw Pact invasion, university student Jan Palach set himself on fire on the steps of the National Museum (above). Following the 17 November 1989 beating of students on Národní třída, thousands gathered here in anger, night after night. A week later, in a stunning mirror-image of Klement Gottwald's 1948 proclamation of communist rule from the balcony of the Kinský Palace in the Old Town Square, Alexander Dubček and Václav Havel stepped onto the balcony of the Melantrich building to a thunderous and tearful ovation, and proclaimed the end of communism in Czechoslovakia.

At the top of the square is Josef Myslbek's muscular equestrian **statue of St Wenceslas** (sv Václav), the 10th-century pacifist Duke of Bohemia. Flanked by other patron saints of Bohemia he has been plastered over

SOUTHERN NOVÉ MĚSTO

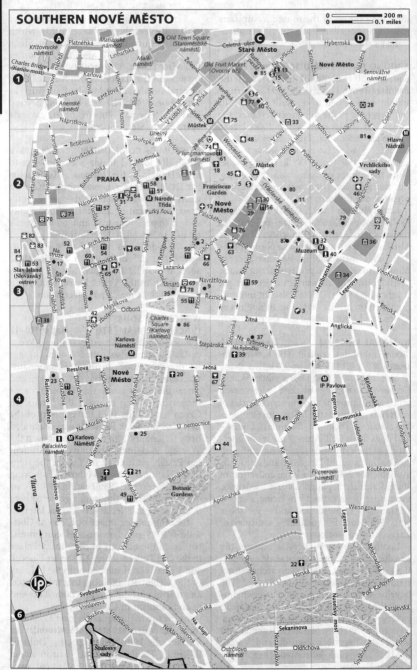

with posters and bunting at every single one of the square's historical moments. If you've got a date with a Praguer, chances are they'll want to meet you under the horse's tail.

The square has become a monument to consumerism, a gaudy gallery of cafés, shops, money-changers, cabbies and pricey hotels. If you like Times Square or Leicester Square, this is your kind of place.

LUCERNA PASSAGE   Map pp110–11

The most elegant and convoluted of Nové Město's many arcades, or *pasáž*, runs beneath the Lucerna Palace at Štěpánská 61, bounded by Štěpánská, Vodičkova and V jámě. The buildings fronting the arcade on Vodičkova – U nováků and Fortuna – are among Prague's finest Art Nouveau façades. The arcade was designed by Václav Havel, the ex-president's grandfather, so it's no surprise Havel chose to walk through this *pasáž* on his way to proclaim the end of communism. The Lucerna complex includes theatres, a cinema, shops, a rock club and cafés. Outside the cinema, David Černý's commentary on Czech history hangs from the ceiling.

CHURCH OF OUR LADY OF THE SNOWS   Map pp110–11

If you haven't had enough medieval architecture in Staré Město, head for the Gothic **Church of Our Lady of the Snows** (kostel Panny Marie Sněžné) at the bottom end of Wenceslas Square. Karel IV began its construction in the 14th century, but only the chancel was ever completed, which is why it looks taller than it is long. Karel had intended it to be the grandest church in Prague – the nave is higher than that of St Vitus and the altar, an extravagance of black and gold, is the city's tallest. It was a Hussite stronghold, echoing to the sermons of Jan Želivský – these days it has a strict 'no talking' rule.

While you're here, rest your feet in the **Franciscan Garden** (Františkánská zahrada; ✆7am-10pm Apr-Sep, 7am-8pm Oct, 8am-7pm Nov-Mar), formerly part of a monastery and now a peaceful, rigorously groomed park where office workers scoff a quick sandwich and read the paper.

ALONG NÁRODNÍ TŘÍDA

Národní třída is central Prague's 'high street', a row of mid-range shops and grand government buildings whose stateliness is somewhat obscured by rushing traffic.

At Národní 40, fronting Jungmannovo náměstí, is an imitation Venetian palace known as the dům Látek (Cloth House) or **Adria palác** (Map pp110–11); you'll have seen a lot of heavily decorated buildings in Prague, but this one takes the cake. Beneath it is the Adria Theatre, original home of Laterna Magika and meeting place of Civic Forum in the heady days of the Velvet Revolution.

The **memorial** (Map pp110–11) reading '17.11.89' with hands making peace signs, on the wall near No 16, is in memory of the students clubbed here on that date.

Across the road at No 7 is the fine Art Nouveau façade (by Osvald Polívka) of the **Viola Building** (Map pp98–9), former home of the Prague Insurance Company, with the huge letters 'PRAHA' around five circular windows.

On the southern side at No 4, looking like it has been bubble-wrapped by Christo, is **Nová Scéna** (Map pp110–11), the 1983 'New National Theatre' building, home of Laterna Magika (see Entertainment p144). Finally, facing the Vltava across Smetanovo nábřeží, is the **National Theatre** (Národní divadlo; Map pp110–11), the neo-Renaissance flagship of the Czech National Revival, funded entirely by private donations. Architect Josef Zítek's masterpiece burned down within weeks of its 1881 opening, but, incredibly, was funded again and restored in less than two years. You have to attend a performance to get inside.

Across from the theatre is the **Kavárna Slavia** (Map pp98–9), once the haunt of theatre and literary types, but now largely living on its past glory. The river views are still just as lovely, though.

MASARYKOVO NÁBŘEŽÍ   Map pp110–11

About 200m south of the National Theatre along Masarykovo nábřeží is a series of stunning **Art Nouveau buildings** between Nos 26 and 32 – kitty gargoyles, Mucha-esque Nouveau sgraffito and gorgeous balconies are worth looking for. No 32, once the East German embassy, is now occupied by the Goethe Institut.

Opposite this is **Slav Island** (Slovanský ostrov), a sleepy sandbank with river views and gardens, named after Slav conventions held here since 1848. Around the northern tip of the island there are three little boat-hire places (see Activities p123). In the middle of the island is a 19th-century meeting hall, now the Gastro Zofin restaurant (see Eating p137). At the southern end is **Šitovská věž**, a 15th-century water tower (once part of a mill) with an 18th-century onion-dome roof, and a children's playground featuring arcane playthings seemingly sourced from Soviet-era torture manuals.

Beneath the tower is the **Mánes Gallery** (☎ 224 931 410; Masarykovo nábřeží; adult/child 40/20Kč; ☼ 10am-6pm), established in the 1920s by a group of artists headed by painter Josef Mánes as an alternative to the Czech Academy

---

STUDENT SACRIFICES

On 16 January 1969, university student Jan Palach set himself on fire on the steps of the National Museum in protest at the Soviet invasion of Prague. He staggered down the steps in flames and collapsed beneath the statue of King Wenceslas. The following day around 200,000 people gathered in the square in his honour. A cross has since been placed in the pavement below the steps of the National Museum in his memory.

Jan took four agonising days to die, and his body was buried in Olšany Cemetery in Žižkov (p122). A shrine of flowers and candles near the top of Wenceslas Square (Map pp110–11) marks the spot where he fell. Jan wasn't the only one to kill himself in protest at the invasion: Josef Hlvaty died on 25 January; Miroslav Malinka and Blanka Nachazelova on 22 January; Jan Zajic drank acid and set himself alight on 25 February outside Wenceslas Square 39; and on April 4 a civil servant and former Communist Party member, Evzen Plocek, publicly took his own life.

The street entering Jan Palach Square from the north is called 17.listopadu (17 November), which now has a dual meaning. It originally honoured students killed in an anti-Nazi demonstration in 1939. Exactly 50 years later, students marching along Národní třída in memory of that day were clubbed by police. The national outrage triggered by this event pushed the communist government towards its final collapse a few days later. There's a memorial plaque reading '17.11.89' with hands making peace signs inside the arcade at Národní 16.

of Arts; it's still a great place to find out what's happening right now in Czech art.

CHARLES SQUARE
(KARLOVO NÁMĚSTÍ)   Map pp110–11

At over seven hectares, **Charles Square** is Prague's biggest square – actually it's more of a park. Presiding over it is the baroque 1678 **Church of St Ignatius of Loyola** (kostel sv Ignáce), designed by Carlo Lurago for the Jesuits. Inside see the 'Mary in a rock garden', diorama-style Chapel of Our Lady of Lourdes.

The square's historical focus is the **New Town Hall** (Novoměstská radnice) at the northern end, built when the 'New Town' was new. From its windows several of Sigismund's Catholic councillors were flung to their deaths in 1419 by followers of the Hussite preacher Jan Želivský. 'Defenestration' (the act of throwing someone out of a window) got its meaning, Czechs got a new political tactic, and the Hussite Wars were off to a flying start. The **tower** (admission 30Kč; ☯ 10am-6pm Tue-Sun) was added 35 years later.

The baroque palace at the southern end of the square belongs to Charles University. It's known as **Faust House** (Faustův dům) because, according to a popular story, Mephisto took Dr Faust to hell through a hole in the ceiling here. During the 16th-century reign of Rudolf II, court alchemist, con-artist and Irishman Edward Kelley also lived here while pretending to work at turning lead to gold.

CHURCH OF SS CYRIL &
METHODIUS   Map pp110–11

In June 1942, Czech paratroopers flew in from England to assassinate Reinhard Heydrich, the Nazi Governor of Bohemia and Moravia, known as the Butcher of Prague. When they'd done the job, they hid out in the baroque **Church of SS Cyril & Methodius** (kostel sv Cyril a Metoděj; Resslova & Na Zderaze) until they were betrayed by a colleague and hunted down by the Nazis – the outer wall beneath the plaque commemorating them still bears bullet scars. In savage revenge for the assassination, the Nazis randomly obliterated the village of Lidice (p158), west of Prague. The church itself was designed in the 1730s by Kilian Dientzenhofer and Paul Bayer.

RAŠÍNOVO NÁBŘEŽÍ   Map pp110–11

If you've taken a boat on the river you've no doubt wondered what's up with that entirely modern, curvy building with the ball on its head. Emerging from between its Art Nouveau neighbours, the joyfully daring **Dancing Building** (Tančící dům; Rašínovo nábřeží 80) was designed by Czech Vlado Milunć and American Frank Gehry, who originally called it the 'Astaire & Rogers Building'. Completed in 1996, it's an excellent addition to the ageing skyline.

A little further south along Rašínovo nábřeži is the **František Palacký Monument** (Palackého náměstí), which no-one can accuse of being understated. Stanislav Sucharda's extraordinary statue is an Art Nouveau swarm of haunted bronze figures around a stodgy statue of the 19th-century historian and giant of the Czech National Revival.

EMMAUS MONASTERY   Map pp110–11

Emmaus Monastery (klášter Emauzy; Vyšehradská 49) was completed in 1372 for a Slavic order of Benedictines. Its Gothic St Mary Church (kostel Panny Marie) was damaged by Allied bombs in February 1945; the striking, very modern sweeping spires, added in the 1960s, look distinctly out of place, but the more you look at them the better they get.

Across Vyšehradská is the 1739 **Church of St John of Nepomuk on the Rock** (kostel sv Jana Nepomuckého na Skalce), one of the city's most beautiful Dientzenhofer churches. Just south on Na slupi are large, peaceful **botanic gardens** (Botanická zahrada; ☯ 10am-5pm Jan–mid-Mar, 10am-6pm mid-Mar–Nov, 10am-4pm Nov-Dec).

EAST OF CHARLES SQUARE
(KARLOVO NÁMĚSTÍ)   Map pp110–11

This area is full of hospitals and clinics, and is a pleasant, quiet, leafy neighbourhood to wander through. On Na Rybníčku II is one of Prague's only three surviving Romanesque rotundas, the **Rotunda of St Longinus** (rotunda sv Longina), built in the early 12th century. Closed to the public and scrawled with graffiti, it looks lost and forlorn in its bed of weeds.

One of the city's finest baroque houses is **Vila amerika** (Ke Karlovu 20). This 1720, French-style summerhouse, again designed by Kilian Dientzenhofer (and once slated to be a museum of the architect's work), is now the **Antonín Dvořák Museum** (admission 40Kč; ☯ 10am-5pm Tue-Sun). If you have a passing interest in the composer, you might enjoy browsing the exhibits while listening to his work. It's a great place to buy a Dvořák CD, as the staff at the store give excellent advice.

At the southern end of Ke Karlovu is a little church with a big name, **Church of the Assumption of the Virgin Mary & Charlemagne** (kostel Nanebevzetí Panny Marie a Karla Velikého), founded by Charles IV in 1350 and based on Charlemagne's burial chapel in Aachen. In the 16th century it acquired its ribbed vault, whose revolutionary unsupported span was attributed by some to witchcraft.

Below the church you can find some of Nové Město's original fortifications, and look out at the Nusle Bridge (Nuselský most), vaulting the valley of the Botič creek to Vyšehrad, with six lanes of traffic on top and the metro inside.

Vyšehrad
Map p115

Archaeologists know that various early Slavonic tribes set up camp near Hradčany and at Vyšehrad (High Castle), a crag above the Vltava, but Vyšehrad alone is regarded as Prague's mythical birthplace. According to legend, the wise chieftain Krok built a castle here in the 7th century. Libuše, the cleverest of his three daughters, ran the joint until her subjects complained – they wanted a male ruler, despite the troubles Libuše predicted would result. Taking as her king a ploughman named Přemysl, she founded the Přemyslid line of Czech rulers. War broke out almost immediately; on her deathbed she predicted the rise of a great city, Praha.

Vyšehrad may in fact have been settled as early as the 9th century. Boleslav II (ruled 972–99) may have lived here for a time. There was certainly a fortified town by the mid-11th century. Vratislav II (ruled 1061–92) moved here from Hradčany, beefing up the walls, and adding a castle, the St Lawrence Basilica, the Church of SS Peter & Paul and the Rotunda of St Martin. His successors stayed until 1140, when Vladislav II returned to Hradčany.

Vyšehrad then faded until Karel IV, aware of its symbolic importance, repaired the walls and joined them to those of his new town, Nové Město. He built a small palace and decreed that coronations of Bohemian kings should begin with a procession from here to Hradčany.

Nearly everything was wiped out during the Hussite Wars. The hill remained a ruin –

except for a township of artisans and traders – until after the Thirty Years' War, when Leopold I refortified it.

The Czech National Revival generated new interest in Vyšehrad as a symbol of Czech history. Painters painted it, poets sang about the old days, Smetana set his opera *Libuše* there. Many fortifications were dismantled in 1866 and the parish graveyard was converted into a national memorial cemetery.

Vyšehrad retains a place in Czech hearts. Since the 1920s the old fortress has been a quiet park, with splendid views of the Vltava and Nusle valleys. It's a great place to stroll, shake off the urban blues and take in a bit of Prague's mythical flavour. There's still plenty of excavation going on, and more ruins may be visible by the time you read this.

A good booklet about Vyšehrad's buildings is available from the Casemates, St Lawrence Basilica and the Vyšehrad Gallery.

THE VYŠEHRAD COMPLEX

Most visitors enter Vyšehrad through the **Tábor Gate** (Táborská brána), where they find a sign with extensive rules about ways in which they may and may not use the grass. Inside are remains of another gate (brána Špička), an **information office** (🕑 9.30am-5pm Nov-Mar, 9.30am-6pm Apr-Oct), a café, and the **Leopold Gate** (Leopoldova brána), the fort's most elegant – both gates date to the post-Thirty Years' War refortification.

Vratislav II's little **Rotunda of St Martin** (Rotunda Sv Martina) is Prague's oldest standing building. In the 18th century it was used as a powder magazine. The door and frescoes date from a renovation in about 1880.

Nearby are a 1714 **plague column** and the baroque **St Mary Chapel in the Ramparts** (kaple Panny Marie v hradbách), dating from about 1750; and behind them the remains of the 14th-century **Church of the Beheading of St John the Baptist** (kostelík Stětí sv Jana Křtitele).

In the park across the road from the former New Archdeaconry (Nové děkanství) is a **stone cluster** of three phalli, made of a stone not found in this region. They may have been part of a prehistoric sundial or solstice marker.

If you enjoy making pilgrimages to the graves of your heroes, then the **Vyšehrad Cemetery** (Vyšehradský Hřbitov; 🕑 8am-5pm Nov-Feb, 8am-6pm Mar-Apr, 8am-7pm May-Sep, 8am-4pm Oct)

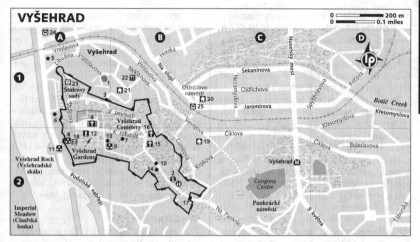

VYŠEHRAD

0 |====| 200 m
0 |====| 0.1 miles

INFORMATION		Old Archdeaconry	13 A2	EATING	(pp132–9)
Grial Internet Café	1 A1	Penguin Tenis	14 B2	Snack Bar	(see 13)
Information Centre	2 B2	Plague Column	(see 16)	U Neklana	22 B1
		Remains of the Church of the Beheading of			
SIGHTS & ACTIVITIES	(pp88–123)	St John the Baptist	(see 16)	DRINKING	(pp139–41)
Brick Gate	3 A1	Remains of Špička Gate	(see 2)	Café	(see 2)
Church of SS Peter & Paul	4 A1	Rotunda of St Martin	15 B2		
Cubist House at Libušina 3	5 A1	St Mary Chapel in the Ramparts	16 B2	ENTERTAINMENT	(pp141–4)
Cubist Houses at Rašínovo Nábřeží 6–10	6 A1	Tábor Gate	17 B2	Summer Theatre	23 A1
Former New Archdeaconry	7 B2	Vyšehrad Gallery	18 A2		
Foundations of Charles IV's Palace	8 A2			TRANSPORT	(pp146–51)
Foundations of St Lawrence Basilica	9 A2	SLEEPING	(pp125–32)	Tram Stop	24 A1
Leopold Gate	10 B2	Hotel Amadeus	19 B2	Tram Stop	25 B1
Libuše's Bath	11 A2	Hotel Union	20 B1		
Myslbek Statues	12 A2	U Šemíka Hotel	21 B1		

is your one-stop Czech shop. Composers Smetana and Dvořák, writers Karel Čapek, Jan Neruda and Božena Němcová, painter Alfons Mucha and sculptors Josef Myslbek and Bohumil Kafka are all here. A directory of big names is at the entrance. In between the stars, the graves of the lesser known are a real showcase of headstone design. The Prague Spring music festival kicks off every 12 May, the anniversary of Smetana's death, with a procession from his grave to the Municipal House.

Vratislav II's **Church of SS Peter & Paul** (Kostel Sv Petra a Pavla; adult/child 20/10Kč; ☺ 9am-noon & 1-5pm Mon, Wed & Sat, 9am-noon Fri, 11am-noon & 1-5pm Sun, closed Tue & Thu) has been built and rebuilt over the centuries, culminating in a neo-Gothic makeover by Josef Mocker in the 1880s. The towers were added in 1903; the beautiful Art Nouveau frescoes inside – very unusual in this baroque-obsessed city – were painted in the 1920s, largely by František and Marie Urban. Each chapel has an English label explaining its story and artist.

Beside the church are the **Vyšehrad Gardens** (Vyšehradské sady), with four statues by Josef Myslbek, based on Czech legends of mythological Vyšehrad. Libuše and Přemysl are in the northwestern corner; in the southeast are Šárka and Ctirad. From May to August, open-air concerts are held here at 2.30pm on Sunday, with anything from jazz to oompah to chamber music.

Within the Vyšehrad's ramparts there are many vaulted **casemates**. At the 1842 **Brick Gate** (Cihelná brána), 20Kč will buy you a guided tour through several of these chambers, now used as a historical exhibit and for storing four of Charles Bridge's original baroque statues (other originals are at the Lapidárium in Holešovice).

If you want to see the ruined foundations of the 11th-century Romanesque **St Lawrence Basilica** (bazilika sv Vavřince; admission 5Kč; ☺ 11am-6pm), ask for the key in the snack bar by the Old Archdeaconry. In front of the southwestern bastion are the foundations of a small **palace** built by Charles IV, and then dismantled in 1655. Perched on the bastion is the **Vyšehrad Gallery** (Galérie Vyšehrad; ☎ 241 410 348; www.praha-vysehrad.cz; admission 10Kč; ⏰ 9.30am-5pm), which holds temporary exhibitions and often sells the artworks at very reasonable prices. Below the bastion are some ruined guard towers poetically named '**Libuše's Bath**'.

In the northwestern corner is an open-air **Summer Theatre** (Letní scéna; admission 35Kč; ⏰ 5pm Thu) where you can catch a concert or cultural show.

There are a few spots to eat around the complex, though a picnic lunch is definitely a good option. You can grab a sausage with bread or a marinated cheese (25Kč and 30Kč) and a beer at the Archdeaconry snack bar.

The simplest way to get to Vyšehrad is by metro. Exit Vyšehrad metro station on the Hajé-bound side, towards the Congress Centre – you'll see brown tourist signs directing you to 'Vyšehrad', where you'll enter through the Tabor Gate. There's more climbing if you walk up from tram No 7, 18 or 24 on Na slupi (from Karlovo nám metro), through the Brick Gate. Check out the fine views of the Nusle valley from the northeastern bastion. A quicker, steeper route is up the long stairs from tram No 3, 7, 16 or 17 on the riverside drive – the stairs come out by the Vyšehrad Cemetery.

CUBIST ARCHITECTURE

If you've taken the trouble to come out to Vyšehrad, don't miss a clutch of Prague's famous Cubist buildings in the streets north of the Brick Gate. Cubist architecture, with its eye-catching use of elementary geometric forms, is more or less unique to the Czech Republic, particularly Prague.

One dramatic villa, designed by Josef Chochol, the dean of Czech Cubist architects, is at Rašínovo nábřeží 6–10, just before the street tunnels beneath Vyšehrad rock. Others by Chochol are a very well-preserved freestanding house at Libušina 3, and the clean lines of an apartment block at Neklanova 30 – look for the U Neklana restaurant (see Eating p137). All date from around 1913.

Holešovice   Map pp82–3

With its wide, leafy streets, grimy buildings and air of just going about its daily business, Holešovice is a real contrast to central Prague. Up-and-coming in the late 1990s, Holešovice apparently called a halt to development before the malls and multiplexes started moving in – consequently, you'll find a few good modern restaurants, bars and cafés, plenty of old *hospodas* (pubs) and an easily accessible atmosphere of 'so this is what Prague is *really* like'.

This patch of the city in the Vltava's 'big bend' sprang from two old settlements – Holešovice and the fishing village of Bubny – little hamlets opposite the bustling city until industry arrived in the mid-19th century. When the Hlávkův Bridge was built in 1868, linking the area to Nové Město, the population swelled. A horse-drawn tram, a river port and the Fairgrounds followed, and the area became a part of Prague in 1884.

FAIRGROUNDS

This vast exhibition area is the venue for a big and popular annual fair *(Matějská pouť)* in February and March, when it's full of rides, fairyfloss, and half of Prague having fun. Some of the buildings went up in 1891 for the Terrestrial Jubilee Exposition, including the Prague Pavilion (Pavilón hlavního města Prahy), which houses the Lapidárium and the Palace of Industry (Průmuslový palác).

It's a popular weekend destination, a great spot for a sausage, a beer and some *dechovka* (Bohemian brass-band music). The whole complex is closed on Monday during the day. **Křižík Fountain** (Křižíkova fontána; ☎ 220 103 280; www.krizikovafontana.cz; admission 200Kč; ⏰ 8, 9, 10 & 11pm) performs computer-controlled acts of water gymnastics to music – expect treats like the soundtrack from *Jurassic Park* or *Pearl Harbor*, or you might get a bit of Smetana or Dvořák (the *Prague Post* has weekly details of the programme).

While the gullible saps are marvelling at the replica statues on the Charles Bridge, you could be at the **Lapidárium** (☎ 233 375 636; adult/child 20/10Kč; ⏰ noon-6pm Tue-Fri, 10am-12.30pm & 1-6pm Sat & Sun) checking out the real thing. This is a repository of some 400 sculptures from the 11th to the 19th centuries, removed from Prague's streets and buildings to save them from demolition or pollution.

Get to the Fairgrounds on tram No 12, 15 or 17 from nádraží Holešovice metro station and get off at the Výstaviště stop.

STROMOVKA PARK

West of the Fairgrounds, this is Prague's largest park. In the Middle Ages it was a royal hunting preserve, and is referred to as Royal Deer Park (Královská obora). Rudolf II had rare trees planted and several lakes dug (fed from the Vltava by a still-functioning canal). You can get here across the Vltava via Císařský ostrov.

CENTRE FOR MODERN & CONTEMPORARY ART

The National Gallery's massive **Centre for Modern & Contemporary Art** (☎ 824 301 003; Dukelských hrdinů 47; adult/child 1 fl 50/100Kč, 2 fls 70/150Kč, 3 fls 100/200Kč, 4 fls 120/250Kč; ☯ 10am-6pm Tue-Sun, 10am-9pm Thu) has seemingly collected every work of modern Czech art, plus a fair swathe of other big names from the rest of Europe. If you don't have the time or money to see the full collection (it would take a whole day to see it properly), you can choose to do the gallery a floor at a time. Highlights include Czech Cubists, Art Nouveau, Mánes' portraits and Mařak's landscapes, social realism and Karel Pauzer's grotesque *Dog Family*. Your ticket lasts a whole day, and you can go in and out as much as you want. Take tram No 12, 15 or 17 west from Nádraží Holešovice metro station, two stops to Veletržní.

NATIONAL TECHNOLOGY MUSEUM

For hands-on fun, visit the **National Technology Museum** (Národní technické muzeum; ☎ 220 399 111; Kostelní 42; adult/child 70/30Kč; ☯ 9am-5pm Tue-Sun). The giant main hall is full of old trains, planes and automobiles, including 1920s and '30s Škodas. There are also some great old motorbikes and bicycles. You can take a tour down a mineshaft, or learn about photography, astronomy or timepieces. From the Vltavská metro station, take tram No 1 or 25 three stops to Letenské náměstí and walk down Nad štolou and Muzejní streets.

LETNÁ

Letná is a vast park between Hradčany and Holešovice, with playgrounds, tennis courts, meandering paths packed with Rollerbladers, and an outdoor **beer garden** with postcard-perfect views of the city and the Vltava bridges. In 1261 Přemysl Otakar II held his coronation celebrations here.

The present layout dates from the early 1950s, when a 30m, 14,000-tonne statue of Stalin, the biggest monument to the man in the Eastern bloc, was erected by the Czechoslovak Communist Party, only to be blown up in 1962 when Kruschev took over. Today, in its place, stands a peculiar giant **metronome** – if you stand in Old Town Square facing up Pařížská you can see it ticking out time against the sky. The terraced area around the metronome is a wonderland of rail slides and 50/50s, adored by local skateboarders.

Letná used to be the site of May Day military parades, similar to those in Moscow. In late 1989, some 750,000 people demonstrated here in support of what became known as the Velvet Revolution. In 1990 Pope John Paul II gave an open-air Mass here to more than one million people, most of whom were probably looking for the beer garden.

Smíchov   Map p118

In Smíchov, Prague changes before you at the speed of time-lapse photography. Five years ago tourists might have crossed over to this dirty, rough neighbourhood to get a taste of the real Prague; these days real equals shopping malls, multiplexes and construction, construction, construction. Tourist attractions are few and far between, which means the beautiful, grubby baroque and Art Nouveau buildings are uncluttered with souvenir stores. The swarming, shopping masses clot around Anděl metro station; the northern end of Smíchov is a happening enclave of sushi restaurants and modern theatre. Head to the southern end to get the old-school version; the rail yards, old pubs and Staropramen brewery (just follow your nose) still have the air of 1838 Smíchov, when the suburb became Prague's industrial quarter.

MOZART MUSEUM AT BERTRAMKA

You'll need more than a passing interest in Wolfgang Amadeus to get the most out of this **museum** (☎ 257 316 753; www.bertramka.cz; Mozartova 169; adult/child 90/50Kč; ☯ 9.30am-6pm Apr-Oct, 9.30am-4pm Nov-Mar), where they're keen to remind you that Prague liked Mozart before anyone else thought of it. Mozart finished *Don Giovanni* while staying here. The museum has a couple of instruments the master may once have played, and lots of information about local musicians Mozart was involved with. Take tram No 4, 6, 9, 12 or 14 from the Anděl metro station.

Vinohrady   Map p119

The suburb of Vinohrady is southeast of the National Museum and main train station.

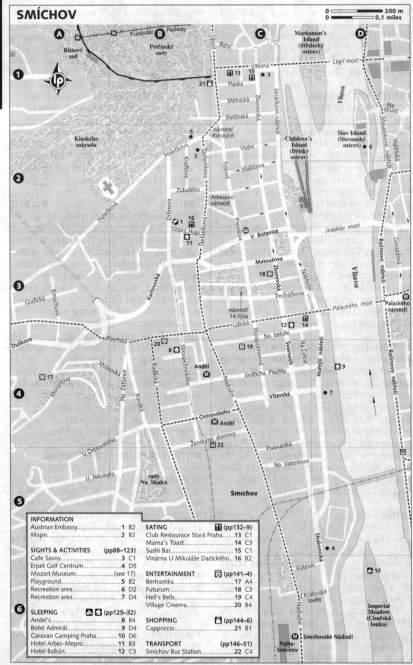

SMÍCHOV

0 ____ 200 m
0 ____ 0.1 miles

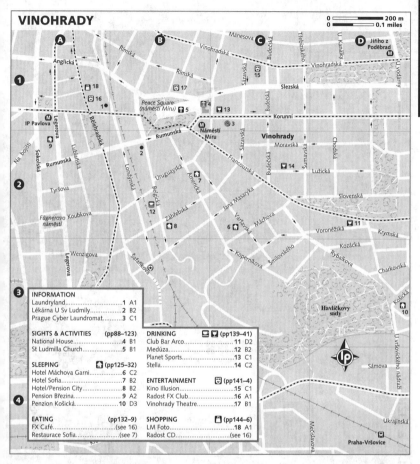

VINOHRADY

0 ——————— 200 m
0 ——————— 0.1 miles

The name refers to vineyards that grew here centuries ago; even as recently as 200 years ago there was little urbanisation. Now the tree-lined streets are peppered with little cafés and bars, and the buildings have all had a good scrubbing and a fresh coat of paint – it's one of the prettiest of Prague's inner suburbs. There's not a lot to see here, but walking the Parisian-style streets from náměstí Míru to Havlíčkovy sady is a very pleasant way to spend a few hours.

PEACE SQUARE (NÁMĚSTÍ MÍRU)
Vinohrady's physical and commercial heart is Peace Square (náměstí Míru), dominated by the brick, neo-Gothic **St Ludmilla Church** (Kostel sv Ludmily) – the church steps are

a popular meeting spot. Right behind it at No 9 is the neo-Renaissance **National House** (Národní dům), with exhibitions and concert halls. On the northern side of the square is the 1909 **Vinohrady Theatre** (Divadlo na Vinohradech), a popular drama venue.

Žižkov
Map pp120–1
Named after the Hussite hero and formidable military commander Jan Žižka, who whipped Holy Roman Emperor Sigismund and his army on a hill here in 1420, Žižkov has always been a rough-and-ready neighbourhood, working-class and full of revolutionary fizz well before 1948. One of the first protests of the Velvet Revolution took place here, in Škroupovo nám. Žižkov has some

PRAGUE

NORTHERN NOVÉ MĚSTO, KARLÍN & ŽIŽKOV

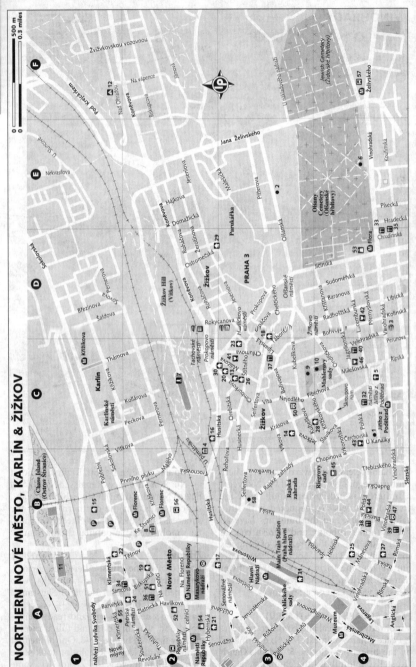

500 m
0.3 miles

INFORMATION		
CKM Travel	1	C4
Foreigners' Police & Passport		
Office	2	E3
Laundryland	(see 18)	
Pl@neta Internet Café	3	D4
SIGHTS & ACTIVITIES	(pp88–123)	
Army Museum	4	B2
Church of the most Sacred Heart of		
Our Lord	5	C4
Jan Palach's Grave	6	E4
Jan Žižka Monument	7	C2
Miminka	(see 10)	
Museum of the City of Prague	8	B2
National Memorial	(see 9)	
Old Jewish Cemetery	9	C3
Playground	(see 45)	
TV Tower	10	C4
Winter Sports Stadium	11	A1
SLEEPING	(pp125–32)	
Alfa Tourist Service	(see 17)	
Autocamping Žižkov	12	F1
Bílý Lev	13	C3
Clown & Bard Hostel	14	C4
Hilton Hotel	15	B1
Hostel Elf	16	C2

Hostel Jednota	17	A2
Hotel Golden City	18	D3
Hotel Harmony	19	A2
Hotel Kafka	20	C3
Hotel Meteor Plaza	21	A2
Hotel Opera	22	B1
Hotel Prokopka	23	C3
Kolej Petrská	24	A2
Mary's Accommodation Agency	25	B4
Pension Prague City	26	C3
Stop City Accommodation		
Agency	27	B4
Strawberry Hostel	28	C4
Studio Henri	29	D2
U Tří Korunek	30	C3
Vesta Hostel	31	A3
EATING	(pp132–9)	
Akropolis Café-Restaurant	(see 50)	
Buon Giorno Pizzeria	32	C4
Crazy Daisy Restaurant	33	D4
Hacienda Mexicana Restaurant	34	A2
Infinity Restaurant & Music Bar	35	D4
Kavárna Imperial Café	36	A2
Mailsi	37	C3
Pastička	38	B4
Tiger Tiger	39	B4
U Sloupu	40	C4

DRINKING	(pp139–41)	
A-Club	41	C3
Hapu	42	D4
James Bond	43	C4
Maler	44	B4
Park Café	45	B4
Piano Bar	46	C4
ENTERTAINMENT	(pp141–4)	
Cinema City	(see 53)	
Gejzee..r	47	B4
Guru Music Club	48	D3
Matrix Klub	49	D2
Palác Akropolis	50	C3
SHOPPING	(pp144–6)	
Bílá Labuť Department Store	51	A2
Hudy Sport	52	A2
Palác Flóra	53	D4
Second Hand Land	54	A2
TRANSPORT	(pp146–51)	
Avis	55	A1
Florenc Bus Station	56	B2
Želivského Long-Distance Bus Stand	57	F4
OTHER		
Petrol Station	58	B3

very unbaroque sights, loads of pubs and clubs, and a great deal of grungy panache.

ŽIŽKOV HILL

The famous battle of 1420 took place on this long mound – known then as Vitkov – separating Žižkov and Karlín districts. These days the area feels more like a monument to the communist era, with its blocky, grandiose buildings and statuary.

From Florenc or the main train station, walk along Husitská; after the first railway bridge, climb to the left up U památníku. To your right you'll see the **Army Museum** (Armádní muzeum; ☎ 220 204 924; U památníku 2; adult/child 30/15Kč; ⌚ 9.30am-6pm Tue-Sun); its exhibits on the history of the army and the resistance movement in WWII are in Czech only, but excellent temporary exhibits have English texts.

At the top of the hill, Bohumil Kafka's 1941 **statue** of a fearsome, bandaged Jan Žižka wields his beating weapon from atop a vein-popping horse: Kafka must have had some terrifying nightmares during its design.

Behind Žižka, the over-the-top **National Memorial** (Národní památník) was completed around 1930 as a memorial to the Czechoslovak 'unknown soldier', but later hijacked as a mausoleum for communist leader Klement Gottwald (the embalming didn't take, and when old Klement started rotting the memorial was closed and he was buried elsewhere). The outside of the memorial is covered in bas-reliefs glorifying the worker and soldier, but you can only

visit the inside on the first Saturday of the month at 2pm: call **Prague Information Service** (☎ 602 664 078) to find out more.

TV TOWER

The 216m, white **TV Tower** (Televizní Věž; ☎ 267 005 778; www.tower.cz; Mahlerovy sady 1; adult/child 150/30Kč; ⌚ 11am-11.30pm) is visible from everywhere. It's worth getting up close to this '80s vision of the future for a good look at the faces of David Černý's bizarre sculpture *Miminka*. While the outside of the tower is one of the city's highlights, the inside is a wash-out. Views through the grubby windows are bigger but not necessarily better than those from St Vitus Cathedral or Petřín Tower.

OLD JEWISH CEMETERY & MUSEUM

The foundations of the TV Tower were excavated in an old **Jewish cemetery** (☎ 224 819 456; Mahlerovy sady; admission 20Kč; ⌚ 9am-1pm Tue & Thu), which operated between the closing of Josefov, at a time of plague outbreak, and the opening of the cemetery near Želivského metro, in 1890. The remaining gravestones have been crowded into this tiny yard – apparently 40,000 people have been buried here. To get into the cemetery outside opening hours, call and request an appointment.

CHURCH OF THE MOST SACRED HEART OF OUR LORD

With its perforated brickwork, stocky, looming clock tower and ultrasimple interior, this is probably Prague's most original church, its brawny charm reminiscent of a solid, rough factory worker downing his first beer of the afternoon. The **church** (Kostel Nejsvětějšího Srdce Páně; náměstí Jiřího z Poděbrad, Žižkov) was built in 1932 by Slovenian Josef Plečnik (who made the eyebrow-raising modern additions to Prague Castle).

OLŠANY CEMETERY & JAN PALACH'S GRAVE

A world away from the insanity of Old Town Square, the inhabitants of **Olšany Cemetery** (Olšanské hřbitovy; ☎ 267 310 652; Vinohradská 2807; admission free; ☼ 8am-6pm Mar-Apr & Oct, 8am-7pm May-Sep, 8am-5pm Nov-Feb) rest in some serious peace. This cool, green cemetery overgrown with ivy is Prague's main burial place, founded in 1680 during a plague epidemic.

Jan Palach, the student who set himself on fire in January 1969 (see boxed text p112) in protest at the Soviet invasion, is buried here (though for nearly 20 years he was moved elsewhere by the government to stop his grave becoming a protest site). It's worth visiting the Museum of Communism (p109) first to find out more about him. To find his grave, enter the main gate and turn right – it's about 50m along on the left of the path.

JEWISH CEMETERY

The grave of **Franz Kafka**, in this quiet, ivy-covered modern cemetery, is a pilgrimage spot for hundreds of visitors, covered in pebbles and little notes. The **cemetery** (Židovské hřbitovy; ☼ 9am-5pm Sun-Thu, 9am-2pm Fri, closed Jewish holidays) opened around 1890 when the previous Jewish cemetery – now at the foot of the TV Tower – was closed. The entrance is beside Želivského metro station, and the grave of Kafka and his parents is to the right, in front of the third gate (section 21). There are holocaust memorials just inside the main gate. Men should cover their heads (yarmulkes are available for loan at the gate).

Northwest Outskirts   Map pp82–3

DEJVICE

Not the happiest of chappies, artist František Bílek sculpted tortured monuments to his metaphysical religious beliefs, many of which you can see at the **Bílkova Villa** (☎ 224 828 244; Mickiewiczova 1; adult/child 50/40Kč; ☼ 10am-6pm Tue-Sun mid-May–mid-Oct, 10am-6pm Sat & Sun mid-Oct–mid-May). Bílek built the villa in 1911 as a house for himself and his family; these days it houses

some of the furniture he designed, and the City Gallery of Prague's collection of his dramatic work. To get there, walk south from Hradčanská metro down Badeniho.

STAR SUMMER PALACE

In 1530 Ferdinand I established a hunting reserve on a verdant hill east of White Mountain; it's now a little chunk of walled forest amid the suburbs, crisscrossed by secluded paths. In 1556 one Archduke Ferdinand of Tyrol built a Renaissance summer palace here in the shape of a six-pointed star. Inside the **Star Summer Palace** (Letohrádek hvězda; adult/child 30/10Kč; ☼ 9am-5pm Tue-Sun May-Sep, 10am-6pm Tue-Sun Oct) there's a small museum dedicated to the chateau, the Battle of White Mountain and artists Mikuláš Aleš and Alois Jirásek. Upstairs, the floor is fragile and you'll be asked to wear giant slippers – the potential for fun is almost infinite. Take tram No 25 from Hradčanská metro or No 22 from Malostranská towards Bílá hora and get off at the second-last stop, Malý Břevnov.

ACTIVITIES

Raising a glass is the most popular local cardiovascular activity, and if you're only here a few days you might as well go with the flow. Those who can't bear another day off the treadmill should try centrally located **Fitness Týn** (Map pp98-9; ☎ 224 808 295; Týnská 21, Staré Město; casual workout 85Kč) gym, which also has aerobics (60Kč) and spinning (100Kč) classes. Most of the chain, top-end hotels have gyms that can be used on a casual basis, but it will cost you around 500Kč.

Prague's Range Rover drivers love **Erpet Golf Centrum** (Map p118; ☎ 257 321 229; www.erpet.cz; Strakonická 2860/4, Smíchov; ☼ 10am-11pm Mon-Fri, 9am-11.30pm Sat & Sun). Entry to the outdoor swimming pools costs from 300/200Kč per adult/concession. Tennis court hire starts at 180Kč per hour, while squash is 200Kč. Erpet also has sauna, Jacuzzi and massage. Call if you want to swing a golf club.

Prague has lots of free **recreation areas**. The one in Smíchov (Map p118; Hořejší nábřeží) has a skate park, a basketball hoop, a small soccer pitch and a good kids' playground. The one on Children's Island (Dětský ostrov; Map p118), just south of Most Legii (access is from Janáčkovo nábřeži) has a playground, skate park, soccer pitch, concrete table tennis tables and a strange combination boules-ten pin bowling game. It's open from 9am to 8pm daily from April to October and 10am to 6pm the rest of the year.

Clay tennis courts in the Vyšehrad historic grounds are managed by **Penguin Tenis** (Map p115; ☎ 241 407 619; Vyšehrad complex, Vyšehrad). Call for rates and reservations.

Rollerbladers and **skateboarders** should head to Letná (Map pp82–3). The paths here are a very popular after-work in-line skating area, while the plinth of the metronome echoes to the p'kaks of local skateboarders.

Rent a **rowing boat** (from 60Kč per hour per person) or **pedal boat** (80Kč) from the northern end of Slav Island (Slovanský ostrov; Map pp110–11). The rental spots are generally open from 10am to 8pm in summer, and close when the weather gets bad. Only one (Slovanka, on the western side of Slav Island) rents a pedal boat shaped like a swan – you'll pay 100Kč per person for the privilege of floating around in this beauty. None of the boats can be taken beyond the upstream and downstream weirs. All the boat rental spots sell beer, of course.

Prague may be the only place in the world where you can combine indoor **bouldering** and beer – leave it to the Czechs to come up with this one. To use the bouldering wall at **Boulder Bar's** (Map pp110-11; ☎ 222 231 244; www.boulder.cz in Czech; V Jámě 6; ☼ 8am-10pm Mon-Fri, noon-10pm Sat & Sun), call ahead to reserve a spot.

In winter, an ice-skating rink is set up at the feet of Jan Hus in the Old Town Square – little kids and silly adults will enjoy being guided around the rink by university students dressed as princesses and jesters.

THE ROYAL WAY WALKING TOUR

The Royal Way (Královská Cesta) is the ancient coronation route to Prague Castle, and it's a real greatest hits of Prague sightseeing tour. Start the walk at náměstí Republiky. The Art Nouveau **Municipal House** (1; p106) is

facing the square. Beside it is the 15th-century **Powder Tower** (2; p106). Go under the tower and west into Celetná; heading west towards Old Town Square, this street is an open-air museum of pastel baroque façades.

Turn off the Royal Way, north into Královdvorská. This area, the **Royal Court** (3; Králův dvůr), was once the royal stables. On U Obecního domu is the restored Art Nouveau **Hotel Paříž** (4; p128), built in 1907. Turn left into Jakubská; at its western end is **St James Church** (5; p104), famous for its pipe organ and acoustics.

The entire block across from the church was once a medieval inn, the **Týn Court** (6; p103), and has now been renovated. Turn right and go around it by way of the quiet Týnská passage, where you can see the beautiful north door of the **Týn Church** (7; p103). Turn left behind it to return to Celetná and the Royal Way, and you're in **Old Town Square** (8; p102).

Beyond the **Old Town Hall** (9; p102) is **Little Square** (10; Malé náměstí; p105). Bear left, then right into Karlova. All along the right side of Karlova is the **Klementinum** (11; p104) and its churches.

You're now looking at the Old Town tower of **Charles Bridge** (12; p101). Cross the bridge, through the crowds of tourists, hawkers and pickpockets, and the rows of baroque statues, and soak up the views of Prague Castle.

The western end of Charles Bridge crosses the island of **Kampa** (13; p96), separated from Malá Strana by the Čertovka channel. Walk beneath the Malá Strana bridge towers and you're on Mostecká.

Distance: 3.5km, with some steep climbs up to the castle.
Duration: Two hours to one day, depending on how many buildings you look inside.

At the top of Mostecká is Malá Strana Square (Malostranské náměstí), bisected by trams and centred around one of Prague's finest baroque structures, the **Church of St Nicholas** (**14**; p95). Cross the square to Nerudova, one of Prague's most picturesque streets. On many of Nerudova's mostly baroque façades there are colourful emblems that have given these buildings their popular names.

Continue along Úvoz to the **Church of St Roch** (**15**; p93) and the **Strahov Monastery** (**16**; p93) behind it, then backtrack via Loretánská to Hradčanské náměstí and the entrance to **Prague Castle** (**17**; p88). Don't miss the view of the city from the corner of the square, with Petřín Hill off to the right.

PRAGUE FOR CHILDREN

Prague probably isn't the most exciting destination for kids – baroque architecture, castles without battlements or armour or crossbows, churches, and museums of Jewish history don't generally get the youngsters all fired up. However, there are a few sights around town that kids might enjoy. **Petřín** (p96) has a mirror maze that cracks kids up, a playground and the replica Eiffel Tower. The **National Technology Museum** (p117) has plenty of hands-on entertainment, while the **National Museum** (p109) is good for those who like stuffed animals and skeletons. There's a big **toy museum** (p91) and the very medieval **Old Royal Palace** (p91) at the castle.

Prague has lots of good **playgrounds** – there are several on islands in the Vltava, one in the Kinský Gardens in Malá Strana, a huge one in Letná, one near the Hotel Romantik in Hradčany and one by the river in Smíchov. Many kids enjoy renting a boat on the river; if your kids have skateboards or in-line skates with them, take them to Letná. **Minor Theatre** (p144) hosts traditional marionette shows for kids.

If you'd rather leave the kids behind while you hit the town, most top-end and many mid-range hotels have **babysitting** services – call ahead to see whether yours does.

QUIRKY PRAGUE

Sculptor David Černý, a big success in the US, has made a huge effort to make Prague a more interesting, less precious place. Most of his efforts have been thwarted – the giant statue of a naked, masturbating man he had planned for the roof of the National Theatre

somehow never got approval – while others, like his *Pink Tank*, a revolutionary nose-thumbing piece created during the communist era, have been removed, but there are at least three of his works you can visit.

The TV Tower in Žižkov crawls with the giant babies of *Miminka*; the Lucerna Passage is home to his interpretation of Wenceslas Square's Václav statue; while his *Hanging Around* caused complaints to the police after it was installed on the roof of a house in Jilská, Staré Město. There's more information, including plans for the future, at www.davidcerny.cz.

TOURS

Thanks to its small size and excellent public transport system, Prague is very easy to get around by yourself, and if you already know a lot about the city a tour is probably a waste of time and money. If you want to know what Prague has to offer, don't have much time or have mobility problems the more-mainstream bus tours give a good overview of the city. The walking and specialised culture tours are a good idea if you want to learn more about a particular aspect of Prague.

City Walks (☎ 222 244 531, 608 200 912; www.prague walkingtours.com) A variety of walking tours, including a Franz Kafka tour, a pub walk, Prague by bike and a nightly Ghost Walk. Tours start from 300/250Kč per adult/student. Pick-up Astronomical Clock.

Martin Tour (Map pp98-9; ☎ 224 212 473, 603 454 994; www.martintour.cz; Štepanska 61, Nové Město) Bus tours with headphone commentary (which means you can't ask questions) of Prague sights (two hours 350Kč), river cruises, trips to Terezín, Karlovy Vary, Karlštejn, Konopište, Kutná Hora, Český Krumlov and Dresden. Some tours involve walking; commentary tends to gloss over the interesting details. Pick-up Staroměstské nám.

Prague Master (☎ 607 820 158, 603 813 541; info@ praguemaster.com) This small company runs tailor-made, individual walking and driving tours and specialises in tours for people in wheelchairs and people with lots of questions. Prices start at 300Kč per person. Driving tours include Bohemia's back roads, Tabor, Český Krumlov, Telc, Jihlava and Třebíč. You choose the pick-up point.

Pragotur (Map pp98-9; ☎ 224 482 562; guides .pis@volny.cz; Old Town Hall, Staroměstské nám, Staré Město) The Prague Tourist Board's guide service, provides tailor-made walking tours from 500Kč per person for three hours. Tours include architecture, history, Art Nouveau and Jewish culture.

Precious Legacy Tours (Map pp98-9; ☎ 222 321 951, 602 214 088; www.legacytours.net; Maiselova 16, Staré

Město) Jewish culture tours of the Jewish Quarter (620Kč, three hours) and Terezín (1100Kč, six hours), plus tailored tours to other destinations in the Czech Republic and central Europe.

Premiant City Tours (☎ 296 246 070, 606 600 123; www.premiant.cz; Plackého 1, Staré Město) Bus tours of Prague sights (two hours 380Kč), river cruises, trips to Karlštejn, Kutná Hora, Konopiště and Český Krumlov. Well-informed guides and lots of detail; some tours involve walking. Pick-up Na Příkopě 23, Nové Město (Map pp98-9).

Silver Line through Golden Prague This self-guided walking tour designed by the Prague Information Service (PIS; Map pp98-9) takes in 38 sights in Staré Město, Malá Strana, Hradčany and Nové Město. The comprehensive guide booklet is available at PIS for 156Kč.

FESTIVALS & EVENTS

Throughout summer, Prague can barely move for festivals. Keep an eye on *Houser*, the *Prague Post* and posters to see what's happening while you're in town. Updates on festivals can be found at www.prague-info.cz and www.prague.tv. Some regularly scheduled events include the following:

Open-air cinema festival (☎ 266 712 746; www.stre lak.cz in Czech) Throughout summer, films are shown outdoors on Marksmen's Island (Střelecký Ostrov) – screenings include English-language films and German and French art house classics, as well as recent releases and Czech favourites.

Prague Spring (Pražské Jaro; ☎ 257 312 547; www .festival.cz; Hellichova 18, Malá Strana) Prague's biggest festival drawcard begins on 12 May with a procession from Smetana's grave at Vyšehrad to the Municipal House, and a performance of *Má vlast*. The festival of classical music contin-ues until 2 June. The cheapest tickets are available from the box office, open from 10am to 6pm Monday to Friday from April to 12 May, and until 5pm during the festival. For a guar-anteed seat, though, you will have to book by mid-March.

Vinobraní From 1 August, you'll see signs popping up around the city advertising burčák: it's slightly fermented grape juice, the first product of the wine harvest. Prague toasts burčák for a few days in late September at náměstí Míru in Vinohrady, traditionally a wine-growing area.

SLEEPING

There are hundreds of hotels in Prague, but the incredible demand for beds means this is one of Europe's most expensive places to stay. During high season (see p431) it pays to reserve ahead.

Staré Město, Nové Město and Malá Strana – the tourist centres – have the greatest variety and charge the most. Vinohrady has a lot of mid-range, smaller hotels, and is a very

pleasant place to stay, within easy reach of the centre and with lots of restaurants and bars. Žižkov has hostels and budget hotels as well as a few mid-range options, and is popular with younger travellers – it's a bit grungy, and has tons of bars and clubs. Holešovice and Vyšehrad are both good op-tions for mid-range hotels within easy reach of the centre, though there's less going on in these suburbs than in Vinohrady.

Camping is prohibited on public land and most campgrounds are on the outskirts of Prague – we've listed some of those that are closer in.

In summer, many schools and universities convert themselves to hostels – look for big, yellow 'Travellers Hostel' banners. We've generally only listed year-round hostels.

Touts swarm on the arrival platforms of the main and Holešovice train stations offering private rooms. Check the location and the transportation: some are right out in the suburbs. Prices start around 500Kč per person if you're sharing entrance and bathroom with the family. If you want to organise a private room ahead of time, some accommodation agencies handle them.

Apartments are an increasingly popular option. If you're staying more than a week, they can be very good value, particularly as you can cook meals at home. We've listed agencies that handle apartments – email them with your requirements and how much you're prepared to pay, and they'll let you know what your options are.

In Prague, we've divided accommoda-tion into budget (all hostels and camp sites, and hotels charging less than 1300Kč a double), mid-range (hotels charging be-tween 1300 and 4500Kč a double) and top end (4500Kč a double or more).

Accommodation Agencies

Agencies are a good for private rooms or apartments or if you show up in peak sea-son and can't find a bed. If you're booking a hotel it's cheaper to do it direct.

Alfa Tourist Service (Map pp120-1; ☎ 224 230 037; Opletalova 38, Nové Město; ✆ 9am-5pm Mon-Fri) Accommodation in student hostels, *pensions*, hotels and private rooms.

AVE (☎ 251 551 011; www.avetravel.cz) Walk-in booking offices at the main train station, Holešovice train station, the airport and PIS branches; efficient and helpful, with hostel, *pension* and hotel rooms and a few private rooms.

Happy House Rentals (Map pp98-9; ☎ 222 311 855; Soukenická 8, Nové Město; ⏱ 9am-5pm Mon-Fri) One of Prague's friendliest, most helpful agencies, Happy House rents out apartments and rooms all over the city in all price ranges.

Maja Rentals (☎ 608 513 567; www.majarentals.com; ⏱ 11am-8pm) Good value short- and long-term apart-ment rentals in the centre and suburbs. No office, call the mobile phone number to make inquiries.

Mary's (Map pp120-1; ☎ 222 253 510; www.marys.cz; Italska 31, Vinohrady; ⏱ 9am-9pm) Private rooms, hostels, *pensions*, apartments and hotels in all price ranges in Prague and surrounding area.

GAY & LESBIAN PRAGUE

For a city where it seems like every third person is making out in public, Prague is notable for the lack of gay affection displayed on its streets. While there are no laws against homosexual-ity in the Czech Republic – the age of consent is 15, the same as for straights – public opinion seems to be lagging behind legislation.

Amigo magazine's website (www.amigo.cz) has English-language listings. Tourist services, accommodation, listings and a bulletin board can be found at www.praguegaycity.com. Lesba (www.lesba.cz - Czech only) has lots of information in Czech. Gay Iniciativa (http://gay.iniciativa.cz - Czech only) is a gay and lesbian support service. Probably the most comprehensive informa-tion source is Gay Guide Prague (www.gayguide.net/europe/czech/prague), with online forums, events, accommodation, tours, newsletters and support groups.

In April, the lesbian Aprilfest (www.lesba.cz/apriles) is a week of happenings; on the third Sunday in May there's a candlelit gay pride march in Prague.

Gay-owned accommodation includes **Pension Arco** (Map p119; ☎ 271 740 734; Voroněžská 24/172, Vinohrady; s/d from 950Kč) and **Studio Henri** (Map pp120-1; ☎ 271 773 837; www.studiohenri.cz; Jeseniova 52, Žižkov; d from 2310Kč; P ⏱ ⏱), a four-person apartment with a whirlpool.

Rainbow Travel (☎ 220 910 855; www.rainbowtravel.cz) runs tours in Prague and throughout Bo-hemia. Restaurants Down Town Café Praha (see Eating p136) and U Rybíček (see Eating p136) are both gay-owned. There are Internet cafés at U Rybíček and Pension Arco.

Soccer players of all (or no) skill levels might enjoy having a kick around with Prague's informal gay football team (http://gaysport.kluci.cz/e_index.html). There are primarily male nude beaches at Seberak Lake (take the C metro to Kačerov, then the Seberak bus) and Šarka Lake (take the A metro to Dejvická, then tram 26 to the end of the line).

Social Scene

The gay scene in Prague changes fast – check out one of the listings services above before you head out. Be a little picky if you're planning to take someone home from one of these clubs: Prague has had a recent spate of robberies and even a few murders perpetrated by young male prostitutes who pick up expats and travellers in gay bars.

A-Club (Map pp120-1; ☎ 222 781 623; Miličova 25, Žižkov; ⏱ 7-10pm Wed-Thu, 7pm-5am Fri & Sat) A women-only club (men can visit if they come with a female friend), A-Club hosts meetings and social happenings during the week and gets a bit livelier on the weekend. You can book the whole club on days they're not open.

Club Bar Arco (Map p119; ☎ 271 740 734; Voroněžská 24/172, Vinohrady; ⏱ 8am-midnight) A quiet little spot in genteel Vinohrady, popular with older chaps. There's also a *pension* here and an Internet café.

Friends (Map pp98-9; ☎ 221 635 408; Náprstkova 1, Staré Město; ⏱ 4pm-3am) This welcoming music and video bar has excellent coffee and wine, and DJs after 10pm.

Gejzee..r (Map pp120-1; ☎ 222 516 036; Vinohradská 40, Vinohrady; ⏱ 9pm-5am Thu-Sat) Prague's big-gest gay and lesbian club, with two bars and a huge dance floor.

Maler (Map pp120-1; ☎ 222 013 116; www.maler-club.cz - Czech only; Blanická 28, Vinohrady; ⏱ 9am-11pm Mon-Thu, 9-4am Fri & Sat, 1-10pm Sun) You'll find Prague's hippest lesbians at this 'secret ladies' club'.

Piano Bar (Map pp120-1; ☎ 222 727 496; Milešovská 10, Žižkov; ⏱ 5pm-midnight) Tucked away in a Žižkov cellar, Piano Bar is homely and relaxed.

Stella (Map p119; ☎ 224 257 869; Lužická 10, Vinohrady; ⏱ 8pm-5am) Probably the most popular gay bar in town, Stella is intimate and candlelit. You have to ring the doorbell to get in.

Stop City (Map pp120-1; ☎ 222 521 233; www.stopcity .com; Vinohradská 24, Vinohrady; ☯ 10am-9pm Apr-Oct, 11am-8pm Nov-Mar) Specialising in private and *pension* accommodation in the Vinohrady and Žižkov areas.

Top Tour (Map pp98-9; ☎ 224 819 111; www.top tours.cz; Rybná 3, Staré Město; ☯ 1-7pm Mon-Fri) Apartments and rooms in central Prague.

Vesta (Map pp120-1; ☎ 224 225 769; Hlavní Nádraží), Hostels, including its own Hostel Vesta at the main train station, and Hotel Kafka in Žižkov.

Hradčany & Malá Strana   Map pp94–5
BUDGET

Hostel ESTEC (☎ 257 210 410; estec@jrc.cz; blok 2, Vaníčkova 5, Strahov; s/d/tr 400/600/900Kč; ☯ year-round) One of several Strahov student dormitories offering traveller accommodation. This one is recently renovated and is a good deal cheerier than its neighbours. Take bus No 143, 149 or 217 from Dejvická metro to Kolej Strahov.

Hostel Sokol (☎ 257 007 397; hostelsocool@seznam .cz; 3rd fl, Hellichova 1; dm 350Kč; ☒) Sokol is accessed via a courtyard from Všehrdova 42 (take the metro to Malostranská and then tram No 12, 22 or 23 two stops south). While the location is choice the rooms are ultrabasic and crowded.

MID-RANGE

Hotel Sax (☎ 257 531 268; www.sax.cz; Jánský vršek 328/3; s/d 3100/3700Kč; P ☒ ▣) In a quiet, atmospheric corner of Malá Strana, eclectically furnished Hotel Sax has huge baths, big flat-screen TVs, primary-coloured leather couches, striking abstract photography and some of the chintziest bedrooms in Prague. It's very reasonably priced for the area and has a great ambience.

TOP END

Romantik Hotel U raka (☎ 220 511 100; www.rom antikhotels.com/prag; Černínská 10; s/d 6200/6900Kč; P ☒ ☒) Totally secluded but within an easy walk of Strahov and the castle, this tiny six-room hotel in an 18th-century wooden house with its own walled garden is the epitome of privacy. The owners have managed to blend 18th-century atmosphere with entirely modern fittings – each room is unique. Children under 10 are not allowed. You have to reserve a room well in advance.

Kampa Hotel Best Western (☎ 257 320 508, reservations ☎ 271 750 275; www.euroagentur.cz; Všehrdova 16; s/d/tr 4900/5800/7500Kč; P ☒ ☒) Overflowing with jovial, pastel-toned medieval atmosphere, Kampa Hotel is littered with suits of armour and halberds; its medieval-themed feasting hall (dining room to you and me) is just downright nuts. Unfortunately, the 'bring in the jesters' ambience doesn't extend to the rooms, which are clean and comfortably nondescript (although there are no signs forbidding pillow jousting, so use your own discretion).

Hotel Questenberk (☎ 220 407 600; www.questen berk.cz; Úvoz 15/155; s/d €168/240; P ☒ ☒ ▣) Once Strahov Monastery's hospital, this brand-new hotel is close to the castle and the Loreta. Its very pleasant rooms are sunny and furnished with old-fashioned opulence. There's an Internet connection in every room if you have your own laptop.

Other recommendations:

U Páva (☎ 257 533 360; www.romantichotels.cz; U lužického semináře 32; s/d from 5400/5900Kč; P ☒ ▣) Gothic detailing and heavy, dark furniture throughout, some rooms have stained glass and magical views of the castle.

U krále Karla (☎ 257 531 211; Úvoz 4; s/d incl breakfast from 5000/5500Kč; P ☒) You can't really get closer to the castle than this hotel, right at the base of the walls. Rooms are spacious and regal.

Hotel Hoffmeister (☎ 251 017 111; www.hoffmeister.cz; Pod Bruskou 7; s/d €190/245; P ☒ ☒ ▣) Little architectural details and original drawings make this quiet, personal boutique hotel a cut above average. The Jacuzzi baths in every room don't hurt either.

Staré Město & Josefov   Map pp98–9
BUDGET

Hostel Týn (☎ 224 828 519; www.hostel-tyn.web2001.cz; Týnská 21; dm/d/tr 400/1100/1350Kč; ☒) With its great central location, clean, comfortable rooms and spotless bathrooms, Hostel Týn is very good value. Rooms don't include breakfast.

Hostel Dlouhá (☎ 224 826 662/3; www.travellers.cz; Dlouhá 33; dm/s/d/tr 370/1120/1240/1440Kč; P ▣) The only Travellers' Hostel that is open year-round (if you're visiting in summer, you can book one of four other centrally located hostels by calling Dlouhá). The big dorm is a bit dark and grim, but smaller dorms are bright and clean if a little cramped (each bed has its own reading lamp, a nice touch). Self-contained apartments go for 2100Kč to 3000Kč, depending on the number of beds you need. There's also a bar with pizza and a jukebox.

Pension Unitas (☎ 224 221 802; www.unitas.cz; Bartolomějská 9; s/d/tr from 1000/1100/1600Kč; ✗) In space rented from a convent that was once a Czech secret police jail, rooms are quiet (but cramped), and have share bathrooms. Václav Havel was held here for a day, and if it's available you can stay in the very cell (No P6). Rooms for four/five go for 1850/2000Kč. If you don't want to share a bath, singles/doubles/triples are 1100/1400/1750Kč.

MID-RANGE

Hotel Antik (☎ 222 322 288; www.hotelantik.cz; Dlouhá 22; s/d 3590/3990Kč) A delightful little hotel, Antik has brand-new fittings in a 15th-century building (no lift). The 12 rooms are cosy (ask for one with a balcony), there's a little garden and the staff are lovely. An attached coffee shop is strewn with more of the eponymous antiques.

Hotel Ungelt (☎ 224 828 686; www.ungelt.cz; Malá Štupartská 1; d incl breakfast 4431Kč; P ◻) This apartment hotel dates to the 12th century – it has a lot of serious, old-fashioned class, including wooden floors with rugs instead of the usual chain hotel carpet monstrosities. All rooms are self-contained and have their own living room and kitchen.

Hotel Cloister Inn (☎ 224 211 020; www.cloister -inn.com; Konviktská 14; s/d/tr 4000/4200/5000Kč; P ✗ ◻) The Cloister Inn's refurbished convent rooms were once part of the still-operational St Bartholomew Church. While some architectural touches remain from the convent, they're a little overwhelmed by the hotel's overly cheery rumpus-room colour scheme. It's a comfortable place, and if you can snag one of the top-floor executive rooms, you'll also get air conditioning and a fax machine.

Other recommendations:

Hotel U klenotníka (☎ 224 211 699; www.uklen otnika.cz; Rytířská 3; s/d 2500/3300Kč; ✗) This friendly central hotel has no lift, but you get the *Guardian* with your breakfast and the rooms are comfortable and deco-rated with unique art.

Hotel Expres (☎ 224 211 801; expres@zero.cz; Skořepka 5; s/d/tr 2600/2800/3400Kč) Clean and modern, this centrally located hotel has sunny rooms at very reason-able prices. Rooms with shared bathrooms are cheaper.

Pension U Lilie (☎ 222 220 432; www.pensionulilie.cz; Liliová 15; s/d from 1850/2800Kč) You're right in the heart of things in this slightly scruffy but friendly hotel.

Hotel Mejstřik (☎ 224 800 055; www.hotelmejstrik.cz; Jakubská 5; d from 4000Kč; P ◻) This small boutique

hotel in a reasonably quiet back street has striking furnish-ings and a garden that puts it ahead of the crowd.

TOP END

Hotel Paříž (☎ 222 195 195; www.hotel-pariz.cz; U Obecního domu 1; d from €170; P ✗ ◻ ◻) This splendid Art Nouveau building is now a historic monument. There's atmosphere galore, and no expense spared on the plush fittings. If you're planning to stay in a top-end hotel, this should definitely be at the top end of your list.

Northern Nové Město

BUDGET

Hostel Jednota (Map pp120-1; for reservations call Alfa Tourist Service ☎ 224 230 038; www.alfatourist.cz/ ejednota.html; Opletalova 38; dm/s/d incl breakfast 350/550/750Kč) Don't be put off by the glum Soviet-style lobby: the rooms at Jednota are bright, airy, well laid-out for maximum privacy and thoroughly 21st century. It's a pity this hostel, near the main train station, is open only in summer. There are cooking facilities and a bar.

Kolej Petrská (Map pp120-1; ☎ 222 315 189, reserva-tions ☎ 224 930 010; Petrská 3; s/d 500/960Kč) Groups of three Spartan rooms share a kitchen, bath-room and separate toilet in this functional hostel. Staff members are friendly and help-ful, each room has a phone, and breakfast can be had for an extra 70Kč.

MID-RANGE

Hotel Opera (Map pp120-1; ☎ 222 315 609; www.hotel -opera.cz; Těšnov 13; s/d 3650/4200Kč; ✗ ◻) The bathrooms here are so new they hurt your eyes. While the rooms themselves are clean and comfortable, the furnishings have a mismatched, grandmotherly feel. Gym, sauna, bar and restaurant are on premises. Prices include breakfast, and discounts are available in July and August.

Hotel Harmony (Map pp120-1; ☎ 222 319 807; www.hotelharmony.cz; Na poříčí 31; s/d incl breakfast 2400/ 3400Kč; ✗) The rooms here are sparklingly clean, simple and comfortable and the staff business-like and friendly: it's good value for money. Three-person apartments go for 3600Kč; all prices include breakfast in the pleasant, inexpensive restaurant.

Hotel Meteor Plaza (Map pp120-1; ☎ 224 192 130, 224 192 559; www.hotel-meteor.cz; Hybernská 6; s/d incl breakfast €89/99; P ✗) For a Best Western, the Meteor is quite upmarket, and definitely slicker and more modern than others in the price range. If you have your own laptop, you can access the Internet from your room. There's a bar, restaurant, gym and hairdresser in the hotel.

Botel Albatros (Map pp98-9; ☎ 224 810 541/7; fax 224 811 214; nábřeží Ludvíka Svobody; s/d/tr 2160/2700/3240Kč; **P**) Spartan cabins with tiny shower and toilet are no great bargain in summer, but not too bad with the low-season discount. German businessmen love this floating hotel. It has a restaurant and café, and connections by tram No 3 to Wenceslas Square.

TOP END

Hilton (Map pp120-1; ☎ 224 841 111; www.prague .hilton.com; Pobřežní 3; s/d from €278; **P** ✕ ✕ ⧉ ⧉) They pull no punches in Prague's biggest hotel: four restaurants, a bar, high-speed Internet in every room, bathrooms with separate toilets, chock-full minibars, baby-sitting service, TVs with Playstation and a huge gym with a spinning room. Fifteen of the rooms are wheelchair accessible. Want to stay in the room Mick Jagger and Bill Clinton use when they're in town? It has its own sauna and will set you back €1087. The hotel is in a lousy location by the freeway in Karlín, but who cares?

Southern Nové Město & Vyšehrad
BUDGET

Hostel Klub Habitat (Map pp110-11; ☎ 224 921 706; hostel@iol.cz; Na Zderaze 10; dm incl breakfast from 400Kč; ✕ ⧉) You'll find absolutely no frills at friendly, tidy Habitat, but beds in the eight-bed dorm are very affordable. If you want to luxe it up, you'll pay 450Kč for the four-bed dorms. Bathrooms are clean.

Hostel U Melounu (Map pp110-11; ☎ 224 918 322; info@hostelmelounu.cz; Ke Karlovu 7; dm 380Kč) One of the prettier hostels in town, U Melounu is in a historic building in a quiet back street amid clinics and the botanic gardens (and a short walk from Vinohrady's restaurants and bars). It's about a 10-minute walk south of IP Pavlova metro, or take bus No 504 or 505 down Sokolská.

MID-RANGE

Hotel 16 U sv Kateřiny (Map pp110-11; ☎ 224 920 636; www.hotel16.cz; Kateřinská 16; s/d incl breakfast from 2500/3400Kč; **P** ✕ ⧉) Near the Botanic Gardens and about 10 minutes' walk from Karlovo nám metro station, the very

friendly boutique Kateřiny is quiet, clean and very comfortable. There's a peaceful terraced garden out the back (try to get a back room if you don't mind having twin beds) and a small bar. Recommended.

Hotel Amadeus (Map p115; ☎ 224 937 569; www .dhotels.cz site; Slavojova 8; s/d/tr 2400/2700/3650Kč; **P** ✕ ⧉) You can just about smell the paint in this comfortable new hotel. Rooms in the front block are spacious; those in back a little more cramped. One room has disabled access and the hotel's four two-storey, four-person suites (4750Kč) are air conditioned.

Other recommendations:

U Šemíka Hotel (Map p115; ☎ 224 920 736; www .usemika.cz; Vratislavova 36; s/d from 1700/2300Kč; **P** ✕ ⧉) This very friendly little hotel, right below the Vyšehrad cliffs, has brand new beds and a couple of spacious, air-conditioned apartments.

Hotel Koruna (Map pp110-11; ☎ 224 932 229; www.korunahotel.cz; Opatovická 16; s/d incl breakfast 2300/3350Kč; ✕) The Koruna's main draw is its great location – close to all the action but in a quiet back lane relatively unaffected by rowdy tourists.

Hotel Union (Map p115; ☎ 261 214 812; www.hotelunion .cz; Ostrčilovo náměstí 4; s/d/tr 2815/3380/4495; **P** ✕) Rooms in this 1906 hotel are appropriately old-fashioned: a little dowdy, but perfectly clean and not too worn.

TOP END

Interhotel Ambassador Zlatá Husa (Map pp110-11; ☎ 224 193 111; www.ambassador.cz; Václavské náměstí 5-7; s/d US$240/265; **P** ✕ ✕ ⧉) There are plenty of luxury touches at this 1911 hotel right on Wenceslas Square. Every bath has a Jacuzzi and each bathroom has a separate shower. Bedrooms are decorated in Queen Anne style – it's a little prissy, but at least it has some character.

Hotel Adria (Map pp110-11; ☎ 221 081 111; www.adria.cz; Václavské náměstí 26; s/d €180/220; **P** ✕ ✕ ⧉) Recently refurbished, the Adria is classy, very private and particularly suitable for business visitors. Enjoy the *Wall Street Journal* with breakfast (not included in the tariff).

Hotel Esplanade (Map pp110-11; ☎ 224 501 111; www.esplanade.cz; Washingtonova 19; d from €149; **P** ✕ ✕ ⧉) The soaring marble lobby gives the impression you're in for something special, but unfortunately only those who can upgrade to an apartment get the luxury treatment. Otherwise, expect clean and comfortable rooms convenient to the station, opera and Wenceslas Square.

Holešovice   Map pp82–3
BUDGET
Sir Toby's Hostel (☎ 283 870 635; www.sirtobys.com; Dělnická 24, Holešovice; dm/s/d/tr 325/750/1050/1200Kč; **P** **✕** **⌨**) New, clean rooms and cheerful, friendly staff make this a great place to stay out in Holešovice. If you want a private bathroom, add 50Kč to the cost; for breakfast, add 60Kč. Wheelchair-bound travellers should call ahead to check whether a room can be prepared. From Nádraží Holešovice metro station/Praha-Holešovice train station, take tram No 12 or 14 or night tram No 54 east two stops to Dělnická.

MID-RANGE
Hotel Splendid (☎ 233 375 940; www.hotelsplendid.cz; Ovenecká 33, Holešovice; s/d/tr 1820/2450/2990Kč; **P** **✕** **✕**) In a quiet little side-street, the Splendid may be the only mid-range hotel in Prague that is apparently entirely free of Ikea-style furniture. It's a little worn around the edges, but the friendly, comfortable Splendid's mid-'80s décor has a certain charm. There are five wheelchair-accessible rooms. Take westbound tram No 1 or 25 three stops from Vltavská metro station.

Hotel Belvedere (☎ 220 106 111; www.europehotels.cz; Milady Horákové 19, Holešovice; s/d/tr from 2250/3150/3900Kč; **P** **✕** **✕**) In a great location in the heart of Holešovice, near transport and restaurants, the Belvedere has comfortable rooms, some wheelchair-accessible rooms and a very pleasant, relaxed atmosphere. Take westbound tram No 1 or 25 two stops from Vltavská metro station.

Smíchov
BUDGET
Caravan Camping Praha (Map p118; ☎ 257 317 555; www.caravancamping.cz; Císařská louka 162; tent/car/caravan 90/90/150Kč; ☉ year-round; **P**) At the tip of quiet Císařská louka island, this narrow strip of grass has fine views across to Vyšehrad. The camp site has a restaurant (open in summer) and a shop. From Smíchovské nádraží metro and train station, take tram No 12 two stops south to Lihovar, cross the freeway and walk down the slip-road by the petrol station – it's about a 10-minute walk.

MID-RANGE
Hotel Kavalír (Map pp82-3; ☎ 257 216 565; Plzeňská 177; s/d 2100/2900Kč; **P**) This homy hotel is away from the madding crowds – and unfortunately away from restaurants and bars – in western Smíchov. All the rooms are comfortable and snug, but ask for one away from Plzeňská, which is a pretty noisy road. Take tram No 4, 6, 7, 9 or 10 or night tram No 58 four stops west from Anděl metro to Kavalírka.

Hotel Balkán (Map p118; ☎ /fax 57 32 71 80; Svornosti 28; s/d incl breakfast 1600/2200Kč) At the grungier southern end of Smíchov, the Balkán's rooms are dark and a bit sombre, but clean with TV, phone and bathroom. Close to Anděl and bridges across the river, it's good value.

Other recommendations:
Botel Admirál (Map p118; ☎ 257 321 302; www.admiral-botel.cz; Hořejší nábřeží 57; s/d 2710/2840Kč; **P**) The Admiral floating hotel has compact, well-designed rooms (a little overpriced for what you get), a terrace overlooking the water and a restaurant with more brass ship fittings than Nelson's fleet.
Hotel Arbes-Mepro (Map p118; reception ☎ 251 116 555, reservations ☎ 257 210 410; www.arbes-mepro.cz; Viktora Huga 3; s/d incl breakfast 2400/2900Kč; **P** **✕**) Recently refurbished, the slightly stuffy Mepro has large, comfy rooms and big baths.

TOP END
Andel's (Map p118; ☎ 296 889 688; www.andelshotel.com; Stroupežnického 21; s/d €220/250; **P** **✕** **✕** **⌨**) Nowhere sums up new Smíchov quite like Andel's. This sleek, so-now-it's-almost-tomorrow boutique hotel has DVD and CD players, Internet access, and modern abstract art in every room. Bathrooms are a wonderland of polished chrome and frosted glass. There's a gym and a salon and rooms designed for wheelchairs. Kids under 12 stay free. Go now before it gets dated.

Troja   Map pp82–3
Northwest of Holešovice, over the Vltava, Troja is out by the zoo.

BUDGET
Autocamp Trojská (☎ 283 850 487; autocamp-trojska@iol.cz; Trojská 157, Troja; site per person/tent 115/75Kč; ☉ year-round) The most expensive of a string of camp sites in the quiet northern suburb of Troja; this one has the most facilities. Take bus No 12 from Dejvická metro to Kazanka bus stop.

Camp–Pension Herzog (☎ 283 850 472; info@camperzog.cz; Trojská 161, Troja; per person/tent 80/80Kč; ☉ Apr-Oct) Another of the Troja camp sites,

Herzog is set in an orchard, charges 55Kč per person for students and has a kitchen. Take bus No 12 from Dejvická metro to Čechova škola bus stop.

Žižkov   Map pp120–1
BUDGET
Hostel Elf (☎ 222 540 963; www.hostelelf.com; Husitská 11; dm/s/d/tr 260/700/820/1140Kč) Friendly, bright and cheerful, Hostel Elf has lots of nooks and crannies where you can get some quiet time, as well as a very convivial terrace and lounge room. Nine-bed dorms are comfortable and well laid-out. Some doubles have their own bathrooms, but the shared bathrooms allow a lot of privacy.

Other recommendations:
Strawberry Hostel (☎ 222 726 007; Slavíkova 22; dm 400, d per person 500Kč; P) Clean, spacious dorms have five or fewer beds, the breakfast room is large and sunny and the staff friendly. There are daily city tours (100Kč) and regular concerts. The only drawback is the prison-style showers and that it's open only in summer.
Clown & Bard Hostel (☎ 222 716 453; www.clownandbard.com; Bořivojova 102; dm 250–400Kč, d per person 450Kč; P ☺) You're guaranteed a party in Clown & Bard's 36-bed dorm – if you want things quieter, pay a little more for five-seven person rooms, some of which have their own kitchen and bath. The ever-popular if basic and slightly grubby Clown has a café, a bar, friendly, knowledgeable staff and good tours.
Autocamping Žižkov (☎ 267 314 862; info@prazackak.cz; Za Žižkovskou vozovnou 17; sites per person/tent 150/100Kč; ☼ May-Aug) Basic camping facilities in a school sports ground. Take tram No 1, 9 or 16 to Vápenka.

MID-RANGE
Hotel Prokopka (☎ 222 781 647; www.osf.cz/hotelprokopka - Czech only; Prokopova 9; s 800-1000Kč, d 1300-1500Kč; P ☺) Super-friendly and excellent value, Prokopka's rooms have their own bath and kitchen or share facilities with one other room; rooms on the top floor are smaller but have balconies. Rooms have phone but no TV (there's a lounge with a shared TV). There's also a laundry room and a backyard. Students – who should call ahead – can get rooms from 350Kč to 500Kč per person.
Hotel Golden City (☎ 222 711 008; www.goldencity.cz; Táboritská 3; s/d/tr incl breakfast 1150/1450/1750Kč; P ☺ ☺) Rooms are comfortable and reasonably priced with satellite TV and phones; some have air conditioning. There's free and unlimited Internet.

Hotel Kafka (☎ 222 781 333, reservations ☎ 224 617 118; vesta@atlas.cz; Cimburkova 24; s/d/tr incl breakfast 1700/2200/2600Kč; P ☒) Quiet, simple rooms with telephone and bath are very reasonably priced and can take up to five people (3100Kč). Self-contained apartments across the street go for 2500Kč to 3800Kč, depending on the number of occupants. Dogs can stay for 150Kč; call if you want to reserve parking.
U tří korunek (☎ 222 781 112; www.3korunky.cz; Cimburkova 28; s/d/tr 1900/2900/3900Kč; P) This very pleasant hotel was recently renovated and is comfortable and spotless. Every room has phone, satellite TV and a toilet separate from the bathroom; four rooms have disabled access.
Bílý Lev (☎ 222 780 430; fax 222 780 465; Cimburkova 20; s/d/tr 1500/2500/3100Kč; P) There are lots of options on this street, and though this place is fine it should probably be your last choice of the three. The hotel itself is a bit rundown, but the rooms, while small, are clean and nicely furnished. Some share bath, and all have satellite TV and phone.
Pension Prague City (☎ 222 782 483; www.praguecity.cz; Štítného 13; s/d/tr 1300/1600/1900Kč; P) A nice little *pension* that's recently opened; has clean, comfortable rooms with bath and TV.

Vinohrady   Map p119
BUDGET
Penzion Košická (☎ 271 742 483, reservations ☎ 222 511 777; Košická 12; dm/d 420/620Kč) A fair hike from anywhere, but with plenty of neighbourhood atmosphere, Košická is friendly and well-kept. The dorms are cosy and have comfy beds. If you want to stay in the hotel portion of the *pension*, you'll pay 2600Kč for a double. You can walk there from náměstí Míru metro, or pick up the No 22 or 23 tram and get off at Ruská.
Hotel/Pension City (☎ 222 519 282; www.hotelcity.cz; Belgická 10; d incl breakfast 1670Kč; ☒) In a charming corner of Vinohrady, two blocks from náměstí Míru metro station, you can't go wrong staying at the Pension City. Plain rooms with bath, satellite TV and telephone are good value – if you don't mind sharing a bath with one other room, you can get a double for 1160Kč.

MID-RANGE
Pension Březina (☎ 296 188 888; www.brezina.cz; Legerova 41; s/d 1800/2000Kč; ☒ ☺) Comfortable,

large rooms in this converted apartment block with a small garden still retain traces of their Art Nouveau past. Most rooms have their own Internet connections – rooms without Internet and with shared bath start at 1100Kč. Try to get a back room as Legerova can be noisy.

Hotel Sofia (☎ 224 255 711, reservations ☎ 251 556 457; www.avetravel.cz; Americká 28; s/d incl breakfast €55/70; ℗) Traces of Bulgarian ambience add to the character of this otherwise simple but comfortable hotel. Rooms include TV and phone.

Hotel Máchova Garni (☎ 222 510 107, reservations ☎ 222 511 777; www.dhotels.cz; Máchova 11; s/d incl breakfast 2100/2350Kč) In a quiet street close to transport, this very comfortable hotel has all the modern fittings without being too try-hard. Four-person rooms go for 3400Kč.

Dejvice & Northwest Outskirts
Map pp82–3

BUDGET
Hostel Orlík (☎ 224 311 240; Terronská 6, Dejvice; dm 250Kč) Simple beds in clean dorms in a pleasant neighbourhood at a very reasonable price. Walk east on Evropská from Dejvice metro station, through the traffic circle and continue on Československé armády until you hit Terronská on the left; it should take about five minutes.

Camp Hostel Džbán (☎ 235 358 551; www.camp.cz /dzban; Nad lávkou 5, Vokovice; tent per person 90Kč plus 15Kč tax, car/dm 90/265Kč; ℗ ⊠) About a 15-minute walk from the tram (take No 20 or 26 seven stops from Dejvická metro to Nádraží Veleslavín), this camp site and hostel is part of the Aritma sports complex. Facilities include a natural swimming pool, exchange office, shop, restaurants, tennis courts and gym. Four-person bungalows go for 1000Kč.

TOP END
Hotel Crowne Plaza (☎ 224 393 111; www.crowneplaza .com; Koulova 15, Dejvice; s/d from €280; ℗ ⊠ ⊠ ⊠) Come for the décor rather than anything else. Rooms here are standard top-end chain style, with all the necessities but not too many luxuries. However, the 1957 Soviet-style building, covered in bas reliefs and frescoes of the noble worker and topped with a green star, is really something special. The hotel has 24 wheelchair-accessible rooms.

EATING
You can barely turn around without tripping over a restaurant in Prague. Ten years ago you could only get pork and dumplings in this city, and it was hard work finding that. These days, if you can imagine eating it, some entrepreneurial Praguer is cooking it. Vegetarian food is widely available, though finding anything vegan is still next to impossible; Italian, French, Indian, Moroccan, Lebanese, seafood, Thai, Greek, Chinese, pizza and Icelandic are all on offer, as is the sort of fusion food filling plates in San Francisco, Sydney and London. And if you want pork and dumplings, you can pick up a pub lunch for around 60Kč, or pay 350Kč for a luxurious gourmet version made with the freshest ingredients by the best chefs.

Prices soar as you approach Old Town Square and Malostranské náměstí, and it's rare that quality soars accordingly, but you can find plenty of good, reasonably priced food in side streets even near the biggest tourist centres. Restaurants are generally open by 10am or 11am, and close at 11pm or midnight.

Hradčany
Map pp94–5

As you'd expect from an area where tourists are trapped, tired and hungry, prices at the castle are out of control, and you won't get good value for your money. If it's a nice day, think seriously about bringing a picnic, or just packing a few energy bars or pieces of fruit to see you through until you can get to somewhere decent. Elsewhere in Hradčany there are some good options.

MID-RANGE
Malý Buddha (☎ 220 513 894; Úvoz 46; mains 60-160Kč; ⊙ 1-10.30pm Tue-Sun; ⊠) Like stepping into a Saigon temple, Malý Buddha is all tinkling music, oriental knick-knacks and an atmosphere of enforced peace. The food is mostly Vietnamese influenced, with lots of vegetarian offerings and an interesting selection of 'healing' wines, though it doesn't mention which is recommended for cobblestone-inflicted blisters.

TOP END
U zlaté hrušky (☎ 220 515 356; Nový svět 3; mains 400-480Kč; ⊙ 11.30am-3pm & 6.30pm-midnight) Tucked down a blissfully quiet winding lane behind

---

AUTHOR'S CHOICE

Country Life (Map pp98-9; ☎ 224 213 336; Melantrichova 15, Staré Město; mains 75-150Kč; ☽ 8.30am-7pm Mon-Thu, 8.30am-6pm Fri, 11am-6pm Sun, closed Sat) Prague's best health-food shop and vegetarian salad and sandwich bar has vegetarian pizza and goulash too. Food is sold by weight, and you should be able to fill up for under 80Kč. The original Old Town branch has sit-down service at the back, while the **newer branch** (Map pp110-11; Jungmannova 1, Nové Mešto), on the corner with Vodičkova, is cafeteria style. Both get densely crowded at lunch time, so go early or get a takeaway.

   Dahab (Map pp98-9; ☎ 224 827 375; Rybná 28, Staré Město; mains 100-200Kč; ☽ noon-1am) Tagines, couscous and a great North African/Middle Eastern atmosphere. Smoke apple-flavoured tobacco through a water pipe for 150Kč, or settle back in the kilim-covered lounge room. The pistachio couscous is excellent. There's a snack bar *(yalla)* out the front, where you can get similar dishes cheaper, and to take away. They're open from 10am to 8pm Monday to Friday, and between 2pm and 6pm everything is 20% off.

   Vinárna v zátiší (Map pp98-9; ☎ 222 221 155; Liliová 1, Staré Město; mains 395-795Kč; ☽ noon-3pm & 5.30-11pm) One of Prague's best restaurants, and one of the few top places focusing on traditional, delicious, gourmet Czech food. There's a two-course lunch menu, including one drink, for 495Kč, or you can lash out on the dinner menu for 1075Kč (pay 600Kč extra, and the *vinárna* will match local wines to the dishes). The vegetarian menu – all mains are 395Kč – is original and interesting.

   U Pinkasů (Map pp110-11; ☎ 221 111 150; Jungmannova nám 16, Nové Město; mains 100-180Kč) If you do some sort of complicated equation matching cost against quality, this has to be the best Czech food in Prague. You'll eat every scrap of dumpling on your plate, and wish you had one more to sop up that last bit of goulash. The roast pork and sauerkraut is excellent, and the service is friendly and professional. There's a small garden out the back, under the walls of the Church of Our Lady of the Snows, and a basement pub that stays open until 4am.

---

the Loreta, this wood-panelled gourmet restaurant specialises in duck (though it does charmingly offer a menu 'for guests who are not able to eat a duck', but with no vegetarian options).

   Peklo (☎ 220 516 652; Strahovské nádvoří 1/132; mains 280-400Kč; ☽ 11am-midnight; ✖) This subterranean restaurant serves up fine pan-European cuisine in the pretty, secluded grounds of the Strahov Monastery. The name means 'hell', referring to the fact that monks once did penance here, but it's anything but penitential now.

Malá Strana   Map pp94–5
BUDGET

Hostinec U tří zlatých trojek (Tomášská 6; mains 45-160Kč) Amid the overpriced tourist traps around Malá Strana, this place serves good, solid, typical Prague pub grub at surprisingly low prices. Goulash is 89Kč; cheesy vegetarian dishes go for 65Kč to 90Kč.

   Café St Nicholas (☎ 603 954 171; Malostranské náměstí 9; ☽ 10am-7pm) This may come as a surprise to you, but here in the heart of Europe it's next to impossible to find a good slice of cake. Stop searching and

pull up seat at St Nick's – delicious cakes, pastries and desserts, most in the 55Kč to 70Kč range, are accompanied by good coffee and a window on to the bustling crowds of Malá Strana.

   Restaurace Bar Bar (☎ 257 312 246; Všehrdova 17; mains 75-110Kč; ☽ noon-midnight Sun-Thu, noon-2am Fri-Sat) Great for a quick feed after a few beers, Bar Bar has huge salads and tasty crepes, including a lemon and sugar crepe for 13Kč.

   Bohemia Bagel (☎ 257 310 831; Újezd 18; mains 60-120Kč; ☽ 9am-midnight Sun-Thu, 9-2am Fri-Sat) Endlessly popular with travellers, Bohemia Bagel is like a little outpost of America. Bagels, quiches, soups, salads and all-you-can-drink soft drinks and coffee, as well as the Internet café, keep people coming back over and over. It's also a great place to meet people. There's another **branch** (Map pp98-9; Masná 2, Staré Město) that is also an Internet café.

MID-RANGE

U sedmi Švábů (☎ 257 531 455; Jánský vršek 14; mains 95-280Kč) This rather silly but utterly charming medieval-themed restaurant is in a small lane behind Nerudova 31. Czech standards, with quite a few vegetarian dishes, are served in an authentic, electricity-free atmosphere – all the illumination is provided by candles, which means you can't really see what you're eating. Mead is 35Kč a goblet.

Hergetova Cihelna (☎ 257 535 534; Cihelná 2b; mains 120-490Kč; ⏰ 9-2am) They're all about superlatives at this brand new sibling for renowned restaurant Kampa Park: Prague's longest bar, Prague's best pizza chef, Prague's most stunning view of Charles Bridge while eating tiramisu… Fair enough: they did bother to import the pizza chef from Napoli. And the views are gorgeous too, with a sweeping terrace perched right above the river. And, OK, the bar is pretty long, and it does have 50 brands of beer.

Bakeshop Diner (☎ 257 534 244; Lázeňská 19; mains 120-250Kč; ⏰ 7am-10pm) Pale wood, red leather, good-looking staff, top-notch coffee and excellent baked goods all add up to a very pleasant way to while away a few hours, just out of the Charles Bridge crush. Try one of the burgers or salads, or turn up Thursday to Saturday nights for live acoustic music.

TOP END

Mazlova vinárna U malířů (☎ 224 510 269; Maltézské náměstí 11; mains 390-1580Kč; ⏰ 11.30am-midnight) This upscale French restaurant in a 16th-century building is all class: linen tablecloths and silver and glassware glisten beneath a vaulted ceiling covered in frescoes. The prix fixe three-course menu St Hubert serves a selection of the best for 1190Kč.

Kampa Park (☎ 257 532 685; Na Kampě 8a; mains 325-700Kč; ⏰ 11.30am-?) You know that you're in professional hands when a restaurant refuses to close until the last guest feels like leaving. This superb restaurant serves up award-winning cross-cultural cuisine with a view of the river and the Old Town; in winter, an enclosed garden lets you take in the view without pain. Plenty of vegetarian dishes and over 150 wines, plus the incredible décor, add up to a big night out.

Other recommendations:

Pálffy Palác Club Restaurace (☎ 257 530 522; Valdštejnská 14; mains 475-585Kč) Renowned for its palatial baroque atmosphere (largely due to being in a palace), this restaurant serves delicious traditional gourmet dishes and fine wines.

U modré kachničky (At the Blue Duckling; ☎ 257 320 308; Nebovidská 6; mains 280-480Kč; ⏰ noon-4pm & 6.30-11.30pm) The Duckling is on a quiet side street, perfect for a romantic evening. It serves good Czech game or fish and vegetarian dishes, but its speciality, of course, is duck.

Josefov   Map pp98–9
BUDGET

Pivnice U Milosrdných (☎ 222 327 673; Milosrdných & Kozí; mains 60-120Kč; ⏰ 10am-10pm Mon-Fri, 11am-10pm Sat) Solidly typical Czech and always packed – particularly at lunchtime – with local office workers and old Prague men, this *pivnice* serves all the Czech favourites, including a 65Kč goulash with bacon dumplings.

Žíznivý pes (Thirsty Dog; ☎ 222 310 039; Elišky Krasnohorské 5; mains 95-130Kč; ⏰ 11-2am Mon-Fri, 2pm-2am Sat & Sun) Part of the British pub diaspora, the Thirsty Dog serves burgers, pastas, pizza and English-style curries, with plenty of vegetarian options, in a laid-back and laddish atmosphere.

MID-RANGE

Pizzeria U Golema (☎ 222 328 165; Maiselova 8; mains 60-180Kč; ⏰ 11am-midnight) While the connection between Golems and Italian food is none-too-clear, this is still a good place for a spot of lunch and dinner during your trawl around Josefov. There's a small Jewish menu.

TOP END

King Solomon (☎ 224 818 752; Široká 8; meals from 400Kč; ⏰ noon-11pm Sun-Thu, noon-sundown Fri, closed Sat) The kosherest restaurant in town, King Solomon serves carefully prepared meals in a lovely glassed conservatory. While the restaurant is closed to walk-in traffic on Shabbat, you can call ahead for meals at that time. A catering service can deliver kosher meals to your hotel.

Staré Město   Map pp98–9
BUDGET

Pivnice Radegast (Templová 2, off Celetná; mains 60-190Kč; ⏰ 11-12.30am) Don't expect smiles and flirtatious behaviour from your waiter; do expect your beer and food to turn up quick smart (and do expect to pay a cover if you don't wave away the bread and sauces left on your table). This has to be the cheapest place in the neighbourhood (the 'Prague dessert' is 15Kč and actually pretty good)

FUNNY, I DON'T REMEMBER ORDERING THAT

Keep in mind that nothing comes for free in Prague restaurants – if the waiter offers you fries with that, and you accept, you'll be charged for them. Bread, tomato sauce, mustard, vegetables…everything has a price tag. Many restaurants also have a cover charge or couvert, which every diner must pay regardless of what they eat and even if they eat nothing. Some places also charge a deposit on glasses. It's not a plot, it's just the way things are done.

If the menu has no prices, ask for them. Don't be intimidated by the language barrier; know exactly what you're ordering. If something's not available and the waiter suggests an alternative, ask for the price. Immediately return anything you didn't order and don't want, such as bread, butter or side dishes; don't just leave it to one side.

Check your bill, as there's a chance it will contain things you didn't order. If you pay with a credit card, keep track of it. See that the date and price are clear and correct on the sales slip, complete the 'total' box yourself, add a currency symbol before it with no space in between, and be sure only one sales slip is imprinted.

Most importantly, though, don't let paranoia ruin your meal. The majority of overcharging happens at tourist-oriented restaurants in the very centre. If you're not eating in Old Town Square or Wenceslas Square, or if you're at a place run by young Czechs, you're unlikely to have problems.

and it does all the Czech classics. It's always packed. Have a game of coaster tick-tack-toe while you eat.

Beas Vegetarian Dhaba (Týnská 19; meals 68-83Kč; 8.30am-8pm Mon-Fri, 10am-6pm Sat & Sun) Tucked in a courtyard off Týnská, this little dhaba makes one vegetarian curry a day and serves it with rice, salad, chutneys and raita for 68Kč, or you can add a drink and dessert for 83Kč. It's good value, and a great place to meet Czechs of an alternative bent.

Giallo Rossa Pizzeria (604 898 989; Jakubská 1; pizzas 70-130Kč; 10am-midnight) Half of Prague seems to be lining up at the take-away counter here come lunch time. Huge pizza slices go for 70Kč. If you'd rather sit down, there's a restaurant by the storefront; there's Internet access upstairs.

MID-RANGE

Red, Hot & Blues (222 314 639; Jakubská 12; mains 150-400Kč; 9am-11pm) If you've been dying for a great hamburger or a spicy serve of rice and beans, come on in, sugar. Most of the menu comes from New Orleans (including Louisiana bread pudding), but there are also other American classics on offer. There are nightly jazz and blues gigs (7pm to 10pm), and a small adjoining store selling hot sauce and all the other Orleanian necessities.

Klub architektů (224 401 214; Betlémské náměstí 5; mains 150-220Kč) Part of a slightly smug complex dedicated to modern architecture, architektů draws the crowds with its atmospheric stone-cellar dining room and inventive, reasonably priced dishes. As well as plenty of vegetarian options, architektů also has a couple of (apparently) vegan dishes. Upstairs, the outdoor café by Betlémská Kaple has serviceable salads and light meals.

Reykjavík (224 229 251; Karlova 20; mains 165-300Kč) Always packed, thanks to its primo corner location, Reykjavík may specialise in Icelandic seafood – like the salmon in tarragon cream sauce – but lots of punters come here for the burgers instead.

Zlatý Dvůr (224 248 602; Husova 9; mains 190-290Kč; noon-midnight) Jazz, goulash and beer is what they advertise, and that's what you'll get – daily live jazz of the George Benson variety, six kinds of goulash (including Mexican goulash with beans) and – this being Prague – great beer.

Au Gourmand Café (Na příkopě 25; 10am-7pm Mon-Fri, 10am-5pm Sat) Au Gourmand's patisserie has a joyously bewildering array of cakes and its caffè latte is among the best in town.

TOP END

Le Saint-Jacques (222 322 685; Jakubská 4; mains 400-800Kč; noon-3pm & 6pm-midnight) An excellent French restaurant with pleasant service. It's not quite good enough to justify the prices, but delicious anyway.

Nové Město

BUDGET

The sausage stands lining the sides of Wenceslas Square will rustle you up a hot dog or *smažený syr* (fried cheese) for 25Kč; wash it down with a shot of vodka or rum for 15Kč, or beer in a plastic cup for 20Kč (also useful for obliterating the memory of that mysterious chunk you found in your sausage). They are greatly loved for performing life-saving food-application procedures on drunk tourists and locals at all hours.

U Sportovce Pivnice (Map pp98-9; ☎ 222 816 609; Soukenická 4; mains 60-130Kč) Good Czech food at good Czech prices in an atmosphere to please your dirty old uncle. There's football on the TV and corny, lewd comics on the wall; the food on the table is solid and tasty and the beer is 19Kč. Try the beef with lemon, cranberries and dumplings, or the big plate of fruit dumplings.

Kavárna Imperial Café (Map pp120-1; ☎ 222 316 012; Na poříčí 15; mains 80-150Kč; 9am-midnight Mon-Thu, 9-1am Fri-Sat, 9am-11pm Sun) All right, it's a tourist trap, but it's certainly a charming one. Not only do you get a free doughnut with every coffee, you can also shell out 1943Kč for a bowl of yesterday's doughnuts, plus a licence to throw them at everyone else in the café (though the menu warns you must be 'sorbet' – sober? – and over 21 to do so).

Pizzeria Kmotra (Map pp110-11; ☎ 224 915 809; V jirchářích 12; pizzas 80-130Kč) A great spot to wash down good, ungreasy pizzas with cheap beer. The crowds can get out of control by 8pm, so try to snag a table before then.

MID-RANGE

Dynamo (Map pp110-11; ☎ 224 932 020; Pštrossova 29; mains 105-240Kč) Don't be put off by the funky font, spearmint-green décor or notice-me light fittings – there's more to Dynamo than hipster flash. The cook here has some bright ideas, and throws together unusually fresh ingredients in all kinds of interesting ways. The menu includes liver with baked apples and sage, the chicken salad is delicious and the staff are friendly and unpretentious. It's a great place for a girls' night out.

Příčný řez (Map pp110-11; ☎ 222 233 283; Příčná 3; mains 65-180Kč) A modern take on traditional Czech pub food (but still in that old-style České atmosphere), Příčný řez's signature dishes include a deliciously rich duck with lime and tarragon sauce and chicken stuffed with ham, cheese and basil. There are lots of vegetarian options, and on weekends an American-style brunch is served from 11.30am to 4.30pm.

Tulip Café (Map pp110-11; ☎ 224 930 019; Opatovická 3; mains 99-135Kč; 11am-midnight Mon-Thu, 11am-2am Fri-Sat, 11am-11pm Sun) Big, comfortably padded booths, friendly and attentive service, a spacious back courtyard and a menu of great-value dishes make this a popular spot for young professional Czechs. Food includes pizzas and pastas, satay tofu burgers, tandoori chicken and fish and chips – the cooking isn't always spot on, but there are lots of fresh vegetables and vegetarian dishes. It's one of the few restaurants in Prague that puts a little thought into the music they play.

U Rybiček (Map pp110-11; ☎ 224 918 885; Gorazdova; mains 100-250Kč; 8am-11.30pm) Gay-friendly U Rybiček is a fish restaurant and so much more. The cocktail bar here serves all the classics at reasonable prices, or you can use the Internet for 1Kč per minute. Little plates of grilled meats go for 43Kč, and vegetarian dishes for around 90Kč.

Down Town Cafe Praha (Map pp110-11; ☎ 224 411 276; Jungmannovo náměstí 21; mains 65-110Kč; 10am-11pm) Affecting a ridiculously hip attitude – does any other café have a 'wait-staff hair styled by...' credit in its menu? – Down Town nonetheless makes a mean and massive baguette. In a cute little square off Wenceslas, this gay-friendly café concentrates on sandwiches, but also has cakes and a huge list of cocktails, complicated coffee derivatives and teas. Take a seat on the shady terrace and enjoy the eye candy.

Hacienda Mexicana restaurace (Map pp120-1; ☎ 221 851 095; Mlynářská; mains 100-270Kč;) While it's probably never been within 1000 miles of a Mexican, the food at Hacienda is a pretty good approximation of Tex-Mex (though less than spicy). The cheery fiesta décor might make you forget where you are – or maybe that was the margaritas.

Restaurant of India (Map pp110-11; ☎ 224 227 073; Štěpánská 63; mains 145-260Kč; 11.30am onwards) The curries here actually taste like curries, the delicious *sabzi* (80Kč) is packed full of real vegetables, and the basic *pullao* (40Kč) is studded with crunchy hazelnuts.

Titanic Steak House (Map pp110-11; ☎ 296 226 282; Štěpánská 22; mains 90-250Kč; 11am-11pm

RICHARD NEBESKÝ

Hotel Slovan (p186) in the spa town of Františkovy Lázně

MARTIN MOOS

Ossuary Chapel of All Saints (p164), Sedlec,
near Kutná Hora

The castle (p73) and village of Karlštejn

RICHARD NEBESKÝ

Krumlov Chateau (left) and the old town of Český Krumlov (p219)

Náměstí Přemysla Otakara II, the centre of České Budějovice (p213)

The giant sandstone rock towers of Adršpach-Teplice Rocks (p262)

Trosky Castle (p259), atop basalt peaks, Český ráj

Mon-Sat, 3-11pm Sun) Oddly named – perhaps the food goes down nicely? – this is a cool and quiet place with a range of steaks and sauces.

Restaurace U medvídků (Map pp98-9; ☎ 224 211 916; Na Perštýně 5-7; mains 180-220Kč; ✕ noon-10pm; ✕) This is a touristy beer hall plus wine bar plus nonsmoking restaurant plus outdoor garden, all with the same meaty Bohemian menu. It has a much more pleasant atmosphere than many of Nové Město's beer halls.

Gastro Zofin (Map pp110-11; ☎ 224 934 548; Slovanský ostrov; mains 130-170Kč; P) The food's nothing special – an assortment of average Czech and international dishes – but the island is green and quiet, and the outdoor terrace includes a small playground to keep the kids occupied while you nap over a lunchtime Budvar.

Ark Thompson (Map pp110-11; ☎ 224 917 583; Vyšehradska 43; mains 70-235Kč; ✕ 10am-11pm Mon-Fri, 1-11pm Sat, 3-11pm Sun) Located by the Botanic Gardens, Ark Thompson has terrible suburban-modern décor and German MTV on the television, but soldier on! The great baguettes (50Kč to 70Kč) are worth it.

TOP END

Restaurant Pod Křídlem (Map pp110-11; ☎ 224 951 741; Národní 10; mains 310-450Kč; ✕ 1pm-midnight Mon-Fri, 11.30am-midnight Sat & Sun) With its gourmet take on the Czech classics, classy and modern Pod Křídlem draws plenty of locals along with the tourists. There's a good selection of Czech wine, plus live jazz at the weekends.

Vyšehrad   Map p115

U Neklana (☎ 224 916 057; Neklanova 30; mains 89-120Kč) Reminiscent of a suburban veterans' club restaurant, U Neklana has an unpretentious charm that is somehow enhanced by the poker machines and hits-of-the-'80s soundtrack. The menu is mostly Czech and European: it's no haute cuisine, but the service is friendly and portions are huge. U Neklana occasionally screens live English football and has a regular 'travesty show' (99Kč).

Holešovice

Hong Kong Chinese (Map pp82-3; ☎ 233 376 209; Letenské náměstí 5; mains 85-200Kč; ✕ 10.30am-4pm & 5.30-11pm) There are a lot of Chinese res-

taurants in Prague, but this is one of the better ones. There's an immense menu of dishes and an Asian grocery store on the premises. Take tram No 1, 3 or 25 from Vltavská metro station to the Letenské náměstí stop.

Restaurant Corso (Map pp82-3; ☎ 220 806 541; Dukelských hrdinů 48; mains 120-300Kč; ✕ 9am-11pm) Very good international and Czech dishes in an old-fashioned interior. The lunch menu is a real bargain: three courses, coffee and two drinks for 300Kč. Take tram 12, 15 or 17 west from Nádraží Holešovice metro station, two stops to Veletržní.

Hanavský pavilón (Map pp94-5; ☎ 253 323 641; Letenské sady; mains 550-700Kč; ✕ 11.30-1am) Tuxedoed waiters glide between diners at this overpriced but gorgeous restaurant. Originally built for the 1891 Prague Exposition, the pavilón still has some of the best views in town. It also has some hysterical dinner music – the resident Casio maestro is a whiz. Take tram No 18 from Malostranská metro station, one stop to Chotkovy sady, then walk a little way through the park, towards the river.

Smíchov   Map p118
BUDGET

Mama's Toast (☎ 251 511 277; Lidická 11; sandwiches 12.90-35Kč; ✕ 8am-8pm Mon-Fri, 1-6pm Sat) Nové Mesto style at Smíchov prices. Tiny Mama's Toast displays a cabinet full of bite-size open Czech sandwiches or *cheblíčky* (12.90Kč) as though they were precious jewels. Choose from caviar, salami, egg salad and others, or splash out on a gigantic baguette for 35Kč. Eponymous toasted sandwiches go for 25Kč to 30Kč.

MID-RANGE

Vinárna U Mikuláše Dačického (☎ 257 322 334; Viktora Huga 2; mains 150-300Kč; ✕ 4pm-1am Mon-Fri, 6pm-1am Sat & Sun) Dimly lit and classy, this *vinárna* feels like the perfect place to take a mistress or plan a hit. Specialising in steaks, it also does a line in traditional Czech.

Club restaurace Stará Praha (☎ 251 510 217; Vítězná 11; mains 70-200Kč) Traditional Czech food in a homy setting. Try one of the special plates, like duck, dumplings and sauerkraut (98Kč), and finish off with ice cream and eggnog (49Kč). Vegetarians can choose from several cheesy and eggy mains (55Kč to 70Kč).

TOP END

Sushi Bar (☎ 603 244 882; Zborovská 49; mains 390-900Kč; ⏰ 10am-10pm Mon-Sat) Crammed with affluent locals at lunch time, the Sushi Bar sources its very fresh fish from its seafood store next door. It's not among the world's great sushis, but beautifully presented plates of 18 pieces of *maki* are priced at 690Kč. Lunch specials start at 350Kč. Budget for the non-negotiable 50Kč per person cover, which gives you an appetiser and a warm towel.

Dejvice Map pp82-3

U cedru (☎ 233 342 974; Národní obrany 27; mains 200-300Kč) If you're dying for a bit of tabouli or kofte, this is the place to go. An excellent Lebanese restaurant, U cedru serves plates of delicious morsels including chopped lamb, tabouli salad, stuffed vine leaves and more.

Budvarka (☎ 224 314 838; Wuchterlova 22; mains 65-170Kč) The bonhomie spills out of this place and onto the street. Popular with both locals and tourists, Budvarka serves friendly Czech meals and reasonably priced beer, and on Saturday night it has live bands.

Pizzeria Grosseto (☎ 233 342 694; Jugoslávských partyzánů 8; mains 70-150Kč) An incredibly popular Italian restaurant, overflowing with students and office workers at any given lunch time. Bookings are recommended. Most pizzas – wood-fired and good quality – are under 135Kč, or you can upgrade to pasta for less than 150Kč.

Vinohrady

BUDGET

Restaurace Sofia (Map p119; ☎ 603 298 865; Americká 28; mains 55-150Kč; ⏰ noon-11pm) If you're not going to make it to Bulgaria on this trip, don't fret: Restaurace Sofia whips up Bulgarian classics like buttered tripe, beef tongue fried in butter, mixed grill and *musaka* (Bulgarian for 'moussaka'). If you like this sort of thing, you'll love it – if you don't, at least it will revive your enthusiasm for goulash.

MID-RANGE

FX Café (Map p119; ☎ 224 254 776; Bělehradská 120; mains 100-170Kč; ⏰ 11.30-2am) Vegetarians who've been subsisting on fried cheese for weeks will be beside themselves when they see this hip, comfortable café's extensive and delicious menu. Everyone else will breathe a sigh of relief at the freshness and variety of the ingredients.

Pastička (Little Mousetrap; Map pp120-1; ☎ 222 253 228; Blanická 25; mains 110-200Kč; ⏰ 11-1am Mon-Fri, 5pm-1am Sat & Sun) They may not have the greatest cuisine in the world, but the Czechs sure can name a dish: Pastička offers 'Robin's hit the bull's eye', 'pungent chicken' and 'stray lambkin cutlets'. The lambkins are so pink and juicy, you can't help but be glad they strayed. There's also a vegetarian menu. Cosy and friendly, this neighbourhood basement pub is decorated with a century's worth of industrial design detritus.

Tiger Tiger (Map pp120-1; ☎ 222 512 048; Anny Letenské 5; mains 155-270Kč; ⏰ 11.30am-11pm Mon-Fri, 5-11pm Sat & Sun) If you're after a spicy kick in the trousers, Tiger Tiger can help you out. Plenty of chilli, plenty of fresh ingredients and a 100Kč lunch menu make this Thai place a popular spot.

Žižkov Map pp120-1

BUDGET

Akropolis Café-Restaurant (☎ 296 330 990; Kubelíkova 27; mains 70-180Kč; ⏰ 11.30-1am) Beside the Palác Akropolis club, this popular café offers tasty meals, including lots of vegetarian options, at very good prices. The décor is charmingly oddball, though the air is ridiculously, almost unbearably, smoky.

MID-RANGE

Infinity Restaurant & Music Bar (☎ 272 176 580; Chrudimská 2a; mains 100-280Kč; ⏰ 11am-midnight Mon-Fri, noon-midnight Sat & Sun; ⚅) Bottle blondes, fresh from the gym upstairs, pick at French grilled duck with fruit compote and chestnuts at this modern fusion restaurant. Lots of salads, a few vegetarian pastas, a large wine list and young, cheerful staff make it a pleasure to dine here. There's also a bar downstairs, open from 6pm, that has DJs some nights and the beautiful people most nights.

Mailsi (☎ 060 346 6626; Lipanská 1; mains 145-200Kč; ⏰ noon-3pm & 6-11.30pm) Prague's first Pakistani restaurant is recommended for the courteous service, good food and modest prices (though prawns add around 100Kč to the price of a dish). There's a subcontinental grocery next door.

Crazy Daisy Restaurant (☎ 267 310 378; Vinohradská 142; mains 125-220) The tree growing in the middle of the room and the canopy of stars above your head set the scene at this popular little eatery opposite Flora metro station. The Czech–French fusion food is a little overpriced, but the service is friendly and the décor is great.

U Sloupu (☎ 222 713 151; Lucemburská & Velehradská; mains 70-220Kč; ☺ closed Sun) U Sloupu's slightly worn Art Deco interior and white-shirted waiters make this feel like a good place to take your grandmother. The chicken with prunes and caramel sauce is excellent, and could easily pass for dessert.

Buon Giorno Pizzeria (☎ 222 727 697; Slavíkova 6; mains 80-130Kč; ☒) There's a good chance you'll be waiting for a table at this popular neighbourhood eatery. The pizzas are a cut above the Prague average, with crisp crusts and dried red pepper.

Skalka   Map pp82–3
Hop on the metro green line and head east past Vinohrady and Žižkov and you eventually wind up in Skalka.

U Kašpárka (☎ 225 795 007; Dubečská 4/74; mains 80-120Kč; ☺ noon-1am) If you're only going to make one excursion out to the suburbs, go to U Kašpárka. A great, fun atmosphere, surprisingly good, fresh Czech and Italian food, an English-language menu and a lively, young local crowd make it worth the trip to the end of the A line. Take the metro to Skalka, then walk north on Úvalská, turn left on V Rybníčkách and follow it until you hit Dubečská. The walk should take about five minutes.

Self-Catering
There are corner stores (*potraviny*) and supermarkets everywhere. The best bets are Julius Meinl, which you'll find all over the centre, and Delvita, which you'll find further out. The five million people shopping in **Tesco** (Map pp110-11; Národní) at one time all seem to have left their manners at the door, but this supermarket has just about anything you'll need.

If you don't need to buy everything in one place, fruit and vegetable stores (*ovoce-zelelina*) have better and cheaper produce than the supermarkets, though the selection is smaller and the opening hours shorter. Delis (*lahůdky*) sell all kinds of cold meats

and cheeses, as well as great little Czech open sandwiches (*chlebíčky*) with ham, egg or salami, which go for less than 20Kč each. Bakery food isn't that good in Prague, and is generally stale or greasy, but the omnipresent Paneria chain has sandwiches, salads and pastries which aren't bad; Michelské pekárny, which is also all over town, is better than average.

There aren't many open-air produce markets in the city. The biggest one near the centre is the **daily market** (Map pp110-11; Havelská), south of Old Town Square, but you have to pick through a lot of souvenirs to get to the food. There's also a **daily market** (Map pp110-11; above Národní třída metro station) behind Tesco; and a selection of **fruit and veg stands** (Map pp82-3; Václavkova) in Dejvice, near Hradčanská metro and Laundry Kings.

Note that some perishable supermarket food items bear a date of manufacture (*datum výroby*) plus a 'consume-within…' (*spotřebujte do…*) period, whereas others, such as long-life milk, will have a stated minimum-shelf-life (*minimální trvanlivost*) date (after which freshness of the product is not guaranteed).

DRINKING
Once the preserve of traditional Czech pubs and *kavárna*, Prague is now awash with cocktail bars of all stripes, arty cafébars and pretty much any variation on the drinking theme you can think of. Traditional pubs are generally open from 11am to 11pm, while bars tend to be open noon to 1am during the week; they may stay open until 4am or 5am on weekends. For fancy cocktail bars, head to the centre; grungy, youthful pubs are out in Žižkov; traditional Czech pubs are everywhere.

Hradčany & Malá Strana   Map pp94–5
Bazaar (☎ 257 535 050; Nerudova 40) It's possible we dreamed this place. Nestled under the castle wall, Bazaar is a multifloored warren of dim candle-lit nooks and crannies, Arabian-nights'-style canopied beds complete with hookahs (no: hook*ahs*), barstools in the form of swings and a sweeping roof-garden with a view over the rooftops of Malá Strana. The drinks aren't cheap – a small *pivo* will knock you back 40Kč – but the atmosphere more than makes up for it.

PRAGUE

AUTHOR'S CHOICE

Park Café (Map pp120-1; Riegrovy sady, Vinohrady) Sometimes you want the simple things in life: a cheap beer, a sausage with bread and mustard, and 500 other people who want the same thing. At its best in warm weather, this outdoor beer garden on top of precipitous Riegrovy Park has all that, plus awesome night-time views of the castle, a big screen showing sport and plenty of chances to play table football and table hockey with half of Prague. It looks like a safe spot to smoke pot, but don't: there are undercover cops.

Medúza (Map p119; ☎ 222 515 107; Belgická 17, Vinohrady; ⏰ 11am-1am Mon-Fri, noon-1am Sat & Sun) The perfect Prague coffee house. Medúza's old, worn furniture, dark wood, armchairs and antique sugar bowl on every table are practically begging you to sink into a Kafka novel or indulge in a conversation on the nature of self. Coffees and teas of all types, plenty of alcohol (including Velvet on tap), pancakes and massive banana splits will sustain you through the most bohemian moments.

Tato Kojkej (☎ 257 323 102; Park Kampa; ⏰ 10am-midnight) Strewn with comfy couches and scattered with artwork, this café/bar/gallery in a low-ceilinged former mill on Kampa must be one of the cosiest drinking spots in Malá Strana. To find Tato, look for the water wheel and the big yellow woman.

Letní bar (Marksmen's Island/Střelecký Ostrov; ⏰ noon-midnight) Basically a shack serving Budvar in plastic cups (20Kč), Letní is the place to pick up a beer before hitting the beach at the northern end of the island, or settling in for a starlit screening at the Open-air cinema festival (see Festivals & Events p125).

Pivnice pod Petřínem (5 Hellichova) A classic Prague beer hall experience – the *pivo* comes fast and cheap, the bartender is a grump, it's so smoky in here you can barely see.

U zavěšeného kafe (The Hanging Coffee; ☎ 060 529 4595; Radnické schody 7; ⏰ 11am-9pm) This lively, crowded café/bar cranks up the classic rock tunes and serves remarkably cheap beer for the area. There's original art on the walls and a huge menu of Czech pub food (60Kč to 175Kč).

Josefov
Map pp98–9

Ocean Drive (☎ 224819089; V Kolkovně 7; ⏰ 7pm-2am) Take the pulse of hip Josefov at Ocean Drive. Have more than a couple of the swishly mixed cocktails and you may be wondering whether you got on the plane to Malibu Beach by accident. Plenty of blue backlighting, pleather and members of the gorgeous elite make this a place to be seen.

Palírna Igor Sevčík (Rámová 1071; ⏰ 10am-10pm) If you're keen to try slivovice, there's no better place to start than Palírna Igor Sevčík, a temple to the fiery brew. This tiny, stylish place seemingly stocks every available brand, and the walls are decorated with murals of slivovice through the seasons.

Staré Město
Map pp98–9

If you like a quiet drink with the locals, then Staré Město is not the neighbourhood for you. On weekends, it's the haunt of marauding British stag parties, but if that doesn't bother you, or if you like your boozing rowdy, then there are plenty of options.

U zlatého tygra (The Golden Tiger; ☎ 222 221 111; Husova 17; ⏰ 3-11pm) It's not easy finding anything approaching an authentic Czech pub in this neighbourhood, but Bohumil Hrabal's old local fits the bill. It's smoky, boozy and you'll see plenty of Czech blokes in sandals and socks. The tiger-inspired interior decoration is also great, in a totally ridiculous way.

Chateau (☎ 222 316 328; Jakubská 2; ⏰ noon-3am Mon-Thu, noon-4am Fri, 4pm-4am Sat, 4pm-2am Sun) When this raucous place gets fired up you can barely hear yourself think, but who needs thinking anyway? Bar service is fast and friendly, there are all kinds of bizarre happenings going on outside the bathroom and it's often so crowded you'll be drinking on the pavement (if the bouncers let you). Embrace your inner lad and enjoy.

Marquis de Sade (☎ 224 817 505; Templová 8; ⏰ 11-2am) Slightly calmer than its near neighbour, Chateau, the Marquis cashes in on its former-brothel ambience with plenty of velvet, a salo(o)n atmosphere and art on the walls. By 11pm you won't be able to see any of it for the crowds. This is a popular spot for a tipple of absinthe.

Trosca Bar (Martinká 5; ⏰ 3pm-midnight Mon-Fri, 5pm-midnight Sat & Sun) Not your average Old-Town bar, Trosca's cheap beer, dilapidated furniture, execrable bathrooms, ironic art, beyond-sticky floor, black-clad long-haired regulars and death-metal soundtrack are almost the exact opposite of a quiet 85Kč Pilsner Urquell opposite the Astronomical Clock. It sounds scary, but it isn't at all.

Nové Město
Map pp110–11

Novoměstský pivovar (☎ 222 232 448; Vodičkova 20; 8am-11.30pm Mon-Fri, 11.30am-11.30pm Sat, noon-10pm Sun) Breweries are all the rage in New Town, and like many of the others this one draws a lot of tourists. It's considerably cheaper than most though (28Kč for 0.5L), and the food is very good, including a delicious *svíčková* (cream sauce with beef and dumplings). If you'd like to eat a roast piglet or goose, call the day before.

Pivovarský dům (☎ 296 216 666; Lípová 15) There's no problem finding cheap beer in vast quantities in Prague, but the House of Brewing prefers quality. This totally unpretentious microbrewery – one of the few that's not on the tour-group track – makes an awesome traditional lager (26.50Kč for 0.5L) as well as flavoured beers including cherry and banana (26.50Kč for 0.3L). The coffee beer is a synergistic miracle. If you want to take a tour of the brewery (50Kč), call ahead.

Boulder Bar (☎ 222 231 244; V Jámě 6; 2pm-midnight Mon-Fri, 4pm-midnight Sat & Sun) The Czechs like beer with everything – beer with hiking, beer with pedal boats, beer with breakfast. Now they have beer with rock climbing. The bouldering wall at this popular little bar is open 8am to 10pm Monday to Friday, and noon to 10pm Saturday and Sunday; call ahead if you want to use it.

Velryba (The Whale; ☎ 224 912 484; Opatovická 24) Young Czechs and plenty of backpackers keep this place jumping. The front room is more café than bar. The back room is all about intense conversations over a Fernet citrus.

Jazz Café č. 14 (☎ 224 920 039; Opatovická 14) Imagine The Prodigy dressed up as Chet Baker – it might be something like Jazz Café č. 14. This dim little bar/coffee shop in a back alley serves coffee, booze, cigars, bar snacks and really good cake.

Vinohrady & Žižkov

James Bond (Map pp120-1; ☎ 221 449 732; Polská 7, Vinohrady; 4pm-1am Mon-Sat, 4-11pm Sun) Operating under the motto 'Mixing Enjoy and Girls', James Bond must be Prague's most self-consciously hip cocktail bar. With stylishly uncomfortable pleather seating, fish tanks and plenty of back-lit plexiglass, it serves cocktails to American expats taking a meeting and local hipsters SMSing like their lives depend on it. The kitchen hasn't quite grasped the concept, which means you can order porridge as a bar snack.

Planet Sports (Map p119; ☎ 224 255 005; Korunní 5, Vinohrady; 4pm-5am) Planet Sports' odd opening hours allow homesick Americans to watch live baseball and football. The staff at this new bar are really eager to please, and will try to hunt down any sporting event you care to watch. Check out the soccer goals in the men's bathroom.

Hapu (Map pp120-1; ☎ 222 720 158; Orlická 8, Žižkov; 6pm-2am Mon-Sat) Low-ceilinged, plush-chaired, dimly lit and tiny, with a comprehensive cocktail list, local wines, several kinds of scotch and friendly staff who wield a mean shaker.

ENTERTAINMENT

For reviews, an up-to-the-minute directory of venues and day-by-day listings, consult the 'Night & Day' section of the *Prague Post*. The weekly *Houser* magazine (www.houser.cz in Czech), available free from venues, bars and cafés, is in Czech but easy to decipher. Websites are an even better bet: www.badpoint.com specialises in clubbing; Prague TV (www.prague.tv) has two English-language entertainment listings; www.techno.cz and www.rave.cz (both in Czech) list club happenings and www.freemusic.cz has the latest on live bands.

There are ticket consolidators on nearly every street corner in Staré and Nové Městos. They're convenient and they usually take credit cards, but you'll pay around 10% mark-up over buying direct from the venue. Ask if there are discounts for students, seniors or the disabled. **BTI** (Bohemia Tickets; Map pp98-9; ☎ 224 227 832; www.ticketsbti .cz; Na příkopě 16, Nové Město; 10am-7pm Mon-Fri, 10am-5pm Sat, 10am-3pm Sun) and **Ticketpro** (Map pp98-9; ☎ 296 328 888; www.ticketpro.cz; Salvátorska 10; 9am-12.30pm & 1-5.15pm Mon-Fri) cover the most venues and events – the addresses given here are head offices, but you can find outlets all over town or order on the web.

Cinema

There's been a multiplex building boom in Prague in the last few years, and you'll have no problem finding a first-run Hollywood movie in English with Czech subtitles. The big operators have squeezed out a lot of the smaller cinemas, so seeing art-house has become more difficult. Admission is from around 90Kč to 160Kč.

The closest multiplexes to the centre are the **Village Cinemas** (Map p118; ☎ 251 115 111; www.villagecinemas.cz in Czech; Radlická 1E, Smíchov) at Anděl, **Palace Cinemas** (Map pp98-9; ☎ 257 181 212; www.palacecinemas.cz; Na Příkopě 22, Nové Město) at Slovanský dům, and **Cinema City** (Map pp120-1; ☎ 255 742 021; www.cinemacity.cz in Czech; Vinohradská & Jičínská, Žižkov) at Palác Flóra. Art-house cinemas close to the centre include the **Kino Lucerna** (Map pp110-11; ☎ 224 216 972; Lucerna Building, Vodičkova 36, Nové Město), **Kino Illusion** (Map p119; ☎ 222 520 379; Vinohradská 48, Vinohrady) and **Kino Kotva** (Map pp98-9; ☎ 224 828 316; náměstí Republiky 8, Staré Město).

Classical Music, Opera & Ballet

There are around six concerts of one kind or another almost every day in summer, a fine soundtrack to the city's rich, visual delights. For information on current performances, ask at PIS, one of the ticket consolidators or check the 'Day & Night' lift-out of the *Prague Post*. The following are some major venues.

Bertramka (Mozart Museum; Map p118; ☎ 257 316 753; www.bertramka.cz; Mozartova 169, Smíchov) Hosts afternoon and evening garden concerts of music by Mozart and other composers (summer only).

Municipal House (Obecní dům; Map pp98-9; ☎ 222 002 101; www.obecni-dum.cz; náměstí Republiky 5) Classical concerts in the Smetana Hall, one of Prague's most stunning venues. The box office is open 10am to 6pm daily.

National Theatre (Národní divadlo; Map pp110-11; ☎ 224 913 437; Národní 2, Nové Město) Mainly opera, ballet and high-brow theatre. The box office is next door at Nová Scéna, and is open from 10am to 6pm Monday to Friday, and from 10am to 12.30pm Saturday and Sunday. There is wheelchair access.

Rudolfinum (Map pp98-9; ☎ 224 893 111; www.ceskafilharmonie.cz; Alšovo nábřeží 12, Staré Město) Home of the Philharmonic. The box office is open from 10am to 6pm Monday to Friday, and for one hour before performances; there is wheelchair access.

Prague State Opera House (Státní opera Praha; Map pp110-11; ☎ 224 227 266; www.opera.cz; Legerova 75, Nové Město) Opera and ballet performances. The box office is on U Divadla, open from 10am to 5.30pm daily (closed Saturday and Sunday from noon to 1pm).

Estates Theatre (Map pp98-9; ☎ 224 215 001; Ovocný trh 1, Staré Město) Hosts *Don Giovanni* by **Opera Mozart** (☎ 271 741 403; www.mozart-praha.cz; Sevastopolská 14) at 8pm every night during summer: anyone who's been to a high school production of *Godspell* will be familiar with the production values. Other opera and classical productions year-round.

Daily chamber concerts, solo performances and organ recitals in the city's various churches are good value at 350Kč to 500Kč. There are several cathedrals and churches frequently used as concert venues:
Bethlehem Chapel (Betlémská kaple; Map pp98-9; Betlémské náměstí 1, Staré Město)
Chapel of Mirrors (Zrcadlová kaple; Map pp98-9; Klementinum, Mariánské náměstí, Staré Město)
Church of St Francis (Kostel sv Františka; Map pp98-9; Křížovnická náměstí, Staré Město)
St Giles Church (Kostel sv Jiljí; Map pp98-9; Husova, Staré Město)
St Nicholas Church (kostel Sv Mikuláše) Staré Město (Map p98; Old Town Square, Staré Město); Malá Strana (Map p94; Malostranské náměstí, Malá Strana)
Spanish Synagogue (Španělská Synagóga; Map pp98-9; Vežeňská 1, Staré Město)

Clubs

With few exceptions, Prague's dance clubs cater to teenagers weaned on MTV Europe and techno/tribal beats – if you want to dance to anything other than hip-hop, R&B or house, you'll have to look long and hard. Most venues open late (after 10pm) and keep the music going until 4am or 5am. Clubs have notoriously short life spans; check *Houser* weekly magazine or www.badpoint.com for up-to-date listings.

Roxy (Map pp98-9; ☎ 224 826 330; www.roxy.cz; Dlouhá 33, Staré Město; cover charge 150Kč; ⊗ 1pm-1am) The Roxy is an excellent, atmospheric space for dancing, live music, chatting or just having a few drinks. This decrepit old theatre has been refitted in industrial/futuristic style; there's a gallery and a small, *Matrix*-style Internet café upstairs. Say hi to the polar bear for us.

Radost FX Club (Map p119; ☎ 224 254 776; Bělehradská 120, Vinohrady; cover charge 100Kč; ⊗ 10pm-

5am) Radost's recent face-lift has made it Prague's most comfortable, gorgeous and stylish venue for lounge, soul, R&B, Buddha nights, house and alternative. Radost seems to be moving away from commercial dance and into performance and unusual DJs.

Futurum (Map p118; ☎ 257 328 571; www.music bar.cz; Zborovská 7, Smíchov; ☺ 8pm-3am) Designed for those who were living in a communist country when Roxette was all the rage, Futurum's twice-weekly '80s and '90s parties (80Kč) might be your only chance to dance to the Beastie Boys, Nirvana, Madonna and Right Said Fred all in one place. See all the videos you wish you'd forgotten and have a great deal of fun despite yourself. Occasional live bands.

Other recommendations:

Karlovy Lázně (Map pp98-9; ☎ 222 220 502; Novotného lávka, Staré Město; cover charge 100Kč; ☺ 9pm-5am) This is central Europe's biggest club: four floors of dance, all of them unremarkable. Girls travelling by themselves may find the meat-market atmosphere a bit much, or they may get lucky.

Matrix Klub (Map pp120-1; ☎ 222 780 423; www .matrixklub.cz; Koněvova 12, Žižkov; ☺ 8pm-4.30am Tue-Sat) DJs, parties and occasional live shows. Take bus No 133 or 207 from Florenc metro, or night bus No 504 from IP Pavlova metro.

Palác Akropolis (Map pp120-1; ☎ 296 330 911; www.palacakropolis.cz; Kubelíkova 27, Žižkov) Akropolis has a very alternative reputation, but most of the time expect DJs spinning hip-hop. Shows after 8pm. Whatever is on, the venue is great.

Jazz & Blues

Prague has a lot of places claiming to be jazz bars – like marionettes and tiny glass bottles, jazz has become a mainstay of the tourist industry. But most of what you'll actually hear is blues, or jazz of a very tame variety. Most of the clubs listed have good jazz CD stores on the premises. Cover charges are 100Kč to 150Kč unless otherwise stated. The *Prague Post* 'Night & Day' lift-out has listings of who's playing when.

Železná Jazz Club (Map pp98-9; ☎ 224 239 697; www.jazzclub.cz; Železná 16, Staré Město; ☺ 3pm-1am) Keeping it a bit more real than many other jazz clubs, Železná, in a renovated stone cellar, has atmosphere to burn and a calendar that features some daring original jazz. Music starts at 9pm Monday to Saturday and 8pm Sunday.

U Malého Glena (Map pp94-5; ☎ 257 531 717; Karmelitská 23, Malá Strana; ☺ 8-2am) Restaurant and bar by day, U Malého Glena dishes up hard-swinging local jazz or blues bands from 9pm to at least midnight most nights. The kind kitchen focuses on food for drunk people: baked potatoes, sandwiches and lots of other soft, easy-to-eat things at very decent prices.

Reduta Jazz Club (Map pp110-11; ☎ 224 912 246; Národní 20, Nové Město; ☺ 5pm-12.30am) Founded under communism, this is the classic old-school venue this side of the river. There's live jazz here from 9pm daily and the ticket office is open to 5pm weekdays and 8pm Saturday.

U Staré paní Jazz Lounge (Map pp98-9; ☎ 603 551 680; www.jazzinprague.com; Michalská 9, Staré Město; ☺ 7pm-2am) Jazz or blues kicks off at 9pm every night, then winds up by midnight, when DJs playing world music take over the stage. ISIC and Go25 cardholders get one free drink.

Rock & Other Music

While Prague was once a thriving live music scene, the influx of hotels and affluent apartment buyers into the centre of town has meant a tightening of noise restrictions and the death of many venues. These days you often have to head out to the 'burbs for live music, or make do with cover bands and revival acts tailored for the tourist market.

Guru Music Club (Map pp120-1; ☎ 222 783 463; www.guruclub.wz.cz in Czech; Rokycanova 29, Žižkov; cover charge 50Kč; ☺ 11am-5am) Guru takes rock seriously, with hardcore, 'emocore', 'pig beat' and open mikes almost every night of the week. DJs fill the gaps. Take bus No 163 from Flora.

Malostranská beseda (Map pp94-5; ☎ 257 532 092; Malostranské náměstí 21, Malá Strana; ☺ 5pm-1am) Anything from hard rock to bluegrass, theatre and screened cartoons is the scene here. Music from 8pm.

Other recommendations:

Hells' Bells (Map p118; ☎ 257 320 436; Na Bělidle 27/302, Smíchov; ☺ 5pm-3am Mon-Sat, 5pm-11.59pm Sun) Hells' Bells has live metal on the weekends and head-banging ambience during the week.

Rock Café (Map pp110-11; ☎ 224 933 947; Národní 22, Nové Město; ☺ 10-3am Mon-Fri, 8pm-3am Sat & Sun) A stripped-down venue for DJs and live rock. Mainly features tribute bands. Music from 8.30pm.

Strahov 007 (Map pp94-5; ☎ 257 211 439; Block 7, Strahov dormitory complex, Strahov; ☻ 7.30pm-1am Mon-Sat) Raw music (and venue) – heavy rock, punk, hip-hop and alternative bands (or DJs). Take bus No 143, 149 or 217 from Dejvická metro station, or walk from the top of the funicular railway. Music from 8pm.

Sport

FOOTBALL (SOCCER)

SK Slavia Praha and AC Sparta Praha are leading teams in the national league. Matches are mostly on Sunday afternoons. The season runs from September to December and March to June. Tickets cost around 90Kč and you can usually pick up a ticket at the stadium just before the game.

Slavia's stadium is under reconstruction for the next few years; until then they're using the **Strahov Stadium** (Map pp94-5; ☎ 257 213 290; Diskařská 100, Strahov) – catch the No 176 bus from Karlovo nám metro. **Sparta Stadium** (Map pp82-3; ☎ 220 57 03 23; Milady Horákové 98, Bubeneč) is opposite Letná Park, and is very convenient to the beer garden for post-game drinks; take tram No 1, 8, 25 or 26 one stop east from Hradčanská metro.

When the Czech Republic is playing international matches, a big screen is set up in Old Town Square and the place is packed with yelling, flag-waving fans.

ICE HOCKEY

One of the best national teams is HC Sparta Praha. You can see them play in winter at the **HC Sparta Sports Hall** (Map pp82-3; U Sparty, Bubeneč) next to the Sparta stadium; take tram No 1, 8, 25 or 26 one stop east from Hradčanská metro. Other games are played at **HC Apex Praha's zimní stadion** (winter stadium; Map pp120-1; ☎ 0602 291 372; Hlávkův most, Holešovice). The ice hockey season runs from September until early April, and cheap tickets are available at the rinks for the mainly weekend games.

Theatre

Prague has no shortage of theatre shows, though most serious drama is in Czech. English-language theatre is dominated by black-light theatre, where live or animated actors in phosphorescent costumes do their thing on a stage lit only by ultraviolet lights.

Laterna Magika (Magic Lantern; Map pp110-11; ☎ 224 914 129; Nová Scéna, Národní 4; tickets from 600Kč) Prague's most famous theatre happening, this multimedia show interweaving dance,

opera, music and film is unique. If it's sold out, you may be able to get a no-show ticket half an hour beforehand. The box office is open from 10am to 8pm Monday to Saturday.

National Marionette Theatre (Národní divadlo marionet; Map pp98-9; ☎ 224 819 322; www.mozart.cz; Puppet Kingdom, Žatecká 1; adult/child 490/390Kč) It might sound silly, watching life-size marionettes perform Mozart's *Don Giovanni*, but it's one of the longest-running shows in town so they must be doing something right. The box office is open from 10am to 8pm.

Other venues:

Estates Theatre (Stavovské divadlo; Map pp98-9; ☎ 224 215 001; Ovocný trh 1, Staré Město) Some plays include simultaneous translation on headphones.

Image Theatre (Map pp98-9; ☎ 222 329 191; Classic Club, Pařížská 4; tickets 400Kč) Mime and black-light theatre, box office open from 9am to 8pm.

Minor Theatre (Divadlo Minor; Map pp110-11; ☎ 222 231 351; Vodičkova 6, Nové Město) Children's puppet theatre has shows at 9.30am on most weekdays; wheelchair access.

SHOPPING

Prague's main shopping streets are Wenceslas Square and three streets around the edge of Staré Město: Na příkopě, 28.října and Národní třída. Here you should be able to find almost anything you need. Prague's tourist specialities are marionettes, glass and garnets (and, apparently, Bob Marley T-shirts and Native American dream catchers: we've listed a few of the better tourist outlets. Antique books and homewares also make great souvenirs, and the small streets of Staré Mesto are thick with antikvariat.

Antiques & Bric-a-Brac

Art Deco Galerie (Map pp98-9; ☎ 224 223 076; Michalská 21, Staré Město; ☻ 2-7pm Mon-Fri) All kinds of gorgeousness, mostly Art Deco, fills this well-ordered and very reasonably priced store. A great selection of glassware, clocks, china, jewellery and dresses, with many things under 600Kč.

Bríc á Brac (Map pp98-9; ☎ 224 815 763; Týnská 7, Staré Město; ☻ 10am-6pm) An Aladdin's cave of old household items and trophies and toys and cigar boxes and typewriters and stringed instruments and... Despite the junky look of this place, the knick-knacks are surprisingly expensive.

Eduard Čapek (Map pp98-9; Dlouhá 32, Staré Město; ☻ 10am-6pm Mon-Fri) You may not need a door knob, rusty bed springs or a cracked teapot, but drop in anyway at the old hardware/houseware shop founded before WWI and doing a roaring trade ever since. Promotional badges from Czech companies start at 10Kč.

Cameras, Film & Processing

LM Foto (Map p119; ☎ 224 252 463; Bělehradská 124, Vinohrady; ◷ 9am-7pm Mon-Fri, 10am-1pm Sat) LM has most brands of black and white film and professional colour in 35mm and 120 rolls. The processing is also excellent.

Jan Pazdera (Map pp110-11; ☎ 224 216 197; Vodičkova 28; ◷ 10am-6pm Mon-Fri) This place overflows with second-hand cameras, some of them looking well over 100 years old, and darkroom gear.

Ceramics, Glass & Crystal

Tupesy lidová keramika (Map pp98-9; ☎ 224 210 728; Havelská 21, Staré Město; ◷ 10am-7pm) Charming ceramic household goods featuring naive floral designs from Southern Moravia are for sale here.

Obchod U Sv Jiljí (Map pp98-9; ☎ 224 232 695; Jilská 7, Staré Město; ◷ 10am-5pm) Offbeat ceramics, as well as a selection of high-quality, unique marionettes.

Moser (Map pp110-11; ☎ 224 211 293; Na příkopě 12, Nové Město; ◷ 10am-8pm Mon-Fri, 10am-7pm Sat & Sun) Prague's most prestigious glassmaker has been around since 1857. You may not be able to afford any of the gorgeous fripperies on display, but treat the place like a museum and visit anyway.

Balnys Spa (Map pp98-9; ☎ 222 222 123; Náprstkova 4, Staré Město; ◷ 10am-6pm Mon-Fri) Modern glass featuring semi-precious stones that are quite unlike what you'll find at most souvenir shops in town. This store also stocks original black-and-white photos and pen-and-ink drawings of Prague.

Kubista (Map pp98-9; ☎ 224 236 378; Ovocný trh 19; ◷ 10am-6pm) In the Cubist House of the Black Madonna, Kubista stocks all kinds of Cubist-influenced ceramics starting at around 1400Kč. It also has furniture from 100,000Kč, and books and postcards featuring Cubist design.

Clothing & Jewellery

Second Hand Land (Map pp120-1; ☎ 241 711 995; Hybernská 5, Nové Město; ◷ 9am-6pm Mon-Fri, 10am-2pm Sat) When the kids have dirtied everything they own, when you absolutely must have a

T-shirt featuring some form of Czech logo, or if you just feel like stocking up on frocks without spending three weeks' beer money, head to Second Hand Land. T-shirts start around 40Kč; dresses start from 150Kč.

Devátá Vlna (Ninth Wave; Map pp98-9; ☎ 224 917 773; Pasáž Metro, Národní 25, Nové Město; ◷ 11am-7pm Mon-Sat, 10am-7pm Sun) Young Prague designers Dita Ladovská and Kateřina Kašparová whip up extremely wearable, affordable street wear for gals – skirts, hoodies, trousers and some very cute dresses and swimsuits. It also stocks covetable T-shirts from other local designers.

Mýrnyx Týrnyx Eclectiks (Map pp94-5; ☎ 224 923 270; Saská Ulicka, Malá Strana; ◷ 11am-7pm) Carefully selected second-hand clothes for chaps and lasses share rack space with original designs for brave fashionistas. Mýrnyx represents designers from the Czech Republic and Germany.

Granát Turnov (Map pp98-9; ☎ 222 315 612; Dlouhá 28-30, Staré Město) One of the biggest manufacturers and stockists of silver and gold garnet jewellery in Prague. The semi-precious Czech garnet – usually a red stone – is supposed to replace sadness with joy: its effectiveness probably depends on who's doing the buying.

Department Stores & Malls

If there's one difference between the Prague of today and the Prague of, say, 1999, it's the vast quantity of shopping malls that have sprung up in the last few years. Na příkopě, 28 řijna and Národní have a slew of gleaming arcades and multistorey malls, and the area around Anděl metro, in Smíchov, is sprouting malls like mushrooms after rain.

Palác Flóra (Map pp120-1; cnr Vinohradská & Jičínská, Žižkov; ◷ 8am-midnight except Christmas) You could be anywhere in the capitalist world in this shiny, glittering paean to consumerism. Slick cafés share floor space with girly emporia of tiny T-shirts and sparkly makeup. There's a giant Albert's supermarket on the bottom floor.

Roya (Map pp110-11; cnr Vodičkova & Řeznická, Nové Město; ◷ 9.30am-7pm) This mall is all about mums and babies, featuring maternity wear, some runway-worthy tots' fashion and plenty of toys.

Bílá Labuť (Map pp120-1; ☎ 224 811 364; Na poříčí 23, Nové Město; ◷ 9am-8pm Mon-Fri, 9am-6pm Sat,

10am-6pm Sun) The old-school option: this is less a shopping destination than a cultural experience. There's everything you'd expect in a department store, but less of it, cheaper, of dubious quality and oddly arranged.

Tesco (Map pp110-11; ☎ 222 003 111; Národní 26, Nové Město; ⏱ 8am-9pm Mon-Fri, 9am-8pm Sat, 10am-8pm Sun) In Prague, the answer to the question 'where can I get a [insert difficult-to-find item of your choice]?' is invariably, 'try Tesco'. Four floors of department store, and Prague's best-stocked and least-pleasant supermarket have everything covered. The supermarket is open from 7am to 10pm Monday to Friday, 8am to 8pm Saturday and 9am to 8pm Sunday.

Gifts & Souvenirs

Manufaktura Malá Strana (Map pp94-5; ☎ 257 533 678; Mostecká 17); Staré Město (Map pp98-9; Melnatrichova 17); Staré Město (Map pp98-9; cnr Karlova & Husova) There are Manufakturas all over town, mostly in Staré Město and Malá Strana. All feature quality traditional handcrafts – the bulk of their stock is wooden toys, but they also have ceramics, textiles, soaps, candles and knick-knacks.

Fun Explosive (Map pp98-9; ☎ 224 236 369; Jilská 14, Staré Město; ⏱ 10am-7pm) You'll have seen Fun Explosive's bright, cartoony t-shirts in stores around town, but this is the mother lode. T-shirts, mugs, calendars, posters, original art and other assorted bits and bobs.

Music

If it's jazz you're after, most jazz clubs (p143) sell excellent selections of CDs, and knowledgeable staff can provide good advice.

Bontonland (Map pp110-11; ☎ 224 473 080; Václavské náměstí, Nové Město; ⏱ 9am-8pm Mon-Sat, 10am-7pm Sun) Prague's music megastore, in the basement of the Koruna building, stocks classical, jazz, folk, soundtracks, rock, metal, Czech pop compilations and a limited selection of vinyl. Bontonland also has an Internet and Playstation café, DVDs, books, T-shirts and tickets for shows.

Radost CD (Map p119; ☎ 224 252 741; Bělehradská 120, Vinohrady; ⏱ 10am-7pm) A great selection of hip-hop, dance, reggae, jazz, rock classics and independent artists – finally get a copy of that Kool Keith or White Stripes album that's come out since you've been on the road.

Trio (Map pp98-9; ☎ 222 322 583; Franz Kafka nám 3, Staré Město; ⏱ 10am-7pm Mon-Fri, 10am-6pm Sat & Sun) A great little shop specialising in classical CDs. It also has collections of Jewish music and Czech and Slovak folk.

Cappriccio (Map p118; ☎ 257 320 165; Újezd 15, Smíchov) Pick up the score for *Don Giovanni* or *From the New World* at this eclectic sheet music shop. Those who don't play might enjoy the books of country music favourites – who doesn't want to learn *Rhinestone Cowboy* in Czech?

Sporting Goods

Hudy Sport (Map pp98-9; ☎ 224 813 010; Havličkova 11, Nové Město; ⏱ 9am-6.30pm Mon-Fri, 9am-1pm Sat) Hudy is a huge outdoor shop with all the latest in fleece, Gortex, backpacks, rock-climbing gear, skis, stoves, shoes, sleeping bags and accessories. Six other Hudys are scattered around the city.

Giga (Map pp98-9; Mýslbek Shopping Centre, Na příkopě, Nové Mesto; ⏱ 9.30am-7pm) Balls, boots, flippers, jog bras and no end of Nike and Puma street wear – Giga has three floors of sportswear and equipment.

GETTING THERE & AWAY

Air

Prague Ruzyně, the Czech Republic's only international airport, is on the western outskirts of the city.

The arrivals hall has a Travelex currency-exchange office as well as several ATMs. The accommodation agency AVE is reliable; the Čedok desk has upper-end accommodation. A DP office sells metro tickets. Eurotel and T-Mobile rent phones and sell SIM cards. There is a 24-hour, left-luggage office (50Kč daily per bag). There are several airline and ticket-consolidator desks in the departures hall.

ČSA (Map pp98-9; ☎ 220 104 111; V celnici 5, Nové Město; ⏱ 7am-6pm Mon-Fri, 7am-3pm Sat & Sun) has several flights a day to Brno and Ostrava and numerous international connections.

Bus

INTERNATIONAL

Nearly all international buses leave from the Florenc station (Map pp120–1), outside the Florenc metro station. Most Eurolines services depart from Želivského bus station, but its London and Germany services use Florenc. At least one of the four ticket

PRAGUE

windows (AMS) sells both domestic and international tickets; try ticket window No 5.

Overall it is much simpler to book through a good travel agency (see Information p87). The price is the same, and you're more likely to get discounts.

DOMESTIC

All domestic, long-distance buses and most regional services (such as those for excursions around Prague) use Florenc station (Map pp120–1). Some regional buses depart from stands near metro stations Anděl, Dejvická, Černý Most, Hradčanská, Nádraží Holešovice, Radlická, Roztyly, Smíchovské Nádraží, Zlinčín and Želivského.

Agencies don't book seats on domestic buses, but they can tell you which stand is best for a particular trip or whether you should take the train instead. **ČSAD's information line** (☎ 1034; ☼ 6am-8pm), Florenc's **information window** (☎ 900 11 90 41, 900 11 90 44; ☼ 6am-9pm) and ČSAD's **online schedule** (www.jizdnirady.cz) are useful planning tools. At Florenc, the information window is No 8, and is open from 6am to 9pm daily. If you get no joy there, try the friendly Tourbus travel agency in a corridor off the main hall.

At Florenc in the central hall and outside at stands Nos 1 and 2, there is a maze of charts on the wall; they include clear instructions in English, and though they're time-consuming to figure out, they do make sense. See the list of bus (p456) and train (p461) timetable symbols for more information. You can buy your own regional timetables from one of the ticket counters.

Short-haul tickets are sold on the bus. Long-distance domestic tickets are sold from AMS counters Nos 11 to 13. Since ticketing is now computerised at **Florenc** (☼ 6am-8pm), **Želivského** (☼ 7.30am-noon Mon-Fri, 1-5pm Sat), **Roztyly** (☼ 7.30am-noon Mon-Fri, 1-5pm Sat), **Knížecí** (☼ 7.30am-noon Mon-Fri, 1-5pm Sat) and **Černý Most** (☼ 7.30am-noon Mon-Fri, 1-5pm Sat), you can book ahead from 10 days to 30 minutes prior to your departure.

There are generally more departures in the morning. Buses, especially if full, sometimes leave a few minutes early, so be there about 10 minutes before departure time. Many services don't operate on weekends, so trains are a better bet then.

Florenc has a **left-luggage office** (úschovna zavazadel; ☼ 5am-11pm).

Car & Motorcycle

For information on car rental, documents, road rules and fuel, see the Transport chapter (p456).

Train

INTERNATIONAL

Most international trains arrive at the main station, Praha hlavní nádraží (Map pp120–1), which is three blocks from Wenceslas Square.

International trains between Berlin and Budapest often stop at Praha-Holešovice (metro nádraží Holešovice; Map pp82–3) on the northern side of the city.

International tickets, domestic and international couchettes and seat reservations are sold on level 2 of the main station at the even-numbered windows from 12 to 24 (except 14) to the right of the stairs up to level 3.

If you'd like to let someone else do the ticket-buying work, try a travel agent (see Information p87) or go to any train station and look for the state railway office, ČD (České dráhy). In Prague, information about connections is available on ☎ 221 111 122 or www.cd.cz. Station foyers have timetables on rotating drums.

DOMESTIC

Most domestic trains arrive at the main station or Masarykovo nádraží, two blocks north of it. Others where you might end up are Praha-Dejvice (two blocks from metro station Hradčanská), Praha-Smíchov (adjacent to metro Smíchovské nádraží), Praha-Vysočany northeast of the centre (take bus Nos 185, 209, 259 or 278 to/from metro station Českomoravská) and Praha-Vršovice (tram No 24 to/from Wenceslas Square).

Hlavní nádraží handles domestic trains to Benešov (52Kč, one hour, 49km), České Budějovice (204Kč, 2½ hours, 169km), Cheb via Plzeň (250Kč, four hours, 220km), Karlovy Vary via Chomutov (274Kč, four hours, 199km – quicker and more affordable by bus from the main bus station Florenc – 150Kč), Košice (970Kč, 10 hours, 708km), Mariánské Lázně (224Kč, three hours, 190km), Plzeň (140Kč, two hours, 114km – or buses from Florenc – 110Kč) and Tábor (130Kč, 1½ hours, 103km).

Trains going to Brno (140Kč, 3½ hours, 257km – or buses from Florenc – 120Kč) and Bratislava (5½ hours, 398km) may leave from either Hlavní nádraží, Holešovice or Masarykovo nádraží.

Trains to Kutná Hora (98Kč, 1½ hours, 73km) depart from Holešovice or, more frequently, Masarykovo nádraží. Karlštejn trains (46Kč; 34 minutes, 29km) always depart from Smíchov.

At the main station, domestic tickets *(vnitrostátní jízdenky)* are sold on level 2 at the odd-numbered windows from 1 to 23 to the left of the stairs.

MAIN TRAIN STATION

You disembark at level 3 into a swarm of currency-exchange desks, accommodation offices and people offering places to stay. Get your bearings and a map at the helpful **PIS booth** (Level 2; ☼ 9am-7pm Mon-Fri, 9am-4pm Sat & Sun).

If you've got a few minutes to spare, make your way up to the top floor and you can have a look at the fading Art Nouveau elegance of the original (and mostly abandoned) building designed by Josef Fanta and built between 1901 and 1909. Levels 3, 2 and 1 are the modern extension beneath Wilsonova třída. Buses are on the roof top of the modern section, which is also the car park. Taxis are found outside the northern and southern end, and there are several metro station entrances on level 2. Public-transport information is available at the DP booth beside the northern metro entrance. Level 1 has a 24-hour left-luggage office, day-use lockers and baggage check-in counter – if you leave your luggage in your locker longer than 24 hours, it will be removed and placed in the left-luggage office and you'll be fined.

The station is closed from 1am to 3am, so don't try to sleep here then. At night it's a bad place to hang around anyway. Accommodation close to the station includes Hostel Jednota (p128), Hostel Elf (p131) and the Hotel Esplanade (p129).

GETTING AROUND

Prague's compact historical centre is best appreciated on foot, with the help of good, cheap public transport. Pollution, traffic congestion and vibration damage to old buildings have led to the construction of pedestrian-only zones and restrictions on vehicular traffic.

To/From the Airport

City bus No 119 does the run from Ruzyně airport to the Dejvická metro station every 10 minutes (15 minutes on weekends) from 4.25am to 11.40pm (buy a 12Kč ticket from DP in the arrivals hall, from the yellow machine at the bus stop or from the driver for 15Kč – exact amount required). The trip takes about 45 minutes, including the metro trip to/from the city centre.

Cedaz Microbuses (☎ 220 114 296) charges 360Kč to take one to four people to one address – see the desk in the arrivals hall. Call to book a return transfer to the airport at a 20% reduction, or be at nám Republiky on the hour and half-hour from 5.30am to 9.30pm for a 90Kč trip.

Airport Cars (☎ 220 113 892; www.airport-cars.cz) runs officially sanctioned taxis with polite drivers. It is 600Kč per person to hotels around Malá Strana and Old Town Square, with a 20% discount for the return trip.

A regular taxi fare to the airport should be 450Kč from the vicinity of Old Town Square, but some unscrupulous taxi drivers will charge much more. Only taxis sanctioned by the airport can collect passengers at the airport arrivals hall – they will all try to charge horribly inflated prices.

Bicycle

Prague is not a brilliant place to ride a bike. Traffic is heavy, pollution can be choking and there are no bicycle lanes. The cobblestones loosen your teeth, and tram tracks are treacherous, especially when wet. But a bike is a great way to get out of town – there are some good paths along the Vltava valley into the parks that surround the city.

If you want to buy a bike, many of the city's bazaars have low-grade second-hand cycles for around 1000Kč. You'll need a good lock for the wheels and frame: bikes are a popular target. Spare parts are available in the city's many bike shops. You can take your bicycle on the metro for an extra 6Kč. You must keep it near the last door of the rear carriage, and only two bikes are allowed in. You can't do it at any time when the carriage is full, nor if there's already a pram in the carriage.

BICYCLE RENTAL

Praha Bike (Map pp98-9; ☎ 732 388 880; www.praha bike.cz; Dlouhá 24, Staré Město; ☼ 9am-7pm) Good, new bikes with lock, helmet and map, plus free luggage storage. Two-hour rentals start at 220Kč, or 540Kč for six hours. Also offers student discounts and group bike tours.

City Bike (Map pp98-9; ☎ 776 180 284; Královdorská 5, Staré Město; ☺ 9am-7pm) Two-hour tours start at 450Kč. Much better value is the four-hour tour plus two-hour free ride for 500Kč. Nine hours of free riding is 700Kč. City Bike also has skydiving (US$130) and bungee jumping (700Kč).

Car & Motorcycle

Driving in Prague is no fun. Trying to find your way around while coping with trams, lunatic drivers and pedestrians, one-way streets and police on the lookout for a little handout, will make you wish you'd left the car at home. Try not to arrive or leave on a Friday or Sunday afternoon or evening, when half the population seems to head to and from their weekend houses.

Central Prague has many pedestrian-only streets. They are marked with Pěší zóna (Pedestrian Zone) signs, and only service vehicles and taxis are allowed in these areas.

CAR RENTAL

Mainstream agencies charge over 2000Kč per day for unlimited mileage and collision waiver; A-Rent charges slightly less. All have airport pick-up points (where you pay an extra 400Kč surcharge) and most do not charge extra for one-way rentals.

A-Rent Car Thrifty (Map pp110-11; ☎ 24 22 98 48; Washingtonova 9, Nové Město)
Avis (Map pp120-1; ☎ 221 851 225; Klimentská 46, Nové Město)
CS-Czechocar (Map pp110-11; ☎ 221 637 423; Rathova passage, Na příkopě 23, Nové Město)
Europcar (Map pp98-9; ☎ 224 810 515; Pařížská 28, Staré Město)
Hertz (Map pp110-11; ☎ 222 231 010; Karlovo nám 28, Nové Město)

Local companies charge less than the multinationals, though they may not speak great English. Typical rates for a Škoda Felicia at the time of writing were 700Kč to 1200Kč per day with unlimited kilometres and collision waiver; many ask for a deposit of 5000Kč.

Alimex ČR (Map pp110-11; ☎ 800 150 170; www.alimexcr.cz; Wenceslas Square, Václavské náměstí, Nové Město)
Secco Car (Map pp82-3; ☎ 220 802 361; www.seccocar.cz; Přístavní 39, Holešovice)

EMERGENCIES

For emergency service, the Czech automobile and motorcycle club, **ÚAMK** (Automotoklub; ☎ 1230) has 'Yellow Angels' (Žlutý andělé) that provide 24-hour nationwide assistance.

Another outfit offering round-the-clock repair services nationwide is **Autoklub Bohemia Assistance** (ABA; ☎ 26 14 91), which also has a **Prague information centre** (Map pp110-11; ☎ 222 241 257; Opletalova 29, Nové Město; ☺ 8am-noon & 12.30-4.30pm Mon-Fri).

PARKING

Meter time limits range from two to 24 hours at around 40Kč per hour. Parking in one-way streets is normally only allowed on the right-hand side. Traffic inspectors are strict, and you may be towed.

There are several car parks at the edges of Staré Město and around the outer city near metro stations. Most are marked on the SHOCart GeoClub 1:20,000 Praha and Žaket city maps.

Public Transport

Prague has a marvellous integrated public transport system – it's cheap, clean, convenient and safe, runs all night and will take you pretty much anywhere you need to go. The system includes the metro (underground), trams and buses.

The metro runs from 5am to midnight. To change lines, look for a sign that's the colour of the line you want to transfer to, and follow the arrows. The orange 'výstup' signs indicate exits.

Regular trams and buses run from 4.30am to 11.30pm. After midnight, night trams and buses fill in the gaps, though they may run as infrequently as every 40 minutes. The most-used night trams pass through Karlovo nám and by Národní třída metro (where you'll also find lots of fast food to stave off hunger while you wait) – ask your hotel which night tram you need, or grab a copy of the night tram/bus timetable from a DP office (see the following Information section).

INFORMATION

There are DP ticket offices in all metro stations, plus DP information centres in Muzeum and Můstek (☺ 7am-9pm) and Karlovo náměstí and nádraží Holešovice (☺ 7am-6pm). The DP information centres

PRAGUE

PRAGUE METRO

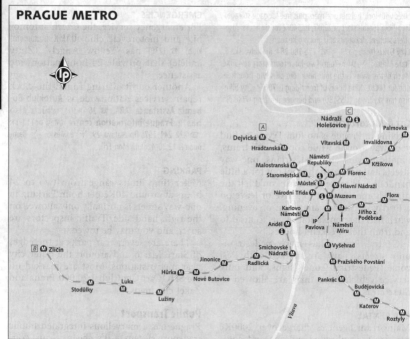

and **Prague Public Transport head office** (Map pp110-11; ☎ 296 191 817; www.dpp.cz; Na bojišti 5, Nové Město; ☺ 6.30am-6.30pm Mon-Fri, 7.30am-noon Sat) sell tickets, maps and timetables for day and night services.

TICKETS & PASSES
One ticket covers all transport. A basic ticket costs 12Kč and lasts 60 minutes (5am to 8pm weekdays) or 90 minutes (8pm to 5am weekdays and 24 hours on weekends). There is also a short-hop 8Kč ticket that can be used for only 15 minutes on buses and trams, or for riding the metro no more than four stations; it's invalid on night trams and buses. Tickets for kids aged six to 15, bikes and big bags cost 6Kč; kids under six ride free.

Ticket machines – found in metro stations and at some tram stops – are simple to use and include instructions in English. Choose the type of ticket you want (it's probably a 12Kč ticket), then press that button for as many tickets as you want – the screen will show what you owe. Feed in some coins (the machine will give change) and wait for your change and tickets. It's

not a bad idea to buy a few tickets at a time, as you can validate them when you need them later. Tickets are also available at Trafiky shops, newsstands and DP offices.

When you're ready to use it, validate your ticket by sticking it in the little yellow machine at the top of the metro escalator or inside the bus or tram – you only need to validate each ticket once, no matter how many times you use it to transfer.

Short-term passes aren't very good value; you're unlikely to take enough trips to justify the 24-hour (70Kč) or three-day (200Kč) tickets, though they have the advantage of convenience. The seven-day (250Kč) and 15-day (280Kč) passes are better value. One-month (420Kč) and three-month (1150Kč) tickets are sold between the 25th and 8th of the month in the DP office at Na bojišti 5 (near metro station IP Pavlova), or from DP ticket counters at about half the city's metro stations. You need to bring a passport photo and fill in a form – if you can take a Czech-speaker with you you'll have a much easier time. The Prague Card (see boxed text p88) includes three days of transport.

anywhere tourists predominate is much the same as wearing a T-shirt that says, 'Please rip me off'; even Czechs aren't immune. It's rare for a cabbie to use his meter – if a driver does it without being asked, tip him. If you must flag a cab, establish the fare beforehand or insist on having the meter turned on.

You're better off calling a radio-taxi, as they're better regulated and more responsible. From our experience the following companies, all with 24-hour service, have honest drivers, some of whom speak English:

AAA Radio Taxi (☎ 233 113 311)
Airport Cars (☎ 220 113 892)
Halo Taxi (☎ 244 114 411)
ProfiTaxi (☎ 261 314 151)

At the time of writing, the maximum rate was 30Kč flag fall plus 22Kč per kilometre, or 4Kč per minute if stalled in traffic. On this basis, a trip within the centre should cost 100Kč to 150Kč; the airport should cost 450Kč.

Regulations say the meter must be zeroed when you get in, and fares must be displayed. At the end of the journey the driver must give you a meter-printed receipt showing company name, taxi ID number, date and times of the journey, end points, rates, the total, the driver's name and his signature. Get one before you pay, and make sure it has all these things in case you want to make a claim.

There's no telephone number you can use for complaints. If something goes wrong, mail your receipt and the cab's licence number to Prague City Hall, Mariánské nám 2, 110 01 Praha 1 – it won't get your money back, but the driver will get nailed.

Tickets are inspected very regularly, and if you're caught without a valid ticket you'll be fined 400Kč.

Taxi

Prague's unscrupulous, corrupt taxi drivers are legendary. While the city has begun work on cleaning up the system, it's still better avoided. Flagging a cab on the street

---

DEVEŘE SE ZAVÍRAJÍ

The Prague metro is really a sight in itself. A joy to travel on (it's not even too horrible at peak hours) and incredibly affordable, the 49-station network includes 50km of track. Every carriage is a cross-section of the local and tourist population, a jumble of fashions and languages with a few groping couples thrown in – it's great for people-watching.

Construction began in the '70s, with the A line. The floods in 2002 almost wiped out the system, with many stations filled to road-level with water – look for little plaques on station escalators showing where the water rose to. Many of the central stations are strikingly decorated: náměstí Míru and Malostranská have the most gorgeous colours, while Karlovo nám has fabulously futuristic wall-coverings. The very Soviet venting systems above every station are also worth a look.

Your first complete Czech phrase will probably be *Ukončete výstup a nástup, dveře se zavírají* (Finish getting on and off, the doors are closing) – after three days of metro travel you'll be saying it in your sleep. As the train pulls away the announcer says, *Příští stanice...* (The next station is...), perhaps noting that it's a *přestupní stanice* (transfer station).

Central Bohemia

In many ways, Central Bohemia is the garden of Prague: a rolling, rural region that has been both the great escape for generations of hard-working urbanites and the backdrop for some of the country's most adventurous and opulent aristocratic grand designs. Scattered with the fortresses and architectural playthings of successive kings and princes, as well as a smorgasbord of parks, picture-postcard villages and hiking trails, this is indeed the capital's grand and gleaming back yard.

In fact, a trip through Central Bohemia is like a good rummage in the national jewellery box. Karlštejn, Kutná Hora, Konopiště; the roll call reads like a 'what's what' of central Europe's architectural treasures, covering a smorgasbord of styles and making up for a million pages of unread history.

With many of the sights within an hour's journey of Prague, even Central Bohemia's back roads can clog up with tour buses and eager weekenders come summertime. But their proximity to the capital can also be their beauty. As the buses and caravans roll out at nightfall, many of the towns and villages once again belong to the locals and an overnight stay will immerse you in the region's blissful serenity – Central Bohemia's true, although sometimes elusive, highlight.

HIGHLIGHTS

- Prepare to be dazzled by Kutná Hora's unique **Cathedral of St Barbara** (p162)
- Wander among the dead in Sedlec's ghoulish **ossuary** (p164)
- Check out the castles at **Karlštejn** (p156), **Český Šternberk** (p156) and **Konopiště** (p155)
- Admire the views and sample the wines in the pretty village of **Mělník** (p159)
- Turn off the highway and explore the beautiful back roads around **Mělník** (p159)

Castles & Chateaux

There are at least six castles or chateaux that you can visit in Central Bohemia. The two most popular, Karlštejn and Konpiště are covered in more detail in the Castles and Chateaux special section on p71.

Take note of opening times before you go. Most of the region's castles, chateaux and other historical monuments are open Tuesday to Sunday during summer, but are closed the first working day after a holiday and also from November to March. A few open on weekends in April and October, with Karlštejn and Křivoklát having a much longer season than most. At any sight where a guided tour is required the ticket offices close an hour or so before the official closing time.

Most admit visitors only in guided groups, though they will often let you pay the Czech price (typically around 60Kč) and lend you a written English narrative. If you want to catch every detail, be prepared to fork out from 70Kč to 200Kč for an English-language tour (available at major tourist sights).

The **National Monuments Institute** (☎ 274 008 154; www.stc.npu.cz - Czech only) produces a *State-owned Castles and Chateaux in Central Bohemia* brochure, covering most chateaux in the region and listing current contact details and opening times. It is available in tourist offices in Prague and throughout the region.

Tours

If you're short on time or want to let someone else make the plans, Prague-based tour companies have a range of all-day excursions from the capital during the summer months. Tour operators include:

Prague Sightseeing Tours (☎ 224 314 661; www.pstours.cz; Klimentská 52, Staré Město, Prague) Tours include: Konopiště (810Kč), Karlštejn (890Kč), Kutná Hora (890Kč).

Martin Tour (☎ 224 212 473; www.martintour.cz; Štepanská 61, Nové Město, Prague) Tours, using head-phones rather than guides, include: Konopiště (800Kč), Kutná Hora (800Kč).

PRŮHONICE

As landscaped parks go, **Průhonice** (admission free; ⊙ 8am-7pm Apr-Oct, until 5pm Nov-Mar), just

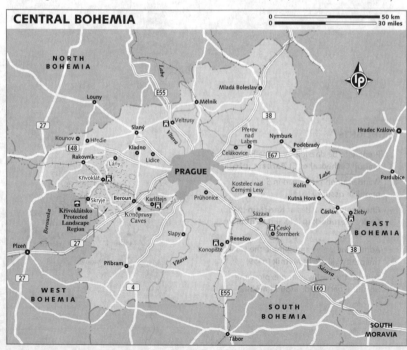

CENTRAL BOHEMIA

0 — 50 km
0 — 30 miles

southeast of Prague, has long been one of Europe's finest. The 2002 floods took a heavy toll here, closing many sections, but the gardens are now on the road to recovery. On weekends Průhonice is packed with day-tripping Czech families, but on a weekday morning you could have it to yourself.

The **chateau** in the grounds is occupied by the Botanical Institute of the Czech Academy of Sciences and is largely closed to the public; you can book tours in advance (☎ 271 015 235).

Getting There & Away
On weekdays, buses leave hourly from Prague's Opatov metro station, on the C line (17Kč, 20 minutes). On weekends services are reduced.

KONOPIŠTĚ
Dating from 1300 Konopiště chateau earned its place in European history courtesy of its last owner, Archduke Franz Ferdinand d'Este, whose 14 June assassination triggered WW1. The French-style chateau now sports the neo-Gothic face-lift instigated by the Archduke in the 1890s and remains one of Bohemia's more romantic chateaux.

For more information on Konopiště, see the Castles & Chateaux special section on p74.

Orientation & Information
Konopiště is south of Prague. The nearest town is Benešov. Its train and bus stations are opposite one another and about 250m from the town square, Masarykovo náměstí (turn left out of the train station, then right at Tyršova).

The castle is 2km away in the opposite direction from town, a fine walk through the estate. Cross the bridge over the railway lines, turn first left into Ke stadiónu and third right down Spartakiádní. Drivers can go straight down Konopišťská from the bridge. On weekdays there are at least three buses a day between Benešov and Konopiště castle.

Sleeping & Eating
KONOPIŠTĚ
Hotel Nová Myslivna (☎ 317 722 496; www.hotelmyslivna.zde.cz; d incl breakfast 500Kč; **P**) The bizarre angular roof of this place clashes with the softer lines of the castle, but its location by the chateau car park is unbeatable.

BENEŠOV
Hotel Atlas (☎ 317 724 771; hotelatlas@quo-reklama.cz; Tyršova 2063; s/d incl breakfast 742/864Kč) It's sterile and functional, but the rooms here are spotless and comfortable.

Hotel Pošta (☎ 317 721 071; hotel-posta@quick.cz; Tyršova 162; s/d incl breakfast 310/620Kč) Once grand, this large hotel is now looking rather threadbare. The rooms have been priced accordingly though.

Sport Hotel (☎ 317 722 919; Hraského 1913; per person 170Kč; **P**) In the winter stadium (*zimní stadion*), off Hrázského to the east, this has basic beds in Spartan surrounds.

Hostinec U zlaté hvězdy (☎ 317 723 921; Masarykovo náměstí; mains 80-120Kč) Snug, inn-style Bohemian snacks can be had at this central *pivnice* (beer hall).

Getting There & Away
There are regular trains from Prague (64Kč, one hour). Most trains to and from Tábor and České Budějovice also stop here.

Coaches depart from Florenc and Roztyly metro station every two to three hours (45Kč, 1¼ hours).

SÁZAVA MONASTERY
Sázava Monastery (Sázavský klášter; ☎ 327 321 177; adult/concession 30/15Kč; ⏰ 9am-noon & 1-6pm Tue-Sun May-Aug, until 5pm Sep, until 4pm Sat & Sun only Apr & Oct) was founded in the 11th century as a centre of orthodox Christianity; it was the first place in Bohemia to conduct services in Old Church Slavonic, though the brethren were booted out of Bohemia a few decades later. Rebuilt in the 13th century and defaced by a heavy-handed baroque renovation, it served as a private chateau in the 19th century.

Star of the show is the monastery's **Gothic chapter hall**, rediscovered under whitewash and masonry during excavations in the 1940s, and restored in the 1970s. All the baroque renovations were meticulously scraped away to reveal the original Gothic chamber, complete with fragmentary frescoes like those at Prague's Emmaus Monastery (another former centre of the Slavonic liturgy).

These ancient bits are really the only reason to drop by on your way to/from Český Šternberk (see the following section).

While the compulsory tours are in Czech, English-language text is available.

Getting There & Away

Get off the train to/from Český Šternberk at Sázava Černé Budy. Go behind the station, cross the tracks, descend the hill, cross the Sázava river and make for the monastery church steeple. It's an 800m-walk – a sign by the station that puts it at 4.5km presumably predates the bridge over the river.

ČESKÝ ŠTERNBERK

pop 100

The hulking 13th-century Šternberk Castle, southeast of Prague, is encompassed by humpbacked hills and thick walls of pine forest, making it not only impenetrable but, before the tarmac road, almost impossible to locate as well. It succumbed to heavy baroque remodelling in the 17th and 18th centuries, but traces of its darker Gothic personality remain, lending it all the broody grandeur of vampire mythology.

The scenery on the train journey up the Sázava river valley – deep woods, steep contours and limestone crags – is itself worth the ride.

Orientation

Don't get off at Český Šternberk station, but one stop further at Český Šternberk zastávka, across the river from the castle. A road and a shorter footpath climb around behind the castle.

Šternberk Castle

Šternberk's (☎ 317 855 101; www.hradceskysternberk .cz - Czech only; adult/concession 50/35Kč, or in English 120/80Kč; ☼ 9am-6pm Tue-Sun Jun-Aug, until 5pm May & Sep, until 4pm Sat & Sun only Apr & Oct) interior is bit of a let down after the castle's imposing façade. The rather slow 45-minute tour reveals an Italian baroque renovation, very heavy on stucco. Such highlights as there are include the rococo **St Sebastian Chapel** (kaple sv Šebastiána) and the **Yellow Room**, with sweeping vistas over the countryside. From here you can see trees marking out a 17th-century, French-style park across the river, the only part of a planned Šternberk chateau that was completed before the money ran out.

Sleeping

Hotel Vesna (☎ 317 855 102; fax 317 855 151; s/d incl breakfast 400/800Kč; P) At a quiet spot on the river, a 25-minute trek downstream on the castle side, this is a pleasant, if slightly crumbly place to soak up the resounding hush of this beautiful region.

Getting There & Away

There are trains to/from Prague's main station Hlavní nádraží (98Kč, 2¼ hours) or Benešov (for Konopiště, 64Kč, 1½ hours); most train services to Český Šternberk zastávka require a change at Čerčany.

KARLŠTEJN

pop 800

Karlštejn, southwest of Prague, is in such good shape these days it wouldn't look out of place on Disney's Main St. The crowds come in theme-park proportions as well (it is best to book ahead), but the peaceful surrounding countryside offers views of Karlštejn's stunning exterior that rival anything you'll see on the inside. For more information, see the Castles & Chateaux special section on p73.

Orientation & Information

It's a 500m walk from the station to the village (turn right), and another 800m up to the castle through a gamut of souvenir stalls selling everything from giant rubber spiders to African woodcarvings.

Walks

On a red-marked path east from Karlštejn village it is 7km via Mořinka (not Mořina) village into the **Karlík Valley** (Karlické údolí), a nature reserve where you may find the remains of Charles IV's **Karlík Castle**, abandoned in the 15th century. Karlík village, 1km down the valley, has a 12th-century rotunda. A road and a green-marked trail run 1.5km southeast from there to Dobřichovice, on the Prague–Beroun train line.

From Srbsko, one train stop west of Karlštejn, another red trail climbs up the wooded Bubovický valley, 8km to the ridgetop **Monastery of St John Under the Rock** (klášter sv Jan pod Skálou), allegedly once an StB (secret police) training camp. About 1.5km further, on a blue-marked trail, just beyond the highway, is Vráž, where you can catch buses back to Beroun or to Prague.

Either walk can be done in about three hours.

Sleeping & Eating

Penzión U královny Dagmar (☎ 311 681 614; d incl breakfast 1400Kč) Close to the castle and a rung –

or two – up the price ladder, this slick place has all the creature comforts and a top-notch eatery.

Pension & Restaurant U Janů (☎ 311 681 210; info@ujana.cz; s/d incl breakfast 700/1000Kč) On the road up to the castle, this atmospheric place has dark wood décor and a decent dollop of authentic charm. The restaurant's good, but the staff can be grumpy.

Ubytovna (☎ 311 681 221; dm 120Kč; **P**) On the main road, next to the sports ground and Pap Oil garage, this has basic beds at knockdown prices.

Autokemp Karlštejn (☎ 311 681 263; tent per person 60Kč; **P**) On the northern side of the river, 500m west of the bridge, this has a top location and staff can help organise a canoe for a paddle on the river.

Other recommendations:

Pension Slon (☎ 311 681 550; s/d incl breakfast 500/1000Kč) Away from the crowds, behind the station (follow the elephant signs).

Restaurant Česká hospoda (mains 60-150Kč) Cheap(ish) Czech eats en route to the castle.

Getting There & Away

Trains depart hourly from Prague's Smíchov station (40Kč, 35 minutes). There are return departures from Karlštejn until about 10pm.

BEROUN

pop 17,500

Beroun's recent makeover has made the most of the old town gates and 14th-century walls, and has brought the town a pleasant, almost Mediterranean feel. Southwest of Prague, Beroun is now an attractive base for exploring Křivoklát, Karlštejn, the Koněprusy Caves and the hiking trails of the Berounka river basin.

Orientation & Information

The town's main square, Husovo náměstí, is 500m north of the train station. A not-very-useful **municipal tourist office** (☎ 311 654 321; mic@muberoun.cz; Husovo náměstí 69; 8.30am-12.30pm & 1-6pm Mon-Fri, until noon Sat) is on the southeastern corner of the square. **ČSOB** (Husovo náměstí 38) has a currency exchange and ATM. The bus station is east of the square, past the tourist office and across the river.

Sleeping & Eating

Hotel Parkan (☎ 311 624 372; rtot@iol.cz; Horno-hradebni 162; s/d incl breakfast 1200/1600Kč; **P**) In a quiet pedestrianised alleyway off Husovo's southwestern corner, this has lashings of class and excellent rooms with satellite TV.

Hotel Český dvůr (☎ 311 621 411; hotelceskydvur@centrum.cz; Husovo náměstí 86; s/d 350/600Kč) It's a bit rickety, but this passable place is slap-bang in the heart of the action and there's a decent in-house Asian restaurant.

There is a **camp site** (☎ 311 623 294; Vančurova 1126; tent per person 60Kč; **P**) 800m northeast of Husovo across the river.

Restaurace Na Baště (Hornohradebni; mains 90-130Kč) Just across from Hotel Parkan, and also competing for the window box of the year award, this cosy Czech place has good food and plenty of character.

Billiard Club U Brány (☎ 311 623 724; Husovo náměstí) Under Prague Gate (Pražské Bráné), this offers lively crowds, pool tables, a terrace for sipping coffee and...erm...neon trim.

Getting There & Away

From Prague it's a beautiful train ride along the Berounka river (64Kč, 45 minutes). Express trains leave about every two hours from Prague's Hlavní nádraží, while local trains leave more frequently from the Smíchov station. There are also trains to Křivoklát (40Kč, 35 minutes).

KONĚPRUSY CAVES

Human bones, the remains of a woolly rhino and a forge for counterfeiting coins are some of the oddities to be found in the guts of these impressive 600m-deep limestone **caves** (Koněpruské jeskyně; adult/concession 80/40Kč; 8am-5pm Jul-Aug, until 4pm Apr-Jun & Sep, until 3pm Oct) southwest of Prague. Take a pullover: it's a constant, chilly 10°C, and you'll be down there for 45 to 60 minutes.

There's no food to speak of except a snack bar at the caves.

Buses run the 6km from Beroun's train station to the caves at 9.25am, 11.10am, 1.40pm and 3.55pm, returning at 9.40am, 11.20am, 1.55pm and 4.10pm. The trip takes 10 minutes.

It's worth checking these times with the Beroun tourist office or with the **bus company** (☎ 311 637 081) before you go.

KŘIVOKLÁT

pop 650

Křivoklát, west of Prague, is a drowsy village beside the Rakovnický potok river. Half the pleasure of visiting Křivoklát Castle is getting there – by train up the wooded Berounka valley.

Although the castle was once a celebrated hunting lodge, the region is now included in the Křivoklát Protected Landscape Region and is a Unesco 'biosphere preservation' area.

The valley is dotted with holiday bungalows and hemmed in by limestone bluffs. On weekdays you'll find none of the crowds associated with places like Karlštejn.

Orientation

From Hotel Sýkora in Křivoklát village, climb up the road about 500m to the castle turn-off.

Křivoklát Castle

With origins stretching back to the 12th century, **Křivoklát** (☎ 313 558 120; www.krivoklat.cz; adult/concession 60/35Kč, or in English 120/70Kč; ◷ 9am-noon & 1-5pm Tue-Sun Jun-Aug, until 4pm May & Sep, until 3pm Apr & Oct, until 3pm Sat & Sun only Mar, Nov & Dec) is one of the oldest Czech castles, surviving seemingly endless renovations as a prettified chateau with roots in the whimsy of 19th-century Romanticism. Its **chapel** is one of the Czech Republic's finest, with unaltered late-Gothic interiors full of intricate polychrome carvings. The altar is decorated with angels carrying instruments of torture – a legacy of the castle's 16th century role as a political prison.

Right under the chapel are the **prison** and **torture chambers**. The **Knights' Hall** features a permanent collection of late-Gothic religious sculpture and painted panels. Across one end of the 1st floor is the 25m-long **King's Hall**, the second-biggest Gothic hall in the republic, after Vladislav Hall in Prague Castle. There is also a **library** of 52,000 volumes. The full tour takes about 70 minutes.

If you've got the gear and an extra day or two, consider walking the fine 18km trail (marked red) southwest up the Berounka valley to Skryje. It starts on the western side of Rakovnický potok near the train stop.

Sleeping & Eating

Hotel Sýkora (☎ 313 558 114; d incl breakfast 900Kč; Ⓟ) This family-run place, with a decent restaurant and beer hall, has comfy rooms with shared bathroom and a friendly atmosphere. It's in Křivoklát village itself.

Pension restaurace U Jelena (☎ 313 558 530; Hradební 53; d incl breakfast 1500Kč; Ⓟ) Across the road, this modern place is slightly more polished and rather less rustic.

There are camping grounds about 3km up the Berounka river from Křivoklát at Višňová, across the river at Branov (cross at Roztoky) and at Skryje.

Getting There & Away

The best trains run from Prague's Hlavní nádraží and Smíchov stations via Beroun. Plenty of trains run to Beroun, the key is making sure there's a good connection from there. Expect a trip from Prague of at least 1¾ hours each way (98Kč).

LIDICE

When British-trained, Czechoslovak paratroops assassinated Reichsprotektor Reinhard Heydrich in June 1942, the Nazis took a savage revenge. Picking – apparently at random – the mining and foundry village of Lidice, 18km northwest of Prague, they proceeded on 10 June to obliterate it from the face of the earth. All its men were shot, all the women and the older children shipped to the Ravensbrück concentration camp, and the younger children farmed out to German foster homes. The village was systematically burned and bulldozed so that no trace remained. Of its 500 inhabitants, 192 men, 60 women and 88 children eventually died.

The atrocity electrified the world and triggered a campaign to preserve the village's memory. The site is now a green field, eloquent in its silence, dotted with a few memorials and the reconstructed foundations of a farm where most of the men were murdered.

Nearby is a **museum** (www.lidice-memorial.cz; adult/concession 50/20Kč; ◷ 9am-6pm Apr-Sep, until 4pm Oct-Mar) that recreates the village in photographs and text, and also has chilling SS film of its destruction.

Getting There & Away

Lidice is on the bus line to Kladno, half an hour from Prague (18Kč). Buses leave Prague from opposite Hotel Diplomat, by Dejvická metro station. Direct (*přímý spoj*) services to Kladno don't stop at Lidice, but anything serving Buštěhrad does: about every hour on weekdays, every two hours on Saturday and every two or three hours on Sunday.

KOUNOV STONES

The **Kounov Stones** (Kamenné řady u Kounova), west of Prague, are a grid of over 2000 small menhirs (standing stones), dating from Neolithic (late Stone Age) times. Their exact use is a mystery, but they were most likely part of an astronomical calendar-observatory. They're similar to sites found around Western Europe, but are the only array of its kind in central Europe.

This is only for those with a real interest in such sites. Stonehenge it's not – most of the stones are less than a metre across, and buried in tall grass in a forest. Over the years many bigger ones have been taken for building materials.

Getting There & Away

Getting there is a pain without a car. Kounov village is 6km west of Hředle, which is 10km north of Rakovník. Or it's 45 minutes by bus from Rakovník (34Kč); from Prague's Hradčanská bus stop at the metro station buses leave hourly for Rakovník (55Kč; 1½ hours).

At Kounov, turn north by a pond; 1.5km up the hill, past the train line there is a signposted trailhead at an intersection. Take the road on your right and follow the horizontal, blue-line trail. After walking for 2km up the track, fork right onto a nature trail with diagonal green markings for 1.5km, then go through the woods and around an open field. At the other side of the field is a house near which are signboards for the nature trail. The stones are at nature-trail signboard No 7.

MĚLNÍK

pop 19,500

Pretty Mělník, north of Prague, sprawls over a rocky promontory surrounded by the flat sweep of Bohemia's modest wine-growing region. Staunchly Hussite in its sympathies, the town was flattened by Swedish troops in the Thirty Years' War, but the castle was rebuilt as a prettier, less threatening chateau and the centre retains a strong historical identity. Modernity has caught up with the town's trailing edge, bringing a clutch of factories to its outskirts, but views from the castle side are untouched and Mělník remains a good bet for a spot of wine-tasting bacchanalia far from the bustle of the capital.

Orientation

Turn right out of the bus station and take the first left on Jaroše, which climbs up to the old town. Beyond the old gate tower, bear right into náměstí Míru, an arcaded square lined with pastel-tinted Renaissance and baroque façades. Take the first left along Svatováclavská to Mělník Chateau and the Church of SS Peter & Paul.

Information

The **tourist information centre** (☎ 315 627 503; infocentrum@melnik.cz; náměstí Míru 11; ☼ 9am-5pm May-Sep, Mon-Fri only Oct-Apr) sells maps and historical guides, and can help with accommodation.

KB (náměstí Míru 26) has an ATM and exchange desk.

Sights

CHATEAU

The Renaissance **chateau** (zámek Mělník; ☎ 315 622 121; adult/concession 60/30Kč; ☼ 10am-6pm) was acquired by the Lobkovic family in 1739. They opened it to the public in 1990.

You can wander through the former living quarters, crowded with the family's rich collection of baroque furniture and 17th- and 18th-century paintings. Additional rooms have changing exhibits of modern works and a fabulous collection of 17th-century maps detailing Europe's great cities.

Another tour descends to 14th-century **wine cellars** where you can taste the chateau's wines (70/110Kč for two/six wines). A shop in the courtyard sells the chateau's own label.

CHURCH OF SS PETER & PAUL

This 15th-century Gothic **church** (kostel sv Petra a Pavla), with baroque furnishings and tower, is worth a look. Remnants of its Romanesque predecessor have been incorporated into the rear of the building.

The old crypt is now an **ossuary** (admission 30Kč; ☼ 9.30am-12.30pm & 1.15-4pm Tue-Sun), packed with the bones of some 10,000 people dug up to make room for 16th-century plague victims, and arranged in macabre patterns.

REGIONAL MUSEUM

The ho-hum **regional museum** (☎ 315 630 922; www.muzeum-melnik.cz - Czech only; náměstí Míru 54; adult/concession 20/10Kč; ☼ 9am-noon & 1-5pm Tue-Sun) has exhibitions on viticulture, folk architecture and children's toys.

Sleeping & Eating

Hotel U Rytířů (☎ 315 621 440; jansladecek@seznam.cz; Svatováclavská 17; d incl breakfast 2100Kč) Right next to the castle, this opulent little place has plush, apartment-style rooms with all the trimmings.

Penzión V podzámčí (☎ 315 622 889; hrzi@post.cz; Seiferta 167; s/d incl breakfast 650/1300Kč) This reasonably central place (three blocks from náměstí Míru, to the left as you face the chateau) has modestly modern rooms above a Bohemia crystal shop.

Autocamp Mělník (☎ 315 623 856; fax 315 626 568; Klášterní 717; tent per person 65Kč; **P**) The camping ground is northeast of the centre.

Restaurace Sv Václav (☎ 315 622 126; Svatováclavská 22; mains 150Kč) Dark wood décor, cigar humidors, red leather seats and quality Czech fare conspire to make this one of Mělník's best restaurants.

Drinking

Noční Bar Díra (☎ 315 624 700; náměstí Míru) This Irish-style bar is a good spot for a pre- (or post-) dinner Guinness.

The best local white and red wines are both called Ludmilla, after the saint and grandmother of St Wenceslas. One of the best places to taste and buy them is in the chateau or at **Moravenka Vinoteka** (☎ 315 625 614; Palackého 136), just off Míru.

Getting There & Away

On weekdays, buses (36Kč, 45 minutes) run to Mělník every 30 to 60 minutes from Prague's nádraží Holešovice metro station, and less often from Florenc bus station. At weekends Florenc is your best bet.

VELTRUSY

This primly symmetrical chateau north of Prague was built in the early 18th century as a summer retreat for the aristocratic Chotek family. As the Choteks collaborated with the Nazis in WWII, the Czechoslovak government seized the chateau and expelled them.

Sadly, the chateau was badly damaged during the 2002 floods and is closed for repairs until further notice. Check with tourist information in Prague for the latest opening times.

PŘEROV NAD LABEM

In this village east of Prague is the **Labe River Region Ethnographic Museum** (Polabské národopisné muzeum; ☎ 325 565 272; adult/concession 40/20Kč; ◷ 9am-5pm Tue-Sun Apr-Oct), the oldest of Bohemia's open-air museums of traditional architecture. It was established in 1895, soon after the first museum of its type opened in Stockholm (the Swedish word for such a museum, skansen, has stuck). Contrived as skansens are, they are a unique aid to visualising past times.

This one was started around a Přerov house that was already here: the 'Old Bohemian Cottage', which is dressed in herringbone timber-cladding and carved ornaments. Other buildings have been brought in piecemeal from around the region: over a dozen houses, as well as belfries, pigsties and decorated beehives. Staff tend gardens and raise bees using traditional methods. An English-language brochure is 20Kč extra.

Infrequent buses run via Mochov to/from Prague's Černý Most (20Kč, 30 minutes).

KUTNÁ HORA

pop 22,000

Now dwarfed by 21st century Prague, Kutná Hora once marched in step with the capital and, with a little help from fate, might even have stolen its crown as the heart and soul of Bohemia. Enriched by the silver ore that ran in threads through the surrounding hills, the medieval city once enjoyed explosive growth, becoming the seat of Wenceslas II's royal mint in 1308 and the residence of Wenceslas IV just under 100 years later. But while boomtime Kutná Hora was Prague's undisputed understudy, the town tripped out of history when the silver mines began to splutter and run dry in the 16th century; a demise hastened by the Thirty Years' War and certified by the devastating fire of 1770. While the capital continued to expand, its sister city largely vanished from sight.

Which is not to say everyone has forgotten about it. Largely reminiscent of Prague 400 years ago, modern Kutná Hora is an A-list tourist attraction, luring visitors with a smorgasbord of historic sights and more than a touch of nostalgic whimsy. Standing on the ramparts surrounding the mighty Cathedral of St Barbara, looking out across rooftops eerily reminiscent of Prague's Malá Strana, it's all too easy to indulge in spot of melancholic what-could-have-been.

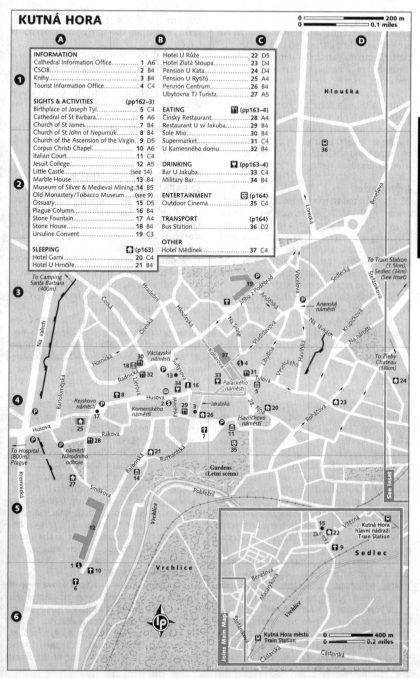

KUTNÁ HORA

INFORMATION	
Cathedral Information Office	1 A6
ČSOB	2 B4
Knihy	3 B4
Tourist Information Office	4 C4

SIGHTS & ACTIVITIES	(pp162–3)
Birthplace of Joseph Tyl	5 C4
Cathedral of St Barbara	6 A6
Church of St James	7 B4
Church of St John of Nepumuk	8 B4
Church of the Ascension of the Virgin	9 D5
Corpus Christi Chapel	10 A6
Italian Court	11 C4
Jesuit College	12 A5
Little Castle	(see 14)
Marble House	13 B4
Museum of Silver & Medieval Mining	14 B5
Old Monastery/Tobacco Museum	(see 9)
Ossuary	15 D5
Plague Column	16 B4
Stone Fountain	17 A4
Stone House	18 C3
Ursuline Convent	19 C3

SLEEPING	(p163)
Hotel Garni	20 C4
Hotel U Hrnčíře	21 B4

Hotel U Růže	22 D5
Hotel Zlatá Stoupa	23 D4
Pension U Kata	24 D4
Pension U Rytířů	25 A4
Penzión Centrum	26 B4
Ubytovna TJ Turista	27 A5

EATING	(pp163–4)
Čínský Restaurant	28 A4
Restaurant U sv Jakuba	29 B4
Sole Mio	30 B4
Supermarket	31 C4
U Kamenného domu	32 B4

DRINKING	(pp163–4)
Bar U Jakuba	33 C4
Military Bar	34 B4

ENTERTAINMENT	(p164)
Outdoor Cinema	35 C4

TRANSPORT	(p164)
Bus Station	36 D2

OTHER	
Hotel Mědínek	37 C4

Orientation

The historic centre is compact enough to see on foot. Most attractions lie between the central square, Palackého náměstí, and the Cathedral of St Barbara in the southwestern corner of town.

The bus station is 500m north of the town centre. Although there's a train station near Kutná Hora's old town, trains from Prague stop only at Sedlec, 3km to the northeast.

The user-friendly town centre has almost too many signs. Quite a few places accommodate disabled visitors.

Information

The helpful **tourist information office** (informační centrum; ☎ 327 512 378; www.kh.cz; Palackého náměstí 377; ☯ 9am-6pm May-Sep, until 4pm Mon-Fri Oct-Apr) can arrange accommodation, tours and guides. It also has Internet access (1Kč per minute) and an attached **alchemy museum** (muzeum alchymie; adult/concession 30/20Kč; ☯ 10am-5pm) – if you're really bored.

ČSOB (Husova 108) has an exchange desk and ATM; the **post office** (Husova 149) is nearby.

Knihy (82/6 Jakubská) has a good selection of maps and the **hospital** (okresní nemocnice; ☎ 327 503 111; Kouřimská) is about 1km west of the main square.

Sights

ITALIAN COURT

The **Italian Court** (Vlašský dvůr; ☎ 327 512 873; guide@mu.kutnahora.cz; Havlíčkovo náměstí; adult/concession 70/50Kč; ☯ 9am-6pm Apr-Sep, 10am-5pm Mar & Oct, 10am-4pm Nov-Feb) gets its name from the Italian experts brought in by Wenceslas II to kick-start the Royal Mint here. A palace, chapel and tower were added a century later by Wenceslas IV, who subsequently decided to move in. When the mint closed in the early 18th century it became the town hall. The guided tour (with translated text) is worth it for a look at the few historical rooms open to the public.

The oldest remaining part, the (now bricked-up) niches in the courtyard, were **minters' workshops**. The original **treasury rooms** now hold an exhibit on coins and minting.

In Wenceslas IV's **Audience Hall** are 19th-century murals of two important events that took place here: the 1471 election of Vladislav II Jagiello as king (the angry man in white is Matthias Corvinus, the loser), and an agreement between Wenceslas IV

and Jan Hus (then rector of Charles University) to alter the university's German/Czech ratio.

About all that remains of Wenceslas IV's **Chapel of SS Wenceslas & Vladislav** (kaple sv Václava a Vladislava) is the oriel (bay window), which is best seen from the courtyard – although the 1904 Art Nouveau interior renovation is very striking.

The **Galérie Félixe Jeneweina**, just inside the courtyard, has changing art exhibits with the same opening hours as the mint.

ITALIAN COURT TO CATHEDRAL OF ST BARBARA

Around the corner from the Italian Court is the colossal **Church of St James** (kostel sv Jakuba), begun in 1330 but only completed a century later. Passing south of the church, you come to **Ruthardská**, a venerable and very photogenic lane running up beside the old town walls. It's named after Rožina Ruthard who, according to local legend, was sealed alive in a closet by her medieval burgher father.

At the top of the lane is the **Little Castle** (Hrádek), originally part of the town's fortifications. It was rebuilt in the 15th century as the residence of Jan Smíšek, administrator of the royal mines, who grew rich from silver he illegally mined right under the building. It's now the **Museum of Silver & Medieval Mining** (☎ 327 512 159; muzeum@kutno horsko.cz; Barborská 28; adult/concession 60/30Kč; ☯ 9am-6pm Tue-Sun May, Jun & Sep, from 10am Jul & Aug, 9am-5pm Apr & Oct). If you get off on small spaces, you can also descend into Smíšek's mine for 50Kč extra. During the summer months it is best to book in advance.

The approach to the cathedral up Barborská passes 13 crumbling **Gothic statues** and a congregation of knick-knack stalls, *á la* Prague's Charles Bridge. The former **Jesuit College** (1700) is the biggest in the Czech Republic after Prague's Klementinum.

CATHEDRAL OF ST BARBARA

The miners' guilds of Kutná Hora pipped Prague in the cathedral department: their Gothic **Cathedral of St Barbara** (chram sv Barbory; ☎ 776 363 938; adult/concession 30/15Kč; ☯ 9am-5.30pm Tue-Sun May-Sep, 9-11.30am & 1-4pm Apr & Oct, 9-11.30am & 2-3.30pm Nov-Mar), dedicated to the patron saint of miners, is one of the finest Gothic churches in Europe.

Work was started in 1380, interrupted during the Hussite Wars and abandoned in 1558 when the silver began to run out. It was completed in neo-Gothic style as late as the end of the 19th century.

Inside, eight **ambulatory chapels** surround the main altar, some with vivid frescoes – including mining scenes – dating from the 15th century. The lofty, bright ceiling vault is covered in a tangle of ribs, stars and floral patterns, and the coats of arms of the miners' guilds and local nobility. The northwest chapel has an eye-popping mural of the *Vision of St Ignatius*.

On the hillside below the cathedral is the less exciting **Corpus Christi Chapel** (kaple Božího těla; adult/concession 20/10Kč; 10am-6pm May-Sep, 10am-5pm Apr & Oct, 10am-4pm Nov-Mar), built in the 14th century.

Tickets for both are available from a small information office at the end of Barborská.

OTHER SIGHTS
From the Jesuit College, walk through náměstí Národního odboje and turn left on Husova to see bits of the **old city walls**. Return along Husova, via Rejskovo náměstí, with its 1495 Gothic **Stone Fountain** (Kamenná kašna) to the baroque former **Church of St John Of Nepomuk** (kostel sv Jana Nepomuckého; adult/concession 20/10Kč; 10am-5pm).

Cross via Lierova to Radnická. The Gothic confection at No 183 is the **Stone House** (Kamenný dům), a burgher's house dating from 1490, now home to a **museum** (adult/concession 40/20Kč; 9am-6pm Tue-Sun May, Jun & Sep, 10am-6pm Jul-Aug, 10am-5pm Apr & Oct) with exhibitions on mining, burghers' culture and 17th- to 19th-century life.

East and then south is Šultysova, once part of the town's medieval marketplace, lined with handsome townhouses, in particular the **Marble House** (dům U Mramorů) at No 173. At the bottom of the street is a 1715 **plague column**.

Across Palackého náměstí, walk down Tylova to No 507, the museum and **birthplace of Josef Tyl** (Tyluv dům; 327 512 159; adult/concession 30/15Kč; 3-5pm Mon-Fri), the 19th-century playwright who wrote *Kde domov můj?* (Where Is My Home?). This became part of the Czech national anthem.

Cross the square again to Kollárova and turn right on Jiřího z Poděbrad. Two blocks

down is the former **Ursuline Convent** (klášter Voršilek), with a 1743 **chapel** by Kilian Dientzenhofer.

Sleeping
Hotel Zlatá Stoupa (327 511 540; zlatastoupa@iol.cz; Tylova 426; s/d incl breakfast 1200/1800Kč;) The ace of plush (well, here at least) has excellent rooms with period furniture and satellite TV.

Pension U Rytířů (327 512 256; Rejskovo náměstí 123; s/d 300/600Kč) In a 14th-century building, this offers a taste of the good old days with a warm atmosphere and creaking floors.

Hotel U Hrnčíře (327 512 113; Barborská 24; d incl breakfast 1000Kč) This beautifully ornate pink townhouse has stylish rooms and an adventurous kitchen – pre-order your whole piglet on a spit now!

Penzión Centrum (327 514 218; kv.info.kh@pha.pvtnet.cz; Jakubská 57; s/d incl breakfast 700/1000Kč) Tucked away off the main drag, this has snug rooms and a sunny (at least when the sun's out) garden.

Ubytovna TJ Turista (327 512 960; náměstí Národního odboje 56; dm 150Kč;) This attractive, central hostel has space in four-bed rooms. It gets very busy and reception opens erratically – book ahead.

Camping Santa Barbara (327 512 051; tent per person 70Kč;) The camp site is northwest of town off Česká, near the cemetery *(hřbitov)*.

Other recommendations:
Pension U Kata (327 515 096; Uhelná 596; s/d 250/400Kč) Out of the way, but very cheap.
Hotel Garni (327 514 618; kh_hotels@iol.cz; Havlíčkovo náměstí 513; d incl breakfast 990Kč) Small and intimate with creature comforts.

Eating & Drinking
Sole Mio (327 515 505; cnr Václavské náměstí & Česká; pizza 80-110Kč) Sunflowers, dried sheaves of corn and a collection of porcelain suns bring more warmth to this place than a clutch of scorching summer days. And the pizza's not bad either.

Čínský restaurant (327 514 151; náměstí Národního odboje 48; mains 70-250Kč) In a plush, historic building, this is more upmarket than most, with a wide range of Chinese classics. It's closed on Sunday and Monday.

Restaurant U sv Jakuba (327 512 275; Vysokostelská 104; mains 60-150Kč) This is unabashedly touristy, but the garden terrace is pleasant and the eclectic menu is distinctly multilingual.

U Kamenného domu (☎ 327 514 426; Lierova 4/147; mains 70-150Kč) This cheerful bar/eatery has had a crack at going stylish, with muslin drapes and fresh flowers creating a colourful, floaty feel. The food's reliable.

Other recommendations:

Bar U Jakuba (Palackého náměstí) Has Guinness on tap.

Military Bar (☎ 602 478 942; Husova) Booze and music until 5am (weekends).

Supermarket (potraviny; cnr Palackého náměstí & Tylova).

Entertainment

An **outdoor cinema** (kino) sets up shop during the summer months in the gardens below the Italian Court. Ask tourist information for details.

Getting There & Away

Around 70km southeast of Prague, the fastest route to Kutná Hora is Highway 12 via Kolín and Sedlec; the prettiest is route 333 via Kostelec.

Several daily fast trains go to Kutná Hora hlavní nádraží (main station) in Sedlec, including seven departing from Prague's main station (98Kč, one hour). Each has a good connection by local train (10Kč, eight minutes) to Kutná Hora město station, adjacent to the old town.

Long-distance buses leave from Prague's Florenc station, departing approximately seven times each weekday (70Kč, 1¼ hours). There are also some local buses from Prague's Želivského metro station; however, there are very few services on Sunday and virtually none on Saturday.

For all bus and train times and prices, visit www.idos.cz.

Getting Around

Local buses on Masarykova go to/from Sedlec and the train station about hourly on weekdays, less often on weekends. Buy a ticket from the driver (6Kč).

Hotel Mědínek (☎ 327 512 741; Palackého náměstí) rents out bikes for 50/250Kč per hour/day.

AROUND KUTNÁ HORA
Ossuary Chapel of All Saints

The home of a ghoulish ossuary, Sedlec is little more than a drab suburb of Kutná Hora. Sedlec's medieval boom-time was ignited when a 13th-century abbot came back from Jerusalem with a pocketful of earth and sprinkled it on the local monas-

tery's graveyard. The Cistercian monastery, Bohemia's earliest, had been around since 1142, but when the plague struck demand for grave plots skyrocketed. With tens of thousands already buried here, the bones began to pile up and the small 14th-century **All Saints' Chapel** (kaple Všech svatých) was soon pressed into service as an **ossuary** (adult/concession 30/20Kč; ⏲ 8am-6pm Apr-Sep, 9am-noon & 1-5pm Oct, 9am-4pm Nov-Mar).

When Joseph II abolished the monasteries, the Schwarzenberg family bought this one, and in 1870 a Czech woodcarver named František Rint laughed in the face of death by indulging in an extraordinarily imaginative flurry of bone art. Largely immune to decay, his work is still visible in the ossuary today; a ghoulish congregation of bone crosses, chalices, coats of arms and even an extraordinary chandelier made from every bone in the human body. Rint even signed his name in bones, at the foot of the stairs. Multilingual tour sheets give you the low-down.

Down on the main road is the monastery's **Church of the Ascension of the Virgin** (kostel Nanebevzetí Panny Marie), which was renovated at the beginning of the 18th century by Giovanni Santini in his 'baroque-Gothic' style, unique to Bohemia. It was once again closed for renovations at time of writing but should open again shortly. Nearby, the old monastery is now part of a Phillip Morris tobacco factory, which has a small **tobacco museum** (Muzeum Tabaku; admission free; ⏲ 10am-4pm Mon-Fri).

SLEEPING

Hotel U růže (☎ 327 524 115; hotelruze@khora.cz; Zámecká 52; s/d incl breakfast 1100/1300Kč) If you can ignore the rumbling of tour bus engines, this atmospheric hotel has a nice garden and comfortable rooms.

GETTING THERE & AWAY

The ossuary is 2km northeast of Kutná Hora and can be reached by local bus. Some buses stop by the church, and some opposite the ossuary, two blocks up Zámecká from the church.

Žleby Chateau

Dating from around 1289, the first castle to stand here was flattened by the Hussites during the wars of the early 15th century.

Žleby has since worn a variety of architectural faces, acquiring its latest romanticist look between 1849 and 1868 at the behest of its then owner, Karel Vincent Auersperg. Typically chocolate box in appearance, modern-day Žleby sports all the required fairy-tale accoutrements, from pastel décor to gleaming spires.

The Auerspergs lived here until 1945, when they fled to Austria, leaving everything behind. The **chateau** (☎ 327 398 121; www.stc.npu.cz - Czech only; ☺ 8am-5pm Tue-Sun May-Aug, from 9am Sep, 9am-4pm Sat & Sun only Apr & Oct) is therefore in immaculate – and authentic – shape, offering a glimpse of how the other half lived in Czechoslovakia in the early 20th century.

Inside it's all armour and mounted firearms, wood panelling and leather wallpaper, rococo flourishes and a treasure trove of old furniture. Highlights include the **Knights' Hall**, with a huge baroque cupboard and rows of Czech and German glass; the **Duchess Study**, with a replica Rubens on the ceiling and a fantastic door of inlaid wood; and the kitchen, fitted out with the 19th-century's most up-to-date equipment.

There are two tours: Tour 1 (adult/concession 50/20Kč) takes in the romanticist interior, the chapel and kitchen, while Tour 2 (75/40Kč) also includes access to the large tower, including sweeping views of the surrounding area.

GETTING THERE & AWAY
The chateau is accessible from Kutná Hora by bus (40Kč, one hour). There are at least half a dozen morning connections, but you must change at Čáslav. Get off at Žleby náměstí, the square at the foot of the chateau. Check return times, as buses stop around 5pm.

KOLÍN
pop 31,000
A glimpse of Czech life, minus the Central Bohemian crowds, can be had in this sluggish, seldom-visited town east of Prague on the Labe river. Plans to build a $1.3 billion car plant here look set to change Kolín's economic fortunes and probably its lazy charm to boot.

The town centre is next to the river, an 800m walk from the adjacent bus and train stations. The **tourist information office** (městské informační centrum; ☎ 321 712 021; Na Hradbách 157; ☺ 9am-noon & 1-5pm Mon-Fri, until 3pm Sat & Sun) also offers Internet access.

ČSOB (Karlovo náměstí) has an exchange counter and ATM.

Sights
Kolín has a picturesque central square (Karlovo náměstí) with a baroque **Marian column** (1682) and **fountain** (1780) in the middle. A block away on Brandlova is the towering **Gothic Church of St Bartholomew**. The **Regional Museum** (regionální muzeum Kolní; adult/concession 15/8Kč; ☺ 9am-noon & 2-4pm Tue-Sun) is next to this church.

Festivals & Events
The **Kmochův Festival** (www.kmochuv-kolin.cz - Czech only) of brass-band music in June is Kolín's festival highlight.

Sleeping & Eating
The tourist office staff can help with cheap accommodation and private rooms.

Hotel U Rabina (☎ 321 724 463; rabin.pension@worldonline.cz; Karolíny Světlé 151; s/d incl breakfast 1020/1450Kč) Just north of the church, this has snug period-style rooms and a decent restaurant.

Hotel American (☎ 321 713 824; Kovářská 101; s/d 300/600Kč) This place has simple but conveniently located rooms above a raucous beer hall. It is just around the corner from the main square.

Stoletá (Kutnohorská 33; mains 50-120Kč) Dark wood, pub-style décor, Guinness on tap and a spread of Czech bar food make this a good all-round haunt come nightfall.

Getting There & Away
Buses run regularly to Kutná Hora (15Kč, 15 minutes), and Prague (56Kč, one hour). Kolín is also a major junction on the Prague–Košice train line, with frequent services to and from Prague (88Kč, 45 minutes).

North Bohemia

North Bohemia is both a beauty and a beast. While its quieter corners offer some of the country's most spectacular landscapes and its historic towns a clutch of fine cultural monuments and museums, the region remains the industrial heart of the Czech Republic and its factories, mines and chimneys are rarely far from view.

Stick to the main roads and first impressions may well be of a landscape crisscrossed with freeways, electricity pylons and sooty buildings, a region with plenty of industrial oomph, but very little worth getting a camera out for. If you make the effort to go exploring, however, the reality is very different. While North Bohemia does bear the rugged features that come with centuries of hard graft, the area is a Pandora's box, containing some of the country's more unique treasures, as well as some of its grimiest industrial eyesores. In fact, while many areas of the Czech Republic specialise in picture-postcard town squares and fairy-tale chateaux, North Bohemia's attractions have a wilder, grittier edge, ranging from the imposing Napoleonic fortress of Terezín, which later became a Nazi concentration camp and today contains the fascinating Museum of the Ghetto, to the sublime landscapes and rambling opportunities of the Sandstone Rocks of Labe. Even the large river port of Děčín, once choked with coal smoke, has evolved into a lively city surrounded by a clutch of heavily forested hills, where 21st century Czech life can be sampled away from the madding crowds of tour groups and souvenir vendors.

NORTH BOHEMIA

HIGHLIGHTS

- Confront the region's darker side in the fortress of **Terezín** (p169), a former Nazi concentration camp

- Wander through the prehistoric canyons and rock formations of the **Sandstone Rocks of Labe** (p178) to the colossal Pravčická Gate

- Relax among the sleepy streets of **Litoměřice** (p171)

- Sample Czech urban life away from the crowds in the river port of **Děčín** (p174)

- Soak up the splendour of **Ploskovice Chateau** (p174)

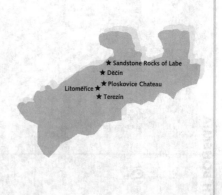

★ Sandstone Rocks of Labe
★ Děčín
★ Ploskovice Chateau
Litoměřice ★
★ Terezín

NORTH BOHEMIA

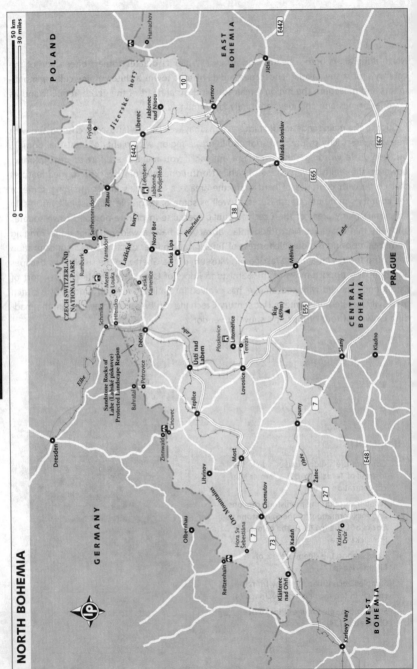

TEREZÍN

pop 2900

It is perhaps no coincidence that Terezín (Theresienstadt in German) and terror share the same first three letters. A massy bulwark of stone and earth, this immense fortress was built in 1780 by Emperor Joseph II with a single purpose in mind: to keep the Prussians out. Ironically, when the Germans took control of Terezín during the WWII, this role was reversed and the walls were employed as a grim holding pen for Jews bound for extermination camps. While the surviving structure has all the presence of the country's other chocolate-box chateaux, it has none of their refinement. After the rich, gentrified structures of many Czech towns, Terezín is a stark, but profoundly evocative monument to a darker aspect of central Europe's past.

The bleakest phase of Terezín's history began in 1940 when the Gestapo established a prison in the Lesser Fortress. Evicting the townspeople from the Main Fortress the following year, the Nazis subsequently transformed the structure into a transit camp, through which some 150,000 European Jews eventually passed en route to extermination camps. For most, conditions were appalling. Between April and September 1942 the ghetto's population increased from 12,968 to 58,491, leaving each prisoner with only 1.65 sq m of space and causing disease and starvation on a terrifying scale. In the same period, there was a fifteen-fold increase in the number of deaths within the prison walls.

Ironically, Terezín later became the centre-piece of one of Nazism's more extraordinary public-relations coups. Official visitors to the fortress, which was billed as a kind of Jewish 'refuge', saw a town with a Jewish administration, banks, shops, cafés, schools and a thriving cultural life – it even had a jazz band – a charade that twice completely fooled international observers.

The reality was a relentlessly increasing concentration of prisoners, regular trains departing for the gas chambers of Auschwitz, and the death by starvation, disease or suicide of some 35,000 Jews.

Though lacking the immediate horror of places like Auschwitz, Terezín has a potent impact and is an easy day trip from Prague.

Orientation

Public buses stop at náměstí Československé armády, the central square area of the town within the Main Fortress. The Lesser Fortress is an 800m-walk east across the Ohře river. In between is a huge tour-bus parking lot.

Information

Pretty much all the information you need can be picked up from the museum (see the following section).

Česká Spořitelna (náměstí Československé armády) has an ATM and exchange desk. There is also a post office near the northern side of náměstí Československé armády.

Sights

Tickets for Terezín's fascinating, sights can be purchased at the **Museum of the Ghetto** (Muzeum ghetta; ☎ 416 782 576; manager@pamatnik-terezin.cz; Komenského; ☯ 9am-6pm May-Sep, until 5.30pm Oct-Apr) – or from each of the other venues – and cost 180/140Kč (adult/concession) for combination entry to the Museum of the Ghetto, Magdeburg Barracks, the Crematorium and the Lesser Fortress, or 160/130Kč (adult/concession) for the Museum of the Ghetto and Magdeburg Barracks only. The museum has good multilingual self-guide pamphlets, a large selection of books for sale, and guides for hire (some of them ghetto survivors).

MAIN FORTRESS

From the ground, the sheer scale of the knot of walls and moats that surround the **Main Fortress** (hlavní pevnost) is impossible to fathom – mainly because the town is actually inside them. In fact, when you first arrive by bus or car, you may be left thinking that the central square looks no different to 101 other small town centres. Take a peek at the aerial photograph in the Museum of the Ghetto on Komenského, or wander past the walls en route to the Lesser Fortress, however, and a very different picture begins to emerge.

At the heart of the Main Fortress, is the squared-off, boxy town of Terezín. There's little to look at except the chunky, 19th-century **Church of the Resurrection**, the arcaded **commandant's office**, the neoclassical administrative buildings on the square and the surrounding grid of houses with their awful secrets.

TEREZÍN

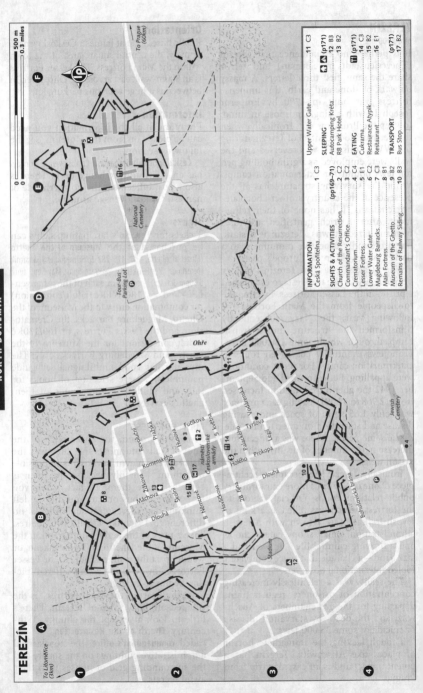

To Litoměřice
(3km)

To Prague
(60km)

500 m
0.3 miles

Ohře

National
Cemetery

Tour-Bus
Parking Lot

Jewish
Cemetery

Stadium

Revoluční
Pražská
Husova
Fučíkova
Komenského
Tyršova
náměstí
Československé
armády
Ziźkova
Máchová
Školní
Palackého
Leģí
Prokopa
B. Němcové
Havlíčkova
28. října
Holého
Dlouhá
5. května
Vodárenská
Bohušovická brána
Dlouhá

INFORMATION	
Česká Spořitelna...........................	1 C3

SIGHTS & ACTIVITIES	(pp169–71)
Church of the Resurrection............	2 C2
Commandant's Office......................	3 C2
Crematorium..................................	4 C4
Lesser Fortress..............................	5 E1
Lower Water Gate..........................	6 C2
Magdeburg Barracks.......................	7 C3
Main Fortress................................	8 B1
Museum of the Ghetto....................	9 B2
Remains of Railway Siding..............	10 B3
Upper Water Gate.........................	11 C3

SLEEPING	(p171)
Autocamping Kréta.........................	12 B3
RB Park Hotel................................	13 B2

EATING	(p171)
Cukrárna.......................................	14 C3
Restaurace Atypik..........................	15 B2
Restaurant.....................................	16 E1

TRANSPORT	
Bus Stop..	17 B2

South of the square are the anonymous remains of a **railway siding**, built by prisoners, on which loads of further prisoners arrived – and left. Two **water gates** (for access to the river) remain.

The main attraction here is the absorbing **Museum of the Ghetto** (Muzeum ghetta; ☎ 416 782 576; manager@pamatnik-terezin.cz; Komenského; 9am-6pm May-Sep, until 5.30pm Oct-Apr), which has two branches. The main museum, on Komenského by the highway, explores the rise of Nazism and life in the Terezín ghetto, using the discarded bric-a-brac of the time to startling and evocative effect. Erected in the 19th century to house the local school, the museum building was later used by the Nazis to accommodate the camp's 10- to 15-year-old boys. The haunting images painted by these children still decorate the walls.

A newer branch is in the former **Magdeburg Barracks** (Magdeburská kasárna; cnr Tyršova & Vodárenská), which served as the seat of the Jewish 'government'. Here you can visit a reconstructed dormitory for prisoners, and look at exhibits on the extraordinarily rich cultural life – music, theatre, fine arts and literature – that somehow flourished against this backdrop of fear.

Both museum branches are open from 9am to 6pm (until 5.30pm October to April), and are closed Christmas Eve to Boxing Day and New Years Day.

There is also the **Crematorium** (Kramatorium; 10am-5pm Sun-Fri Mar-Nov) in the Jewish Cemetery just off Bohušovická brána about 1km south from the main square in Terezín. There is another small exhibit here.

LESSER FORTRESS

You can take a self-guided tour of the **Lesser Fortress** (malá pevnost; 8am-6pm May-Sep, until 4.30pm Oct-Apr) through the prison barracks, isolation cells, workshops and morgues, past execution grounds and former mass graves. It would be hard to invent a more menacing location and it is while wandering through the seemingly endless tunnels beneath the walls that you can fully appreciate the vast dimensions of the fort. The Nazis' mocking concentration-camp slogan, *Arbeit Macht Frei* (work makes you free) hangs above a gate. In front of the fortress is a National Cemetery, founded in 1945 for those exhumed from mass graves.

Sleeping & Eating

Only committed history buffs, and the pathologically ghoulish, are likely to want to stay the night here.

RB Park Hotel (☎ 416 782 260; Máchova 162; s/d 210/400Kč) This central place is rough and ready, but the best bet in the Main Fortress area.

A camping ground, **Autocamping Kréta** (☎ 482 782 473; tent/hut 70/150Kč) is open April to mid-September by the stadium west of the Main Fortress.

Restaurace Atypik (☎ 416 782 780; Máchova 91; mains 60-100Kč) Atypik by name, but rather typical by nature, this bustling place offers all the predictable local favourites, with an emphasis on stodge and unapologetic meatiness.

Cukrarna (náměstí Československé armády; snacks 20-50Kč) Coffee break? Here's the place for a no-fuss, no-frills caffeine fix.

In addition to the burger joints and hot-dog vendors at the tour-bus car park, there's a **restaurant** (dishes 30-70Kč) in the former German officers' mess in the Lesser Fortress. There are also restaurants at Autocamping Kréta and RB Park Hotel.

Getting There & Away

Buses leave from Prague's Florenc bus station (25Kč, one hour) every hour or two.

Buses leave Terezín from the northeastern corner of náměstí Československé armády and run to and from Litoměřice station (3km away) roughly hourly (10Kč, 10 minutes). The last bus leaves Terezín at 6.30pm.

LITOMĚŘICE
pop 26,000

After wandering wide-eyed through Terezín, Litoměřice is your chance to exhale. Although only a few kilometres to the north of the region's infamous fortress, this quaint riverside town is a million miles from its horrors. Pastel pinks and intricate gables jostle for dominance on the main square and the town's lively bars and restaurants play host to some vibrant, after-hours action.

Once stridently Hussite, Litoměřice saw much of its Gothic face levelled during the Thirty Years' War and today the town's unassuming castle plays second fiddle to a clutch of effete Renaissance houses and impressive churches (many by esteemed 18th century architect, Ottavio Broggio).

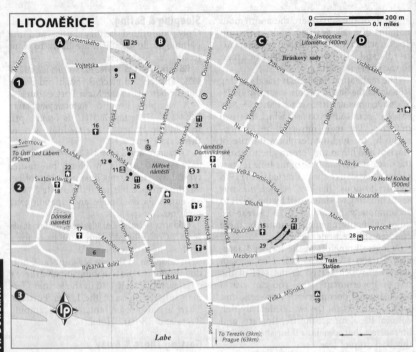

LITOMĚŘICE

But there are more than photo opportunities here. While the main square oozes old-world charm, Litoměřice is no fossil. In fact, in this youthful community, it's not a museum that occupies the old town bastion, but a bar.

Orientation

Litoměřice sits at the confluence of the Labe and Ohře rivers. From the train station or adjacent bus station, the old centre begins just across the road to the west, past the best preserved of the 14th-century walls. Walk down Dlouhá to the central square, Mírové náměstí.

Information

Internet Club Centrum (☎ 416 736 060; 1st fl, Mírové náměstí 125; 1Kč per min) A lively Internet café and bar.

Jonas Knihkupectví (jonas@kna.cz; Mírové náměstí) This bookshop sells maps.

KB bank (Mírové náměstí 37) Has an ATM and exchange desk.

Main post office (cnr Osvobození & Na Valech) Two blocks north of Mírové náměstí.

Nemocnice Litoměřice (☎ 416 723 111; Žitenická) This hospital is 1km northeast of the centre.

Tourist information office (městské informační centrum; ☎ 416 732 440; www.litomerice.cz - Czech & German only; Mírové náměstí 15/7; ⏱ 8am-6pm Mon-Sat, until 4pm Sun May-Sep, 8am-4pm Mon-Fri, until 11am Sat

Oct-Apr) Is in the town hall and can help with accommodation. From April to October it also offers sightseeing tours for 50Kč per person.

Sights

MÍROVÉ NÁMĚSTÍ

Dominating this attractive square is the Gothic tower of **All Saints Church** (kostel Všech svatých), built in the 13th century and 'Broggio-ised' in 1718. Beside it, with multiple gables, pointy arches and a copper-topped tower, is the handsome, Gothic **Old Town Hall** (Stará radnice), with a small **town museum** (Okresní Vlastivědné Muzeum Litoměřice; adult/concession 20/10Kč; ☒ 10am-5pm Tue-Sun) inside. From May to September it is possible to join a Czech (and occasionally English) tour to visit 366m of the **catacombs** (historické sklepy; ☎ 416 734 306; adult/concession 25/10Kč; ☒ 10am-5pm). The entrance is through the Radniční sklípek restaurant.

Most striking is the 1560 Renaissance **House at the Black Eagle** (dům U Černého orla; Mírové náměstí 12), covered in sgraffito biblical scenes and housing the Hotel Salva Guarda. A few doors down is the present town hall, in the 1539 **House at the Chalice** (dům U Kalicha; Mírové náměstí 15/7), with a massive Hussite chalice on the roof. This building also houses the tourist information office. The piece of baroque fruitcake is the **House of Ottavio Broggio**.

An interesting local art exhibit is housed in the **Museum and Gallery of Litoměřice Diocese** (muzeum a galerie litoměřické diocéze; ☎ 416 732 382; Mírové náměstí 16; adult/concession 20/10Kč; ☒ 9am-noon & 1-6pm Tue-Sun Apr-Sep, until 5pm Oct-Mar). The collection runs through several beautiful old burgher's houses and includes modern art, as well as works from St Stephen Cathedral.

AROUND THE SQUARE

Another Broggio original, built for the Jesuits, is just south of the square: the pink-and-white **Church of Annunciation of Our Lady** (kostel Zvěstování Panny Marie).

West of the square is another house with a Broggio face-lift, now home to the worthwhile **North Bohemia Fine Arts Gallery** (Severočeská galerie výtvarného umění; ☎ 416 732 382; Michalská 7; adult/concession 32/18Kč; ☒ 9am-noon & 1-6pm Tue-Sun Apr-Sep, until 5pm Oct-Mar). It displays work from the 14th to 20th centuries, but its pride and joy is a set of panels on the life of the Virgin from the *Litoměřice Altar-*

piece, one of Bohemia's most famous works of Renaissance art, by the anonymous 'Master of Litoměřice' (whose work also graces Prague's St Vitus Cathedral).

Other Litoměřice monastery churches of the Counter-Reformation include the remains of the **St Michael Church** (kostel sv Michala), west of the fine arts gallery, the **St James Church** (kostel sv Jakuba), which is northeast of the square on náměstí Dominikanské, and **St Ludmilla Church** (kostel sv Ludmily), southeast of the centre.

CATHEDRAL HILL

Southwest of Mírové náměstí is the weedy Dómské náměstí, site of an ancient Slavic fortress and, despite its abandoned appearance, the town's historical heart. On the way (along Dómská from the fine arts gallery), don't miss Broggio's finest work, the little **St Wenceslas Church** (kostel sv Václava; 1716).

At the top of Cathedral Hill (dómský pahorek) is the town's oldest church, the huge **St Stephen Cathedral** (katedrála sv Štěpána), built in the 11th century and rebuilt in the 17th. Spacious and Romanesque in shape, a tall arch reaches out to an 1880s belfry. Behind it is the renovated former **Bishop's Palace**.

CASTLE

The town's heavily reconstructed, 14th-century **castle** is north of Mírové náměstí, up Lidická, and was closed at time of writing. It was never a very interesting building to begin with and it now has a massive, ugly **cultural centre** (dům kultury) attached to it like a barnacle.

Sleeping

The tourist information office can help with private rooms from 250Kč per person.

Hotel Salva Guarda (☎ 416 732 506; hotel.restaurant@salva-garda.cz; Mírové náměstí 12; s/d 920/1450Kč; ☒) With a legacy stretching back to 1576 (and they won't let you forget it), this is the place for passing VIPs. The lights don't seem to get switched on much, but slick service and old school charm earn a clutch of gold stars.

U Svatého Václava (☎ 416 737 500; usvatehovaclava@hotmail.com; Svatovaclavská 12; s/d incl breakfast 600/1000Kč) Tucked away in the shadow of St Wenceslas Church, this pretty villa houses a tip-top *pension* with sauna, well-equipped rooms and a homey apron-toting owner who whips up a fine breakfast.

Labe Hotel (☎ 416 735 436; hotel_labe@volny.cz; Vrchlického 292/10; s/d incl breakfast 520/840Kč; P) You may find yourself a long way from the ground in this *1984*-style tower block, but while the building itself has fewer frills than a clean-cut kaftan, it does have 11 floors of comfy, well-priced rooms with bathrooms and TV.

Hotel Koliba (☎ 416 732 861; koliba@post.cz; Českolipská; s/d 300/600Kč) Slightly back from the road (the entrance is opposite the shiny Hennlich office), about 1km east of the centre, this decent place seems eerily empty. Still, the price is right and it sure is quiet.

Autocamp Slavoj (☎ 416 734 481; tent/bungalow 70/200Kč; P) On an island called Střelecký ostrov (Marksmen Island), directly south of the train station, this pleasant camp site is open May to September.

Eating & Drinking

Music Club Viva (☎ 606 437 783; Mezibrani; mains 80-200Kč) Housed in the beautiful old town bastion, this hip, music-oriented eatery juggles old and new with stylish aplomb. With a cocktail bar below, decent restaurant fare above and creaking wood beams galore, this is the favoured haunt of town's upwardly mobile.

Time Out (☎ 416 731 660; Jezuitská 1; mains 70-180Kč) Sports on the telly, crowds at the bar, beer on tap and a stage set for late night frolics, this lively bar/restaurant also offers a top-notch range of pastas, salads and meaty grills.

Pizzeria Sole (☎ 416 737 150; Na Valech 56; pizza 60Kč) The dodgy window décor may not holler 'Italia!', but the pizzas are cheap and cheerful at this snug little diner.

Radniční sklípek (☎ 416 734 306, Mírové náměstí 21; mains 50-150Kč) Plenty of basement beer-supping from the old school here. Line your stomach from a menu packed with hearty local favourites.

Pekárna Kodys & Hamele (Novobranská 18) Cakes and stickies from the Willy Wonka school of baking can be had from here.

Getting There & Away

There are bus connections between Litoměřice and Terezín (only 3km away) roughly hourly (10Kč, 10 minutes).

Buses from Prague's Florenc station (61Kč; 1¼ hours) to Ústí nad Labem stop here hourly.

The train trip is very tedious.

For all bus and train times and prices, visit www.idos.cz.

PLOSKOVICE
pop 344

Ottavio Broggio may have left a starburst of churches behind him, but his secular works are few and far between. The chateau here is a notable exception and makes a worthwhile diversion for those wanting to get to the bottom of the celebrated architect's work. It has more personality than any of his churches in Litoměřice, the more so for the deliciously excessive rococo interior renovations by painter Josef Navrátil, part of an 1850s overhaul for Emperor Ferdinand V.

Chateau

The guided tour of the **chateau** (☎ 416 749 092; adult/concession 40/20Kč; 🕙 9am-6pm Tue-Sun Jul-Aug, until 5pm May, Jun & Sep, until 4pm Apr & Oct) takes in about 10 rooms used by the emperor and empress (the tour's in Czech, but you can borrow an English text if there aren't enough people for an English-language tour). Highlights include the emperor's ostentatious bedroom, with unusual bidet, and the stunning main hall at the rear, with murals by Václav Vavřinec Reiner representing the four corners of the world. Most of the chateau's other murals are by the immodest Josef Navrátil: on the ceiling of the empress' study he painted himself beside her favourite sculptor, Benvenuto Cellini.

At the rear is a stately, manicured garden, complete with peacocks.

Getting There & Away

Irregular buses link Litoměřice and Ploskovice (11Kč, 20 minutes). Take a bus bound for Třebušín, but check return times with the driver as times may not be posted in Ploskovice.

DĚČÍN
pop 53,000

Recently emerging from a decades-old chrysalis of soot and grime, the Labe river port is a good example of the region's gradual regeneration, with the Department of the Environment holding it up as a fine example of a city

THE BLACK TRIANGLE

The Black Triangle (černý troûhelník) is a brown coal basin roughly spanning 70km of the North Bohemian countryside between Klášterec nad Ohří and Ústí nad Labem. The topsoil has been removed from large swaths of the land, and the brown coal mined. The resulting huge craters make the landscape look as if asteroids have crashed down here.

Brown coal is the most toxic fossil fuel, and the region burns up much of the extracted coal in factories and power stations, which belch plumes of white and yellowish smoke like a volcano. This results in acid rain, which has destroyed many of the trees in the Ore Mountains (Krušné hory). Life expectancy is several years lower than the national average here. In 1996 the so-called smog season (October to March) included 45 days when the air quality was outside the government's maximum safety level.

Things are improving now, but more than 100 villages in the vicinity of Most have been destroyed – their populations relocated – to make the way for these mines, and it will be many years yet before the landscape recovers.

'going green'. The landscape remains rather different from the one settled by the Slavic Děčané tribe (who gave the town its name) centuries ago, but some dramatic crags and hills (cut through with trails) surround the centre and moves are being made to preserve what little history remains around the main square. Either way, the city is primarily a jumping-off point for the nearby Sandstone Rocks of Labe (Labské pískovce), where fresh air and stunning vistas come as standard.

Orientation

The town has two distinct centres – Děčín proper, on the east bank of the Labe, and Podmokly on the west, at the foot of Shepherd's Wall (Pastýřská stěna). The Děčín side has the town's few historical attractions, while Podmokly has the train and bus stations.

Information

Dezka (☎ 412 531 333; dezka@space.cz; Prokopa Holého 8; ☯ 9am-5pm Mon-Fri, until noon Sat), in Podmokly, acts as the local tourist office.

There are post offices south of the train station on the corner of Podmokelská and Poštovní in Podmokly, and at náměstí Svobody on the Děčín side.

ČSOB has branches on the corner of Zbrojnická and Československých legií in Podmokly and on the corner of Řetězová and Radniční in Děčín. Both have ATMs.

Sights

OLD TOWN & CHATEAUX

A small but pretty section of old-town Děčín has been preserved at the eastern foot

of the castle. The centrepiece is the **Church of the Ascending Holy Cross** (kostel povýšení sv Kříže), with its high-domed, Romanesque exterior and its frescoed, baroque interior. From here a walled avenue, the so-called Long Ride (Dlouhá jízda), climbs to the castle, with a separate, covered walkway along one side.

Děčín's one real historical attraction is its huge, brooding **chateau** (zámek Děčín; ☎ 412 531 153) founded in 1305 by the Přemysl King Václav III. The 'baroquefied' Renaissance chateau inside is said to have 'as many rooms as the year has days'. Among its distinguished visitors was Frédéric Chopin, who composed a waltz (in A flat major) here in 1835. The castle passed into the hands of the Czechoslovak state in 1932, before becoming a garrison for German, and then Soviet troops. The Soviet army upped sticks and left in 1991, but the Long Ride, with high grey walls on either side and streetlamps above, retains an intimidating Stalinist air. At time of writing, the chateau's interior was closed for renovations, but you can still visit the attached **Regional Museum of Děčín** (Oblastní Muzeum v Děčín; adult/concession 30/15Kč; ☯ 9am-noon & 1-5pm Tue-Sun), which delves into local history and hosts temporary exhibitions.

Console yourself with the very beautiful **Rose Gardens** (Růžová zahrada; adult/concession 12/6Kč; ☯ 9am-8pm May-Sep) beside the castle, accessible from the Dlouhá jízda, or via a footpath from the church to a rear entrance.

STONE BRIDGE

Those people interested in art history might like to visit the melancholy **stone**

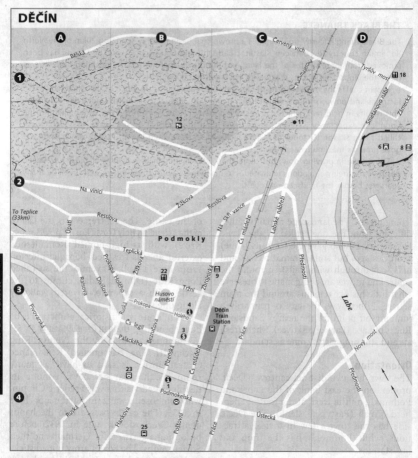

DĚČÍN

footbridge over the Ploučnice river, with a slowly crumbling, baroque sculptural group by Jan Brokoff (whose work also decorates Charles Bridge in Prague). The footbridge is south of the castle, surrounded by weeds and traffic flyovers on U starého mostu.

SHEPHERD'S WALL
On the Podmokly side, walk up Žižkova to this **cliff**, with a startling bird's-eye view over the castle and Děčín side. A small **zoo** (☎ 412 531 164; adult/concession 50/30Kč; ☼ 8am-6pm Apr-Sep, until 4pm Oct-Mar) is just behind the little chateau at the top.

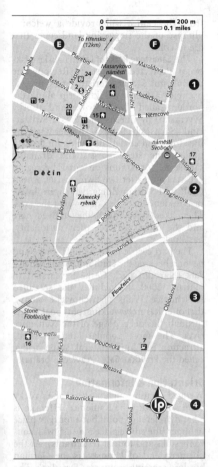

new swimming area has rapid pools, slides, saunas and a bar.

Sleeping

Dezka can help with cheap accommodation and private rooms from 250Kč per person.

Hotel Česká koruna (☎ 412 516 104; ceska.korun .decin@quick.cz; Masarykovo náměstí 6; s/d incl breakfast 880/1160Kč) A clutch of European flags and a splash of colour courtesy of the window boxes promise a slicker service here. And this three-star offering largely delivers, with a decent eatery and well-equipped rooms.

Hotel Pošta (☎ 412 511 544; Masarykovo náměstí 9; d with shared/private bathroom 340/600Kč) There's enough beer-hall rumpus downstairs to shake the foundations of this place, but the functional rooms above are well-priced and surprisingly peaceful. Reception is upstairs, on the first floor.

Pension Nela (☎ 412 517 026; nela.dc@iol.cz; U starého mostu 4; s/d incl breakfast 800/1000Kč; P) In a bizarre location, among the strands of a spaghetti junction, this is nevertheless a cosy, homey place, with a spacious garden. Rooms come with satellite TV and the owners promise that the scary dogs are quite safe.

Hotel Faust (☎ 412 518 859; www.hotel.cz/faust; U Plovárny 43; s/d incl breakfast 650/1050Kč; P) A collection of the devil's-own 1970s furniture counts against this otherwise passable lakeside haunt. It's ageing, but well-placed.

Ubytovna Termospol (☎ 412 514 151, 602 441 623; 17 Listopadu 380/5; per person 120Kč) This unmarked place is the cheapest in town, so long as you can get hold of the owner first. Unsolicited arrivals may well find themselves lingering on the doorstep.

Eating

Hospoda Retro 33 (☎ 412 510 400; Radniční 10; mains 50-150Kč) Retro bric-a-brac and clutter give this place an Irish pub feel. The food's good and there's a lively buzz come nightfall.

Caffe Paralod (☎ 412 519 866; Tyršova 347; pizza 80Kč) It looks like a boat from the bridge and it will feel like one if you have too many cocktails on the sun terrace. Decent pizza and coffee draw big crowds.

Restaurace Arizona (☎ 412 538 311; Husovo náměstí 9; mains 60-150Kč) Yee-hah Tex-Mex ambience, steaks, grills and ice-cold beers are the staples here.

P&K Lahůdky (☎ 412 510 280; Masarykovo náměstí; snacks 30Kč) This deli plates up quick, stand-up

REGIONAL MUSEUM

In an 18th-century palace, in the north of Podmokly, is the interesting **Regional Museum** (okresní muzeum; Československé mládeže 1; adult/concession 30/15Kč; ⏲ 9am-noon & 1-5pm Tue-Sun). The best displays focus on the castle (including its earlier versions and various royal and aristocratic owners) and shipping on the Labe (the latter is good for kids too, very hands-on). Who'd have guessed that for 200 years until 1886, some Labe boats pulled themselves along a 720km chain between Mělník (Central Bohemia) and Hamburg?

Activities

Plavecký Areál Děčín (☎ 412 704 211; Oblouková 1400; adult/concession 60/30Kč; ⏲ 10am-6pm) This glossy

NORTH BOHEMIA

snacks, while its sister outfit, **P&K Lahůdky Jídelna** (mains 45Kč; � 10am-3pm Mon-Fri), just around the back, serves up super cheap meat-and-two-veg in bright blue and orange sit-down surrounds.

Delvita supermarket on Tyršova provides for self-caterers.

Entertainment

Kino Sneznik (☎ 412 531 431; www.kass.cz - Czech only; Podmokelská 1070/24) Near the bus station, the cinema shows a decent selection of English language films (60Kč).

Music Club Magnet (☻7pm-4am) Down a small un-named alleyway off Radniční, this is a favoured haunt of Děčín's night owls.

Getting There & Away

Dopravní Podnik Města Děčína (DPMD; ☎ 412 531 400) runs most of the long-distance buses out of the main bus terminal (which sits on an un-named road through a park). It has seven buses a day to/from Prague's Florenc station (85Kč, 1¾ hours). There are also four buses a day to Hřensko (15Kč, 30 minutes), for the Sandstone Rocks of Labe.

Trains (☎ 412 503 481) take a little longer to get to Prague (162Kč, two hours), but also run to cities elsewhere in Europe, including Dresden (390Kč).

For all bus and train times and prices, visit www.idos.cz.

Getting Around

Most municipal bus lines run between the train station (Podmokly) and Masarykovo náměstí (Děčín). Bus tickets are available from automated machines on the bus (8Kč).

SANDSTONE ROCKS OF LABE

North of Děčín, the road rolls through the precipitous Labe valley to Hřensko (12km away on the German border), where the entire North Bohemian watershed, along with a steady stream of tourists, empties into Germany through a tight slot in the rolling hills. Garden gnome aficionados will tell you that lawn ornaments are a whole lot cheaper in Poland and the Czech Republic than in Germany and Hřensko is literally inundated with souvenir stalls selling them – along with bottles of Becherovka. While Hřensko itself is just another touristy border settlement, a short walk

from the centre will provide a welcome glimpse of the staggering landscapes that are to come.

The **Sandstone Rocks of Labe** (Labské pískovce) Protected Landscape Region, one of Bohemia's characteristic 'rock towns', occupies a 5km by 35km strip along the border. Called 'Czech Switzerland' (Český Švýcarsko) by Czechs and 'Saxon Switzerland' (Sächsische Schweiz) by Germans, the meadows and chalets do look a bit Swiss – though the steep gorges and dramatic sandstone formations do not. The region gets its name after two Swiss artists, Anton Graff and Adrian Zingg, who were living in Dresden when they discovered the area. They liked it so much they moved here and the moniker, after their nationality, has stuck.

The part east of the road to Hřensko and beyond became the **Czech Switzerland National Park** (Národní park České Švýcarsko) in January 2000. It includes the so-called Jetřichovice Walls (Jetřichovické stěny), that offer leisurely walking, plus boat jaunts through the deep gorge of the Kamenice river. The most popular (and crowded) attraction is a huge, natural, stone bridge called the **Pravčická Gate** (Pravčická brána).

Orientation & Information

Wedged picturesquely at the Labe's rocky confluence with the Kamenice, Hřensko is a handy reference point but a touristy place to linger (the entire place is awash with souvenir stalls and tourist restaurants). At the northern end of Hřensko is the German border crossing towards Dresden. The tourist information office, at the turn-off east up the Kamenice valley, was being renovated at time of writing, but may soon reopen. **Hudy Sport** (☎ 412 554 086; Hřensko 131) is east of the centre and offers camping equipment, maps and (sometimes) well-informed advice (the staff can range from very helpful to very offhand).

A road and several walking trails roughly follow the Kamenice from Hřensko to Česká Kamenice. Along or near it, the villages of Mezná, Mezní Louka, Vysoká Lípa and Jetřichovice offer food, accommodation and access down into the gorge or up into the rocks.

The maps to have, especially if you're walking, are SHOCart's *Českosaské Švýcarsko*

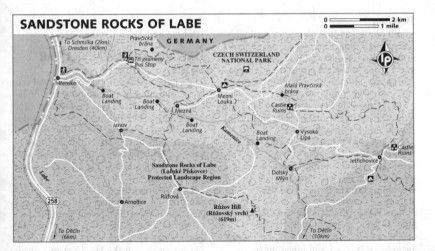

SANDSTONE ROCKS OF LABE

(Czech-Saxon Switzerland) 1:50,000 or the official *Národní Parky Česke Švýcarsko* 1: 25,000.

Activities

The Sandstone Rocks of Labe are a great option for independent climbers. There are no organised climbs as such.

WALKING TOURS

If you're short on time, a well-worn **nature trail** (*naučná stezka*), marked with a green diagonal slash, lets you take in the region's highlights in one long day. From Hřensko it runs beside the road for 3km to a bus stop at Tři prameny, 2km up to the **Pravčická brána** natural bridge and 6km back to the road at Mezní Louka. From there it plunges 2.5km into the **Kamenice gorge** below Mezná and returns to Hřensko – part of the way by boat (see the following section). A variation that skips the gorge is the yellow-marked trail from Mezná back to Tři prameny.

A 'grand tour' of the Jetřichovické stěny is a red-marked, high trail that follows the nature trail from Hřensko to Mezní Louka (6km by road; the trail itself may be longer as it doesn't follow a straight line) and then continues to Jetřichovice (15km), with options to spend the night at Mezní Louka or Vysoká Lípa. Additional attractions en route include a smaller stone bridge, the **Malá Pravčická brána**, and **castle ruins** north of Vysoká Lípa and also just east of Jetřichovice.

A shorter alternative follows a blue-marked trail from Mezní Louka down into the Kamenice gorge at Dolský Mlýn, and a yellow trail back out to Jetřichovice.

Pravčická Brána

With postcard views south to the 619m cone of **Růžov Hill** (Růžovský vrch), this 30m-high natural stone bridge is one of Europe's finest. If you don't want to walk all the way there, get off a Hřensko–Vysoká Lípa bus at Tři prameny and walk up for 2km – a 50Kč fee is payable on the way in.

Kamenice Gorge

You can break your hike with a placid float on the dammed-up stretches of the Kamenice river above and below Mezná. Whatever the weather up above, it's mossy, damp, cool and more than a little Jurassic at the bottom of this spectacular canyon.

If you're just interested in the boat trip, you still have to walk: 2km from Hřensko to the lower end; a very steep, sharp 1.5km below Mezná to the middle two boat landings; or 3km down a blue trail from Mezní Louka to the upper end. From the upper end you could also continue southeast to Vysoká Lípa or Jetřichovice.

Each stretch is 50Kč and takes 20 to 30 minutes; just wait at the landing and a boat will be along, normally within half an hour. The boats run daily from May to August and on weekends in April, September and October.

Sleeping

You'll hardly go 2km along the road without seeing '*Zimmer frei*' signs. Some villages also have camp sites, fairly cheap *pensions* and pricier hotels. In Hřensko, accommodation can be difficult to find in summer; it wouldn't hurt to book ahead.

All of these places serve meals and are either plush hotels or inn-style pubs with rooms above a restaurant/bar.

Hostinec and Penzión U Emigranta (☎ 412 554 196; Hřensko 43; s/d incl breakfast 450/900Kč; P) This fairy-tale, yellow timber lodge is on the quiet eastern edge of Hřensko and sits by a babbling stream on the road through the Kamenice Gorge.

Hotel Praha (☎ 412 554 006; hotel.praha@volny.cz; s/d incl breakfast 1400/2100Kč; P ⊠ ⬚) The poshest place in town delivers top-notch rooms, sycophantic service and piped music.

Pension Lugano (☎ 412 554 146; fax 412 554 156; Hřensko; s/d incl breakfast 450/900Kč) This pleasant place is closer to the centre, with a busy eatery, snug rooms and enough flowers to give a honeybee hay fever.

Mezní Louka has **Hotel Mezní Louka** (☎ 412 554 220; d incl breakfast 1050Kč; P) and **Camp Mezná Louka** (☎ 412 554 084; camping per person 50Kč, bungalow 350Kč; P). Mezná has **Penzión Na Vyhlídle** (☎ 412 554 065; s/d 400/750Kč; P) and private rooms in handsome half-timbered houses. Vysoká Lípa also has private rooms. About 1.5km south of pretty Jetřichovice is a camping ground.

Getting There & Away

Buses run from Děčín to Hřensko (14Kč, 30 minutes) and from Děčín via Česká Kamenice to Jetřichovice (23Kč, one hour) every two or three hours. The last bus from Hřensko to Děčín leaves at 6.15pm.

BORDER CROSSING

At time of writing, there were no buses on the German side; check with the tourist information office in Děčín. The nearest are 11km inside Germany at Schmilka, which go to Dresden. Some trains between Děčín and Dresden stop at Schöna, on the German side of the river, opposite Hřensko.

Getting Around

Buses run between Hřensko and Mezná four times a day (12Kč, 20 minutes). If you're driving, there is a hefty 5000Kč fine if you park anywhere on the road between Hřensko and Mezní Louka.

JABLONNÉ & LEMBERK CHATEAU
pop 3800

The chateau of Lemberk (or Löwenberg; 'Lion Mountain'), on the outskirts of Jablonné v Podještědí, was founded in 1240 by Havel Markvartic, head of a North Bohemian feudal aristocratic family. Its best-known resident was Havel's frail Moravian wife, Zdislava, beatified in 1907 (and now slated for sainthood) for her exemplary Christian life.

Later owners turned the castle into a comfortable Gothic and then Renaissance chateau. It owes its present baroque face to Albrecht of Wallenstein, the Habsburg general who grew rich on confiscated Hussite property, and the family of one of his officers who contrived to keep the castle after Wallenstein's murder.

The last private owners, the Auerspergs (who also owned Žleby Chateau in Central Bohemia), lent the castle to the German army during WWII.

Though out of the way as a trip from Prague, it's worth visiting en route to/from Děčín or Český ráj in East Bohemia. You and the occasional Zdislava pilgrims should have it more or less to yourself.

Orientation & Information

The chateau is in the hamlet of Lvová on the outskirts of Jablonné v Podještědí, midway between Česká Lípa and Liberec. It's a 500m climb up through scented woods from the Lvová stop on the Česká Lípa–Liberec train.

Alternatively, get off the bus or train at Jablonné, make for the domes of St Lawrence Church a few hundred metres up the hill, have a look in at the mummies in the crypt and then walk 3.5km northeast on a green-marked trail to the chateau.

There is a **tourist information office** (informační centrum; ☎ 487 762 441; náměstí Míru) offering private rooms and local info near the St Lawrence Church in Jablonné.

St Lawrence Church & Mummies

This big church on náměstí Míru is **St Lawrence Church** (kostel sv Vavřince), completed in 1722, and is apparently where Zdislava is buried. Beneath the building is a **crypt** (krypta;

☎ 487 762 105; adult/concession 30/20Kč; ☉ 9-11am & 2-4pm Tue-Sun May-Sep, at 11am, 2pm, 3pm & 4pm only Sat & Sun Apr & Oct) with mummified corpses dating from the 17th and 18th centuries, amazingly well preserved thanks to a clever ventilation system.

Lemberk Chateau

A 45-minute, Czech-language tour (foreign text available for 20Kč extra) of the **chateau** (zamék Lemberk; adult/concession 40/20Kč; ☉ 9am-4pm Tue-Sun May-Sep, 9am-3pm Sat & Sun only Apr & Oct) takes in a big, open-hearth kitchen, chapel, rooms full of furniture and church furnishings, and a great upstairs hall that has a ceiling with 70 panels (dating from 1608) depicting German proverbs and Aesop's fables. There are also several rooms with breathtaking exhibits on Zdislava.

A few rooms are used for changing exhibitions. Check these out, as it may give you the chance to look at the most interesting part of the chateau, a little upstairs baroque chapel beside the castle tower – and possibly the tower too. Outside the gate are several preserved North Bohemian half-timbered houses.

Sleeping & Eating

The tourist office staff can organise cheap rooms in Jablonné.

Pension Lemberk (☎ 776 863 213; d incl breakfast 1000Kč; ℗) This brand new place in Lvová, opposite the train station and close to the chateau, offers bright, airy doubles, warm welcomes and decent dinners.

You camp at **Kopaliště Kemping** (☎ 487 762 343; tent/bungalow per person 45Kč/150Kč; ℗), just north of the train station and highway.

Restaurace Lev (☎ 487 762 800; náměstí Míru; mains 60-120Kč) Opposite the tourist office on Jablonné's main square, this local inn has oodles of rustic Bohemian charm, a garden and scrumptious local specialities.

Getting There & Away

Jablonné is on long-distance bus routes linking Karlovy Vary (in West Bohemia), Děčín, Liberec and the Krkonoše resorts (in East Bohemia). One bus a day (except Sunday) makes the three-hour trip from Prague's Florenc station (75Kč). All buses stop at the train station.

Trains are limited, with occasional links to Liberec, Cheb and Děčín.

NORTH BOHEMIA

West Bohemia

West Bohemia is, perhaps, the flipside of the capital's coin. If Prague is a city of excesses, the region's spa towns are for making amends; if Prague's vistas are getting too grey, its sunflower fields will inject the colour; if Prague is swamped with crowds, its mountains and forests will swallow them up.

And so the tourists flood in. Most head for Karlovy Vary, biggest of the spa towns, where visitors drink, bathe in and dream about the waters that bubble up through its elegant streets. After the broody guts of Prague, Karlovy Vary and its sister spas, Mariánské Lázně and Františkovy Lázně are spotless, serene and slow-paced, becoming more so with each sip of potent Becherovka liqueur – the so-called 13th spring of Karlovy Vary and the real reason why so many spa town visitors leave feeling elated.

But there's plenty more beyond the spas. The woodland of Šumava, which runs along the German border, makes up the country's biggest national park and here, as in the Ore mountains and Slavkov forest further north, the outdoorsy can lose themselves for weeks, surfacing only to visit the region's beautiful villages, of which Loket is surely the most spectacular.

Thankfully, it's not all about relentless self-betterment though, and for every visitor sipping from a jug of spring water, there is another thirstily chugging down West Bohemia's real liquid gold, Pilsner Urquell. After days spent hiking, bathing and rehydrating, West Bohemia's own big city and famed brewery town, Plzeň is the perfect place to undo all that good.

HIGHLIGHTS

- Wallow in the waters, or simply soak up the sophistication in the butter-yellow spa town of **Mariánské Lázně** (p189)

- Indulge in the flicks at Karlovy Vary's vibrant July **International Film Festival** (p197)

- Drink one of the world's best beers, Pilsner Urquell, on the streets of its vivacious hometown, **Plzeň** (p200)

- Visit the quaint town of Loket nad Ohří and its impressive **Gothic castle** (p199)

- Head off the beaten track into the villages of the traditional **Chodsko region** (p208)

★ Karlovy Vary
Loket nad Ohří

★ Mariánské Lázně

★ Plzeň

Chodsko
★ region

WEST BOHEMIA

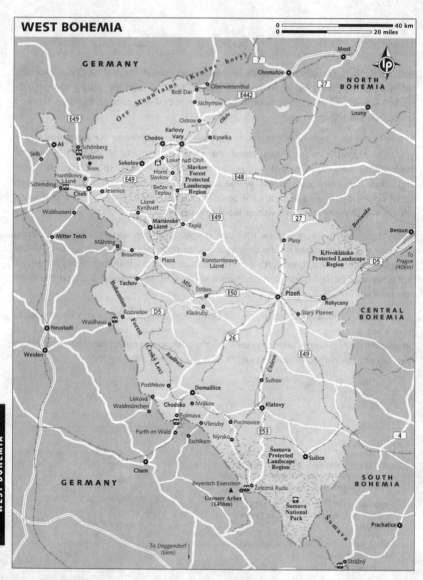

WEST BOHEMIA

0 — 40 km
0 — 20 miles

GERMANY

Ore Mountains (Krušné hory)

Most
Chomutov
Oberwiesenthal
Boží Dar
Jáchymov
Ostrov
Ohře
Louny
Karlovy
Chodov Vary
Kyselka
Loket nad Ohří
Sokolov
Horní **Slavkov**
Slavkov **Forest**
Protected
Bečov n. **Landscape**
Teplou **Region**
Lázně
Kynžvart
Marlánské
Lázně Teplá
Plasy
Beroun
Křivoklátsko
Protected Landscape
Region
To
Prague
(40km)
Mitter Teich
Mähring
Broumov
Planá
Konstantinovy
Lázně
Mže
Tachov
Štříbro
Pilzeň
Rozvadov
Kladruby
Starý Plzenec
Waidhaus
CENTRAL
BOHEMIA
Neustadt
Radbuza
Weiden
Bohemian Forest
Český Les
Úhlava
Postřekov
Domažlice
Švihov
Lišková
Waldmünchen Chodsko Mrákov
Folmava Klatovy
Všeruby Pocinovice
Furth im Wald
Nýrsko
Eschlkam
Šumava
Protected
Landscape
Region
Sušice
Cham
GERMANY
Beyerisch Eisenstein Železná Ruda
Grosser Arber
(1456m)
Šumava
National
Park
Prachatice
To Deggendorf
(6km)
Strážný

E49
Aš Schönberg
Selb Vojtanov
Soos
Františkovy
Lázně
Schirnding Cheb Jesenice
Waldsassen
Rokycany
E49
E48
E49
27
D5
E50
D5
26
E53
4
7
E442
27
NORTH
BOHEMIA
SOUTH
BOHEMIA

FRANTIŠKOVY LÁZNĚ
pop 6000

Pristine and perfectly put together, the clean lines and sparkling streets of Františkovy Lázně are so prim they could pass as their own parody; a kind of spa town theme park where reality appears to have ground to a halt and huddles of tourists wander through a tidy procession of cafés, souvenir stalls and springs.

Beethoven and Goethe rank among the spa's most celebrated patrons, but the waters here are best-known for the treatment of female infertility. Whether or not a cure is on the cards, this is a unique little place.

Orientation

Get off the long-distance bus at the 'Sady' (gardens) stop, opposite Hotel Centrum. From the train station it's 600m southwest down Nádražní and across the Municipal Gardens (Městské Sady) to the centre. The centre, focusing on the pedestrianised main street, Národní, is pathologically signposted.

Information

The **Town Information Centre** (Městské Informační Centrum; ☎ 354 543 162; Ameriká 2; ☼ 6am-6pm Mon-Fri, 8am-2pm Sat & Sun) offers maps and accommodation advice.

For spa cures and accommodation, contact **Františkovy Lázně AS** (☎ 354 542 970; Jiráskova 17; per person from 1200Kč; ☼ 9am-5pm Mon-Fri, until noon Sat).

Česká spořitelna (Anglická 7) has an exchange and ATM. There is a **post office** (Boženy Němcové) and **library** (Dr Pohoreckého 8; ☼ 9am-noon & 2-4pm Mon-Fri, until noon only Tue), by the Municipal Museum, has Internet access.

Sights & Activities

Aside from the relentlessly neoclassical façades, all painted the same two shades of yellow (presumably by decree), there is the parish **Church of the Ascension of the Cross** (kostel Povýšení sv Kříže) on Ruská, and the town's central spring, the **Františkův pramen**, at the southern end of Národní.

If these haven't stirred you, neither will the exhibits on the spa's history at the **Municipal Museum** (Městské muzeum; Dr Pohoreckého 8; adult/concession 30/15Kč; ☼ 10am-5pm Tue-Sun).

About 2km southwest of the city centre you can rent a boat on **Rybník Amerika**, or swim at **Rybník Jadran**. Between April and September a **mini-train** (mikrovláček; adult/concession 20/10Kč; ☼ 10am-4.30pm) runs to the lakes and back every half-hour or so from a terminal outside Milano Penzion on Máchova.

Six kilometres northeast of town, in the hamlet of Hájek, is **Soos Nature Reserve**, featuring peat-bogs and mud volcanoes.

Sleeping

The Town Information Centre can help with private rooms. Accommodation here is affected by seasonal variation; these are average peak season prices – they *may* fall by as much as 20% out of season.

Autocamping Amerika (☎ 354 542 518; tent 60Kč) Open May through September, the camp

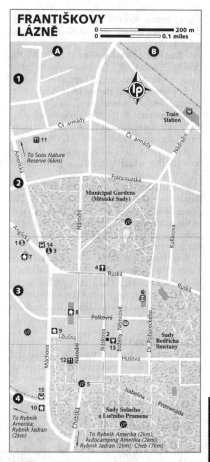

FRANTIŠKOVY LÁZNĚ

site is beside Rybník Amerika. It also has double/quad bungalows (320Kč/600Kč) and a restaurant.

Milano Penzión and Kavarna (☎ 354 542 521; Máchova 8; s/d 350/500Kč; **P**) The best cheap sleeps in town can be found here, where an enthusiastic English-speaking owner offers a selection of snug modern rooms over his café.

Hotel Centrum (☎ 354 543 156; spahotel@centrum.cz; Anglická; s/d incl breakfast €29/49; **P**) Slightly away from the push-and-shove of the tourist superhighway, this little modern number has all the usual trimmings in business class surrounds.

Hotel Tři Lilie (☎ 354 208 900; trililie@franzensbad.cz; Máchova; incl breakfast s/d 1500/2300Kč; **P** ✗ ✗) Some 'luxury' spa hotels have all the charm of a trauma ward. Not so here, where quality rooms, attentive staff, polished décor and B-list celebrity guests come as standard.

Hotel Slovan (☎ 354 542 841; slovan.frl@cmail.cz; Národní 5; incl breakfast 1050/1650Kč) The bowels of this central place lack the sparkle of the façade, with frumpy (in extremis) brown décor. The rooms are large and comfortable though.

Eating & Drinking

Saloon Bažina (CS Armady 2; steaks 120Kč) If you feel like washing down your mineral water with a decent cut of red meat, this pine-trimmed 'saloon' serves the closest town gets to Tex-Mex tucker. It even has the requisite confederate flag outside.

Vídeňska Kavárna (☎ 354 543 162; Národní 1; snacks 50Kč; mains to 400Kč) Taking pride of place on the main drag, this chic café, attached to the Ingo Casino, whips up a mean smorgasbord of monumental ice creams and decadent coffees. The attached formal restaurant is one of the finest in town.

Pivnice U Pošty (Boženy Němcové) If all the yellow paint is giving you cataracts, this cosy dark wood hideaway is the place to catch up with the local crowd, talk shop and swill beer over light snacks.

Hotel Slovan (☎ 354 542 841; Národní 5; mains 100Kč) The décor may be frumpy, but at least this place serves old-fashioned portions at old-fashioned prices. Choose from a restaurant, a café and a *vinárna* (wine bar).

Getting There & Away

The bus is faster, more direct and more frequent than the train. One daily bus comes direct from Prague via Karlovy Vary (160Kč, 3½ hours); about three a day come from Plzeň (65Kč, 1¼ hours). For additional long-distance options, and international connections, go via Cheb, which has buses to Františkovy Lázně every 30 minutes (11Kč, 15 minutes).

CHEB

pop 34,000

A bridgehead between nations, Cheb (pronounced 'kheb') stands astride a European fault-line, with traditions and aspirations that have as much in common with Germany as they do with the Czech Republic. A hot-bed of support for Germany's claim to the Sudetenland in the 1930s, Cheb was badly impacted post-WWII, when the town's German population was brutally expelled.

But Cheb's civic schizophrenia has left behind a fine historic and architectural legacy. Today the slightly crumbly centre is refreshingly opposed to the contrived, neoclassical character of the nearby spas. Here, winding streets and a unique red-brick fortress take centre stage in a town filled with hidden oddities.

But Cheb is no fairy tale. Buildings are still stained with the soot from decades of heavy industry and after dark prostitutes ply the streets for custom: two more sides to this town's fragmented personality.

Orientation

From the adjacent bus and train stations it's 1km west and northwest along Svobody to the old town's sloping, triangular, main square, náměstí krále Jiřího z Poděbrad (King George of Poděbrady Square).

Information

Infocentrum (☎ 354 422 705; infocentrum.cheb@email .cz; náměstí krále Jiřího z Poděbrad 33; ⏰ 9am-6pm Mon-Fri, until noon Sat) sells maps, guidebooks, theatre and concert tickets, and can organise guides.

Česká spořitelna (náměstí krále Jiřího z Poděbrad) has an ATM and exchange desk.

The post office (Slikova 15) is just south of the main square.

Sights

NÁMĚSTÍ KRÁLE JIŘÍHO Z PODĚBRAD

The main square has a selection of architectural treats. Pick of the bunch is the tangle of teetering 16th-century former Jewish mer-

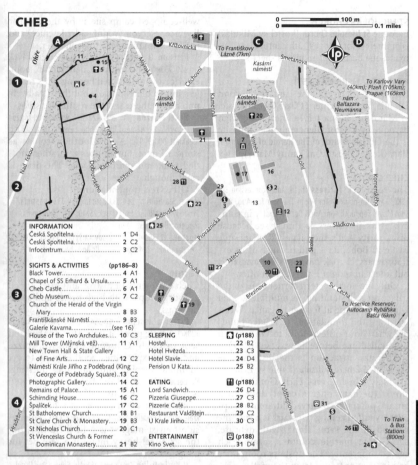

CHEB

0 — 100 m
0 — 0.1 miles

INFORMATION	
Česká Spořitelna............................	1 D4
Česká Spořitelna............................	2 C2
Infocentrum...................................	3 C2

SIGHTS & ACTIVITIES	(pp186–8)
Black Tower.....................................	4 A1
Chapel of SS Erhard & Ursula......	5 A1
Cheb Castle.....................................	6 A1
Cheb Museum..................................	7 C2
Church of the Herald of the Virgin	
Mary..	8 B3
Františkánské Náměstí.....................	9 B3
Galerie Kavarna.....................(see 16)	
House of the Two Archdukes....	10 C3
Mill Tower (Mlýnská věž)...........	11 A1
New Town Hall & State Gallery	
of Fine Arts..............................	12 C2
Náměstí Krále Jiřího z Poděbrad (King	
George of Poděbrady Square)..13 C2	
Photographic Gallery..................	14 C2
Remains of Palace.........................	15 A1
Schirnding House...........................	16 C2
Špalíček...	17 C2
St Batholomew Church.................	18 B1
St Clare Church & Monastery.......	19 B3
St Nicholas Church........................	20 C1
St Wenceslas Church & Former	
Dominican Monastery...........	21 B2

SLEEPING	(p188)
Hostel..	22 B2
Hotel Hvězda................................	23 C3
Hotel Slavie..................................	24 D4
Pension U Kata.............................	25 B2

EATING	(p188)
Lord Sandwich.............................	26 D4
Pizzeria Giuseppe.........................	27 C3
Pizzeria Café................................	28 B2
Restaurant Valdštejn....................	29 C2
U Krale Jiriho...............................	30 C3

ENTERTAINMENT	(p188)
Kino Svet......................................	31 D4

chants' houses called **špalíček** ('the Block'). Another late-Gothic refugee is **Schirnding House** (Schirndingovský dům; náměstí Krále Jiřího z Poděbrad 508), with its crow-step gables.

Among the 18th-century baroque stars are the **New Town Hall** (Nová radnice; adult/concession 50/25Kč; ☼ 9am-noon & 12.30-5pm Tue-Sun), incorporating the **State Gallery of Fine Arts** (Státní galerie výtvarného umění; admission incl in town hall fee) with changing exhibits of modern Czech art. Also note the **House of the Two Archdukes** (dům U dvou arcivévodů; náměstí Krále Jiřího z Poděbrad 26/471), at the top of the square, once the town's oldest inn and now a music shop and restaurant.

North on Kamenná is **St Wenceslas Church** (kostel sv Václava), which once operated as a **Dominican monastery** and a small **photographic gallery** (Galerie Fotografie; Kamenná 2; admission free; ☼ 10am-6pm Tue-Fri, until 5pm Sat).

CHEB MUSEUM
Wallenstein met his sticky end while staying at the pink Renaissance **Pachelbel House** (Pachelblův dům; náměstí Krále Jiřího z Poděbrad 492) at the northern end of the square. It is now the **Cheb Museum** (Chebské muzeum; ☎ 354 422 386; adult/concession 50/25Kč; ☼ 9am-12.30pm & 1-5pm Tue-Sun).

The highlight is a gallery of 20th-century paintings of the town, which show Cheb's decline quite graphically. There is also a mock-up of the bedroom where Wallenstein was run through, a moment re-enacted in multiple illustrations.

WEST BOHEMIA

ST NICHOLAS CHURCH

Baroque **St Nicholas Church** (kostel sv Mikuláš) is of interest for its age (13th century), its Romanesque basilica plan and its sheer size.

FRANTIŠKÁNSKÉ NÁMĚSTÍ

On the eastern of the square, beyond Dlouhá, is the former **St Clare Church** (kostel sv Klára) and monastery, a fine piece of high baroque by Kristof Dientzenhofer. Opposite is the Gothic **Church of The Herald of the Virgin Mary** (kostel Zvěstování Panny Marie).

CHEB CASTLE

The red-brick **fortress** (hrad; adult/concession 30/ 15Kč; ☉ 9am-noon & 1pm-6pm Tue-Sun Jun-Aug, until 5pm May & Sep, until 4pm Apr & Oct), mostly in ruins except for its towers, is a must-see because of its rarity – it's the biggest Romanesque castle in Bohemia – and because of its extraordinary chapel. No tours are available, but a text in pidgin English is on offer.

Only the northeastern corner walls of the palace are still standing, its multiple-arched windows hinting at former elegance. Westward are the foundations of a later building where four officers loyal to Wallenstein were killed just before he was (see p187).

The star attraction is the little, square **Chapel of SS Erhard & Ursula** (kaple sv Erharda a Uršuly). In the very early-Gothic lower storey (perhaps once a crypt) four thick granite pillars, each carved differently, support a vaulted ceiling. Upstairs is a sublime version of the same thing, with delicate, late-Gothic marble columns, again each carved differently. The upstairs room once had its own entrance from the castle.

Above the moat-bridge, the dusty, thick-walled **Black Tower** (Černá věž) offers views of the river, old-town rooftops and distant apartment blocks from its 18.5m top. In an adjacent building is a tantalising **archaeological exhibit** on Chebsko (the Cheb region), unfortunately without English captions.

To appreciate the scale of the fortifications, take the steep path leading down to Křížovnická, past the round, late-Gothic **Mill Tower** (Mlýnská věž) and the stretch of town walls.

Sleeping

Autocamp Rybářská Bašta (☎ 354 431 951; berdychp@ quick.cz; tent/bungalow per person 50/200Kč; **P**) Around 6km east of the city centre at Dřenice, this well-equipped camp site is by the popular Jesenice reservoir (vodní nádrž Jesenice) and is open from mid-May to September.

Pension U kata (☎ 354 423 465; Židovská 17; s/d 450/900Kč) The spit-polished, picture book exterior is a bit of a red herring – it's rather less immaculate inside – but there's a lively pub atmosphere and the rooms are snug.

Hotel Hvězda (☎ 354 422 549; www.hotel-hvezda .cz - Czech only; náměstí krále Jiřího z Poděbrad 4; s/d incl breakfast 600/900Kč) A top location comes as standard here, but so does the rather mottled pink and maroon décor. The price is right though.

Other recommendations:

Hotel Slavie (☎ 354 433 216; fax 354 433 494; třída Svobody 75; s/d incl breakfast €25/40; **P**) Functional, modern, bland, but clean.

Hostel (☎ 354 423 401; Židovská 7; per person 150Kč; ☉ 8am-noon & 4-8pm) No frills and cheap beds.

Eating

Cheb has plenty of bistros and cafés aimed at tour groups, with high prices and small helpings.

Pizzeria Giuseppe (☎ 354 438 200; Jateční 18; pizza 120Kč) A little piece of Italy, stone-baked and sent to Cheb, Giuseppe's cooks up pizza and Italian specialties good enough to get Mamma weeping and waistlines bursting.

Pizzerie Café (☎ 354 436 143; Jakubská 1; pizza 70Kč) is half the price, with half the frills.

Restaurant Valdštejn (☎ 354 442 561; náměstí krále Jiřího z Poděbrad; mains 75-150Kč) This square-side tourist magnet is a flick frumpy, but the schnitzel-heavy menu is a safe bet for a big feed.

U Krale Jiriho (cnr náměstí krále Jiřího z Poděbrad & Březinova; mains 50-75Kč) It may be in the guts of the House of the Two Archdukes, but this raucous beer hall (watch out for the lewd cartoons on the wall) is rather rougher than the façade suggests. The goulash is cheap though and it's often full of locals.

Other recommendations:

Galerie Kavarna (náměstí krále Jiřího z Poděbrad; coffee 20Kč) A pleasant café in the Schirnding House.

Lord Sandwich (třída Svobody 28; burgers 25Kč) For no-frills snacks.

Entertainment

Most of the so-called 'night clubs' around town are brothels/strip joints. A night at the movies in **Kino Svet** (☎ 354 437 722; Májová 29), however, is usually pretty safe.

Getting There & Away

There are four buses a day from Prague (160Kč, three hours) and at least seven each from Karlovy Vary (50Kč, one hour) and Mariánské Lázně (30Kč, 30 minutes). Regional buses run between Cheb and Františkovy Lázně (11Kč, 15 minutes) every hour or so.

Express trains from Prague (250Kč, three hours) are less frequent but faster than the bus. For shorter trips – eg from Plzeň, Františkovy Lázně or Karlovy Vary – there are several fast trains a day, though they're pricier than ordinary trains and the bus.

Cheb is also a convenient point for international train connections.

For all bus and train times and prices, visit www.idos.cz.

MARIÁNSKÉ LÁZNĚ
pop 16,000

A necklace of neoclassical and Art Nouveau elegance laid out along a slot in the rolling Slavkov Forest, Mariánské Lázně is the best placed of the region's spa towns. With a whole range of walking trails and fresh mountain air on tap, this is the spot for those who need more than just water – however pure – to stave off lost youth.

Founded by a local physician in the early 19th century, Mariánské Lázně (formerly Marienbad) retains the aura of an overgrown sanatorium. Things move at a leisurely, almost geriatric pace and a faint whiff of hospital disinfectant hangs in the air.

But behind the white coats, stairlifts and stethoscopes, there is a glitzier side to discover. Long favoured by central Europe's A-list celebrity set, Mariánské Lázně once drew the likes of German poet JW Goethe (who, at 72, wrote of his love for a 16-year-old local hotelier's daughter in the *Marienbad Elegy*), Franz Kafka (who visited shortly before succumbing to tuberculosis in 1924) and even Britain's King Edward VII. The ageing celebrities have now largely dissipated, but some of the money, much of the splendour and a fair flick of the town's reputation for fun and frolics remain. Of all the spa towns, this is the place to sin (a little) and repent in equal measure.

Orientation

Mariánské Lázně stretches for 4km along Hlavní třída. From the adjacent bus and train stations at the southern, 'business' end of town, it's 2km on trolleybus No 5 to the spa area's main bus stop, opposite the Hotel Excelsior.

The spa area is a network of paths, parks and 39 therapeutic springs – centred on the photogenic Colonnade (Kolonáda) and surrounded by streets of plush hotels and mansions. Mírové náměstí has a summer *kavárna* (café) and an open-air stage. The spa is at the southern toe of the Slavkov Forest (Slavkovský les) Protected Landscape Region.

Parking is largely confined to pricey car parks – there is a multistorey near Hotel Europa (12Kč per 30-minute period during the day and 4Kč at night).

Information

City police office (☎ 158; Ruská) Is behind the town hall.
Infocentrum (☎ 354 622 474; infocentrum@marianske lazne.cz; Hlavní 47; ☼ 9am-noon & 1-6pm) Sells theatre tickets, maps and guidebooks. It also has a guide service and can advise on accommodation. Internet access is available here.
KB bank (Hlavní třída 132) and **ČSOB** (Hlavní třída 81) Have ATMs and exchange desks.
Marienbad Spa Hotels Information Office (☎ 354 655 550; www.marienbad.cz; Masarykova 22; ☼ 9am-5pm Mon-Fri, until noon Sat) Manages and books eight of the biggest spa hotels and has information on spa packages (from €75 per person/per night).
Post office (Poštovní) Located about 200m south of the main bus stop.
Town Library (Městská Knihovna; ☎ 354 622 115; Hlavní 370/3; ☼ 9-11am & 1-6pm Mon-Fri) Charges 1kč per minute for Internet access.

Sights & Activities
HLAVNÍ TŘÍDA & RUSKÁ

On the 2nd floor of **Chopin House** (dům F Chopina), in dům U Bílé labutě, is a little **museum** (Hlavní 47; adult/concession 30/15Kč; ☼ 2-5pm Tue-Thu & Sun) to Frédéric Chopin, who stayed here in 1836.

There are two churches on Ruská (both reachable by stairways from Hlavní). The 1901, red and yellow **St Vladimír Church** (kostel sv Vladimíra; Ruská 347-9; admission 20Kč; ☼ 8.30am-noon & 1-5pm May-Oct, 9.30-11am & 2-4pm Nov-Apr) is a plush, Byzantine-style Orthodox church with an amazing porcelain iconostasis.

Prim and equally striking is the 1879 neo-Gothic **Anglican Chapel** (Anglikánský kostelík; adult/concession 20/10Kč; ☼ 9am-noon & 1-4pm Tue-Sun), which is further up the block.

MARIÁNSKÉ LÁZNĚ

0 _____ 500 m
0 _____ 0.3 miles

INFORMATION
ČSOB Bank	1	B2
Infocentrum	2	B2
KB Bank	3	B3
Marienbad Spa Hotels Information Office	4	C2

SIGHTS & ACTIVITIES (pp189–91)
Ambrožův Spring	5	C2
Anglican Chapel	6	B2
Chopin Haus	7	B2
Church of the Assumption of the Virgin Mary	8	C2
Colonnade (Kolonáda)	9	C2
Cross Spring	10	C2
Ferdinandův Spring	11	C5
Forest Spring	12	B1
Goethovo Náměstí	13	C2
Karolinin Spring	14	C2
Library	15	B4
Mariin Spring	16	C2
Monument to the US Army	17	C2
Motorcycle Race Track	18	B6
Municipal Museum	19	C2
New Baths	20	C2
Prelátův Spring	21	D6
Public Pool	22	B4
Rudolfův Spring	23	C5
Singing Fountain	24	C2
St Vladimir Church	25	B3
Watchtower	26	C3

SLEEPING (p192)
Hotel Bohemia	27	B2
Hotel Cristal Palace	28	B3
Hotel Europa	29	B2
Hotel Haná	30	B5
Hotel Helvetia & Pivnice	31	B4
Hotel Koliba	32	D2
Hotel Kossuth	33	B2
Hotel Richard	34	B3
Start Motel & Camp Site	35	B6
TJ Lokomotiva	36	B6

EATING (pp192–3)
China Restaurant	37	B3
Filip 1	38	B3
Restaurace Jalta	39	B2
U Zlaté Koule	40	C2

DRINKING (pp192–3)
Irish Pub	41	B3
New York Restaurant	42	B4
Pueblo Mexicana	43	B5
Scottish Pub Highlanders	44	B4

ENTERTAINMENT (p193)
Kino Slava	45	B4
NV Gogol Theatre	46	B2

TRANSPORT (p193)
Bus Station	47	A6
Cable Car	48	D3
Main Bus Stop in Spa Area	49	B3

OTHER
Kolonada Oplatky	50	C2

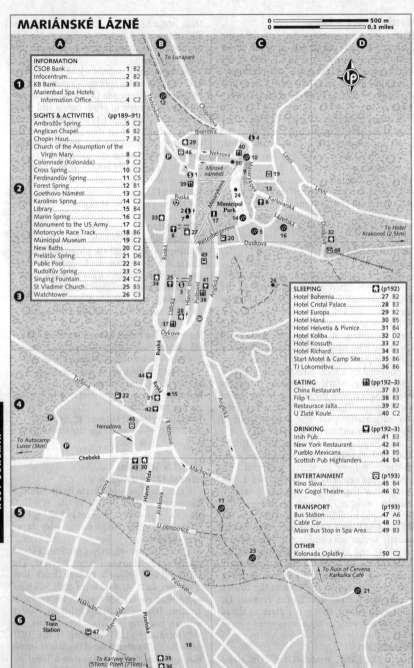

To Lunapark
To Hotel Krakonoš (2.5km)
Ibsenova
Nehrová
Mírové náměstí
Ruská
Municipal Park
Karlovarská
Lázeňská
Duškova
Reitenbergerova
Dyková
Tyršova
Ládícká
Hlavní třída
Anglícká
Nerudova
B Němcové
Máchova
Chebská
Husova
Komenského
Jiráskova
Hlavní třída
U nemocnice
To Autocamp Luxor (3km)
To Ruin of Červena Karkulka Café
Palackého
Nákladní
Plzeňská
Train Station
To Karlovy Vary (51km); Plzeň (71km)
Trebízkého
Chopinova
Masarykova
Lesní
Poštovní

WEST BOHEMIA

AROUND THE COLONNADE
The beautifully restored cast-iron **Colonnade** (Kolonáda), east of the municipal park, is the spa's visual centrepiece. From a little bandstand inside, concerts – and not just the oom-pa-pa variety – are presented two or three times a day in the high season.

In its own whitewashed pavilion by the northern end of the Colonnade is **Cross Spring** (Křížový pramen; 🕑 6am-6pm), the spa's first spring, where heavy drinkers can buy little plastic drinking cups (3Kč), or choose from a whole host of souvenir, porcelain mugs. At the other end is the crowd-pleasing **Singing Fountain** (Zpívající fontána), leaping and spraying to recorded classical music every two hours all day.

Statues in the squeaky-clean municipal park (no dogs, no bicycles, no smoking – drinking seems to be allowed) include a **monument** to the liberation of the town by the US army on 6 May 1945.

GOETHOVO NÁMĚSTÍ
This manicured square, edged with extravagant late-19th- and early-20th-century buildings, probably looks much as it did when King Edward VII et al patronised the surrounding hotels.

At the site of a house where Goethe stayed (the square is named after him) on his last visit to Mariánské Lázně, is a ho-hum **Municipal Museum** (Městské muzeum; Goethovo náměstí 11; adult/concession 40/20Kč; 🕑 9am-noon & 1-5pm Wed-Sun), although it does give a good overview of the town's history (with Czech captions). Ask staff to put on the 30-minute video in English for you before you go through.

Opposite is the bulky, eight-sided **Church of the Assumption of the Virgin Mary** (kostel Nanebevzetí Panny Marie), built in 1848 in 'neo-Byzantine' style.

HIKES
A dozen trails wind through the surrounding woods, past pavilions and springs. Wilderness it isn't (some paths are even signposted with cardiac, energy-use data!) but pleasant it is. The routes are shown on some city maps, and on map-boards at the south end of the Colonnade.

A popular trail climbs to **Hotel Panoráma**, round past an old stone **watchtower** (100 steps up to a sweeping view over the trees) and on to the ruin of **Červená karkulka Café**.

Mortals can descend from here to buses on Hlavní (total less than 4km). Those here for the cure can carry on for a 7km round trip.

An easier loop trail heads north past Forest Spring (Lesní pramen) to Lunapark.

BATHS & SWIMMING
Tourists can soak in spring water at the **New Baths** (Nové lázně; 🕾 354 644 111; Reitenbergerova 53; admission 150Kč; 🕑 3-8pm). It also has a 'hydrotherapy' pool (admission 240Kč; 🕑 open to men on Mon, Wed & Fri pm & women on Tue, Thu, Fri am & Sat am), or choose from a host of other treatments.

You can also take a splash in the **public pool** (plavecký stadión; 🕾 354 623 579; Tyršova 617; adult/concession 50/20Kč; 🕑 11am-9pm Mon-Sat), southwest of the city centre.

Walking Tour
From the bus stop on Poštovní, cross north into the municipal park, past the **memorial to the American liberation (1)** of Mariánské Lázně in WWII. On the far side is the centrepiece of the spa, the **Colonnade (2)**, along with the popular **Singing Fountain (3)**.

East beyond the Colonnade is Goethovo náměstí, with several venerable hotels, the octagonal **Church of the Assumption of the Virgin Mary (4)** and the **Municipal Museum (5)**. Detour east on Karlovarská and south on Dusíkova to the folksy Koliba Restaurace, from where a **cable car (6)** (adult/concession 30/15Kč; 🕑 9am-6pm Tue-Sun May-Sep) sometimes (it was experiencing 'technical difficulties' at time of writing) climbs to Hotel Krakonoš. The wooded

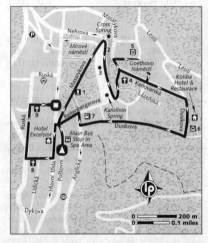

hills for some 1.5km southward are laced with hiking trails.

Walk west along Reitenbergerova, past the **New Baths (7)**, where even tourists can enjoy a mineral swim and a massage (spas are normally restricted to paying guests of spa hotels. In this instance, you can just walk in and soak in the waters). Cross Hlavní, head south past the Hotel Excelsior and climb the steps up to the Orthodox **St Vladimír Church (8)**. Some 200m north on Ruská is an **Anglican Chapel (9)**. Return down to Hlavní on another set of steps.

Festivals & Events

The town has a lively summertime cultural life, including the opening of the spa season in May, a week-long **Frédéric Chopin Music Festival** (☎ 354 622 617; www.chopinfestival.cz) in mid-August, the **Mozart Festival** in October and frequent outdoor concerts. It bears no relation whatever to Alan Resnais' proto-psychedelic 1960s film, *Last Year at Marienbad*.

Sleeping

Mariánské Lázně has over three dozen hotels, but prices tend to be (Prague) high and extremely seasonal – the prices quoted here are high season summer rates (expect discounts of up to 30% off season). Infocentrum can help with private rooms from 350Kč per person with breakfast, and hotels.

Drivers staying at most of the central hotels should plan on the extra cost of overnight parking.

BUDGET

Autocamp Luxor (☎ 354 623 504; tent/bungalow per person 60/200Kč; P) This decent site, located in Velká Hleďsebe (2km west along the Chebská road, then 1km south) is open May to September. It's easy to get to with a car, or take trolleybus No 6 from the town centre to Velká Hleďsebe and walk from there.

TJ Lokomotiva (☎ 354 623 917; Plzeňská 9; dm per person 150Kč; P) This bargain basement sports centre has inexpensive dorm beds. You must arrive and register between 7am and 3pm weekdays – but even then you may not find anyone about.

Hotel Kossuth (☎ 354 622 861; kossuth@iol.cz; Ruská 77; d with shared/private bathroom incl breakfast 700/970Kč) Things are a little moth-eaten here, but the rooms have a few years in them yet.

Hotel Europa (☎ 354 622 063; fax 354 625 408; Třebížského 2; d with shared/private bathroom incl breakfast 900/1500Kč; P) Gloating over a surprisingly hot location for a cheap(ish) hotel, Europa juggles some seriously cheery staff with décor that is homogenous at best. Overall, a safe bet though.

Start Motel (☎ 354 622 062; Plzeňská; s/d 395/664Kč; P) This prefab motel is blueprint spit-and-sawdust, but remains one of the cheaper options in town. Even so, it's only worth considering as a last resort.

MID-RANGE

Hotel Richard (☎ 354 696 111; hotelrichard@tiscali.cz; Ruská 487/28; incl breakfast s/d 2100/3100Kč; P ⊠ ⊠ ⊠) Taking a brave step away from the trademark yellow façade theme, this shiny new hotel, daubed a camp shade of pink, has spotless new facilities and slick service.

Hotel Koliba (☎ 354 625 169; hotel-koliba@xercom.cz; s/d incl breakfast 1200/1710Kč; P) Tucked away, up among the pines, this Swiss-style chalet is one for the mountain lovers, with heaps of hush and a fair serving of Alpine ambience.

Hotel Helvetia (☎ 354 620 161; fax 354 622 378; Hlavní 230; s/d incl breakfast 1500/1900Kč) This place is rather ho-hum, but it is sufficiently close to the centre to warrant a few nights' stay. If it's full, there's more of the same at **Hotel Haná** (☎ 354 622 753; Hlavní 260; s/d incl breakfast €40/50).

TOP END

Hotel Cristal Palace (☎ 354 615 111; www.cristalpalace.cz; Hlavní 61; s/d incl breakfast 3080/4070Kč; P ⊠ ⊠ ⊟ ⊠) With more glass than class, this shiny business hotel has everything you could possibly need (and a little more to boot), served up in slick, modern surrounds.

Hotel Bohemia (☎ 354 610 111; hotel.bohemia@orea.cz; Hlavní 100; s/d incl breakfast 2450/3580Kč; ⊠) In the fancy façade stakes, this beautiful old hotel comes a clear top. Conservative four-star comfort come as standard on the inside too.

Eating & Drinking

Eating grandly is all part of 'the cure' and Mariánské Lázně is full of elegant, high-priced restaurants.

U Zlaté Koule (☎ 354 624 455; Nehrova 26; mains 300Kč) A stunning cocktail of five-star class and snug, beer cellar informality, this swish eatery was voted Czech Restaurant of the Year 2003. Creaking wood beams, sparkling glassware and antiques create the atmosphere, while the game-rich menu whips up the 'wow' factor.

Restaurace Jalta (☎ 354 150 603; Hlavní; mains 65Kč) Local food at local prices is the motto at this popular no-frills diner. It's on the first floor, above a clothes shop.

China Restaurant (☎ 354 626 819; Lidická 125; mains 120Kč) This carbon-copy Chinese offers typically good Chinese fare at typically reasonable prices.

Irish Pub (☎ 354 620 828; Poštovni 96; Guinness 55Kč) In a courtyard behind Hlavní 96 (follow signs to 'Irish Pub'), this snug Celtic offering is perfect for late nights and a good Irish feed. Scots may prefer to give their custom to **Scottish Pub Highlanders** (Ruská), which comes with Internet access and a William Wallace memorial.

Other recommendations:
Pueblo Mexicano (☎ 354 620 318; Chebská; mains 70-150Kč; ☺ 5pm-5am) Spicy food, salsa nights and disco action.
Filip 1 (☎ 354 626 161; Poštovni 96; mains 100-150Kč) Czech food without the tourist mark-up.

Entertainment

NV Gogol Theatre (Divadlo NV Gogola; ☎ 354 622 036; Třebízského 106) Check the programme here for musical and theatrical performances. Many events are also held at **Chopin Haus** (Hlavní třída 47) and there are regular daily Colonnade concerts at the **Spa Colonnade** from May to September. For details ask at Infocentrum.

New York Restaurant (☎ 354 623 033; Hlavní třída 233; ☺ until 2am) Jazz bands play this snug bar venue most evenings from 8pm.

Kino Slava (☎ 354 622 347; www.marianskelazne .com/kino; Nerudova 437) Cinema-goers can catch the latest Hollywood blockbusters here.

Getting There & Away

Half a dozen fast trains a day run from Prague (224Kč, three hours) all via Plzeň (100Kč, 1¼ hours), and more from Cheb (40Kč, 30 minutes). Buses from Prague (132Kč, three hours), Plzeň (65Kč, 1½ hours) and Cheb (25Kč, 25 minutes) are less frequent (up to five a day) and take as long as the train. The train journey from Karlovy Vary (76Kč, 1¾ hours) is slow but scenic.

> **OPLATKY**
>
> Locals believe the correct way to take your spring water is from the 'spa cup' or *lázeňský pohárek*, and kill the taste with big, round, sweet wafers called *oplatky*. Oplatky are sold for about 5Kč each at a few spa hotels or speciality shops; you can pick them up at **Kolonada Oplatky** (cnr Nehrova and Masarykova).

AROUND MARIÁNSKÉ LÁZNĚ
Teplá Monastery
pop 3100

Founded in 1193, the **Premonstratensian Monastery** (Premonstrátský klášter; ☎ 354 392 264; tour in Czech/English 50/100Kč; ☺ 9am-4pm Mon-Sat, 11am-4.30pm Sun May-Oct; until 3pm Nov-Apr, closed Jan) at Teplá was one of the richest landowners in Bohemia in the 16th century. Among its holdings was Mariánské Lázně itself.

Though a bit run-down now (it served as an army barracks during the Communist years), it boasts a sturdy Romanesque-Gothic church that has survived almost intact from 1232; and the second-largest library in the country, with some 80,000 books.

Organ and chamber concerts are held here in summer, and on 14 July there is an annual procession by former political prisoners, incarcerated by the Nazis and Communists.

Klášterní hospice (The Cloister Inn; ☎ 354 392 264; fax 354 392 312; s/d incl breakfast 890/1580Kč; P) Part of the monastery itself, this rather glossy hotel has some swish rooms that are anything but monastic.

GETTING THERE & AWAY

There are eight trains a day to/from Mariánské Lázně (28Kč, 30 minutes). By car, take the Karlovy Vary road for 7km and turn east.

KARLOVY VARY
pop 60,000

However you look at it, Karlovy Vary is a town quite literally built on water and the foundations run deep. The elixir vitae for the tens of thousands who flock here annually to bathe, drink and steam themselves stupid, water has brought beautiful, butter yellow Karlovy Vary all the splendour of a boom-time oil town, but with a whole lot less mess.

Effete, haughty and sophisticated, this is the oldest and most grandiose of the Bohemian spas, a living monument to opulent 19th- and early-20th-century architecture and a magnet for tourists, health-seekers and the arts in equal measure. Those arriving on spec may be disappointed to discover that popping into a steam inhalation session or diving into a scalding sulphur bath isn't really possible without an appointment, but anyone can drink the mineral-rich water until their teeth float; and winers, diners and arts aficionados can always find something to do between drinks.

History

It may look like a monument to order and enlightened good sense today, but legend has it that Karlovy Vary's springs were stumbled upon by pure chance. In fact, strictly speaking, they were discovered by a dog, which fell into the first of the town's springs while out on a hunting trip with Emperor Charles IV. The loss of the dog was negligible when set against the possible profits to be made from the warm springs and in 1358 Charles had a hunting lodge built near the largest, granting the town status as 'Charles Spa' shortly afterwards.

The town soon became a magnet for European aristocrats, who flocked to the growing watering hole in the hope of purging themselves of the digestive disorders that were the fashion of the day: Russian Tsar Peter the Great, Frederick I of Prussia and Empress Maria Theresa all made a splash in the early years.

Its popularity was further enhanced when Dr David Becher invented Becherovka, a potent herb liqueur, while analysing the composition of the town's waters in around 1790, thus giving people the opportunity to get sozzled and better simultaneously. Unsurprisingly, the liqueur remains the mainstay of Karlovy Vary's souvenir industry today.

Attracting a growing population of aristocrats, with plenty of money, and plenty of time to kill between treatments, Karlovy Vary soon became a centre for the arts as well. The playwright Johann Schiller honeymooned here, and Goethe returned 13 times. Visiting composers included Bach, Beethoven, Brahms, Wagner, Tchaikovsky, Schumann, Liszt and Grieg. Here Dvořák's symphony *From the New World* premiered

in 1884. The spa hosts an annual Dvořák Autumn Festival in September.

As the money poured in, the buildings went up and the 'neo'-style and Art Nouveau structures that graced the skyline in the late 19th and early 20th centuries remain in fabulous condition today.

Orientation

The business end of town is centred on Dr Bechera, while the spa sprawls for 3km up the Teplá Valley, in the northern corner of the Slavkov Forest (Slavkovský les).

Trains from Cheb, Plzeň and Prague, and most international connections, arrive at the upper station (horní nádraží), also called main station (hlavní nádraží), 400m from the other side of the Ohře. Those from Mariánské Lázně and the south use the lower station (dolní nádraží), on the spa side of the Ohře.

Long-distance buses and international buses to Germany use stands by the lower train station. The main junction for city and regional buses is on Varšavská.

MAPS

Infocentrum sell a useful *Karlovy Vary* map (30Kč), as well as one incorporating the surrounding area. Both are published by Paret.

Information

BOOKSHOPS

Nava (TG Masaryka 12) This bookshop also sells a selection of regional maps.

EMERGENCY

Tourist Police (Cizinecká policie; ☎ 974 366 803; Závodu míru 16, Stará Role) Reached on bus No 3 from Tržnice bus station.

INTERNET ACCESS

VIR Net (☎ 776 597 426; TG Masaryka; ☯ 10am-10pm) Charges 80Kč per hour for Internet access.

INTERNET RESOURCES

The town's website www.karlovyvary.cz is another useful resource, with a history of the town and plenty of useful contacts.

MEDIA

Promenáda (www.promenada.cz; 15Kč) is a monthly multilingual booklet full of information on spa history, cultural events, transport and other practicalities.

KARLOVY VARY

0 —————————— 400 m
0 —————————— 0.2 miles

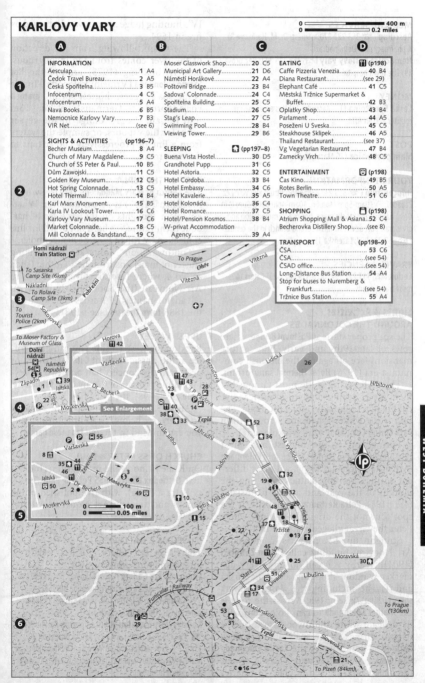

WEST BOHEMIA

MEDICAL SERVICES
Aesculap (☎ 353 222 870; náměstí Dr. M. Horákové 8) A pharmacy near Dolni nádraží.
Nemocnice Karlovy Vary (☎ 353 115 111; Bezručova 19) The town hospital.

MONEY
Česká Spořitelna (TG Masaryka 14) Has an exchange counter and an ATM.

POST
Main post office (TG Masaryka 1)

TOURIST INFORMATION
Infocentrum (☎ 353 232 838; infocentrum.kv@volny.cz; Západni; ☺ 9am-5pm Mon-Fri, 10am-4pm Sat & Sun) Is in Dolni nádraží and stocks maps, books accommodation and gives transport advice. It has a second branch in the centre (☎ 353 224 097; Lázeňska 1).

TRAVEL AGENCIES
Čedok (☎ 353 222 994; Dr. Bechera 21-23) Caters to most travel needs.

Sights & Activities
AROUND THE COLONNADES
The spa proper starts at **Poštovní Bridge**, where rows of late-19th- and early-20th-century mansions face off against the blockish communist-era (1976) **Hotel Thermal** sanatorium.

The 13th Spring is the most famous but there are 15 springs housed in or near five colonnades (kolonády) along the Teplá. The first is the whitewashed and wrought-iron **Park Spring Colonnade** (Sadová kolonáda).

Further on is the biggest and most popular, the neo-Renaissance **Mill Colonnade** (Mlýnská kolonáda; 1881), with five different springs, rooftop statues depicting the months of the year and a little bandstand (see p198). **Petra Restaurant**, opposite, is the spot (but not the original building) where Peter the Great allegedly stayed in 1711.

Straight up Lázeňská is a gorgeous Art Nouveau building called **dům Zawojski** (1901). Nearby you can do some very upmarket window shopping along Lázeňská and Tržiště including the **Moser glasswork shop** (Tržišteʾ 7); see p198. Across the road is the **Market Colonnade** (Tržní kolonáda) with its delicate white 1883 woodwork; one of its two springs is the spa's oldest, **pramen Karla IV**. Behind this is the **Castle Colonnade** (Zámecká kolonáda) and a castle tower, the **Zámecká věž**, erected in place of Charles

IV's hunting lodge after it was destroyed by fire in 1604.

The steam billowing from the direction of the river comes from the incongruous, modern building (1975) around the **Hot Spring Colonnade** (Vřídelní kolonáda). Inside is the spa's biggest, hottest spring, **pramen Vřídlo** (Sprudel to Germans), belching 15m into the air. People lounge in the geyser room for the vapours, or sample the waters from a line of progressively cooler taps in the next room.

EAST OF THE TEPLÁ
The **Church of Mary Magdalene** (kostel sv Maří Magdaléná; 1737) is across the river. Whatever your thoughts on the excesses of baroque architecture, it's hard not to fall for this confection by Kilian Ignatz Dientzenhofer.

Southward on Moravská is a striking cluster of mansions from neo-Gothic (such as No 4, where Dvořák stayed in 1879) to Art Nouveau (the Spořitelna building on Divadelní náměstí). Across the square is the 1886 **town theatre** (see p198).

UPPER VALLEY
Back on the western side you can have coffee at the classic **Elephant Café** (see p198) or peek into the concert hall and two-storeyhigh dining rooms of the gigantic **Grandhotel Pupp** (see p198), the spa's first hotel.

About 500m past the Pupp is the **Municipal Art Gallery** (see below) and a little further still, you can unwind in the **Zen Japanese garden**.

CHURCH OF SS PETER & PAUL
On Krále Jiřího, is the incongruous but deluxe **Orthodox Church of SS Peter & Paul** (kostel sv Petra a Pavla), with five polished onion domes and vaguely Art Nouveau exterior murals.

MUSEUMS & GALLERIES
There's an art gallery and four relatively interesting museums in town:
Municipal Art Gallery (Galerie Umění; ☎ 353 224 387; Goethova stezka 6; adult/concession 30/15Kč; ☺ 9.30am-noon & 1-5pm Tue-Sun) Features a modest collection of 20th-century Czech art.
Karlovy Vary Museum (Krajské muzeum Karlovy Vary; ☎ 353 226 252; Nová Louka 23; adult/concession 30/ 15Kč; ☺ 9am-noon & 1-5pm Wed-Sun) With exhibits on Karlovy Vary history and natural history, Czech glasswork and church furnishings.

Golden Key Museum (muzeum Zlatý klíč; ☎ 353 223 888; Lázeňská 3; adult/concession 20/10Kč; ☺ 9am-noon & 1-5pm Wed-Sun) Boasts paintings of the spa by Viennese artist Wilhelm Gause.

Jan Becher Museum (Jan Becher muzeum; ☎ 353 170 156; TG Masaryka 57; adult/concession 100/25Kč; ☺ 9am-5pm) Deals with all things Becherovka, the town's famed herbal liqueur.

Moser Museum of Glass (Sklářské muzeum Moser; ☎ 353 449 455; Kpt Jaroše 19; admission free; ☺ 8am-5.30pm Mon-Fri, until 3pm Sat) Offers a history of glass-making in the area, as well as visits to the Moser Factory glass works (book in advance; admission 50Kč; ☺ 9am-1pm Mon-Fri).

HIKING & BATHING

For light relief, climb steeply up from the Teplá into fragrant woods filled with statues and decaying pavilions.

It's about 1.5km from the Grandhotel Pupp to a hilltop **viewing tower** (vyhlídka vez; adult/concession 10/5Kč; ☺ 9.15am-5.45pm), with the garden **Diana restaurant** (☎ 353 222 872). The woods on the way to the lookout are peppered with monuments, including one to that old bourgeois Karl Marx, who visited Karlsbad three times between 1874 and 1876.

Alternatively, you can ride a **funicular railway** (lanovka; single/return 30/50Kč; ☺ 9am-6pm) from behind Grandhotel Pupp. The trip to Diana takes five minutes. **Stag's Leap** (Jelení skok), the promontory where Charles IV's dog made its famous discovery, is 500m northeast from an intermediate stop on the funicular. Another lookout tower is on **vyhlídka Karla IV**, south of Grandhotel Pupp.

If you're feeling lively, it's 17km on a blue-marked trail, via the Diana lookout, along the Ohře to the romantic castle and village of **Loket nad Ohří** (see p199).

For a quick dip, the **pool** (Hotel Thermal, IP Pavlova; admission 40Kč; ☺ 9am-9.30pm) at Hotel Thermal offers simple swimming, or a range of spa treatments.

Festivals & Events

The **Karlovy Vary Film Festival** (www.kviff.com), held in July, always features the year's top films as well as attracting plenty of (B-list) stars. It is rather behind the pace of the likes of Cannes, Venice and Berlin but is well worth the trip. Among the many other cultural events are the **Jazz Festival** in May and the **Dvořák Autumn Festival** in September.

Sleeping

Accommodation is as dicey and pricey as in Prague, especially in the peak film festival month of July. Budget accommodation is at a premium.

Prices quoted are for high season (May-September, plus Christmas and New Year). During low season discounts of up to 40% are available.

Expect to pay 'spa tax' (15Kč per bed per night).

ACCOMMODATION AGENCIES

Čedok (☎ 353 222 994; Dr. Bechera 21-23) can suggest private rooms from 350Kč per person, but you may need to stay for three or more nights. **W-privat** (☎ 353 227 768; wprivat@volny.cz; náměstí Republiky 5) can also arrange private rooms (from 350Kč). Also try Infocentrum.

BUDGET

Rolava (☎ 353 332 212; tent per person 60Kč; ℗) On a little lake of the same name, this camp site is 3km northwest of town. Take bus No 12 from Tržnice bus station five stops to Třeboňská stop.

Sasanka (☎ 353 590 130; tent/5-bed bungalow 65/490Kč; ℗) This quiet camp site is in Sadov, 6km north on the road to Ostrov. It also has bungalows.

Buena Vista Hostel (☎ 353 239 002; hostel@premium-hotels.com; Moravská 42; dm per person 188Kč) In a town where cheap sleeps are like gold dust, this is a little piece of bullion. There's a terrace, a pool table, a small café and beds in four- or six-bed rooms.

Hotel/Pension Kosmos (☎ 353 225 476; www .hotelkosmos.cz; Zahradní 39; s/d incl breakfast 650/1250Kč) Mostly clean and polished – although the views are spoilt by the hulk of the Thermal Hotel – this is a reliable cheapie. It also has better, renovated rooms for 990/1500Kč.

Hotel Kavalerie (☎ 353 229 613; kavalerie@volny.cz; TG Masaryka 43; s/d incl breakfast 629/1225Kč) Smiling staff and cosy rooms come as standard in this cheerful place above a café.

MID-RANGE

Hotel Embassy (☎ 353 221 161; embassy@mbox.vol.cz; Nová Louka 21; s/d incl breakfast 2020/2980Kč) Blooming window boxes and oodles of fairy-tale charm make for a page from a 19th-century picture book. Warm welcomes and snug rooms put the cherry on the cake.

Hotel Astoria (☎ 353 335 111; www.astoria-spa.cz; Vřídelní 23; s/d incl breakfast €43/66; ✗ ⊠ ⊠) This opulent spa hotel offers all the treatments coupled with top-notch modern comforts.

Hotel Kolonáda (☎ 353 345 555; www.kolonada.cz; IP Pavlova 8; s/d incl breakfast €88/121; ✗ ⊠) Slap bang in the middle of the spa, this place has lashings of class (shame about the plaster colonnade) and facilities galore.

Also recommended:

Hotel Cordoba (☎ 353 230 473; www.hotel-cordoba.com; Zahradní 37; s/d incl breakfast €30/50) A functional backup.

Hotel Romance (☎ 353 222 646; www.hotelromance.cz; Tržiště 37; s/d incl breakfast €55/80) Wonderful outside, more ordinary inside.

TOP END

Grandhotel Pupp (☎ 353 109 111; www.pupp.cz; Mírové náměstí 2; s/d incl breakfast €110/140; ℗ ✗ ✗ ⊠ ⊠) Grand with a double-decker 'G', Karlovy Vary's most salubrious address has held the number one spot in the sophistication stakes for some 300 years.

Eating

Food prices, especially in and around the colonnades, will come as a shock unless you've just arrived from Prague. And check your bill: 'mistakes' happen.

You can buy *oplatky* (see the boxed text p193) at the Městská tržnice supermarket by the bus stop on Varšavská, or at many locations across town.

Zamecky Vrch (☎ 353 221 321; Zamecky Vrch 14; mains 200Kč) Dangling pots and pans, wooden beams and assorted 19th-century clutter add lashings of charm to this upmarket, local specialty eatery.

Posezeni u Sveska (☎ 353 232 276; Stará Louka 10; mains 150Kč) This atmospheric, inn-style eatery boasts plenty of dark wood décor and scrumptious gamey mains. It's tucked away behind the promenade – look out for the two model pipe-smoking war heroes on the bench outside.

Caffe Pizzeria Venezia (☎ 353 229 721; Zahradní 43; pizza 110Kč) Decent pizza, coffee-sipping crowds and Ferrari flags for that 'authentic' Italian look are the norm here.

Steakhouse Sklipek (☎ 353 229 197; Zeyerova 1; steaks 150Kč) The US meets Italy in this bar-style steakhouse. Big grills and booths come as standard.

Vg Vegetarian Restaurant (☎ 353 229 021; IP Pavlova 25; mains 60–100Kč) This little place offers some light relief for vegetarians traumatised by all the tourist-style meat feasts.

Other recommendations:

Thailand Restaurant (☎ 723 011 893; Tržiště 37; mains 90–150Kč) For Thai and Chinese.

Elephant Café (☎ 353 223 406; Stará Louka 30; coffee 35Kč) Town's chic, old school tea room.

Entertainment

Town Theatre (Městské Divadlo v Karlových Varech; ☎ 353 225 801; www.mdkv.cz - Czech only; Divadelní náměstí 2) The main theatre stages a range of performances throughout the year. Tickets (80Kč to 500Kč) are available from the theatre, or from Infocentrum.

Karlovy Vary Symphony Orchestra (☎ 353 228 707; www.kso.cz; IP Pavlova 14) The town's orchestra stages a regular programme of concerts. See its website or *Promenáda* for details. From mid-May to mid-September **concerts** are also held in the **Mill Colonnade** from Tuesday to Sunday.

Rotes Berlin (☎ 353 233 792; Jaltská 7; ☾ until 3am) This club/bar hosts regular gigs ranging from jazz nights to Depeche Mode tribute parties.

Čas kino (☎ 353 223 272; TG Masaryka 3) Cinema lovers can get their flick fix here.

Shopping

Becherovka distillery shop (☎ 353 170 156; TG Masaryka 57; ☾ 9am–5pm) This shop is next to the Jan Becher museum (see p197), and is the place to stock up on the goodies from the 13th spring – you'll find the Becherovka a fair bit cheaper here than in other souvenir shops.

Moser glasswork shop (☎ 353 235 303; Tržiště 7; ☾ 9am–5pm Mon–Sat). If you can't make it to the factory (see p197), on the Cheb road in the western outskirts, this is the spot to pick up the glasses for your Becherovka, among other things.

Karlovy Vary porcelain is also well known, and not just those funny spa cups. The top local name is Pirkenhammer.

Getting There & Away

AIR

ČSA (☎ 353 225 760; www.czechairlines.com; Mírové náměstí 2) flies to Prague twice weekly (990Kč). It has a booking office in the Grandhotel Pupp.

BUS & TRAIN

Regular **ČSAD** (☎ 353 913 550; Terminal Dolni Nádraží) buses run to Prague (150Kč, two hours) and are much quicker than the trains (☎ 353 913 559; 275Kč, four hours).

Asiana (☎ 353 360 413; 2nd fl, Atrium Shopping Centre, IP Pavlova) also runs buses to Prague Florenc (130Kč, two hours) and the airport every two hours.

A seat reservation *(místenka)* is recommended for Prague (a day or two ahead) and for international connections (a week or more).

There are also departures to Nuremberg and Frankfurt once a week (you need to book this one as it does not stop in Karlovy Vary if there are no bookings), and Amsterdam once a week, from the lower train station.

For all bus and train times and prices, visit www.idos.cz.

Getting Around

Local buses run at 20- to 30-minute intervals; routes are posted at the stop on Varšavská. Bus tickets (8Kč) are sold in kiosks and from machines at major stops, or cost 12Kč from the driver.

Bus No 11 runs hourly from Karlovy Vary horní nádraží train station to the Tržnice bus station at the market, then over the hills to Divadlo náměstí and the Vřídelní Colonnade.

TAXIS & PARKING

A 24-hour taxi service is **Willy Taxi** (☎ 800 100 154).

A large, partially underground car park is next to Thermal Sanatorium on IP Pavlova (40/80Kč for two/24 hours).

LOKET NAD OHŘÍ

pop 3200

If size matters, Loket is the exception. A cluster of houses in sweet-shop pinks, greens and blues huddled around a fairy-tale castle, this tiny village stands on a loop in the river Ohře so extreme it almost makes an island. In fact, 'JW Goethe's favourite town' (as the tourist bumph likes to describe it) is so pretty, if you saw it in a film you'd think it was a painted backdrop.

Loket's German name is Elbogen, and it's been famous by that name since 1815 for the manufacture of porcelain, as have the neighbouring towns of Horní Slavkov (Schlackenwald) and Chodov (Chodan). You can look at some fine examples in the town and do a bit of shopping too.

Orientation & Information

The bus from Karlovy Vary provides a cinematic look at the town, almost completely circling it on approach.

The local **tourist information office** (Infocentrum; ☎ 352 684 123; www.loket.cz; TG Masaryka 12; ⏰ 10am-noon & 1-5pm) is by the bridge.

Česká spořitelna (TG Masaryka 101) has an exchange counter.

At the end of July, the **Loket Summer Cultural Festival** features opera performances in the open-air theatre below the castle walls (contact Infocentrum for details).

Sights

CASTLE

The chocolate-box **castle** (hrad Loket; ☎ 352 684 104; adult/concession 70/35Kč; ⏰ 9am-4.30pm May-Oct, until 3.30pm Nov-Apr) was built on the site of an earlier Romanesque fort, of which the only surviving bits are the tall square tower, and fragments of a rotunda and palace. Its present late-Gothic look dates from the late 14th century. From 1788 until 1947 it was used (and abused) as the town prison. The town, not the state, did the impressive restoration work in the 1970s.

A tour isn't necessary, and the English text on the castle's history has little on the exhibits inside – several cutaway sections from archaeological work on the castle and two rooms full of luscious ceramics are barely enough to whet the appetite. Check out the postcard views of the village and forest from the tower.

OTHER ATTRACTIONS

The narrow, curving square, náměstí Masaryka, has its fair share of handsome Gothic façades. But one of the most eye-catching buildings is the recently renovated, neo-Gothic **Hostinec Bílý kůň** (White Horse Inn), where Goethe stayed.

In the early-baroque **town hall** (radnice), you can visit the town's vaguely interesting (for bookbinders) **bookbinding museum** (adult/concession 30/15Kč; ⏰ 10am-1pm & 2-6pm). Ceramics junkies can also get a fix wandering around the town's **ceramics showrooms**, including a shop selling Loket's own Epiag brand.

Two old gate towers (Černá Vež and Robičská Vež) are still standing. Join in the Czech fascination with lookout towers and climb the **Black Gate Tower** (Černá Vež; TG Masaryka; admission 15Kč; ⏰ 9am-5pm), which houses

WEST BOHEMIA

a small art gallery and wine shop and offers some tip-top photo opportunities. Outside the gate towers is the tiny baroque **St Anne Chapel** (kaple sv Anny), now empty.

The red-and-white **Church of St Wenceslas** (kostel sv Václava), dating in its present form from the early 18th century, is on your way to the castle.

Sleeping & Eating
Hostinec Bílý kůň (☎ 352 685 002; TG Masaryka 8; s/d incl breakfast 900/1200Kč) Goethe used to be partial to suite 103, but recent renovations have sharpened things up a bit, creating a look that's more 'new millennium' than 'olde-worlde'. Prices go up by 20% in summer.

Hotel St Florian (☎ 352 685 109; TG Masaryka 70; incl breakfast €27 per person) Sporting a new coat of lemon paint, this charming little hotel boasts bright, airy rooms and a flourish of blooming window boxes.

Penzion 72 (☎ 352 684 918; www.penzion72loket .cz - Czech only; Kostelni 72; s/d €13/22) Right in the shadow of the castle, on a postcard pretty cobbled lane, this little *pension* has cosy rooms with modern trimmings. **Pension Mirka** (☎ 352 684 383; s/d €12/20), next door, has more of the same.

There are several restaurants around town, but **Hostinec Bílý kůň** has one of the best.

Getting There & Away
Buses link Loket with Karlovy Vary's lower train station (20Kč, 25 minutes). There are seven departures per day on weekdays, fewer on weekends. The tedious train trip requires a change at Sedlo.

You could even walk from Karlovy Vary, on a very fine 17km trail (marked blue) beside the Ohře (see p197).

PLZEŇ
pop 175,000

Beer and cars don't mix – just ask your local law enforcement officer. In Plzeň, however, it is a very different story. As the home of the Škoda Engineering Works and the brewery responsible for world-renowned Pilsner Urquell beer, the Czech Republic's fourth biggest city is a dynamic industrial centre with a global reputation forged in two very different fields. Most tourists, along with a good portion of the local population, are more interested in the one you can drink than the one you can drive,

and Plzeň rises to the challenge. Peppered with bars and restaurants – as well as a fair spread of more cultural pursuits – Plzeň is a vibrant city with an enthusiastic taste for cold beer and good times.

Despite its spectacular main square, Plzeň is considerably swarthier than the spa towns further north. But after the bus parks, sanatoriums and souvenir stalls of fairy-tale Karlovy Vary, it is also a city grounded firmly in the real world, revealing a side to West Bohemia otherwise hidden behind a barricade of ice creams, tour groups and shelves of Becherovka. Spend some time here then, and it is impossible not to fall in love with the region's rougher side.

History
Founded as West Bohemia's administrative capital in 1295 by Přemysl King Václav II, the fortified, solidly Catholic Plzeň grew quickly, becoming Bohemia's third largest town after Prague and Kutná Hora by the 14th century.

Among other things, Václav II granted to some 260 Plzeň burghers the exclusive right to brew beer. By the time of the Thirty Years' War there were 26 separate basement breweries, each with its own beer hall – though many of the products were not particularly drinkable. In 1842 the crafty brewers pooled their experience, installed 'modern' technology and founded a single municipal brewery, with spectacular results. Their golden beer, labelled Plzeňský Prazdroj (*prazdroj* is old Czech for 'the original source' – Pilsner Urquell in German), is now one of the world's best, and most imitated, beers.

At the same time, Plzeň began to industrialise. The Škoda Engineering Works was founded in 1869 and prospered as a manufacturer of armaments. Since WWII it has been known mainly for the ubiquitous Škoda car, as well as locomotives and industrial machinery. In the midst of post-1989 euphoria, Volkswagen offered Škoda a staggering US$1 billion development loan, and the German car manufacturer now has a majority share in the company.

Orientation
Plzeň sits near the confluence of four sizable rivers, two of which, the Mže and the Radbuza, flow past the old town centre.

The central bus station (centrální autobusové nádraží) is west of the town centre, 1km down Husova to the main square, náměstí Republiky. The main train station (hlavní nádraží) is the same distance on the other side; turn right under the tracks and left (west) on Americká, and cross the Radbuza, and the second, third and fourth right turns will take you into náměstí Republiky.

Information
CULTURAL CENTRES
American Center Plzeň (☎ 377 237 722; www .americancenter.cz; Dominikánská 9; 🕑 9am-10pm) Mainly a business-resource centre, with a restaurant/bar and CNN news.

INTERNET ACCESS
American Center Plzeň(☎ 377 237 722; www .american center.cz; Dominikánská 9; 🕑 9am-10pm) Charges 39Kč per hour.
Internet Kavarna (☎ 377 222 146; Tylova 6, 1st fl; 🕑 9am-9pm) Charges 1Kč per minute.
City Information Centre (městské informační středisko; ☎ 378 032 750; www.plzen-city.cz; náměstí Republiky 41; 🕑 9am-6pm) Charges 2Kč per minute.

MONEY
Česká Spořitelna (náměstí Republiky) By the Archdeacon's House, this has an ATM and exchange counter.
ČSOB (cnr Sady 5 kvetna & Františkánská) Just south of the main square.

POST
Main post office (Solní) Is west of the main square.

TOURIST INFORMATION
City Information Centre (městské informační středisko; ☎ 378 032 750; www.plzen-city.cz; náměstí Republiky 41; 🕑 9am-6pm) Reserves accommodation, organises guides, sells maps and changes money.

TRAVEL AGENCIES
CKM (☎ 377 236 393; ckm_plzen@volny.cz; Dominikánská 1; 🕑 8am-6pm Mon-Thu, until 5pm Fri) Books international travel and cheap accommodation.

Sights & Activities
NÁMĚSTÍ REPUBLIKY
Plzeň's main square, náměstí Republiky, is the hub of the city's lively and attractive old town. It is particularly notable for the gigantic Gothic **St Bartholomew Church** (kostel sv Bartoloměje), which towers over the surrounding façades from the centre of the square. Have a look inside at the delicate marble 'Pilsen Madonna' (dating from about 1390) on the main altar, or climb 301 steps to the top of the **tower** (adult/concession 20/10Kč; 🕑 10am-6pm depending on weather) for serious views.

Plzeň is less plastered with baroque façades than many Bohemian towns. The best Renaissance structures in the old centre are in and around the square. Check out **Chotešov House** (náměstí Republiky 106/13) and around the corner the delightful old **Gerlach House**.

One of the most charming buildings in Bohemia is Plzeň's **old town hall** (Staroměstská Radnice; admission free; 🕑 8am-6pm). The bottom four floors, built in 1558, are pure Italian Renaissance. A few years later the top floor, tower, multiple gables and little brass flags were added; all it needs is a liveried ensemble doing trumpet fanfares from the roof. The sgraffito on the front also dates from the 16th century. There is also a model of the old city centre here. In front is a 1681 **plague column** (one Czech tourist brochure calls it a 'plaque column').

The 1710 **Archdeacon's House** (Arciděkanství; náměstí Republiky 234/35) by Jakub Auguston, a local boy, is on the western side.

The southern half of the square becomes a boisterous **open market** every Friday.

UNDERGROUND PLZEŇ
The extraordinary **Museum of Plzeň's historical underground** (Plzeňské historické podzemí; ☎ 377 225 214; Perlová 4; adult/concession 45/25Kč; 🕑 9am-5pm Tue-Sun Jun-Sep, Wed-Sun Apr, May, Oct & Nov) is a web of passages under the town.

The earliest were probably dug in the 14th century – perhaps for beer production, or defence; the latest date from the 19th century. Of an estimated 11km excavated in the 1970s and '80s, some 500m are open to the public.

Plzeň's wealthier set used to have wells in their cellars. Over-use led to severe water shortages until a municipal water system was established in the 15th century. When wells dried up they were often filled with rubbish and buried; these have yielded an amazing trove of artefacts. The tunnels are dotted with exhibits of wooden water pumps, mining tools, pewter, pottery and – to the surprise of some historians – Czech glass dating back to the 14th century.

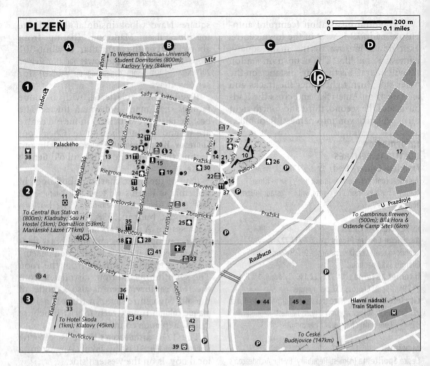

PLZEŇ

A good English text is available, but bring extra clothing (it's chilly); a torch (flashlight) will let you peer into the eeriest corners. The last tour is at 4.20pm.

ASSUMPTION CHURCH & FRANCISCAN MONASTERY

South of the square on Františkánská is the **Assumption Church** (kostel Nanebevzetí Panny Marie), entered past an unusual crucifix with a clean-shaven Christ nailed to the cross by only one hand and one foot.

In the former **Franciscan monastery** (klášter Františkánů), next door, is the **Diocese Museum** (Diecésní muzeum; Františkánská 11; adult/concession 40/20Kč; 10am-6pm Tue-Sun Apr-Sep) with tours of a fine collection of church statues. The real reason to visit is to see the little **St Barbara Chapel** (kaple sv Barbory) on the the cloister's eastern side: unaltered since it was built in the 13th century, it bears the remains of frescoes from as early as the 15th century.

ELSEWHERE AROUND NÁMĚSTÍ REPUBLIKY

The streets of Nový Plzeň's original chessboard layout are good for browsing.

At least three buildings – two on Solní and one on náměstí Republiky – bear bright murals by Mikuláš Aleš, a central figure of the so-called 'National Theatre generation' of the Czech National Revival.

At the end of Pražská is a stone **water tower** (vodárenská věž) dating from 1530 and part of the first town water system (this tower supplied fountains in the square until the beginning of the 20th century). Opposite is a former arcade of medieval **butchers' stalls** (masné krámy), which is now part of the **West Bohemian Gallery** (377 223 759; Pražská 13; adult/concession 20/10Kč; 10am-6pm Tue-Fri, from noon Sat, 10am-5pm Sun), with changing exhibits of modern Czech art.

Heading out through a town gate that's no longer there, you cross the **Prague Bridge** (Pražský most) over a moat that's no longer there. Turning left brings you to some weedy, reconstructed bits of the old town walls.

South of the square on Smetany is the very baroque **St Anne Church** (kostel sv Anny), another work by Jakub Auguston. The former **Premonstratensian monastery** next door is now part of a State Science Library.

PRAZDROJ (PILSNER URQUELL) BREWERY

Across the Radbuza is the **brewery** (pivovar; ☎ 377 062 888; www.prazdroj.cz; U Prazdroje 7; admission 120-180Kč; ⊙ 10.30am, 12.30pm, 2pm & 3.30pm Mon-Fri Jul-Aug, 12.30pm & 2pm only Sep-Jun) that put Plzeň on the map, entered through the gate that has graced the label of its beer since 6 October 1842. Individual visitors can join an interesting (for beer aficionados) one-hour tour with a film, visits to the brewing rooms and chilly fermentation cellars, and, of course, beer-tasting. You can also visit at the weekend, but you have to book ahead.

Head east on Pražská, then cross the river and bear left on U Prazdroje; the gate is near a pedestrian bridge, 750m from náměstí Republiky.

Through a similar gate 500m on is the **Gambrinus brewery**. Sorry, no tours here.

GREAT SYNAGOGUE

The neo-Renaissance **Great Synagogue** (Velká synagóga; ☎ 602 441 943; Sady Pětatřicátníků 11; admission 50Kč; ⊙ 11am-5pm Sun-Fri), across Sady Pětatřicátníků, is the third largest in the world, built in 1892 by the 2000 or so Jews who lived here then. English tours cost 50Kč extra.

MUSEUMS & GALLERIES

The **Brewery Museum** (☎ 377 235 574; Veleslavínova 6; admission 60Kč; ⊙ 10am-6pm; until 4pm Oct-Mar) offers an insight into how beer was made (and drunk) in the days before Prazdroj was founded. Highlights include a mock-up of a 19th-century pub, a tiny working model of a steam brewery and a collection of beer mats. All have English captions, bless 'em, and there's a good English text. Guides cost 40Kč extra.

The **West Bohemian Museum** (Západočeské muzeum; ☎ 377 236 460; Kopeckého sady 2; adult/concession per exhibit 20/10Kč; ⊙ 9am-5pm Tue-Sun) fills a magnificent agglomeration of buildings. In the basement the original armoury (zbrojnice) features a weapons collection; the ground floor has changing exhibits; and the 2nd floor houses an exhibit of glass and porcelain in the magnificent Art Nouveau Jubilee Hall (Jubilejní sál).

The **Town Art Gallery** (Galerie Města Plzně; ☎ 378 035 310; Dominikánská 3; adult/concession 20/10Kč; ⊙ 10am-noon & 1-6pm Tue-Sun) hosts art and design exhibitions.

The **Ethnographic Museum** (náměstí Republiky 106/13; adult/concession 20/10Kč; ⊙ 9am-5pm Tue-Sun) has a small, vaguely interesting collection.

Festivals & Events

Plzeň was liberated by the US army two days earlier than the rest of the country and so celebrates the national **Liberation Day** holiday two days earlier, on 6 May. Celebrated with perennial gusto, the event features a huge parade of Czechs dressed in WWII army surplus. There is also an **International Folk Festival** in mid-June.

Sleeping

The tourist information office and CKM have private rooms for around 300Kč per person.

BUDGET

Bílá Hora (☎ 377 534 905; tent/bungalow per person 80/180Kč; **P**) and **Ostende** (☎ 377 534 905; tent/bungalow per person 80/180Kč; **P**) have bungalows and are open from May to September. They're on opposite sides of Velký Bolevecký rybník, a lake about 6km north of the city centre and accessible (tediously) by bus No 20 from near the train station.

Sou H (☎ 377 382 012; Vejprnická 56; per person 289Kč; **P**) This year-round hostel (*ubytovna*) is 3km west of town but easily accessible on tram No 2 (direction: Skvrňany) from the train or bus station. A range of cheap beds are available.

Western Bohemian University (☎ 377 259 814; Bolevecká 30; s/d 280/400Kč; **P**) The university has student rooms, some with private bathrooms, during summer. Take tram No 4 two stops north from the Great Synagogue.

MID-RANGE

Pension City (☎ 377 326 069; fax 377 222 976; Sady 5 kvetna 52; s/d incl breakfast 900/1200Kč; **P**) On a quiet street, this pretty, perennially popular place has helpful English-speaking staff, plenty of polished trimmings and a blooming array of window boxes.

Penzion v Solní (☎ 377 236 652; pension.solni@post.cz; Solní 8; s/d 600/1020Kč) Snug and homey, this small, newly-renovated place has a few cosy, modern rooms.

Pivnice U Salzmannů (☎ 377 235 855; fax 377 235 476; Pražská 8; s/d from 550/750Kč) This traditional beer hall features plenty of foam-soaked moustaches and a small number of cheap rooms. There are also more salubrious rooms for 1350/1500Kč.

Hotel Rosso (☎ 377 226 473; recepce@hotel-rosso.cz; Pallova 12; s/d incl breakfast 1080/1980Kč; **P**) Mediterranean style counts in this hotel's favour. The rooms are bright and charming.

Another place to try is the ordinary but central **Pension K** (☎ 377 329 683; hotelk@atlas.cz; Bezručova 156/13; s/d 890/1350Kč).

TOP END

Hotel Continental (☎ 377 235 292; mail@hotelcontinental.cz; Zbrojnicka 8; s/d with shared/private bathroom 860/1460Kč, incl breakfast 1580/2150Kč) Although struck by an Allied bomb during WWII, this historic place retains some attractive Art Deco features and has put up such luminaries as Gerard Depardieu and John Malkovich. There are also better, renovated rooms for 2450Kč.

Hotel Škoda (☎ 377 420 252; fax 377 421 322; náměstí Českých bratří 10; s/d 1380/1950Kč) A little more 'old' Škoda than 'new' Škoda, this ageing place one kilometre from the centre is still a decent backup.

Also recommended is **Hotel Central** (☎ 377 226 757; hotel-central@iol.cz; náměstí Republiky 33; s/d incl breakfast 1550/2390Kč).

Eating & Drinking

Plzeňská bašta (☎ 377 237 262; Riegrova 5; mains 100Kč) This local institution, supported by a network of ancient wood beams, has oodles of personality, lashings of beer and plates of local, meaty grub.

Denní Bar & Pizzerie (☎ 377 237 965; Solní 9; pizza 65Kč) This wee pizzeria draws big lunchtime crowds with its cheerful ambience and scrumptious Italian tucker.

U Mansfelda (cnr Dřevěna & Křížíkovy sady; mains 70-120Kč) This raucous modern pub sports brass fittings, a sun terrace and pub grub in lively surrounds.

Rhodos (☎ 608 131 204; Bezručova 20; mains 120Kč) Brighter than a line in Benidorm beachwear, this Greek tavern has warm welcomes and tasty, healthy cooking. They may even let you smash the plates.

Dominik Jazz Rock Café (☎ 377 323 226; Dominikánská 3; mains 100Kč) Student-style pub fare, crowds of local twentysomethings and groovy music are the staple at this bar/restaurant. It's open until 2am most nights.

Zach's Pub (☎ 377 223 176; Palackého náměstí 2) Late nights, Guinness and fish and chips are all on the menu at this lively bar

Also recommended:

Long Feng Čínská (☎ 377 222 084; Americká 8; mains from 59Kč) For Chinese.

Slunečnice (Jungmanova 10; sandwiches 35Kč) For fresh, tasty baguettes and buffet-style snacks.

Entertainment

CLUBS

For dancing until the early hours try:

Dance Club 28 (☎ 608 701 470; Prokopova 28)
Music Club 21 (☎ 377 220 860; Prokopova 21)

THEATRE & MUSIC
JK Tyla Theatre (☎ 378 038 001; www.djkt-plzen
.cz - Czech only; Prokopova 14) Plzeň's main theatre
stages regular performances.
   Konzervatoř (Conservatory; Kopeckého sady 10) The
majority of classical concerts are held here.
   Kino Elektra (☎ 377 270 243; www.elektra-plzen
.cz - Czech only; Americká 24) Film buffs can catch a
flick before heading to the attached **Rock Bar
Elektra** for late night drinks and tunes.

Getting There & Away
There plenty of direct buses (60Kč, 1½
hours) and trains (140Kč, 1¾ hours) daily
to/from Prague.
   To and from Karlovy Vary, buses are
quicker (59Kč, 1¾ hours) and more frequent
(about eight a day) than the train (no direct
services).
   For České Budějovice, the train (162Kč,
1¾ hours) is usually quicker, but more expensive than the bus (96Kč, 2½ hours).
   For all bus and train times and prices,
visit www.idos.cz.

Getting Around
You can buy tickets (8Kč) for the buses,
trolleybuses and trams from kiosks and
tabák shops, or from machines at major
stops. There are also day passes available
(40Kč per day).

AROUND PLZEŇ
Kladruby
pop 750
A Benedictine abbey was founded here
in 1115 by Prince Vladislav I. Following
repeated plundering in the Thirty Years'
War, the Counter-Reformation abbots undertook a major face-lift of the buildings
by two of the most prominent Bohemian
artists of the time, Giovanni Santini and
Kilian Ignatz Dientzenhofer.
   The main attraction is the **Abbey Church
of the Holy Virgin**, rebuilt between 1712 and
1726 by Santini in an extraordinary 'baroque Gothic' style seen nowhere outside
Bohemia (an earlier Santini work in this
style is the abbey church at Sedlec, near
Kutná Hora). Bohemia abounds in fine but
often repetitive architecture; here is something very different.

The church has the original floor plan
of a Romanesque basilica, the longest in
Bohemia (85m). The church itself, Santini's
design from the fantastically complex vaulting right down to the pews, is an improb-
able marriage of baroque flamboyance and
Gothic severity that would verge on tongue-
in-cheek if it weren't so beautiful. At the
front to the left is the **tomb of Vladislav I**, one
of the few Přemysl rulers not buried either
at Prague Castle or Zbraslav.
   The standard tour also includes the
cloisters, with several dozen allegorical
sculptures from the workshop of the celebrated baroque sculptor Matthias Bernard
Braun. Of the monastery buildings themselves (not on the tour), the west wing is
the **Old Prelature** (Abbot's residence), now
a church library. The baroque east wing is
the so-called **New Convent**, built to a design
of Dientzenhofer between 1729 and 1739,
and now beautifully renovated.
   The **abbey** (☎ 374 631 773; kladruby@mybox.cz;
adult/concession 40/25Kč; ☼ 9am-4pm Tue-Sun May-
Sep, Sat & Sun Apr & Oct) hosts hourly group
tours in Czech (foreign text available for
40Kč extra). There are two circuits: Tour I
includes the monastery and church, while
Tour II takes in the chateau.

GETTING THERE & AWAY
Kladruby village is about 35km west of
Plzeň, just south of Stříbro. Getting there
without a car is tricky. There is one daily
bus to and from Prague via Plzeň (90Kč, 2¼
hours). Changing buses at Stříbro gives you
additional options from Plzeň.
   From Kladruby's main square, walk (in
the direction of the parish church) 1.5km
to the monastery.

KLATOVY & AROUND
pop 23,000
Fine views of the Šumava mountains herald
Klatovy's place as the gateway to this pristine,
romantic region. A sleepy renaissance square
provides more than enough for a few hours
of meandering, but the town, which was
founded in 1262, is really just a stopover en
route to bigger (and more beautiful) things.

Orientation & Information
The main train station and the bus station are
about 1.5km from the central square, náměstí
Míru. Take bus No 1 or 2 from either one.

Infocentrum Pergolia-Tour (☎ 376 313 515; pergolia.tour@worldonline.cz; náměstí Míru 63; ☼ 9am-noon & 1-5pm Mon-Fri), beside the old town hall, has info on Klatovy and the Šumava area.

KB (cnr náměstí Míru & Křížová) changes money and has an ATM.

The **main post office** (Domažlická) is west of the centre. You can get online at **Internet Café** (Václavská 19; ☼ 12pm-12am).

Sights & Activities
BLACK TOWER & AROUND
The **Black Tower** (Černá věž; adult/concession 20/10Kč; ☼ 9am-noon & 1-5pm Tue-Sun May-Sep, until 4pm Apr & Oct), at the hub of the old town, was completed in 1557, and given the present roof in 1872 after the old one blew off in a storm – it has also burnt down three times.

Next door is the late-16th-century **town hall**. The handsome neo-Renaissance façade was added only in 1925, by architect Josef Fanta.

JESUIT CHURCH & JESUIT HOSTEL
Opposite the Black Tower is the sober-faced **Church of the Immaculate Conception & St Ignatius**, worth a visit for its extraordinary trompe l'oeil frescoes. Towering over the tiny main altar is a painting of the immense altar and domes the Jesuits probably wished they could have had.

Across Balbínova is the former **Jesuit hostel**. After the Jesuits were forced out of Bohemia, the two-block-long building was subdivided into a school, brewery and an army barracks. It's now a shopping mall.

CATACOMBS
Klatovy's most popular, and ghoulish, attraction lies beneath the Jesuit church: **catacombs** (adult/concession 40/20Kč; ☼ 9am-noon & 1-5pm May-Sep, Sat & Sun only Oct-Apr) with over 200 corpses in surprisingly good condition (for corpses), including Jesuit monks and many of the region's 17th- and 18th-century luminaries. The secret to their preservation was clever, natural air-conditioning, although the arrival of tourists in recent years raised the humidity and temperature just enough for the cadavers to resume their decay; many had to be buried.

APOTHECARY MUSEUM
A few doors down the western side of náměstí Míru is the **White Unicorn Apothecary**

(U bílého jednorožce), with its original, lavish, rococo furnishings from the 17th and 18th centuries. It was a working pharmacy until the 1960s, and is now a **museum** (☎ 376 313 109; adult/concession 40/20Kč; ☼ 9am-noon & 1-5pm Tue-Sun May-Oct) offering guided tours. If there are fewer then five of you, you are advised to book ahead.

Next door is an **art gallery** (Galerie U bílého jednorožce; ☎ 376 312 049; náměstí Míru 149; adult/concession 25/10Kč; ☼ 10am-noon & 1-5pm Tue-Sun) with mostly modern exhibits.

WHITE TOWER & ARCHDEACON'S CHURCH
East of náměstí Míru is another of Klatovy's great towers, a Renaissance belfry called the **White Tower** (Bílá věž). Nearby is the town's oldest church, the early-Gothic (16th century) **Archdeacon's Church of the Nativity of Our Lady**, restored to its present state by Josef Fanta early in the 20th century.

A block east is one of the surviving bastions of the **old town walls**. Another, a round bastion called **Okrouhlice**, is beside a path between Balbínova and Komenského.

ŠUMAVA MOUNTAINS
The ancient Šumava range along the border begins southeast of Klatovy and boasts some of Bohemia's most pristine mountains. It now forms one of the Czech Republic's newest national parks and lies mainly in South Bohemia (see p226).

Sleeping
There are plenty of private rooms (ask Infocentrum Pergolia-Tour for help), and a **camp site** (☎ 376 313 200; Dr Sedlaka; tent per person 60Kč; Ⓟ), open May to September, north of town.

Hotel Mivet Sport (☎ 376 310 910; Domažlická 609; per person with shared/private bathroom 240/295Kč; Ⓟ) Noisy quads and triples come attached to a sauna and popular, smoky beer hall. It's a 1.2km walk from the town centre (west on Domažlická, north on Nerudova), or you can take bus No 2 to the Zimní Stadion stop.

Penzión U Hejtmana (☎ 376 317 918; fax 376 310 650; kpt Jaroše 145; s/d 280/560Kč) Glamour is not the strong suit of this tidy little place, but the rooms (with private bathrooms) are very good value.

Jockey Club Pension (☎ 376 313 060; cnr Vídeňská & Podbránská; s/d incl breakfast 670/1040Kč; Ⓟ) We'll

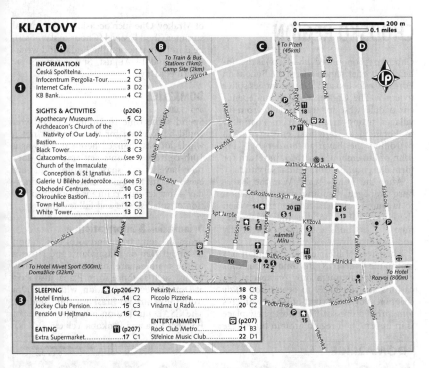

KLATOVY

wager that this place sports more horse photos per sq metre than anywhere else in the country. The restaurant is a bit naff, but the rooms are spotlessly clean.

Also recommended are:

Hotel Rozvoj (☎ 376 311 609; fax 376 315 442; Prochazkova 110/IV; d 500Kč) For good-value basic sleeps.

Hotel Ennius (☎ 376 320 567; fax 376 320 564; Randova 111; s/d incl breakfast 630/945Kč) A good quality mid-ranger.

Eating

Střelnice Music Club (☎ 376 322 366; Pražská 122; mains from 59Kč) Sanded wood floors (still unsullied by beer stains), sparkling brass fittings and kit pub paraphernalia bring the class to this spacious drinking/eating den.

Vinárna U Radů (☎ 376 314 594; cnr Pražská & Československých legií; mains 70-100Kč) The faded publicity shots in the window don't do much to add to the charm of this popular local eatery, but the local dishes provide a fix of reliably tasty stodge.

Piccolo Pizzeria (☎ 376 315 887; náměstí Míru; pizza 65Kč) Even the pizza isn't all that Italian in this '80s-style eatery, but it does pack out

with loyal – and impressively heavy smoking – local punters.

Other recommendations:

Pekařstvi (Rybníčky 64; cakes 20Kč) The sweet-toothed will find an antidote for every cake craving here.

Extra Supermarket (cnr Pražská & Dobrovského) For self-caterers.

Entertainment

Rock Club Metro (Vančurova 57) and **Střelnice Music Club** (☎ 376 322 366; Pražská 122) both host live bands.

Getting There & Away

In general, bus is the most convenient way to get here from Prague (110Kč, three hours) about twice a day; Plzeň (40Kč, one hour) five times; and Domažlice (32Kč, 45 minutes) five times. If you're carrying on south to Železná Ruda on the German border, trains are better, with four fast ones daily.

Getting Around

Infocentrum Pergolia-Tour (see p186) rents out mountain bikes for 190/250Kč per half/full day.

CHODSKO REGION

Chodsko (pronounced 'khodsko') is the Bohemian border region where the Bohemian Forest (Český les) and Šumava ranges splice together. The Chods, a sturdy, independent people who are traditionally from 11 villages sitting in an arc from Postřekov to Pocínovice, were first entrusted with patrolling the Bavarian border by King John of Luxembourg in 1325, in return for formal exemption from feudal servitude.

After the Thirty Years' War the Habsburgs reneged, handing over the region to favoured courtiers and generals. When these refused to honour the old agreements, the Chods took up arms, briefly and disastrously.

Their way of life, neither Bohemian nor Germanic, survives in unique customs and speech, although only on special occasions are you likely to hear Chod *dudy* (bagpipes) or catch sight of Chod women's long printed dresses. The most likely place is in upper Chod region around the village of Mrákov. One such occasion is the annual summer Chod Festival (Chodské slavnosti), held in Domažlice on the Friday and weekend around 14 August, St Lawrence's (sv Vavřinec) Day.

DOMAŽLICE
pop 11,000

Spend some time in Domažlice and you could be forgiven for thinking that not a whole lot has changed here since it was a 10th-century customs settlement. It does now have its fair share of communist-era eyesores, but the quiet (unless it's Wednesday – market day) centre is a pretty collection of small streets and tall towers.

Orientation & Information

From the joint train and local bus station it's about 1km on Masarykova and Husova to the main square, náměstí Míru. A few trains, such as those from Planá, also stop at Domažlice město station, which is 500m from the centre via Jiráskova and Chodská. The ČSAD bus station is on the corner of Poděbradova and Prokopa Velikého.

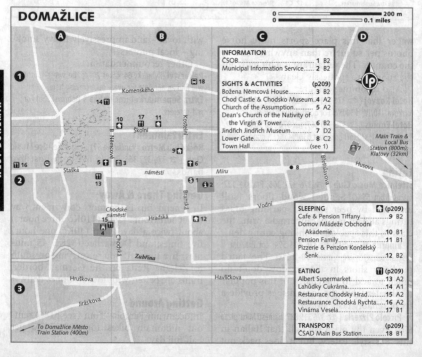

DOMAŽLICE

0 — 200 m
0 — 0.1 miles

INFORMATION	
ČSOB....................................	1 B2
Municipal Information Service......	2 B2

SIGHTS & ACTIVITIES	(p209)
Božena Němcová House..............	3 B2
Chod Castle & Chodsko Museum..4	A2
Church of the Assumption...........	5 A2
Dean's Church of the Nativity of the Virgin & Tower,.................	6 B2
Jindřich Jindřich Museum...........	7 D2
Lower Gate..............................	8 C2
Town Hall.............................	(see 1)

SLEEPING	(p209)
Cafe & Pension Tiffany................	9 B2
Domov Mládeže Obchodní Akádemie..........................	10 B1
Pension Family........................	11 B1
Pizzerie & Penzion Konšelský Šenk..................................	12 B2

EATING	(p209)
Albert Supermarket..................	13 A2
Lahůdky Cukrárna.....................	14 A1
Restaurace Chodsky Hrad..........	15 A2
Restaurace Chodská Rychta.......	16 A2
Vinárna Vesela........................	17 B1

TRANSPORT	(p209)
ČSAD Main Bus Station..............	18 B1

Main Train & Local Bus Station (800m); Klatovy (32km)

To Domažlice Město Train Station (400m)

WEST BOHEMIA

The **Municipal Information Service** (městská informační centrum; ☎ 379 725 852; www.idomazlice.cz; náměstí Míru 51; ☺ 7.30am-5pm Mon-Fri 9am-noon Sat Jun-Sep, until 4pm Mon-Fri Sep-May), in the town hall, can also advise on accommodation.

ČSOB, next door, changes money and has an ATM.

The **post office** (Stašska) is just west of the main square.

Sights & Activities
NÁMĚSTÍ MÍRU

The narrow, 500m-long square is almost closed at the eastern end by the 13th-century **Lower Gate** (Dolní brána) and a Gothic **gatehouse**.

Dominating the square is the slightly leaning tower of the **Dean's Church of the Nativity of the Virgin** (Děkanský kostel Narození Panny Marie), a little gem in cream and gold by Kilian Ignatz Dientzenhofer. It's a long climb up the 56m **tower** (adult/concession 20/10Kč; ☺ 9am-noon & 1-5pm Apr-Oct), but the views of the Šumava are fine.

Across the square is the neo-Renaissance **town hall**. A block west is a house where the Czech writer **Božena Němcová** lived and worked between 1845 and 1847, beyond it the Gothic monastery **Church of the Assumption** Nanebevzetí Panny Marie).

CHOD CASTLE & CHODSKO MUSEUM

Southwest of the square, and as old as Domažlice itself, is the town **castle** (adult/concession 35/15Kč; ☺ 9am-noon & 1-5pm Tue-Sun Apr-Oct, 10am-noon & 1-3pm Mon-Fri Nov-Mar). There is a lapidarium in the basement with statues and parts of façade decorations from the old castle; other rooms have rich exhibits of local folklore including bagpipes and dresses.

JINDŘICH JINDŘICH MUSEUM

You can get a good look at some aspects of the Chod lifestyle – such as handicrafts, clothing, a typical home – at a little **museum** (Husova; adult/concession 20/10Kč; ☺ 10am-noon & 1-5pm 15 Apr-15 Oct) based on the collections of a composer named Jindřich Jindřich, who lived here in the 1960s. It's just outside the Lower Gate.

Sleeping & Eating

Domov mládeže Obchodní akademie (☎ 379 722 386; B Němcové 116; dm per person 140Kč) Basic dorm beds are on offer here, but phone ahead as reception isn't always staffed.

Pizzerie & Penzion Konšlský Šenk (☎ 379 720 200; Vodní 33; s/d incl breakfast 580/960Kč) This terracotta place brings a flick of warm Mediterraneana to the streets of Domažlice. With a garden and fab pizzas to boot, why leave?

Café & Pension Tiffany (☎ 379 725 591; pension .tiffany@quick.cz; Kostelní 102; s/d incl breakfast 400/800Kč) Friendly, English-speaking Otto offers pleasant rooms over his groovy, colourful café.

Vinárna Vesela (☎ 602 263 652; Školní 109; s/d 400/600Kč) This moody cellar bar is perfect for cheap eats, lazy tipples and well-priced sleeps (upstairs).

Restaurace Chodsky Hrad (☎ 379 776 010; Chodské náměstí 96; mains 80-150Kč) Its location by the castle sucks in the crowds, but the local speciality food is tasty rather than touristy and the pleasant atmosphere comes on the house.

Other recommendations:

Lahůdky Cukrárna (B Němcové; snacks 15Kč) For super cheap snacks and coffees.

Albert Supermarket (cnr Staška & Chodská) For self-caterers.

Getting There & Away

Regular trains (76Kč, 1½ hours) and buses (54Kč, 1½ hours) run to Plzeň. There are also less frequent train (204Kč, three hours) and bus (96Kč, three hours) services to Prague. Bus (32Kč, 58 minutes) and train (52Kč, 50 minutes) also run to Klatovy.

WEST BOHEMIA

South Bohemia

South Bohemia is a land of lakes, forests and fields, sprinkled with quaint villages that mix a Bavarian or Austrian flavour with Czech baroque folk motifs. Watching it race by from the window of a Český Krumlov-bound tour bus, it is easy to forget that there is more to this beautiful and varied region than the spectacular little town that has become the region's undisputed, but mildly over-pampered, starlet. In fact, Český Krumlov's draw is so profound these days that the needle of the tourist compass seems to point forever south, to only those streets and squares overlooked by its fairy-tale chateau. But while Český Krumlov remains the region's populist drawcard, there is plenty more besides. Whether you dream of rambling over deserted hills, paddling down crystal rivers or simply propping up the bar of some of the continent's most esteemed beer halls, South Bohemia has something to tickle every fancy.

Flowing north from the Šumava mountains, the Vltava river bisects South Bohemia and is an obvious starting point for any journey, joining the dots of South Bohemia's tourist trail and bringing with it enduring traces of Austrian and German culture. Cutting north past Rožmberk's chateau, Český Krumlov and the dynamic brewery town of České Budějovice, the Vltava is an A-list attraction in itself, lined with picturesque villages and riverside beer halls, and ideal for those who want to hire a boat and watch the beautiful landscape drift by.

But while the tourist brochures wax lyrical about Český Krumlov and the region's unspoilt countryside, the region is at its most idiosyncratic when you take a step or two from the beaten track. From the photogenic former Hussite stronghold of Tábor to remote little Slavonice, where the hands of the town clock never seem to move, South Bohemia's less-visited communities and quieter corners offer some of the most colourful insights into the manifold Czech identity found anywhere in the country.

HIGHLIGHTS

- Soak up the festival atmosphere of **Český Krumlov** (p219), one of central Europe's prettiest towns

- Watch the beautiful landscapes of South Bohemia drift by while canoeing down the **Vltava** (p221)

- Make a pilgrimage to **České Budějovice** (p213), home of the original Budweiser beer

- Take in the history in the former Hussite stronghold of **Tábor** (p238)

- Escape the crush in the remote village of **Slavonice** (p245)

SOUTH BOHEMIA

SOUTH BOHEMIA

SOUTH BOHEMIA

0   30 km
0   20 miles

To Vienna (40km)

SOUTH MORAVIA

CENTRAL BOHEMIA

WEST BOHEMIA

AUSTRIA

GERMANY

Šumava

To Plzeň (14km)

E65
E59
E551
E49
E55
E49
E49
E55
E49
19
33
4
4

Humpolec
Pelhřimov
Jihlava
Dačice
Slavonice
Kamen
Červená Lhota
Jindřichův Hradec
Nová Bystřice
Granetten
Halámky
Neunagelberg
Gmünd
Chýnov
Tábor
Soběslav
Veselí nad Lužnicí
Třeboňsko Protected Landscape Region
Rožmberk
Třeboň
Braňná
Nepomuk
Trocnov
České Velenice
Žofínský prales Protected Landscape Region
Dolní Dvořiště
Milevsko
Sezimovo Ústí
Bechyně
Týn nad Vltavou
Vltava
Hluboká nad Vltavou
Dobrá Voda
Kaplice
Rybník
Dolní Dvořiště
Wollowitz
Horní Dvořiště
Orlík nad Vltavou
Žďákov
Zvíkovské Podhradí
Písek
Temelín
Čičenice
Netolice
Ohrada
Holašovice
České Budějovice
Boršov nad Vltavou
Třísov
Divoká
Zlatá Koruna
Klet' (1083m)
Blanský Les Protected Landscape Region
Rájov
Český Krumlov
Rožmberk nad Vltavou
Studánky
Weigetschlag
Mirotice
Kestřany
Otava
Slanik
Strakonice
Protivín
Kratochvíle
Prachatice
Husinec
Černá v Pošumaví
Horní Planá
Frymburk
Dolní Vltavice
Lipno n Vlt
Vyšší Brod
Lake Lipno
Vítkův Kámen (1053m)
Blatná
Vimperk
Boubín (1362m)
Horní Vltavice
Lenora
Šumava Protected Landscape Region
Horní Planá
Plechý (1378m)
Nýrsko
Svihov
Hojsova Stráž
Klatovy
Železná Ruda
Sušice
Nepomuk
Strážný
Philippsreut
Kvilda
Šumava National Park
Švarcenberský kanál
Grosser Arber (1456m)

ČESKOBUDĚJOVICKO REGION

ČESKÉ BUDĚJOVICE

pop 100,000

České Budějovice jostles with Plzeň in the practically religious struggle to produce the Czech Republic's best beer, rising to notoriety as the birthplace of the original Budvar (Budweiser) and still prized as the home of one of Europe's finest tipples.

Like Plzeň, South Bohemia's capital is a vibrant city, big enough to escape the more touristy 'toy town' attributes of nearby Český Krumlov, but still small enough to ensure that its pretty old heart isn't choked by the industry on its boundaries.

More green than grey, the region's biggest city is a patchwork of tight alleys, broad parks and gaping squares, offering a slightly scruffy – and reliably rowdier – take on the country's perennial old town blueprint. It may still have the air of an overgrown village, but after an overdose of South Bohemian rusticity this is the place to indulge in a shot of (quietish) urban living and a sample or two of South Bohemia's amber aqua vitae.

History

The marshy site, ideal for the defence of a medieval fortress, was selected by King Přemysl Otakar II in 1265 as a royal town and a bulwark against powerful local families.

Its ancient predecessor, the village of Budivojovice, was at the present site of the Church of St Procopius & John the Baptist (kostel sv Prokopa sv Jana Křtitele), north of the centre in the suburb of Pražské sídliště. As old as the town are the Dominican Monastery and Church of the Sacrifice of the Virgin, and náměstí Přemysla Otakara II.

By the 14th century České Budějovice was the most powerful town in Southern Bohemia. Its many fine Renaissance buildings testify to its wealth from trade and silver mining. It remained staunchly royalist and Catholic during the Hussite Wars, though it was never attacked by Hussite armies. The royal mint was established here in the late 16th century.

Prosperity continued until the Thirty Years' War, when a disastrous fire (in 1641)

destroyed half the town. The silver also began to run out and the royal mint was closed.

České Budějovice only began to recover with the establishment of a major school in 1762 and a bishopric in 1785. Industry arrived in the 19th century. The first railway train on the continent rode out from here to Linz, Austria, in 1832.

After WWI the southern part of South Bohemia was given to Czechoslovakia, although over half of its population was German. Though Germans and Czechs had coexisted peacefully here for centuries, the Germans were nevertheless all expelled from České Budějovice in 1945.

Orientation

From the adjacent bus and train stations, it's a 1km-walk west down Lannova třída to náměstí Přemysla Otakara II, the centre of town.

Parking is considerably cheaper outside the old town.

Information

INTERNET ACCESS

Internet cafés charge 40Kč to 60Kč per hour:
Internet Café Babylon (☎ 728 190 461; 5th fl, náměstí Přemysla Otakara II 30; ⏲ 10am-10pm Mon-Sat, 1-9pm Sun)
Na Půdě (☎ 387 313 529; Krajinská 28; ⏲ 9am-10pm)

LEFT LUGGAGE

The left-luggage office at the bus station is open from 7am to 7pm weekdays and until 2pm Saturday; and at the train station from 5am to noon and from 12.30pm to 7pm daily.

MEDICAL & EMERGENCY SERVICES

24-hour pharmacy (☎ 387 873 103) At the hospital.
Hospital (nemocnice; ☎ 386 355 555; B. Němcové 54)
Jihočeský autoklub (☎ 386 356 566; Žižkova třída 13) Offers motoring assistance.
Police station (☎ 387 621 304; Pražská 5) Has a section for foreigners.

MONEY

Česká spořitelna (cnr náměstí Přemysla Otakara II & U Černé věže') Changes money and has an ATM.
KB (Krajinská 19) Changes money and has an ATM.

POST

Main post office (Pražská 69) Open 24 hours. There is another branch on Senovážné náměstí.

ČESKÉ BUDĚJOVICE

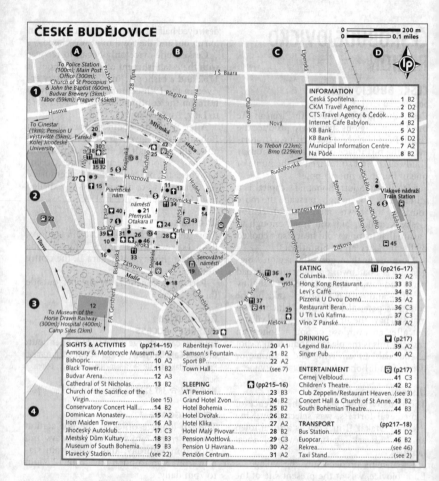

INFORMATION
Česká Spořitelna	**1** B2
CKM Travel Agency	**2** D2
CTS Travel Agency & Čedok	**3** B2
Internet Cafe Babylon	**4** B2
KB Bank	**5** A2
KB Bank	**6** D2
Municipal Information Centre	**7** A2
Na Půdě	**8** B2

SIGHTS & ACTIVITIES   (pp214–15)
Armoury & Motorcycle Museum	**9** A2
Bishopric	**10** A2
Black Tower	**11** B2
Budvar Arena	**12** A3
Cathedral of St Nicholas	**13** B2
Church of the Sacrifice of the Virgin	(see 15)
Conservatory Concert Hall	**14** B2
Dominican Monastery	**15** A2
Iron Maiden Tower	**16** A3
Jihočeský Autoklub	**17** C3
Městký Dům Kultury	**18** B3
Museum of South Bohemia	**19** B3
Plavecký Stadion	(see 22)
Rabenštejn Tower	**20** A1
Samson's Fountain	**21** A2
Sport BP	**22** A2
Town Hall	(see 7)

SLEEPING   (pp215–16)
AT Pension	**23** B3
Grand Hotel Zvon	**24** B2
Hotel Bohemia	**25** B2
Hotel Dvořák	**26** B2
Hotel Klika	**27** A2
Hotel Malý Pivovar	**28** B2
Pension Mottlová	**29** C3
Pension U Havrana	**30** B2
Penzión Centrum	**31** A2

EATING   (pp216–17)
Columbia	**32** A2
Hong Kong Restaurant	**33** B3
Levi's Caffé	**34** B2
Pizzeria U Dvou Domů	**35** A2
Restaurant Beran	**36** C3
U Tří Lvů Kafirna	**37** C3
Víno Z Panské	**38** A2

DRINKING   (p217)
Legend Bar	**39** A2
Singer Pub	**40** A2

ENTERTAINMENT   (p217)
Cernej Velbloud	**41** C3
Children's Theatre	**42** B2
Club Zeppelin/Restaurant Heaven	(see 3)
Concert Hall & Church of St Anne	**43** B2
South Bohemian Theatre	**44** B3

TRANSPORT   (pp217–18)
Bus Station	**45** D2
Euopcar	**46** B2
Rekrea	(see 46)
Taxi Stand	(see 2)

TOURIST INFORMATION & TRAVEL AGENCIES

Municipal Information Centre (Městské Informarční Centrum; ☎ 386 801 413; www.c-budejovice.cz; náměstí Přemysla Otakara II 2; ☯ 8.30am-6pm Mon-Fri, until 5pm Sat, 10am-4pm Sun) Books tickets, tours and accommodation.

CTS (☎ 386 360 543; 1st fl, náměstí Přemysla Otakara II 38; ☯ 9am-noon & 1-5pm Mon-Fri) Stocks maps and can help with private accommodation.

Čedok (☎ 387 763 253; náměstí Přemysla Otakara II 39; ☯ 9am-5pm Mon-Fri) Has a few accommodation ideas, but is most helpful for bus, train and plane tickets.

Sights & Activities
NÁMĚSTÍ PŘEMYSLA OTAKARA II

This eclectic jumble of arcaded buildings, centred on **Samson's Fountain** (Samsonova

kašna; 1727), is actually the broadest plaza in the Czech Republic, spanning 133m. Prize among the architectural treats is the formerly Renaissance 1555 **town hall** *(radnice)*, which received a baroque face-lift in 1731 courtesy of AE Martinelli. The allegorical goody-goody figures on the town hall balustrade – Justice, Wisdom, Courage and Prudence – are matched by a rather exotic foursome of bronze dragon gargoyles.

Just off the square on U Černé věže is the dominating, 72m Gothic-Renaissance **Black Tower** (Černá věž; ☎ 386 352 508; adult/concession 20/ 10Kč; ☯ 10am-6pm Tue-Sun Apr-Oct), built in 1553. You can climb its 225 steps (yes, we counted them) for fine views of the city centre. The tower's two bells – the Marta (1723) and

Budvar (1995; a gift from the brewery) – are rung daily at noon and will turn your head to ash if you are climbing the tower at the time.

Beside it is the popular local wedding venue, the **Cathedral of St Nicholas** (katedrála sv Mikuláše), built as a church in the 13th century, rebuilt in 1649 and made a cathedral in 1784.

AROUND THE OLD TOWN

The old town is surrounded by Mlýnská stoka, the Malše river and extensive gardens where the walls once stood. Only a few bits of the Gothic fortifications remain, including **Rabenštejn Tower** (Rabenštejnská věž; cnr Hradební & Panská; adult/concession 40/20Kč; 10am-6pm Mon-Fri, 9am-noon Sat), which you can poke your nose into; and the 15th-century **Iron Maiden Tower** (Železná pana; Zátkovo nábřeží), a squat and crumbling former prison.

Along Hroznová, on Piaristické náměstí, is the **Church of the Sacrifice of the Virgin** (kostel Obětování Panny Marie) and a former **Dominican Monastery**, which has a splendid pulpit. You enter the church from the Gothic cloister. Beside the church is a medieval armoury (zbrojnice) that was later used to store salt until it could be sent down the Vltava to Prague; and the small **South Bohemian Motorcycle Museum** (Jihočeské Motocyklové; 387 200 849; Piaristické náměstí; adult/concession 40/20Kč; 9am-5pm Wed-Sun), which has a fine collection of Czech Jawas and a handful of wonderful WWII Harley-Davidsons.

Return up to Česká, turn right and follow it to Radniční. Another right onto Biskupská takes you past the 18th-century **bishopric** (biskupství; admission free; 8am-6pm May-Sep). It is accessible through a small gate in the wall.

Follow Zátkovo to dr Stejskala. Pass the **South Bohemian Theatre** (Jihočeské divadlo) and continue to JV Jirsíka and turn right into Dukelská, where you'll find the **Museum of South Bohemia** (Jihočeské muzeum; 387 929 328; adult/concession 45/10Kč; 9am-12.30pm & 1-5.30pm Tue-Sun), with its extensive collection on history, books, coins, weapons and wildlife.

A small **Museum of the Horse-Drawn Railway** (Památky koněspřežní železnice; 386 354 820; Mánesova 10; 9am-12.30pm & 1-5pm Tue-Sun) is south of the centre, near the Koh-i-noor factory, but a serious interest in horses, railways, or preferably both, is a prerequisite.

BUDVAR BREWERY

Touring the modern **Budvar brewery** (pivovar; 387 705 341; cnr Pražská & K Světlé; adult/concession with tasting 88/38Kč, without tasting 70/20Kč; 9am-5pm) with all its sights, smells and science is actually a whole lot less interesting than sampling its product in one of the city's many beer halls. Nevertheless, a pilgrimage to the home of Budvar, several kilometres north of the city (take bus No 2), deserves its place on any South Bohemian travel itinerary. Visitors are advised to book the 80-minute tour in advance by phoning the brewery, or organising it through the tourist information office. However, individuals can just turn up for the 2pm tour (Monday to Friday only). There is a 30Kč surcharge at weekends.

If all this proves too much for you, you can always put your feet up in the attached **Budvar beer hall** (10am-10pm).

Sleeping

Accommodation can get tight in July and August, so book in advance. Prices also fluctuate seasonally – these are high (summer) season rates. In the low season you could possibly expect a discount of as much as 25% (although each hotel has its own rules).

BUDGET

Hostels

The **municipal information centre** (Městské Informarční Centrum; 386 801 413; www.c-budejovice.cz; náměstí Přemysla Otakara II 2; 8.30am-6pm Mon-Fri, until 5pm Sat, 10am-4pm Sun) and **CKM Travel Agency** (387 424 505; Lannova třída 63; 9am-5pm Mon-Fri), near the train station, can arrange accommodation in dormitories from 120Kč per person. All of the listed tourist offices (see p213) can also help with private rooms for about 300Kč.

Kolej jihočeské university (387 774 201; Studentská 800/15; d 350Kč; P) During the holidays, the university offers basic doubles with shared bathroom and no breakfast.

Pension U výstaviště (387 240 148; U výstaviště 17; s/d 250/500Kč; P) Things are basic here, but it's about the closest thing to a traveller's hostel in town and there's a communal kitchen for DIY eating. It's 30 minutes west from the city centre by bus No 1 or 14 from outside the bus station to the fifth stop (U parku); the pension is about 100m up the right-hand street.

Camping

Motel Dlouhá Louka Autocamp (☎ 387 203 601; Stromovka 8; tent/s/d 65/550/950Kč; **P**) This motel and camp site is a 2km walk southwest of town (take bus No 6 from in front of Městský dům kultury). You can camp May to September, or take a rather uninspiring motel room year round.

Stromovka Autocamp (☎ 387 203 600; tent/3-bed bungalow 50/500Kč; **P**) Just past Dlouhá Louka Autocamp, this has so-so bungalows and ample tent space. There are only a few showers here so the queues can be long. It's open April to October.

MID-RANGE

Small private *pensions* around town are often a better deal than the hotels.

Penzión Centrum (☎ 387 311 801; penzion_restaurant@centrum.cz; Biskupská 130/3; s/d incl breakfast 800/1000Kč) Gigantic rooms with satellite TV, helpful staff and fresh modern décor are the main drawcards at this super central place.

Hotel Bohemia (☎ 386 360 691; hotel-bohemia@volny.cz; Hradební 20; s/d incl breakfast 1290/1690Kč) Occupying a couple of old burghers' houses on a quiet street, this snug little number offers elegant comfort for shallow(ish) pockets.

AT Pension (☎ 387 312 529; Dukelská 15; s/d 500/800Kč) It doesn't look like the dowdy pink décor has been updated since 1910 (the date over the door), but this homely place gets high marks for friendliness.

Other recommendations:

Pension U Havrana (☎ 387 318 132; Panská 13; s/d 350/700Kč) Rooms above a raucous beer hall.

Pension Mottlová (☎ 386 357 135; Alešova 5; s/d 350/700Kč) Offers a couple of cheap rooms with shared bathroom.

TOP END

Hotel Klika (☎ 387 318 171; hotel@hotelklika.cz; Hroznová 25; s/d incl breakfast 1450/1950Kč) On the water's edge, with traces of the 14th-century walls still visible in the restaurant, this newly refurbished place stylishly blends old world charm and modern functionality. The rooms, all sanded wood and bright décor, are light and airy.

Hotel Malý Pivovar (☎ 386 360 471; musil@budvar-hotel.cz; Karla IV 8-10; s/d incl breakfast 1950/2650Kč; **☒ ☒**) A glass-topped, 1980s-style atrium takes pride of place, but the smart, stylish rooms are the biggest selling point.

Grand Hotel Zvon (☎ 387 311 384; ghz@hotel-zvon.cz; náměstí Přemysla Otakara II 28; 1750/2400Kč; **☒ ☒**) Borderline swanky with slightly haughty staff, this place is a little faded and promises more on the outside than it delivers inside. However, the newly refurbished rooms (add 50% to listed prices) remain really quite opulent.

Hotel Dvořak (☎ 386 253 140; dvorakcb@genea2000.cz; náměstí Přemysla Otakara II 36; s/d incl breakfast 2000/2300Kč; **☒ ☒**) Cleanliness verging on the pathological is a plus, but this new well-equipped place is distinctly lacking in atmosphere.

Eating

CAFÉS

U Tři Lvů Kafirna (☎ 386 351 985; U tři lvů 4; snacks 45Kč) New Ageist in extremis, this cosy little place features water pipes, ambient tunes, Asian-style seating and more varieties of leaf than attended the Boston Tea Party.

Levi's Caffé (Kanovnická 4; coffee 30Kč) The doors have only recently opened on this minimalist, chichi coffee house. Head up to the 1st floor, place yourself in one of the giant windows and get down to some serious people watching.

RESTAURANTS

Try the local carp, which is on many restaurant menus.

Columbia (☎ 387 315 915; Česká 30; mains 100-150Kč) Presumably named after the Space Shuttle (the dishes contain enough calories to launch a rocket), this fabulously friendly, fantastically snug café/restaurant serves up a plethora of meaty Bohemian specialities in throbbing surrounds. Book ahead at weekends and order only one starter if you don't want to move up a waist size.

Restaurant Beran (☎ 386 359 559; Žižkova 3; mains 100-250Kč) A 1/20th scale model of the Leaning Tower of Pisa holds up the roof, a ceramic dog cocks its leg against the bar and a full-size model ram glowers at inbound customers – the décor of this cellar bar/restaurant may be quirky, but the Italian-meets-Texicana food gets a resounding 'yee-hah!'

Pizzeria U Dvou Domů (☎ 777 696 948; Panská 17; pizzas 100Kč) There's not much more to this little place (it seats about eight) than a wood-fired oven, some sublime smells and a man who knows his pizza. If you can't get a seat, pick your toppings, grab a Budvar and gobble it up in the nearby park.

Hong Kong Restaurant (☎ 387 312 846; Široká 25; mains 100-200Kč) Housed in immaculately renovated premises (spot the red banners), Hong Kong's menu has also had a face-lift. On a good day, it can even give the view from the Star Ferry a run for its money.

Víno z Panské (☎ 387 318 511; Panská 14; mains 100-150Kč) On the 1st floor, above a wine shop, this quiet little wine bar offers intimate eats for those who miss their grapes.

Drinking

Singer Pub (☎ 386 360 186; Česká 55) Presumably named after the brand of sewing machine that graces most of the tables (the late night singing is not worth remembering), this tub-thumping Irish bar is a top place to kick off an evening.

Legend Bar (Radniční 9) The motorcycle theme is a little strained, but this dingy and perennially lively drinking den is chock-a-block with rockers until the wee small hours of the morning.

Entertainment

BARS & CLUBS

Černej velbloud (☎ 386 360 528; www.cernyvelbloud .com - Czech only; U tří lvů 4) Purportedly specialising in 'archaic revival', this is in fact a good honest rock venue featuring regular live bands and a fair few camel (*velbloud* means 'camel') motifs.

Club Zeppelin (3rd fl, náměstí Přemysla Otakara II 38) By day this is the more innocent Restaurant Heaven; by night Club Zeppelin provides yet more leather-clad, late night action.

DRAMA, CLASSICAL MUSIC & CINEMA

South Bohemian Theatre (Jihočeské Divadlo; ☎ 386 356 643; www.jihoceskedivadlo.cz; dr Stejskala 23) The city's main theatre presents plays (usually in Czech), operas and concerts.

Children's Theatre (Malé divadlo; ☎ 386 352 508; Hradební 18) Child-oriented puppet shows and the like are the norm here.

Chamber Philharmonic Orchestra of South Bohemia (☎ 386 353 561; www.music-cb.cz; Kněžská 6) Staging most of its performances out of the Church of St Anne, this is the first stop for classical music lovers.

Conservatory (konzervatoř; ☎ 386 110 410; Kanovnická 22) This Stalinist shoebox also hosts classical music performances.

Cinestar (☎ 385 799 999; www.cinestar.cz - Czech only; Obchidní Centrum Čtyři Dvory) One kilometre west of the centre, this state-of-the-art multiplex stages all the latest cinema releases (65Kč).

SPORT

Budvar Arena (☎ 386 107 111; FA Gerstnera) Ice hockey matches are staged here from September to April. Contact the tourist information office for details.

Plavecký Stadion (☎ 387 315 784; ⏱ 10am-6pm) Just across the river, on a small island, this sports hall has swimming pools and saunas open to the public.

Getting There & Away

All bus and train times and prices can be checked at www.idos.cz.

BUS

From České Budějovice, direct buses (☎ 386 354 444) go to Prague Roztyly (134Kč, 2½ hours), Jihlava (90Kč, 2½ hours), Tábor (54Kč, one hour) and Český Krumlov (26Kč, 50 minutes).

TRAIN

There are fast, direct trains (☎ 387 854 361) to Plzeň (162Kč, two hours), Tábor (88Kč, one hour), Prague (204Kč, 2½ hours) and Jihlava (162Kč, 2½ hours).

Twice a day there are trains to and from Linz, Austria (2¼ hours, 125km). Three times a day you can go to Linz with a change of trains at the border stations (Horní Dvořiště and Summerau). Connections with trains between Prague and Vienna are made at České Velenice, 50km southeast of České Budějovice. Two daily trains run to and from Vienna (Franz-Josefsbahnhof) with a change in Gmünd.

Getting Around

The city is well connected by bus (8Kč). The main **taxi stand** (☎ 800 141 516; Lannova 1) is by the train station.

To rent a car, talk to **Čedok** or visit **Europcar/Rekrea** (☎ 387 312 290; Široká 12; ⏱ 9am-5pm Mon-Fri).

Bikes (190Kč per day), rafts (650Kč per day) and canoes (180Kč per day) can be hired at **Sport BP** (☎ 387 318 439; Sokolovský ostrov 1; ⏱ 9am-noon & 1-6pm Mon-Fri, until 11.30am Sat). Expect to pay a 1500Kč deposit.

SHOCart GeoClub's *Českobudějovicko* (1:75,000) map shows local cycle routes.

AROUND ČESKÉ BUDĚJOVICE
Trocnov

The birthplace of Hussite hero Jan Žižka is 12km southeast of České Budějovice and has a small **museum** (☎ 387 995 345; adult/concession 25/10Kč; ☻ 9am-5pm Tue-Sun May-Sep) dedicated to him. From Budějovice there are at least six daily buses (12Kč, 28 minutes).

Holašovice

South Bohemia is well known for its ornate, 19th-century 'folk baroque' country houses and barns. Some of the best examples are in the tiny village of **Holašovice**, a Unesco site 15km west of České Budějovice.

Traditionally, holidays and festivals have been celebrated in just such a setting, around a large square complete with a pond and a chapel, and each spring maypoles are still erected in many villages to celebrate the end of winter. There are about four daily buses from České Budějovice (13Kč, 30 minutes).

Kratochvíle

This attractive Renaissance **chateau** (☎ 388 324 380; tours in Czech/English 50/100Kč; ☻ 9am-5.15pm Tue-Sun Jun-Aug, until 4.15pm May & Sep, 9am-4pm Sat & Sun Apr & Oct) was completed in 1589 for the Rožmberk family, and is decorated inside with stucco reliefs and murals based on classical mythology. Kratochvíle is also home to an interesting **Museum of Animated Film**, with examples from notable Czech producers like Jiří Trnka and Hermína Týrlová.

You can take a bus to Netolice from České Budějovice (20Kč, one hour) or Prachatice (13Kč, 30 minutes), and walk the remaining 1.5km.

HLUBOKÁ NAD VLTAVOU
pop 4800

Crowned with a stunning chateau, which is visible for miles around, this little village draws visitors from across the country. Most tourists head off once the castle tour is over, however, making Hluboká a pleasant place to stay if accommodation is tight in nearby České Budějovice.

Information

The **tourist information centre** (☎ 387 966 164; www.hluboka.cz; Masarykovo 35; ☻ 10am-5pm) publishes a useful map listing all local accommodation options.

Česká spořitelna (Masarykovo 38) changes money and has an ATM.

Chateau

See p72 for a full description of Hluboká nad Vltavou's chateau.

South Bohemian Aleš Gallery

This exquisite **gallery** (Alšova jihočeská galérie; ☎ 387 967 041; adult/concession 60/15Kč; ☻ 9-11.30am & 12.30-6pm) is to the right of the castle gate, in a former riding school (*jízdárna*). On display is a fabulous permanent collection of Czech religious art from the 14th to 16th centuries, plus 17th-century Dutch masters and changing exhibits of modern art.

JAN ŽIŽKA

Hussite Count Jan Žižka was born in Trocnov, just outside České Budějovice, in 1376. He spent his youth at King Wenceslas IV's court and fought as a mercenary in Poland, but returned to the Czech kingdom at the beginning of the Reformation and became the leader of the Taborites (see p238). His military genius was responsible for all the Hussite victories, from the 1420 Battle of Žižkov onwards. After losing both eyes in two separate battles, Žižka eventually died of the plague in 1424.

Žižka's army was highly organised and was the first to use a system of wagons with mounted artillery – the earliest tanks in history. These vehicles allowed him to choose where to draw up position, taking the initiative away from the crusaders and making them fight where he wanted. The technique proved almost invincible.

The Hussites successfully saw off their enemies for a decade following Žižka's death, but were defeated by a combined army of the rival Hussite faction of the Utraquists and the Holy Roman Empire in 1434. Surprisingly, Žižka's invention was not incorporated into other armies until Sweden's King Gustavus II Adolphus adopted it two centuries later.

Sleeping & Eating

The tourist information centre can recommend private rooms. Also watch for 'Zimmer frei' or 'privát' signs along Masarykovo.

Hotel Štekl (☎ 387 967 491; stekl@bohemiagold.cz; s/d incl breakfast 3200/3500Kč; P 🛇 🖳) Just across from the castle entrance, this opulent place is almost as plush as the chateau itself.

Hotel Bakalář (☎ 387 965 516; Masarykova 69; s/d incl breakfast 900/1400Kč) Back in the village proper, this ordinary place has functional rooms and a useful bike hire outfit.

Autokemping Křivonovska (☎ 387 965 285; tent/bungalow per person 60/200Kč; P) Three kilometres north of Hluboká at Křivonovska, this decent place has bungalows and is open from 15 May to September.

Pizzerie Ionia (☎ 387 963 109; Masarykova 33; pizza 80Kč) By the tourist office, this has al fresco dining and a wide selection of Italian staples.

Getting There & Away

Buses run from České Budějovice to Hluboká's main square every 30 to 60 minutes (14Kč, 20 minutes).

AROUND HLUBOKÁ

The baroque **Ohrada Chateau** (☎ 387 865 340; adult/concession 40/20Kč; 🕑 8.30am-2pm Tue-Sun Apr & Oct, until 5pm May & Sep, until 6pm Jun-Aug) is 2km southwest of Hluboká. A former Schwarzenberg hunting lodge, it is now a museum of hunting and forestry, featuring wildlife, hunting trophies and some unsettling furniture made from antlers. There is a small **zoo** attached.

Public transport is not very regular, but the castle is a pleasant walk from Hluboká.

ČESKÝ KRUMLOV

pop 15,000

If anywhere symbolises the idiosyncratic beauty of small town Middle Europe, it is Český Krumlov. Capped with the second-largest chateau in the country, this achingly beautiful little town is a labyrinth of lanes and squares lifted straight out of the book marked 'chocolate box clichés'. Wrapped up in the tight arcs of the Vltava river and cut through with some serious olde-worlde magic, this is the place to live the picture postcard idyll.

Earning its place on Unesco's World Heritage list in 1992, Český Krumlov has

a reputation on the tourist circuit that far outstrips its size, attracting an endless carnival of visitors. On the one hand, this influx has brought in busloads of cash, resulting in a starburst of fancy restaurants, boutique hotels and, perhaps most importantly, restoration work. On the other, it has meant that the town sometimes feels like it is going to buckle under the sheer weight of all the coaches.

But while the town does become a whirlwind of trinket shops, tour groups and street performers come the summer months, there is no danger of Český Krumlov losing its charm. You will no longer get this little place to yourself, but you will always feel part of its seemingly endless festival.

Orientation

Český Krumlov has an irregular shape and is tricky to navigate; the chateau tower and Church of St Vitus are helpful landmarks.

From the main bus station it's a short walk southwest to the Inner Town (Vnitřní Město), centred on náměstí Svornosti. The Lazebnický Bridge (Lazebnický most) takes you to Latrán, a warren of shops beneath the chateau.

The main train station is in the northern part of Český Krumlov, 1km from the chateau (turn right from the station, take the first left and continue downhill on třída Míru).

If you're driving, note that parking in the old town is permit-only (ask if your hotel can issue you with one). There are public car parks just outside the centre.

Information

INTERNET ACCESS

Internet cafés charge around 60Kč per hour. Options include:

Café Internet (☎ 380 712 219; Zámek 57; 🕑 9am-9pm) Next to Unios Tourist Service.

Infocentrum (☎ 380 704 622; infocentrum@ckrf.ckrmlov.cz; náměstí Svornosti 1; 🕑 9am-8pm)

LAUNDRY

Laundromat Lobo (☎ 380 713 153; Latrán 73; 🕑 8am-8pm) Offers self-service washing machines and dryers.

LEFT LUGGAGE

Unios Tourist Service (☎ 380 712 219; tourist.service@unios.cz; Zámek 57; 🕑 9am-6pm) Can store baggage for 100/300Kč per hour/day.

SOUTH BOHEMIA

ČESKÝ KRUMLOV

0 ▬▬▬▬▬ 200 m
0 ▬▬▬▬▬ 0.1 miles

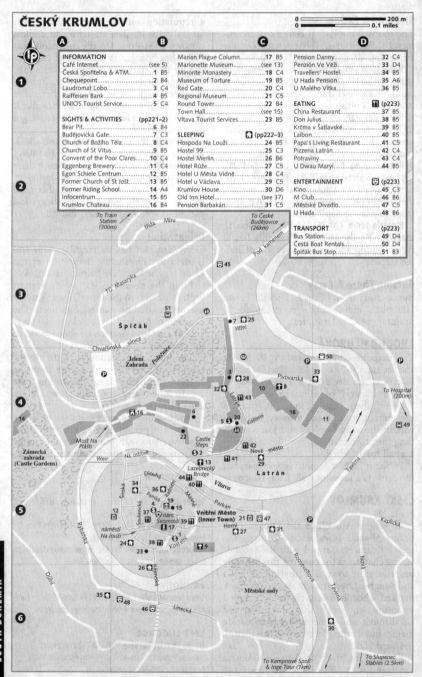

INFORMATION
Café Internet ....(see 5)
Česká Spořitelna & ATM............**1** B5
Chequepoint.............................**2** B4
Laudromat Lobo.......................**3** C4
Raiffeisen Bank.........................**4** B5
UNIOS Tourist Service...............**5** C4

SIGHTS & ACTIVITIES **(pp221–2)**
Bear Pit..................................**6** B4
Budějovická Gate.....................**7** C3
Church of Božího Těla..............**8** C4
Church of St Vitus....................**9** B5
Convent of the Poor Clares......**10** C4
Eggenberg Brewery.................**11** D4
Egon Schiele Centrum..............**12** B5
Former Church of St Jošt..........**13** B5
Former Riding School...............**14** A4
Infocentrum............................**15** B5
Krumlov Chateau.....................**16** B4

Marian Plague Column.............**17** B5
Marionette Museum................(see 13)
Minorite Monastery.................**18** C4
Museum of Torture..................**19** B5
Red Gate................................**20** C4
Regional Museum....................**21** C5
Round Tower...........................**22** B4
Town Hall...............................(see 15)
Vltava Tourist Services.............**23** B5

SLEEPING 🏠 **(pp222–3)**
Hospoda Na Louži...................**24** B5
Hostel 99................................**25** C3
Hostel Merlin..........................**26** B6
Hotel Růže.............................**27** C5
Hotel U Města Vídně...............**28** C4
Hotel u Václava......................**29** C5
Krumlov House........................**30** D6
Old Inn Hotel..........................(see 37)
Pension Barbakán...................**31** C5

Pension Danny........................**32** C4
Penzión Ve Věži......................**33** D4
Travellers' Hostel....................**34** B5
U Hada Pension.......................**35** A6
U Malého Vítka.......................**36** B5

EATING 🍴 **(p223)**
China Restaurant.....................**37** B5
Don Julius...............................**38** B5
Krčma v Šatlavské...................**39** B5
Laibon...................................**40** B5
Papa's Living Restaurant..........**41** C5
Pizzeria Latrán........................**42** C4
Potraviny...............................**43** C4
U Dwau Maryl.........................**44** B5

ENTERTAINMENT 🎭 **(p223)**
Kino.......................................**45** C3
M Club...................................**46** B6
Městské Divadlo......................**47** C5
U Hada...................................**48** B6

TRANSPORT **(p223)**
Bus Station.............................**49** D4
Čestá Boat Rentals..................**50** D4
Špičák Bus Stop......................**51** B3

MEDICAL & EMERGENCY SERVICES
Hospital (nemocnice; ☎ 380 761 911; Hřbitovní 424)
One block east of the bus station.
Police (☎ 158; náměstí Svornosti 1)

MONEY
Banks with ATM and change facilities
include:
Česká Spořitelna (cnr náměstí Svornosti)
Chequepoint (Latrán 5) Changes money (no ATM) until late.
Raiffeisen Bank (náměstí Svornosti 15)

POST
Post office (Latrán 81) Also has an exchange office.

TOURIST INFORMATION
Infocentrum (☎ 380 704 622; infocentrum@ckrf.ckrum
lov.cz; náměstí Svornosti 1; 🕑 9am-8pm) Books accommodation and concert tickets, sells maps, and organises
guided tours. It also has audio guides to the town (100Kč
per hour) and Internet access.
Unios Tourist Service (☎ 380 712 219; tourist.servic@
unios.cz; Zámek 57; 🕑 9am-6pm) This private information office provides a similar service.
Vltava Tourist Services (☎ 380 711 988; ckvltava@
ckvltava.cz; Kájovská 62; 🕑 9am-7pm) Books accommodation and arranges fishing, canoeing, horse riding etc.

Sights
LATRÁN & KRUMLOV CHATEAU
Krumlov Chateau, (see p74) the city's most
photogenic sight, looms high above the old
town.

Just off Latrán you will find the **Minorite
Monastery** and **Convent of the Poor Clares** (Minor-
itský klášter; adult/concession 40/20Kč; 🕑 10am-noon &
12.30-6pm), which can be accessed through a
gate at the end of Klášterni. English text is
available for those wanting to explore the
interior, or you can escape the crowds for
a quiet stroll through the gardens.

The former armoury is now the **Eggen-
berg Brewery** (☎ 380 711 426; obchod@eggenberg.cz;
Latrán 27; tours with/without tasting 130/100Kč), built
in 1630 and now provider of much of
Krumlov's beer. Tours must be booked in
advance.

INNER TOWN
Travelling south from the chateau along
Latrán you pass the former **Church of St Jošt**
(kostel sv Jošta) on the way to Lazebnický
Bridge, from where the Inner Town opens
up. The church now houses a small **Marionette Museum** (Latrán 6; adult/concession 70/40Kč;

🕑 10am-6pm) – for puppet fetishists only.
Turning right into Parkán takes you to
Na ostrově, a small island with good views
across the river to the chateau.

Below the square, in a pretty former
brewery, is **Egon Schiele Centrum** (☎ 380 704 011;
www.schieleartcentrum.org; Široká 70-72; adult/concession
180/105Kč; 🕑 10am-6pm). This excellent private
gallery was established in 1993 and houses a
respectable retrospective of Viennese painter
Egon Schiele (1890–1918), who lived briefly
in Krumlov in 1911, raising local hackles by
hiring young girls as nude models. For this
and other sins he was eventually driven out.
On a rotating basis, it also houses temporary
exhibitions of other A-list artists.

Continue on Široká and Na louži, and
turn left to náměstí Svornosti, with its 16th-
century **town hall** and **Marian plague column**
(Mariánský sloupek), erected in 1716. Several
buildings have valuable stucco and painted
decorations, such as the hotel at No 13 and
the house at No 14. Near Infocentrum you
will also find the requisite **Museum of Torture**
(cnr náměstí Svornosti & Radniční; adult/concession 80/40Kč;
🕑 9am-8pm) displaying the usual clutch of
ghoulish implements.

Back at the square, follow Horní uphill
and past Kostelní to the 14th-century **Church
of St Vitus** (kostel sv Víta). Continue on
Horní past the 1588 **Jesuit College** (Jesuitská
kolej), now housing the plush Hotel Růže.

Up on the left is the **Regional Museum**
(Regionální muzeum v Českém Krumlové; ☎ 380 738 473;
www.muzeum.ckrumlov.cz; Palackého 21; adult/concession
60/30Kč; 🕑 10am-12.30pm & 1.30-6pm Tue-Sun Apr-Oct,
9am-noon & 12.30-4pm Tue-Sun Nov-Mar), featuring
folk art from the Šumava region, archaeology, history, fine arts, furnishings and
weapons. The highlight is a room-sized,
ceramic model of Český Krumlov as it was
in 1800.

Activities
In summer, you can rent canoes, kayaks
and rafts for paddling or drifting on the
Vltava – some hostels also rent tyre inner
tubes. Companies will usually offer one-
way transport to towns upriver, where you
will pick up your boat for the trip back to
Český Krumlov. The journey takes about
seven hours from Vyšší Brod, five hours
from Rožmberk, or three from Branná.
There are plenty of beer gardens and camp
sites en route if you want to take things

more slowly. You can also head north from Český Krumlov to Zlatá' Koruna (five hours) and Boršov nad Vltavou (nine hours). Prices are much of a muchness and come in at about 700Kč per day for an open canoe and 1200Kč per day for a much bigger raft. Reliable companies offering this service include **Čestá Boat Rentals** (☎ 602 453 661), which is by the P3 car park, and **Inge Tour** (☎ 380 746 139; www.ingetour.cz; Kemp Nové Spolí) in the Nové Spolí camp site, 2km south of the centre on the east bank.

There are plenty of other outdoor activities available.

Slupenec Stables (☎ 380 711 052; info@slupenec.cz; Slupenec 1; ☼ 9am-6pm Tue-Sun) has horses for trips and lessons (one/11 hours 250/1800Kč). The stables are 2.5km south of town and activities can also be booked through the tourist information offices.

Bikes can be hired for 300Kč per day from Unios Tourist Service and Vltava Tourist Services (see p221).

Festivals & Events
Infocentrum sells tickets to major festivals, including the **Chamber Music Festival** in late June and early July, the **International Music Festival** during August (for more information see www.czechmusicfestival.com) and **Jazz at Summer's End Festival** at the end of August. The **Pětilisté růže** (Five-Petalled Rose) **Festival** in mid-June features two days of street performances, parades and medieval games (expect a small admission fee).

Sleeping
There are literally thousands of beds, but accommodation can still get tight in summer. Prices fluctuate dramatically, with rates dropping by as much as 40% during winter. These are high (summer) season rates.

BUDGET
Expect to pay from 400Kč per person for a private room, often with breakfast included. Inquire at the various tourist information offices.

Hostel 99 (☎ 380 712 812; hostel99@hotmail.com; Věžní 99; dm/d 300/600Kč) Lodged in the guts of the old town walls, this popular place has oodles of charm and features everything from laundry and bike hire, to Internet access and barbecues. If you're bankrupt you can even just crash on a couch (100Kč).

Krumlov House (☎ 380 711 935; info@krumlov hostel.com; Rooseveltova 68; dm/d 250/600Kč) Also packed with facilities (including free rubber rings for river floating), this is a slightly quieter affair, located just outside the fray.

Travellers' Hostel (☎ 380 711 345; krumlov@trav ellers.cz; Soukenická 43; dm/d 250/600Kč) This institution is the most central hostel option and its barn-like bar packs out come nightfall. On the downside, the rooms are a bit scruffy and if your bed's near the action, you'll need some serious earplugs.

Kemp Nové Spolí (☎ 380 728 305; tent per person 55Kč; Ⓟ) On the right (east) bank of the Vltava, about 2.5km south of town, this spartan camp site is seriously busy. It's open June to August.

Other recommendations:
Hostel Merlin (☎ 606 256 145; Kájovská 59; dm 250Kč) Ramshackle but cosy.
U Hada (☎ 606 957 697; u.hada@seznam.cz; Rybářská 37; dm/d 300/600Kč) Just around the corner from its nightclub namesake.

MID-RANGE
Pension Barbakán (☎ 380 717 017; www.barbakan.cz; Horní 26; d incl breakfast from 1100Kč) The views from the terrace restaurant of this elegant *pension* are enough to give you vertigo. Luckily, the plush, individually styled rooms are the perfect place to recover.

U Malého Vitka (☎ 380 711 925; vitekhotel@ email.cz; Radniční 27; d incl breakfast 1450Kč) This stylishly refurbished offering combines medieval monastic charm with 21st-century comfort. Curiously quirky, you can choose from a variety of rooms named after fairy-tale characters, from Tit Ivanka to Slug Viky.

Hospoda Na Louži (☎ 380 711 280; hotel@nalouzi .cz; Kájovská 66; d incl breakfast 1200Kč) This Schiele-era oak-panelled inn literally oozes old world cheer, with fabulous beer, authentic early 20th-century décor and some cosy rooms.

Hotel u Václava (☎ 380 715 094; uvaclava@quick.cz; Nové Město 25; d 2200Kč) This stylish boutique hotel has seven delightful rooms dripping with drapes and soft furnishings.

Other recommendations:
Pension Danny (☎ 380 712 710; daniel.sedlak@ worldonline.cz; Latrán 72; d incl breakfast 800Kč) Small and brightly furnished.
Penzión Ve Věži (☎ 380 716 972; Nové Město 28; d incl breakfast 1000Kč) For eccentric sleeps in a Gothic tower.

TOP END

Hotel Růže (☎ 380 772 100; info@hotelruze.cz; Horní 154; s/d incl breakfast 3400/5200Kč; P X X 🗔 🗦) This palatial hotel fills the old Jesuit college and boasts everything you could possibly want – and a bit more besides. It is only let down by the congregation of dodgy medieval mannequins in the lobby.

Old Inn Hotel (☎ 380 772 500; info@hoteloldinn.cz; náměstí Svornosti; s/d incl breakfast 2100/3800Kč; X X 🗦) Hotel Růže's sister hotel offers a slightly dumbed-down version at a slightly deflated price. The rooms are still properly posh though, the location is unbeatable and you can use the pool at Hotel Růže.

Hotel u Města Vídně (☎ 380 713 915; info@hmv.cz; Latrán 77; s/d €89/109; X X) Business-style comfort comes at the expense of old-fashioned atmosphere here, but the sparkling new rooms are perennially reliable.

Eating & Drinking

Krčma v Šatlavské (☎ 380 713 344; Horní 157; mains 100-150Kč) Darker than the inside of a cow, with roaring fires in every corner, this medieval-style barbecue cellar (it really isn't as naff as it sounds) serves tip-top slabs of meat and its wine out of earthenware goblets. Open-air grill-ups with live music are a weekly speciality. Book ahead.

Laibon (Parkán 105; mains 70-150Kč) One of town's rare meat-free zones, this snug veggie oasis whips up all the great couscous, pasta and Czech (erm...dumplings with cream sauce) favourites.

U Dwau Maryí (☎ 380 717 228; Parkán 104; mains 80-175Kč) This idiosyncratic, medieval-style haunt serves up surprisingly delicious Dark Ages pub grub (including vegetarian dishes) in a riverside setting. It's also the place to slurp down the country's oldest beer.

Pizzeria Latrán (☎ 380 712 651; Latrán 37; pizza 100Kč) Top-notch pizza comes straight from the wood-fired oven here. The drifting smells attract locals and tourists in equal numbers.

China Restaurant (☎ 737 460 072; náměstí Svornosti 14; mains 100-250Kč) The murals say 'medieval Europe', the food says 'authentic Chinese', the bill says 'touristy'. All in, a good bet.

Don Julius (☎ 380 712 310; Kájovská; mains 120-250Kč) With a spitting and smoking central fireplace, lots of bare stone and bric-a-brac

a-plenty, this is a cosy place to tuck into meaty grills and local specialities.

Papa's Living Restaurant (☎ 380 711 585; Latrán 13; mains 100-250Kč) Bloody steaks, lip smacking ribs, scrumptious salads and riverside views are served up here against a backdrop of colourful Mediterraneana.

Potraviny (supermarket; Latrán 55) Picnic? This is the place to come.

Entertainment

CLUBS

U Hada (☎ 606 957 697; Rybářská 37; ☾ until 3am) Has it been dubbed 'the snake pit' because everyone leaves legless? Apparently not. In fact, it is because they keep snakes under the bar. Either way, expect serious frolics until a flick before dawn.

M Club (☎ 380 716 850; Rybářská 40; ☾ until 3am) DJs, pool tables and slump seating provide enough dusk-until-nearly-dawn entertainment for you not to have to bother wasting money on a hotel.

THEATRE & CINEMA

Městské divadlo (☎ 380 711 775; www.divadlo.ckrumlov.cz; Horní 2) The town theatre has performances most weeks.

Kino (☎ 380 711 892; Špičák 134) This central cinema shows the latest releases in English (60Kč).

Getting There & Away

Seven buses (120Kč, three hours) and one direct train (224Kč, 3¾ hours) run to/from Prague daily. Buses run all day to/from České Budějovice (26Kč, 50 minutes) and seven times a day to/from Rožmberk nad Vltavou (22Kč, 40 minutes). About eight local trains a day run to České Budějovice (46Kč, one hour), where you can change for further onward trains to Prague.

For travel information, contact Infocentrum or visit www.idos.cz.

AROUND ČESKÝ KRUMLOV
Blanský Les

The **Blanský Les** Protected Landscape Region is good hiking territory, particularly near the summit of the **Kleť** (1083m); in winter it is a ski resort. A year-round **chairlift** climbs to the summit from the car park above Krasetín, 2km from Holubov, where the Český Krumlov–České Budějovice train stops.

Kleť can also be reached on foot via a green-marked trail from near Český Krumlov's main train station. Other trails are marked on SHOCart's GeoClub *Českobudějovicko* (1:75,000) map.

Zlatá Koruna
pop 600

Above the Vltava is the wee village of Zlatá Koruna and a well-preserved Gothic **monastery** (Cisterciácký klášter; adult/concession 85/40Kč; ☉ 9am-noon & 1-5pm Tue-Sun), founded in 1263 by Přemysl Otakar II to demonstrate his power in the region.

Originally called the Saintly Crown of Thorns, the monastery in later, wealthier days was renamed the Gold Crown (Zlatá Koruna). The walled complex also houses a **Museum of South Bohemian Literature** (Památník písemnictví jižních Čech).

The entire complex – entered at the rear through a functioning convent – can be visited on regular guided tours (minimum five people; last tour 4.15pm).

INFORMATION
Infocentrum (☎ 380 743 173; ☉ 9am-1pm & 2-5pm Tue-Sun) has maps of the area and can help with accommodation. It is in the Obecní Urad, just before the monastery.

SLEEPING & EATING
There are private rooms here and in the adjacent village of Rájov, a 1.5km downhill walk south.

Pension Koruna (☎ 380 743 194; Zlatá Koruna 26; s/d incl breakfast 350/700Kč) Attached to the only real restaurant in town, this inn-style place has comfy rooms.

Zlatá Koruna Kemping (☎ 380 743 333; tent per person 60Kč) Open May to September, this slightly scruffy camp site is just across the bridge at the bottom of town.

GETTING THERE & AWAY
Regular buses run to/from Český Krumlov (12Kč, 15 minutes).

Around Zlatá Koruna
The brawny, ruined **Dívčí kámen**, a castle on an outcrop above the Vltava, was founded by the Rožmberks in 1349 but abandoned in 1541. It's an easy 4km walk on a red-marked trail by the river, north from Zlatá Koruna.

TŘEBOŇ
pop 9000

Although largely off the tourist circuit, Třeboň is known not only for its picturesque old centre and surviving defensive walls, but also as a spa town. The narrow main square has some fine baroque and Renaissance façades, and Třeboň's chateau is worth a peek. Don't forget to try the flavoursome local fish and another delicacy, Regent beer.

Orientation
Old Třeboň is entered through its venerable gates. From the main square, Masarykovo náměstí, it's easy to find your bearings.

The main train station is northwest of the old town, a 1.5km-walk or a local bus ride away. There's also a smaller station the same line, Třeboň Lázně, 800m northeast. The bus station is 1km due west, off Svobody.

Information
The **tourist information office** (Informační středisko; ☎ 384 721 169; info@iks.tbnet.cz; Masarykovo náměstí 103; ☉ 9am-6pm Mon-Fri, 9am-noon Sat & Sun) can help with private accommodation – it closes erratically in winter.

Česká spořitelna (Masarykovo náměstí 100) changes money and has an ATM. The **main post office** (Seifertova 588) is west of the main square.

Sights
AROUND MASARYKOVO NÁMĚSTÍ
The main attractions are the Renaissance and baroque houses on the square and within the town walls, which date from 1527. Don't miss the **town hall** on the square, and **St Giles Church** (kostel sv Jiljí) and the **Augustine Monastery** (Augustinský klášter) on Husova. The **brewery** (pivovar; Trcnovské náměstí) has been home to Regent beer, one of Bohemia's oldest and best beers, since 1379. The brewery itself is closed to the public, but it does have a smoky and raucous *pivnice* (beer hall) for sampling the product.

TŘEBOŇ CHATEAU
The **chateau** (zámek; ☎ 384 721 193; ☉ 9am-5.15pm Tue-Sun Jun-Aug, until 4pm Apr-May & Sep-Oct) includes a **museum** with a small collection of furniture and weapons. There are three tour routes to choose from, ranging from 45Kč to 60Kč (double that in English). Enter through a gate (opposite Březanova)

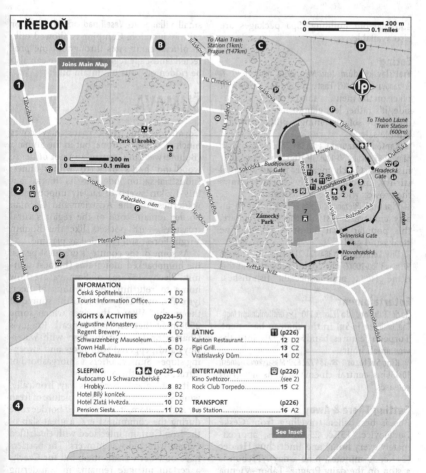

TŘEBOŇ

Park U hrobky

INFORMATION
Česká Spořitelna.................... 1 D2
Tourist Information Office..........2 D2

SIGHTS & ACTIVITIES (pp224–5)
Augustine Monastery................3 C2
Regent Brewery.......................4 D2
Schwarzenberg Mausoleum......5 B1
Town Hall..............................6 D2
Třeboň Chateau......................7 C2

SLEEPING (pp225–6)
Autocamp U Schwarzenberské
Hrobky.............................8 B2
Hotel Bílý koníček...................9 D2
Hotel Zlatá Hvězda................10 D2
Pension Siesta.......................11 D2

EATING (p226)
Kanton Restaurant...................12 D2
Pipi Grill..............................13 C2
Vratislavský Dům....................14 D2

ENTERTAINMENT (p226)
Kino Světozor.....................(see 2)
Rock Club Torpedo.................15 C2

TRANSPORT (p226)
Bus Station...........................16 A2

See Inset

from Masarykovo náměstí or via the courtyard off Rožmberská. The ticket office is in the tower. The last tour is 45 minutes before closing.

SCHWARZENBERG MAUSOLEUM
Many Schwarzenbergs have taken their last rest in this 1877, neo-Gothic **mausoleum** (Švarcenberská hrobka; adult/concession 30/20Kč, in English 60/30Kč; ☼ as chateau) in Park U hrobky, on the other side of the pond from Třeboň. It's a pleasant area for a picnic.

Sleeping
Autocamp U Schwarzenberské hrobky (☎ 384 72 24 36; tent per person 60Kč; P) South of town near the Schwarzenberg Mausoleum, this pleasant camp site is open from May to September only.

Pension Siesta (☎ 384 724 831; penzionsiesta@tiscali.cz; Hradebni 26; s/d incl breakfast 400/800Kč) Clinching pole position right on the edge of the canal, this pleasant spot comes with bags of charm and a warm welcome.

Hotel Bílý koníček (☎ 384 721 213; Masarykovo náměstí 97; s/d incl breakfast 800/1000Kč) Built in 1544, this small square-sided hotel comes with a Renaissance front, bike hire and passable rooms. There is also a restaurant on the premises (see the following section).

Hotel Zlatá Hvězda (☎ 384 757 111; mailbox@zhvezda.cz; Masarykovo náměstí 107; s/d incl breakfast 1500/1900Kč) The main square's smartest offering has plush rooms set in a photogenic

430-year-old building. Spa packages are also available.

Eating
Vratislavský dům (cnr Masarykovo náměstí 97 & Březanova; pizza 90Kč) Tasty pizzas take pride of place on the menu of this terrace eatery. Inside, it's rather less glamorous, with a load of frumpy sofas seemingly pilfered from a jumble sale.

Kanton Restaurant (☎ 384 722 563; Masarykovo náměstí 87; mains 50-120Kč) Offering a peculiar fusion of Czech meat feast and oriental stir-fry, this cheap and cheery eatery draws the crowds with its eclectic menu.

Pipi Grill (Březanova; mains 80-160Kč) Set in an airy courtyard just off the main square, this popular local haunt whips up fine steaks and grills.

Bílý koníček (☎ 384 721 213; Masarykovo náměstí 97; mains 100-200Kč) The crowds suggest that this is the place to opt for speciality fish dishes.

Entertainment
Rock Club Torpedo (Zámek 110; ⊙ until midnight Mon-Thu, until 2am Fri-Sat) In the chateau basement, Torpedo features bands and DJs into the wee small hours.

Kino Světozor (☎ 384 722 850; Masarykovo náměstí 103) This central cinema screens new(ish) releases.

Getting There & Away
Bus is best when travelling from České Budějovice (15Kč, 25 minutes, approximately every hour) and Jindřichův Hradec (21Kč, 30 minutes, nine a day). Třeboň is a stop on the daily Prague–Tábor–Vienna train line. On a local train from Tábor, you must normally change at Veselí nad Lužnicí; the whole trip from Tábor takes about an hour and costs 40Kč.

AROUND TŘEBOŇ
A good **forest walk** begins at Masarykovo náměstí, following a green-marked trail east out of Třeboň. This joins a blue-marked trail that runs northeast to Na kopečku, past **Rožmberk Pond**, through Stará Hlína to **Hodějov Pond**. From here a yellow trail runs west to Smítka, where it joins a red trail heading north to Klec and a primitive camp site.

From there, for nearly 20km, the red trail runs north, past more ponds, forests and small villages to **Veselí nad Lužnicí**, a major railway junction. Camping is allowed only in official camp sites throughout the protected landscape region. This route can also be ridden on your mountain bike.

ŠUMAVA

Cornfields and trunk roads may cover much of Middle Europe, but in the Šumava (Böhmerwald in German), a knot of dense woodland harks back to wilder times. Industrialisation has left its mark, but this 125km sweep of largely unpopulated wilderness on the Austrian and German border remains one of the region's rural treasures, with pockets like the Boubín Virgin Forest still regarded as pristine.

As some of the country's grandest peaks, the humpbacked mountains (highest summit: Plechý 1378m) of Šumava are now home to returning populations of deer, lynx and owl. They are also the source of the mighty Vltava, the river which some 250km further on rolls beneath Prague's Charles Bridge. Cut through with waterways and peppered with lakes and sweeping slopes, Šumava offers a smorgasbord of attractions for the outdoorsy.

It hasn't always been this way. Ironically, while Šumava is now the very picture of fresh air and freedom, it was a closed border zone during the communist era: a great slab of the Iron Curtain, interlaced with electrified barbed wire and watchtowers. The barriers have now been dismantled, but for Czechs a certain intrigue remains in wandering through a former forbidden zone.

The Boubín Virgin Forest region has been a nature reserve since 1858. The 1630-sq-km Šumava Protected Landscape Region (Chráněná krajinná oblast, or CHKO) was established in 1963. In 1990 Unesco declared this a biospheric reservation. The adjacent Bavarian Forest gained this status in 1981, and together they comprise central Europe's largest forest complex. In April 1991, 685 sq km of the CHKO became the Šumava National Park (Národní park Šumava). This and the CHKO now make up the biggest, single, state-protected area in the Czech and Slovak Republics.

Most of the Šumava is now open for trekking (*turistika*). The mountainous terrain

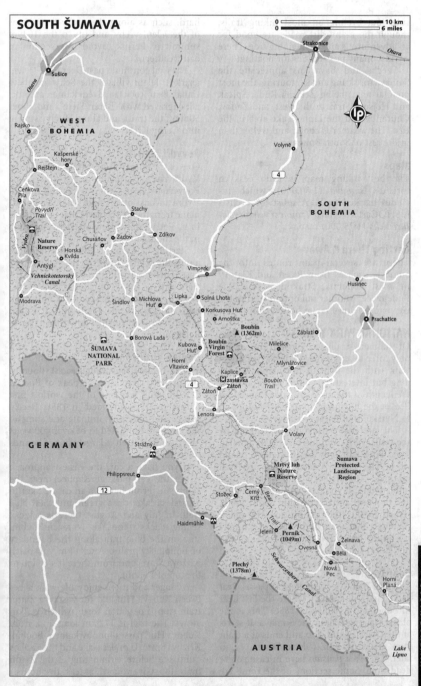

SOUTH ŠUMAVA

| 0 | | 10 km |
| 0 | | 6 miles |

rules out cycling on most hiking trails, though the many dirt roads are good for an adventurous and challenging ride. There are also many possibilities for boating.

Czechs and Bavarians appreciate the Šumava for skiing and ski touring, the most popular areas being Železná Ruda, Špičák and Hojsova Stráž in the west, and Zadov, Churáňov and the Lipno Lake area in the east. The weather is cooler and wetter than in the rest of South Bohemia.

Maps

The best hiking map is Klub českých turistů's *Šumava* (1:50,000), which includes marked trails. A must for cyclists is SHOCart's *Šumava Trojmezí velká cyklo-turistická* (1:75,000) map.

Getting There & Away

There are several train routes into the Šumava, such as from Plzeň and Klatovy in West Bohemia, Strakonice or České Budějovice. Another rail option is from the German side on Prague-bound trains.

NATIONAL PARK WALKS

Of the many trails to choose from, we list only three here; it's easy to devise your own walk with the help of the maps. A very long but interesting walk is along most of the length of the national park, from Nová Pec, at the northern tip of Lake Lipno, up to Nýrsko, southwest of Klatovy.

The national park must be entered by the trails, with camping only at designated sites. Fires can only be lit at those camp sites. The colour-coded trails are well marked with distance and walking-time information. If you pass a trail intersection and don't see a marker within about 300m, return to the intersection and try again. Also note that some of the reserve is totally off-limits: watch for 'Vystup zakázán' (do not enter) signs.

Bear Trail

The **Bear Trail** (Medvědí stezka) passes **Bear Rock** (Medvědí kámen), where the last bear in Bohemia was killed in 1856. This is the oldest walking trail in the Šumava. It starts at the Ovesná train stop and ends at a train stop in Černý Kříž (Black Cross), 14km later. There's a *pension* here in case you're dead tired. Some sections of the route are hard, such as along the rocky formations of the Jelení vrchy and up to the 1049m summit of Perník (avoid this section in bad weather).

The trail continues past Deer Lake (Jelení jezírko), Jelení village, the Schwarzenberg Canal, Bear Rock (Medvědí kámen memorial; engraved with 'Bären Stein', and about 50m off the trail), and along Hučivý stream into Černý Kříž.

Povydří Trail

One of the Šumava's best trails is along the Vydra river, especially in the area called Povydří, between Čeňkova Pila and Antýgl. Vydra means 'otter', and the river got its name from the many otters that used to live in it. Today, only a few otters live high up in the mountains.

Starting at Čeňkova Pila, the trail goes along the Vydra to Modrava, taking you past Turnerova hut (*chata*), Antýgl, the right side of the Vchnickotetovský Canal, Rokyta and finally to Modrava. This is an easy and very scenic 14km trail. It is also possible to start further down the river at Rejštejn.

Boubín Virgin Forest

The 46-hectare **Boubín Virgin Forest** (Boubínský prales), surrounds the peak of Boubín (1362m) and was one of the world's first nature reserves, founded in 1858. Beech, spruce and pine predominate and some of the trees are estimated to be over 400 years old; the forest itself is largely out of bounds to visitors.

If you have a car, the easiest approach is via the car park at Kaplice, near the camp site. From here it's an easy 2.5km to U pralesa lake, on a green and then blue trail. In July and August there is a kiosk selling snacks at the lake. To reach Boubín, stay on the blue trail along the boundary of Boubínský prales. After 6km you reach Křížová Smrč, and from there it's 1.5km to the top of Boubín.

A longer and more enjoyable walk is between Kubova Huť and the zastávka Zátoň train stop (not Zátoň town, which is 2km away). The trail is 17.5km long and, from Kubova Huť, passes Johnův kámen, Boubín, Křížová Smrč, U pralesa lake and the Kaplice camp site before terminating at the Zátoň train stop. Give yourself at least five hours.

Sleeping & Eating

There is plenty of accommodation in the region, but private rooms are often the best bet – houses will often have '*Zimmer frei*' signs in the window. There's little to see in the region's towns, so you won't be missing anything by staying in the wilds.

Kubova Huť is a ski resort in the winter and is literally teeming with resorts, *pensions* and private rooms.

Irma Hotel Armika (☎ 388 436 326; hotel.armika@iol.cz; s/d incl breakfast 1000/1180Kč; P X ⚡ ⚡) The modern Alpine design is in keeping with the ski resort theme and the facilities (including a solarium and tennis courts) promise a comfortable stay. It can feel a little deserted in summer though.

Horní Vltavice, a little further south, has a few uninspiring hotels.

Camp TJ Vltava (☎ 388 436 198; ou.hvltavice@tiscali.cz; tent/bungalow 60/360Kč; P) This riverside camp site draws plenty of hikers and there are bungalows (sleeping four) for when a squall rolls in off the hills.

Volary mainly offers private rooms but is one of the region's dingiest towns.

Pension Kuboňová (☎ 388 333 795; Soumarská 408; s/d incl breakfast 400/700Kč; P) At the Lenora end of town, on the approach road, this little *pension* has comfy rooms.

Lenora's *pensions* are hard to find from the train station (head 10 minutes downhill to the main road).

Hotel Zámeček Lenora (☎ 388 438 861; mains 70-150Kč) Strangely, this 'hotel', in an attractive former hunting lodge, wasn't offering rooms at the time of writing. Still, it is the best place in town for a good feed, with a grand selection of local specialities (mostly meaty).

Pension Lenora (☎ 388 438 813; s/d incl breakfast 450/800Kč) Just across the road, this is undoubtedly the most attractive place to stay in Lenora.

Try **Pension Kizek** (☎ 388 582 527; s/d incl breakfast 400/800Kč) at Rejštejn. Further on at Čeňkova Pila is **Pension Bystřina** (☎ 388 599 221) and a basic camp site. In Antýgl there is only **Autocamp Antýgl**, open from May to October. In Modrava there is **Penzion Arnika** (☎ 388 599 349; d 350Kč), but facilities are shared.

Getting There & Away

Up to eight trains a day run between Volary and Strakonice (98Kč, two hours), stopping at Lenora and two other stations – zastávka Zátoň and Horní Vltavice, both of which are about 10km from their respective towns (Kubova Huť and Vimperk). From Volary you can get direct trains to Horní Planá (40Kč, 35 minutes) and Český Krumlov (88Kč, 1¾ hours).

On weekdays there are six runs on the very scenic, 21km Vimperk to Lenora route, via Kubova Huť and Horní Vltavice. Between Sušice and Modrava a bus runs once or twice a day.

BORDER CROSSINGS

There are border crossings to Germany south of Vimperk. A 24-hour vehicle and pedestrian crossing at Strážný, to Philippsreuth, can be reached by local bus from Horní Vltavice. Another at Stožec, to Haidmühle, is for pedestrians and cyclists only, and is open from 9am to 9pm.

ROŽMBERK NAD VLTAVOU

pop 400

On a steep hillock above a hairpin bend in the Vltava river, Rožmberk is one of South Bohemia's prettiest castles and can doubtless be expected to star in a medieval action movie in the not-too-distant future. Relatively – for somewhere near Český Krumlov – empty of tourists, the unassuming, quaint little town at its base is mainly visited by passing canoeists, who stop for a beer here on their lazy way from Vyšši Brod north.

The so-called **Upper Castle**, built in the mid-13th century, was destroyed by fire in 1522; the only reminder today is the crumbling **Jakobín Tower** in the trees above. The 1330s **Lower Castle** (☎ 380 749 838; hradrozmberk@cz.gin.cz; adult/concession 140/80Kč, in English 140/80Kč; ☼ 9am-4.15pm Tue-Sun Jun-Aug, until 3.15pm May & Sep, 9am-3.15pm Sat & Sun Apr & Oct) was rebuilt in Renaissance style in the 1550s. It's said to be haunted by a ghost called the White Lady (Bílá paní), the long-suffering wife of one of the Rožmberks.

After the Battle of the White Mountain the castle came into the hands of the Buquoy family. All the paintings, sculpture, porcelain, furniture, weapons and some particularly nasty torture instruments are all from their era. The treat of the tour is the Banquet Hall, covered in 16th-century Italian frescoes. One fresco, behind a grille, is encrusted with jewels confiscated during the Thirty Years' War.

Sleeping & Eating

The village below has some private rooms (look for signs with *privát* or *ubytování*) starting from 350Kč per person.

Hotel u Martina (☎ 380 749 745; s/d incl breakfast 350/700Kč) A white horse prances over the entrance of this riverside hotel, which offers bright rooms, a top-notch eatery and oodles of rustic charm. It is right on the main square, next to Hotel Růže.

Hotel Růže (☎ 380 749 715; recepce@hotelruze.rozemberk.cz; s/d incl breakfast 800/1250Kč) Snaps of happy-looking honeymooners assert this hotel's position as the best in town. There's also a good riverside restaurant.

Penzion Adler (☎ 380 749 844; s/d incl breakfast 380/700Kč) Small and snug, this is just south of the main square but reels in the lunch-time crowds with its intimate terrace eatery. The rooms are basic but reliably comfortable.

Penzion Romantik (☎ 380 749 906; penzion .romantik@cmail.cz; s/d incl breakfast 580/980Kč) Pathologically clean, this sparkling new place is 200m before the main square, on the Český Krumlov road.

Hotel Studenec (☎ 380 749 818; hotel.studenec@ post.cz; s/d 450/900Kč; P) This excellent place, 1.5km along the road to Český Krumlov, has 'wow' views and a serious collection of stag heads. It also hires out canoes and bikes.

Kemp Rožmberk (☎ 380 749 816; tent 60Kč; P) North of the castle, across the river from the Český Krumlov road, this pleasant camp site has the perfect riverside setting.

There is a supermarket on the main square for provision purchasing.

Getting There & Away

Seven buses a day come from Český Krumlov (22Kč, 40 minutes) continuing on to Vyšší Brod.

VYŠŠÍ BROD
pop 2500

Vyšší Brod's drawcards are a large central square and an even larger Cistercian monastery. Stop – along with the hordes of Austrian day-trippers – on your way through to somewhere else. It's only 8km to the Austrian border and 24km to Český Krumlov.

Information

Infocentrum (☎ 380 746 627; náměstí 104; ⏲ 9am-1pm & 1.30-5.30pm) organises accommodation and sells maps.

Sights
CISTERCIAN MONASTERY

This fortified **monastery** (cisterciácký klášter; ☎ 746 674; cist.klaster@vtssibrod.cz; adult/concession 60/40Kč, in English 120/100Kč; ⏲ 9.30-11.30am & 1.15-4.15pm Tue-Sat, 1.15-4.15pm Sun Apr-Sep) was founded by Vok Rožmberk in 1259, though it was not completed until the late 14th century. It successfully withstood two Hussite assaults in the 15th century. Later owners were the Eggenbergs and the Schwarzenbergs. It was closed by the Communists in 1950 and its monks imprisoned. After nearly half a century of neglect major repairs began in 1990.

It has one of Bohemia's finest Gothic buildings, the **Chapter House** (Kapitulní síň), completed in 1285, its roof supported by a single pillar. A highlight is its 70,000-volume **library**, founded with the monastery. The Large Library Hall is entered by a secret door through a bookcase in the Small Library Hall. Note the gold leaf, rococo ceiling.

In the monastery grounds, there is also a three-storey **Postal Museum** (poštovní muzeum; adult/concession 40/20Kč; ⏲ 9am-noon & 1-5pm Tue-Sun Apr-Oct), for serious letter junkies.

Activities

If you're interested in paddling down the Vltava, **Inge Tour** (☎ 380 746 139; info@ingetour.cz; Miru 379) operates out of the **Inge Penzión**, right below the monastery, and hires out canoes and rafts for the one-way trip to Rožmberk and Ceský Krumlov. Prices come in at around 700Kč per day for an open canoe and 1200Kč per day for a much bigger raft.

Sleeping & Eating

Pod hrází (☎ 380 746 427; tent/bungalow per person 60/200Kč; P) This camp site is between the monastery and the river and is open May through September.

Café/Penzión Alpská Růže (☎ 380 746 315; villa@volny.cz; náměstí 73; s/d incl breakfast 450/900Kč) Wonderful smells drift out of this arty café/ *pension*, where the cakes are to die for. If you eat 'til you drop the rooms are fab too.

Hotel Panský dům (☎ 380 746 669; info@hotel panskydum.cz; Miru 82; s/d incl breakfast 650/1300Kč) Just off the main square, this place has been around since the Empire (the Austrian one) – you can admire its many incarnations in a photographic display in the lobby. Its latest face is goblin green, but the rooms are smart and modern.

Inge Penzion (☎ 380 746 139; fax 380 746 953; Miru 379; s/d incl breakfast 370/740Kč; P) Throbbing with passing canoeists, this crowded spot is lively, if not relaxing. The rooms are well priced and hit the spot after a day's paddling. There is also a good restaurant.

Getting There & Away
The town is on a rail spur on the well-serviced České Budějovice–Austria line. There are at least 11 trains a day from Rybník (20 minutes), and it's about 1¼ hours from there to České Budějovice (45Kč).

Frymburk-bound buses run about seven times a day from Český Krumlov via Rožmberk nad Vltavou to Vyšší Brod (40Kč, one hour).

BORDER CROSSINGS
Two 24-hour vehicle and pedestrian crossings to Austria are near Vyšší Brod: Studánky to Weigetschlag, and Dolní Dvořiště to Wullowitz.

LAKE LIPNO
pop 500
Visitors come from miles around to splash in Lake Lipno, but there's not a whole lot here but the largest artificial body of water in the Czech Republic and an awful lot of ice-cream stalls. Backing up behind a dam 8km west of Vyšší Brod, this huge watery expanse is a worthwhile stop-off if you are into waterspouts.

Orientation
The largest town along the lake is Horní Planá, a major centre with accommodation, shops and transport. The smaller towns of Frymburk and Černá v Pošumaví can also be used as bases to explore the area.

Information
KIC Infocentrum (☎ 380 738 008; náměstí 8; ☼ 9am-6pm May-Aug, until 4pm Oct-Apr), in Horní Planá, sells hiking and cycling maps, arranges accommodation, and fields most transport and activities questions. It also has Internet access (2Kč per minute).

Activities
Boats, windsurfers, bikes and skis (in winter) are available from rental outfits across the area. Speak to KIC Infocentrum (see above) about the best deals.

Sleeping & Eating
Along the lakefront, especially the eastern shore, there are literally dozens of camp sites and *pensions*, but few hotels. Without a booking in July or August, your only hope is a camp site, most of which open from May to September. Prices plummet outside the summer season.

HORNÍ PLANÁ
There are plenty of hotels on the main square, but they are quite a hike from the lake itself.

Autocamping U pláže (☎ 337 736 190; Lipno nad Vltavou; tent/bungalow per person 65/200Kč; P) Down by the ferry dock, about 1km from the main square, Autocamping U pláže has a pleasant lakeside location and two-person bungalows.

Hotel Na Pláži (☎ 337 738 374; info@hotel-plaz.cz; s/d incl breakfast 540/980Kč; P) Nearby, this new development is also right by the lake's edge. It's a bit sterile, but the rooms are some of the best in the area.

ČERNÁ V POŠUMAVÍ
The lakeside strip here is literally inundated with camp sites.

Autokemping Jihočeského Autoklubu (☎ 380 744 125; tent/bungalow per person 60/180Kč; P) This camp site gets seriously busy, but there's always lots going on.

Hotel Swing (☎ 380 744 294; www.hotelswing.cz; s/d incl breakfast 600/1000Kč; P) Well signposted from the main road, this out-of-the-way place is 3km along the lake's edge in a quiet spot away from the crowds. It's a bit dowdy, but peace-and-quiet comes at a price here.

FRYMBURK
The most pleasant place to stay, Frymburk has the feel of a bustling market town.

Maxant (☎ 380 735 229; maxant@iol.cz; s/d incl breakfast 900/1350Kč) Right on the main square, this is one of the posher places, with painted shutters, blooming window boxes and a crowded terrace café. It also sports a solarium and massage parlour.

Markus (☎ 380 735 418; markus.frymburk@c-box.cz; s/d incl breakfast 680/1080Kč) Nearby, this pretty place offers slightly less for...slightly less.

Camping Frymburk (☎ 380 735 284; tent 80Kč) North of town, this also has two-, three- and four-bed huts (400/450/500Kč).

Getting There & Away

About five buses a day run from Horní Planá through Černá v Pošumaví and Frymburk to Lipno nad Vltavou (24Kč, 40 minutes). Many continue to Český Krumlov (34Kč, 1¼ hours).

Up to five trains a day travel from České Budějovice (88Kč, two hours) to the Volary stop. From Volary, trains go to Prachatice (40Kč, 40 minutes) and beyond eight times a day.

Getting Around

Apart from local buses, ferries make regular crossings from Horní Planá, Dolní Vltavice and Frymburk. From June to September there is a boat service from Lipno nad Vltavou to Horní Planá via Přední Výtoň, Frymburk and Černá v Pošumaví.

PRACHATICE

pop 12,000

Nestled in a divot chipped out of the South Bohemia hills, Prachatice is a schizophrenic little town, juxtaposing an arc of grimy Stalinist concrete with one of the most evocative and best preserved Renaissance centres in the region. Ringed by an almost unbroken 14th-century defensive wall, which has kept developers as well as more ancient enemies at bay, old Prachatice is one of the few towns that really is prettier than its postcard. Although small, it is surrounded by beautiful woodland, providing plenty of diversions for a relaxing long weekend.

History

The town of Prachatice was founded in the 13th century as a trading post along the important Golden Trail (Zlatá stezka), bringing salt from Bavaria in return for Czech grain. Hussites under General Jan Žižka conquered it in 1420; as a reward for its later return to the royalist fold in 1436, King Sigismund made it a royal town.

After a fire in 1507, Prachatice, by then in the hands of the Rožmberks, was rebuilt; most of the Renaissance structures to be seen today come from that time. Petr Vok, the last of the Rožmberks, sold it to Rudolf II in 1601, but the town sided with the Protestants during the rebellion of the Czech nobles, and in 1620 it was heavily damaged by one of Rudolf II's generals, Buquoy. During the rule of later aristocratic families Prachatice stagnated, though one result of the neglect was the survival of the town walls.

Orientation

The main train station is at the end of Nádražní, the continuation of Zvolenská, a 500m-walk east of the old town. The main bus station is a bit closer, on the corner of Nádražní and Nebahovská.

Part of the old town is pedestrianised – there is a car park at the northern end of Velké náměstí.

Information

Infocentrum (☎ 388 312 563; www.prachatice.cz; Velké náměstí 1; ☺ 8am-6pm Mon-Fri, 10am-noon & 1-4pm Sat & Sun Jun-Sep, limited hrs out of season) can also organise accommodation.

ČSOB (Nádražní 67) has an exchange desk and an ATM.

The **post office** (cnr Pivovarská & Malé náměstí) is just north of the old town.

Club 111 (☎ 388 315 888; Křišťanova 111; ☺ 10am-midnight) is a small sports bar with Internet access.

The **hospital** (nemocnice; ☎ 388 600 111; Nebahovská) is 500m east of the centre.

Sight & Activities

Coming from the bus or train station, along Zvolenská and Malé náměstí, you are faced with the 14th-century **town walls**, which were beefed up in 1620. On the left is the **Chapel of St John of Nepomuk** (kaple sv Jana Nepomuckého).

Enter the old town and historic Velké náměstí through the **Lower Gate** (Písecká brána). Through the gate, on the left behind the heavily decorated **Heydl House** (Heydlův dům), at No 30, is the 16th-century **Literary School** (Literátská škola), where Jan Hus is said to have studied.

In front of you is the 14th-century **St James Church** (kostel sv Jakuba), with a little park behind it. The house on the south side, at No 31, bears a sgraffito depicting the Last Supper.

At Velké náměstí 41 is **Rumpál House** (Rumpálův dům), a former brewery covered with Renaissance battle scenes. Opposite are the **Old Town Hall** (Stará radnice; 1571) and the neo-Renaissance **New Town Hall** (Nová radnice; 1903), both covered in sgraffito.

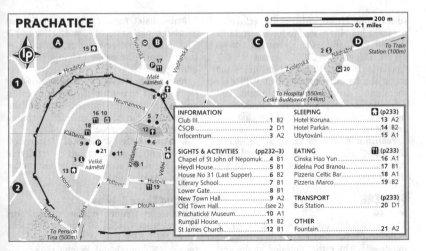

PRACHATICE

0 ———— 200 m
0 ———— 0.1 miles

INFORMATION		SLEEPING	(p233)
Club III	1 B2	Hotel Koruna	13 A2
ČSOB	2 D1	Hotel Parkán	14 B2
Infocentrum	3 A2	Ubytování	15 A1
SIGHTS & ACTIVITIES	(pp232–3)	EATING	(p233)
Chapel of St John of Nepomuk	4 B1	Cinska Hao Yun	16 B1
Heydl House	5 B1	Jidelna Pod Branou	17 B1
House No 31 (Last Supper)	6 B2	Pizzeria Celtic Bar	18 A1
Literary School	7 B1	Pizzeria Marco	19 B2
Lower Gate	8 B1		
New Town Hall	9 A2	TRANSPORT	(p233)
Old Town Hall	(see 2)	Bus Station	20 D1
Prachatické Museum	10 A1		
Rumpál House	11 B2	OTHER	
St James Church	12 B1	Fountain	21 A2

The **Prachatické Museum** (☎ 388 311 419; Velké náměstí 13; adult/concession 40/15Kč; ☼ 9am-5pm Tue-Sun) was built as a palace in 1572 by the Rožmberks and still has the town's finest façade, plus a collection of arms and old postcards.

Festivals & Events

Prachatice goes fairly wild during the mid-June **Gold Trail Festival** (Slavnosti zlaté stezky), with medieval costumes, fencing tournaments and fireworks. An annual **folk music festival** is held on the last Saturday in February.

Sleeping & Eating

Infocentrum can help with private rooms (from 300Kč per person).

Ubytování (☎ 602 474 270; Starokasárenská 192; dm per person 200Kč) Just north of the centre, this basic hostel is about the cheapest in town.

Hotel Koruna (☎ 388 310 177; koruna@c-box.cz; Velké náměstí 48; s/d incl breakfast 650/950Kč) In a side alley just off the main square, this has plenty of old-school charm, with a traditional-style cellar restaurant, comfy rooms and a photogenic Renaissance façade. Does it have a fake suit of armour on display? Oh yes.

Hotel Parkán (☎ 388 311 868; pavel.hlavac@iol.cz; Věžní 51; s/d incl breakfast 690/990Kč; ☒ ☒) With roots in the 14th century and a good chunk of its superstructure built into the town walls, this is surely the most salubrious address in town. The terrace, overlook-ing the park, is a particularly fine spot for a sundowner.

Pizzeria Marco (☎ 388 316 950; Husova 106; mains 80-110Kč) Uniformed staff, drifting basil aromas and warm Med-style décor make this a snug spot for a bite.

Jídelna Pod Branou (Malé náměstí 24; ☼ 7am-2pm) They forgot the frills when decorating this place, but the pick-and-point buffet is a good choice for no-fuss breakfasts and lunches.

Other recommendations:

Pension Tina (☎ 388 319 318; Pod Lázněmi 318; s/d 350/550Kč) A homely, chalet-style pension.

Pizzeria Celtic Bar (☎ 388 310 048; Velké náměstí; mains 60-70Kč; ☼ until 5am Fri-Sat) Cheap pizzas, late drinks and loud tunes.

Cinska Hao Yun (☎ 721 912 759; Velké náměstí 10; mains 90Kč) Sizzling woks and passable Chinese.

Getting There & Away

There are 12 buses a day to Prague (120Kč, 2½ hours), 15 to České Budějovice (34Kč, one hour) and departures all day to Husinec (10Kč, 10 minutes) and Vimperk (21Kč, 40 minutes).

Prachatice is on a minor train line from Volary to Čicenice (45 minutes away, 11 trains a day), where it joins the České Budějovice–Plzeň main line.

HUSINEC

pop 500

The small village of Husinec, 5km north of Prachatice, is known for the **Jan Hus House** (dům Jana Husa), where the reformist preacher Jan Hus is said to have been born around 1371, and its small **museum** (☎ 388 331 284; adult/concession 20/10Kč; ☼ 9am-noon & 1-4pm Tue-Sun May-Sep). In early July this is the scene of a **Jan Hus commemoration**, with a remembrance ceremony, cultural events and exhibitions. The main square, Prokopovo náměstí, has a large **statue of Hus** that was erected in 1958.

Penzión u Blanice (☎ 388 331 062; Komenského 38; s/d 350/600Kč) Next to the river and near the bus terminal, this is reasonable for sleepovers.

VIMPERK
pop 8100

This is a pleasant town with a castle majestically perched on a hill – but not much else. The **castle**, founded at the end of the 13th century but incinerated after a lightning strike in 1857, is still extremely dilapidated, but the views make a climb up the **Vlček Tower** (Vlčkova věž; admission 5Kč) worthwhile. There's also a small **museum** (adult/concession 20/5Kč; ☼ 9am-noon & 1-4pm Tue-Sun May-Oct), with some so-so glass (Vimperk is a centre for glass manufacturing) exhibits. Bohemia's first calendar was printed here in 1484, but you get the feeling that not much has happened since.

The town grew around the castle, prospering from trade along the so-called Golden Trail (Zlatá stezka) between Bavaria and Bohemia. Some Gothic and Renaissance houses remain in the square, along with the Gothic **Black Tower** (Černá věž).

Orientation & Information

The train and bus stations are 3km from the castle and old town; turn left onto the highway and continue downhill. Buses to town are frequent in the morning, less so in the afternoon.

The **tourist information office** (městské informační středisko; ☎ 388 411 894; náměstí Svobody 8; ☼ 9am-5pm Mon-Fri, until 4pm Sat & Sun) is on the main square.

Sleeping & Eating

Autocamp Volnik (☎ 388 415 316; Jiraskova 278; tent 60Kč; Ⓟ) This camp site, 2km from the train station (follow signs to Zdíknov), is the closest to the centre. It is open from June to August.

Amber Hotel Anna (☎ 388 412 050; anna@lconsulting.cz; Kaplířova 168; s/d incl breakfast 1300/1800Kč) The service is rather haughty, but this has town's most glamorous lodgings by quite a margin.

Hotel Vltava (☎ 388 411 469; hotel.vltava@volny.cz; Kaplířova 64; s/d incl breakfast 410/710Kč) Someone's gone crazy with the Formica here and the receptionist can be elusive, but the rooms are central and reasonably priced.

Restaurace Lotte (☎ 388 514 034; Rožmberská 4; mains 80-180Kč) Bright, light and cheerful, this first floor eatery serves good honest tucker to a constantly full house.

Getting There & Away

Buses are less frequent but faster than trains to Strakonice (24Kč, 40 minutes), Prachatice (21Kč, 35 minutes), České Budějovice (48Kč, 1¾ hours) and Prague (86Kč, 2¼ hours).

Vimperk is about an hour from either end of the Strakonice–Volary train line, with about eight trains a day (50Kč) through beautiful mountain and forest scenery.

ŽELEZNÁ RUDA & AROUND

The name of this popular Šumava ski resort means 'Iron Ore', which hints at its 16th-century mining origins. The main thing to do now, however, is walk.

Orientation

The train station for the village of Železná Ruda is 2km from the German border, at an elevation of about 750m.

Along the road to Nýrsko, a green-marked trail climbs (4km in all) north to Špičák, a ski area in a saddle (Špičácké sedlo) at about 1000m. About 7km beyond the saddle, at 900m, is another village and ski area, Hojsova Stráž.

Hiking

About 2.5km from the village towards the saddle is a year-round **chairlift** to a lookout tower at the summit of **Pancíř** (1214m). Alternatively, there's a red-marked trail up to it from the saddle.

From Špičák you can also climb to the Šumava's two largest glacial lakes. The 18-hectare **Black Lake** (Černé jezero) is 4.5km to the northwest on a yellow-marked road. Smaller **Devil's Lake** (Čertovo jezero) is 2.5km southwest of the saddle, by trail only. Both lakes are on a red-marked trail that continues northwest along the border for 25km.

Sleeping
There are plain camp sites 1km northeast of Železná Ruda on the road to Čachrov; and at Brčálník, about midway between Špíčácké sedlo and Hojsova Stráž.

There are plenty of hotels, although private rooms are better value (watch for signs).

Getting There & Away
Železná Ruda is easiest to reach by train from Plzeň (120Kč, 2½ hours, about 10 direct trains a day) or Klatovy (64Kč, one hour, 12 a day). About half of these continue across the border to Bayerisch Eisenstein; the border is open 24 hours.

PÍSECKO REGION

PÍSEK
pop 30,000
Gold earned Písek it's name – quite literally. At the hub of a traditional gold-panning area (Písecko), the town takes its name from the Czech word for the sand *(písek)* from which the gold was separated. These days, factories jostle for space with the attractive historic buildings that date from the town's heyday, but the centre is well worth a quick wander and the Otava river is spanned here by Bohemia's oldest bridge. For those who want to dig away at the town's history, Písek also boasts one of the region's best museums.

History
The town and castle, plus a church and monastery, were founded in 1243 by Přemysl Otakar II. The town prospered from its position on the Golden Trail trading route, and Charles IV established salt and grain storage houses here. Písek backed the Hussites, but was taken and virtually emptied by Habsburg forces early in the Thirty Years' War. It enjoyed a kind of rebirth with the logging trade in the late 18th century.

The poet Frána Šrámek (1877–1952), who has inspired a number of directors to make films in the town, lived here.

Orientation
The train and bus stations are near each other, 1km south of the city centre. To get to the centre walk up Nádražní, turn right at Budovcova, left at Chelčíkeho, cross Alšovo náměstí, and take Jungmannova to the main square, Velké náměstí.

Information
Infocentrum (☎ 382 213 592; www.icpisek.cz - Czech only; Heydukova 97; ☉ 10am-noon & 1-5pm Mon-Fri, until noon Sat) is just off Velké náměstí. It has Internet access (1Kč per minute).

KB (Velké náměstí) has an exchange desk and ATM.

Sights
The 13th-century castle was never rebuilt after a 1510 fire. Only the original right wing remains today, hidden inside a courtyard just off the main square. Nowadays, it houses the superb **Prácheňské historické muzeum** (☎ 382 211 113; Velké náměstí 114; adult/concession 30/10Kč; ☉ 9am-6pm Tue-Sun Mar-Sep, until 5pm Oct-Feb), with first-rate displays on the Nazi and communist eras.

Next door is the baroque **town hall**, which replaced the castle's left wing. **Putim Gate** (Putimská brána) is the only section left from the castle's original fortifications.

There are some finely decorated Renaissance and baroque houses on Velké náměstí and Jungmannova. Mikuláš Aleš (see p237) designed the sgraffito decoration of the **Hotel Otava**. Most enjoyable is a walk along the Otava near the stone **Kamenný Bridge**, which dates from the second half of the 13th century and is the oldest in Bohemia (even predating Prague's Charles' Bridge).

The city power station, on the river east of Velké náměstí, houses the suspiciously Soviet-sounding **Technical Museum of Public Lighting and Power Supply** (☎ 382 271 105; Podskalí; adult/concession 30/10Kč; ☉ 9am-noon & 1-4pm Tue-Sun Jun-Sep). Crowded it is not.

Festivals & Events
The Písecko region's preoccupation with gold-panning is celebrated in early August with a **panning championship**, that is held anywhere between Slaník, a few kilometres east of Strakonice, and Kestřany, near Písek. In early June there is also the **Písek Historical Festival**.

Sleeping

Municipal Ubytovna (☎ 382 214 644; Dr M Horákové 1748; dm per person 150Kč; **P**)) Just over 1km east of the main square, down Budá and left into Harantova, this hostel is cheap and clean.

Hotel Pod skálou (☎ 382 214 753; Podskalí 156; s/d incl breakfast 400/700Kč) Down a cobbled lane and right by the riverbank, this has a lovely location even if the place itself is a little lacking in glamour.

Hotel Bílá růže (☎ 382 214 931; fax 382 219 002; Šrámkova 169; s/d incl breakfast 1100/1300Kč) Just off Velké náměstí, this is one of town's flashiest options, with comfortable rooms. Most of the 'flash' dates from the 1980s and it also advertises 'Dancing' (or 'Dancig' if you're coming from the south).

Other recommendations:

Hotel Amerika (☎ 382 219 357; Richarda Weinara 2375; s/d incl breakfast 1330/1980Kč) Once upmarket, now fast fading.

Pension u Kloudů (☎ 382 210 802; Nerudova 66; s/d 500/850Kč) *Pension* comfort over a busy bar.

Eating

Pizzeria Maestro Appetito (☎ 383 211 222; Drlíčon 147; mains 80-150Kč) Facing the church on one of town's prettier squares (south of Velké náměstí), this place whips up a mean pizza. The comfy terrace seats are ideal for sampling the result. It also delivers.

U Zlatého Býka (☎ 382 221 286; Kocínova 1; mains 80-200Kč) This offers steaks, steaks and still more steaks, served up in a trendy(ish) interior, or out on the sunny terrace. Head south off Velké náměstí down Frán Štrámka.

Restaurace U Přemysla Otakara II (☎ 382 212 132; Velké náměstí 114; mains 60-150Kč) A smarter breed of beer hall, with slightly fewer foam-soaked moustaches, less smoke and marginally better food. Bohemian specialties bulk out the menu.

Julius Meinl supermarket (cnr Velké náměstí & Jungmannova) For self-caterers.

Getting There & Away

Direct trains run throughout the day to Plzeň (140Kč, two hours), České Budějovice (64Kč, 1¼ hours) and Tábor (76Kč, 1½ hours). Other services change at Ražice or Protivín.

Quicker buses also run to České Budějovice (42Kč, 50 minutes), Prague (80Kč, 1½ hours) and Orlik (23Kč, 40 minutes).

For all bus and train times and prices, visit www.idos.cz.

STRAKONICE

pop 25,000

Blowing its way to notoriety on the back of the bagpipes (*dudy* in Czech), which were made here, this industrial town later took to manufacturing notoriously guttural ČZ motorbikes. No doubt feeling at home here, the gregarious General Patton based himself in Strakonice when the US army liberated parts of Bohemia in 1945.

Orientation & Information

The train and bus stations are about 1km southeast of the city centre.

Ciao (☎ 383 323 400; Zámek 1; ☼ 8am-6pm Mon-Fri) doubles as the tourist information office.

Česká spořitelna (Velké náměstí 55) changes money and has an ATM.

Sights

In the remains of the derelict **castle** (Strakonický hrad; admission free; ☼ 9am-5pm Tue-Sun Jun-Aug, 8am-4pm May, Sep & Oct) is the **regional museum** (muzeum Středního Pootaví Strakonice; adult/concession 30/20Kč; ☼ as castle) with exhibits on gold panning and local industry, including a collection of *dudy*. As always, there is also a **tower** (adult/concession 10/5Kč) to climb.

Of Velké náměstí's sgraffitoed buildings, the finest is the former **town hall** by Mikuláš Aleš; others are the **municipal headquarters** (městký úřad) and **Investiční banka**.

Festivals & Events

In mid-August the castle hosts an **International Bagpipe Festival** (Mezinárodní dudový festival).

Sleeping & Eating

Autokemping Podskalí (☎ 383 322 024; tent/3-bed hut 60/345Kč; **P**) Open May to September, this camp site is a long walk west out of town and past the castle, along the Otava. You can also catch buses 380160 and 380130 from the station or the castle (10Kč).

Amber Hotel Bavor (☎ 383 321 300; bavor@lconsulting.cz; Kostelecká 1379/16; s/d incl breakfast 1100/1500Kč; **P**) A card-carrying member of the shoebox school of architecture, this nevertheless has business standard rooms, a sauna and a gym. It is by the river, near the castle.

Hotel Bílá Růže (☎ 383 321 946; info@hotelruzest.cz; Palackého náměstí 80; d 800Kč) Across the main road from the castle, back towards Velké náměstí, this place is plain, but pleasantly passable.

Tsing Tao (☎ 723 306 488; Palackého náměstí 80; mains 60-120Kč) Right next to Hotel Bílá Růže, this place cooks up a decent Chinese.

Pekast (cnr Palackého náměstí & SV Markéty) This bakery does a decent line in cakes, pastries and baguettes.

Getting There & Away

There are regular direct trains to Plzeň (98Kč, one hour), Blatná (40Kč, 44 minutes), Písek (34Kč, 33 minutes) and České Budějovice (76Kč, 50 minutes). Buses are a bit cheaper on the same routings and are the best bet for Prague (72Kč, 1¾ hours).

BLATNÁ

pop 6800

Blatná's name comes from the district's *blata* (fens) that were drained and made into ponds. The town's sole attraction is its castle, which is worth a look if you're driving through the area. General Patton stayed in the castle in May 1945. The Communists didn't allow the town's liberation by US forces on 5 May to be celebrated, but since 1990 it has been, with gusto.

The **tourist information office** (informační centrum; ☎ 383 420 389; JP Koubka 4; ☻ 9am-5.30pm Mon-Fri, 9am-1pm Sat, 2-5pm Sun) can also help with accommodation.

Sights

The 13th-century **castle** (Vodní hrad; ☎ 383 422 934; adult/concession 70/50Kč, in English 140/70Kč; ☻ 10am-4pm Tue-Sun Jun-Sep, 10am-4pm Sat & Sun Apr, May & Oct) was rebuilt several times before a major makeover in the mid-19th century. A 50-minute tour takes in the **Hunting Room** (Lovecký sál), with furniture made from stag horns. The castle is connected by a bridge to the large **English Garden** (anglický park), ideal for picnics.

The **Cathedral of the Virgin** (chrám Panny Marie), across from the castle on náměstí Míru, is one of Bohemia's most valuable, late-Gothic structures.

Sleeping & Eating

The tourist information office can suggest private rooms.

Hotel Beranek (☎ 383 422 231; JP Koubka: s/d 200/400Kč) Opposite the tourist office, this central place is cheap but glum.

U Bílého Lva (náměstí Míru 210; mains 50-80Kč) Between tourist information and the castle, this Czech-style eatery serves hearty fare in crumbling historical surrounds.

Getting There & Away

Regular trains link Blatná and Strakonice (40Kč, 45 minutes). To/from Plzeň, change at Nepomuk. There are infrequent buses to Prague (70Kč, 1½ hours).

AROUND BLATNÁ

About 11km east of Blatná is **Mirotice**, the birthplace of Mikuláš Aleš (1852–1913). Aleš was the foremost artist of Bohemia's so-called 'National Theatre generation', which focused on folk themes from Czech history. His designs decorate houses in Písek, Plzeň and Strakonice; and the house where he was born is now a small **museum** (adult/concession 25/10Kč; ☻ 10am-4pm Tue-Sun Apr-Oct) dedicated to him. The museum is down Mikoláše Aleše, which runs from the southern corner of the main square.

The village is just west of the Písek–Březnice road, with several buses a day travelling the 20km to Písek (13Kč, 30 minutes).

ORLÍK NAD VLTAVOU

Though still one of the finest castles in the republic, Orlík has been vigorously renovated to the point of sterility; in summer it's also oppressively crowded. (The nearby Zvíkov castle offers a more authentic experience; see p238). Orlík's main asset is its setting – on a cliff-lined bay encircled by trees. The castle was once high above the Vltava, but the Orlík dam has filled the valley almost to the castle's lower walls.

The town of Orlík is 500m north of the castle.

Orlík Castle

The original, early-Gothic **castle** (☎ 382 275 101; adult/concession 60/30Kč, in English 130/60Kč; ☻ 9am-5pm Tue-Sun May-Aug, until 4pm Apr, May & Oct) dates from the 13th century. After fires in 1514 and 1802, it was rebuilt and extended. The last Czech owner, Krištof ze Švamberka, lost the castle after the Battle of the White Mountain, when it fell into Austrian hands; the Schwarzenbergs held it from 1719 until 1945, when it was seized by the state.

In 1992 it was returned to the Schwarzenbergs, and the one-hour castle tour is mainly about them. The highlight is a magnificently carved wooden ceiling that took four years to complete. In the thickly wooded gardens is the **Schwarzenberg Mausoleum** (Švarcenberská hrobka). A number of hiking trails start from here.

From late June to August and less often in May and September, **Quarter** (☎ 382 275 333) runs five boats a day to the dam (adult/concession 80/40Kč, one hour) and Zvíkov Castle (adult/concession 80/40Kč, 50 minutes). Tickets can be bought from the boats, which depart from just below the castle. The castle cash desk has timetables.

Small boats also offer short cruises of the lake.

Sleeping & Eating

Restaurace U Cvrků (☎ 382 275 124; s/d 160/320Kč) This inn, in the centre of the village, offers pub grub and basic rooms.

Restaurace U Toryka (☎ 382 275 181; mains 65-195Kč) In the shadow of the castle, this place caters to the tourist crowd, serving a spread of tasty, slightly overpriced mains.

Getting There & Away

Up to five daily Prague–Písek buses stop near Orlík Castle; Orlík is about 1½ hours from Prague (80Kč).

ZVÍKOV CASTLE

pop 250

This small Gothic **castle** (☎ 382 285 676; adult/concession 50/20Kč; ☙ 9am-noon & 1-5pm Tue-Sun Jun-Aug, until 4pm May & Sep, 9.30am-noon & 12.30-3.30pm Sat & Sun Apr & Oct), built by the Přemysl princes in the 13th century, commands a better position than Orlík. The castle sits high above the lake, at the point where the Otava and Vltava rivers enter. During the rebellion of the Czech Estates in 1618, a garrison of 140 men successfully defended the castle against 4000 Habsburg troops. Unlike many Bohemian castles, it retains a medieval look.

A self-guided tour takes in furniture, weapons and a frescoed ballroom, plus a chapel with an altar featuring the Deposition of Christ and Veneration of the Three Kings (Oplakávání Krista a Klanění Tří králů), all in one painting.

Sleeping

Unless you have a car, it is difficult to see both Zvíkov and Orlík castles without stay-

ing the night. At the village of Zvíkovské Podhradí, a walk of just over 1km south from Zvíkov Castle, there are private rooms available.

Hotel Zvíkov (☎ 382 899 659; fax 89 96 55; s/d 1000/1400Kč; ☐) Also in the village, this has plush rooms and a decent restaurant.

Getting There & Away

Up to seven buses a day cover the 19km from Písek to Zvíkovské Podhradí (12Kč). Alternatively, it is a fine 14km walk on a marked trail beside the lake between the castles of Zvíkov and Orlík, or you can take a boat (see the Orlík castle section earlier). Cyclists have to use the minor road further inland.

NORTHEASTERN REGION

Blood and religion fleck the history of this predominantly rural corner of Bohemia in equal measure. As the hub of the Hussite movement, led by Jan Žižka and Prokop Holý, the area was central to the Protestant sect's struggle with the Catholic authorities.

While the Hussite stronghold of Tábor still projects an air of medieval militarism, the region, which includes the Českomoravská vysočina (Czech-Moravian highlands), is rather more peaceful these days – a sedate landscape of gently rolling cornfields and quiet village squares.

Highlights of the area include its historic heart, Tábor, the chateau of Červená Lhota and the sleepy village of Slavonice.

TÁBOR

pop 37,000

Founded on ideology and subsisting through warfare, the former Hussite bastion of Tábor has a long tradition of staunch independence and ironfisted defiance. The legions of tourists today descending on the town's tight alleyways and gabled squares are rather less threatening than the Catholic armies that once marched against it, but Tábor retains a proud sense of history, boasting one of the best-preserved and most idiosyncratic old centres in Bohemia.

With a steep hillside dropping off into dense woodland on three sides of the old

SOUTH BOHEMIA

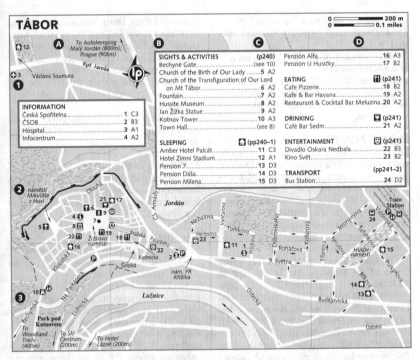

TÁBOR

INFORMATION
Česká Spořitelna	1 C3
ČSOB	2 B3
Hospital	3 A1
Infocentrum	4 A2

SIGHTS & ACTIVITIES (p240)
Bechyně Gate	(see 10)
Church of the Birth of Our Lady	5 A2
Church of the Transfiguration of Our Lord on Mt Tábor	6 A2
Fountain	7 A2
Hussite Museum	8 A2
Jan Žižka Statue	9 A2
Kotnov Tower	10 A3
Town Hall	(see 8)

SLEEPING (pp240–1)
Amber Hotel Palcát	11 C3
Hotel Zimni Stadium	12 A1
Pension 7	13 D3
Pension Dáša	14 D3
Pension Milena	15 D3
Penzión Alfa	16 A3
Penzión U Husičky	17 B2

EATING (p241)
Cafe Pizzerie	18 B2
Kafe & Bar Havana	19 A2
Restaurant & Cocktail Bar Meluzina	20 A2

DRINKING (p241)
Café Bar Sedm	21 A2

ENTERTAINMENT (p241)
Divadlo Oskara Nedbala	22 B3
Kino Svět	23 B2

TRANSPORT (pp241–2)
Bus Station	24 D2

town, Tábor's natural defences are as formidable today as they would have been when the Hussites first set up shop here some 600 years ago. But while the town's picture postcard appeal is blatantly apparent, Tábor is no fossil. With a youthful *joie de vivre* permeating its streets, it remains as vibrant as it is venerable.

History
Archaeological evidence suggests that Tábor was a Celt settlement in around 100 BC. A castle and town called Hradiště were established by Přemysl Otakar II in the 13th century, only to be burned down in 1277 by the Víteks. In the 14th century the lords of Sezimové z Ústí built a castle here, of which all that remains is the single Kotnov Tower.

God's Warriors, the Hussites, founded Tábor proper in 1420 as a military bastion in defiance of Catholic Europe. The town was organised according to the biblical precept that 'nothing is mine and nothing is yours, because the community is owned equally by everyone'. New arrivals threw all

their worldly possessions into large casks at the marketplace and joined in communal work. This extreme nonconformism helped to give the word Bohemian the connotations we associate with it today. Planned as a bulwark against Catholics in České Budějovice and further south, Tábor is a warren of narrow streets with protruding houses that were intended to weaken an enemy attack. After the Taborites' defeat at the Battle of Lipany in 1434, the town's significance declined.

Orientation
The old town is a 500m west from the train and bus stations through Husův park and along 9. května. The latter runs to náměstí FR Křižíka, from where Palackého and Pražská lead through the old town to Žižkovo náměstí.

Information
The post office is in the pink building just off Žižkovo náměstí.
Amber Hotel Palcát (☎ 381 252 901; 9. května 2471; ⏰ 24hrs) Charges 50Kč per hour for Internet access.

ČSOB (náměstí FR Křižíka) Has an exchange and ATM.
Česká spořitelna (třída 9. května 10) Has an exchange
and ATM.
Hospital (nemocnice; ☎ 381 608 111; Kpt. Jaroše) Is
northwest of the old town.
Infocentrum (☎ 381 254 755; www.tabor.cz; Žižkovo
náměstí 2; ☘ 8.30am-7pm Mon-Fri, 10am-4pm Sat &
Sun May-Sep, 9am-4pm Mon-Fri Oct-Apr) Also books
accommodation.

Sights & Activities

Start on Palackého and go west past the **Divadlo Oskara Nedbala** (Oskar Nedbal Theatre)
to the handsome main square, Žižkovo
náměstí. On every side it's lined with late-
Gothic, Renaissance and baroque houses;
and in the middle is a **fountain** (1567) with a
statue of the Hussite commander Jan Žižka,
and two stone tables that the Hussites probably used for religious services.

On the square's northern side is the
**Church of the Transfiguration of Our Lord on
Mt Tábor** (kostel Proměnění Páně na hoře
Tábor), built between 1440 and 1512 and
known for its vaulting and the neo-Gothic
altar. May to September (and the rest of
the year on weekends and holidays if the
weather is good) its **tower** (adult/concession 15/
10Kč) is open for a sweeping view of Tábor.

The other imposing building on Žižkovo
náměstí is the early-Renaissance **town hall**
(1521), now the **Hussite Museum** (Husitské
muzeum; ☎ 381 252 245; adult/concession 60/30Kč;
☘ 8.30am-5pm Apr-Oct, Mon-Fri only Nov-Mar), with
a copy of a peasant wagon mounted with
cannons – the ingenious prototype tank
invented by Jan Žižka. Also here is the
entrance to a 650m stretch of **underground
passages** (podzemní chodby; adult/concession 40/20Kč;
☘ as museum), which is open for visits only
when a group of five people forms. The
passages, constructed in the 15th century
as refuges during fires or times of war, were
also used to store food and to mature beer.

The archipelago at Žižkovo náměstí 22,
beside the town hall, leads into Mariánská
and then Klokotská, which runs southwest to **Bechyně Gate** (Bechyňská brána),
now a small **historical museum** (adult/concession
40/20Kč; ☘ 8.30am-5pm May-Sep) focusing on
peasant life.

Kotnov Castle, founded here in the 12th
century, was destroyed by fire in 1532; in the
17th century the ruins were transformed into
the current brewery. The remaining 15th-
century **Kotnov Tower** (adult/concession 20/10Kč;
☘ 8.30am-5pm May-Sep) can be climbed from
the Bechyně Gate museum for a sweeping
view of Tábor and the Lužnice river.

Tábor is surrounded by woodland and a
number of marked **trails** cut into the forest of Tynska, just across the river from
Bechyňská.

Ski Centrum (☎ 381 255 772; Bechyňská 398) rents
bikes (100Kč per day) and rafts (450Kč per
day).

Festivals & Events

The annual **Hussite Festival of Tábor**, held on
the second weekend in September, features
food, drink and locals dressed in Hussite
costumes.

Sleeping

Infocentrum can help with seasonal hostel
(from 150Kč) and private room (from
200Kč) accommodation.

Autokemping Malý Jordán (☎ 381 235 103; tent
60Kč; Ⓟ) This camp site is 1km north of the
town near Lake Jordán. A few buses (Nos
20 or 21) a day come from the main train
station. It is open from mid-June to September.

Pension Milena (☎ 381 254 755; milena.sport@
volny.cz; Husův náměstí 529; s/d 300/400Kč) This hostel-
style place is seemingly entirely constructed
out of Formica, but the en suite rooms are
spotless if simple.

Penzión Alfa (☎ 381 256 165; art-in@seznam.cz;
Klokotská; s/d 400/700Kč) This pretty little place
has a groovy, American Indian-themed café
below and a few large snug rooms above.
Book ahead as in summer it packs out before you can say 'Jan Žižka'.

Penzión u Husičky (☎ 381 256 419; Tržní 274;
s/d incl breakfast 700/900Kč) Large modern rooms
and monumental breakfasts are served up
above a health food store here. Try and get
there before 5pm when the shop shuts and
the owner vanishes.

Hotel Lázně (☎ 381 202 511; lazne@genea2000.cz;
Čelkovice 44; s/d incl breakfast 1800/2000Kč; Ⓟ ☒ ☒)
This candy floss pink place, right on the
river's edge, is Tábor's newest, smartest
offering, with satellite TV, smiley staff and
an endless loop of muzak.

Other recommendations:
Hotel Zimni Stadium (☎ 381 231 088; tzmtzs@tzmt
.cz; Václava Soumara; dm/d 135/720Kč; Ⓟ) Dorms and
doubles in cheerily cheap surrounds.

THE HUSSITES

When Jan Hus was burned for heresy at Constance in 1415, the consequences were far greater than the Catholic authorities could have foreseen. His death caused a religious revolt among the Czechs, who had seen Hus' adoption of the Czech mass as a step towards religious and national self-determination. Hus himself had not intended such drastic revolution, focusing on a translation of the Latin rite, and the giving of bread and wine to all the congregation instead of to the clergy alone. But for many the time was ripe for church reform.

Hus was born around 1372 in Husinec, South Bohemia. From a poor background, he managed to become a lecturer at Charles University in Prague and in 1402 was ordained a preacher. He dreamt of a return to the original doctrines of the church – tolerance, humility, simplicity – but such a message had political overtones for a church that treated forgiveness as an opportunity to make money.

Tried on a trumped-up charge of heresy at Constance, in present-day Germany, Hus was burned at the stake on 6 July 1415. The trial was doubly unjust, in that Hus had been given safe conduct by the Holy Roman Emperor Sigismund.

In Bohemia many nobles offered to guarantee protection to those who practised religion according to Hus' teachings, and Hussite committees became widespread. The movement split over its relationship with the secular authorities, with the moderate Utraquists siding in 1434 with the Catholic Sigismund.

The more radical Taborites, seeing themselves as God's warriors, fought the Catholics in every way. As the military base for the Hussites, Tábor – named after the biblical Mt Tabor – was successfully defended by a mainly peasant army under Jan Žižka (see p218) and Prokop Holý.

The movement also attracted supporters from other Protestant sects in Europe. Many converged on Tábor and many of the groups joined against the crusading armies of the Holy Roman Empire.

Hussite ideals were never extinguished in Bohemia. Although the Utraquists became the dominant force after defeating (with the help of Sigismund's Catholic forces) the Taborites at the Battle of Lipany in 1434, the peace guaranteed religious freedom for the movement. It took almost 200 years before Protestantism was suppressed in the Czech Lands by the Catholic Habsburg rulers following the Battle of the White Mountain.

Pension Dáša (☎ 381 256 253; pensiondasa@volny.cz; Bílkova 735; s/d incl breakfast 700/990Kč; **P**) Upmarket *pension* with gym and sauna.

Pension 7 (☎ 381 252 039; Bílkova 783; s/d incl breakfast 400/600Kč) Simple, homely place with shared bathrooms.

Eating & Drinking

Kafe & Bar Havana (☎ 381 253 383; Žižkovo náměstí 17; mains 60-200Kč) Downtown Dublin meets Little Havana in this vivacious bar/eatery, where cocktails and Tex-Mex food bulk out the menu. The clocks here all tell different times so it's always time for your first margarita.

Restaurant & Cocktail Bar Meluzina (☎ 381 254 180; Radnická; mains 100-200Kč) Through the little archway to the left of the museum, this snug little place offers a sunny (when the sun's out) terrace, oodles of Czech speciality dishes and an atmospherically gloomy interior for drinks.

Café Pizzerie (☎ 381 254 048; Kostnická 159; pizza 60-90Kč) Small and lively, this is a friendly spot for Italian.

Café bar Sedm (Žižkovo náměstí 7) The favoured haunt of Tábor's artsy twentysomethings, this trendy little bar features decent beer and lively nights (it stays open until 2am weekends).

Entertainment

Divadlo Oskara Nedbala (☎ 381 254 701; www.div adlotabor.cz - Czech only; Palackého) Tábor's theatre is closed over the summer, but stages a bit of everything the rest of the year.

Kino Svět (☎ 381 252 200; náměstí FR Křižíka 129) This cinema has a limited programme of populist favourites (65Kč).

Getting There & Away

Bus (☎ 381 253 898) is generally the best way in and out of Tábor. Direct services include: Prague (78Kč, 1½ hours), České

SOUTH BOHEMIA

Budějovice (54Kč, one hour), Jihlava (66Kč, 1½ hours) and Brno (140Kč, three hours). Most services to Plzeň are via Prague or České Budějovice, but there is one direct service a day (114Kč, 2½ hours). For Telč, you will have to change in Jihlava.

Trains (☎ 381 484 111) also make the run to Prague (130Kč, 1½ hours), but they are generally more expensive and less convenient.

For all bus and train times and prices, visit www.idos.cz.

AROUND TÁBOR
Chýnov Cave
At the **Chýnov Cave** (Chýnovská jeskyně; ☎ 361 809 034; adult/concession 40/20Kč; 9am-4.30pm Tue-Sun Jul-Aug, until 3.30pm May, Jun, Sep & Aug) a narrow passage descends 37m to the colourful stalagmites formed by slowly dripping, mineral-laden water.

The cave is a 3km walk on a blue-marked trail northeast from the train station at Chýnov, itself four stops east of Tábor on the Pelhřimov line.

Soběslav
pop 7350
During the Hussite Wars Soběslav, 18km south of Tábor, was Oldřich Rožmberk's main defensive stronghold against the Hussite armies.

The main attractions of this small town are its two double-naved Gothic churches: **St Vitus Church** (kostel sv Víta) and the **Church of our Lady** (kostel Panny Marie). The latter is notable for its tower, built in 1487, and an elaborate vaulted ceiling in the crypt.

BECHYNĚ
pop 5700
A quiet spa town, largely off the beaten track, Bechyně has been revitalised in recent years with the renovation of its beautiful castle. Standing over the precipice of the Smutná creek (there are vertiginous views coming into town over the bridge from Tábor), the chateau backs onto an impressive square featuring a few worthwhile sights of its own.

Orientation & Information
The adjacent bus and train stations are 500m southwest from the castle and the main square, náměstí TG Masaryka.

CK Avanti Travel (☎ 381 213 822; ckavanti@volny.cz; Libušina 151; 9am-5pm Mon-Fri, until noon Sat) is just off the main square and doubles as the local tourist information office.

Sights & Activities
CASTLE
The **castle** (☎ 381 213 143; adult/concession 90/50Kč, in English 150Kč; 10am-5pm Tue-Sun 18 May-Sep) is one of many founded by Přemysl Otakar II and later owned by a parade of noble families, including the Rožmberks. After years of dereliction, it was recently returned to its original owner and following hefty reconstruction now looks in fabulously fine fettle. You can visit large portions of the interior, including its impressive weapons collection, Black Kitchen (the historic kitchen complete with all the old cooking paraphernalia) and portrait galleries as part of a 50-minute tour.

In the castle grounds, you can also visit the **Vladimír Preclík Museum** (muzeum Vladimíra Preclíka; adult/concession 50/30Kč; as castle), which offers an interesting insight into the life of this famous Czech writer/sculptor. The attractive grounds are perfect for a picnic and host an annual **summer cultural programme**.

MUSEUMS & CHURCHES
In the 15th century the town grew famous for its ceramics. The large **South Bohemian Aleš Gallery** (Alšova Jihočeská galerie; adult/concession 30/15Kč; 9am-noon & 12.30-5pm Tue-Sun May-Sep), in a former brewery just off náměstí TG Masaryka, features a seemingly endless and really quite interesting display of modern (and more traditional) ceramics from across the USA and Europe.

The small **Firefighting Museum** (Hasičské muzeum; adult/concession 20/10Kč; 9am-noon & 1-5pm Tue-Sun May-Sep), in a former synagogue on the main square, displays several wonderful old fire engines but not much else.

The nearby **Franciscan Church**, with fine vaulting and a dazzling clock tower, is open for services only.

Sleeping & Eating
Check in with tourist information (see above) for cheap private rooms, or contact **Vinarna u Hradeb** (☎ 381 211 799; Libušina 151) next door.

Penzión & Vinarna u Pichlů (☎ 381 211 022; jiri.fuka@quick.cz; d incl breakfast 550Kč) This snug pub by the Firefighting Museum offers a decent informal restaurant, a broody mock-Gothic interior and some tidy little rooms.

Hotel Panska (☎ 381 212 550; hotel.pankska@iol.cz; s/d incl breakfast 990/1490Kč; P ☒ ☒) The town's glitziest opening, also on the main square, oozes modern functionality and is especially disabled-friendly. It also has a popular restaurant.

Getting There & Away

Ten trains a day come from Tábor (34Kč, 47 minutes). Buses are faster to Tábor (24Kč, 40 minutes) and České Budějovice (36Kč, 52 minutes).

KÁMEN

pop 125

The Czech word for rock (*kámen*) lends itself to the great boulder that Kámen Castle sits on. Founded in the 13th century, the castle was renovated in the 17th century in early-baroque style.

Apart from a few historical displays, the castle's main attraction is a **Motorcycle Museum** (muzeum Motocyklo; adult/concession 40/20Kč; ☼ 9am-noon & 1-5pm Tue-Sun May-Sep, until 4pm Sat & Sun Apr & Oct), featuring Czech motorbikes from 1899 to the 1960s, including late-model Jawas and ČZs, in their time among the best in the world.

Getting There & Away

Up to five daily buses run to/from Tábor (32Kč, one hour).

PELHŘIMOV

pop 17,000

Slow-moving and pretty, this industrial centre still has a fine catalogue of Renaissance and baroque houses. While it makes a pleasant stop-off en route to somewhere else, it isn't really worth a special trip.

Orientation & Information

The train station is 1.5km south of the old town; to reach it turn left onto Nádražní, follow it past the bus station (keep sharp left) and take Poděbradova left up to the main square.

The **tourist information office** (☎ 565 326 924; ic@kzpe.cz; Masarykovo náměstí 1; ☼ 9am-12.30pm & 1-5pm Jun-Sep, until 4pm Mon-Fri Oct-May) is helpful. Nearby **Česká spořitelna** has an ATM.

Sights

Most Renaissance houses on and around the square were rebuilt in baroque style after a devastating fire in 1766. One at Masarykovo náměstí 13 was given a striking cubist face by Pavel Janák in 1913.

Also on the square is the ho-hum **Pelhřimov Museum** (muzeum vysočiny Pelhřimov; ☎ 565 323 184; adult/concession 30/15Kč; ☼ 9am-noon & 12.30-5pm Tue-Sun Apr-Sep, Tue-Fri Oct-Mar). In the courtyard behind the museum a statue of St Václav guards the entrance to a tiny castle, completed in 1554 for the Lords of Říčany, which now houses an extension of the Pelhřimov Museum (same times and prices).

Just north of the castle is the **Church of St Bartholomew** (kostel sv Bartoloměj), with its 61m **lookout tower** (vyhlídkova věž; adult/concession 15/10Kč; ☼ as museum).

Sleeping & Eating

The information office has a list of cheap *pensions* and hotels.

Domov mládeže ubytovna (☎ 565 323 537; Friedova 1464; dm 160Kč) This basic hostel offers no-frills accommodation in rooms with two or three beds.

Hotel Slavie (☎ 565 321 540; slavie@iol.cz; Masarykovo náměstí 29; s/d incl breakfast 600/800Kč; P) A few rungs up the comfort ladder, this mid-ranger sports decent rooms with TV and the faintest whiff of formality.

Cukrarna u Radnice (Masarykovo náměstí; pastries 30Kč) This square-side café is *the* place to kick back with a coffee and watch the action on the main square.

Getting There & Away

Buses run reasonably frequently to Jihlava (32Kč, 40 minutes). Long-distance buses run to Prague (70Kč, two hours, up to five a day) and Brno (90Kč, two hours, up to six a day). Pelhřimov is on the Jihlava–Tábor train line, an hour from Tábor (76Kč, ten trains a day) and 1¼ hours from Jihlava (64Kč). There are also buses to Jihlava (32Kč, 45 minutes).

JINDŘICHŮV HRADEC

pop 21,800

Who would have guessed that quiet Jindřichův Hradec was in the Middle Ages one of Bohemia's most important towns? Its central square and lakeside chateau, situated between the Nežárka river and

SOUTH BOHEMIA

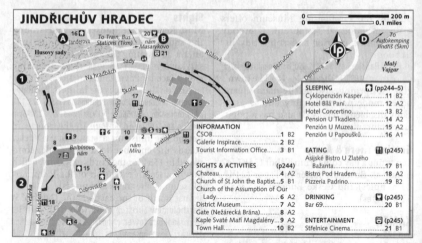

JINDŘICHŮV HRADEC

0 —————— 200 m
0 —————— 0.1 miles

INFORMATION	
ČSOB......................................1	B2
Galerie Inspirace......................2	B2
Tourist Information Office.......3	B2

SIGHTS & ACTIVITIES	(p244)
Chateau...................................4	A2
Church of St John the Baptist...5	B1
Church of the Assumption of Our	
Lady....................................6	A2
District Museum......................7	A2
Gate (Nežárecká Brána)..........8	A2
Kaple Svaté Maří Magdalény...9	A2
Town Hall..............................10	B2

SLEEPING	(pp244–5)
Cyklopenzión Kasper...........11	B2
Hotel Bílá Paní....................12	A2
Hotel Concertino.................13	B2
Pension U Tkadlen...............14	A2
Penzión U Muzea................15	A2
Penzión U Papoušků............16	A1

EATING	(p245)
Asijské Bistro U Zlatého	
Bažanta..............................17	B1
Bistro Pod Hradem..............18	A2
Pizzeria Padrino..................19	B2

DRINKING	(p245)
Bar 69................................20	B1

ENTERTAINMENT	(p245)
Střelnice Cinema.................21	B1

Vajgar lake, are striking. The town, prospering from its position on a trade route from Austria, suffered three great fires in 1435, 1773 and 1801; the result is a broad spectrum of architecture from the 15th to the 19th centuries. Of course, some people come simply to gawk at the world's largest mechanised nativity scene.

Orientation & Information

The adjacent bus and train stations are 1km from the city centre; to reach the main square walk south down Nádražní, turn left past a church onto Klášterská and continue south down Panská to the main square, náměstí Míru.

The **tourist information office** (Informační Středisko; ☎ 384 363 546; www.jh.cz; Panská 136; ☯ 8am-6pm Mon-Fri, until noon Sat & Sun Jul-Aug, 8am-5pm Mon-Fri, until noon Sat Sep-Jun) also arranges accommodation.

Galerie Inspirace (☎ 384 362 375; náměstí Míru 138/1) has Internet access at the back of the shop.

ČSOB (náměstí Míru) has exchange and ATM facilities.

Chateau

For a full description of the town's chateau, see p73.

Sights

AROUND THE OLD TOWN

Sections of the old **town walls** still remain. To the west is the gate, **Nežárecká brána** (1466).

The main square (náměstí Míru) has several late-Gothic, Renaissance and baroque houses, the most notable being the sgraffitoed **Langrův dům** (náměstí Míru 139) and its vaulted archway.

The **Church of the Assumption of Our Lady** (kostel Nanebevzetí Panny Marie), behind the **town hall**, has a good cycle of 17th-century frescoes and photogenic views from its **tower** (adult/concession 10/5Kč; ☯ 10am-noon & 1-4pm). The **Church of St John the Baptist** (kostel sv Jana Křtitele; 10Kč; ☯ 9am-noon & 12.30-4.30pm Jun-Aug) is the oldest church in town and is noteworthy for some 600-year-old frescoes, including one of St Louis of Toulouse.

DISTRICT MUSEUM

The Jesuit seminary opposite the former Jesuit college on Komenského now houses the **District Museum** (muzeum Jindřichohradecka; ☎ 384 363 660; adult/concession 40/20Kč; ☯ 8.30am-noon & 12.30-5pm Jun-Sep, Tue-Sun Apr, May & Oct). The foremost attraction is an extraordinary, **mechanical nativity scene** completed by one Tomáš Krýza in 1756, after 60 years of labour. The scene comprises over 1000 handcrafted figurines and fills an entire room.

Sleeping

BUDGET

Penzión U tkadlen (☎ 384 321 348; fax 384 326 076; Pod hradem 7/IV; per person 280Kč) Housed in an atmospheric, traditional-style building in a restful spot down by the canal, this has

SOUTH BOHEMIA

two- and three-bed rooms and oodles of rustic charm.

Autokemping Jindřiš (☎ 384 326 758; behoun@ cbox.cz; Jindřiš 15; tent 65Kč) In the village of Jindřiš, this is 5km east from town on a train from the main station.

MID-RANGE

The tourist information office books private rooms for about 200Kč per person.

Hotel Bílá paní (☎ 384 363 329; Dobrovského 5; s/d incl breakfast 600/1000Kč) Daubed with frescoes and dripping with understated style, this has a top-notch location near the castle and lashings of choccie box charm.

Penzión u Papoušků (☎ 384 362 235; Na Příkopě 188/11; d incl breakfast 900Kč) Sporting a startling new lick of bright blue paint, this cheerful place has pleasant rooms and a popular Chinese-meets-Italian eatery below.

Cyklopenzión Kasper (☎ 723 760 915; náměstí Míru; s/d 550/1100Kč) In a quiet cranny just off the main square, this butter yellow place has cosy beds for weary cyclists – and anyone else for that matter.

Penzión U muzea (☎ 384 361 698; umuzea@jhweb .cz; Balbinovo náměstí 17/1; s/d incl breakfast 500/950Kč; P) The décor's frumpy here, but there's billiards, a sun terrace and parking (very handy in summer).

TOP END

Hotel Concertino (☎ 384 362 320; svihalek@concert ino.cz; náměstí Míru 141/1; s/d incl breakfast 990/1700Kč; P ✗ ❋) Oozing chain hotel reliability, this four-star number offers the glitziest bed in town – and the prices aren't too bad either.

Eating & Drinking

Bistro Pod Hradem (☎ 384 362 203; Pod hradem; mains 80-150Kč; ☼ from 4pm) With a wooden terrace teetering on the canal's edge, this is a top spot for romantic waterside dining.

Asijské Bistro u Zlatého Bažanta (Panská 97; mains 50Kč) This pick-and-point Chinese buffet is fine for inexpensive Asian eats.

Pizzeria Padrino (☎ 777 660 870; náměstí Míru 158; mains 90Kč) There's a sad absence of trademark jumbo pepper grinders, but the tasty pizza and pasta dishes keep the crowds coming anyway.

Bar 69 (☎ 384 361 918; Jarošovská; ☼ 5pm-1am) The mojitos keep things lively in this local hipster bar.

Entertainment

Střelnice cinema (☎ 384 351 405; náměstí Masarykovo) This central cinema shows films nightly.

Classical music concerts are held across town. Ask tourist information for the latest programme.

Getting There & Away

Reasonably regular buses make the run to Telč (36Kč, one hour), Tábor (44Kč, 1½ hours), Slavonice (35Kč, 1¼ hours), České Budějovice (40Kč, 1¼ hours), Brno (130Kč, three hours) and Prague (160Kč, four hours).

Jindřichův Hradec is on the train line between České Budějovice (88Kč, one hour) and Jihlava (90Kč, 1¼ hours). Useful services also run to Tábor (76Kč, one hour) and Prague, via Veselí (184Kč, three hours).

For all train and bus times and prices, visit www.idos.cz.

ČERVENÁ LHOTA

This romantic, faded pink **chateau** (☎ 384 384 228; adult/concession 50/25Kč, in English 100/50Kč; ☼ 9.30am-5.15pm Tue-Sun Jun-Aug, until 4pm May & Sep, 9am-4pm Sat & Sun Apr & Oct) sits on an outcrop in the middle of a lake. It got its name ('Red Lhota') in 1641 due to its innovative, bright-red roof tiles. The 14th-century Gothic fortress was rebuilt into a Renaissance castle that was later adapted in baroque style. In the second half of the 18th century the jovially-named German composer Karl Ditters von Dittersdorf lived here. Červená Lhota makes an excellent day trip from Jindřichův Hradec. Tours of the interior run every hour or so (last tour 45 minutes before closing).

Getting There & Away

On weekdays there are four daily buses from either Soběslav or Jindřichův Hradec, each about half an hour away (20Kč). Weekend transport is sporadic.

SLAVONICE

pop 2600

On the very cusp of the former forbidden zone, Slavonice was as close to Austria as Czechs were permitted to live during the chilliest days of the Cold War. These days, the tourists drift across the border unhindered, stopping off for a lazy lunch in Slavonice before heading off to destinations further north. With origins stretching back to 1277, historic Slavonice is a spectacular, soporific little town, surrounded by blueprint rolling countryside.

While Slavonice is now listed by Unesco as an historical town preserve, many of the surrounding villages were evacuated and destroyed during the communist era. The castle at the village of Maříž near Slavonice was destroyed for a different purpose – the making of a film for a western company – but is a worthwhile diversion for those eager to get a handle on how this region must have looked when tanks and electric fences, rather than combine harvesters and cornfields, were the norm here. Ask at the tourist office for details.

Orientation

From the train station it's 400m northeast along Nádražní to Slavonice's old town. The bus station is 200m north of the main square, náměstí Míru.

The **tourist office** (☎ 384 493 320; www.slavonice -mesto.cz; náměstí Míru 480; ☉ 9am-6pm Jun-Sep, 10am-4pm Mon-Fri Oct-May) also has **Internet** access.

Sights

The town's architectural treasures are around náměstí Míru, Horní náměstí and Boženy Němcové. The **sgraffito at Horní náměstí 88** depicts the Habsburgs and figures from Greek mythology. The 1599 **town hall** stands out, as does the Gothic **Church of the Assumption of Our Lady** (kostel Nanebevzetí Panny Marie), surrounded by 14th- to early-16th-century houses on náměstí Míru. As ever, you can climb the church **tower** (Navštivte věž; adult/concession 15/10Kč; ☉ 9am-6pm May-Aug, Sat & Sun only Apr & Sep) for fine vistas.

Also on the square is a small **museum** (městské muzeum; adult/concession 15/10Kč; ☉ 9am-noon & 1.30-5pm Tue-Sun Jun-Aug, until 4pm May & Sep)

with some artefacts from the medieval village of Pfaffenschlag.

Sleeping & Eating

Hotel u Růže (☎ 384 493 004; www.dumruze.cz; náměstí Míru 452; s/d 900/1400Kč; ☒ ☒ ☒) This little place has heaps of elegant style and a buffet lunch of trimmings including a (microscopic) pool, billiards, bike hire and a sauna. Some of the rooms also come with kitchenettes.

Hotel Arkáda (☎ 384 408 408; info@hotelarkada.cz; náměstí Míru 466; s/d incl breakfast 450/900Kč) Just across the square, this modern hotel has some pleasant, newly renovated rooms above a rather incongruous mini casino.

Ubytování (☎ 384 493 432; náměstí Míru 468; per person 200Kč) Two doors up from Arkáda (look out for the 'Penzión' banner), this simple place has some of the cheapest beds in town. Ring the 'Součkovi' buzzer.

Besídka (☎ 384 493 292; Horní náměstí 522; mains 100Kč) This cheerful bar/restaurant is housed in a prettified sgraffito building and whips up ice-cold beers and glorious local fare.

La Petite Mort (náměstí Míru; coffees 25Kč) At the foot of the Church of the Assumption of Our Lady, this hip, hole-in-the-wall café throws together top-notch coffee, frappés and a mean tiramisu.

Getting There & Away

Slavonice is at the end of a minor train line that goes through Telč in South Moravia (33Kč, one hour) to Kostelec u Jihlavy. The bus from Prague takes 3½ hours to Dačice (120Kč), where you must change for Slavonice (30 minutes).

BORDER CROSSING

Just over 1km south of Slavonice is a vehicle and pedestrian border crossing, to Fratres in Austria (6am to 10pm daily).

East Bohemia

Rocks, rather than Renaissance squares, are the aces in East Bohemia's hand. And there are plenty to choose from. From the mighty Krkonoše range, which marks the border with Poland and appears to prop up the skies of most of northern Bohemia, through the rugged sandstone towers of Adršpach-Teplice, to the ruin-strewn hills and vistas of Český ráj, East Bohemia is an idiosyncratic region peppered with natural wonders. For skiers, ramblers and climbers alike, these ragged landscapes – which culminate in Sněžka (1602m), the Republic's highest summit – are one of the country's great attractions, offering trails and slopes a-plenty and enough mountain air to put you into hibernation.

But that's not to say there's nothing to do in the towns. While East Bohemia's upland resorts are predominantly functional – presumably the gigantic dimensions of the surrounding landscapes are just too intimidating for the bland lines of Stalinist architecture to compete with – the region's lowlands boast a string of vibrant, historic cities. From the schizophrenic provincial capital, Hradec Králové, with its awesome old town square and Art Nouveau façades, to quieter Pardubice, with its picture-postcard historic hub, East Bohemia seems to have a tower for every peak and a church for every valley.

HIGHLIGHTS

- Hump it up 1602m-high **Sněžka** (p268), the Czech Republic's highest peak

- Wander through picture-postcard landscapes capped with ruins in **Český ráj** (p257)

- Conquer the Wolf Gorge hiking trail and sandstone rock formations of the **Adršpach-Teplice Protected Landscape** (p262)

- Sip coffee and watch the world go by on Pardubice's pristine **Renaissance square** (p253)

- Explore the many layers of **Hradec Králové's** (p249) architectural heritage

★ Sněžka

★ Adršpach-Teplice Protected Landscape

★ Český ráj

★ Hradec Králové

★ Pardubice

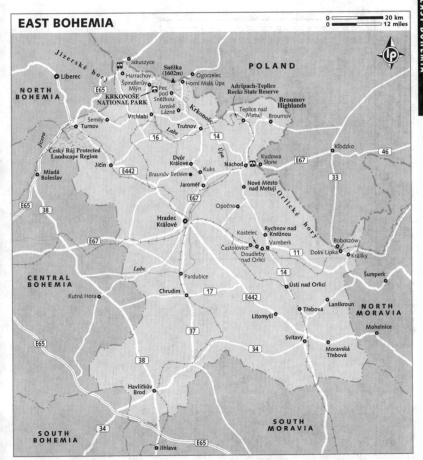

HRADEC KRÁLOVÉ

pop 100,500

Fortress walls gave Hradec Králové its one-time potency, but they also stifled its early growth. Many of the old fortifications have now gone, but the boundary between the city's historic heart and the grand sprawl of its latter-day expansion runs across the cityscape like a fault line. In Staré Město, the old town clusters around the appropriately named Big Square (Velké náměstí), a photogenic sweep surrounded by a buffet lunch of Gothic, Renaissance and baroque façades. Cross the river, however, and the city's New Town (Nové Město) is a very different bag, shaking up some grandiose monuments to Art Nouveau with a motley band of communism's bleakest monsters. As an administrative centre, modern Hradec Králové has something of a workaday, bureaucratic feel, but with a regular stream of tourists, plenty of bars and restaurants and a decent collection of sights and museums, there's plenty of life in the old workhorse yet.

History

Two rivers and a hill: the ideal foundations for a fortified town. And it didn't take long for the local warlords to notice. By the 9th century, a stronghold had been constructed at the confluence of the Labe and Orlice rivers and within 300 years the fledgling city had become the administrative centre of East Bohemia.

HRADEC KRÁLOVÉ

Money flooded in and by the 14th century it was one of Bohemia's most important cities, becoming the seat of the kingdom's widowed queens (the name means 'Queens' Castle') – a mixed blessing, as the immense fortifications that followed soon began to strangle further growth.

Although overrun by Swedish troops during the Thirty Years' War, Hradec Králové's reputation as a stronghold remained and with the merging of the Austrian and Hungarian thrones in the 19th century, its defences were once again bolstered, this time against the Prussians. Fortunately for Hradec Králové, the Prussians avoided the city when they marched south in 1866, trouncing the Austrians just east of the centre instead.

In the following decades the walls were pulled down. Thus released, Hradec Králové expanded explosively, guided by some farsighted planning. Nové Město, the 'new town', bears both the Art Nouveau and severe functionalist imprint of Bohemia's leading turn-of-the-century architects, particularly Jan Kotěra and his student Josef Gočár.

Orientation

Staré Město, the old town, is squashed between the Labe and Orlice rivers. Nové Město begins west of Československé armády.

From the train and bus stations it's a 400m walk east into the heart of Nové Město, or about 1km to Staré Město. Trolleybus Nos 2, 3 and 7 go from the train station to the edge of Staré Město.

Information

EMERGENCY
Foreigners' Police office (☎ 158; Riegrovo náměstí) By the train station.

INTERNET ACCESS
Internet cafés charge from 30Kč per hour.
Informační centrum (☎ 495 580 492; Velké náměstí; ☺ 10am-5pm daily May-Sep, 10am-5pm Mon-Fri Oct-Apr)
OK Net (Gočárova 32/806; ☺ noon-midnight Mon-Thu, noon-7pm Fri, 2-7pm Sat, 2-10pm Sun)

MEDICAL SERVICES
Hospital (nemocnice; ☎ 495 831 111; Sokolská) Is 500m south of the old town.

MONEY
Česká Spořitelna (cnr Československé armády & Palackého) Has an exchange desk and ATM.

POST
Main post office (Zamenhofova) Opposite the train station. Another **post office** (Tomkova) is near Velké náměstí.

TOURIST INFORMATION
Tourist information centre (Informační centrum; ☎ 495 580 492; www.ic-hk.cz; Velké náměstí; ☺ 10am-5pm May-Sep, Mon-Fri Oct-Apr) Sells maps, helps with accommodation and has Internet access. There is another **branch** (☎ 495 534 492; Gočárova 1225) in Nové Město.

Sights
STARÉ MĚSTO
The old town's architectural heart is at the west end of Velké náměstí (also known as Žižkovo náměstí). The oldest structure here is the brick Gothic **Church of the Holy Spirit** (kostel sv Ducha), founded in 1307. Dour outside, the church is plain and lofty inside, illuminated by decorative stained glass.

Next door is the 68m Renaissance **White Tower** (Bílá věž; adult/concession 15/10Kč; ☺ 9am-noon & 1-5pm Tue-Sun), built in 1589 and no longer very white. The tower's original, 16th-century clock was ruined by a storm in 1828; the current clock dates from a 1993 renovation. Climb the tower to see (but hopefully not hear) the 9.8-tonne **Augustine Bell** (cast in 1506). Next door is the plain baroque **St Clement Chapel** (kostel sv Klimenta).

Facing the square, the twin-towered, 15th-century, **former town hall** (radnice) has been converted into commercial office space. To the south of the square, at the end of a row of pastel-painted former canons' residences, is the **municipal brewery**.

Sturdy arcades line the north side of the square; opposite is the Jesuits' **Church of the Assumption of the Virgin** (kostel Nanebevzetí Panny Marie), light and pretty inside in spite of its baroque baggage. This and the adjacent **Jesuit College** and **Bishop's Palace** date from the 17th century, when a bishopric was established in Hradec Králové. Tucked beside the church is a Josef Gočár addition, a staircase down to Komenského ulice.

A definite highlight of Hradec Králové is the regional **Gallery of Modern Art** (Galérie moderního umění; Velké náměstí 139-140; adult/concession 25/10Kč; ☺ 9am-noon & 1-6pm Tue-Sun). In the handsome, Art Nouveau building (designed by

Osvald Polívka) is a superb collection of late-19th- and 20th-century Czech painting and sculpture, as well as changing modern exhibitions.

The eastern extension of Velké náměstí is the less-photogenic Malé náměstí (Little Square), also known as Husovo náměstí.

NOVÉ MĚSTO – EAST OF THE RIVER

Nové Město begins from Československé armády, although the strip east of the Labe is more neglected than the clean-cut neighbourhoods west of the river.

Where Palackého meets the river is the **East Bohemia Regional Museum** (Krajský muzeum vychodních Čech; ☎ 495 512 462; www.muzeumhk.cz - Czech only; Eliščino nábřeží 465; adult/concession 30/15Kč; ◷ 9am-noon & 1-5pm Tue-Sun), a graceful, Art Nouveau building of red brick, designed by Kotěra, with seated giants on either side of the door. Inside are old photos, clockworks, mammoth bones and a fascinating scale model of Hradec Králové dating from 1865, showing the fortress that bound the town for four centuries.

Down at the confluence of the two rivers is **Jiráskovy sady**, a wooded park which features a 16th-century **wooden church** brought from Ukraine in 1935.

NOVÉ MĚSTO – WEST OF THE RIVER

Gočár's showpiece square, boxy Masarykovo náměstí, is overtly tidy and thoroughly functional, best showing his wider vision for the city. Nowadays it's linked by a pedestrianised mall to the livelier Baťkovo náměstí.

To the south are several brick school buildings designed by Gočár between 1925 and 1928. The most interesting is the **State Grammar School** (Státní gymnázium), with a severe façade reminiscent of an open book. Nearby is another arresting Gočár work, the wedge-shaped Protestant **Ambrosian Chapel** (Ambrožů sbor).

On náměstí 28.října, hunt down the functionalist **Church of the Blessed Heart of Our Lord** (kostel Božího Srdce Páně), with a dramatic arched space inside.

Sleeping

The tourist office has a list of private rooms (starting at 250Kč per person). The nearest camping ground is at Stříbrný rybník, about 5km east of the centre (take bus No 17).

BUDGET

Two multistorey hostels offer accommodation year-round, though they're often fully booked by workers from local construction sites:

Ubytovna Astra (☎ 495 211 133; paulinapatkova@ atlas.cz; Vocelova 802; dm per person 140Kč) With basic shared rooms.

Ubytovna ZVU (☎ 495 511 175; havlova@hotelovydum.cz; Heyrovského 4; dm/s/d 170/ 240/340Kč) With dorms and private rooms.

MID-RANGE

Penzion Nové Adalbertinum (☎ 495 063 111; fax 495 063 405; Velké náměstí 32; s/d incl breakfast 790/1190Kč) You can't beat the location of these large, airy rooms housed in the former Jesuit college. The atmosphere's a bit monastic, but standards are religiously high.

Hotel Stadión (☎ 495 514 664; fax 495 514 667; Komenského 1214; s/d incl breakfast 670/770Kč; **P**) It looks like a bus station, but the rooms are clean and in an otherwise expensive town, the prices are fair.

Pension U sv Lukáše (☎ 495 518 616; fax 495 511 652; Úzká 208; s/d incl breakfast 1000/1400Kč) The snug rooms in this pretty yellow townhouse have more old-world charm than most. There's also a cosy eatery below.

Other recommendations:

Pod Věží Penzion (☎ 495 514 932; Velké náměstí 165; s/d incl breakfast 990/1250Kč) Sparkling new and central.

Penzion U Jana (☎ 495 514 604; penzionujana@ volny.cz; s/d incl breakfast 798/1155Kč) A pleasant, welcoming *pension*.

TOP END

Hotel U královny Elišky (☎ 495 518 052; fax 495 518 872; Malé náměstí 117; s/d incl breakfast 2400/2800Kč; **P** ⊠ ⊠ ⊠) The old town's plushest hotel has plenty of polished style and all the mod-cons, including a fitness centre, pool and sauna.

Eating & Drinking

Kavárna U Knihomola (☎ 495 516 089; Velké náměstí 26; mains 70-150Kč) The city's lively young things troop to this vibrant bar/restaurant to indulge in its fabulously large steaks, sandwiches and salads. It's open until 2am on Friday and Saturday.

Černý kůň (☎ 603 202 438; Malé náměstí 10-12; mains 120Kč) Sanded floors and pine tables give this traditional pub-style eatery a fresh, up-to-date look. Expect all the Bohemian staples.

Escobara (☎ 608 140 741; Karla IV 611; mains 150Kč) This stylish place whips up pastas, grills and cocktails in trendy bar-style surrounds. Despite the name, there isn't a hoodlum in sight.

Cuba Libre (Malé náměstí 14-15; ☿ closed Sun) The clichéd Che portraits invite political debate at this groovy café and gallery.

Other recommendations:

China Restaurant (☎ 495 516 072; Velké náměstí 164; mains 70Kč) For quality Chinese favourites.

Tesco Department Store (Dukelská) For supermarket shops.

Entertainment

Filharmonie Hradec Králové (☎ 495 211 375; www.fhk.cz; Eliščino nábřeží 777) The city orchestra stages regular classical concerts.

Klicperovo divadlo (☎ 495 514 590; Dlouhá 98) Theatre (usually Czech) is on the programme here.

Kino Centrál (☎ 495 213 613; Karla IV 774) This cinema shows Czech and foreign films.

Getting There & Away

Direct **buses** (☎ 495 521 742) link Hradec Králové with Prague (72Kč, 1½ hours) and Brno (89Kč, 2½ hours), with departures all day.

There are about 12 **fast trains** (☎ 495 537 555) a day to Prague (140Kč, 1½ hours), three to Brno (204Kč, 2½ hours) and dozens to Pardubice (34Kč, 30 minutes).

You can check all bus and train times and prices at www.idos.cz.

PARDUBICE

pop 92,000

Semtex and oh-so-delicate Renaissance façades may make uneasy bedfellows in any other context, but here they form the twin foundations of East Bohemia's second city. With the infamous explosives factory in its outer suburb of Semtim and an immaculately preserved Renaissance square at its heart, Pardubice is a peculiar cocktail of wedding-cake romanticism and bleak modernity; a chocolate-box village surrounded by a rumbling, smoking city. The grey sweep of 'new' Pardubice is unlikely to play a starring role in anyone's holiday snaps, but the town's rougher edges are all too easy to tune out while propping up the counter of a café in the exquisite old square, or strolling through the beautiful castle grounds. With plenty of good hotels, Pardubice remains an appealing base for exploring the wider region as well as a worthwhile day-trip destination in its own right.

History

Founded around 1340, Pardubice caught the noble eye of the Moravian Pernštejn family when they took ownership of the whole region in 1491. After giving it a bit of a makeover, the new landlords moved into the town's castle soon after and over the next century, with the help of Italian artisans and the unexpected assistance of two devastating fires, built Pardubice a glossy new Renaissance face. Though only a fraction of the Pernštejns' legacy still stands today (thanks to the work of a Swedish siege army in the Thirty Years' War), the town centre remains achingly pretty.

Orientation

Míru, the artery of 'new' Pardubice, is an 800m walk east along Palackého from the bus and train stations (or take any bus or trolleybus). On the east side of náměstí Republiky is a Gothic gate-tower into the old centre, Pernštýnské náměstí.

Information

The **tourist information office** (☎ 466 612 474; info@pardub.cz; Míru 61; ☿ 9am-7pm) has maps and accommodation information.

Česká spořitelna (náměstí Republiky) has an ATM and exchange desk. **Česká Pojišťovna** (Míru 2647) also has a 24-hour exchange machine.

Grand Internet Café (☎ 777 671 393; cnr náměstí Republiky & Míru; ☿ 9am-6pm Mon-Sat) is on the 3rd floor of the large, tiled Grand Shopping Mall.

The **main post office** is on Míru.

Sights & Activities
NÁMĚSTÍ REPUBLIKY

This modern square is home to three of Pardubice's oldest and most interesting buildings. The most arresting, with its picturesque gablets and needle-thin tower, is **St Bartholomew Church** (kostel sv Bartoloměj), dating originally from the 13th century. Its present form dates from about 1515, when it was rebuilt after being razed by the Hussites.

At the other end of the square is the fine Art Nouveau **Municipal Theatre** (Městské

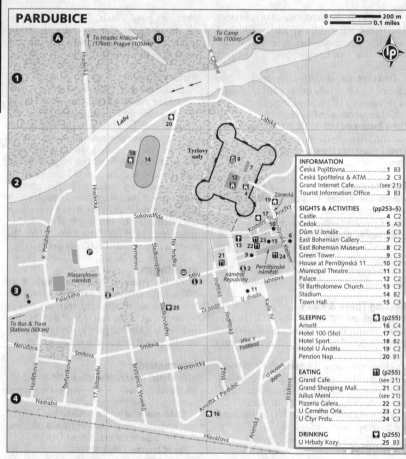

PARDUBICE

0 —— 200 m
0 —— 0.1 miles

To Hradec Králove (17km); Prague (105km)

To Camp Site (100m)

Labe

Labská

Tyršovy sady

Zámecká

Sukovatřída

Kostelní sv. Anežky

Masarykovo náměstí

náměstí Republiky

Pernštýnské náměstí

Jahnova

Miru

To Bus & Train Stations (600m)

Palackeho

Sládkovského

U divadla

U Husova sboru

Jiříka z Poděbrad

Hronovická

Jindřiška

Za pastři

Karla IV.

Jiráskova

Arnošta z Pardubic

Hlaváčova

INFORMATION
Česká Pojišťovna.....................1 B3
Česká Spořitelna & ATM.........2 C3
Grand Internet Cafe.........(see 21)
Tourist Information Office........3 B3

SIGHTS & ACTIVITIES   (pp253–5)
Castle......................................4 C2
Čedok......................................5 A3
Dům U Jonáše..........................6 C3
East Bohemian Gallery.............7 C2
East Bohemian Museum............8 C2
Green Tower.............................9 C3
House at Pernštýnská 11..........10 C2
Municipal Theatre..................11 C3
Palace....................................12 C3
St Bartholomew Church..........13 C3
Stadium.................................14 B2
Town Hall...............................15 C3

SLEEPING   (p255)
Arnošt....................................16 C4
Hotel 100 (Sto).......................17 C2
Hotel Sport.............................18 B2
Hotel U Ánděla.......................19 C2
Penzion Nap...........................20 B1

EATING   (p255)
Grand Cafe........................(see 21)
Grand Shopping Mall...............21 C3
Julius Meinl.......................(see 21)
Pizzeria Galera.......................22 C3
U Černého Orla.......................23 C3
U Čtyr Prstu...........................24 C3

DRINKING   (p255)
U Hrbaty Kozy........................25 B3

divadlo). On the eastern side, brandishing flags and pointy gables, is the 16th-century **Green Tower** (Zelená brána; admission 15Kč; ☺ 9am-noon & 1-5pm May-Sep, Sat & Sun only Oct), which you can climb for views over the town's two faces.

PERNŠTÝNSKÉ NÁMĚSTÍ

This cobbled square is one of Bohemia's most handsome, completely enclosed by bright Renaissance buildings, including a genial, neo-Renaissance **town hall**. The square's most notable façade is the 18th-century, snow-white, stucco relief of Jonah being swallowed by the whale, on the house called **dům U Jonáše** (☎ 466 510 003; adult/concession 30/10Kč; ☺ noon-6pm Tue-Fri, 10am-6pm Sat & Sun), which contains a small gallery.

Walk through the narrow alleys to the north and east of the square, beneath bulky stone arches supporting heavily sloping, virtually arthritic, Renaissance-era buildings. Among the most venerable of these is the **house at Pernštýnská 11**, more or less unchanged since the 16th century.

PARDUBICE CASTLE

The **castle** (zámek; admission 40Kč; ☺ 10am-6pm Tue-Sun), filled with courting peacocks and a solitary gobbling turkey (no dogs!), is accessible from Zámecká, north of Pernštýnské náměstí. Inside is the renovated **palace**, featuring some exquisite Renaissance murals of Moses receiving the Ten Commandments and Samson and Delilah. Opposite, in two smaller wings, are a superb gallery and a museum, both included in the entrance fee. The **East Bohemian Gallery** (Východočeská galérie) has a permanent collection of 19th- and 20th-century Czech art, including unexpected modern sculptures around the grounds. A rather immodest exhibit on the role of the Pernštejns in Czech history is featured in the **East Bohemian Museum** (Východočeská muzeum).

Sleeping

Tourist information can help with private rooms, or there is a camping ground just north of the river opposite the castle. Prices are generally high.

Arnošt (☎ 466 613 668; Arnošta z Pardubic 675; s/d 450/600Kč; **P**) A recent makeover has brought a sprinkling of sparkle to this hostel-style place; it has also pushed up prices. The basic rooms are spotless and good value though.

Hotel U anděla (☎ 466 535 656; Zámecká 24; d incl breakfast 1000Kč; **P**) The rooms are snugger than a rug bug in this stylish, traditional-style inn.

Hotel 100 (Sto) (☎ 466 511 179; fax 466 501 825; Kostelní 100; d incl breakfast 1000Kč; **P**) In a restored burgher's house in the heart of the old town, this friendly place is both a little bit dated and a little bit special.

Penzion Nap (☎ 466 512 650; penzion.nap@tiscali.cz; U Stadionu 2030; s/d incl breakfast 650/850Kč; **P**) Near the stadium and opposite the river, this offers warm welcomes but slightly crumbly rooms.

Hotel Sport (☎ 466 512 062; info@hotelsport.cz; Sukova Třída 1735; s/d incl breakfast 750/850Kč; **P**) Also out by the stadium, this has blockish, functional style and reliable standards.

Eating & Drinking

Pizzeria Galera (☎ 466 530 083; Pernštýnské náměstí; pizza 100Kč) Poppy tunes, colourful yellow décor and big crowds put the jazz into this top-notch Italian. The thin-crust pizzas are huge and very tasty.

U Čtyr Prstu (☎ 466 516 709; Pernštýnské náměstí; dishes 50-150Kč) The coffees and cakes go down a treat at this little terrace café, where the people-watching possibilities are all part of the appeal.

U Hrbaty Kozy (☎ 466 611 734; Sladkovského 507) A certain leap of faith is required to find this snug Irish pub – it's downstairs in a seemingly empty garage – but the daring

---

SEMTEX

Invented in 1966 by Stanislav Brebera, who was only paid a couple of hundred dollars for his efforts, Semtex plastic explosive has been manufactured by Pardubice's Explosia factory for more than 30 years. Widely used by commercial miners, who can buy it under license for as little as US$6 per kg, Semtex is odourless, highly versatile and devastatingly efficient (a mere 250g can down an airliner), making it an attractive proposition for terrorists, who will pay as much as $1400 per kg on a booming black market. Despite bolstered security at the Pardubice factory today, nearly 700 tonnes, enough for 1.5 million of the bombs that brought down the Pan-Am airliner over Lockerbie, was exported to Libya in the 1970s. Much of this may still be within its shelf-life.

---

are rewarded with a pleasant little watering hole.

Grand Café (☎ 603 493 277; náměstí Republiky) Cocktails and Pardubice's twentysomethings come together to lively effect in this airy café/bar. It also serves coffee and snacks.

Other recommendations:

U černého orla (☎ 466 511 611; Pernštýnské náměstí; mains 60-110Kč) For cheap Bohemian favourites.

Julius Meinl (cnr Míru & náměstí Republiky) The supermarket is in the Grand Shopping Mall.

Getting There & Away

Pardubice is 30 minutes from Hradec Králové by bus (22Kč) or train (34Kč). Buses go about every half hour, trains go hourly. Tickets are available from machines in the station.

There are over a dozen direct trains daily from Pardubice to Olomouc (two hours, 184Kč).

A visit is feasible as a day trip from Prague, best by fast train (130Kč, 1¼ hours, about hourly). ČSAD buses take two hours but are a bit cheaper.

OPOČNO

Plots, schemes and intrigue put an interesting spin on this beautiful castle, which looms over the village of Opočno, 25km northeast of Hradec Králové.

There was a Přemysl fortress at Opočno by the 11th century, but after a later owner,

Jan Městecký, abandoned the Hussite cause, it was trashed by disciples of the Hussite military hero Jan Žižka.

In the 16th century the fortress was converted by the Trčkas, one of Bohemia's richest families, into the neo-Romanesque chateau you see today. The last of the line, Adam Erdmann Trčka, was killed in 1634 in the course of a plot to assassinate Ferdinand II. The emperor then sold the chateau to the Italian Colloredo family, who lived in it right up until 1945.

In 1813, King Friedrich Wilhelm II of Prussia, Austrian Chancellor Metternich and Russian Tsar Alexander II met here in the course of forming their 'Holy Alliance' against Napoleon.

The prettified, pastel **chateau** (🕓 9-11.30am & 12.30-6pm Tue-Sun Jul-Aug, until 5pm May, Jun & Sep, until 4pm Sat & Sun only Apr-Oct) is impressive partly because it still looks lived-in. The owner at the start of the 20th century, Josef II Colloredo-Mannsfeld, filled one end of the castle with his hunting trophies and artefacts from Africa and the Americas. Tours (in Czech) cost 40/20Kč (adult/concession), or 60/30Kč including a diversion into the armoury. The last tour is 1¼ hours before closing.

All that remains of the older fortress is one cylindrical tower. The baroque houses around the chateau are worth a peek, as is the surrounding **Zámecký park** (🕓 7am-8pm).

Orientation & Information

The joint train and bus stations are 1.5km west from the castle: follow Nádražní to Kupkovo náměstí then veer right on Zámecká. The chateau is a 400m climb from Opočno's renovated central square.

Penzión Orchidea (☎ 602 112 787; Komenského 75; s/d 700/1200Kč; P) is the best of the bunch in a town with very few passable accommodation options. For a cheap Czech lunch try the beer hall **U slunce**, off Kupkovo náměstí on the road to the chateau.

Getting There & Away

Buses run from Hradec Králové every hour or so (32Kč, 40 minutes). From Prague there are three buses a day (96Kč, 2¾ hours).

ČASTOLOVICE & AROUND

The 13th-century stronghold of Častolovice, 31km southeast of Hradec Králové, was renovated as a Renaissance chateau at the end of the 16th century; it passed into the hands of the Šternberk (Sternberg) family in 1694, and then into the hands of the state at the end of WWII. The Šternberks reclaimed it in the 1990s, repairing the Communist-era pillage and opening some of its 150 rooms to visitors. They still live here.

Highlights of the **chateau** (adult/concession 60/30Kč; 🕓 9am-6pm Tue-Sun May-Sep, Sat & Sun only Apr & Oct) tour include a vast Knights' Hall with biblical scenes on the ceiling, the family's fine collection of 17th- to 19th-century furniture and portraits of every one of the Czech kings. The chateau is surrounded by a sedate, English-style park. The last tour (in Czech) is an hour before closing and English text is available.

The chateau makes an easy excursion from Hradec Králové, or you could make a long day trip full of chateaux and castles, including those at **Kostelec** and **Doudleby nad Orlicí** (respectively about 2km and 7km beyond Častolovice on Hwy 11), and at **Rychnov nad Kněžnou** (a few kilometres on to Vamberk and 5km north on Hwy 14). In fact there are some 30 castles and chateaux, from Romanesque to Renaissance, in a 50 sq km area around Hradec Králové.

Getting There & Away

Buses run about hourly from Hradec Králové (37Kč, 35 minutes). All the castles (except Rychnov) are on the railway line from Hradec Králové.

At least two buses a day go to Častolovice from Prague Florenc (96Kč, 2½ hours). There are also a few direct trains (184Kč, 2¼ hours).

KUKS

Few of the region's sights are as ghoulish as **Kuks** (☎ 499 692 161; www.kuks.cz - Czech only; tours adult/concession 50/25Kč, or in English 100/50Kč; 🕓 9am-noon & 1-5pm Tue-Sun May-Aug, until 4pm Sep, until 3pm Sat & Sun Apr & Oct), the spooky carcass of a fine baroque building on the banks of the Labe river. While the present structure would surely hold its own as a devilish lair in a Hammer House of Horror flick, Kuks was originally constructed in the early 18th century as an immodest monument to art patron Franz Anton von Sporck's bulging bank balance. Having discovered a mineral spring on his land, 30km north of Hradec Králové, Sporck set out to make an impression on his neighbours, erecting a deluxe spa complex, complete with baths, infirmary, chapel, racecourse, theatre, gardens, guesthouses and a chateau. The concerts, salons, hunts and lavish parties at this upper-class 'resort' briefly made it a rival to the West Bohemian spa-towns.

The party ended in 1740, two years after Sporck's death, when a massive flood washed away many of the buildings and destroyed the spring. All that remains today are the **chapel** and **infirmary**, a big staircase leading nowhere, and a fine collection of **statues** by Matthias Bernard Braun (1684–1738), one of Bohemia's masters of baroque sculpture. All of these remains are included on the 45-minute guided tour, and with broader renovations underway more attractions may open shortly.

Non-Czech visitors are rare at Kuks. Consider stopping if you're in the area, otherwise give it a miss.

Braunův Betlém

About 3km west of Kuks is **'Braun's Bethlehem'**, an alfresco 'gallery' with several extraordinary religious sculptures – hermits, saints and biblical scenes, some with little grottoes behind them – all but one by Braun, hewn directly from the rock outcrops scattered through the woods. This is all that remains of another Sporck project, which once had fountains and chapels as well.

Getting There & Away

Buses come from Hradec Králové (32Kč, 30 minutes) about hourly, stopping at Kuks village, across the Labe from the infirmary. South of the infirmary is a whistle stop on the railway line.

To get to Braunův Betlém, walk west on a red-marked path from Kuks village or on a yellow path from the infirmary. By car, drive 3km west from Kuks village to Žíreč, turn left, cross the railway and climb for 2km to a car park on the far side of the woods; it's an 800m walk from there.

ČESKÝ RÁJ

Český ráj (Czech Paradise) is a maze of low hills, sandstone 'rock towns' and volcanic basalt fingers, all set against a backdrop of gently rolling woods and farmland. Threaded with walking trails, Český ráj rises gradually northward into the foothills of the Krkonoše mountains, dotted at the highest points with ruined castles. Spend a few days hiking here and it's easy to see why the landscape inspired poets, sculptors and painters of the Czech National Revival, and why it's so popular with Czech holiday-makers.

A small part (92 sq km) was designated the Bohemian Paradise Protected Landscape Region in 1955, though 'Český ráj' is used loosely for a much wider area.

There are two so-called 'gateways' to Český ráj – Turnov and Jičín. Of the two, Jičín is by far the more interesting and appealing. A road and a railway line link the two towns, and there's plenty to see and do within walking distance of the train stations.

Information

Tourist offices in Jičín and Turnov stock maps, and can book accommodation.

SHOCart has a large-scale map of *Jizerské Hory a Český ráj* (1:100,000, sheet No 203) as well as the more detailed *Český ráj Mladoboleslavsko* (1:50,000, sheet No 21). The best map for cyclists is SHOCart Active's *Český ráj – Veľká Cykloturistická* (1:50,000, sheet No 112). The best map for the Prachovské skalý formations is Geodézie ČS' *Plán města Jičín – Prachovské skalý* (1:7000), which looks like a cheap leaflet (but isn't). There's also a 1:10,000 map of *Prachovské skály* (Prachov Rocks) by Kartografie Praha.

Walks

A good, short option is to take a bus from Jičín to the Prachovské skalý formations, where there are enough walking trails to occupy a morning or afternoon.

Option two is to take a train from Jičín or Turnov to Hrubá skála and see Trosky Castle, the Hruboskálské skalní město rock formations and Valdštejn Castle (13km total) before returning on a train via Turnov Město.

The most direct (red) trail from Jičín to Turnov is about 32km, possible in one long day for fit hikers. If you've got the gear, it's worth taking a leisurely two or three days, camping en route.

Bikes can be hired for around 250/1000Kč per day/week.

EAST BOHEMIA

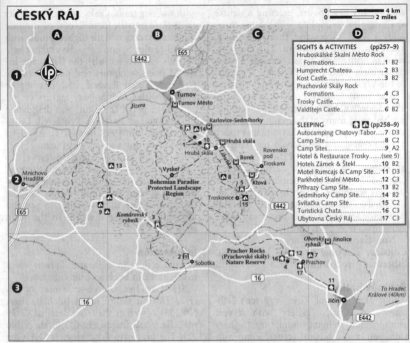

ČESKÝ RÁJ

SIGHTS & ACTIVITIES	(pp257–9)
Hruboskálské Skalní Město Rock	
Formations	1 B2
Humprecht Chateau	2 B3
Kost Castle	3 B2
Prachovské Skály Rock	
Formations	4 C3
Trosky Castle	5 C2
Valdštejn Castle	6 B2

SLEEPING	(pp258–9)
Autocamping Chatovy Tabor	7 D3
Camp Site	8 C2
Camp Sites	9 A2
Hotel a Restaurace Trosky	(see 5)
Hotels Zámek & Štekl	10 B2
Motel Rumcajs & Camp Site	11 D3
Parkhotel Skalní Město	12 C3
Přihrazy Camp Site	13 B2
Sedmihorky Camp Site	14 B2
Svitačka Camp Site	15 C2
Turistická Chata	16 C3
Ubytovna Český Ráj	17 C3

Getting There & Away

During the day, trains run from Hradec Králové to Jičín (76Kč, one hour) and Turnov (110Kč, two hours) every hour or two. Buses also make the run from Hradec Králové to Jičín (50Kč, one hour) and Turnov (70Kč, 1¾ hours).

A local train chugs between Turnov and Jičín (40Kč, 45 minutes) about every two hours, and local buses service all the villages that aren't near the railway line.

From Turnov, there is also a tourist bus which runs six routes through Český Raj. Routings are available from tourist information offices or are published in the annual *Český ráj* newspaper (10Kč), which is available at tourist information offices.

PRACHOVSKÉ SKÁLY

This is the biggest *skalní město* (rock town) – a labyrinth of sandstone pinnacles, caves and passages – in Český ráj. The rocks are accessible (admission 25Kč) via colour-coded hiking trails from two points on the minor road beyond Motel Rumcajs: Ubytovna Český ráj (red trail) and the Turistická chata (green,

yellow and red trails). All three trails meet up. A full loop on the green trail takes up to two hours and covers the main sights.

Sleeping & Eating

Accommodation here is overrun in summer, when you're better off booking ahead from Jičín.

Autocamping Chatovy Tabor (☎ 493 591 929; tent per person 50Kč) This camp site is just southwest of Jinolice.

Ubytovna Český ráj (☎ 493 524 626; per person 120Kč; P) This is super simple and super cheap but fine for hostel veterans.

Turistická chata (☎ 493 524 641; per person 200Kč; P) More substantial, this has a little Hansel and Gretel charm and a popular restaurant. It opens from mid-April to September.

Parkhotel Skalní město (☎ 493 525 011; parkhotel@iol.cz; s/d incl breakfast 800/1360Kč; P) The sharpest tool in the box, this upmarket place has tended lawns and comfy rooms.

Getting There & Away

From Turnov, there is a tourist bus which runs six routes through Český Raj. Routes are available from tourist information offices or are published in the annual *Český ráj* newspaper (10Kč), available at tourist information offices.

From Jičín, local buses also run right past these places about every two hours; stops are labelled 'Holín (Prachov Skalní město)' to the hotel or 'Holín (Turistická chata)'. Or you could walk it, a relatively easy 8km hike from Rumcajs Motel at Jičín.

HRUBÁ SKÁLA & AROUND

Another 'rock town', Hruboskálské skalní město is a dull uphill hike from the Hrubá skála train station; turn right across the tracks and follow the blue trail 3km to the Hotel Štekl car park. From here, take the red trail southeast to **Trosky Castle** (6.5km) or northwest to **Hruboskálské skalní město** (1.5km) and **Valdštejn Castle** (another 1.5km).

Valdštejn Castle (adult/concession 20/10Kč; 9am-4.30pm Tue-Sun May-Sep, until 4pm Sat & Sun Apr & Oct), dating from the 13th century, was used variously by Hussite rebels, bandits and Albrecht of Wallenstein (Valdštejn), and has now been renovated.

Sleeping

Sedmihorky camp site (481 391 162; tent per person 80Kč) About 1.5km from the Karlovice-Sedmihorky train stop, this pretty spot has a pond with a little beach. It is open from April to October.

Guarding the trail heads are two year-round hotels:

Hotel Zámek (481 389 681; hrskala@iol.cz; s/d incl breakfast 640/920Kč; P) In an atmospheric castle, this also has better 'luxury' rooms (s/d 1420/2190Kč).

Hotel Štekl (481 389 684; karel.zima@hotel-stekl.cz; s/d incl breakfast 600/900Kč) A reliable back-up.

Getting There & Away

From Turnov, there is a tourist bus which runs six routes through Český Raj. Routings are available from tourist information offices or are published in the annual *Český ráj* newspaper (10Kč), available at tourist information offices.

By train, the most convenient access to Hruboskálské skalní město is from the stations at Hrubá skála or Turnov Město (red trail; 5.5km). Express trains do not stop at either station, but at least 10 daily local trains serve Turnov–Jičín and Turnov–Hradec Králové (via Jičín).

KOST CASTLE

Kost Castle (admission 40Kč; 8am-noon & 1-5pm Tue-Sun May-Aug, from 9am Sep, until 4pm Sat & Sun Apr & Oct) lies 15km west of Jičín, on a minor road a few kilometres from the village of Sobotka. Dramatically situated atop a crag overlooking a tranquil pond, Kost is one of the best-preserved Gothic castles in Bohemia. It can be reached via a 6.5km hike on a red trail from Sobotka, or a 10km red or green trail from Hruba Skála.

TROSKY CASTLE

Like a pair of extinguished cigar butts, the crooked towers of **Trosky Castle** (www.trosky.cz - Czech only; adult/concession 35/25Kč; 8.30am-6pm Tue-Sun May-Aug, until 4pm May, Sep & Oct) teeter on twin basalt towers, setting the scene for one of the most dramatic ruins in the country. Built around 1380 by Honoratus of Vartenburg, the strategically placed castle has changed hands frequently over the centuries; in addition to its many lawful owners was a gang of 15th-century robbers who terrorised the countryside for several years.

The higher tower is called Panna (the Maiden), and the other is Bába (the Granny). Panna and some lower walls were restored in the early 1990s and the views, from 514m above sea level, are awesome whether you are looking up at the castle from the main road, or down across the plains from the towers themselves.

At the foot of the towers, and just as grey, is the sprawling **Hotel & Restaurace Trosky** (481 382 290; s/d 350/700Kč; P). Alternatively, follow the green trail 1km south to the very basic **Svitačka camp site**, priced at 50Kč per person.

Getting There & Away

The odd bus from Turnov stops below the hotel, from where it's 500m up to the castle. Better alternatives for walkers are local trains (not express) to Ktová plus a 2km hike up the green trail, or to Borek plus a 4km walk up a blue trail. It's also possible to walk from Hruboskálské skalní město.

JIČÍN

Little more than a fading photocopy of 101 prettier Bohemian towns, pleasant Jičín is nevertheless a useful jumping off point for the wider region. One of the town's biggest fans was Wallenstein (Valdštejn),

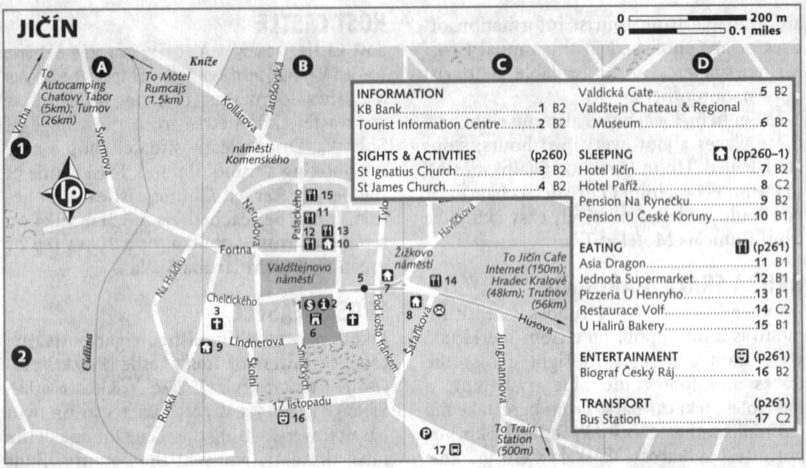
JIČÍN
0 200 m
0 0.1 miles
To Autocamping Chatovy Tabor (5km); Turnov (26km)
To Motel Rumcajs (1.5km)
Kníže
Vrcha
Švermova
Kollárova
Jarošovská
náměstí Komenského
Nerudova
Palackého
Tylova
Havlíčkova
Fortna
Valdštejnovo náměstí
Žižkovo náměstí
To Jičín Cafe Internet (150m); Hradec Kralové (48km); Trutnov (56km)
Husova
Na Hrádku
Chelčického
Lindnerova
Pod koštem
Pod koštofránkem
Šafaříkova
Jungmannova
Cidlina
Ruská
Školní
Smiřických
17 listopadu
To Train Station (500m)
INFORMATION
KB Bank....1 B2
Tourist Information Centre....2 B2
SIGHTS & ACTIVITIES (p260)
St Ignatius Church....3 B2
St James Church....4 B2
Valdická Gate....5 B2
Valdštejn Chateau & Regional Museum....6 B2
SLEEPING (pp260–1)
Hotel Jičín....7 B2
Hotel Paříž....8 C2
Pension Na Rynečku....9 B2
Pension U České Koruny....10 B1
EATING (p261)
Asia Dragon....11 B1
Jednota Supermarket....12 B1
Pizzeria U Henryho....13 B1
Restaurace Volf....14 C2
U Halírů Bakery....15 B1
ENTERTAINMENT (p261)
Biograf Český Ráj....16 B2
TRANSPORT (p261)
Bus Station....17 C2

a Habsburg general who decided he liked Jičín so much he had an old castle transformed into an ostentatious residence here between 1625 and 1633.

Orientation

Husova, the main drag, is a block north of the bus station, or 700m north of the train station. Head west along it towards Žižkovo náměstí and continue beneath the red-topped gate-tower into the main square, Valdštejnovo náměstí. Both of the squares and much of Husova have been pedestrianised.

Information

The useful **tourist information centre** (městské informačni centrum; ☎ 493 534 390; www.jicin.org; Valdštejnovo náměstí; 9am-5pm Mon-Sat, 9am-6pm Sun Jun-Sep, 9am-5pm Mon-Fri, 9am-1pm Sat Oct-May) sells hiking maps, books accommodation and has transport schedules. It also rents bikes for 250/1000Kč per day/week.

Jičín Café Internet (1st fl, Husova 1058) charges 1Kč per minute and is east of the main square, as is the **post office** (Šafarikova 142).

KB (Valdštejnovo náměstí), adjacent to tourist information, has an ATM and exchange counter.

Sights

You can enjoy a bird's-eye view of town from the Gothic **Valdická Gate** (adult/concession 15/10Kč; 9am-5pm Jun-Aug, 2-5pm Tue-Sun Apr, May & Sep) on Valdštejnovo náměstí. You enter the square past the unsteepled Jesuit **St James Church** (kostel sv Jakuba), which has a Renaissance façade and a baroque interior.

The square and its Renaissance façades are dominated by the chateau built by Valdštejn's Italian architects. A rather uninspiring **regional museum** (okresní muzeum; adult/concession 50/30Kč; 9am-5pm Tue-Sun) fills eight halls of the chateau, with archaeology, local history and art exhibits.

A block west of the square is the big, crumbling Gothic **St Ignatius Church** (kostel sv Ignác).

Sleeping

Motel Rumcajs (☎ 493 531 078; Koněvova 331; tent/hut per person 50/260Kč, motel room s/d 250/400Kč; P) About 1.5km northwest on the Sobotka road, this camp site also has a restaurant, huts and motel rooms.

Hotel Paříž (☎ 493 532 750; fax 493 534 510; Žižkovo náměstí 3; s/d with shared bathroom 300/450Kč, s/d with private bathroom 750/890Kč; P) Facilities are frugal here, but the Spartan rooms are reasonably comfortable. The rooms with private bathroom are better.

Hotel Jičín (☎ 493 544 250; fax 493 544 251; Havličkova 21; s/d incl breakfast 800/1200Kč; P) This glossy new place has blooming flower boxes, well-equipped rooms and walls emblazoned with military memorabilia. There's a good restaurant below.

Other recommendations:

Pension Na rynečku (☎ 493 534 857; rynecek@post.cz; náměstí Svobody 19; d incl breakfast 950Kč) Fresh décor on a crumbling square.

Pension U české koruny (☎ 493 531 241; Valdštejnovo náměstí 77; s/d incl breakfast 450/900Kč) Basic, but homy ambience.

Eating

U Dělové Koule (☎ 493 544 250; Havlíčkova 21; mains 90-200Kč) Hotel Jičín's atmospheric eatery has bags of charm and some scrumptious Bohemian specialities.

Pizzerie U Henryho (☎ 493 531 924; Čelakovského; pizza 60-90Kč) Kiddie-friendly and popular, this has filling pizza featuring a choice of 34 toppings.

Restaurace Volf (cnr Havlíčkova & Husova; mains 60-170Kč) Venison is the speciality here, but there are plenty of veggie dishes on offer and a selection of sickly sundaes to finish.

Other recommendations:

Asia Dragon (cnr Palackého & Židovská; mains 40Kč) For cheap, Asian eats.

U Halířu (cnr Palackého & Na Příkpech) Takeaway bakery treats.

Jednota (Valdštejnovo náměstí) For supermarket supplies.

Entertainment

Biograf Český ráj (☎ 493 532 823; 17 listopadu 47) English-language films make the rounds at this cinema.

Getting There & Away

To get to Jičín from Prague it's best to go by bus (77Kč, 1½ hours). To access the Adršpach-Teplice Rocks there is one bus daily from Jičín to Trutnov (one hour, 59Kč) and an extra four Monday to Friday.

TURNOV

Turnov has plenty of cheap lodgings and is a convenient, if dull, Český ráj gateway.

Orientation

The town square is náměstí Českého ráje. The train station is about 1km west, across the river on Nádražní. Regional buses (to/from Jičín, for example) stop at the big bus station by the river; Prague and other long-distance buses deposit you by the train station.

Information

The **information centre** (☎ 481 366 256; info@ turnov.cz; náměstí Českého ráje; ☉ 8am-6pm Mon-Fri, until 4pm Sat, until 2pm Sun Jul & Aug, until 5pm Mon-Fri, until noon Sat Sep-Jun) stocks hiking maps and books local and regional accommodation. It also has a couple of Internet terminals (1Kč per minute).

ČSOB (náměstí Českého ráje) has an exchange desk, and **KB** (Palackého 192) has an ATM. The **main post office** (Skálova) is just off the main square.

Sleeping & Eating

The information centre can help with private rooms and other cheap places.

Pension U sv Jana (☎ 481 323 325; Hluboká 142; s/d incl breakfast 600/900Kč) There's a café downstairs and a restaurant on the first floor, but finding someone to sell you one of the comfortable rooms can be a hike in itself.

Hotel Alfa (☎ 481 320 078; Palackého 211; d incl breakfast 600Kč) The crumbly lobby is a bit

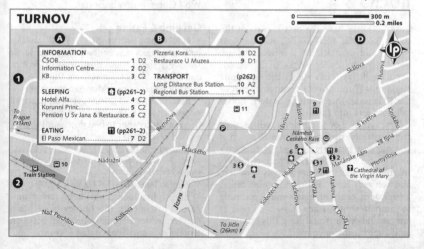

TURNOV

0   300 m
0   0.2 miles

INFORMATION	
ČSOB	1 D2
Information Centre	2 D2
KB	3 C2

SLEEPING	(pp261–2)
Hotel Alfa	4 C2
Korunní Princ	5 C2
Pension U Sv Jana & Restaurace	6 C2

EATING	(pp261–2)
El Paso Mexican	7 D2

Pizzeria Kora	8 D2
Restaurace U Muzea	9 D1

TRANSPORT	(p262)
Long Distance Bus Station	10 A2
Regional Bus Station	11 C1

To Prague (91km)

Náměstí Českého Ráje

Cathedral of the Virgin Mary

Train Station

To Jičín (26km)

off-putting, but the rooms are passable at this reliable back-up option.

Korunní Princ (☎ 481 324 212; hotel.korunni.princ@centrum.cz; náměstí Českého ráje 137; s/d incl breakfast 920/1240Kč; **P**) This happily tops the pops in town's accommodation stakes, offering an excellent Italian restaurant, polished rooms and a warm atmosphere.

El Paso Mexican (☎ 604 284 147; Markova; mains 70-150Kč) An airy terrace and typical Tex-Mex interior set the scene for some good, spicy specialties.

Pizzeria Kora (cnr náměstí Českého Ráje & 5 května; pizza 50Kč) More amateur dramatics than old school operatics, this no-frills Italian offers cheap wine and cheaper pizza.

Restaurace U Muzea (Skálova; 50-100Kč) It's tasty, but you may need an extra belt-hole to accommodate the hearty, dumpling-friendly fare whipped up here.

Getting There & Away

There are direct trains to/from Prague (130Kč, 2½ hours), and around 10 buses (85Kč, two hours) a day.

From Turnov, there is also a tourist bus which runs six routes through Český Raj. Routings are available from tourist information offices or are published in the annual *Český ráj* newspaper (10Kč), available at tourist information offices.

ADRŠPACH-TEPLICE ROCKS

Český ráj may have the best known of the Czech Republic 'rock towns', but the most rugged and dramatic rock formations are the Adršpach-Teplice Rocks (Adršpašsko-Teplické skály). They lie in the Broumov Highlands (Broumovská vrchovina) east of the Krkonoše, in a knob of Eastern Bohemia that juts into Poland.

You can hike or stroll along well-marked paths, scramble up for a view over 20 sq km of luscious deep pine forest, or get together with local guides for some serious rock-climbing. In summer the trails are heavily trodden, and you may have to book accommodation a week or more ahead, unless you're planning to camp; in winter, when snow can linger as late as mid-April, you'll have this stunning landscape mostly to yourself.

There are actually two clusters of formations: Adršpach Rock Town (Adršpašské skalní město) and Teplice Rock Town (Teplické skalní město). They now comprise a single state nature reserve, some 15km east of Trutnov.

At each 'rock town' you pay 50/20Kč (adult/concession) admission; try to pick up an *Adršpašsko-Teplické skály a Ostaš* (1: 25,000) trail map.

TEPLICE ROCK TOWN

About 200m west of the Teplice nad Metují-Skály train station is a car park and the Hotel Orlík. From here a blue-marked trail climbs the valley of the **Skalní potok** (Rocky Stream), making a 7km loop through some of the more impressive formations.

About 1km along, those not subject to vertigo or shortness of breath can detour by stairs and ladders to the **Střmen look-out**. This and neighbouring formations were the site of a 13th-century wooden castle, destroyed in 1447 when the Hussites hiding in it were defeated.

Two scenic trails continue along the valley floor to **Teplice Rock Town**. Here you can follow walkways through narrow rock clefts, to the cool, ferny **Sibiř** (Siberia) **gorge**.

From the blue loop-trail's west end, follow the green then another blue trail 4km to a yellow trail, which meanders 3km north up **Vlčí rokle** (Wolf Gorge) to connect with Adršpach. A yellow trail that starts just before Střmen and continues 4km north up Wolf Gorge is much shorter.

Sleeping & Eating

Autokemping Bučnice (☎ 491 581 387; www.autokemp.wz.cz - Czech only; tent/bungalow per person 40/120Kč; **P**) About 300m northwest of Teplice nad Metují-Skály train station, this also has bungalows. It's open May to September.

Hotel Orlík (☎ 491 581 025; orlik@hotel-cz.com; s/d incl breakfast €13/26; **P**) It's often packed, but this is a handy spot to bed down and there's a good restaurant.

Penzión pod Ozvěnou (☎ 604 965 110; s/d 200/400Kč; **P**) Nearby, this has basic rooms with shared bathroom.

Pension Tara (☎ 491 581 122; s/d 500/1000Kč; **P**) With Alpine looks, well-kept lawns and garden ornaments, this homey place has a quieter, wilder setting on the road between Hotel Orlík and Teplice nad Metují.

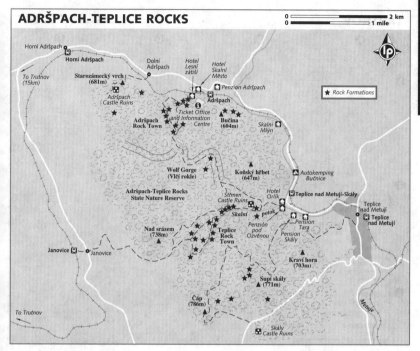

ADRŠPACH-TEPLICE ROCKS

0 — 2 km
0 — 1 mile

Horní Adršpach

Horní Adršpach

To Trutnov
(15km)

Starozámecký vrch
(681m)

Dolní
Adršpach

Hotel
Lesní
zátíší

Hotel
Skalní
Město

Penzion Adršpach

Adršpach
Castle Ruins

Adršpach

★ Rock Formations

Ticket Office
and Information
Centre

Adršpach
Rock Town

Bučina
(604m)

Skalní
Mlýn

Wolf Gorge
(Vlčí rokle)

Koňský hřbet
(647m)

Autokemping
Bučnice

Adršpach-Teplice Rocks
State Nature Reserve

Střmen
Castle Ruins

Hotel
Orlík

Teplice nad Metují-Skály

Teplice
nad Metují

Skalní   potok

Teplice
nad Metují

Nad srázem
(738m)

Teplice
Rock
Town

Penzión
pod
Ozvěnou

Pension
Tara

Pension
Skály

Janovice   Janovice

Kraví hora
(703m)

To Trutnov

Čáp
(786m)

Supí skály
(771m)

Skály
Castle Ruins

Metuje

Skalní Mlýn (☎ 491 586 961; adrspach@skalni-mlyn .cz; s/d incl breakfast 550/1000Kč; P) If you have your own transport, or a lively pair of legs, this place is about halfway between Teplice nad Metují-Skály and Adršpach and has oodles of traditional charm, a delightful riverside setting, a restaurant and snug rooms.

ADRŠPACH ROCK TOWN

These rock formations are easiest to reach from Adršpach train station. The green trail makes a 2.5km loop past the Czech Republic's tallest sandstone towers. You can make a good cross-country hike south on the yellow trail (via Wolf Gorge) to the Teplice nad Metují-Skály train station.

There is a small **information office** (☎ 491 586 012; www.skalyadrspach.cz; ⏲ 8am-12.30pm & 1-5.30pm) by the train station.

Sleeping & Eating

Both these places offer good discounts for stays of more than one night.

Hotel Lesní zátíší (☎ 491 586 018; grofit@ mbox.vol.cz; s/d incl breakfast 600/1200Kč; P) The rock trail begins so close to the front door

of this place you can almost fall out of bed onto it. That is if you can bring yourself to leave the comfy rooms. The restaurant throbs at lunchtime.

Penzion Adršpach (☎ 491 586 102; fax 491 586 106; s/d incl breakfast 600/1200Kč; P) Sparkling new, rather than overtly atmospheric, the rooms here are modern and there's a garden and restaurant. It's 300m from Adršpach station on the road to Teplice.

Getting There & Away

Regular trains make their way from Trutnov to Teplice nad Metují (46kč, 1¼ hours) via Adršpach (34Kč, one hour).

TRUTNOV

Trutnov is little more than an opportunity to regroup before changing trains for Teplice.

Orientation

The main square, Krakonošovo náměstí, is 500m southeast of the bus station along Horská, and a bit further along from the train station across the Úpa river.

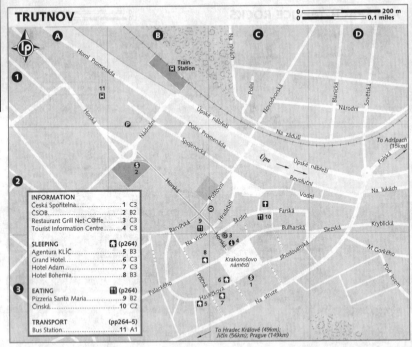

TRUTNOV

INFORMATION
Česká Spořitelna..................................1 C3
ČSOB...2 B2
Restaurant Grill Net-C@ffe.................3 C3
Tourist Information Centre.................4 C3

SLEEPING   (p264)
Agentura KLÍČ.....................................5 B3
Grand Hotel..6 C3
Hotel Adam..7 C3
Hotel Bohemia....................................8 B3

EATING   (p264)
Pizzeria Santa Maria...........................9 B2
Čínská...10 C2

TRANSPORT   (pp264–5)
Bus Station..11 A1

To Adršpach (15km)

To Hradec Králové (49km);
Jičín (56km); Prague (149km)

Information

Trutnov's **tourist information centre** (☎ 499 818 245; Krakonošovo náměstí 72; ☼ 9am-6pm Mon-Fri, 9am-noon Sat) has hiking maps and a list of private rooms.

ČSOB (cnr Horská & Nádražní) and **Česká Spořirelna** (Krakonošovo náměstí 20/16) both have exchange counters and ATMs.

Restaurant Grill Net-C@ffe (☎ 499 810 470; Krakonošovo náměstí 72) has Internet access for 1kč per minute.

Sleeping & Eating

The best cheap option is a private room – inquire at the information centre or **Agentura KLÍČ** (☎ 499 818 308; Halíčkova 15; ☼ 9am-5pm Mon-Thu, 9am-3pm Fri). Otherwise, hotels are quite expensive.

Hotel Bohemia (☎ 499 329 242; ales.antos@tiscali.cz; Palackého 81; s/d 720/920Kč) This three-star offering is one of the better bets, with pleasant, spacious rooms.

Grand Hotel (☎ 499 819 144; Krakonošovo náměstí 120; s/d incl breakfast 490/900Kč) Grand on the outside, not so on the inside, this still has okay rooms at fair prices.

Hotel Adam (☎ 499 811 955; fax 499 811 957; Havlíčkova 10; s/d 1010/1450Kč; (P)) A welcome sauna earns this smart place a few extra gold stars. Discounts of up to 30% are available at the weekend.

Pizzeria Santa Maria (Na vrchu; pizza 70Kč) Checked tablecloths and plastic vines bring this lively place a flick of Italian charm. There's also a sun terrace – but not a single giant pepper-grinder in sight.

Restaurant Grill (☎ 499 810 470; Krakonošovo náměstí 72; mains 50-150Kč) A streetside terrace provides plenty of airy seating for big grills, big coffees and big ice creams.

Čínská (☎ 499 814 234; Školní 156; mains 60-160Kč) This mid-range Chinese place has all the old favourites.

Getting There & Away

Buses run to Trutnov throughout the day from Prague (131Kč, 2½ hours), Hradec Králové (55Kč, 1¼ hours) and the main Krkonoše centres.

There are trains to the rocks every two hours or so, stopping at Teplice nad Metují (46Kč, 1¼ hours) and Adršpach (34Kč, one hour). Note that most express trains do not stop at Teplice nad Metují-Skály; change to a local train at Teplice nad Metují or walk.

KRKONOŠE

In a country of undulating hills and pancake plains, the Krkonoše ('Riesengebirge' in German) range is the true roof of the Czech Republic. Capped by Sněžka (1602m), the nation's highest summit, these rolling giants are covered in thick spruce forest and cut through with shallow valleys, grandly staking out both the Polish border and one of the country's few true wildernesses.

Not that they are out of reach. In fact, quite the opposite is true. Renowned (at least locally) for good skiing and walking opportunities, the mountains are now peppered with resorts and interlaced with roads; even the hallowed summit of Sněžka is accessible by chairlift. But the 363 sq km Krkonoše National Park (Krkonošský národní park) isn't just for those who want to experience things the easy way. Once the snow melts, the region's villages, often cloaked in a fine mist of drizzle, have a habit of looking rather washed out, but the dense woods and tall summits away from the developments still offer up plenty of year-round magic for those with a pack and a stiff pair of boots.

Orientation
Most 'villages' in the park are functional resorts with innumerable places to sleep and eat. The main centres are Harrachov for skiing and Špindlerův Mlýn and Pec pod Sněžkou for walking.

Vrchlabí is sometimes referred to as the park's 'gateway', but in fact the bigger resort centres inside the park have better information, and it's easy to reach many of them directly from Prague and Hradec Králové.

Information
National park information centres in the main towns have brochures, maps and accommodation advice. For up-to-date trail and weather information, go to the nearest Mountain Rescue Service (Horská služba) in Špindlerův Mlýn or Pec pod Sněžkou.

Kartografie Praha has a *Krkonoše* (1: 50,000) map with details of the main cen-

tres and colour-coded hiking trails. There is also a two-part, 1:25,000 map.

Activities
There are walking trails galore, including the red-marked Cesta česko-polského přátelství (Czech-Polish Friendship Trail) along the border ridge. Couch potatoes, and travellers with children, can get up into the high country year-round via chairlifts at Pec pod Sněžkou (to the summit of Sněžka) and Špindlerův Mlýn, and via a cable car at Janské Lázně.

Link roads, some with limited (or no) public motor access, are a treat for cycling enthusiasts. And of course there's skiing in winter. It's possible to rent ski equipment at Harrachov, Vrchlabí, Špindlerův Mlýn and Pec pod Sněžkou. A day's ski pass costs around 350Kč.

Sleeping
There are literally hundreds of hotels and chalets in the park. The hotels tend to be full year-round, but in the summer many chalets at lower elevations are used for *pension* or private accommodation. For two people, figure on about 800Kč and up, with breakfast, but prices can skyrocket in ski season – quoted prices are for the cheaper summer season.

The local word for a mountain hut, chalet or hotel is *bouda* (*b.* on maps), a term originally used for shepherds' huts. Other more-or-less equivalent Czech terms are *chata* and *chalupa*. There are some comfortable, and popular, *boudy* along the high-elevation trails. You should try to book these at least a few days ahead; inquire at a park information centre.

Getting There & Away
Buses are the most convenient way into the Krkonoše, with numerous daily direct services from Prague to Pec pod Sněžkou

---

WARNING

Despite the relatively modest elevations, it's usually windy and extremely cold year-round at the higher elevations. Even in summer, mountain fog creates a hypothermia risk (see p464 for details). Don't go up without the appropriate gear.

(142Kč, 3½ hours) and Špindlerův Mlýn (125Kč, three hours), and others via Hradec Králové, Vrchlabí and Trutnov. There are also direct buses between Pec pod Sněžkou and Brno (200Kč, five hours).

The nearest fast-train junctions are Vrchlabí and Trutnov, with connections to Harrachov, Rokytnice nad Jizerou and Svoboda nad Úpou.

Getting Around

There are regular hourly buses between Vrchlabí and Špindlerův Mlýn (20Kč, 25 minutes). Getting to Pec pod Sněžkou from Vrchlabí or Špindlerův Mlýn usually means a change at Trutnov or Svoboda.

VRCHLABÍ

Although billed as the gateway to the peaks, Vrchlabí actually feels a long way from the wilds. Despite an unsightly suburban sprawl, however, it's an okay place to get organised and you will probably have to make a transport connection here at some point.

Orientation & Information

The town straggles inconveniently along the Labe for several kilometres. From the adjacent bus and train stations it's 1.5km north (cross the river and take the second right on Slovanská, which becomes Krkonošská) to the town centre at náměstí Masaryka. Náměstí Míru, overlooked by a church tower, is a further 200m north.

The **town information centre** (☎ 499 451 111; Krkonošská 8; 🕑 9am-6pm Mon-Fri, 9am-noon Sat) is south of náměstí Masaryka; a **Česká Spořitelna** (Krkonošská) with an ATM and exchange desk is another 30m south. A **park information centre** (☎ 499 421 474; náměstí Míru; 🕑 9am-4pm Mon-Sat) has maps and brochures.

You can check your email at **Internet Café** (1st fl, Krkonošská 182; 🕑 10am-11pm Mon-Sat, 1-11pm Sun), right opposite the tourist office.

Sleeping & Eating

Sportovní hala (☎ 605 518 190; per person 200Kč; 🅿) This sports centre, just over the river from the bus station, is the best bet for cheap sleeps. Call ahead though.

Hotel Gendorf (☎ 499 429 629; hotelgendorf@ gendorf.cz; Krkonošská 153; s/d 850/1200Kč; 🅿 ⊗ 🔲) Vrchlabí's slickest offering has very good value rooms, polished service and spotless surrounds. There's also a good restaurant.

Klasika (☎ 499 421 260; náměstí Masaryka; s/d 450/900Kč) This atmospheric Italian restaurant has a wood-fired pizza oven, a good night-time buzz and can organise private rooms elsewhere.

Vejsplachy camp site, open June through September, is several kilometres southwest of the centre on Pražská třída, the road to Prague. There are 'Zimmer frei' signs across town.

Getting There & Away

Vrchlabí is connected by regular buses to Prague (113Kč, 2½ hours) and Hradec Králové (64Kč, 1½ hours). Buses run frequently all day to Špindlerův Mlýn (20Kč, 25 minutes) and (usually indirectly) to Pec pod Sněžkou (one hour).

ŠPINDLERŮV MLÝN

With the highest hotel density of just about anywhere in the country, Špindlerův Mlýn has more in common with a theme park than a functioning town. Views tend to be of high-rise hotels rather than mountain peaks, but there are countless accommodation options and come winter, this becomes the largest recreation centre in the region: forget about the vistas and get out on the slopes.

Orientation & Information

From the bus stop, the **Mountain Rescue Service** (Horská služba; ☎ 499 433 230; Svatopetrska) is 500m east, after a right turn at the **post office**.

There are dozens of information offices. **Infocentrum** (☎ 499 433 148; www.spindleruv-mlyn.cz; Predni Labska 47; 🕑 8am-7pm) is 200m north of the bus stop and can help with accommodation. A second, private **Information Centre** (☎ 499 433 407; www.spindl.com; Svatopetrska 297; 🕑 9am-6pm) is just before the mountain-rescue office and has Internet access. Both can advise on skiing, cycling and other activities.

Sights & Activities

A **chairlift** runs northwest to the top of Medvědín (1235m) for 60/100Kč one way/return, and another runs south up Pláň (1196m).

You can hike up to the **Labe headwaters** on a blue-marked trail heading north and northwest. At the top of a nasty 200m ascent at the end of the valley is the Labská bouda chalet; the **source of the Labe** (pramen

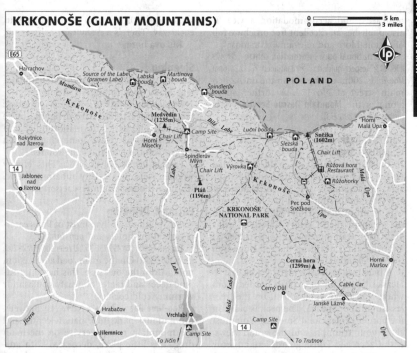

KRKONOŠE (GIANT MOUNTAINS)

Labe on maps) is about 800m further on, along the red trail. Return to Špindlerův Mlýn on the red trail south via Horní Mísečky, or on a green trail east via Martinova bouda, making a round-trip of five or six hours.

Sleeping & Eating

There are dozens of hotels and *pensions* in and around town – shop around or ask at the information centre.

Penzion ABM (☎ 499 433 255; fax 499 433 332; Svatopetrska; s/d incl breakfast 500/1000Kč) This typical *pension* has reliable rooms and helpful staff.

Savoy (☎ 499 433 221; hotel@savoy.cz; Predni Labska; s/d 450/600Kč; P) An architectural medley of mock-Tudor-meets-Alpine-chalet, this looming hotel is rather less glamorous than its London namesake but offers decent rooms at okay prices – they go up by 40% in winter. It is behind Infocentrum.

Autokemp (☎ 499 523 534; tent per person 60Kč; P) About 1.5km up the valley road from the bus stop, this camp site is open from May to September.

Eating out is pretty much confined to the hotels, but **Pavilon**, in the same building as Infocentrum, does a decent pizza.

Getting There & Away

There are at least a dozen buses a day to and from Vrchlabí (20Kč, 25 minutes) and Prague (125Kč, three hours).

Getting Around

A bus runs from the Špindlerův Mlýn bus stop up the Labe valley to Špindlerův bouda on the main Krkonoše ridge (1100m). See tourist information for the latest timetable.

PEC POD SNĚŽKOU

Known to its friends as plain old 'Pec', this has some of the best skiing in the Czech Republic and an enviable location beneath the country's highest peak. It's not the Alps, but then you're not paying Alpine prices.

Orientation & Information

Veselý Výlet (Jolly Jaunt; ☎ 499 736 130; www.vesely vylet.cz - Czech only; ⊙ 8.30am-6pm), near the bus stop, is a little gallery with excursion ideas, postcards, and accommodation advice. It also publishes an excellent free brochure full of regional lore and relevant excursions.

The **national park information centre** (☎ 499 896 213; tespec@quick.cz; ⏰ 8am-noon & 12.30-6pm Mon-Fri) is 200m up the hill on the un-named main street at No 172. A further 400m along is the **Mountain Rescue Service** (Horská služba; ☎ 499 896 233).

Sights & Activities
CLIMBING SNĚŽKA

In the 19th century you could get carried up Sněžka for six gold coins and 40 Kreutzers. Today, unless you take the chairlift, it is a three-hour climb or a five-hour round trip. From near the Hotel Horizont, climb the green-marked Čertový schody (Devil's Staircase) trail northwest to a chalet at Výrovka, then north up the red ridge trail to Luční bouda chalet.

A blue trail crosses a marshy area east to Slezská bouda on the Polish border, from where you make your assault on the treeless summit of Sněžka. The peak is bang on the border (Poles call it Śnieżka). You must share your triumph, and the grand views, with Czech and Polish guards and an army of tourists who have come up the easy way, by chairlift from both sides.

From Sněžka, take the yellow ridge trail south to chalets at Růžohorky, and then descend along a steep green trail back to Pec.

If you can't handle the climb, walk 300m back from the bus stop and about 1.5km up the valley of the Úpa to the chairlift (*lanovka*), and ride right to the top. The two-stage trip (100Kč return) takes half an hour each way. There's a restaurant halfway up, at Růžová hora.

Sleeping

The hillsides above Pec are thick with chalets, many open to tourists in summer

Pension Nikola (☎ 499 736 151; nikola-pec@volny.cz; s/d incl breakfast 450/900Kč) This delightful place overlooks the park information office and has lashings of cosy Alpine charm, with carved wood décor and snug rooms.

Pension Doulik (s/d 400/800Kč) This creaky wooden *pension* is rickety but atmospheric. It's near the mountain rescue service.

Eating & Drinking

As in Špindlerův Mlýn, most of Pec's eateries are in the hotels and *pensions*.

Enzian Grill (☎ 499 736 357; U Zeleneho Potoka 209; mains 100-150Kč) On the main road about 250m uphill from the bus stop, this has snug Alpine décor and plates of hearty goulash for warming cold cockles.

Rag-Time Bar (U Zeleneho Potoka 213) Between the national park information centre and the mountain rescue service on the main drag, this little place, decorated with animal pelts and ski-slope bric-a-brac, keeps the town ticking over with its lively happy hours (7pm to 8pm).

Getting There & Away

There are regular buses to Pec from Trutnov (25Kč, 30 minutes), Hradec Králové (70Kč, two hours) and Prague (142Kč, 3½ hours).

North Moravia

CONTENTS

With a map in one hand and a history book in the other, it is all too easy to wrongly presume that North Moravia is the Czech Republic's weed-ridden back yard – a province too far geographically from the parties and pleasantries of the capital and too close historically to the country's overheated weapons and mining industries. Make this mistake at your peril. While pockets of the region are permeated with a certain sootiness, North Moravia offers a wild, rugged portrait of the Czech Republic, with dynamic and largely unvisited cities and, in the Jeseníky range, some of the nation's least tamed mountains. After the seemingly endless round of chocolate-box Renaissance squares served up in other parts of the country, these harsher lines can be as refreshing as cold beer on a summer's afternoon.

While looming Ostrava – with its legendary nightlife – is North Moravia's administrative hub and largest city, the university town of Olomouc is surely its highlight, providing the truest sense of what Prague would be like without the crowds: in a word, fabulous. Miraculously missing a slot on the received tourist trail A-list, Olomouc's broody streets offer some of the finest cityscapes in central Europe, as well as a clutch of its least-visited sights.

But it's not all bricks and mortar. The wilds of the Jeseníky mountains remain relatively untraversed and the village of Štramberk and the *skansens* of Rožnov pod Radhoštěm offer some of the best insights into traditional wooden architecture in the country.

HIGHLIGHTS

- Indulge in the history – and university town nightlife – of **Olomouc** (p272), the country's most underrated city

- Admire the proletarian **astronomical clock** (p272) of Olomouc's magnificent town hall

- Take a step into the past among the traditional wooden buildings of **Štramberk** (p281) and Rožnov pod Radhoštěm's **Walachian Open-Air Museum** (p283)

- Paint the town red in the clubs and bars of Ostrava's raucous **Stodolní ulice** (p280)

- Hike up **Radhošť** (p283) and spend a night in the wilds

★ Ostrava

★ Olomouc   ★ Štramberk
                 ★ Radhošť
                 ★ Rožnov pod
                   Radhoštěm

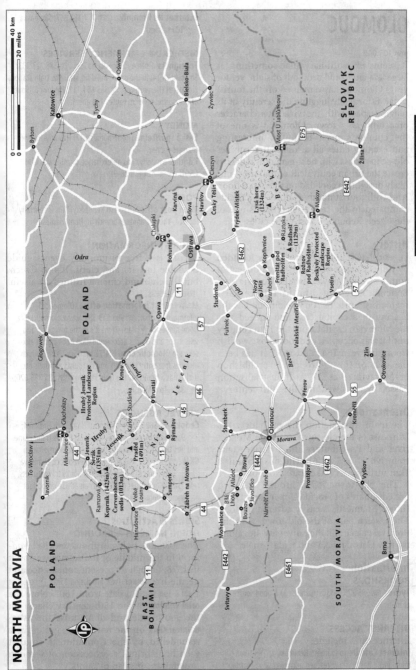

NORTH MORAVIA

OLOMOUC

pop 105,000

It seems extraordinary that something as large as a city could drop out of sight, yet for years Olomouc has remained off the tourist radar. Effortlessly juggling the serenity of its religious past with the vivacious character of a university town, Olomouc is one of the country's most beautiful, interesting and exciting cities all at once. It combines old-school class with next-generation flair to create the urban equivalent of that most unlikely of sights: a cool dad on the dance floor. And with tourist numbers down to a trickle compared to the capital, it remains one of the Czech Republic's best-value cities.

History

Legend has it that Olomouc was founded by Julius Caesar, becoming a major seat of administrative power when Moravia and Bohemia were united in the 11th century, then a bishopric in 1063. Olomouc has the bearing of a capital city, and indeed was the Moravian capital from the 12th century until it was occupied and looted by Swedish troops between 1642 and 1650. It has been the seat of the metropolitan archbishop of Moravia since 1777. Industrialisation passed by until well into the 20th century.

Orientation

The main train station (hlavní nádraží) is 2km east of the old town, over the Morava river and its tributary the Bystřice (take tram No 1, 2, 5 or 6). The bus station is 1km further east (take tram No 5 or 6).

The old town itself, around the two linked squares of Horní (Upper) and Dolní (Lower) náměstí, is easily covered on foot. The eastern part of the old town, with the Přemysl Palace and the university, lies along narrow Ostružinická and třída 1.máje.

Information
BOOKSHOPS

Tycho (☎ 585 225 095; Ostružnická 3) A good source of maps.

INTERNET ACCESS

Internet cafés include:
Internet Café Depo (náměstí Republiky 1; ⏱ 10am-midnight) It has furniture rescued from old railway carriages.

Internet Na Dominika (☎ 777 181 857; Slovenska 12; ⏱ 10am-9pm)

MEDICAL & EMERGENCY SERVICES

Foreigners' Police (Cizinecká policie; ☎ 585 223 333; Smetanova 14) In the police building, near the train station.
Hospital (Nemocnice; ☎ 585 851 111; Pavlova 6) South of the centre, on tram routes 1, 4 and 6.

MONEY

Česká spořitelna (Horní náměstí 17) Has an ATM and changes money.
KB (třída Svobody) Has an exchange counter and ATM.
ČSOB (Dolní náměstí 28-9)

POST

Main post office (náměstí Republiky) This is centrally located. There is another branch on Horní náměstí.

TOURIST INFORMATION

Beristo is a free bi-monthly events guide available in bars and clubs. It's in Czech, but the club and cinema listings are useful nonetheless.
Main tourist information office (Olomoucká informační služba; ☎ 585 513 385; www.olomoucko.cz; Horní náměstí; ⏱ 9am-7pm) It's in the town hall and sells maps and makes accommodation bookings. It also sells the **Olomouc Card** (24/72 hrs 150/220Kč), which includes free entry to sights and discounts at hotels etc. It also has a branch at the train station (☎ 585 785 620; ⏱ 8am-4pm Mon-Fri).

TRAVEL AGENCIES

Čedok (☎ 582 345 974; náměstí Národních Hrdinů 4; ⏱ 9am-6pm Mon-Fri, 9am-noon Sat) Books train, plane and bus tickets and can also help with accommodation.
CKM (☎ 585 222 148; info@ckmolomouc.cz; Denisova 4; ⏱ 9am-noon & 1-5pm Mon-Fri) Books travel tickets, sells ISIC, HI and other cards, and can advise on budget accommodation.

Sights & Activities
HORNÍ NÁMĚSTÍ & AROUND

The splendid, polymorphous **town hall** (*radnice*) in the middle of the square was built in 1378, though its present appearance and needle-like **tower** (věž; admission 15Kč; ⏱ tours at 11am & 3pm Mar-Oct) date from 1607. Note the **oriel window** of the 15th-century chapel on the south side and don't miss the **astronomical clock** on the north side, grotesquely remodelled by the Communists so that each hour brings a procession of wooden proletarians instead of saints.

OLOMOUC

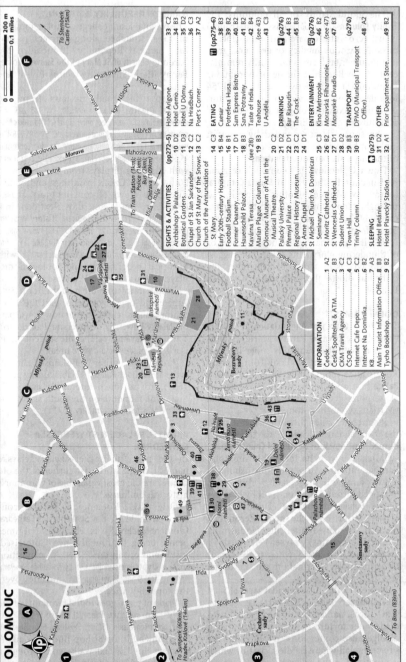

The grand daddy of all columns, the **Trinity Column** (Sousoší Nejsvětější trojice) is just across the square and impossible to miss. A baroque medley of gold and grey, its monumental form is uncannily reminiscent of the Buddhist shrine of Borobudur in Indonesia. Built between 1716 and 1754 to a design by V Render, a local sculptor, it is supposedly the biggest single baroque sculpture in central Europe.

The square is surrounded by a buffet lunch of historic façades and contains two of the city's six baroque **fountains**.

Down Opletalova is Olomouc's original parish church, the vast **St Moritz Cathedral** (chrám sv Mořice). Gothic through and through, it took almost 130 years to complete (from 1412 until 1540). The western tower dates from its 13th-century predecessor. Inside it's an amazing island of peace, or of thundering glory if its organ, the biggest in Moravia, is in action. In September, the cathedral hosts the International Organ Festival.

DOLNÍ NÁMĚSTÍ

The 1661 **Church of Annunciation of St Mary** (kostel Zvěstování Panny Marie) stands out here with its beautifully sober interior. Its antithesis is the opulent 16th-century Renaissance confection, the **Hauenschild Palace** (not open to the public). The square also sports its own **Marian plague column** (Mariánský morový sloup).

Picturesque lanes thread northeast from the two squares, leading to the green-domed landmark of **St Michael Church** (kostel sv Michala), with its incredibly muscular baroque interior. Among the furnishings is a rare painting of a pregnant Virgin Mary. Wrapped around the entire block is an active **Dominican seminary** (Dominikánský klášter). Surprisingly, the square, Žerotínovo náměstí, is named after the landowning family (the Žerotíns) who set Velké Losiny's gruesome 17th-century witch trials in motion (for more information see the boxed text, p278).

Nearby is the tiny round **Chapel of Saint Jan Sarkander** (kaple sv Jana Sarkandra; ☼ 10am-noon & 1-5pm), named after a local priest who died under torture in 1620 for refusing to divulge false confessions. It's built on the site of the jail where he died, part of which is preserved in the cellar.

NÁMĚSTÍ REPUBLIKY & AROUND

The original Jesuit college complex, founded in 1573, stretched along Universitní and into náměstí Republiky. It included the baroque **Church of St Mary of the Snows** (kostel Panny Marie Sněžné), which is full of fine frescoes.

Across the road, upstairs from the **Musical Theatre** (Hudebné divadlo; ☎ 585 223 565; www.divadlohudby.cz - Czech only), is the **Olomouc Museum of Art** (Olomoucký muzeum umění; ☎ 585 228 470; www.olmuart.cz - Czech only; Denisova 47; adult/concession 15/5Kč; ☼ 10am-6pm Tue-Sun), an excellent gallery with changing displays from a collection of 20th-century Czech paintings and sculpture, plus shows of contemporary artists; entry is free on Wednesday. Next door in a former convent, is the **Regional History Museum** (Vlastivědné muzeum; ☎ 585 515 111; www.vmo.cz; náměstí Republiky 5; adult/concession 40/20Kč; ☼ 9am-6pm Tue-Sun Apr-Sep, 10am-5pm Wed-Sun Oct-Mar) with historical, geographical and zoological displays. It is also free on Wednesday.

Detour away from the mad traffic on třída 1.máje and up Křížovského, past the 17th-century **canons' residences** that now house part of **Palacký University** (Universita Palackého). The lively **kavárna** (café) at the student union is a good place for a coffee break.

Around the corner in Biskupské náměstí is the **Archbishop's Palace** (Arcibiskupský palác; 1685), not so much interesting as merely huge. The monolith on the south side of the square is a former **armoury** (1711).

PŘEMYSL PALACE & ST WENCESLAS CATHEDRAL

In the peaceful, pocket-sized Václavské náměstí, in the northeast corner of the old centre, are the most venerable of Olomouc's historical buildings.

Originally a Romanesque basilica, consecrated in 1131, the **St Wenceslas Cathedral** (dóm sv Václava) was rebuilt several times before being thoroughly 'neo-Gothicised' inside and out in the 1880s. An exposition in the **crypt** (krypta; admission by donation; ☼ 9am-4pm Tue-Thu & Sat, 11am-4pm Sun) includes over-the-top reliquaries.

Pride of place goes to the remnants of the early 12th-century **Přemysl Palace** (Přemyslovský palác; adult/concession 15/5Kč; ☼ 10am-6pm Tue-Sun), originally built for Bishop Jindřich Zdík. A detailed English text walks you through a cloister with 15th- and 16th-century frescoes on the original walls, up to the archaeological centrepiece, the bishops' rooms with their Romanesque walls and windows (only rediscovered in 1867) and artistry unequalled elsewhere in the Czech Republic, even in Prague Castle. Downstairs, surviving 16th-century frescoes in the **Chapel of St John the Baptist** (kaple sv Jana Křtitele; 1262) include angels with instruments of torture (a sign of ecclesiastical approval?).

To the left of the palace is the **St Anne Chapel** (kaple sv Anny), and beyond it are the long, yellow walls of the **former deanery** where Wenceslas III, the last of the Přemysl line, was mysteriously assassinated in 1306. This building is now part of Palacký university.

OTHER ATTRACTIONS

In the southwest of the town on Vídeňská are four wonderfully fanciful **early-20th-century houses**. Similar houses are dotted nearby on the edge of **Smetanovy sady**, one of the large parks that enclose the historical centre to the west and east (and which are also worth a stroll through). The **botanical gardens** (botanická zahrada; adult/concession 15/10Kč; ☆ 9.30am-5pm) are in the nearby **Bezručovy sady**.

Sleeping

The tourist information office and CKM can help you with advice on private and hotel rooms.

BUDGET

Poet's Corner (☎ 777 570 730; www.hostelolomouc.com; 3rd fl, Sokolská 1; dm/tw 250/800Kč) Come evening, everyone gathers round the kitchen table for a good banter at this super-friendly, Aussie-run place. Facilities are limited and space is scarce but there's a good buzz and a homey atmosphere.

Hostel Betánie (☎ 585 233 860; fax 585 221 127; Wurmova; s/d 300/450Kč; **P**) This church-run place has a top location, a cosy café and plenty of rooms with shared facilities. It does have a slightly monastic air, but the house rules are far from draconian.

Hostel Plavecký Stadion (☎ 585 427 208; Legionářská 11; d 450Kč; **P**) In a sports hall, with strong whiffs of chlorine wafting up from the pool, this just scrapes by as a budget back-up.

MID-RANGE

Na Hradbách (☎ 585 233 243; nahradbach@quick

.cz; Hrnčířská 3; d 600Kč) On a picture-postcard cobbled street, this tourist-info favourite scoops a whole clutch of gold stars, with comfy rooms and oodles of character.

Hotel u Dómu (☎ 585 220 502; hotel_u_domu@ email.cz; Dómská 4; s/d incl breakfast 1200/1600Kč; **P**) A small, boutique-style place in the shadow of the church spires, this has pleasant rooms and smiling staff.

TOP END

Hotel Arigone (☎ 585 232 350; arigone.olomouc@worldonline.cz; Univerzitní 20; s/d incl breakfast 1600/1950Kč) Swish but small, this newly refurbished hotel has parquet floors, wooden beams and a fair flick of traditional charm.

Hotel Gemo (☎ 585 222 115; gemo@hotel-gemo .cz; Pavelčákova 22; s/d incl breakfast 2390/3290Kč; **P** ✕ ⁂) Olomouc's business-style offering is built on the site of an old burgher's house but errs on the side of frumpy functionality. There are, however, big weekend discounts.

Eating & Drinking

U Anděla (☎ 585 228 755; Hrnčířská 10; mains 100-350Kč) A scattering of seriously interesting clutter, including (if you have a rummage) some Nazi-era tableware, decorates this fabulous traditional-style eatery. The menu should be photocopied and sent out as the blueprint for Moravian cooking everywhere.

Teahouse (☎ 585 233 858; Hrnčířská 12) Spicy odours, 120 types of tea, Chinese prints and water pipes conspire to make this the perfect place to spend long lazy afternoons on a slow-drip caffeine infusion.

Caesar (☎ 585 221 472; Horní náměstí; mains 80-200Kč) The main square's flagship eatery serves up touristy Italian fare on a sunny terrace or in the bowels of the town hall. It is nearly always full.

Potrefena Husa (☎ 585 203 171; Opletalova 1; mains 80-170Kč) The favoured haunt of Olomouc's upwardly-mobile, this chain sports bar boasts plenty of action and tasty grub.

The Crack (☎ 585 208 428; Mlýnská 4; mains from 55Kč) This Irish bar is as Celtic as curry, but there's a lively expat buzz and cheap, cheerful food.

Other recommendations:

Sam Express Bistro (Ztracená 1) For cheap, student-style buffet snacks.

Sana Potraviny (Horní náměstí 9) A supermarket for self-caterers.

Taste of India (☎ 585 208 419; Mlýnská 4; mains 100-200Kč) The fumes say it all at this Indian favourite.

Bar Rasputin (Mlýnská) Russian bar with vodka, Rasputin and all.

Entertainment

Moravské Divadlo (☎ 585 223 531; Horní náměstí 22) The town theatre puts on plenty of shows.

Moravská Filharmonie (☎ 585 206 520; www.mfo.cz; Horní náměstí 23) The local orchestra has a regular programme of concerts.

Kino Metropole (☎ 585 222 466; Sokolská 25) This is one of many cinemas in Olomouc.

Getting There & Away

There are regular buses (80Kč, two hours) and trains (130Kč, 1½ hours) from Ostrava. From Brno, there are about 15 buses (50Kč, 1¼ hours) and five direct fast trains (120Kč, 1½ hours) a day. The best connection from Prague (294Kč, 3¼ hours) is by fast train from Praha hlavní nádraží. You can contact **bus** (☎ 585 313 917) and **train** (☎ 585 785 490) information offices by phone.

From Slovakia, Bratislava has poor bus links but one direct fast train (6½ hours).

For all bus and train times and prices visit www.idos.cz.

Getting Around

Bus tickets cost 6/8Kč and last for 20/40 minutes. You can buy them from *tabák* and newsstands or from the yellow machines at some stops.

A 24-hour transport pass *(denní jízdenka)* for 50Kč is available from the **municipal transport office** (DPMO; cnr Legionářská & Palackého; ☯ 6am-6pm Mon-Fri, 7am-1pm Sat), and at the main bus station.

AROUND OLOMOUC
Šternberk Castle

Fifteen kilometres north of Olomouc, **Šternberk Castle** (Hrad Šternberk; adult/concession 30/10Kč; ☯ 9am-4pm Tue-Sun May-Sep, 9am-3pm Sat & Sun Apr & Oct, 10am-2pm Sat & Sun Nov-Dec), was founded in the late 13th century by the Šternberk family. It received a Renaissance face-lift in about 1480, and its Romantic look from Duke Jan II of Liechtenstein around 1886. It's now open to the public, with historical interiors from Gothic to baroque.

It's about 300m up the hill from the town's main square, Hlavní náměstí. In fact the real landmark here is the **Parish Church of the Annunciation of Our Lord** (farní kostel Zvěstování Páně) on the way up. In contrast to its bombastic baroque façade, the interior is spacious, sparsely furnished and topped with fine murals.

GETTING THERE & AWAY

You can get to/from Olomouc by bus (15Kč, 20 minutes) or train (22Kč, 20 minutes).

Bouzov Castle

For information on Bouzov Castle, see p71. It's best to make Bouzov an overnight trip from Olomouc. There are two buses daily Monday to Friday from Olomouc to Bouzov (44Kč, one hour, 10 minutes) and only one bus daily Monday to Friday in the opposite direction.

Javoříčko Caves

From Bouzov castle it's a 5km walk south on a blue-marked trail (or you can take the occasional local bus) to Javoříčko and the impressive local underground attraction, the **Javoříčko Caves** (Javoříčské jeskyně; admission 40Kč; ☯ 9am-3pm Tue-Sun Apr-Oct).

You can either stay the night (there are basic hotels in Šternberk and near the caves) or continue northeast on a scenic red-marked trail for 8km to Bílá Lhota. Another 4km on are the smaller **Mladeč Caves** (Mladečské jeskyně) at Mladeč, and a further 5km on is Litovel.

JESENÍKY MOUNTAINS

The twin ranges that make up the Jeseníky Mountains also mark the boundaries of one of the country's forgotten spaces. The rugged Hrubý Jeseník rise in the north-western corner of the region and it's here that you'll find Moravia's highest summit, Praděd (1491m) – on a clear day, with a pair of keen eyes and a spot of imagination, you can see both the Krkonoše of Eastern Bohemia and the Tatras of Central Slovakia from its peak. The surrounding Hrubý Jeseník Protected Landscape Region (Chráněná krajinná oblast Hrubý Jeseník) is still home to deer and wild boar. In comparison, the Nízký Jeseník to the southeast are just rolling foothills, topping out at a more modest 700m.

The Hrubý Jeseník have been developed for winter skiing and ski touring, but there are also plenty of walking opportunities. A town of particular historical interest is Velké Losiny, the site of blood-chilling witch trials in the 17th century.

HRUBÝ JESENÍK

This is a great area for walking and trails abound. From Červenohorské sedlo, a 1013m pass on the Šumperk–Jeseník road, which frequent buses pass by all day, it's about 10km southeast on a strenuous red-marked trail to Praděd and on to Petrovy kameny (Peter's Stones). Praděd has a 162m transmitter tower with a **restaurant** in it.

Alternatively, from Červenohorské sedlo take the red ridge-trail west to Šerák (1351m) via Červená hora and Keprník (1423m). There, a year-round cable car descends to Ramzová (or you can walk down on the red trail), with buses and local trains back to Šumperk. This is an easy overnight trip, with *boudy* (huts) at Červenohorské sedlo and on Šerák.

Orientation & Information

Šumperk, Velké Losiny and the village of Ramzová are all convenient bases. The **information centre** (informační centrum; ☎ 584 498 155; www.jesenik.org; Masarykovo náměstí 167; ☼ 9am-5pm Mon-Sat Jun-Aug, 9am-5pm Mon-Fri Sep-May) in Jeseník can help with transport, accommodation and activities information. The map to have is Kartografie Praha's *Jeseníky – turistická mapa* (No 19).

Sleeping

Šumperk, Velké Losiny and Ramzová have plenty of accommodation possibilities. High-country camping is restricted, but there are lots of mountain chalets.

Horský Hotel Červenohorské sedlo (☎ 583 295 101; www.hotel-cervenohorskesedlo.cz - Czech only; s/d incl breakfast 400/800Kč; Ⓟ) Beside the Šumperk–Jeseník road at the crest of the pass, this three-star place has all you need to warm up after a walk.

Sporthotel Kursovní (☎ 583 779 003; s/d incl breakfast 400/800Kč) Just east of the summit of Praděd, this has similar rooms to Horský Hotel Červenohorské sedlo in a wilder setting.

You can also find modestly priced private rooms and *pensions* in nearly every town and village.

Pension Slezský Dům (☎ 584 413 704; www.slezskydum.cz; Lipovská 630; s/d incl breakfast 490/980Kč; Ⓟ) This offers attractive, chalet-style accommodation in Jeseník itself.

Getting There & Away

There are two buses a day from Olomouc to Šumperk (50Kč, 1¼ hours) and half a dozen from Ostrava (110Kč, three hours). At least two run daily from Brno to Šumperk (100Kč, 2¾ hours), with one going on to Ramzová (45Kč, another hour).

From Olomouc there are six daily fast trains to Šumperk (76Kč, one hour) and many slower ones, most continuing to Ramzová. Five daily express trains run from Prague to Šumperk (260Kč, four hours), with local connections from there.

Getting Around

There are only five daily buses (fewer on the weekend) running between Šumperk and Jeseník, via Velké Losiny and Červenohorské sedlo. Direct train connections are not much better, with only four daily trains between Šumperk and Jeseník, via Ramzová, taking two hours. The indirect trains on this line are more frequent but require at least one change, usually at Hanušovice.

THE BOBLÍG INQUISITION

In the 17th and 18th centuries North Moravia was swept by a wave of religious hysteria that makes the Salem witch hunts, happening in the USA at the same time, look like a Sunday outing.

In 1678 the Žerotíns hired František Boblíg to undertake the role of inquisitor in eradicating what they saw as ungodly and superstitious practices.

The inquisitor fulfilled his commission with zeal. Over the course of 15 years, he accused scores of people, mostly women, of witchcraft; many met a grizzly end at the stake. When nobles in Šumperk grew critical of the amount of property that Boblíg and his `judges' were confiscating, he accused them of devilish sympathies as well.

Almost 15 years after they had started, the Žerotíns were persuaded by King Leopold I to take steps to end the persecutions, and the murderous Boblíg was forced to retire. He died of natural causes at an advanced age and was never held to account for the purges.

VELKÉ LOSINY

Velké Losiny, today a minor spa town, was from 1496 to 1802 the seat of the powerful Žerotín family. A factory (with a small museum) established here by the family still produces handmade paper.

Žerotín Chateau

This striking, U-shaped **chateau** (zámek; adult/concession 40/20Kč; ☿ 9am-noon & 1-5pm Tue-Sun May-Aug, 9am-noon & 1-4pm Sep, Sat & Sun only Apr & Oct) is one of Moravia's best preserved Renaissance properties. The group tour in Czech (there's an English text) takes in lots of empire furniture and a 16th-century tiled stove said to be one of the oldest in either republic, as well as portraits of the Žerotíns and paintings collected by them. It steers clear of the actual room – the grotesquely named Hall of Justice – where the infamous witch trials took place (see the boxed text above), and goes into little detail about them.

Getting There & Away

To get to Šumperk, see the preceding section on the Hrubý Jeseník. From there, Velké Losiny is a 20-minute train ride, with about eight departures a day. The chateau is about 1km southwest on a green-marked path from the train station.

OSTRAVA

pop 325,000

Giant, vibrant Ostrava is a working Czech city with little discernible tourist traffic and a face crisscrossed with the hardware of big-time industrialisation. However, while old Ostrava's past is intrinsically linked to the gargantuan Vitkovice steel works, which closed in 1998, the 21st-century city is now busy reinventing itself for this new millennium. As a developing hub for the high-tech and service industries, Ostrava has benefited from a starburst of regeneration projects in recent years, with most energy seemingly going into its booming bar and nightclub scene. While swathes of concrete remain the legacy of the city's industrial boom-time, this modern city is actually one of the greenest in the country, with a whole 30 square metres of parkland per head of population.

Orientation

Ostrava is BIG, but only the central part on the west bank of the river is of interest.

Most trains use the main station, Ostrava hlavní nádraží, from where it's 2.5km south on Nádražní to the centre (tram No 2, 8 or 12). The small Ostrava-střed train station and the main bus station are about 1km southwest of the centre; catch tram No 1, 2 or 14 going north (right) on Vítkovická in front of the bus station.

Information

BOOKSHOPS

Knihkupectví Librex (☎ 596 117 676; Smetanovo náměstí; ☿ 9am-7pm) Has five floors of books, a café and Internet access.

EMERGENCY

Foreigners' Police office (Úřadovna cizinecké policie; ☎ 596 141 111; Ostrčilova 4) Is 200m north of the new town hall.

FOREIGN CONSULATES

Polish consulate (☎ 596 118 074; Blahoslavova 4; ☿ 8.30am-noon Mon-Fri) Issues visas on the same day.

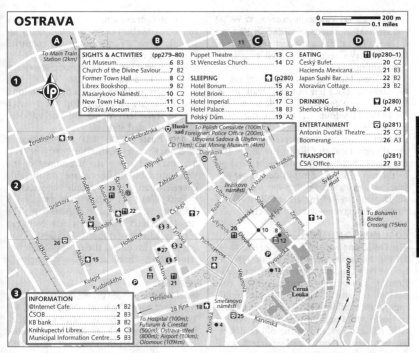

OSTRAVA

SIGHTS & ACTIVITIES (pp279–80)		
Art Museum	6	B3
Church of the Divine Saviour	7	B2
Former Town Hall	8	C2
Librex Bookshop	9	B2
Masarykovo Náměstí	10	C2
New Town Hall	11	C1
Ostrava Museum	12	C3
Puppet Theatre	13	C3
St Wenceslas Church	14	D2

SLEEPING	(p280)	
Hotel Bonum	15	A3
Hotel Brioni	16	C2
Hotel Imperial	17	C3
Hotel Palace	18	B3
Polský Dům	19	A2

EATING	(pp280–1)	
Český Bufet	20	C2
Hacienda Mexicana	21	B3
Japan Sushi Bar	22	B2
Moravian Cottage	23	B2

DRINKING	(p280)	
Sherlock Holmes Pub	24	A2

ENTERTAINMENT	(p281)	
Antonin Dvořák Theatre	25	C3
Boomerang	26	A3

TRANSPORT	(p281)	
ČSA Office	27	B3

INFORMATION		
@Internet Cafe	1	B2
ČSOB	2	B3
KB bank	3	B2
Knihkupectví Librex	4	C3
Municipal Information Centre	5	B3

NORTH MORAVIA

INTERNET ACCESS

Internet cafés include:
@Internet Café (☎ 596 113 456; Škroupova 10;
🕐 9am-10pm Sun-Thu, 9am-3am Fri & Sat)

MEDICAL SERVICES

Hospital (nemocnice; ☎ 596 191 111; Hornopolní) This
is 500m west of the centre.

MONEY

There are banks across town.
ČSOB (Nádražní 10) Has an ATM and exchange counter.

POST

Main post office (Dvořákova) Is three blocks northeast
of Nádražní. There's also a **24-hour post office** (Wat-
tova 1046).

TOURIST INFORMATION

Municipal Information Centre (Městské informační
centrum, or MIC; ☎ 596 123 913; mic@ostrava.cz;
Nádražní 7/686; 🕐 8am-6pm Mon-Fri, 9am-2pm Sat)
This helpful centre also books accommodation. There is a
second branch in the foyer of the **main railway station**
(☎ 596 136 218; 🕐 7am-8.30pm Mon-Fri, 7am-3pm
Sat, 1-8.30pm Sun).

Sights & Activities

In this metropolitan monument to modernity, the oldest public building is the **former
town hall** (Stará radnice) on Masarykovo
náměstí. Inside is the small **Ostrava Museum**
(Ostravské muzeum; ☎ 596 123 760; admission 15Kč;
🕐 9am-5pm Mon-Fri, 9am-1pm Sat & Sun), with exhibitions of regional natural history and
archaeology, including the 20,000-year-old
tiny statue of Petřkovická Venus. It is closed
on Sunday in July and August.

Nearby on Pivovarská is one of Ostrava's
newest public buildings, the **Puppet Theatre**
(divadlo loutek; ☎ 596 114 884; Pivovarská 5), which
sports five giant sculpted puppets around
the entrance – Punch, the King, the Queen,
the Angel and the Devil.

To the east on Kostelní náměstí is
the elegant **St Wenceslas Church** (kostel sv
Václav). The late-Gothic building has a
baroque face on Romanesque foundations.
Two blocks eastwards from Nádražní, on
Československých legií, is a heavy neo-
Renaissance basilica, the parish **Church of the
Divine Saviour** (chrám Božského Spasitele),
which dates from 1889.

Ostrava's **Art Museum** (dům umění; ☎ 596 112 566; Jurečkova 9; adult/concession 50/20Kč; ☺ 10am-1pm & 1.30-6pm Tue-Sat) has a modest collection of 20th-century Czech art, as well as temporary exhibitions.

The **new town hall** (nové radnice; ☎ 596 283 096; Sokolská), about ten minutes' walk north from the town centre, was built from 1929 to 1930. The four statues on the front symbolise the former preoccupations of Ostrava – mining, commerce, science and metallurgy. Find the lift in the lobby (up the stairs ahead and on the right) and go to the top of the 85.6m-tall **clock tower** (věž; adult/concession 20/10Kč; ☺ 10am-7pm Mon-Sun Apr-Oct, 10am-5pm Nov-Mar) for an excellent – and surprisingly green – view of the city.

COAL MINING MUSEUM

The **Coal Mining Museum** (Hornické muzeum; ☎ 596 131 847; adult/concession 60/30Kč; ☺ 9am-6pm Tue-Sun), at Pod Landekem on the north edge of town, is a preserved late 19th-century colliery on the site of Anselm pit. The buildings house exhibits on the history of mining in North Moravia, and you can even don a hard hat and descend to the old coal face. There's also an industrial archaeological trail in the surrounding grounds.

To get there, take tram No 12 from Nádražní to Sad Boženy Němcové, then change to bus No 56 or 34, getting out at Hornické muzeum.

Sleeping

The tourist information office books hotels and can help with private rooms. In general, accommodation prices are high and standards are low.

BUDGET

With a large population of itinerant workers, Ostrava's hostels tend to be rough and ready. Check with tourist information, but the following were the best bets at time of writing. Both are about 1.5km north of the centre, on streets that run off Sokolská.

Ubyovna Sadová (☎ 596 118 369; Sadová 12; dm per person 250Kč; P)

Ubytovna ČD (☎ 596 133 510; Muglinovská 1038; dm per person 180Kč; P)

MID-RANGE

Hotel Brioni (☎ 596 117 848; info@helaxclub.cz; Stodolní; s/d incl breakfast 750/1300Kč) Right in the heart of Ostrava's hip bar district, above one of its liveliest clubs, this temple to insomnia offers a range of cheery, colourful rooms and nocturnal action on tap.

Hotel Bonum (☎ 596 114 050; recepce@t-bonum.cz; Masná 6; s/d incl breakfast 1000/1500Kč) On a much quieter street (it's opposite a police station), just off the city's nightlife strip, this boasts a spread of modern rooms and a decent dose of sophisticated style.

Hotel Palace (☎ 596 158 111; recepce@hotelpalace .cz; 28 října 59; s/d incl breakfast 790/1350Kč) The 'Palace' may yet scoop the misnomer of the year award, but the rooms are considerably cheerier than the grim façade suggests.

Polský dům (☎ 596 122 001; polskydum@volny.cz; Poděbradova 53; s/d incl breakfast 800/1200Kč; P) The *fin de siècle* charm of this Art Nouveau place is fading faster than a decadent's liver, but it remains one of the most popular hotels in town – book ahead.

TOP END

Hotel Imperial (☎ 599 099 099; recepce@imperial.cz; Tyršova 6; s/d incl breakfast 1600/2600Kč; P ☒ ☒ ☒) The city centre's grandest offering is a flick frumpy, but offers a sauna, pool and more creature comforts than you can shake your remote control at.

Eating & Drinking

In Ostrava, a city known for its after-dark revels, eating often plays second fiddle to drinking and dancing. On **Stodolní**, hub of the city's bar and club scene (it even has a website: www.stodolniulice.cz – Czech only), you'll find more than 40 pubs, discos and late night eateries. Wander around and take your pick.

Sherlock Holmes Pub (☎ 605 249 344; cnr Stodolní & Pobialova; mains 80-150Kč) Offering a vaguely continental interpretation of the English pub theme, this snug place has broody wood décor, a lively crowd of locals and good food.

Hacienda Mexicana (☎ 595 133 715; cnr Nádražní & Umělecká; mains 80-150Kč) OK corral looks, sombreros and streams of tequila provide the window dressing for hearty Tex-Mex tucker.

Moravian Cottage (Moravská Chalupa; ☎ 596 124 937; Musorgského 9; mains 90-200Kč) A more sedate ambience and decent Moravian speciality cooking can be found at this popular restaurant.

Other recommendations:

Český Bufet (cnr Zámecká & Masarykovo náměstí; 7am-6.30pm Mon-Fri, 7am-1pm Sat) For cheap and cheerful buffet eats.

Japan Sushi Bar (☎ 777 695 900; Stodolní 6) For the novelty of sushi.

Entertainment

For clubs, head to Stodolní. Try **Boomerang** (☎ 608 707 717; Stodolní 22; from about 10pm-4am Wed-Sat).

The multiplex cinema **Cinestar** (☎ 595 699 999; Novinářská) is in the huge Futurum shopping centre, west of the centre.

The newly constructed **Antonín Dvořák Theatre** (☎ 595 151 111; Smetana náměstí 1) hosts opera, ballet and drama performances.

Getting There & Away

ČSA (☎ 596 122 166; www.csa.cz; Jurečkova 20) has daily flights between Prague and Ostrava for around 3900Kč return.

Trains (☎ 596 185 143) are the easiest way to get between Ostrava and the other big cities. Regular direct services run to Prague (424Kč, 4½ hours), Brno (204Kč, 2¾ hours) and Olomouc (130Kč, 1¼ hours). **Buses** (☎ 596 633 751) to these destinations take marginally longer but are also around half the price.

It's 15km from central Ostrava to the Polish border crossing at Bohumín, linking to Katowice. Buses (15Kč, 25 minutes) and trains (16Kč, ten minutes) make the run. At the main train station you can also catch one of dozens of fast trains passing each day from Prague and Brno to the border. There are also fast trains and buses from Ostrava to the border crossing at Český Těšín (60Kč, one hour), continuing to Kraków.

For all bus and train times and prices visit www.idos.cz.

Getting Around

Mošnov airport is 10km southwest of the centre. Bus No 33 (25 minutes) runs infrequently to the airport daily.

The same tickets are used for all Ostrava's buses, trolleybuses and trams. Buy them in the main train station, at MIC, newsagents and from the orange machines at some stops. They cost 7Kč for 15 minutes, 11Kč for 45 minutes and 32Kč for 24 hours.

WESTERN BESKYDY

Nomadic sheep-farmers, the Vlachs, moved into this region in the 15th century giving their name to Walachia (Valašsko in Czech), the area they came to occupy. By the 18th century, the Vlachs had largely been absorbed into the Habsburg Empire, but these rolling hills retain strong links with their rural traditions, including the carved timber architecture best seen in the *skansens* of Rožnov pod Radhoštěm.

The hills themselves, topping out on Lysá hora (1324m), are delightful for walking and are also popular for winter sports. The map to have is *Kartografie Praha's Beskydy No 42* (1:100,000) trail map.

ŠTRAMBERK

Wood smoke and pine smells are the clichéd trademarks of authentic Walachia. This beautiful village, with its rough-cut, low-gabled timber houses and rolling, forested setting, has both in abundance. In fact, set below the single tower of a ruined castle, the blueprint for Štramberk looks like it might have been pilfered from a fairy story.

Information

The **Municipal Information Centre** (Městské informační centrum; ☎ 556 852 240; mic@stramberk.cz; 9am-noon & 12.30-5pm Tue-Sun) is in the Zdeňka Buriana Museum just below the main square.

Sights

The path up from the north end of the cute village square passes through a stone gate inscribed 'Cuius Regio – Eius Religio – 1111' ('whose place? – his place'). On the slopes are the remains of the Gothic **castle walls**, and at the top you can climb 166 steps to the top of the **tower** (Trúba; adult/concession 20/10Kč; 9am-5pm Tue-Sun Apr-Nov, Sat & Sun only Dec-Mar), which is 508m above sea level, for vertiginous views.

On the village square itself is **Muzeum Štramberk** (☎ 556 701 156; adult/concession 10/5Kč; 9am-noon & 1-5pm Tue-Sun) with exhibits of local archaeology, folk furniture and art. South of the square is the interesting **Muzeum Zdeňka Buriana** (☎ 556 852 240; adult/concession 20/10Kč; 9am-noon & 12.30-5pm Tue-Sun

Jun-Sep), which commemorates the locally born painter, who chose Stone Age people as his subjects.

Further south is the entrance to the **national gardens of Kotouč** (národní sad na Kotoučí). It was here, in the **Šipka cave** (Jeskyně Šipka), that archaeologist KJ Maška found the jawbone of a Neanderthal child in 1880. The discovery became the inspiration for Zdeněk Burian's paintings.

Sleeping & Eating

Penzión Stará Skola (☎ 556 852 697; penzion@zars.cz; s/d incl breakfast 390/780Kč) By the church on the main square, this pretty place has a pleasant garden restaurant and spotless rooms with private shower.

Hotel Šipka (☎ 556 852 181; info@hotelsipka.cz; s/d incl breakfast 700/900Kč) Also on the main square, this mid-ranger is smartish but dark, with a popular eatery and comfortable rooms.

Hotel Gong (☎ 556 721 621; fax 556 852 330; Zauliční 410; s/d 1150/1600Kč; P ≋) Former president Václav Havel stayed here once, and they're proud of it. With a pool, a sauna and a fine Walachian restaurant, this remains the town's most exclusive choice.

While you're in town, try Štramberské uši (Štramberk ears) – conical ginger biscuits with honey and spices, usually served with cream. According to legend, the ears originally belonged to unfortunate Tatar prisoners-of-war.

Getting There & Away

Nový Jičín is a stop for most Olomouc–Ostrava buses, and from there local buses run twice a day to Štramberk (15Kč, 20 minutes). However, the most enjoyable way to get here is on foot through the hills – 8km on a red-marked trail from Nový Jičín město train station, or across the river from Nový Jičín horní nádraží station.

KOPŘIVNICE

A short bus ride from Štramberk lies the industrial town of Kopřivnice, famed for its transport museum. It is also the birthplace of the painter Zdeněk Burian. Today it's mostly known as the home of the vehicle manufacturer Tatra, which produces large trucks.

The popular **Tatra Technical Museum** (Technické muzeum Tatra; ☎ 656 821 415; Záhummení 369; adult/concession 60/25Kč; ✆ 9am-5pm Tue-Sun May-Sep,

9am-4pm Oct-Apr) is housed in purpose-built premises beside the Tatra P-Beam Hotel – you can't miss the red locomotive outside. For fans of old cars, trucks and trains, the Tatra factory has put on a dazzling display of its prized vehicles, including its first car, the 'Präsident' (1897). Tatra products have always had a good reputation for high quality and reliability. The company originally specialised in passenger cars and trucks but in the later days of communist rule most of the production shifted to trucks and limousines, for use mainly by diplomats. As well as a fantastic collection of cars, from the ordinary to the outrageously eccentric, you can also admire the Tatra 815 truck that drove around the world between 1987 and 1990, covering 150,000km and 68 countries.

There are regular buses to Štramberk (10Kč, ten minutes).

ROŽNOV POD RADHOŠTĚM

In 1925 Rožnov pod Radhoštěm ('Rožnov-under-Radhošt') became renowned for its *skansen*, a museum of traditional wooden architecture, which was launched as a showcase for the Walachian way of life. Brought piece by piece from around the Beskydy region, the architectural exhibits caused an immediate stir and continue to do so today. These days, Rožnov is a thriving resort town.

The tourist crush (and hotel crunch), exacerbated by a heavy schedule of contrived 'folk events', changes the face of Rožnov during summer weekends. Stay overnight and arrive at the *skansen* early, however, and you can still have these beautiful exhibits pretty much to yourself.

A completely different kind of culture is on display for about a week around 4 July every year, when Texans of Czech descent pour into Rožnov for a week-long Independence Day jamboree, complete with barbecues, a rodeo and truckloads of Radegast beer. Hotel space is nonexistent then. The folk festivals such as the Easter Traditions or the folk song and dance festival held on the first weekend of July are quieter.

Orientation

From the adjacent train and bus stations it's a 400m walk east across the river to the main square, Masarykovo náměstí.

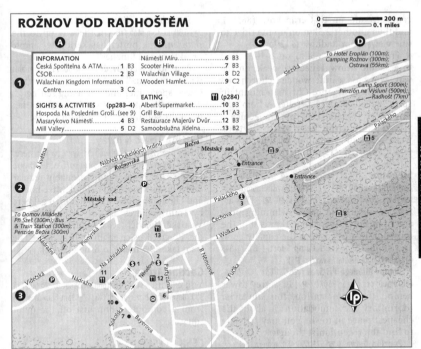

ROŽNOV POD RADHOŠTĚM

INFORMATION
Česká spořitelna & ATM..........1 B3
ČSOB....................................2 B3
Walachian Kingdom Information
Centre.................................3 C2

SIGHTS & ACTIVITIES (pp283–4)
Hospoda Na Posledním Groši..(see 9)
Masarykovo Náměstí..............4 B3
Mill Valley.............................5 D2

Náměstí Míru.........................6 B3
Scooter Hire..........................7 B3
Walachian Village...................8 D2
Wooden Hamlet......................9 C2

EATING (p284)
Albert Supermarket...............10 B3
Grill Bar...............................11 A3
Restaurace Majerův Dvůr.......12 B3
Samoobslužna Jídelna...........13 B2

To Hotel Eroplán (100m);
Camping Rožnov (300m);
Ostrava (55km);

Camp Sport (300m);
Penzión na Výsluní (500m);
Radhošť (7km)

To Domov Mládeže
Při Szeš (300m); Bus
& Train Station (300m);
Penzión Bečva (300m)

NORTH MORAVIA

The *skansen* is about another 800m east on Palackého.

Information

The **Walachian Kingdom Information Centre** (Informační centrum Valašského království; ☎ 571 655 196; www.roznov.cz - Czech only; Palackého 484; ⏰ 8.30am-6pm May-Sep, 9am-3pm Mon-Fri Oct-Apr) can provide a wealth of information about local attractions, transport and accommodation.

Česká spořitelna (cnr Masarykovo náměstí & Lázeňská) and **ČSOB** (Nerudova 2201) have ATMs and exchange counters.

Sights & Activities

WALACHIAN OPEN-AIR MUSEUM

Made up of three separate *skansens*, the **Walachian Open-Air Museum** (Valašské muzeum v přírodě; ☎ 571 757 111; www.vmp.cz) is an impressive effort to keep a grip on the region's architectural and cultural past. Multilingual maps and inventories of the buildings are available at the entrances. Entry to each museum costs 50/25Kč for adult/concession, while a combined ticket is 120/60Kč. Foreign text is 10Kč extra.

The biggest and best of the three *skansens* is the **Walachian Village** (Valašská dědina; ⏰ 9am-5pm May, 9am-6pm Jun-Aug, 10am-5pm Sep), which climbs right up the hillside to a ridge boasting exceptional views. It's a good attempt at reconstructing an entire shepherds' village, right down to the orchards and livestock, which are still raised using traditional methods.

The **Wooden Hamlet** (Dřevěné městečko; ⏰ 8am-6pm Jun-Aug, 8am-5pm Apr, May & Sep, 8am-4pm Nov-Mar) is the most fun, with its Walachian-style *hospoda* (pub) where you can actually get a beer and a good Moravian meal. Other highlights are a pretty church from the village of Větřkovice and a collection of wooden beehives decorated with smirking faces. It is closed from 3 November to 5 December and during Christmas and New Year.

The **Mill Valley** (Mlýnská dolina; ⏰ 8am-5.30pm May-Jun, 9am-6pm Jul-Aug, 9am-5pm Sep) is a fascinating collection of water-driven mills with a working smithy and miller.

WALKING UP RADHOŠŤ

It's 5.5km on a red-marked trail from the Wooden Hamlet museum, past Rožnov campsite and up to Černá hora (885m), and then another 2.5km on up the ridge to fine views from Radhošť (1129m).

From there it's 3.5km on a blue trail to a saddle below Tanečnice peak; on the way, you pass a little wooden church and a stone statue of a pre-Christian mountain spirit called Radegast (after whom the local beer is named). From Tanečnice a year-round chairlift descends to Ráztoka, where you can catch a bus back to Rožnov pod Radhoštěm (15 minutes).

Sleeping

Camping Rožnov (☎ 571 648 001; www.camproznov.cz; tent/bungalow per person 100/280Kč; P ⚲) This attractive family site has a swimming pool and bungalows. It is about 1km east of the museum. Just opposite is the equally good and similarly priced **Camp Sport** (☎ 571 648 011; kempsport-tjroznov@wo.cz; P).

Domov Mládeže Při Szeš (☎ 571 651 248; Zemědělská 500; per person 250Kč; P) In a grey tower behind the train station, this *ubytovna* (dormitory accommodation) is about the cheapest place in town. You may struggle to find the receptionist though.

Penzión Bečva (☎ 571 654 458; majerz@quick.cz; Meziřížská 1652; per person 300Kč; P) Just across the main road, this place is slightly rougher but at least the desk is usually attended.

Horský hotel Radegast (☎ 556 835 130; hotelradegast@hotelradegast.cz; per person incl breakfast 340Kč) Near Radhošť, this chalet is a good bet for those wanting to stay up on the mountain.

Penzión Na Výsluní (☎ 571 648 115; penzion.vysluni@quick.cz; Lesní 642; s/d incl breakfast 580/800Kč; P) At the top of the hill overlooking town, this big *pension* offers plenty of hush, a pleasant location and a decent restaurant.

Hotel Eroplán (☎ 571 648 014; hotel-eroplan@iol.cz; Horní Paseky 451; s/d incl breakfast 1200/1400Kč; P ✗ ✄) The kinetic, comedy bi-plane outside slightly detracts from this hotel's four-star credibility, but there's plenty more on offer for creature-comfort seekers, including a health club and sauna.

Eating

There aren't too many places in town, and most are closed by 9pm.

Grill Bar (☎ 571 654 766; 2nd fl, Masarykovo náměstí 186; mains 70-150Kč) This reliable place dishes up tasty grills-and-things in contemporary surrounds.

Samoobslužna Jídelna (Palackého; mains 49Kč; ☺ 6.30am-3pm Mon-Fri) On the way up to the *skansen*, this buffet has seriously simple breakfasts and lunches.

Restaurace Majerův dvůr (Nerudova 141; mains 60Kč) With a small garden terrace, this offers Czech specialities and a relaxing setting.

Albert (Masarykovo náměstí) The supermarket is on the south side of the main square.

Getting There & Away

Buses are usually the easiest way to get here. There is one daily direct bus to/from Prague (200Kč, 5½ hours) and reasonably regular direct buses from Brno (135Kč, three hours) and Olomouc (60Kč, 1¼ hours). To get here by train requires at least one change at Valašské Meziříčí (13km away) which is on the Prague-Košice main railway line. The train takes 2½ hours to Brno (120Kč).

Getting Around

You can hire **scooters** (půjčovna skútrů; ☎ 602 715 300; Bayerova 52; per day 500Kč; ☺ 9am-5pm Mon-Fri) from a computer shop just off the main square.

ČESKÝ TĚŠÍN

An international border was laid through the middle of this town at the end of WWI using the natural division of the Olše river: to the west is Český Těšín in the Czech Republic, and to the east is Cieszyn in Poland. Most of the original town, and all the interesting historical sights, ended up on the Polish side (refer to Lonely Planet's *Poland* guidebook). The only reason to be here is if you have arrived from, or are off to, Poland.

Orientation

The river is the border, with separate 24-hour crossings for each direction: the Hlavní Bridge (Hlavní most) is for entering the Czech Republic, the Střelniční most for leaving. From the railway tracks on the Czech side, each bridge is about 500m along a street of the same name. Český Těšín's bus station is west of the tracks, via a pedestrian underpass on Hlavní or an automobile underpass on Viaduktova.

Information

The **regional information centre** (regionální informační centrum; ☎ 558 711 866; itesin@grendel.cz; Hlavní 15; ☺ 8am-6pm Mon-Fri, 8am-2pm Sat) has plenty

ČESKÝ TĚŠÍN

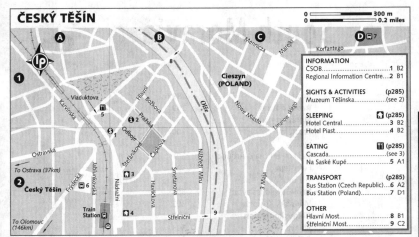

0 — 300 m
0 — 0.2 miles

of information on the region. You can contact the tourist information office in Polish Cieszyn on ☎ 00 48 33 852 3050.

ČSOB (Nádražní 4) has an exchange counter and ATM, as does the **post office** beside the train station.

Sights
Muzeum Těšínska (☎ 558 761 211; Hlavní 15; adult/concession 10/5Kč; ☺ 9am-5pm Tue-Fri, 9am-1pm Sat, 1-5pm Sun) has exhibits on the history and ethnography of the region.

Sleeping & Eating
Hotel Central (☎ 558 713 113; info@hotel-central.cz; Nádražní 10; s/d incl breakfast 650/850Kč) This plush new place has bags of character and about the best bar and restaurant in town.

Hotel Piast (☎ 558 711 560; fax 558 711 564; Nádražní 18; s/d 600/750Kč) In a dazzling shade of yellow, this offers so-so rooms and a looming, local-style restaurant.

Cascada (☎ 558 711 123; Nádražní 18; mains 100-150Kč) Attached to Hotel Central, this has heaps of hacienda charm and decent Tex-Mex food.

Na Saské Kupé (☎ 558 411 855; Sokola Tůmy; mains 90-140Kč) This idiosyncratic little café/restaurant has charming bric-a-brac décor and a good selection of Belgian beers.

Getting There & Away
There are seven fast trains a day to Prague (260Kč, 5½ hours), and seven via Žilina (one hour) and Poprad (three hours) to Košice (4½ hours).

Local trains run to Ostrava (60Kč, one hour) all day.

Buses also leave twelve times a day for Ostrava (45Kč, one hour), where you can change for Olomouc and other destinations. On the Polish side, there is an express bus every hour or two to Katowice, plus several per day for Kraków.

South Moravia

With all the poise of a self-sufficient statelet, South Moravia has a potent sense of identity, acting as a cultural interface between Bohemia and Slovakia, while remaining ever mindful of its own unique character.

For the visitor, this is most apparent in Moravia's thriving folk culture, which sparks into life during the summer festival season. During this time, communities from Telč to Moravské Slovácko don traditional garb, pick up their instruments – and wine glasses – and sing and dance themselves silly, animating ancient traditions in one of the best examples of 'living history' in the Czech Republic.

The backdrop could barely be more spectacular. Studded with historic towns and natural wonders – the incredible caves of the Moravian Karst (Moravský kras) being the best example – South Moravia offers plenty of scope for both committed urbanites and the pathologically outdoorsy. A constellation of photogenic chateaux, counting Pernštejn and Vranov among its brightest stars, is also on offer for the historically minded.

And then there's Brno, the diverse urban heart of Moravia, where communist-era Trabants and new economy Mercedes pass on boulevards lined with grandiose playhouses and old school *pivnice*. Lacking the overtly charismatic cityscapes of Prague, Brno's attractions lie in its countless galleries, museums and theatres; a city of few tourists and, like the rest of South Moravia, a great many artists.

After the heavily trammelled routes of South and West Bohemia, South Moravia is the place to see the big sights while keeping at least one foot off the beaten track.

SOUTH MORAVIA

HIGHLIGHTS

- Take a giant stride into the Renaissance while wandering through **Telč** (p306).
- Indulge in Moravia's vibrant folk culture during **Moravské Slovácko's** summer festival season (p317).
- Soak up the galleries and museums of elegant **Brno** (p290).
- Descend into the bowels of the earth among the caves of the **Moravian Karst** (p299).
- Stand before Mucha's sublime *Slav Epic* in quiet **Moravský Krumlov** (p303).

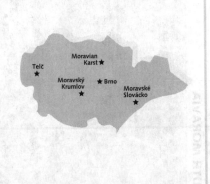

SOUTH MORAVIA

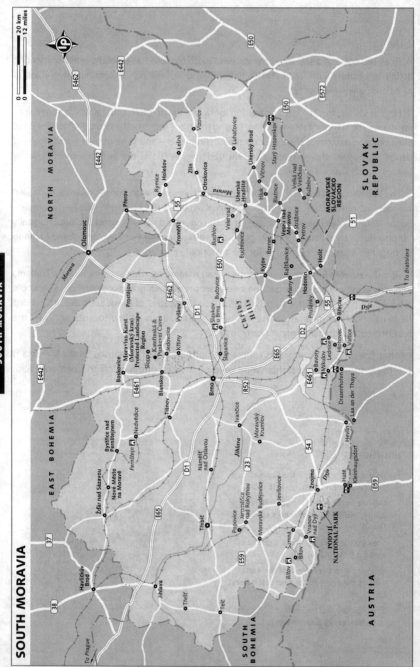

BRNO

pop 385,000
The Czech Republic's second largest city was always going to suffer comparisons with Prague, the city that can do no wrong. But Brno is not interested in living in eclipse. Stately and sophisticated, its broad boulevards have all the airs and graces of a capital, a city where the chatter in the chic terrace cafés is more of Moravia the far-reaching, than Moravia the parochial.

With roots in more recent times, Brno lacks the massive historical importance of Prague. Its largely 20th-century hub is more spacious and considerably less broody. It is also less photogenic. But while central Prague can sometimes feel like a 3-D postcard, Brno is very much a living city, with all the good and bad that comes with it. From its elegant main drag to its scruffier, lively edges, Brno is a great place to sample Czech urban living, away from the standard tourist beat.

With a clutch of museums, galleries and theatres, Brno is a surprisingly effete, culturally minded city, where an endless enthusiasm for the arts, coffee and chatter brings an almost Parisian air to its streets. The flipside of this is that Brno, unlike much of the country, has a reputation for keeping its hair tied tightly up, preferring sophisticated, late-night dining to a good honest knees-up at the local beer hall.

History
The present suburb of Líšeň was a Slav fort, Staré Zámky, at the time of the Great Moravian Empire. Around AD 1000 a settlement was founded on the Svratka river, where the suburb of Staré Brno now stands.

In the 11th century the Přemysl princesses built a castle on Petrov Hill, and the town that grew around it had acquired a defensive wall by the middle of the 13th century. At this time another castle was built on Špilberk Hill. During the reign of John of Luxembourg, Brno became an important centre of arts and trade. In the late 1300s it became Moravia's capital for the first time, and most of Brno's monasteries date from then.

This predominantly Catholic town sided with King Sigismund in the Hussite Wars; the Hussites twice tried to take it but failed. In the mid-15th century Brno sided again with an enemy of the Czechs, Matthias Corvinus (Matyáš Korvín). Later in the 16th century Brno turned Protestant and joined the unsuccessful anti-Habsburg rebellion by the Czech Estates. In the ensuing Thirty Years' War, the town was able to successfully defend itself against the Swedes from 1643 to 1645. After the war Brno underwent extensive baroque reconstruction.

The botanist Gregor Mendel (1822–84) established the modern science of heredity through his studies of peas and bees at the Augustinian monastery in Brno. After the Brno–Vienna railway was completed in 1839, Brno developed into a major industrial centre. As the most important town in the Czechoslovak state after Prague, it also acquired a university and, in the 1920s, some major exhibition buildings.

Orientation
The town is dominated by Špilberk Castle, on the hill of the same name; vying for attention are the spires of the Church of SS Peter & Paul on Petrov Hill.

Brno's main train station (*hlavní nádraží*) is just south of the town centre. Opposite the station is the beginning of Masarykova, a main thoroughfare that leads north to triangular náměstí Svobody, the centre of town. The bus station (*autobusové nádraží*) is 800m south of the train station, beyond the Tesco department store – to get to Tesco go through the pedestrian tunnel under the train tracks, then follow the crowd along the elevated walkway.

Brno's Tuřany airport is 7.5km southeast of the train station.

MAPS
SHOCart's GeoClub 1:15,000 *Brno plán města* is recommended.

Information
BOOKSHOPS
Geokart (Map pp292-3; ☎ 542 216 561; Vachova 8) Stocks maps and travel guides galore.
Knihkupectví Literární Kavárna (Map pp292-3; ☎ 542 217 954; náměstí Svobody 13) Has a decent range of English-language titles.

CULTURAL CENTRE
British Council (Map pp292-3; ☎ 545 210 174; www.britishcouncil.cz; třída Kpt Jaroše) Has a good supply of UK newspapers.

FOREIGN CONSULATE
Consulate General of the Russian Federation (Map p291; ☎ 545 211 617; gkbrnotx@iol.cz; Hlinky 142-b; ⊘ 9am-1pm Mon, Wed & Fri) Opposite the exhibition grounds, 1km west of the city.

INTERNET ACCESS
Internet Centrum (Map pp292-3; 1st fl, Masarykovo 22-24; ⊘ 8am-midnight) Charges 40Kč per hour.
Laundromat @ Bar Pod Balony (Map pp292-3; ☎ 736 277 570; Hybešova 45; ⊘ 10am-midnight) Charges 20Kč per hour.

LAUNDRY
Laundromat @ Bar Pod Balony (Map pp292-3; ☎ 736 277 570; Hybešova 45; ⊘ 10am-midnight) Has plenty of self-service washers and driers, a bar and Internet access.

LEFT LUGGAGE
Left-luggage office (Map pp292-3; per day 20Kč) On the ground floor of the train station, on the right of the concourse if you have your back to the street.

MEDIA
Metropolis (www.netpolis.cz) A free fortnightly events magazine (in Czech), featuring cinema, theatre and club listings.

MEDICAL & EMERGENCY SERVICES
Lékárna Koliště (Map pp292-3; ☎ 545 424 811; Koliště 47) A 24-hour pharmacy.
Tourist Police Station (☎ 974 626 100; Bartošová 1)
Úrazová hospital (nemocnice; Map pp292-3; ☎ 545 538 111; Ponávka 6)

MONEY
KB (Map pp292-3; cnr Kozí & Koblížná)
KB (Map pp292-3; náměstí Svobody 21) Both branches have exchange and ATM services.

PHOTOGRAPHY
Kodak Express (Map pp292-3; ☎ 542 221 541; Josefské 16) Has a one-hour service.

POST
Main post office (Map pp292-3; Poštovská 3/5) One block east of the main square.
Post office (Map pp292-3; Nádražní) By the train station; open 24 hours.

TOURIST OFFICE
Tourist information office (Kulturní a Informační Centrum – KIC; www.kultura-brno.cz) Old Town Hall (Map pp292-3; ☎ 542 211 090; Radnická 8; ⊘ 8am-6pm Mon-Fri, 9am-5pm Sat & Sun) Train Station (Map pp292-3; ☎ 542 221 450; Nádrazvní 6) Mendilanum (Map p291; ☎ 543 242 236; Mendlovo náměstí) The main Town Hall office sells maps and books accommodation.

TRAVEL AGENCIES
Čedok (Map pp292-3; ☎ 542 321 267; Nádražní 10/12)
České dráhy Travel Agency (Map pp292-3; ☎ 542 221 507) In the main train station, this also sells bus tickets to Western Europe.
GTS international (Map pp292-3; ☎ 542 221 996; gts.brno@gtsint.cz; Vachova 4) This youth travel agency sells international air, bus and train tickets.

Dangers & Annoyances
Several cases of pickpocketing are reported daily. According to local police, an area just east of the centre – surrounded by the streets Cejl, Francouzská, Příkop and Ponávka – can be dangerous, especially at night.

Sights & Activities
CITY CENTRE　　　　　　　　　　Map pp292–3
From the main train station, head up Masarykova to Kapucínské náměstí. At No 5 is the **Church of the Holy Cross** (kostel sv Kříže) and the adjoining **Capuchin Monastery** (Kapucínský klášter).

The monastery's ghoulish attraction is its **crypt** (krypta; adult/concession 50/20Kč; ⊘ 9am-noon & 2-4.30pm Tue-Sat, 11-11.45am & 2-4.30pm Sun) – some 150 mummies were deposited here prior to 1784 and the rooms are full of clothed skeletons. It's 10Kč extra for an English text.

Moravian Museum & Around
Turn left out of the monastery to reach the former **Ditrichstein Palace** (Ditrichštejnský palác), which houses the **Moravian Museum** (Moravské zemské muzeum; ☎ 542 321 205; Zelný trh 8; adult/concession 50/25Kč; ⊘ 9am-5pm Tue-Sat). Exhibits straddle the intellectual gulf between extinct life and the medieval village.

In a courtyard around to the right is the **Biskupský Yard Museum** (☎ 542 321 205; Muzejní 1; adult/concession 20/10Kč; ⊘ 9am-5pm Tue-Sat), with the largest freshwater aquarium in the country, plenty on Moravian wildlife and a considerably more soporific section on the history of money.

Cabbages – and plenty of other things – have been bartered for and squabbled over at the **Cabbage Market** (Zelný trh) since the 13th century. There's still a daily market and it remains one of the best places in town for fruit and veg.

BRNO

0 — 1 km
0 — 0.5 miles

A   B   C   D

Kníničky

To Obora Camping;
Hotel Přehrada (2km)

Sadová

Lesná

Králova
Pole

Žabovřesky

Ponava

Černá
Pole

Husovice

Jundrov

Kohoutovice

To Auto Motodrom
Brno CZ (6km)

Veveří

Zábrdovice

Stránice

Pisárky

INFORMATION
Russian Consulate General........1 B3
Tourist Information Office........(see 5)

SIGHTS & ACTIVITIES (pp290–6)
Botanical Gardens....................2 C2
Church of the Assumption of the
  Virgin...................................3 C3
Exhibition Grounds..................4 B3
Mendelianum..........................5 C3
Mitrov Summer Palace.............6 B3
Planetarium.............................7 B2
Vila Tugendhat.........................8 C2
Zoo...9 A1

SLEEPING (pp296–7)
Hotel Boby.............................10 C2
Pension BVV...........................11 B3
Ubytovani Camp TJ Favorit.....12 B3

EATING (pp297–8)
Haribol..................................13 C2

ENTERTAINMENT (p298)
Alterna..................................14 C2
Boby Centrum.....................(see 10)
Radost Puppet Theatre...........15 D3
Stará Pekárna........................16 C2

TRANSPORT (pp298–9)
Main Bus Station....................17 C3

See Central Brno Map (pp292–3)

Trnitá

To Airport
(5km)

Černovice

Komárov

Štýřice

Horní
Heršpice

SOUTH MORAVIA

The unusual **Parnas Fountain** (kašna Parnas) was designed in 1695 by architect JB Fischer von Erlach. Carp were once sold from its waters at Christmas, but today there's only 1Kč coins and the odd cigarette end.

Mozart performed at the nearby **Reduta Theatre** (Reduta divadlo; Zelný trh 4) in 1767, but it is currently closed for restoration.

Cathedral of SS Peter & Paul

From the top of the Cabbage Market take Petrská to Petrov Hill, site of the gargantuan **Cathedral of SS Peter & Paul** (katedrála sv Petra a Pavla). Climb its **tower** (věž; adult/concession 25/20Kč; ☀ 10am-5pm Tue-Sun) for great views of Brno or descend into its rather empty **crypt** (krypta; adult/concession 15/10Kč; ☀ as tower).

The 14th-century cathedral, said to have been built on the site of a pagan temple to Venus, has been reconstructed many times since then. The highly decorated, 11m-high main altar with figures of SS Peter and Paul was carved by the Viennese sculptor Josef Leimer in 1891. The Renaissance **Bishop's Palace** (Biskupská palác; closed to the public) adjoins the cathedral.

Old Town Hall & Around

From Biskupská you can digress left into pleasant **Denisovy Sady** park. Back on Biskupská, turn right onto Starobrněnská and go past the **former brewery**.

On the left, at Mečová 5, is the back of the **Old Town Hall** (Stará radnice; ☀ 9am-5pm). About

CENTRAL BRNO

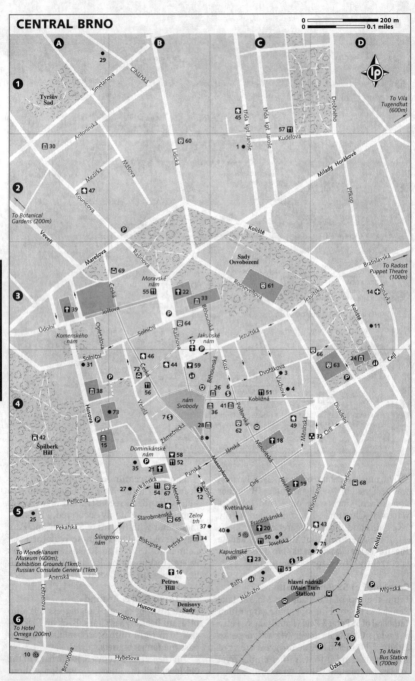

0 — 200 m
0 — 0.1 miles

SOUTH MORAVIA

3m up is what looks like the face of a man. The staple pub yarn goes that a Brno councillor who plotted with the Hussites to surrender the town in 1424 was overheard by Borro, Emperor Sigismund's court clown, while a prisoner of the Hussites. Borro escaped and told the story, and the councillor was sealed alive in the wall.

The original, early-13th-century building, which became the town hall in 1343, has been incorporated into today's structure. A peculiar sight by the entrance on Radnická is a Gothic portal with a crooked middle turret, made by Anton Pilgram in 1510. According to legend, he was not paid the agreed amount by the council and, in revenge, left the turret (above the statue of Righteousness) crooked.

The town hall **tower** (adult/concession 10/5Kč; 🕙 9am-5pm), raised by 5m during repairs in 1905 so as not to disappear among the newly built houses around it, offers magnificent views. For another 20Kč you can also see the town hall's interior, including **Crystal Hall**, **Fresco Hall** and **Treasury**.

The building is full of oddities. Hanging from the ceiling at the entrance is the corpse of a legendary dragon that terrorised the city's waterways. It is, in fact, an Amazon River crocodile, donated by Archprince Matyáš in 1608.

Minorite Monastery & Around
Cross Zelný trh to Květinářská and go over Masarykova into Františkánská, where you'll find the **Church of St Mary Magdalene** (kostel sv Máří Magdalény). Just south of here, turn left into Josefská, and on the right is the **Church of St Joseph** (kostel sv Josefa).

Next head north up Masarykova and turn right into Orlí, at the end of which is the **Měnín Gate** (Měninská brána), built around 1600, with a small **archaeological museum** (☎ 542 214 946; Měnínská 7; adult/concession 20/10Kč; ☺ 9am-6pm Tue-Sun May-Sep, until 5pm Oct-Apr).

From here turn back along Jánská to the **Church of St John** (kostel sv Janů) and the **Minorite Monastery** founded in 1230. The Minorites are the only order in Moravia still in their original quarters.

Náměstí Svobody & Around

A right into Masarykova leads to bustling náměstí Svobody, the city centre's heart.

Here, pride of place goes to the eccentric **House of the Four Mamlases** (dům U čtyř mamlasů; náměstí Svobody 10), where the façade is supported by a quartet of extremely muscled (but clearly moronic) Atlas figures, each struggling to hold up the building and their loincloths at the same time. Created by Germano Wanderley in 1928, the building has provoked a longstanding debate over whether the statues aptly reflect the elegant face of the Moravian capital.

The square dates from the early 13th century, when it was called Dolní trh (Lower Market). Its **plague column** dates from 1680. On the corner of the square and Kobližná is the **Palác Říkovský z Dobrčic**, also known as the House at the Red Ox (dům U rudého vola). At Kobližná 4, the **Schrattenbachův palác** has a niche with a 1637 statue of the Madonna.

Given Moravia's insatiable enthusiasm for tradition, there are probably few better

---

AHEAD OF THEIR TIME

The bells of the Cathedral of SS Peter & Paul disconcertingly ring noon an hour early, at 11am. Legend has it that when the Swedish laid siege to the city in 1645, their commander, General Torstenson, who had been frustrated by Brno's defences for more than a week, decided to launch a final attack, with one caveat: if his troops could not prevail by noon he would throw in his hand.

By 11am the Swedes were making headway but the cathedral tower keeper had the inspired idea of ringing noon early. The bells struck twelve, the Swedes withdrew and the city was saved.

---

places to poke your nose into an **Ethnographic Museum** (Etnografické muzeum; ☎ 542 422 361; Kobližná 1; adult/concession 20/10Kč; ☺ 9am-5pm Tue-Sat). Illustrated with scenes from Moravian country life, this provides a comprehensive insight into the region's traditional culture from the 18th to 20th centuries.

Heading northwards along Běhounská brings you to Jakubské náměstí and the monumentally plain, 15th-century **Church of St James** (kostel sv Jakuba). It has a baroque pulpit with reliefs of Christ dating from 1525. Also here is the baroque tomb of the French Protestant Raduit de Souches, who died leading the defence of Brno in 1645.

But the church's biggest drawcard is a statue near a south-facing window in the church tower. Some think it's a couple engaging in a little slap and tickle, while the official – and perhaps most interesting explanation – is that it depicts Siamese twins.

Dominikánské Náměstí & Around

From náměstí Svobody, Zámečnická leads west to Dominikánské náměstí, a humble square dominated by the **Church of St Michael** (kostel sv Michala), which has an interesting ornate main altar (1759) by Josef Winterhalter.

Also facing the square is the 16th-century **New Town Hall** (Nová radnice) with its impressive frescoes.

Church of St Thomas & Around

The **Church of St Thomas** (kostel sv Tomáše), with a soaring nave in the purest Gothic style, abuts a 14th-century **Augustinian Monastery** that today houses a branch of the **Moravian Gallery** (see the following section).

Along Joštova, past the neo-Renaissance **Assembly** (zemská sněmovna), stands the Evangelical Comenius Church (kostel JA Komenského), better known as the **Red Church** (Červený kostel) for its redbrick exterior; it was built between 1862 and 1867 to a design by H Ferstel. Left down Husova, on the corner of Komenského náměstí, is the **Meeting House** (Besední dům), one of the best works of 19th-century Danish architect Theofil Hansen and now home to the Brno State Philharmonic Orchestra.

Moravian Gallery

If proof were needed that the people of Brno were pathological art lovers, the fact that there are *three* branches of the Moravian Gallery (Moravská galerie) is surely it. Entry to all three galleries is free on the first Friday of the month.

Adjoining the Church of St Thomas, the **Místodržitelský Palace** (☎ 542 321 100; Moravské náměstí 1A; adult/concession 50/25Kč; ☉ 10am-6pm Wed-Sun, until 7pm Thu) hosts a variety of changing exhibitions.

The second branch, the **Applied Arts Museum** (Uměleckoprůmyslové muzeum; ☎ 532 169 111; Husova 14; adult/concession 90/45Kč; ☉ 10am-6pm Wed-Sun, until 7pm Thu) focuses on the evolution of arts and crafts from the Middle Ages to the heyday of Art Nouveau and holds changing, temporary exhibitions as well.

The third branch is up the road, inside the **Pražákův Palace** (☎ 532 169 111; Husova 18; adult/ concession 40/20Kč; ☉ 10am-6pm Wed-Sun, until 7pm Thu). This branch focuses on the Czech Modernist movement and 20th-century art.

ŠPILBERK CASTLE   Map pp292–3
Špilberk Castle may lack fairy-tale good looks, but it has been a crowning feature of the city's skyline for centuries. Founded in the early 1200s, the castle was often used as a residence by the Czech kings, before being modernised in the 18th century and transformed into a military fortress. It was in this form that the castle became 'home' to enemies of the Austro-Hungarian Empire, who were imprisoned in the so-called Prison of the Nations – named after the multinational nature of the rebels kept there. The prison was closed in 1853, but was again put to use by the occupying Nazis in WWII.

Some of Špilberk's casemates *(kasematy)*, the dark, chilly corridors beneath the bastions, are now a **museum of prison life** (☎ 542 123 614; adult/concession 30/15Kč; ☉ 9am-6pm Jul-Aug, 9am-6pm Tue-Sun May, Jun & Sep, 9am-5pm Tue-Sun Oct & Apr). The last entry is 45 minutes before closing time.

The castle itself houses the **Brno City Museum** (Muzeum Města Brna; ☎ 542 123 616; www.spilberk.cz; adult/concession 80/40Kč; ☉ 9am-6pm Tue-Sun May-Sep, 9am-5pm Tue-Sun Apr & Oct, 10am-5pm Wed-Sun Nov-Mar), which hosts permanent exhibitions *(stálé expozice)* on the history of construction, Brno's monuments and town planning, plus a fine arts gallery. You can also climb the **lookout tower** (adult/concession 20/ 10Kč) and admire the rather impressive **chime** (in the second courtyard), which musically sees in the hour from 10am to 6pm – they must turn it off when the tourists leave. Discounted **combination tickets** (adult/ concession 100/50Kč) for the kasematy, lookout tower and exhibitions are also available.

The castle is approachable only on foot, up the hill through the quiet gardens.

On the corner of Pellicova, there is a 1914 **cubist house** by František Uherka. From Husova, walk through Šilingrovo náměstí and left into Dominikánské, with its former **Dominican Monastery** (Dominikánský klášter).

OUTSIDE THE OLD TOWN
Near Špilberk Castle   Map p291
Over Špilberk Hill from the old town, on the corner of Úvoz and Pekařská, is the **Church of the Assumption of the Virgin** (kostel Nanebevzetí Panny Marie), Brno's finest late-Gothic building. Inside is the oldest painting on wood in the Czech Republic, the 13th-century Black Madonna (Černá Madona).

Around the corner at Mendlovo náměstí, in part of the **Abbey of St Thomas**, the **Mendelianum** (☎ 543 424 043; www.mendel-museum.org; Mendlovo náměstí 1; adult/concession 80/40Kč; ☉ 10am-6pm Tue-Sun) is a museum devoted to the daddy of modern genetics, botanist Gregor Johann Mendel (1822–84), who opened up whole new realms of possibility in this area with his pioneering work on the humble garden pea. A former Abbot of St Thomas, Mendel's work went largely unnoticed until after his death, when it was discovered that he had identified the principle of inheritance that governs how characteristics are passed on through the generations. A tour of the abbey costs 60Kč extra.

Take tram No 1 from the train station to Mendlovo náměstí and the museum is through a gate into a garden and second door on your right.

North of the Centre
A short walk from the old town, the small **Leoš Janáček Memorial Museum** (Památník Leoše Janáčka; Map pp292–3; ☎ 542 212 811; Smetanova 14; adult/ concession 30/15Kč; ☉ 1-4pm Mon, 9am-noon Tue-Thu) is dedicated to the composer. Janáček was born in Hukvaldy (North Moravia), but lived in Brno from childhood until his death in 1928. Janáček is the least known of the 'big three' Czech composers, the others being Smetana

and Dvořák. All were exponents of 'musical nationalism', incorporating folk music (very Moravian) into their pieces.

Further north, on adjacent Veveří (to the west), are the **Botanical Gardens** (Botanická zahrada; Map p291; ☎ 541 129 397; ☼ 9am-5pm Mon-Fri, until 3pm Sat & Sun); from the centre take tram No 3 or 13.

Vila Tugendhat (Map p291; ☎ 545 212 118; www.tugendhat-villa.cz; Černopolni 45; adult/concession 80/40Kč; ☼ 10am-6pm Wed-Sun), a modern functionalist building in the suburb of Černá Pole, is the work of the well-known German architect Ludwig Mies van der Rohe (1886–1969), and a shrine for students of modern architecture. Hired by some rich newlyweds to build them a home, Mies turned it into one of the first open-plan houses. Such is its importance that in 2001 it was added to Unesco's list of world cultural and natural heritage sites. At time of writing, tours were by reservation only – phone ahead. Take tram Nos 3, 5 or 11 from Moravské náměstí up Milady Horákové to Černopolní, then walk north.

Exhibition Grounds & Around   Map p291
The **Exhibition Grounds** (Výstaviště), in the suburb of Pisárky (take tram No 1 from the train station), were opened in 1928. They are now a year-round trade-fair venue. In addition to the **Palace of Industry** (Průmyslový palác), other interesting buildings include the **Congress Hall** (Kongresová hala) and Bauhaus-style **New House** (Nový dům).

In the space between Rybářská and Křížkovského, is the quaint **Mitrov Summer Palace** (Letohrádek Mitrovských; Veletržní 19).

Other Museums & Galleries
Yet more contemporary art exhibitions are held at the **City Art Gallery** (dům umění; Map pp292-3; ☎ 542 211 808; Malinovského náměstí 2; adult/concession 40/20Kč; ☼ 10am-6pm Tue-Sun). It's free on Wednesday.

There is also a **planetarium** (Map p291; ☎ 541 321 287; www.hvezdarna.cz) at Kraví hora 2 (tram No 4), and a **zoo** (Zoologická zahrada; ☎ 546 432 311; www.zoobrno.cz; ☼ 9am-6pm) at Bystrc-Mnišī hora (tram Nos 1, 3 or 11).

Festivals & Events
The **Auto Motodrom Brno CZ** (☎ 546 216 406; www .automotodromobrno.cz; Ostravačice, okres Brno) holds events for committed rev-heads through-

out the year, culminating in August's **Moto Grand Prix** (www.motograndprix.com; admission 490Kč). Tickets are available from the circuit, **Čedok** (Map pp292-3; ☎ 542 321 267; Nádražní 10/12) and the **Tourist information office** (Map pp292-3; ☎ 542 211 090; www.kultura-brno.cz; Radnická 8). Brno packs out at this time and hotels can double in price. The racing circuit is just off the D1 road to Prague, 10km west of Brno. It is well signposted.

In early June, Brno celebrates **Brno Days** for four days with shows, exhibitions and fireworks.

Sleeping
In February, April, August, September and October Brno hosts numerous major international trade fairs and hotel rates increase by 40% to 100%. Book ahead.

BUDGET
The information office can help with accommodation in private rooms from around 350Kč.

Hostels
Čedok, the information office and GTS international (see Information p290) can help with accommodation in student dormitories during July and August.

Traveller's Hostel (Map pp292-3; ☎ 542 213 573; brno@travellers.cz; Jánská 22; dm per person incl breakfast 270Kč) As the spot where Gregor Mendel lectured on his discourse in 1865, this is pretty much hallowed ground in Brno. It certainly is for backpackers, who flock here to take advantage of the most central cheap beds in the city.

Hotel Přehrada (☎ 546 210 167; Knínčky 225, Brno Přehrada; dm 180Kč, d with shared/private bathroom 580/780Kč) Open March to November, this has private rooms, or cheap beds if you have a student card. Take tram No 1 from the main train station to the zoo, then cross the road west to náměstí 28 dubna and take bus No 54 to the end.

Camping
Obora Camping (☎ 546 223 334; tent per person 80Kč; ℗) This camp site, at the Brněnská přehrada (Brno dam) northwest of the city centre, opens May to September. To get there from the main train station, take tram No 1 to the zoo then change to bus No 103. The camp site ground is at the seventh stop.

Ubytovani Camp TJ Favorit (Map p291; ☎ 543 211 813; tent/dm per person 70/120Kč; **P**)) Near the exhibition grounds, this has space for tents, plus some basic shared rooms.

MID-RANGE

Pension BVV (Map p291; ☎ 541 159 167; praskova@c-box.cz; Hlinky 28A; s/d incl breakfast 730/980Kč) The extra walk (it's 1.5km west of the centre) is well rewarded at this three-star place, where comfy rooms, perma-smile service and hearty breakfasts come as standard.

Hotel Omega (Map pp292-3; ☎ 543 213 876; hotel@omega.cz; Křídloviská 19b; s/d incl breakfast 600/1000Kč; **P**) This tourist information office favourite is a 1km hike from the centre, but offers some spacious, airy rooms at a reasonable price (for Brno).

Hotel Continental (Map pp292-3; ☎ 541 519 111; info@continentalbrno.cz; Kounicova 6; s/d incl breakfast 1290/1590Kč; **P**) It looks blander than a suet dumpling from the outside, but the retro lobby is kitscher than a rest home for spent Bond villains. The rooms are good too.

Hotel & Pivnice Pegas (Map pp292-3; ☎ 542 210 104; fax 542 214 314; Jakubská 4; s/d 1000/1500Kč) The fabulously moody downstairs bar, full of oompah types, brass fittings and beer stills (they make their own brew), is let down by the slightly dowdy rooms above. It's an interesting place to stay though.

Hotel Avion (Map pp292-3; ☎ 542 214 055; avion@ignet.cz; Česká 20; d with shared/private bathroom 1200/1500Kč; **▣**) Slap bang in the heart of the action, this busy, blockish place sports a bright-coloured façade and a constellation of flashing lights. The rooms are okay.

Also recommended is **Hotel Amphone** (Map pp292-3; ☎ 545 428 310; amphone@brn.czn.cz; trída kpt Jaroše 29; s/d incl breakfast 950/1350Kč) with a quiet location, on an elegant street.

TOP END

Hotel Boby (Map p291; ☎ 541 638 110; hotel@bobycentrum.cz; Sportovní 2; s/d incl breakfast 2450/3640Kč; **P ▢ ▣ ▢ ▣**) The nerve centre of a giant entertainment complex, this stylish place targets a younger, hipper big spender. It's a long way out, but features just about everything you could possibly need, including a strip club.

Hotel Royal Ricc (Map pp292-3; ☎ 542 219 262; hotelroyalricc@brn.inecnet.cz; Starobrněnská 10; s/d incl breakfast 3200/3500Kč; **▢ ▣**) What this opulent place lacks in facilities, it more than makes up for in class. Personal, plush and atmospheric, it oozes once-upon-a-time charm and employs the type of staff that pretend they remember you from last time – even if there wasn't one.

Also recommended is the **Grand Hotel** (Map pp292-3; ☎ 542 518 111; grandhotel-brno@austria-hotels.telecom.cz; Benešova 18-20; s/d €63/92; **P ▢ ▣**) which is increasingly dated, but large and central.

Eating

Potrefená Husa (Map pp292-3; ☎ 542 213 177; Moravské náměstí 8; mains 90-150Kč) Offering a top yuppie combo of cocktails, upmarket bar-style eats and sports on the telly, this popular chain pub attracts a lively young crowd into the wee hours.

Pizza Coloseum (Map pp292-3; ☎ 543 237 318; Dominikánská 3; pizza 150Kč) This upmarket pizzeria features sublime toppings, waiters in white smocks and seating in the shadow of St Michael's. There's also an atmospheric cellar area.

U Staryho Billa (Map pp292-3; ☎ 545 244 453; Kudelova 7; mains 140Kč) Cow skulls, the stars-and-stripes and a model confederate soldier hint at the kind of Tex-Mex fare served up here. It also has a decent cigar and wine list and opens the doors on happy hour from 2.30pm to 5.30pm.

Haribol (Map p291; ☎ 545 215 636; Lužánecká 4; mains 55Kč) Vegetarians can escape the meat feast at this Hare Krishna–run place. The menu is anything but extensive, but the food is cheap and wholesome.

Čhajovna (Map pp292-3; Dominikánské náměstí 6/7; tea 20Kč) A religious theme pervades here, with yoga sessions upstairs, hymns (sometimes) on the stereo and Asian-style seating in a womb-like basement. The one icon everyone here can agree on, however, is the teapot. With more than 40 types on offer, this is a tea drinker's paradise.

Domácí Pečivo Jasa Kavárna (Map pp292-3; ☎ 542 211 146; cnr Masarykova & Nádražní; sandwiches 30Kč) This non-stop bakery and deli has fab baguettes and snacks that taste as good at lunch time as they do at 3am.

Other recommendations:
Bambus (Map pp292-3; Kobližná 13; mains from 60Kč) For pick-and-point Asian eats.
Adria (Map pp292-3; ☎ 542 213 513; Masarykova 31; mains 120-250Kč) For touristy international mains and colossal ice creams.

SOUTH MORAVIA

Stopkova Plzeňská Pivnice (Map pp292-3; ☎ 542 211 094; Česka 5; mains 70-200Kč) The finest exterior in town. Standard Czech favourites inside.

Drinking

Livingstone (Map pp292-3; ☎ 542 210 090; Dominikánské náměstí 5; ☒ until 1am) Appropriately (it is named after an explorer) hidden away through an archway, this raucous bar has Irish pub-style décor complemented by a tank of piranhas, a set of Andy Warhol–themed Laughing Cow prints and a glitter globe. It fills up late.

Sherlock Holmes Pub (Map pp292-3; ☎ 542 214 729; Jakubské náměstí 2; ☒ until 1am) It's a bit glossy for an English theme pub, but this is a popular place for an early doors drink.

Entertainment

Despite a reputation as dullsville, Brno has plenty of things to do at night, but you must hunt around a bit. The free bi-monthly guide, *Metropolis* (www.netpolis.cz), has invaluable listings.

BARS & CLUBS

Sofa (Map pp292-3; Starobrněnská 3; ☒ until 3am) Half gold cave, half cream cave, this club/bar is one for the lounge lizards, featuring cocktails, happy house music and walls decorated with framed (clean) knickers.

Also recommended:

Alterna (Map p291; Kounicova 48, blok B; ☒ until 1am) For rock and punk.

Boby Centrum (Map p291; Sportovní 2) One of the nation's biggest nightclubs – plus much more.

Stará pekárna (Map p291; ☎ 541 210 040; Štefánikova 8; ☒ until 1am) Live bands play jazz to good 'ole rock and roll.

CINEMAS   Map pp292–3

As a centre for the arts, Brno has plenty of cinemas. They include:

Kino Art (☎ 541 213 542; www.kinoartbrno.cz; Cihlářská 19) For art house films.

Palace Cinemas (☎ 543 560 111; www.palacecinemas.cz; Mečova) In the Velký Spalicek shopping centre, this shows all the latest Hollywood releases.

Scala (☎ 542 211 659; Moravské náměstí 3)

CLASSICAL MUSIC
& THEATRE   Map pp292–3

Except in mid-summer when the artists are on holiday, Brno's theatres offer excellent performances. In Brno, you are expected to dress up a bit. The **theatre booking office**

(Národní Divadlo v Brně Prodej Vstupnek; ☎ 841 113 355; www.ndbrno.cz; Dvořákova 11; ☒ 8am-5.30pm Mon-Fri, until noon Sat), behind the Mahenovo, sells tickets for the Mahenovo and Janáček theatres. Following are some major venues:

Janáček Theatre (Janáčkovo divadlo; Sady osvobození) Shows opera and ballet.

Mahenovo Theatre (Mahenovo divadlo; Divadelni) For classical drama (usually in Czech) and operettas.

City Theatre (Městské Divadlo; ☎ 545 321 269; www.mdb.cz; Lidická 16) Hosts Broadway-style musicals and a selection of more sedate plays.

Brno State Philharmonic Orchestra (☎ 542 212 300; www.sfb.cz; Komenského náměstí 8) Holds regular concerts in the Meeting House.

PUPPET THEATRE   Map p291

Radost Puppet Theatre (Radost Divadlo; ☎ 545 321 273; Bratislavská 32) This fabulous theatre puts on shows during the day. It's kids' stuff but great fun nonetheless.

Getting There & Away
AIR

Brno's Tuřany airport is 7.5km southeast of the train station, along Křenová (which becomes Olomoucká). To get to the airport will cost about 80Kč by taxi.

ČSA (Map pp292-3; ☎ 542 210 739; Nádražní 4) has scheduled flights (and buses) from Brno to Prague, where it is possible to get flights to many destinations around the world.

BUS

Two companies, **Český Národní Expres** (☎ 542 211 265) and **Čebus** (☎ 542 216 428) run buses between Prague and Brno (150Kč, 2½ hours). Tickets are available from their offices opposite the Grand Hotel – this is often easier than going all the way to the bus station.

For short trips, buses are faster and more efficient than the trains, especially to Telč (90Kč, two hours), Trenčín, (140Kč, three hours), Znojmo (45Kč, one hour), Strážnice (via Hodonín, 79Kč, 1¾ hours) and Kroměříž (40Kč, 1¼ hours). For more information contact the **bus information line** (☎ 543 212 651). **Euroline** (☎ 224 218 680) buses also connect Brno with German destinations including Dresden (850Kč) and Aachen (1700Kč).

TRAIN

Brno's **train station** (☎ 541 171 111), a major rail hub, has frequent main-line connections to Prague (140Kč, three hours), Bratislava (120Kč, two hours), Vienna (two hours), Budapest (four hours) and Berlin (eight hours). Within Moravia there are direct trains to Břeclav, Jihlava, Třebíč, Žďár nad Sázavou, Blansko, Přerov, Ostrava, and Veselí nad Moravou. You can reserve couchettes or sleepers in the station at ČD centrum to the right of the entrance.

All bus and trains times and prices can be found at www.idos.cz.

Getting Around
MHD (Map pp292-3; Benešova 22; 6am-6pm Mon-Fri, 7am-4pm Sat & Sun) sells tickets and monthly passes for public transport. Single tickets cost 7Kč (valid for 10 minutes), or 12Kč (40 minutes). There are also 24-hour (48Kč) passes. You can also buy tickets from *tabák* shops, or from the orange ticket machines at some tram stops.

City Taxis (☎ 542 321 321) can be called in advance.

Avis (Map pp292-3; ☎ 542 122 670; jiri.tisler@avis.cz; Husova 16) car rental has an office at the Hotel International Best Western.

AROUND BRNO

MORAVIAN KARST
The Moravian Karst (Moravský kras) is a beautiful, heavily wooded hilly area north of Brno, carved with canyons and honeycombed with some 400 caves.

Karst formations are the result of the seepage of faintly acidic rainwater through limestone, slowly dissolving it and, over millions of years, creating hollows and fissures. In caves, the slow drip of this water produces extraordinary stalagmites and stalactites.

Getting There & Away
Unless you have a car, the simplest way in is by train from Brno to Blansko, and by bus from there. Check with tourist information in Brno, for the latest on guided tours from there.

Blansko
pop 22,000
Functional Blansko is little more than a jumping-off point. The only thing of interest in town is a small **museum** (☎ 516 417 221; Zámek 1; adult/concession 40/20Kč; 9am-5pm Tue-Sun Apr-Oct,

Tue-Fri Nov-Mar) in a cute chateau up the hill and across the road from the tourist office.

ORIENTATION & INFORMATION
The main square, náměstí Svobody, is 1km northeast of the train station. From the latter, the bus station is directly across the Svitava river.

The **tourist information office** (Blanenská informační kancelář; ☎ 516 410 470; www.blansko.cz; Rožmitálova 6; 9am-6pm Mon-Fri, until noon Sat) sells maps and advance tickets to the Punkevní and Kateřinská caves, fields transport questions and can help with accommodation. It also has Internet access (40Kč per hour) and bike hire (180Kč per day). ČSOB, with an exchange desk and ATM, is next door.

SLEEPING
The tourist office can book cheap private rooms from 200Kč per person.

Hotel Panorama (☎ 516 418 111; hotel panorama@zm-net.cz; Těchov 168; s/d incl breakfast 880/1180Kč; P) It looks like a chocolate brownie, but this is one of the smartest places in town, with sauna, massage and some slick modern rooms. It is 2km from the centre in Češkovice.

Hotel Probe (☎ 516 414 987; provozni.morava@quick.cz; Husova 1; s/d 480/640Kč; P) The rooms are rather dowdy in this communist-era place, but they are some of the cheapest in town.

GETTING THERE & AWAY
There are 33 trains a day to/from Brno (34Kč, 25 minutes). See Getting There & Away (p300) about getting to the caves. Buses direct from Brno are less frequent.

Skalní Mlýn & the Caves
Skalní Mlýn is the administrative centre for the two most popular caves, Punkevní and Kateřinská. At the far end of the Skalní Mlýn car park are two offices: the first sells train (*vlak* – on wheels) and gondola (*lanovka*) tickets to reach Punkevní Cave and the Macocha Abyss (it's possible simply to walk); the second, called **Ústřední informační služba** (Central Information Service; ☎ 516 413 575; uismk@cavemk.cz) sells the actual entrance tickets to Punkevní and Kateřinská.

Arrive early in summer as tickets sell out. Consider buying Punkevní or Kateřinská tickets in advance from Blansko's tourist office.

PUNKEVNÍ & MACOCHA ABYSS

From the Skalní Mlýn car park, either walk 1km to **Punkevní cave** (Punkevní jeskyně; ☎ 516 418 602; adult/concession 100/50Kč; ☼ 8.20am-3.50pm Apr-Sep, 8.40am-2pm Mon-Fri, until 3.40pm Sat & Sun Oct, 8.40am-2pm Nov-Mar) or pay 30Kč for the 'train' to shuttle you there (every 20 minutes). Once you reach the cave, the 60-minute tour descends 720m and winds through caverns studded with the requisite stalagmites and stalactites, then continues by boat on the underground Punkva river. The tour ends at the bottom of the **Macocha Abyss** (propast Macocha), which is quite wide and almost 140m deep. Visitors either walk to the abyss or – with a prepurchased ticket obtained at the Skalní Mlýn car park – ride the gondola (40Kč).

When the river is low inside the cave, there are also tours involving a reduced boat trip (80/40Kč) or no boat trip (60/30Kč).

Be warned: in summer, tickets for this cave can sell out as much as a week in advance. Book early through the tourist office.

KATEŘINSKÁ CAVE

The **Kateřinská cave** (Kateřinská jeskyně; ☎ 516 413 161; adult/concession 40/20Kč; ☼ 8.20am-4pm Apr-Sep, until 2pm Oct, 10am, noon & 2pm only Feb & Mar) is only 300m from the Skalní Mlýn car park, yet it is much less crowded. The 30-minute tour covers two massive chambers, one of which hosts music concerts on summer weekends.

OTHER CAVES

The least-visited cave is **Balcarka jeskyně** (☎ 516 444 330; adult/concession 40/20Kč; ☼ 7.30am-3.30pm Tue-Fri, 8.30am-3.15pm Sat & Sun Apr-Sep, 7.30am-3.30pm Tue-Fri, 8.30am-2.30pm Sat & Sun Oct, 9am, 11am & 1pm only Feb & Mar), a 2km walk from Skalní Mlýn (or there are a few buses from Blansko). On the way to Balcarka jeskyně is a turn-off to the upper rim of the Macocha Abyss.

The fourth cave, **Sloupsko-Šošůvské jeskyně** (☎ 516 435 335; adult/concession 70/30Kč or for short tour 50/20Kč; ☼ 8am-3.30pm Apr-Sep, 8.30am-1.30pm Oct, 10am, noon & 1pm only Feb & Mar), is near the village of Sloup, and is also the deepest at 1670m. There are two tours: the longer one lasts 1½ hours and the shorter one an hour.

SLEEPING & EATING

Hotel Skalní Mlýn (☎ 516 418 113; smk@smk.cz; s/d incl breakfast 990/1390Kč; P) Opposite the ticket offices, this is the perfect place to warm up after a trip into the bowels of the earth. The restaurant is also good.

Chata Macocha (☎ 516 444 250; dm 230Kč; P) This summer-only hostel has dorm beds near the Macocha Abyss.

GETTING THERE & AWAY

To get there, take a train (33 a day) to Blansko, then walk over to the adjacent bus station. From May to September there are five regular **ČSAD** (☎ 516 418 610) buses between Blansko (stand No 6) and Skalní Mlýn (10Kč, 10 minutes, 7.40am, 9.35am, 11.40am, 3.10pm and 4.50pm). Note that only the first three will get you there in time for the cave tours. The buses return directly (7.55am, 9.50am, noon, 3.25pm and 5pm).

Off-season, buses run to Skalní Mlýn at 7.40am, 3.10pm and 4.50pm only, returning at 7.55am, 3.25pm and 5pm.

On foot it's 5.3km from Blansko's train station to Skalní Mlýn's car park. To get there turn right across the bridge onto the highway, left at Hotel Morava, and follow the signs to Hotel Skalní Mlýn.

PROSTĚJOV

pop 51,000

Prostějov dates back to a castle built here in 1213. A few hours is plenty to see the few sights.

Orientation & Information

From the adjoining train and bus stations, head straight up Svatoplukova for 800m to the main square, náměstí TG Masaryka.

Next to the town hall on the main square is the **tourist information office** (Informační a turistická kancelář; ☎ 582 329 722; www.mestopv.cz; ☼ 8am-5pm Mon-Fri).

Sights

The remains of the pretty **castle** (zámek; Pernštýnské náměstí 8) are 200m north of the main square, but it was closed for restoration at time of writing.

The **town museum** (muzeum Prostějovska; ☎ 582 344 990; náměstí TG Masaryka; adult/concession 20/10Kč; ☼ 9.30am-noon & 1-5pm Tue-Sun), in the **Old Town Hall** (Stará radnice), features shoes, local history and traditional handicrafts.

František Bílek (1872–1941) painted the Stations of the Cross in the **Cathedral of the Ascension of the Holy Cross** (Chrám Povýšení sv Kříže; Filipcovo náměstí). There are also some striking buildings such as the Art Nouveau **Národní Dům** (Vojáčkovo náměstí), which now houses the **town theatre** (☎ 582 333 390) and the 1910 **villa** (náměstí Padlých hrdinů) of the architect E Králík. Both are a short walk northeast of the central square.

Sleeping & Eating

Grand Hotel (☎ 582 332 311; www.grandhotel.cz; Palackého 3/5; s/d incl breakfast 1200/2100Kč; P 🕱) The plushest place in town has slick rooms with satellite TV.

Other recommendations:

Hotel Avion (☎ 582 330 514; hotel_avion@iol.cz; náměstí E Husserla; s/d incl breakfast 550/950Kč; P) Also has rooms with shared bathroom (s/d 350/600Kč).

Hotel Romže (☎ 582 365 493; www.hotelromze.wz.cz; Olomoucká 264; dm/d 200/500Kč; P) Cheap dorms and basic rooms.

Getting There & Away

Trains link Prostějov with Brno (75Kč, two hours) and Olomouc (30Kč, 30 minutes).

Buses are also frequent to Brno (50Kč, 1½ hours) and to Olomouc (20Kč, 25 minutes).

VYŠKOV

Vyškov, on the Haná river, is worth a visit only if you have a *serious* interest in folk museums. The **tourist office** (informační centrum; ☎ 517 301 312; www.vyskov-mesto.cz; Masarykovo náměstí 1; ☉ 8.30am-5pm Mon-Fri) is on the pretty main square.

The oldest building in town is the Gothic **Archbishop's Chateau** (Arcibiskupský zámek), which now houses a **museum** (muzeum Vyškovska; ☎ 517 348 040; mv@muzeum.vyskov.cz; adult/concession 30/15Kč; ☉ 8am-4pm Mon-Fri, 10am-noon & 2-4pm Sat & Sun) that features an interesting section on the folk traditions of the Haná region, including a beehive made from a tree trunk and a mock-up room from a peasant house. It's behind the town hall and through the car park.

Chalupa U městské brány (☎ 517 341 907; Masarykovo náměstí 21; s/d incl breakfast 650/980Kč), on the main square, has snug rooms and an excellent **restaurant** with wood beams and an open fire.

Getting There & Away

Trains run to/from Brno (40Kč, 40 minutes). Buses travel to Prostějov, Kroměříž and Blansko.

SLAVKOV U BRNA & AROUND

pop 5900

Slavkov (Austerlitz) and its surrounds are almost as significant players in the Napoleonic wars as the little Frenchman himself. As the setting for the pivotal Battle of the Three Emperors in 1805, it was here that Napoleon defeated the combined (and superior) forces of Austrian Emperor Ferdinand I and Russian Tsar Alexander I. For more information see the boxed text p302.

Orientation & Information

From Slavkov's train station, turn left onto the highway, go past the bus station, and continue straight up Palackého náměstí to the chateau. The **tourist information office** (Informační regionální centrum; ☎ 544 220 988; info@austerlitz@infos.cz; Palackého náměstí 1; ☉ 9am-5pm Mon-Fri, 10am-4pm Sat & Sun), under the ramp up to the castle, can help with accommodation.

Sights

Napoleon stayed for several days at **Slavkov Chateau** (zámek Slavkov; ☎ 544 221 204; www.zamek-slavkov.cz; ☉ 9am-6pm Jul-Aug, 9am-5pm Tue-Sun May, Jun & Sep, until 4pm Tue-Sun Apr, Oct & Nov), where the treaty with Austria was signed. Built around 1700 to a design by Martinelli, the chateau was enlarged in the mid-18th century and its rooms adorned with stucco decorations and ceiling murals.

You can take a **tour** (adult/concession 50/30Kč, or in English 85/65Kč) of the chateau, or guide yourself through an attached **exhibition** (expozice; adult/concession 45/25Kč), covering pretty much the whole of the Napoleonic wars, except Austerlitz (for that, you have to go to the Cairn of Peace – see below). From December to March, visits are by reservation only (prices 200% more).

Complete the Austerlitz circuit with a trip to **Pracký kopec**, a hill 12km east of Slavkov where the battle was actually decided. At the site is the **Cairn of Peace** (Mohyla míru; adult/concession 40/20Kč; ☉ 9am-6pm Jul-Aug, until 5pm May, Jun & Sep, 9am-5pm Tue-Sun Apr, 9am-3.30pm Tue-Sun Oct-Mar) honouring those who fell and a small **museum** about the battle.

Unfortunately, Pracký kopec is difficult to reach by public transport and hard to find. You can get a bus from Brno's bus station to Prace (nine a day – ask to get off at the Náves stop), from where it is a 1.6km walk south to the top of the hill. On weekends

BATTLE OF AUSTERLITZ

The battle took place 10km west of Slavkov, around the village of Šlapanice, on 2 December 1805 – the anniversary of Napoleon's coronation as emperor. A day before the battle, Napoleon evacuated the Pracký plateau (Pracký kopec; see Sights p301), hoping that the allies would occupy the site. Allied troops advanced on the French through the fog-filled lowlands the next morning, their plan being to attack the French right flank and cut off supply lines from Vienna. But under the cover of fog Napoleon regrouped and when the fog lifted, counter-attacked, recapturing the plateau. By the afternoon the allies were defeated, suffering losses five times higher than the French. Austria signed a peace treaty and the Russian troops returned home.

The Battle of Austerlitz led to the disintegration of the anti-Napoleon coalition and to a new European political map. It is re-enacted annually in December.

it is better to catch one of the more frequent Brno–Slavkov trains (14km, 10 a day), getting off at Poněetovice and walking the 3.5km southeast through Prace.

Sleeping & Eating

Hotel Sokolský dům (☎ 544 221 103; Palackého náměstí 75; s/d incl breakfast 500/800Kč; P) This pleasant, renovated place is the most popular choice in town and plates up decent Czech specialties in its restaurant below.

Hotel Soult (☎ 544 227 148; Nádražní 909; s/d incl breakfast 450/900Kč) This is opposite the train station and a reasonable backup if Sokolský dům is mobbed.

Hostinec U černého lva (Palackého náměstí; mains 70Kč) This typical inn whips up meaty mains on the main square.

Getting There & Away

Slavkov is 21km east of Brno and easily reached by bus (20Kč, 40 minutes) and train (30Kč, 45 minutes).

PERNŠTEJN

If you've overdosed on effete Renaissance chateaux, here is the antidote: a medieval castle with a capital 'C', discarding gilt edges and carved stonework for hard rock and heavy

metal. Dating from the late-13th century, this beautifully preserved Gothic **fortress** (☎ 566 566 101; hrad.pernstejn@iol.cz; ☼ 9am-5pm Tue-Sun Jul-Aug, until 4pm May, Jun & Sep, 9am-3pm Sat & Sun Apr & Oct), high above the small town of Nedvědice, is one of the Czech Republic's most evocative medieval monuments; a link to a time that has otherwise largely crumbled away. From the 1450s to the 1550s it was enlarged and rebuilt in several stages, as the residence of the leading Moravian noble family of Pernštejn, but the beautiful bare bones of the original castle still shine through.

Among the highlights are the small towers, that were part of the original and solid-looking fortifications, and a smorgasbord of renovated rooms, attics, nooks and crannies. A number of tours are on offer. **Tour A** (adult/concession 65/40Kč; 1hr) takes in the main halls of the castle, **Tour B** (150/100Kč; 1½ hrs) covers the 19th-century living areas, **Tour C** (150/100Kč; 1½ hrs) explores the cellars and attics, and **Tour D** (100Kč) shows off the chapel and Cork Tower. At time of writing, all tours were conducted in Czech and only Tour A had English text.

Sleeping

In Nedvědice there are private rooms; look out for 'Zimmer frei' signs.

Pod hradem (☎ 566 566 638; s/d 350/700Kč; P) This pretty *pension* has a great location at the bottom of the road leading up to the castle, but you can't always find anyone to give you a room.

Pension Barborska (☎ 566 566 317; info@barborska.cz; s/d incl breakfast 450/650Kč; P) Blooming window boxes add character to this friendly place by the village pond.

Getting There & Away

There are regular daily trains from Brno to Nedvědice (35Kč, one hour), with a change to a local train at Tišnov.

Without a car the surest way to Pernštejn from Nedvědice is a 2km walk northwest. There are only three daily buses on weekdays and one on weekends.

TIŠNOV

pop 8500

En route from Brno to Pernštejn is the cross-shaped **Porta Coeli Cistercian Convent** (founded in 1233) in the Tišnov suburb of Předklášteří. The church's beautifully carved, Romanesque/Gothic portal dates from the early 13th century. The convent also houses a small **museum** (muzeum Brněnska; ☎ 549 412 293; adult/concession 30/15Kč; ☿ 9am-noon & 1-5pm Tue-Sun). Tours of the convent cost an extra 40Kč in Czech, or 80Kč in English and keep the same hours as the museum (last tour 4pm).

The convent is on the west side of town, across the Svratka river.

NÁMĚŠŤ NAD OSLAVOU
pop 5100

Náměšť is known for its 13th-century **chateau** (☎ 568 620 319; www.zamek-namest.cz; adult/concession 40/20Kč, or in English 80Kč; ☿ 9am-6pm Tue-Sun Jul-Aug, until 5pm May, Jun & Sep, 9am-4pm Sat & Sun Apr & Oct). Its present Renaissance face, largely the work of architect Leonardo Garvi, dates from the 16th century. Highlights include 24 Renaissance and baroque tapestries, and a library adorned with murals.

There are several cheap accommodation options – contact the **tourist information office** (☎ 568 620 493; fax 568 620 338; Masarykovo náměstí 100). **Zámecký pension** (☎ 568 620 301; holy@zamek-namest.cz; d incl breakfast 800Kč), attached to the chateau, has a flick of aristocratic class and a variety of doubles from ho-hum to hey-ho.

Getting There & Away
Náměšť is 26km west of Brno and is easy to reach by bus (36Kč, 45 minutes). The bus station is 300m east from the main square, and the train station is northeast a few minutes further on.

Regular trains also run to/from Brno (64Kč, one hour) and Třebíč (28Kč, 25 minutes).

MORAVSKÝ KRUMLOV
pop 6000

Despite its idyllic location in the valley of the Rokytná river, Moravský Krumlov would be just another entry on a train timetable if it weren't for Alfons Mucha, who was born in the nearby village of Ivančice in 1860. As it happens, this little village is now home to the artist's *Slav Epic*, arguably the finest work of the nation's finest painter. There isn't much else to see, but these 20 canvasses inject more colour into the nation's history than all the books yet written about it.

Mucha Gallery
The **gallery** (☎ 515 322 789; adult/concession 50/20Kč; ☿ 9am-noon & 1-4pm Tue-Sun Apr-Oct) is housed in a slightly moth-eaten Renaissance chateau 300m off the main square. Inspired by Slav history, Mucha's **Slav Epic** (Slovanská Epoje) is unlike the Art Nouveau style of the artist's Paris posters, and yet retains the same mythic, heavily romanticised quality. They border on science fantasy, full of wild-eyed priests, medieval pageantry and battlefield carnage, all under brooding northern skies. Mucha worked abroad for several years, but returned to his newly independent homeland in 1918 and designed some of its banknotes and stamps. No building other than this one could be found to accommodate these huge paintings, which he worked on between 1912 and 1930.

Sleeping & Eating
Hotel Jednota (☿ 515 322 373; náměstí TG Masaryka 27; s/d 300/500Kč; ℗) It's nothing special, but the basic rooms are fine for getting your head down and there's a passable restaurant.

Getting There & Away
The train station is about 2km from náměstí TG Masaryka, though local buses aren't good about meeting the 11 daily trains that come through from Brno (46Kč, one hour). From Brno six buses a day (two on weekends) stop on Moravský Krumlov's main square (36Kč, one hour).

JIHLAVSKO REGION

Hump-backed hills mark the border between Bohemia and Moravia, an undulating region that runs south from Jihlava the whole way to Austria. It includes the pleasant city of Jihlava and the idyllic town of Telč, as well as the chateau at Jaroměřice nad Rokytnou. Gently hilly and dotted with pretty villages, the area is ideal for cyclists.

JIHLAVA
pop 53,000

A big city among rolling hills, Jihlava has a slightly incongruous position amid the pretty landscapes of this largely rural region. But while heavy industry nips its heels, Jihlava sports a fine historical centre,

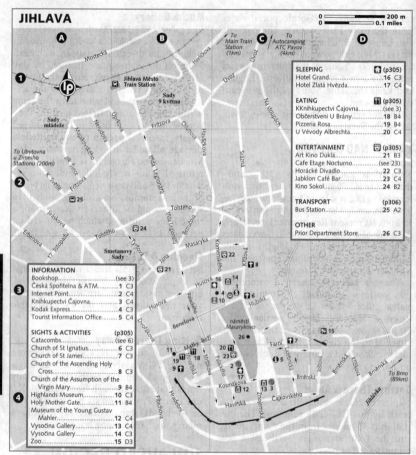

JIHLAVA

SLEEPING	(p305)
Hotel Grand	16 C3
Hotel Zlatá Hvězda	17 C4
EATING	(p305)
KKnihkupectví Čajovna	(see 3)
Občerstvení U Brány	18 B4
Pizzeria Rosa	19 B4
U Vévody Albrechta	20 C4
ENTERTAINMENT	(p305)
Art Kino Dukla	21 B3
Café Etáge Nocturno	(see 23)
Horácké Divadlo	22 C3
Jabklon Café Bar	23 C4
Kino Sokol	24 B2
TRANSPORT	(p306)
Bus Station	25 A2
OTHER	
Prior Department Store	26 C3

INFORMATION	
Bookshop	(see 3)
Česká Spořitelna & ATM	1 C3
Internet Point	2 C4
Knihkupectví Čajovna	3 C4
Kodak Express	4 C4
Tourist Information Office	5 C4
SIGHTS & ACTIVITIES	(p305)
Catacombs	(see 6)
Church of St Ignatius	6 C3
Church of St James	7 C3
Church of the Ascending Holy Cross	8 C3
Church of the Assumption of the Virgin Mary	9 B4
Highlands Museum	10 C3
Holy Mother Gate	11 B4
Museum of the Young Gustav Mahler	12 C4
Vysočina Gallery	13 C4
Vysočina Gallery	14 C3
Zoo	15 D3

including one of the country's largest (36,650 sq metres) town squares – try and ignore the colossal department store. Apart from some photogenic Renaissance façades and crumbling town walls, there's also a good zoo.

Orientation

There are two train stations. The main station (Jihlava hlavní nádraží; for trains to and from Brno, Třebíč and Prague) is 2km north of the centre; take trolleybus A, B or B1 to the main square, náměstí Masarykovo.

The Jihlava město station (for trains to Tábor and České Budějovice) and the bus station (at the corner of Tolstého and Jiráskova) are each a five-minute walk north of the old town.

Information

The **tourist information office** (Turistické informační centrum; ☎ 567 308 034; www.jihlava.cz; náměstí Masraykovo 19; ☻ 8am-5pm Mon-Fri, until noon Sat) arranges accommodation. In July and August it also opens Sunday from 1pm to 5pm.

Česká spořitelna (cnr náměstí Masarykovo & Křížová) has an exchange and ATM.

The **main post office** (cnr náměstí Masarykovo & Komenského) is on the main square. Nearby, **Internet Point** (☎ 800 400 212; 2nd fl, náměstí Masarykovo 37; ☻ 8am-10pm) and **Knihkupectví Cajovna** (☎ 567 312 873; náměstí Masarykovo 21; ☻ 9am-10pm), which is also a bookshop, have Internet access.

Kodak Express (☎ 567 301 250; Komenského 3) has a one-hour service.

Sights

The Gothic **Church of St James** (kostel sv Jakuba), on Jakubské náměstí, has a gilded Renaissance baptismal font, a baroque chapel and the requisite **lookout tower** (adult/concession 20/10Kč; ☺ 10am-1pm & 2-6pm Tue-Sun Jun-Aug). In the 13th-century **Church of the Assumption of the Virgin Mary** (kostel Nanebevzetí Panny Marie), to the west on Minorítská, are some Gothic frescoes and the oldest picture of the town, a 16th-century work showing the defeat of Zikmund Křižanovský z Rokštejna by the local residents in 1402.

In the baroque **Church of St Ignatius** (kostel sv Ignáce; 1689), on náměstí Masarykovo, are an emaciated Christ, some Tepper frescoes on the vaulted ceiling, and a fine main altar. To the left of the church is the entrance to the **catacombs** (historické katakomby; náměstí Masarykovo 64; adult/concession 40/20Kč; ☺ 9am-5pm Jul-Aug, 10am-4pm Apr-Jun & Sep-Oct, 10am-3pm Nov-Dec). Tours are held on the hour except 1pm (minimum three people).

The **Highlands Museum** (Muzeum Vysočiny; ☎ 567 300 091; náměstí Masarykovo 58; adult/child 30/15Kč; ☺ 9am-5pm Tue-Sun) is housed in a late-Gothic villa and includes fine Gothic, Renaissance and baroque interiors, and a display of folk arts and handicrafts.

The **Vysočina Gallery** (Oblastní galerie Vysočiny; adult/concession 25/10Kč; ☺ 9am-5pm Mon-Fri, 10am-4pm Sat & Sun) displays Czech art and sculpture from the 1930s to '60s in two locations: one at Komenského 10, and the other at náměstí Masarykovo 24. Both have the same opening times and admission charges.

At the end of Matky Boží, you can see what remains of the **old town walls**, including the impressive clock tower, the **Holy Mother Gate**, with an archway through to Hradební.

Off the southern end of the square, the **Museum of the Young Gustav Mahler** (Expozice Mladý Gustav Mahler; ☎ 567 309 147; Kosmákova 9; adult/concession 25/10Kč; ☺ 9am-noon & 1-5pm Tue-Fri, from 1pm Sat & Sun Apr-Sep) has a few exhibits relating to the composer's youth.

A real highlight is Jihlava's **zoo** (☎ 567 301 797; Březinovy sady 10; adult/concession 50/30Kč; ☺ 8am-6pm May-Sep, 9am-5pm Apr & Oct, 9am-4pm Nov-Mar), 400m from the main square. Over 400 animals – notably Sumatran tigers, snow leopards and a dozen species of monkeys – are kept in open-air compounds.

Sleeping

Hotel Grand (☎ 567 303 541; info@grandjihlava.cz; Husova 1; s/d incl breakfast 990/1540Kč; ℗) Jihlava's business-style offering has plenty of trimmings, modern-meets-traditional décor and some handy economy rooms (s/d 440/640Kč).

Hotel Zlatá Hvězda (☎ 567 320 782; www.zlatahvezda.cz; náměstí Masarykovo 1096/32; s/d incl breakfast 750/1100Kč) If it's the little things that matter, at least this place makes an effort, with flowers in the rooms, bed and breakfast comfort, and more than the odd smile.

Ubytovna u Zimního Stadionu (☎ 606 190 021; Jiráskova 6; dm 100Kč; ℗) Jiráskova has plenty of cheap hostels (check out Nos 32 and 69 as well).

Autocamping ATC Pavov (☎ 567 210 295; tent/dm per person 70/160Kč; ℗) 4km north of Jihlava, beside the Prague–Brno motorway, this also has a year-round *pension*.

Eating

Knihkupectvi Cajovna (☎ 567 312 873; náměstí Masarykovo 21; snacks 50Kč) This hip ethno-style teahouse oozes incense smells and features scatter cushions, piles of recumbent twentysomethings and decent snacks.

Pizzeria Rosa (☎ 567 300 482; Matky Boží; pizza 85Kč) There's not a whole lot of evidence that Rosa has ever been to the motherland, but the plump pizzas pull a ravenous lunchtime crowd and there's plenty of atmosphere.

Other recommendations:

U Vévody Albrechta (☎ 567 308 074; 1st fl, náměstí Masarykovo 40; mains 70-200Kč) Czech pub décor and hearty local fare.

Občerstveni u Brány (Matky Boží 29; mains 45Kč; ☺ 7.30am-5pm Mon-Fri) A cheap buffet for fly-by diners.

Entertainment

Café Etage Nocturno (☎ 721 639 984; 2nd floor, náměstí Masarykovo 39; ☺ 6pm-2am) Booze plus fish tanks, wicker chairs and oh-so-trendy exposed air vents equals a perennially popular 'soul and funky night bar' (their words, not ours). **Jabklon Café Bar** (☎ 608 811 884), on the next floor down, has live music some nights.

Horácké Divadlo (☎ 567 321 717; Komenskeho 22) Jihlava's swish modern theatre has a regular programme of events.

Kino Sokol (☎ 567 300 801; Tyršova 12) Cinemagoers can see the latest release here. Also try **Art Kino Dukla** (☎ 602 193 918; Jana Masaryka 20).

Getting There & Away

Direct trains run to Brno (80Kč, two hours), Třebíč (64Kč, one hour), Prague (204Kč, 2½ hours) and České Budějovice (162Kč, 2½ hours). Express buses, however, are often quicker and always cheaper: Brno (74Kč, 1½ hours), Prague (84Kč, two hours), Tabor (66Kč, 1½ hours), Telč (32Kč, 30 minutes), Žďár nad Sázavou (38Kč, 1½ hours).

For all bus and train times and prices check www.idos.cz.

ŽĎÁR NAD SÁZAVOU

pop 27,000

Žďár is a bland industrial town, with two hot attractions: the Cistercian Monastery and the Church of St John of Nepomuk (which is a Unesco World Cultural Heritage Site), both by the architect Giovanni Santini. If it weren't for them, it wouldn't be worth getting off the bus.

Orientation & Information

The monastery is 3km north of the adjacent train and bus stations. The central square, náměstí Republiky, is 1km northwest of the stations; follow Nádražní. Local buses pass the monastery from the stations, hourly on weekdays and less frequently on weekends.

Santini Tour (☎ 566 625 808; santini@santini-tour .cz; náměstí Republiky; ☼ 9am-noon & 1-5pm Mon-Fri, until noon Sat), in the Old Town Hall, is central and can help with accommodation. The official tourist office (☎ 566 629 152; itc@zamekzdar.cz; ☼ 9am-5pm Tue-Sun Apr-Sep, 8am-4pm Tue-Sun Oct-Mar) is in the monastery grounds.

Cistercian Monastery

Founded in 1252, the Cistercian Monastery (klášter Cisterciáků; ☼ 9am-5pm Tue-Sun Apr-Sep, 8am-4pm Tue-Sun Oct-Mar) was burned down by the Hussites in 1422. A reconstruction began in 1638, and Giovanni Santini started work here in 1706, though he never completed the project. In it, he attempted to combine the medieval with the baroque in a distinctive dark-and-light style. His Church of the Assumption of the Virgin Mary (kostel Nanebevzetí Panny Marie) contains an altar by Řehoř Thény. The former monastery stables are now a museum devoted to Santini, while another part has an excellent, unique exhibit of historical pianos. You can buy individual tickets to the monastery

(adult/concession 70/35Kč) and the Church of St John of Nepomuk (30/20Kč) or a combined ticket (100/50Kč).

The superb Book Museum (Muzeum knihy; adult/ concession 30/15Kč; ☼ 9am-5pm Tue-Sun Apr-Sep, 8am-4pm Tue-Sun Oct-Mar) on the evolution of writing, calligraphy and printing is also in another part of the monastery.

Church of St John of Nepomuk

A little closer to town, on a hill called Zelená Hora (Green Mountain), is this peculiar but brilliant Santini church (1727) in the shape of a five-pointed star. It's on the Unesco World Cultural Heritage Site list.

According to legend, John of Nepomuk's tongue was cut out for not revealing royal confessions, and he was thrown off Prague's Charles Bridge to his death. Five stars are said to have appeared above the spot where he drowned. Thus the Church of St John of Nepomuk (kostel sv Jana Nepomuckého) is chock-full of 'tongue' motifs, and circles of five stars.

See the above entry, Cistercian Monastery, for times and prices.

Sleeping

Hotel U labutě (☎ 566 622 949; hotelulabute@cbox.cz; náměstí Republiky 70; s/d incl breakfast 450/700Kč) and Hotel Fit (☎ 566 623 508; fax 566 623 761; Horní 30; d incl breakfast 600Kč) offer passable, central rooms.

Getting There & Away

Žďár is on the Brno (110Kč, 1½ hours) to Prague (204Kč, 2½ hours) main line, with about 10 express connections and a few other slower trains a day. There are up to six daily buses to Jihlava (38Kč, 1½ hours).

TELČ

pop 6000

A spot on Unesco's World Heritage List pretty much speaks for itself, but Telč oozes the kind of beauty that provokes sudden outpourings of crass poetry and whimsical diary writing. Barely more than a venerable old square, bordered by covered walkways and watched over by a 16th-century chateau, it is the type of town that gets tourists dreaming about selling their suburban semis and starting a new life in a strange land. Surrounded on three sides by the ponds that used to hold the town's

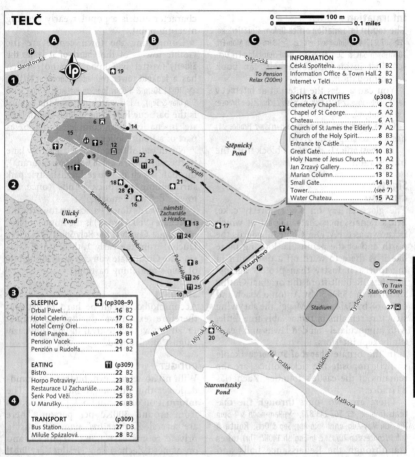

0 — 100 m
0 — 0.1 miles

INFORMATION
Česká Spořitelna.........................1 B2
Information Office & Town Hall.2 B2
Internet v Telči..........................3 B2

SIGHTS & ACTIVITIES (p308)
Cemetery Chapel.......................4 C2
Chapel of St George...................5 A2
Chateau....................................6 A1
Church of St James the Elderly...7 A2
Church of the Holy Spirit............8 B3
Entrance to Castle.....................9 A2
Great Gate..............................10 B3
Holy Name of Jesus Church.....11 A2
Jan Zrzavý Gallery...................12 B2
Marian Column.......................13 B2
Small Gate.............................14 B1
Tower................................(see 7)
Water Chateau.......................15 A2

SLEEPING (pp308–9)
Drbal Pavel...............................16 B2
Hotel Celerin...........................17 C2
Hotel Černý Orel......................18 B2
Hotel Pangea..........................19 B1
Pension Vacek.........................20 C3
Penzión u Rudolfa....................21 B2

EATING (p309)
Bistro.....................................22 B2
Horpo Potraviny......................23 B2
Restaurace U Zachariáše..........24 B2
Šenk Pod Věží.........................25 B3
U Marušky..............................26 B3

TRANSPORT (p309)
Bus Station.............................27 D3
Miluše Spázalová.....................28 B2

SOUTH MORAVIA

secure supply of fish, the historical centre is completely cut off from the more modern section of Telč beyond. A stroll across one of the bridges, therefore, is like taking a wee stride into the Renaissance.

The best time to visit is late July/early August when the town explodes into life during the Prázdniny v Telči folk music festival (www.prazdninyvtelci.ji.cz).

History

Telč was founded in the 14th century by the feudal lords of Hradec as a fortified settlement, with a castle separated from the town by a strong wall. The artificial ponds on each side of Telč provided security and a sure supply of fish. After a fire in 1530,

Lord Zachariáš, then governor of Moravia, ordered the town and castle to be rebuilt in the Renaissance style by Italian masons.

After the death of Zachariáš in 1589, building activity ceased and the complex you see today is largely as it was then. The main square is unmarred by modern constructions, and the **fire hall** (náměstí Zachariáše z Hradce 28) is evidence of local concern to keep it that way.

Orientation

The old centre of Telč, including náměstí Zachariáše z Hradce and the chateau, is nearly surrounded by two ponds. The train and bus stations (one street apart) are 800m southeast of the town centre.

Information

The **tourist information office** (Informační Středisko; ☎ 567 112 407; info@telc-etc.cz; ⏰ 8am-5pm Mon-Fri, 10am-5pm Sat & Sun May-Sep, 8am-5pm Mon-Fri Oct-Apr), just inside the town hall, can book accommodation.

You can access the Internet at **Internet v Telči** (webhouse.cz/telc_folk; náměstí Zachariáše z Hradce; ⏰ 10am-6pm).

Česká spořitelna (náměstí Zachariáše z Hradce 21) has an exchange and ATM.

The **post office** (Staňkova) is a block from the train station.

Sights
CHATEAU

The glacé cherry on a very pretty cake, Telč's Renaissance chateau, part of which is known as the Water Chateau, guards the north end of the peninsula, looking more like it is there to ward off a downturn in the tourist industry than protect against invaders. Rebuilt from the original Gothic structure in 1553–56 by Antonio Vlach and 1566–68 by Baldassare Maggi, the surviving structure remains in remarkably fine fettle, with immaculately tended lawns and beautifully kept interiors.

In the ornate **Chapel of St George** (kaple sv Jiří), opposite the ticket office, are the remains of the castle's founder, Zachariáš z Hradce.

There are two tours through the **chateau** (zámek; ☎ 567 243 821; ⏰ 9am-noon & 1-5pm Tue-Sun May-Aug, until 4pm Apr, Sep & Oct). **Route A** (adult/concession 70/35Kč, in English 140Kč; 1hr) takes you through the Renaissance halls and **Route B** (adult/concession 70/35Kč, in English 140Kč; 45 mins) through the castle apartment rooms. While you're waiting for your guide, visit the local **historical museum** (enter from the chateau courtyard; muzeum vysočiny Jihlava; ☎ 567 243 918; adult/concession 20/10Kč; ⏰ as chateau), with a scale model of Telč in 1895, or the small **Jan Zrzavý Gallery** (galérie Jana Zrzavého; ☎ 567 243 649; adult/concession 30/15Kč; ⏰ as chateau).

OTHER ATTRACTIONS

Telč's stunning town square is bordered on three sides by 16th-century Renaissance houses, built on the ruins of their Gothic predecessors after the 1530 fire. Although it is from another era, the baroque **Marian column** (1717) in the square does not detract from the town's overall character and is a popular early evening meeting point.

Dominating the town centre are the Gothic towers of the **Church of St James the Elderly** (kostel sv Jakuba Staršího), which has a **lookout tower** (věž; adult/concession 15/10Kč; ⏰ 10-11.30am & 1-6pm Tue-Sun Jun-Aug, 1-5pm Sat & Sun May & Sep). Also watching over the square is the baroque **Holy Name of Jesus Church** (kostel Jména Ježíšova), completed in 1667 as part of a Jesuit College.

North out of the square is a narrow lane to the old town's **Small Gate** (Malá brána), through which is a large English-style **park** surrounding the duck ponds (once the town's defensive moat).

Southwards down Palackého towards the **Great Gate** (Velká brána) is the imposing Romanesque **Church of the Holy Spirit** (kostel sv Ducha) from the early 13th century. Outside the Great Gate you can walk along bits of Telč's remaining bastions.

Sleeping

Accommodation can be hard to get and therefore expensive during the annual Prázdniny v Telči festival in late July/early August. Book ahead.

BUDGET

With no hostel in town, budget accommodation is thin on the ground in Telč. The information office can book private rooms from around 300Kč per person. There are several 'Zimmer frei' signs advertising private rooms east along Štěpnická, and on náměstí Zachariáše z Hradce. Try **Drbal Pavel** (☎ 567 243 511; náměstí Zachariáše z Hradce 12; per person 350Kč).

MID-RANGE

Pension Relax (☎ 567 213 126; Pension.relax@post.cz; Na posvátné 29; s/d incl breakfast 430/750Kč) The town's most popular *pension* is a flick east of the centre, but offers a warm welcome and comforts aplenty for those that make the trip.

Pension Vacek (☎ 567 213 099; info@pension vacek.cz; Mlýnská 104; s/d incl breakfast 400/800Kč) This homey little place makes a good backup if Relax is full.

Another place worth trying is **Penzión u Rudolfa** (☎ 567 243 094; náměstí Zachariáše z Hradce 58; s/d 400/800Kč), with *pension* comfort on the main square.

TOP END

Hotel Celerin (☎ 567 243 477; office@hotelcelerin.cz; náměstí Zachariáše z Hradce 1/43; s/d incl breakfast 1400/1600Kč; ✕ 🖭) The rooms in this generally excellent and atmospheric place range from snug traditional to wedding cake Victoriana. Take a look first.

Hotel Černý orel (☎ 567 243 220; www.cernyorel.cz; náměstí Zachariáše z Hradce 7; s/d incl breakfast 1150/1650Kč; ✕ 🖭) This four-star place is disabled-friendly, spacious and – for a town of this size – grandiose.

There is also **Hotel Pangea** (☎ 567 213 122; www.pangea.cz; Na Baště 450; s/d incl breakfast €39/49; 🅿 ✕ 🖭 🖭) which has plenty of facilities but not much character.

Eating

Šenk Pod Věži (☎ 567 243 889; Palackého 116; mains 90-160Kč) Sizzling grills are served up at this perennially lively, traditional-style place. Choose from a lazy terrace out the back, or an atmospheric restaurant inside.

U Marušky (☎ 605 870 854; Palackého; mains 100Kč) Right next door, this is the favoured haunt of Telč's hipper young things, incorporating a vivacious bar-style buzz, with a decent selection of scrumptious eats.

Restaurace U Zachariáše (☎ 567 243 672; náměstí Zachariáše z Hradce; mains 90-200Kč) The terrace here heaves with the tourist crowd, who flock here to tuck into a good selection of Czech and international favourites.

Other recommendations:

Bistro (náměstí Zachariáše z Hradce; mains 45Kč) For supercheap snacks (look for the hamburger sign).

Horpo Potraviny (náměstí Zachariáše z Hradce 65) For supermarket supplies.

Getting There & Away

Frequent buses go from Telč to Jihlava (32Kč, 30 minutes) and Znojmo (90Kč, two hours). Buses from České Budějovice (90Kč, two hours) to Brno (90Kč, two hours) stop at Telč about five times a day. Seven buses a day run to Prague (120Kč, 2½ hours).

Trains from Telč are fairly useless, but do go to Slavonice (40Kč, 40 minutes).

For all bus and train times and prices visit www.idos.cz.

Getting Around

Miluše Spázalová (☎ 567 243 562; náměstí Zachariáše z Hradce 8; per day 150Kč; ☯ 9am-6pm) rents out bikes.

TŘEBÍČ

Pop 40,000

Pollution has scoured the sheen from this industrial city's old centre. Its Jewish ghetto – one of the best preserved in the country – is worth a brief stopover though.

Orientation & Information

The train station is 1km south of the main square, Karlovo náměstí. The bus station is at Komenského náměstí, 500m west of the main square.

The **tourist office** (informační a turistické centrum; ☎ 568 847 070; www.mkstrebic.cz; Karlovo náměstí 53) can book accommodation. **ČSOB** (Karlovo náměstí 21) changes money and has an ATM.

Sights

The castle and former Benedictine Monastery (Klášter benediktínů), around which the town slowly grew, was founded in 1101 and rebuilt shoddily as a **chateau** (zámek; adult/concession 20/10Kč; ☯ 8am-5pm Jul-Aug, 8am-noon & 1-5pm Tue-Sun Apr-Oct, until 4pm Nov-Mar) at the end of the 17th century. Inside, a **museum** (muzeum Vysočiny Třebíč; ☎ 568 840 518) has a small collection of Nativity scenes and pipes.

Also in the complex is the **St Procopius' Basilica** (Bazilika sv Prokopa; ☎ 568 824 692; adult/concession 20/10Kč; ☯ 8-11.30am & 1-5pm Tue-Fri, 1-5pm Sat & Sun May-Sep), with an attractive chancel and carved north portal (Portal Paradisi).

East from the monastery is the former **Jewish ghetto**. The 1639 **Front (Old) Synagogue** (Přední (stará) synagóga; Tiché náměstí) now belongs to the Hussite Church; the **Rear (New) Synagogue** (Zadní (nová) synagóga; ☎ 568 823 005; Subakova 1/44; adult/concession 20/15Kč; ☯ 10am-noon & 1-5pm) has beautifully restored frescoes. The 17th-century **Jewish cemetery** (Židovský hřbitov; admission free; ☯ 8am-6pm), on Hrádek 600m north of the Old Synagogue, is the largest in the country and contains over 11,000 graves, the oldest dating back to 1641.

Sleeping & Eating

Hotel Slavia (☎ 568 848 560; www.hotel-trebic.cz; Karlovo náměstí 5; s/d incl breakfast 500/1200Kč; 🅿) This central, communist-era place is more beast than beauty, but there's a decent restaurant and the rooms are spotless.

Autokemping Poušov (☎ 568 850 641; tent/cottage per person 60/110Kč; 🅿) Situated 2km west of town, and open from May to September, this camp site also has cottages.

SOUTH MORAVIA

Other recommendations:

Penzión u Synagogy (☎ 568 821 665; Subakova 3; s/d incl breakfast 450/650Kč; **P**) Near the Rear Synagogue.

SPŠ Stavební (☎ 568 883 261; Brafova Třída 35; dm 120Kč; **P**) For the cheapest bed in town.

Getting There & Away

Třebíč is on a main line between Brno (88Kč, 1¾ hours) and Jihlava (64Kč, one hour), with about 14 trains a day. There are also buses to Brno (56Kč, 1¼ hours), Jihlava (32Kč, 1¼ hours) and Telč (28Kč, 40 minutes).

JAROMĚŘICE NAD ROKYTNOU

pop 4000

The unassuming small town of Jaroměřice is home to one of Europe's largest baroque chateaux – a typical example of Counter-Reformation architecture in the style fancied by the new nobility, in this case Johann von Questenberg. The visitors come in droves.

A tour of the red-and-white striped **castle** (☎ 568 440 237; zamek_jaromerice@wo.cz; adult/concession 40/20Kč; ☺ 9am-noon & 1-6pm Tue-Sun Jul-Aug, until 5pm May, Jun & Oct, 9am-noon & 1-4pm Sat & Sun Apr & Oct) includes the **Hall of the Forefathers** (Sál předků), with its inlaid wooden ceiling, and the stucco-decorated **Dance Hall** (Taneční sál).

The 18th-century, baroque **St Margaret Church** (kostel sv Markéty), in the castle grounds, boasts a large cupola with a busy fresco by Karel Töpper. The interior can only be seen during services or if you manage to find the caretaker (správce).

In the large French and English-style gardens is a **theatre** where the first Czech opera, *O původu Jaroměřic* (The Origin of Jaroměřice) by František Míča, premiered in 1730.

In August, the chateau hosts the annual **Peter Dvorský International Music Festival** (mezinárodní hudební festival Petra Dvorského). Contact the local **cultural information office** (městské kulturní středisko v Jaroměřicích nad Rokytnou; ☎ 568 440 132; kulturni_stredisko@iol.cz; Komenského 1029) for details.

Sleeping

Opera Hotel (☎ 568 440 230; Komenského náměstí 996; s/d incl breakfast 450/710Kč) This is one of the few options in town, but offers spacious rooms with shower and TV.

Getting There & Away

Jaroměřice, 14km south of Třebíč, is best reached by bus. There are up to five buses a day from Brno (64Kč, 1¾ hours), and 12 from Třebíč (15Kč, 20 minutes) and Moravské Budějovice (13Kč, 15 minutes).

The train station is 2km away in the village of Popovice.

MORAVSKÉ BUDĚJOVICE

Rather less substantial than České Budějovice (its Bohemian counterpart), this small town is best known for its **museum of vanishing and past handicrafts** (adult/concession 40/20Kč; ☺ 9am-5pm Tue-Sun May-Aug), featuring mock-ups of various traditional workshops. Part of the museum is in the town chateau and part in the former butchers' stalls (masné krámy, 1839).

From here, regular trains run to Znojmo (52Kč, 45 minutes).

SOUTH MORAVIAN BORDERLANDS

This is a lowland agricultural and light-industrial region, running along the Austrian border from Znojmo to Břeclav. From the Middle Ages until the end of WWII, much of the borderlands were owned by the Lichtenstein family, who built most of the castles and churches here. Its highlights include the chateaux at Lednice and Vranov, and the small, handsome town of Mikulov.

The region was once home to quite a large German-speaking minority. They were expelled after WWII, leaving a legacy of tidy, prosperous-looking villages. Among Czechs the borderlands are famous for a local delicacy, Znojmo pickled gherkins (Znojemské sladkokyselé okurky). The borderlands also produce excellent wines, the region around Mikulov offering some of the best.

Large parts of southeast Moravia are fairly flat and ideal for cycling. Between Lednice and Valtice is one of the most appealing areas.

ZNOJMO

pop 37,000

A big town with the enduring heart of a village, Znojmo has busy streets and quiet corners in equal measure. On one of the main arteries into Austria, many visitors see little more of Znojmo than its name on a signpost, but the slow-moving centre has a charm all of its own, with a decent spread of grand religious buildings and one of the nation's oldest Romanesque structures.

Orientation

The bus and train stations are 800m from the main square, Masarykovo náměstí. From the bus station go up Tovární, turn left at náměstí Republiky, then right onto Vídeňská. From the train station, walk up 17 listopadu and, at the roundabout (Mariánské náměstí), veer left onto Pontassievská.

Information

The **tourist information office** (turistické informační centrum; ☎ 515 222 552; tic@beseda.znojmo.cz; Obroková 10; ☯ 8am-6pm Mon-Fri, 9am-5pm Sat) also books accommodation. It closes on Saturday afternoon during the winter (October to April).

A second office, next door in the **Town Hall Tower** (Radniční věž; ☎ 515 216 297; Obroková 12; ☯ 9am-1pm & 2-6pm Mon-Fri, until 5pm Sat & Sun) books theatre tickets. It closes on Saturday afternoon and Sunday during the winter (October to April).

Česká spořitelna (Masarykovo náměstí 2) and **Raiffeisenbank** (Obroková 15) exchange money and have ATMs.

The **post office** (Horni náměstí) is north of the centre and there is Internet access (and good vegetarian food) at the groovy **Na Věčnosti** (☎ 515 221 814; Velka Mikulášská 11).

Sights
MASARYKOVO NÁMĚSTÍ & AROUND

The **South Moravian Museum** (Jihomoravské muzeum; ☎ 515 226 529; adult/concession 20/10Kč; Masarykovo náměstí 11; ☯ 10am-6pm Tue-Sat) is on the main square, inside the House of Art (dům umění). The collection includes Czech religious icons, sculpture and temporary art exhibitions. There's another branch at Václavské náměstí (see Other Squares, next).

In the southern part of the square are the **Capuchin Monastery** (Kapucínský klášter) and **Church of St John the Baptist** (kostel sv Jana Křtitele).

North of the square on Obroková looms the handsome and scalable **Town Hall Tower** (Radniční věž; adult/concession 20/10Kč; ☯ 9am-1pm & 2-6pm Mon-Fri, until 5pm Sat & Sun), 66m tall and one of Moravia's best examples of late-Gothic architecture (circa 1448).

Continue along Obroková, then right on Kramářská and through the arch to the old **Chicken Market** (Slepičí třída); at No 2 is the entrance to the **Znojmo Catacombs** (Znojemské podzemí; ☎ 515 221 342; adult/concession 40/20Kč; ☯ 9am-5pm Jul-Aug, until 4pm May, Jun & Sep, 10am-4pm Mon-Sat Apr, 10am-4pm Sat only Oct). In the 14th century the town's cellars were linked by some 27km of tunnels, which were used for storage and defence. These are they.

East on Kramářská is the 13th-century **Church of the Holy Cross** (kostel sv Kříže), part of an active Dominican monastery. The early-Gothic church received a baroque face-lift in the 1780s.

OTHER SQUARES

North of Horní náměstí, via Divišovo náměstí, is Jezuitské náměstí and the Jesuit **Church of St Michael** (kostel sv Michala), a 'baroquefied' Romanesque church at the highest point of the old town.

From here Veselá leads south to Václavské náměstí, where a right turn into Přemyslovců takes you to a former Minorite Monastery, now a branch of the **South Moravian Museum** (Jihomoravské muzeum; ☎ 515 224 961; Václavské náměstí 6; adult/concession 20/10Kč; ☯ 10am-5pm Tue-Sun May-Aug, 9am-6pm Mon-Fri Oct-Apr) with exhibits of crafts and trades, geology, archaeology and oriental weapons.

ST CATHERINE ROTUNDA

The 11th-century **Rotunda of Our Lady and St Catherine** (rotunda Panny Marie a sv Kateřiny; ☎ 515 222 311; admission 90Kč; ☯ 10.15am-5.15pm Tue-Sun Jun-Sep, Sat & Sun only May), one of the republic's oldest Romanesque structures, and the remains of **Znojmo Castle** (☎ 515 222 311; adult/concession 40/20Kč; ☯ 10am-6pm Tue-Sun Jun-Sep, Sat & Sun only May) are along a scenic path that follows the old city walls from the dead-end street of Přemyslovců. On weekends you can get here from Václavské náměstí down Hradní, through the **brewery** (pivovar; closed to the public). Both sites are visited as part of a tour, but the rotunda is only accessible (for a maximum of 15 minutes) when climactic conditions are right. The last tour of the castle is at 5pm.

CHURCH OF ST NICHOLAS

From Hradní take Velká Františkánská to Klácelova and turn right into náměstí Mikulášské. Ahead is the **Church of St Nicholas** (kostel sv Mikuláše), once Romanesque but

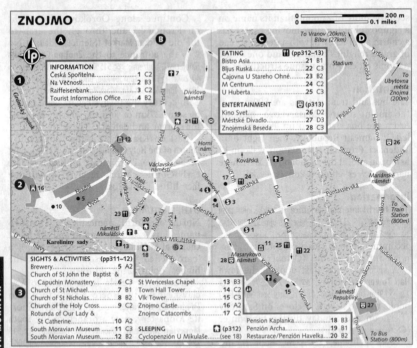

ZNOJMO

0 _____ 200 m
0 _____ 0.1 miles

To Vranov (20km);
Bítov (27km)

INFORMATION
Česká Spořitelna............................1 C2
Na Věcnosti..................................2 B3
Raiffeisenbank...............................3 C2
Tourist Information Office........4 B2

EATING   (pp312–13)
Bistro Asia....................................21 B1
Bljus Ruská...................................22 C3
Čajovna U Stareho Ohné........23 B2
M Centrum....................................24 C2
U Huberta.....................................25 C3

ENTERTAINMENT   (p313)
Kino Svet......................................26 D2
Městské Divadlo.......................27 D3
Znojemská Beseda....................28 C3

SIGHTS & ACTIVITIES   (pp311–12)
Brewery...5 A2
Church of St John the Baptist &
  Capuchin Monastery.............6 C3
Church of St Michael..................7 B1
Church of St Nicholas.................8 B2
Church of the Holy Cross.........9 C2
Rotunda of Our Lady &
  St Catherine.............................10 A2
South Moravian Museum.......11 C3
South Moravian Museum........12 B2

St Wenceslas Chapel................13 B3
Town Hall Tower........................14 C2
Vlk Tower.....................................15 C3
Znojmo Castle...........................16 A2
Znojmo Catacombs..................17 C2

SLEEPING   (p312)
Cyclopenzión U Mikuláše.......(see 18)

Pension Kaplanka.....................18 B3
Penzión Archa............................19 B1
Restaurace/Penzión Havelka...20 B2

To
Ubytovna
města
Znojma
(200m)

To
Train
Station
(800m)

To Bus
Station (800m)

Divišovo
náměstí

Horní
nám.

Václavské
náměstí

náměstí
Mikulášské

Karolíniny sady

Masarykovo
náměstí

náměstí
Republiky

---

rebuilt as the present monumental Gothic structure.

In a side chapel near the entrance is the so-called **'Bread Madonna'**. According to legend, during the Thirty Years' War a box beneath this image was always found to be full of food, no matter how much was removed. Beside the church is the Orthodox **St Wenceslas Chapel** (kaple sv Václava).

Sleeping
The tourist office books private rooms from 300Kč per person.

BUDGET
Cyclopenzión U Mikuláše (☎ 515 220 856; Mikulášské náměstí 8; s/d 200/400Kč) In a serene location, away from the fray, this has basic beds above a cellar-style pub.

MID-RANGE
Pension Kaplanka (☎ 515 242 905; aqua200@volny.cz; U branky 6; s/d 200/400Kč; P) This old white-washed place, with wooden walkways and dreamy vistas, has a variety of rooms from so-so to respectable mid-range (prices

increase accordingly). The garden's perfect for sampling the local vino.

Penzión Archa (☎ 515 225 062; archa@tiscali.cz; Vlkova 4; d 700Kč) The dodgy awning slightly detracts from the olde-worlde atmosphere of this central place, but the rooms are cosy and there's lots of snug, dark-wood décor.

Restaurace/Penzión Havelka (☎ 515 220 138; Mikulášské náměstí 3; d incl breakfast 700Kč) In the shadow of the church, this immaculate *pension* opts for soda-white, holier-than-thou décor – and a Madonna in the garden.

Eating
U Huberta (☎ 515 221 102; Dolní Česká; mains 60-150Kč) This broody eatery puts a 1950s spin on the hunting lodge look, but the Czech food reels in crowds of locals. It also has **rooms** (s/d 450/650Kč).

Bljus Ruská (☎ 515 260 782; Dolní Česká; mains 80-200Kč) It seems strange that Russian food still has a market in the Czech Republic, but a plate of the borscht here goes some of the way towards explaining why it does.

Čajovna U Stareho Ohné (☎ 605 803 702; Staré Město 1; ☻ 3-10pm Mon-Sat) This mellow café

The town hall (p272) and the Marian plague column (p274), Olomouc

Astronomical clock (p272), Olomouc

Detail from the House of Four Mamlases (p294), Brno

Rich sgraffito decoration on house, Telč (p306)

Previous Page:
Statue on Sv Marketa fountain, Telč

mixes one part Zen monastery, two parts teahouse and a portion of fudge brownie to create an antidote to sightseeing fatigue.

Other recommendations:

Restaurace Country (☎ 602 549 759; Masarykovo náměstí 22; mains 90-150Kč) For alfresco steak and ribs.

Bistro Asia (Divišovo náměstí 2; mains 30-45Kč) For cheap Asian eats.

M Centrum (Slepiči třída 7) A supermarket below, a cheap buffet above.

Entertainment

Plays are staged at the **Městské Divadlo** (náměstí Republiky 20) and **Znojemská Beseda** (Masarykovo náměstí 22). For tickets and schedules, visit the Town Hall **tourist information office** (☎ 515 216 297; Obroková 12; ⏰ 9am-1pm & 2-6pm Mon-Fri, until 5pm Sat & Sun).

Kino Svet (☎ 515 224 034; www.illusion.cz; Havlíčkova 7) This cinema shows the latest Hollywood releases.

Znojemský Vinný Sklep (☎ 515 261 872; Horní náměstí 20) This cellar bar is the place to try and buy regional wines.

Na Věčnosti (☎ 515 221 814; Velka Mikulášská 11) A nightly club kicks off here, below the Internet café (see Information p311).

Getting There & Away

Direct buses run to Brno (45 Kč, one hour) and Jihlava (60Kč, 1¾ hours) about five times a day. Two buses also travel to/from Prague (150Kč, three hours). Locally, regular buses go to Moravský Krumlov (40Kč, one hour).

Frequent direct trains run daily to Brno (110Kč, two hours); fewer service Jihlava (120Kč, two hours).

For all bus and train times and prices visit www.idos.cz.

VRANOV NAD DYJÍ

pop 900

West of Znojmo, appearing to rise right out of the plain, is beautiful Vranov Chateau. Closer up you see that it sits atop a cliff over the Dyje river. The chateau can be reached across a bridge, about 1km uphill from the quiet town. See Castles & Chateaux p76 for a full description.

Sleeping & Eating

The **tourist office** (☎ 515 296 285; infocentrumvnd@ volny.cz; Náměstí 47; ⏰ 9am-5pm Mon-Fri, 9am-3pm Sat & Sun Jul-Aug, Mon-Fri only Sep-Jun) can help with private rooms and hostel beds.

Penzión Autokemp U Jelena (☎ 515 224 596; Zámecká 250; dm 160Kč) This is the best, most basic bet, with cheap beds in no-frills surrounds.

Zámecký Hotel (☎ 515 296 101; www.zamecky hotel.cz; s/d incl breakfast 700/1000Kč) Four-star, disabled-friendly and immaculate, this is Vranov's plushest offering – apart from the chateau that is.

Getting There & Away

There are up to nine daily bus connections from Znojmo, 20km away. In July and August only, two daily buses run the 26km to and from Bítov.

BÍTOV

pop 400

The best thing about going to Bitov is the getting there. Surrounded by thickly wooded hills and set above the pea green Dyje river, Bítov has a truly photogenic setting. The original 11th-century **castle** (☎ 515 294 622; bitov@pambr.cz; ⏰ 9am-noon & 1-6pm Tue-Sun Jul-Aug, until 5pm May, Jun & Sep, until 4pm Sat & Sun Apr & Oct) was rebuilt in early-Gothic style, and extended during the 15th to 17th centuries. There are two tours. The first (adult/concession 65/45Kč) takes in the palace, while the second (85/50Kč) lingers over the armoury. Tours in English cost twice as much.

The castle is 3km northwest of Bítov village, and unless you have your own wheels, you must walk (follow the road north from the main square, past Hotel Bítov). If you're driving from Znojmo, don't be fooled by the derelict ruins of **Kornštejn Castle**, a few kilometres southwest of Bítov village; continue past them to Bítov.

Sleeping

Pension U Tesařů (☎ 515 294 616; s/d incl breakfast 400/600Kč; P) This pretty place in the centre of the village has a popular restaurant and tidy rooms.

Autokemping Bítov Horka (☎ 603 958 153; tent/dm per person 60/120Kč; P) Beside the castle near the lake, this is open from June through September and also has hostel accommodation.

Getting There & Away

Buses are infrequent from Znojmo and Jihlava. The best connection is from the train station at Šumná, which is serviced by 13 trains from Znojmo, and five from Jihlava.

SOUTH MORAVIA

MIKULOV
pop 7700

Even a nasty dose of 'pretty village fatigue' can't detract from Mikulov's irresistible chocolate-box charm. Jutting out of the flat surrounding plains on the back of a rocky hillside, the town, topped with its imposing chateau, fully deserves every one of the whimsical travel writing clichés it inevitably generates.

The remains of Mikulov's once thriving Jewish quarter make a fascinating diversion for those that have had their fill of its pretti-fied baroque and Renaissance façades.

Orientation

To get into town from the train station, turn right onto 28 října, left onto Nádražní, and right onto Hraničářu to Piaristů. The bus station is a bit closer to town, on the corner of Piaristů and 28 října.

Information

The **tourist information office** (turistické informační centrum; ☎ 519 510 855; www.mikulov.cz; Náměstí 30; ⏰ 8am-6pm Mon-Fri, 9am-6pm Sat & Sun Jun-Sep,

8.30am-noon & 1-5pm Mon-Fri Oct-May) organises tours and accommodation. **NDC** (☎ 519 511 759; Náměstí 32; ⏰ 8.30am-noon & 1-5.30pm Mon-Fri) has Internet access.

Česká spořitelna (Náměstí 19) has an exchange desk and ATM.

The **post office** (Česká 7) is northeast of the main square.

Sights
CHATEAU

A fortified Slav settlement once stood here, but the present walls and towers are part of a 13th-century castle. The heavy baroque renovations were the work of the Dietrichstein family, who owned it from 1575 until 1945. The **chateau** (☎ 519 510 255; adult/concession 40/20Kč; ⏰ 9am-5pm Tue-Sun May-Sep, until 4pm Apr & Oct) was burned down by the Germans in February 1945, and has been painstakingly restored.

A chateau **museum** (included in price) includes exhibits on folk traditions and winemaking. In the cellar is the largest wine barrel in central Europe, made by Kryštof Secht of Brno in 1643. The barrel has a capacity of 101,000L, though it's now suffering from dry rot.

Other Attractions

The 15th-century **synagogue** (synagóga; ☎ 519 510 255; Husova 11; adult/concession 20/10Kč; ⏰ 1-5pm

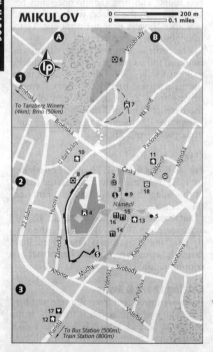

Tue-Sun 18 May-30 Sep) has background on the local Jewish quarter. The **Jewish Cemetery** (Židovský hřbitov; adult/concession 20/10Kč; 9am-5pm Mon-Fri Jul-Aug), founded in the 15th century, is off Brněnská. There are tours every half-hour.

An 'instructive trail' now runs through the Jewish quarter, with information plaques in English. You can pick it up at the end of Husova near Alfonse Muchy. Above the Jewish quarter is **Goat Hill** (Kozí Hrádek) topped with a 15th-century **lookout tower** (adult/concession 5/3Kč; 9am-6pm Apr-Sep).

The town's main square, called simply Náměstí, has many houses of interest, including the **town hall** at No 1 and the sgraffitoed **Restaurace Alfa** (see Eating below) at No 27. At No 5 is the **Dietrichstein Burial Vault** (Dietrichštejnská hrobka; adult/concession 30/15Kč; 9am-5pm Tue-Sun Apr-Oct) with guided tours available.

There is some good **hiking** to be had in the nearby **Pavlovské Hills** (Pavlovské vrchy), while wine lovers can visit **Tanzberg's Bavory Winery** (Vinařství Bavory; ☎ 519 500 040; www.tanzberg.cz), 4km north of Mikulov (on the Brno road), in the village of Bavory (organise visits in advance).

Sleeping

Hotel Rohatý Krokodýl (☎ 519 510 692; rohaty.krokod yl@worldonline.cz; Husova 8; s/d incl breakfast 655/1200Kč;) A good dose of old school swank makes this the town's plushest option.

Pension Prima (☎ 519 511 793; fax 519 510 383; Piaristů 9; s/d 400/600Kč;) Plain, comfortable rooms are available here above an atmospheric, traditional-style pub.

Pension Moravia Centrum (☎ 519 511 644; moravia@pension.com; Poštovní 1; d 700Kč) The location's a bit grey, but this cheerful yellow place has blooming window boxes and a spotless interior.

Ubytovna Národní dům (☎ 519 510 579; Náměstí 9; dm 150Kč) Reception for this central hostel is downstairs in the Admiral Herna. There's one double or plenty of dorm beds.

Eating & Drinking

Restaurace Alfa (☎ 519 510 877; Náměstí 27; mains 90-220Kč) Although housed in the square's most spectacular confection, the interior here is a bit of a letdown. The game specialities are good though, culminating in their *pièce de résistance*, the *Lichtenstein Fleishmix*.

Petit Café (Náměstí 27; crepes 30Kč) Through an archway to the left of Alfa, this courtyard café attracts Mikulov's younger set with its tip-top crepes and coffees.

Party Servis (Náměstí 20) It doesn't even have a name, but this little place is a good spot for cheap breakfasts.

O'Hara (Piaristů 8) The Guinness doesn't travel well (they always say that), but this lively bar has plenty of Irish bric-a-brac and all the usual *craic*.

U Devatero Řemesel (Piaristů 9) Just next door through the archway, this pub has a beer garden and seems to get its ornaments from Czech, rather than Irish, junk shops.

Entertainment

Kino Hvezda Mikulov (Česká) The local cinema shows films on Friday and Saturday. Check with the tourist office for details.

Getting There & Away

There are eight daily trains from Znojmo (64Kč, one hour) and Břeclav (34Kč, 30 minutes) which have direct connections from Brno and Bratislava. Buses are faster from Lednice (24Kč, 30 minutes) and Brno (46Kč, 1¼ hours).

VALTICE

pop 3600

Valtice lies between Břeclav and Mikulov in the heart of Moravia's prime wine region. The town and its chateau were one of the main residences of the Lichtenstein family, who owned it for five-and-a-half centuries. This powerful aristocratic family had almost 100 estates in Moravia, many of which were confiscated from the Protestant Czech Estates when they lost the Battle of the White Mountain in 1620.

Valtice and Lednice are known in the Czech Republic as Lednicko-valtický areál, and the area that encompasses both towns was declared a Unesco World Cultural Heritage Site in 1997 as the most architecturally valuable region in the country.

Orientation & Information

The train station is on the northern edge of town, on the road to Lednice. Buses stop on the main road, where it meets náměstí Svobody. The **tourist information office** (turistické informační centrum; ☎ 519 352 978; www.radnice -valtice.cz; náměstí Svobody 4; 8.30am-12.30pm &

1-5pm Apr-Sep, 7am-3.30pm Mon-Fri Oct-Mar) is on the main square below the chateau.

Sights

The 12th-century **castle** (☎ 519 352 680; adult/concession 50/30Kč; ☺ 9am-noon & 1-5pm Tue-Sun May-Aug, until 4pm Apr, Sep & Oct), on náměstí Svobody, has had face-lifts over the years, and is now recognised as one of the country's finest baroque structures, with work by JB Fischer von Erlach and the Italian architect Domenico Martinelli.

The chateau tour (in Czech with English text) lingers over all the belongings and furnishings left behind when the Lichtensteins fled from the advancing Soviet army in 1945. Of interest are the walls themselves, plastered with 7.5kg of gold. **Vinotéka Vinum Bonum** (☎ 519 352 083), in the chateau, is the place to buy and try local wines.

In front of the chateau is the **Church of the Assumption of the Virgin Mary** (kostel Nanebevzetí Panny Marie) with a Rubens painting behind the main altar.

Next to the tourist office is an interesting (for agriculturalists) **Agricultural Museum** (Národní Zemědělské Muzeum v Praze; adult/concession 20/10Kč; ☺ 9am-4.30pm Tue-Sun Apr-Oct).

Festivals & Events

In July each year, Valtice holds a **Baroque Music Festival** (Zámecké barokní léto; www.radnice-valtice.cz) in many parts of the chateau, complete with a party and fireworks.

Sleeping & Eating

Hotel Hubertus (☎ 627 352 537; hubertusvaltice@email.cz; s/d incl breakfast 1000/1200Kč) The glamour of this place right inside the castle is a little sullied by some frumpy 1950s décor. The location, however, is unbeatable.

Other recommendations:

Penzión Prinz (☎ 519 352 869; prinz@valtice.cz; náměstí Svobody; s/d incl breakfast 600/1000Kč) Colourful, comfortable and cosy.

Vinařský Dům (☎ 519 352 816; náměstí Svobody; mains 90-120Kč) Atmospheric Czech catering.

Getting There & Away

There are regular trains to Mikulov (22Kč, 15 minutes) and Břeclav (22Kč, 15 minutes) with connections to Brno and Zlín. From Mikulov the train continues to Znojmo. There are up to seven buses a day to Lednice (12Kč, 15 minutes).

LEDNICE

pop 2400

It's frigid by name (*lednice* means 'ice-box' in Czech), but this little town literally vibrates with tourists come summer, when crowds flock here to see one of the country's most popular chateaux.

The **information centre** (informační centrum; ☎ 519 340 986; www.lednice.cz; Zámecké náměstí 68; ☺ 9-11am noon-5pm Mon-Fri, 10am-5pm Sat & Sun Apr-Oct) is on the main square.

Sights

Lednice's biggest (well actually its only) drawcard is its ostentatious, 1856 neo-Gothic **chateau** (☎ 519 340 128; szlednice@iol.cz; ☺ 9am-noon & 1-5pm Tue-Sun May-Aug, until 4pm Sep, until 3pm Sat & Sun Apr & Oct) by J Wingelmüller. The Lichtensteins held it from 1582 until 1945, but now the chateau is pretty much in the hands of the visitors queuing up to take one of the tours. There are two to choose from: **Tour 1** (adult/concession 60/30Kč, 45 mins) takes you through a selection of the major rooms, while **Tour 2** (100/50Kč, 45 mins) concentrates on the Lichenstein apartments. There is a 50Kč supplement for tours in a foreign language.

To the right is a **greenhouse** (skleník; adult/concession 40/20Kč) with a collection of exotic flora. The chateau's extensive **gardens** (☺ 5am-11pm May-Sep, 6am-8pm Oct-Apr), complete with lakes and the odd pavilion, are excellent for long summer walks. A highlight is the Turkish-style **minaret** (adult/concession 10/5Kč).

Sleeping & Eating

The information centre can help with bookings for private rooms and hostel beds (from 185Kč per person).

Pension Onyx (☎ 519 340 068; fax 519 340 174; Nejdecká 176; s/d 360/500Kč) Near car park 1, this features a heaving restaurant, spit roasts and decent rooms.

My Hotel (☎ 519 340 135; 21 Dubna 657; d incl breakfast 1995Kč; 🅿 ⊠ 🐾) Grand but soulless, this is the choice for creature comfort cravers.

Apollo (☎ 519 340 414; tent/bungalow per person 60/110Kč; 🅿) 2km south of Lednice on the road to Břeclav, opposite Mlýnský rybník, this camp site opens May to mid-September and has four- and five-bed bungalows.

There is a supermarket on the main square.

Getting There & Away

The train station is in the southern part of town, on the road to Valtice, but buses to Breclav (12Kč, 20 minutes) and Valtice (12Kč, 15 minutes) are more convenient.

AROUND LEDNICE

The flat region around Lednice is fairly easy to explore on foot or by bicycle (though you will struggle to hire a bike nearby). If you can get hold of SHOCart's hiking map *Turistická mapa – Břeclavsko, Pálava* (1:50,000), or its cycling map *Cykloturistická mapa – Pálava, Lednicko-valtický areál* (1:75,000), you can spend an interesting day or two exploring some of the smaller scattered chateaux, temples and pavilions that the Lichtensteins built around Lednice and beyond.

Just over 2km east of Lednice, on a green- or yellow-marked trail through forests and meadows, is the rarely visited but picturesque **Janův Castle** (Janův hrad; adult/concession 40/20Kč; 🕙 9am-5pm Tue-Sun May-Sep, until 4pm Sat & Sun Apr & Oct).

Most of the other buildings can be visited on a red-marked trail south from Lednice. Past the Apollo camping ground, south of Mlýnský rybník, are the **Apollo Temple** (Apollónův chrám; 1817) and the **Nový dvůr Stables** (1890).

Further on, a yellow trail digresses to **Hlohovec** and **Hraniční Chateau** (Hraniční zámek; 1816). On a rise in the southern part of Hlohovec village there are several **wine cellars**, where you can try the local product.

From Hlohovec take the yellow trail joining the dead-straight Valtice–Lednice road to return to Lednice.

MORAVSKÉ SLOVÁCKO REGION

Moravia is at its most colourful in its traditional folk culture – and this is its epicentre. Come summer, when locals don traditional costume to celebrate the region's festival season, the southeastern corner of Moravia erupts in a whirlwind of music, dance and merriment, amounting to one of the most vivid expressions of regional identity seen anywhere in Europe.

Culturally, the inhabitants of this region, which roughly fills the gap between the Chřiby hills (southeast of Brno) and the White Carpathians (over the border in western Slovakia), are neither Moravian nor Slovak, but something in between, drawing on influences and traditions from both sides of the physical divide.

And so the region's special flavour arises not only from a mild climate (incidentally favouring production of the republic's best wine), but also from the character of the people, who seem to have an almost institutionalised proclivity for the arts. Be it the clothes that are worn, the wine that is drunk, the songs that are sung or the houses that are built, the communities of Moravské Slovácko appear to add a little bit of art into every facet of daily life.

Folk dress, heavily decorated with embroidery and lace, includes a head covering and dress for women, hat, shirt (and sometimes a waistcoat) and trousers for men, and boots or leather thongs for both genders. These often differ according to the age of the wearer.

Some of the houses in many villages are still painted in traditional white with a blue band around the bottom, many embellished with painted flowers or birds. Good souvenirs include the famous local pottery, often decorated with floral and other designs, as well as embroidery and woodcarvings.

Wine Cellars

The region's distinctive wine cellars or *vinné sklepy* are generally open for tastings from mid-May through to late September. In places such as Petrov (3km southwest of Strážnice), where they are called *plže* instead of *vinné sklepy*, they are partially underground; in Vlčnov they are more like huts *(vinařské búdy)*.

In some villages wine cellars constitute virtually a separate village, such as at Raštíkovice, where they are north of the village, or at Prušánky. Normally they are within the village boundaries.

Many wine cellars have seating for eager tasters, but take your own containers if you're keen to buy.

Unfortunately, buses around these villages (except to Petrov) are erratic.

Festivals & Events

The best time to see folk dress, and to hear the local music is during a regional festival.

The following are some major ones (more details are given under Strážnice, Blatnice and Vlčnov in this section):

Hluk – Dolňácké festival First weekend of July every four years (next in 2005).

Kyjov – Kyjovsko summer festival On a weekend in mid-August every four years (next in 2007).

Strážnice – International Folk Festival Last weekend in June.

Velká nad Veličkou – Horňácko festival Folk music and dance, on a weekend in the second half of July.

Vlčnov – Ride of the Kings Last weekend of May.

STRÁŽNICE

pop 6000

Strážnice comes into its own during the annual International Folk Festival, one of the best attended in the region. Outside the festival whirlwind, the town is also home to an excellent *skansen*, but has little else of interest. It is best visited as a day trip from Uherské Hradiště.

Orientation

The train and bus stations are near the main square, Předměstí; walk straight out of the train station, turn right onto the main road and follow it for 200m before turning left.

Information

Irra travel agency (☎ 518 332 184; Předměstí 388; 8am-5.30pm Mon-Fri) doubles as the tourist information office.

Česká spořitelna, with exchange desk and ATM, is nearby.

Sights & Activities

Only two of the Renaissance town gates are left from the town's defensive wall. The originally Gothic castle (1261-64) was rebuilt as a neo-Renaissance **chateau** in the mid-19th century, and today it's a **museum** (☎ 518 332 132; adult/concession 35/20Kč; 9am-5pm Tue-Sun Jul-Aug, until 4pm May, Jun, Sep & Oct) which includes good displays on the folk culture of the Slovácko region. From Předměstí walk north on kostelní, turn right and cross náměstí Svobody to Rybářská, and go left up Bzenecka.

Across the road and slightly closer to town is the **skansen** (☎ 518 332 132; Bzenecká 671; adult/concession 40/20Kč; 9am-5pm Tue-Sun Jul-Aug, until 4pm May, Jun, Sep & Oct), with a large collection of Slovácko buildings from the last century, including smithies, wineries

and colourfully decorated beehives. Most houses are furnished.

Půjčovna Lodí Strážnice (☎ 603 371 350; antos .petr@worldonline.cz) hires out canoes (100Kč per hour) and organises boat tours (adult/concession 80/40Kč). They are by the bridge on Rybářská, en route to the chateau.

Festivals & Events

The Strážnice three-day **International Folk Festival** was the first such festival held in the Czech Republic, back in 1945. It gave a major boost to the preservation of traditional culture.

Most of the festivities go on in the chateau's park, including open-air stage performances and impromptu jams, and food stalls with plenty of booze. The entry fee into the park is 120Kč per day or 220Kč for three days. One of the highlights is a procession from the town's main square to the chateau's garden.

Sleeping & Eating

Autokempink Strážnice (☎ 518 332 037; fax 518 332 041; Bzenecká 1533; tent/hut per person 70/110Kč; P) Near the chateau, this also has rooms, bungalows and a buffet – book ahead around festival time. It's open May to October.

Strážnice-Flag (☎ 518 332 059; www.flag.cz; Předměstí 3; s/d 810/1000Kč) It's a bit of a shoebox, but the rooms offer typical three-star comfort.

Turistická Ubytovna (☎ 518 334 501; Bzenecká; dm 120Kč; P) Signposted across the sports field next to the *skansen*, this has basic beds in basic surrounds.

Restaurace Na rynku (náměstí Svobody; mains 50-100Kč) This place near the village centre offers no-fuss Czech fare in pub-style get-up.

Getting There & Away

Direct buses connect Strážnice with Veselí nad Moravou (11Kč, 15 minutes), Hodonín (20Kč, 25 minutes), Uherské Hradiště (26Kč, 45 minutes) and, once a day, Brno (54Kč, two hours).

Trains are pricier, but also run to Veselí nad Moravou (16Kč, 15 minutes), Hodonín (28Kč, 30 minutes) and Uherské Hradiště (34Kč, 45 minutes).

KUŽELOV

Kuželov's Dutch-style **windmill** (admission 20Kč; 9am-noon & 1-5pm Sat & Sun Apr-Oct) dates from 1842 and is one of only a handful (there were 700 in the 19th century) to survive in Moravia. The caretaker will show you how it works, and take you through a little museum full of old furnishings, clothing and utensils.

Buses are scarce, with irregular connections to/from Strážnice (19km) and Veselí nad Moravou (28km).

BLATNICE

Blatnice is 5km west of Veselí nad Moravou, and is known for the **St Anthony Pilgrimage**, which is held on the weekend nearest the period 13 to 16 September. The colourful pilgrimage takes place around the **Chapel of St Anthony** (kaple sv Antonína), built in the 17th century. Many of the pilgrims are dressed in traditional dress, and the songs and music are traditional as well.

VLČNOV

There is little to see in Vlčnov, apart from some decorated houses and the village's 40 or so wine cellars (called *búdy*) – unless you're here for the annual Jízda králů (Ride of the Kings) folk festival.

The closest accommodation is in Uherské Hradiště (15km away), to which there are several daily buses (many more are added during the festival). There is a 75Kč admission fee into the village during the festival.

UHERSKÉ HRADIŠTĚ

pop 27,000

Twin town squares, a brace of interesting museums and a lively buzz make this a good base for exploring the wider region. Although the town sprawls across several kilometres, becoming increasingly grotty around its edges, the historical centre is well preserved. With a reasonably big population and lots of bars and restaurants, there's often plenty going on at night.

Orientation

Uherské Hradiště train station is southwest of the city centre, on the corner of Nádražní and Spojovací, but it's only on a rail link between two main lines. Břeclav–Přerov trains, including from Hodonín and Rohatec, stop in the northern suburb of Staré Město. Brno–Slovakia trains, including those from Kyjov, stop in the southern suburb of Kunovice.

The bus station is at Velehradská třída, near the Centrum department store. To get to the main square, Masarykovo náměstí, walk west along Obránců míru as far as Velehradská and turn left along Krátká and Šromova to the square.

Information

The **tourist information office** (městské informační centrum; ☎ 572 525 528; www.mic.uh.cz; Masarykovo náměstí 21; ☼ 8am-noon & 12.30-6pm Mon-Fri, until 12.30pm Sat) books accommodation and provides Internet access (40Kč per hour).

Česká Pojišťovna (Masarykovo náměstí 34) has an exchange desk and an ATM during office hours. The **post office** (Masarykovo náměstí) is nearby.

Sights
PAMÁTNÍK VELKÉ MORAVY

The archaeological site called **Památník Velké Moravy** (Great Moravia Monument; ☎ 572 543 382;

THE RIDE OF THE KINGS

The Ride of the Kings (Jízda Králů) Festival in Vlčnov features not only folk singing and dancing but also the traditional Ride of the Kings. The ride, which is both a celebration of spring's new crops and a young man's rite of passage, is thought to date back to the old European festival of Whitsuntide. The only other village to do this is nearby Hluk (where it happens only every four years); elsewhere, it died out by the 1940s. The two-day festival happens on the last weekend of May, with the Ride of the Kings on the Sunday.

The king, who must be chaste, is always chosen from among 10- to 12-year-old boys, while helpers can be up to 18 years old. The king may not speak or smile, thus he holds a rose in his teeth throughout the ceremony. He and two helpers dress in women's clothing – which, according to legend, symbolises King Wenceslas' escape from detention, wearing a disguise; the rose is a symbol of his silent escape. The horses are decorated with ribbons and paper flowers. Starting from the home of the king the ride winds through the village, while the helpers, calling out old verses in the king's honour, ask for gifts for him, upon which people stuff money in the helpers' boots.

Jezuitská 1885; adult/concession 20/10Kč; 9am-noon & 12.30-5pm Apr-Nov) is believed to be a major centre of the 9th-century Great Moravian Empire. Many of the artefacts found here – such as jewellery, weapons and ice-skates made from bone – have been collected in the museum. You can also see foundations dating back to the 8th century.

It's in Staré Město, 2km north of the city centre. To get there from the main square walk east on Havlíčkova to the highway (Velehradská třída), turn left and cross the Morava river, continue along Hradištská, turn right into Velkomoravská and take the second left at Jezuitská. Alternatively, take bus No 4 from the bus station on Obránců míru; it stops near this corner, two stops past the bridge.

SLOVÁCKÉ MUSEUM
In addition to an excellent collection of traditional folk dress, the **Slovácké Museum** (572 551 370; Smetanovy sady 179; adult/concession 20/10Kč; 9am-noon & 12.30-5pm) has an unusual example of 'folk art': an exhibit of 17th- to 19th-century shooting targets (from the days of local civil-defence militias) featuring politicians, musicians, mythological characters, animals and birds. It's in Smetanovy Park (Smetanovy sady), behind the cinema, at the intersection of Havlíčkova and the main highway.

The **Gallery of Slovácké Museum** (Galerie Slováckého muzea; 572 552 425; Otakarova 103; adult/concession 20/10Kč; 9am-noon & 12.30-5pm Tue-Sun), just north of the main square, is a branch of the museum exhibiting local art.

Sleeping
Hotel Slunce (572 432 640; recepce@hotelslunce .uh.cz; Masarykovo náměstí 150; s/d incl breakfast 1190/ 1980Kč;) This sparkling new place has jazzy trimmings – like bits of the old structure showing through areas of glass floor – but its super-comfy rooms seem empty.

Hotel Morava (572 551 508; fax 572 552 975; Šafaříkova 855; s/d incl breakfast 500/750Kč) Functionality rules the roost here, but the rooms are good value. Its sister **Hotel Grand** (572 551 511; Palackého náměstí; s/d 750/1150Kč) is a little smarter.

Ubytovna Zimní Stadion (776 809 492; Na Rybníku 957; dm per person 120Kč;) East of the centre, near the museum, this offers rough-and-ready cheap accommodation.

Eating & Drinking
La Provence (572 552 180; Josefa Stancla 149; mains 100Kč) Almighty grills and ice-cold beer are served up in this popular terrace eatery. It is down an alley next to Hotel Slunce.

Corso (672 552 180; Masarykovo náměstí 147) This plain looking café is transformed into the town's liveliest nightspot after dark. Bring on the beautiful people.

Getting There & Away
Trains to/from Hodonín (52Kč, 45 minutes) stop at the Staré Město station, while those to and from Kyjov (52Kč, 50 minutes) use the Kunovice station (see Orientation p319).

There are regular buses to Buchlovice (13Kč, 25 minutes) and Zlín (26Kč, 45 minutes) and less frequent services to Brno (66Kč, 1½ hours) and Mikulov (34Kč, 45 minutes).

Getting Around
City bus No 1 links Staré Město and Kunovice train stations, via the city centre, while bus No 4 connects Uherské Hradiště and Staré Město train stations.

BUCHLOVICE
pop 2400
Baroque **Buchlovice chateau** (575 595 112; adult/concession 50/25Kč; 9am-noon & 12.30-6pm Jul-Aug, until 5pm Tue-Sun May, Jun & Sep, until 3pm Sat & Sun Apr & Oct) was built back in the 1700s, probably to a design by Martinelli, with ornate stucco decorations. On display are the furnishings left behind by the Berchtold family, who fled advancing Soviet forces in 1945. En route to the chateau, you have to pass through a **garden** (adult/concession 10/5Kč) full of preening peacocks.

Sleeping & Eating
The **tourist office** (572 595 996; tic@buchlovice.cz; Svobody 6; 9am-5pm Tue-Sun) can help with cheap accommodation.

Hotel Buchlovice (572 596 021; info@hotel buchlovice.cz; Svobody 426; s/d 950/1550Kč;) This central place has some smart rooms and an excellent restaurant.

Getting There & Away
Infrequent buses stop here en route from Uherské Hradiště (13Kč, 25 minutes) to Kunovice.

SOUTH MORAVIA

BUCHLOV CASTLE

In the Chřiby hills, **Buchlov Castle** (☎ 572 595 161; adult/concession 55/27Kč; ⏰ 9am-6.30pm Jul-Aug, 8am-5.30pm Tue-Sun May, Jun & Sep, until 4.30pm Apr & Oct) was built in the 13th century and, although it's been enlarged, it hasn't been restyled since its founding. The Berchtold family, its last owners, turned it into a museum during the 19th century.

This simple, appealing place has none of the overwrought decoration of the baroque style. Rooms are sparsely furnished but interesting. As in most medieval castles there are plenty of weapons and a few instruments of torture on display.

Hotel Buchlov Park (☎ 572 577 925; info@buchlov park.cz; s/d incl breakfast 1900/2600Kč; **P**) Right next to the castle, this has plenty of creature comforts and organises horse-riding trips (175Kč per hour). Big discounts are available off-season.

Getting There & Away

The castle turn-off is off the Brno highway, 4km west of Buchlovice, though for those on foot or a bike it's uphill all the way. Four daily buses between Uherské Hradiště and Kunovice stop at the castle turn-off, from where it's a pleasant 2km walk through the forest.

VELEHRAD

pop 1400

Not far from Uherské Hradiště, at Velehrad, is the **Cistercian Monastery** (klášter Cisterciáků; ☎ 572 571 130; admission free; ⏰ 7am-6pm). It was long considered, though mistakenly, to have been the archepiscopal seat of St Methodius, who may have died in the area in 885. Pilgrims have flocked to the shrine for centuries, not least Pope John Paul II in 1990.

Under the monastery's church is a **lapidarium** (adult/concession 10/5Kč; ⏰ 9am-4.30pm Tue-Sun Apr-Oct) with the remains of the original basilica.

There are regular buses during weekdays (fewer on weekends) from Uherské Hradiště (10Kč, 20 minutes).

ZLÍNSKO REGION

ZLÍN

pop 90,000

Zlín walked into its slot in Czech history as the home of the famous (among footwear historians/fetishists) Baťa shoe brand. The brainchild of philanthropist shoe millionaire Tomáš Baťa, Zlín was almost entirely planned from scratch – a 'total environment' created to house, feed and entertain the workers at his colossal factory. As with so many utopian projects, 21st-century Zlín now falls well short of the ideal, looking remarkably like 1,001 other less benevolent Stalinist-style schemes. Even so, it's still worth a peek if you're passing through.

Zlín also has a tradition of film-making. Its studios started life promoting Baťa shoes, but more than 2000 films have been made here in the last half-century. Zlín is also the birthplace of playwright Tom Stoppard, born as Thomas Straussler in 1937 (his father worked at the Baťa factory).

Orientation

The train station (Železniční stanice) stands just off Gahurova, south of the river.

SOUTH MORAVIA

THE PEOPLE'S SHOE

Before its present incarnation, humble Zlín was one village among many; an unassuming dot on the map. Its present form, a herringbone pattern of streets radiating from the main thoroughfare, dates from 1894 when Tomáš Baťa, the omnipresent shoe manufacturer, began to expand his enterprise (Baťa had made a fortune from the sale of boots to the Austrian army in WWI). The town grew quickly and between 1910 and 1930 its population trebled to 36,000.

Baťa, and later his son, grew the company into a sizable multinational, and by the early 1930s it had become the world's leading footwear exporter, designing, producing and marketing shoes in 30 countries by 1938.

Tomáš Baťa was killed in a plane accident in 1932, but the company remains a largely family affair. From humble beginnings, it now has 4,700 stores, 60 factories, 50,000 employees and operates in 70 countries.

You can invest in your own pair of local shoes at the **Baťa shop** (Dlouhá 130).

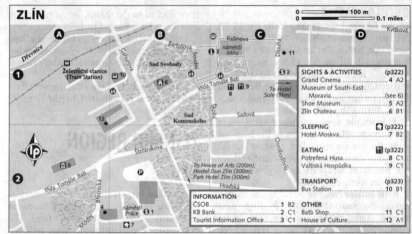

ZLÍN

0 ——————————— 100 m
0 ——————————— 0.1 miles

SIGHTS & ACTIVITIES	(p322)
Grand Cinema	4 A2
Museum of South-East	
Moravia	(see 6)
Shoe Museum	5 A2
Zlín Chateau	6 B1
SLEEPING	(p322)
Hotel Moskva	7 B2
EATING	(p322)
Potrefená Husa	8 C1
Valtiská Hospůdka	9 C1
TRANSPORT	(p323)
Bus Station	10 C1
OTHER	
Baťa Shop	11 C1
House of Culture	12 A1

INFORMATION	
ČSOB	1 B2
KB Bank	2 C1
Tourist Information Office	3 C1

The bus station is about 100m closer to the centre. The town centres on functional náměstí Míru.

Information

The **tourist information office** (Městské informační a turistické středisko; ☎ 577 630 270; www.mestozlin.cz; náměstí Míru 12; ☼ 8am-5.30pm Mon-Fri, until noon Sat) arranges accommodation and provides **Internet access** (1Kč per min).

ČSOB (náměstí Práce) and **KB** (cnr Dlouhá & třída Tomáše Bati) both have ATMs and exchange desks.

Sights

The Zlín Chateau houses the **Museum of South-East Moravia** (Muzeum jihovýchodní Moravy; ☎ 577 004 611; Soudní 1; adult/concession 20/10Kč; ☼ 9am-noon & 1-5pm Tue-Sun), which has displays of local film studios, folk-music instruments and utensils from the Slovácko and Haná regions.

Upstairs is a branch of the **State Gallery** (Galerie Výtvarného Umění ve Zlíně; adult/concession 20/10Kč; ☼ as museum), with permanent displays of 20th-century Czech art and sculpture.

The **Shoe Museum** (Obuvnické Muzeum; ☎ 577 522 225) was closed for renovations at time of writing but is due to open in new premises on třída Tomáše Bati in 2004.

A few 20th-century buildings are also worth a look. František Gahura's **House of Arts** (dům umění; ☎ 577 218 317; náměstí TG Masaryka 2570; adult/concession 15/5Kč; ☼ 9am-5pm Tue-Sun) hosts another branch of the State Gallery, featuring works by Mucha among others.

It's also home to the Zlín philharmonic orchestra.

Another curiosity is the gargantuan **Grand Cinema** (Velké kino; ☎ 577 432 936; www.ateliery.cz; náměstí Práce 2511), built in the 1960s and capable of seating 2000.

Sleeping & Eating

For private rooms (from around 250Kč per person) talk to the information office.

Hotel Moskva (☎ 577 561 111; fax 577 560 111; náměstí Práce 2512; s/d incl breakfast 1000/1200Kč; P ☲) Considered an exceptional example (by Karfík) of 1930s functionalism, this has just about everything, including shops, a bowling alley and an Irish pub. There's also a huge choice of restaurants in its lobby.

Hotel Sole (☎ 577 210 458; www.inext.cz/sole; třída Tomáše Bati 5213; s/d incl breakfast 660/860Kč) Curious name aside (is this a joke?), this typical mid-ranger has decent rooms at a fair price. It is 1km from the city centre towards Slušovice (take bus No 31).

Hostel Duo Zlin (☎ 577 433 112; hostelduozlin@seznam.cz; Růmy 1391; s/d 350/700Kč) Just south of the stadium, this basic place is the poor (cheaper) relative of nearby **Park Hotel Zlin** (☎ 577 056 111; d incl breakfast 1150Kč).

Potrefená Husa (☎ 577 019 555; třída Tomáše Bati 201; mains 120Kč) You can wash down the excellent grills at this groovy sports bar with a buffet lunch of blinding cocktails.

Valtiská Hospůdka (☎ 577 220 393; třída Tomáše Bati 200; mains 100-200Kč) Hearty local fare tops the billing at this cosy Moravian eatery.

Getting There & Away

To go anywhere by train usually requires a change at Otrokovice: the 127km to Brno (100Kč) takes three hours.

Buses are faster. There regular links to Uherské Hradiště (26Kč, 45 minutes), Olomouc (40Kč, 1½ hours) and Kroměříž (35Kč, 55 minutes).

For all bus and train times and prices visit www.idos.cz.

VIZOVICE

pop 4500

As the home of the Jelínek distillery, this small town, 15km east of Zlín, is the source of some of the country's finest slivovice (plum brandy).

The rather ordinary **Vizovice Chateau** (zámek Vizovice; ☎ 577 452 762; adult/concession 40/20Kč; ⏰ 9am-noon & 1-5pm Tue-Sun May-Aug, until 4pm Apr, Sep & Oct), 100m off the main square, does have some good exhibits on traditional trades and crafts.

There are regular daily train and bus connections to/from Zlín.

LEŠNÁ

The attractions of tiny Lešná, 8km north of Zlín, include a Romantic-style chateau and a better-than-average zoo.

Lešná Chateau (zámek Lešná; ☎ 577 914 180; adult/concession 45/35Kč; ⏰ 9am-4pm Tue-Fri, until 5pm Sat & Sun May-Sep, until 3.30pm Sat & Sun Oct, until 5pm Sat & Sun Apr) is an over-decorated concoction of towers and shutters.

The surrounding **zoo** (www.zoolesna; adult/concession 60/30Kč; ⏰ 9am-6pm Tue-Sun Apr-Sep, until 4pm Oct-Mar) is in an English-style park, with 2500 animals largely free to roam within fairly spacious enclosures.

There are hourly buses from Zlín (20Kč, 30 minutes); fewer at weekends.

LUHAČOVICE

pop 5600

Rather less glamorous than West Bohemia's effete spa towns, Luhačovive is more 1970s than 1870s, featuring plenty of blockish communist-era functionality and an everyday, fuss-free feel. It may lack the serene architectural charm of Karlovy Vary et al (the central feature here is a modernist fountain that wouldn't look out of place in the lobby of a corporate HQ), but this is one of Moravia's most pleasant spas, with a serene woodland setting and a friendly, unpretentious atmosphere.

Orientation & Information

Luhačovice snakes along Šťavnice Creek and the main road that runs parallel to it. The train and bus stations are at the southwest end of town; walk out of the stations, turn left onto Masarykova and continue past the police station.

Luha (☎ 577 133 980; www.mesto.luhacovice.cz; Masarykovo 950; ⏰ 9am-5pm Mon-Fri) arranges accommodation and has a good selection of maps. It also opens weekends in July and August.

Sights & Activities

Luhačovice has some fine examples of rustic architecture, incorporating Walachian farmhouse motifs. Among the town's more interesting Tudoresque houses are **Jestřábí dům** and **Vodoléčebný ústav** on L Janáčka, and **Jurkovičův dům** on Dr P Blaha.

The spa follows the creek, lined with trees, spa-hotels and fountains. Perhaps the most visited spas are **Ottovka**, in the gazebo by the tennis courts, and **Aloiska** behind the Palace Sanatorium.

Many spa hotels offer specialised treatment – paraffin packs, four-chamber baths, you name it. The average 'cure' lasts about a week; contact the spa's main office, **Lázně Luhačovice** (☎ 577 682 100; info@lazneluhacovice.cz; Lázeňské náměstí 436).

The **Luhačovice Museum** (Muzeum v Luhačovicích; ☎ 577 132 883; adult/concession 10/5Kč; ⏰ 9am-noon & 1-5pm Tue-Sun Apr-Oct, until 4pm Nov-Mar), next to the tennis courts, has a small collection of painted Easter eggs (kraslice), ceramics, embroidery and other folk art.

Sleeping

There is plenty of accommodation in all ranges, including private rooms from 200Kč per person (Luha can help with these).

Pension Růža (☎ 577 134 202; penzion-ruza@volny.cz; U Šťavnice 256; d incl breakfast 1000Kč) Housed in a pretty, traditional-style villa, this has smart, homey rooms and a small bar.

Hotel Vltava (☎ 577 131 376; jsuransky@iol.cz; Dr Veselého 169; s/d incl breakfast 390/700Kč) With a blindingly blue façade, presumably meant to appeal to water babies, this also has simple rooms at knockdown prices.

Autokemping Luhačovice (☎ 577 133 318; tent/chalet per person 70/120Kč; P) Located at the Údolní Dam (Údolní přehrada), 3km north of town along the creek, or via bus No 7, this is open May to September and also has chalets.

Other recommendations:

Hotel Zálesí (☎ 577 134 060; hotely@zalesi.cz; Zatloukalova 70; s/d incl breakfast 770/1210Kč) Bright and modern.

Hotel Litoval (☎ 577 131 109; nicoma@volny.cz; Dr Veselého 329; d/tr with shared bathroom incl breakfast 350/525Kč) Moth eaten but good value.

Eating

As in all Czech spa towns, sweet wafers (oplatky) are a popular snack. The spa hotels have some of town's smartest eateries.

Restaurace U Šimů (☎ 577 933 759; Masarykova 108; mains 100Kč) This pub-style haunt has meat-heavy local dishes and beer by the bucketful.

Other recommendations:

Samoobslužna (Dr Veselého 195; mains 60Kč; ⏳ until 7pm) The deep-fried and the dumpling reign supreme at this buffet.

Divadelní kavárna (snacks 50Kč; ⏳ until 6pm) A pleasant café.

Getting There & Away

Buses are easier and quicker than trains from most destinations, with up to 11 a day from Zlín (30Kč, 40 minutes) and eight from Uherský Brod (35Kč, 55 minutes).

KROMĚŘÍŽ

pop 30,000

Towns at every corner of the compass seem to be compared with Athens, Venice or Paris, so it only seems right that this pretty corner of Moravia should have its own 'Athens'.

Locally known as Hanácké Athény (the Athens of Haná), this beautiful little town shot to notoriety as the seat of the potent bishops of Olomouc between the 12th and 19th centuries. These days, tourism, rather than religious wrangling, is the order of the day, but the bishops' fabulous baroque chateau remains the town's chief attraction.

History

German colonists began arriving in the 13th century, when the town was fortified. The town was practically destroyed by the Swedes in the Thirty Years' War, but in 1664 the bishops undertook their major baroque construction effort. The

castle was rebuilt by the Italian architects Tencalla and Lucchese to a commission by Charles II of Liechtenstein-Kastlekorn, a bishop. In the mid-18th century, Kroměříž and the chateau were damaged during an occupation by the Prussian army, and later from a fire.

Orientation

If you're arriving at the train or bus stations, get onto Hulínská and cross the river. The interesting bits of town are centred on the chateau and Velké náměstí.

Information

The **tourist information office** (informační centrum; ☎ 573 221 473; www.mesto-kromeriz.cz; Velké náměstí 50; ⏳ 8.30am-5pm Mon-Fri, 9am-1pm Sat & Sun) organises accommodation, rents out bikes (200Kč per day), has a left-luggage office and changes money.

Česká spořitelna (Velké náměstí 43) and **ČSOB** (Riegrovo náměstí 182) both have exchange offices and ATMs.

The main post office is on the corner of Oskol and Denkova. A second branch is in the train station. You can access the Internet at **U M@xe** (☎ 573 331 532; Velké náměstí 39; ⏳ 10am-10pm Mon-Fri, 1-9pm Sat & Sun).

You can develop your snaps at **Foto Mucha** (☎ 573 339 262; Prusinovského 2).

Lékárna v Kovářské (☎ 573 337 425; Kovářská 18) is a central pharmacy.

Sights

ARCHBISHOPS' CHATEAU

North of Velké náměstí is the **Archbishops' Chateau** (Arcibiskupský zámek; ☎ 573 502 011; www.azz.cz; adult/concession 80/50Kč, in English 160/100Kč; ⏳ 9am-5pm Tue-Sun May-Sep, Sat only Apr, Sun & holidays only Oct) with its 84m, baroque tower. It takes 1½ hours to tour the interior, with its rococo ceilings and murals by Franz Anton Maulpertsch and Josef Stern. The **Manský Hall** (Manský sál) has Maulpertsch's skilful ceiling paintings. The best-known room is the **Assembly Hall** (Sněmovní sál), where scenes for the film *Amadeus* were shot. It costs extra to tour the **tower** (adult/concession 40/20Kč) and **Sala Terena** (adult/concession 10/5Kč).

You can also visit the **Chateau Gallery** (Zámecká obrazárna; adult/concession 30/15Kč, with English text 60/30Kč), which has a valuable collection of 16th- and 17th-century paintings. Pride of place goes to Titian's *Flaying of Marsyas*.

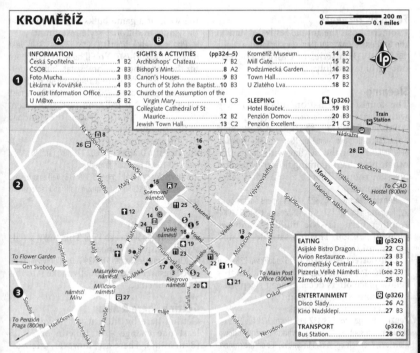

KROMĚŘÍŽ

0 — 200 m
0 — 0.1 miles

INFORMATION
Česká Spořitelna..................1 B2
ČSOB..................................2 B3
Foto Mucha........................3 B3
Lékárna v Kovářské.............4 B2
Tourist Information Office....5 B2
U M@xe.............................6 B2

SIGHTS & ACTIVITIES (pp324–5)
Archbishops' Chateau...........7 B2
Bishop's Mint.......................8 A2
Canon's Houses....................9 B3
Church of St John the Baptist..10 B3
Church of the Assumption of the
Virgin Mary........................11 C3
Collegiate Cathedral of St
Maurice.............................12 B2
Jewish Town Hall................13 C2

Kroměříž Museum...............14 B2
Mill Gate...........................15 B2
Podzámecká Garden...........16 B2
Town Hall..........................17 B3
U Zlatého Lva....................18 B2

SLEEPING (p326)
Hotel Bouček.....................19 B3
Penzión Domov.................20 B3
Penzión Excellent..............21 C3

EATING (p326)
Asijské Bistro Dragon.........22 C3
Avion Restaurace...............23 B3
Kroměřížský Centrál...........24 B2
Pizzeria Velké Náměstí.....(see 23)
Zámecká My Slivna............25 B2

ENTERTAINMENT (p326)
Disco Slady.......................26 A2
Kino Nadsklepí..................27 B3

TRANSPORT (p326)
Bus Station.......................28 D2

SOUTH MORAVIA

Behind the chateau is **Podzámecká Garden** (Podzámecká zahrada; 6.30am-8pm), designed in the 17th century by Lucchese and one of the largest in the country, with 64 hectares of greenery.

Nearby, the **Bishop's Mint** (Biskupskou Mincovnu; Na Sladovnách; adult/concession 10/5Kč; 9am-5pm Tue-Sun May-Sep, Sat & Sun only Oct-Apr) is worth a peek if you're interested in making (in the less interesting sense) money.

AROUND THE OLD TOWN

Leaving the chateau through Sněmovní náměstí, on the right is the **Mill Gate** (Mlýnská brána). On Pilařova is the **Collegiate Cathedral of St Maurice** (Kolegiátní chrám sv Mořice), a seminary built around 1260 and one of the oldest surviving structures in Kroměříž.

Continue on Pilařova to the baroque **Church of St John the Baptist** (kostel sv Jana Křtitele), built 1737–68, which features frescoes by JJ Etgens and Stern.

From Masarykovo náměstí a walk along Jánská back towards Velké náměstí passes a group of colourful **Canon's Houses** (Kanovnické domy) on the left. In the

square, on the corner with Kovářská, is the 16th-century Renaissance **town hall**.

On Velké náměstí, the **Kroměříž Museum** (Muzeum Kroměřížska; 573 338 388; Velké náměstí 38; adult/concession for all exhibitions 60/30Kč, or Max Švabinský only 30/20Kč) has a permanent collection of the works of Max Švabinský (born in Kroměříž in 1873), a specialist in colourful nudes and the designer of many of Czechoslovakia's early postage stamps.

At No 30 is the town's oldest pharmacy (lékárna), **U zlatého lva**, which was established in 1675. The cobblestone square also has a decorative **fountain** and **plague column**.

From Velké náměstí, take Vodní and continue along Farní, past the **Church of the Assumption of the Virgin Mary** (kostel Nanebevzetí Panny Marie). On the left is Moravcova, and halfway down is a reminder of the town's Jewish history, the old **Jewish Town Hall** (Židovská radnice).

A final attraction is the 17th-century, baroque **Flower Garden** (Květná zahrada), with a frequently photographed rotunda by Lucchese and a colonnade by Tencalla. Enter from Gen Svobody, west of the city centre.

Festivals & Events

Kroměříž hosts the annual **Festival of Music in the Gardens & Chateau** (Hudba v zahrádkách a zámku; ☎ 573 321 153), a series of classical concerts during June and July.

Sleeping

The tourist information office can help with private rooms (from 300Kč).

Penzión Excellent (☎ 573 333 023; excellent@ tunker.com; Riegrovo náměstí 164; s/d incl breakfast 600/900Kč) Flying the EU flag with pride, this ornate place has blooming flower boxes and pleasant rooms. There's also a wine cellar for vinophiles.

Penzión Domov (☎ 573 344 744; pensionkm@quick .cz; Riegrovo náměstí 157; s/d incl breakfast 840/1140Kč) Another baroque-style building, another pleasant *pension*. This has satellite TV and ageing, mid-range rooms.

ČSAD Hostel (☎ 517 316 111; Skopalíkova 2385; s/d 200/400Kč; (P)) It isn't clearly marked, but this yellow place offers decent cheap sleeps. It's on bus routes No 1, 2, 6 and 7.

Other recommendations:

Penzión Praga (☎ 573 332 116; Boční 2/704; d 500Kč) Suburban but spotless. Go along Havlíčkova, turn left down Albertova, then left again on Purkynova; it's on the corner of Boční.

Hotel Bouček (☎ 573 342 777; hotel.boucek@seznam.cz; Velké náměstí 108; s/d incl breakfast 800/1300Kč) Top location, dowdy décor.

Eating

Zámecká My Slivna (☎ 573 340 498; Sněmovní náměstí 41; mains 70-200Kč) Hunting apparel decorates the walls and game bulks out the menu at this snug, traditional-style restaurant.

Pizzeria Velké Náměstí (☎ 573 343 460; Velké náměstí 109; pizza 55-75Kč) You'll have to watch out for the dodgy brown floral sofas, but this terrace pizzeria whips up a reasonable Italian.

Avion restaurace (☎ 573 339 446; Velké náměstí 111; mains 55Kč) No frills, no fuss and decent pick-and-point buffet grub is the standard at this popular restaurant.

Other recommendations:

Asijské Bistro Dragon (☎ 602 778 497; Farní 97; mains 60-120Kč) For Asian favourites.

Kroměřížský centrál (☎ 573 335 513; Velké náměstí 37; mains 90-260Kč) For huge mixed grills and regional specialities.

Entertainment

Disco Slady (Na Sladovnách 1576) This town's self-styled 'temple of dance'.

Kino Nadsklepí (☎ 573 339 280; Miličovo náměstí) The latest releases eventually make it to this central cinema.

Getting There & Away

Getting here by train usually requires at least one change – at Kojetín or Hulín (8km away). There are, however, a few direct services to Brno (98Kč, 1¼ hours).

There are regular buses to Zlín (35Kč, 55 minutes), Olomouc (55Kč, 1¾ hours) and Brno (40Kč, 1¼ hours) and infrequent services to Uherské Hradiště (40Kč, 1¼ hours) and Prague (200Kč, four hours).

For all bus and train times and prices visit www.idos.cz.

Slovakia

SLOVAKIA

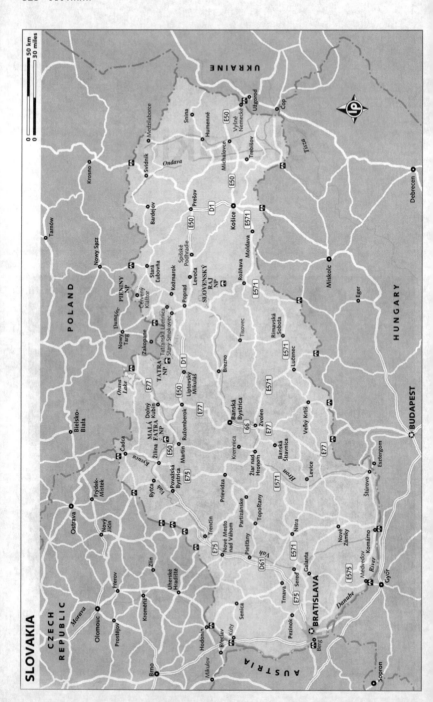

Bratislava

First impressions of Bratislava (Pozsony in Hungarian, Pressburg in German) will probably disappoint. With a bland castle, rather small old town, gargantuan state housing complex south of the Danube and plethora of Communist-era architecture scattered throughout its suburban sprawl, most visitors won't be inspired to stick around for long. But, as the saying goes, don't judge a book by its cover. The Slovak Republic capital, and far and away its largest city, is in fact a vibrant, pulsing city. It encapsulates the best of urban Slovakia, where you can immerse yourself in some of the country's finest museums during the day, choose from an ever-increasing array of international cuisine come evening time and party till dawn in some of its most progressive bars and clubs. It's also a place to relax; Bratislava has yet to attract hordes of tourists, so you'll escape the crowds.

The city is also at the forefront of Slovakia's development and a snapshot of the country's ties with the past and move towards the future. Its close proximity to Western Europe, and its low prices, has attracted many large businesses keen to tap into the Eastern European market. This has in turn attracted many young, energetic Slovaks who know how to work and play hard, adding to the city's buzz. On weekends the streets are packed with them, all eager to enjoy what the city has to offer.

You could easily entertain yourself over two or three days sampling Bratislava's highlights and nightlife and exploring the surrounding area.

BRATISLAVA

HIGHLIGHTS

- Stroll through the picturesque cobblestone streets of the **old town** (p334)

- Admire the Venus of Moravany, one of humankind's earliest attempts at art, in **Bratislava Castle** (p334)

- Take a leisurely river cruise to the cliff-top ruins of **Devín Castle** (p344)

- While away the wee hours in some of the best bars and clubs Slovakia has to offer (p342)

- Wonder at the contrasting architecture of the old town with the Communist-era **New Bridge** and **Petržalka** (p331)

■ TELEPHONE CODE: 02   ■ POPULATION: 452,288

HISTORY

It's hard to believe that Bratislava, the capital of Slovakia, hasn't been very 'Slovak' for long. Officially, it only came into existence in 1919; for 700 years preceding that it was known as Pressburg.

The site of Bratislava has been inhabited, more or less, for the past 4000 years. It was, however, the Celts who first gave the town its kick start by building a large settlement on the site of Bratislava Castle in the 1st century BC. The Romans enjoyed a period of occupation before leaving the area for good in 378, at which time the Slavs moved in. A 5th-century Slav fort – called Breza-lauspurc – grew into an important citadel of the Great Moravian Empire. With the empire's defeat in 906 by the Magyars, this became an administrative centre of the growing Hungarian kingdom.

In the 12th century a royal market was established in the surrounding settlement, and by the 14th century it had become a busy commercial centre at the intersection of several major trade routes. In 1465 King Matthias Corvinus founded the first Hungarian (and Slovak) university here, the Academia Istropolitana.

Then came the Turks. At the Battle of Mohács in 1526 they defeated the Hungarian forces and began their slow march across the plains, finally taking Buda. The Hungarian capital was hurriedly moved to Bratislava in 1536, and the town's heyday began. Wealthy burghers and Viennese aristocrats built grand palaces, many of them still standing. Musical life flourished; frequent visitors included Haydn, Mozart, Beethoven and, later, Liszt.

But the prosperous times did not last forever. With the defeat of the Turks by the Habsburgs, most government functions moved back to Buda and Pressburg fell on hard times. It was not all doom and gloom though; many factories sprang up in the 18th century which helped keep the city's economy afloat. This was somewhat halted during the Napoleonic Wars, when French troops took the city in 1805.

Slovak national awareness began to grow in the 19th century; one of its leading figures, Ľudovít Štúr, lived and published in the city. In the Primatial Palace, Ferdinand V in 1848 signed his name to one of Štúr's demands: the abolition of serfdom.

This was short-lived however, as following the 1867 amalgamation of the Austrian (Habsburg) and Hungarian crowns, a policy of 'Hungarisation' across all of Slovakia made life miserable. After WWI and the collapse of the Austro-Hungarian empire, the Slovaks threw in their lot with the Czechs. On 1 January 1919 the city, with its Slovak name Bratislava, became part of the new Czechoslovakia.

Bratislava's dress-rehearsal as capital came in 1939 when Slovakia was declared a puppet state after Germany invaded Czechoslovakia. The August 1944 Slovak National Uprising (Slovenské národné povstanie or SNP) overthrew this state, but was itself crushed by the Nazis.

With the arrival of the communists, Bratislava was ruthlessly modernised. In 1972, Slovak communist officials cut the ribbon on their pride and joy, the New Bridge (Nový most) and overpass, which had been built over the bulldozed remains of the city's old Jewish quarter. The following year, the vast tower blocks of Petržalka were begun.

On 1 January 1993, Bratislava once again became the capital of Slovakia. Since then, the city centre has been extensively renovated, with the re-cobbling of old town streets and the repainting of historical façades.

ORIENTATION

Most of Bratislava is on the north bank of the Danube. The city's historical heart, the old town (Staré mesto), is a compact, pedestrianised 0.5 sq km bordered by the castle hill, námestie SNP and Hviezdoslavovo námestie. From here Bratislava spreads northeastward in the form of the new town (Nové Mesto) and the bland, high-rise suburbs beyond it. South across the Danube via the striking hypermodern New Bridge (Nový most) is the 'model socialist' suburb of Petržalka, home to some 117,000 Bratislavans.

Bratislava's main train station (Hlavná stanica) is 1km north of the old town. Tram No 1 runs from the station to Hurbanovo námestie (10 minutes), just north of the city centre. Or walk down to Šancová, veer right and cross over the pedestrian bridge, and continue south down Štefánikova for about 1km. A few trains use the Bratislava-Nové Mesto or Petržalka stations, which are less

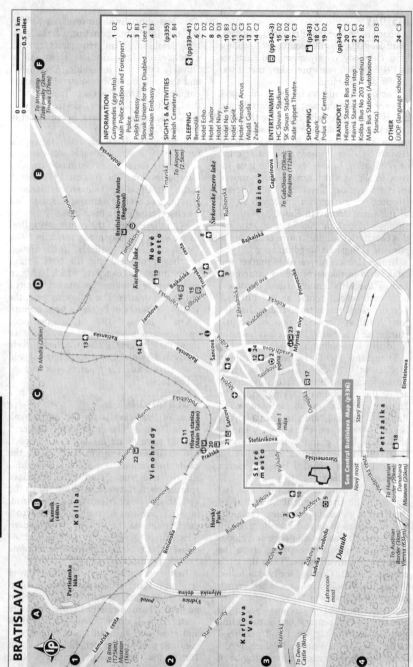

BRATISLAVA IN....

Two Days
Take a morning stroll through the **old town**, stopping for a coffee or light lunch in one of the cafés on **Hlavné námestie**. Make a bee-line for the castle, with a pause at the **Museum of Jewish Culture**. Explore the **Castle** and its museums before enjoying a glass of wine and a meal at **Hradná Vináreň**. Day two, jump on a ferry to **Devín Castle**. In the afternoon head back to town and take in the **Slovak National Gallery**. End the day with an opera at the **Slovak National Theatre**.

Four Days
After exhausting the two-day itinerary, take your time on the third day to see some of the old town's worthwhile museums, such as the **Municipal Museum** and **Primate's Palace**. Climb the **Michael Tower** for fine views of the city and finish off the day with a crisp Slovak beer in one of Bratislava's bars. On day four, take a day trip to the **Danubiana Museum** or to **Modra** for wine tasting.

conveniently located on the northeastern and southern side of the city respectively.

The main bus station (Autobusová stanica) is on Mlynské nivy, a little over 1km east of Kamenné námestie behind a lonely skyscraper; to reach the city centre turn left out of the main doors and make a quick right onto Mlynské nivy (which becomes Dunajská).

Maps
The best map is VKÚ's 1:15,000 *Bratislava* (130Sk), complete with street index, tram and bus routes, 1:5000 scale-plan of the city centre and 1:50,000 scale-map of the surrounding region.

INFORMATION
Bookshops
Eurobooks (Map pp336-7; ☎ 54 41 79 59; Jesenského 5-9) Stocks a range of titles in English, as well as Lonely Planet guides.
Ex Libris (Map pp336-7; ☎ 54 43 24 41; Michalská 4) Quality selection, including a small sample of English titles.
Interpress Slovakia (Map pp336-7; Sedlárska 2) Decent selection of foreign newspapers and magazines.
Knihy Slovenský spisovateľ (Map pp336-7; ☎ 54 43 37 60; Laurinská 2) Sells useful hiking and cycling maps.

Cultural Centres
Czech Cultural Centre (Map pp336-7; ☎ 59 20 33 05; Hviezdoslavovo námestie 8)
British Council (Map pp336-7; ☎ 54 43 10 74; Panská 17)
French Cultural Institute (Map pp336-7; ☎ 59 34 77 77; Sedlárska 7)
Goethe Institut (Map pp336-7; ☎ 54 41 42 59; Konventná 1)

Polish Cultural Centre (Map pp336-7; ☎ 54 43 20 13; námestie SNP 27)

Emergency
Main Police Station and Foreigners' Police (Map p332; ☎ 0961-01 11 11; Sasinkova 23).

Internet Access
An hour online costs anything between 40Sk and 60Sk (some charge up to 2Sk per minute and should be avoided).
Café Online (Map pp336-7; ☎ 0904 999 999; Hurbanovo námestie 5) Probably the largest Internet café in town.
Impetus Call Centre (Map pp336-7; ☎ 54 43 25 58; Nákupné Centrum, Michalská 2) Also has an accommodation service.
Nextra (Map pp336-7; ☎ 58 22 81 11; Cnr Hurbanovo námestie & Michalská; ✆ 9am-6pm Mon-Fri) At 20Sk per hour, one of the cheapest in town.

Internet Resources
Bratislava (www.bratislava.com) Listings, local, national and international news and handy links to other Bratislava and Slovak sites.
In Your Pocket (www.inyourpocket.com/slovakia /bratislava/en) Comprehensive online guide with loads of information on the city.
Bratislava2002 (www.bratislava2001.sk/ang /menu.htm) Some listings are out of date, but solid general information on the city.
Slovak Spectator (www.slovakspectator.sk) Online version of the weekly publication, with current affairs on Bratislava and the rest of Slovakia.

Laundry
Rýchlo Csharen (Map pp336-7; ☎ 52 93 28 88; Tesco Department Store) Two-hour, one-day and two-day services. At least 40Sk per item.

BRATISLAVA

Left Luggage

Main Bus Station (🕙 6am-10pm Mon-Fri, 6am-6pm Sat & Sun) Items up to 15kg/over 15kg 20/30Sk per day.
Main Train Station (🕙 24 hr) Items up to 15kg/over 15kg 25/35Sk per day.

Media

Kam v Bratislave (Where in Bratislava; free) Monthly Slovak-language pamphlet for museums, galleries and theatres.
Propeler (free) Comprehensive coverage of high- and low-brow happenings in this two-weekly Slovak-language magazine.
The Slovak Spectator (35Sk) Weekly English-language paper with good source of information on what's happening in Bratislava.
What's On (40Sk) Monthly English-language magazine listing cultural events, live music and cinema.

Medical Services

24-hour Pharmacy (Map pp336-7; ☎ 54 43 29 52; námestie SNP 20)
Poliklinika (Map pp336-7; ☎ 52 96 24 61; Bezručova 8) Various clinics and emergency services, including dental.

Money

Banks and ATMs Bratislava has a bank and ATM on almost every corner; there are also ATMs in the train and bus stations, and the airport. Most banks within the old centre will cash travellers cheques and exchange foreign currency.
Currency Exchange Booths (zmenareň) A congregation of exchange booths can be found at Kammené námestie (beside the Tesco department store) offering good rates for cash with zero commission. The train station and airport have exchange booths, but the rates aren't very competitive.

Post

Main Post Office (Map pp336-7; námestie SNP 34; 🕙 7am-8pm Mon-Fri, 7am-6pm Sat, 9am-2pm Sun) Letters from abroad are held here for one month.

Telephone

Impetus Call Centre (Map pp336-7; Nákupné Centrum, Michalská 2) Calls to landlines in UK, USA, New Zealand or Australia cost 5.90Sk per minute.
Slovakia Telecom (Slovenské telekomunikacie; Map pp336-7; Kolárska 12) Has a line of public phones outside its front doors. Purchase phone cards at **InfoTel** (Map pp336-7; ☎ 54 43 44 33; námestie SNP 31) or newsstands.

Toilets

Public toilets generally cost between 2Sk and 5Sk.

Tourist Information

Airport Information Desk (☎ 48 57 33 53; 🕙 24 hr)
Bratislava Information Service (BIS; Map pp336-7; ☎ 54 43 37 15; Klobučnícka 2; 🕙 8.30am-6pm Mon-Fri, 9am-6pm Sat & Sun May–mid-Oct, 8am-6pm Mon-Fri, 9am-2pm Sat mid-Oct–Apr) General information about the city. Also has a 24-hour information screen.
Bratislava Information Service (Map p332 ☎ 52 49 59 06; Hlavná stanica; 🕙 7.30am-7pm Mon-Fri, 7.30am-2.30pm Sat & Sun May–mid-Oct, 8am-6pm Mon-Fri, 9am-2pm Sat mid-Oct–Apr) Small office located in the main train station.

Travel Agencies

Satur (Map pp336-7; ☎ 55 41 01 28; Jesenského 9) Arranges air tickets, accommodation and tours in Slovakia, as well as international air, train and bus tickets.

DANGERS & ANNOYANCES

Bratislava is a quite safe city for tourists, and if you're as careful with your belongings as you are at home, then you should have no problems. Pickpockets are known to frequent Kamenné námestie, in particular around the currency exchange booths by the Tesco department store.

SIGHTS

Most of Bratislava's sights are either within the confines of the old town, or within easy walking distance.

Bratislava Castle & Around (Map pp336–7)

Resting 100m above the old town, **Bratislava Castle** (Bratislavský hrad; 🕙 9am-8pm Apr-Sep, 9am-6pm Oct-Mar) is the city's most prominent sight. While many castles in Slovakia have far greater aesthetic appeal (it looks like an upturned bed), this castle's appeal lies in its museums and views.

It took its present shape in the 15th century, when it was beefed up against the Hussites and then heavily remodelled by Maria Theresa in the 18th century. The castle became a seminary and later a military barracks, and was gutted by fire in 1811 and bombed in WWII, only to be rebuilt once again in the 1950s by the Communists.

On the ground floor is the **Treasury of Slovakia** (☎ 54 41 14 44; adult/child 10/5Sk; 🕙 10am-noon, 1-4pm Tue-Sun), a small but important collection of archeological finds. Easily the highlight of the museum (and perhaps Bratislava) is the exquisite mammoth-tusk *Venus of Mora-*

vany, which is a 25,000-year-old fertility statue of a naked woman. Don't blink as you enter the ticket office or you'll miss it.

Taking up a couple of floors is the largest branch of the **Slovak National Museum** (Slovenské národné múzeum; ☎ 54 41 14 44; adult/child 60/30Sk; ☻ 9am-5pm Tue-Sun) which covers folk crafts, furniture, modern art and history, and also includes the all-important ice-hockey hall of fame. The museum allows access to the southwestern tower.

North of the castle but still within the walls is the fun **Museum of Folk Music** (Hudobné múzeum; ☎ 54 41 33 49; adult/child 20/10Sk; ☻ 9am-5pm Tue-Sun), filled with a staggering variety of folk pipes, whistles, drums and more. In summer check the posted schedule of live performances.

From the castle's ramparts you can see Austria (3km southwest) and, on a clear day, Hungary (16km south), although with the New Bridge and the mind-numbingly vast housing estates of Petržalka, the view is not so much beautiful as awesome. The old and new towns stretch to the east.

Squeezed between the castle and the old town is what's left of the old Jewish quarter that was pulled down for the New Bridge. There are a couple of museums worth investigating on Židovská.

Metres from the seething overpass traffic is a handsome, wedge-shaped, rococo burgher's house called the House of the Good Shepherd (dom U dobrého pastiera) after its façade statue. Inside is a small **Museum of Clocks** (múzeum hodín; Map pp336-7; ☎ 54 41 19 40; Židovská 1; ☻ 10am-5pm Tue-Fri, 11am-6pm Sat & Sun May-Sep, 9.30am-4.30pm Tue-Sun Oct-Apr) with a multitude of fancy time pieces. Opposite is the **Decorative Arts Museum** (múzeum umeleckých remesiel) containing some impressively carved furniture. It's open the same hours as the clock museum; entrance to both is adult/child 40/20Sk.

Ahead 50m is the excellent **Museum of Jewish Culture** (múzeum židovskej kultúry; Map pp336-7; ☎ 54 41 85 07; Židovská 17; adult/child 40/20Sk; ☻ 11am-5pm Sun-Fri) with displays in English on Slovakia's much-persecuted Jews.

Historical Centre   (Map pp336–7)
AROUND KAPITULSKÁ
Across from the castle is the 14th-century **St Martin Cathedral** (dóm sv Martina; Rudnayovo námestie; admission free; ☻ 10am-4.45pm Mon-Sat, 2-4.45pm

---

CHATAM SOFER
Born Moshe Schreiber in Frankfurt, Chatam Sofer (1762–1839) moved to Bratislava in 1806 to accept a position of rabbi. Here he founded a yeshiva, a school for rabbis, and in the course of his life trained over 150 rabbis. The school became one of the best known in Europe, and operated up until the first years of WWII when it had to be moved to Israel. After his death, his tomb, located in the city's small **Jewish cemetery** (Map p332; ☎ 0903 265 453; Žižkova; admission 60Sk; by appointment only), became a pilgrimage for Jews from all over Europe. During the Nazi occupation the cemetery was basically buried under rubble, but has recently been reopened to the public and is now Slovakia's most important Jewish site.

Sun), Bratislava's foremost Gothic structure. It's a rather modest building considering this was where at least nine Hungarian Habsburg kings and eight queens were crowned from 1563 to 1830 (the steeple is topped by a golden crown in place of a cross). Inside is a 1734 statue by Georg Raphael Donner, Austria's best-known baroque sculptor, of St Martin cutting off the corner of his cloak for a beggar. The cathedral is constantly undergoing renovations due to vibrations from bridge traffic.

Kapitulská runs north from the cathedral, and is one of the city's oldest, quietest and most romantic streets, which was once lined with the homes of the clergy. At the end is the **Church of the Clarissine Order** (kostol Klarisiek), founded by the Cistercians in the 13th century.

MICHALSKÁ, VENTÚRSKA & PANSKÁ
Collectively Michalská and Ventúrska make up the main street of Bratislava. It's a lively, vibrant avenue of busy cafés and restaurants, lined with beautifully restored baroque palaces, built after the Hungarians moved their capital here. At its northern end facing nearby Hurbanovo námestie is the old town's only surviving watchtower, the **Michael Tower** (Michalská veža; ☎ 54 43 30 44; Michalská 24; adult/child 30/10Sk; ☻ 10am-5pm Tue-Fri, 11am-6pm Sat & Sun), with a 14th-century base, 16th-century top and 18th-century steeple. Go inside for displays

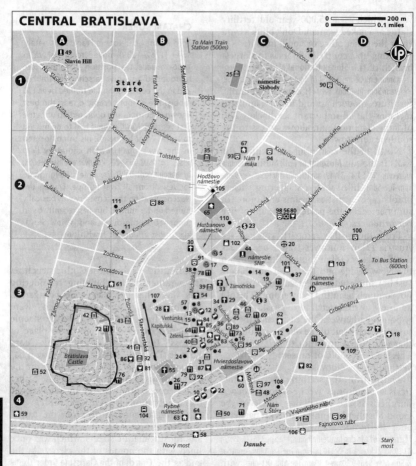

CENTRAL BRATISLAVA

0 _____ 200 m
0 _____ 0.1 miles

of antique swords, armour and guns, and views across the rooftops.

Further south is one of the buildings making up the huge **University Library** (Univerzitná knižnica; Michalská 1) that served as the Hungarian diet, or parliament, in the 18th and 19th centuries.

Another **library building** (Ventúrska 13) has a concert pavilion where nine-year-old Franz Liszt gave his first recital in 1820. Down the street, at Ventúrska 10, is one of several palaces once owned by the Pálffy family. Another child, six-year-old Wolfgang Amadeus Mozart, performed here in 1762; the building is also called **Mozart House** (Mozartov dom). The buildings are generally not open to the public.

At the bottom of Ventúrska turn left onto Panská where you'll see the **City Art Gallery** (☎ 54 43 36 27; Panská 19; adult/child 20/10Sk; ☷ 10am-6pm Tue-Sun) inside the stunning Pálffy Palace (Pálffyho palác). On display is a mix of Slovakian impressionist and postimpressionist art works, plus temporary contemporary art in the basement.

HLAVNÉ NÁMESTIE & FRANTIŠKÁNSKÉ NÁMESTIE

Once the centre and main market of the old town, Hlavné námestie is now a sleek, touristy plaza with a splendid fountain. Among the burghers' houses around it, note the very handsome 1912 Art Nouveau building on the southwestern side.

The square's northern extension is Františkánské námestie. Along its eastern side is the dominant **Church of the Holy Saviour** (kostol Najsvätejšieho Spasiteľa; admission free; ☼ 7am-7pm), a 17th-century Protestant church 'baroquified' by the Jesuits. Immediately north are the **Franciscan Church of the Annunciation** (kostol Zvestovania-Františkáni; admission free) and monastery that give the square its name. The latter, one of Bratislava's oldest churches, was completed in 1297 but thoroughly altered by later renovations. It's normally open only early mornings or late evenings for mass.

Opposite is the 1770 **Mirbach Palace** (Mirbachov palác; ☎ 54 54 15 56; Františkánské námestie 11; adult/child 40/20Sk; ☼ 10am-6pm Tue-Sun), with a small collection of Renaissance religious art, plus modern graphic design on the ground floor.

PRIMACIÁLNE NÁMESTIE

The austere, quiet square behind is dominated by one of Slovakia's finest neoclassi-cal buildings, the **Primate's Palace** (Primaciálny palác; ☎ 54 43 14 73; Primaciálne námestie 1; adult/child 30Sk/free; ☼ 10am-5pm Tue-Sun). Its façade is topped with a 150kg, cast-iron bishop's hat. Enter to see the Hall of Mirrors where Napoleon and the Austrian Emperor Franz I signed the Treaty of Pressburg on 26 December 1805, following the Battle of Austerlitz. In the municipal gallery on the 2nd floor are rare English tapestries from the 1630s.

Next door is one of Bratislava's most appealing buildings, the 14th-century Gothic **Old Town Hall**, complete with Renaissance courtyard and green-roofed neo-Gothic annexe. It's now mostly taken up by the **Municipal Museum** (☎ 54 43 47 42; Primaciálne námestie 3; adult/child 30/10Sk; ☼ 10am-5pm Tue-Fri, 11am-6pm Sat & Sun) which has torture chambers in the casemates and an extensive collection housed in finely decorated rooms. It's also possible to climb its **tower** (adult/child 30/10Sk; ☼ 2-4pm Wed, 3-5pm Sat & Sun).

BRATISLAVA

Hviezdoslavovo námestie to the Danube
Map pp336–7

This narrow, tree-lined square traces a filled-in moat outside the old town walls. It's named after Pavol Orságh Hviezdoslav, Slovakia's favourite poet, whose statue sits in the centre. Presiding over the square is the neobaroque **Slovak National Theatre** (Slovenské národné divadlo; Map pp336-7; ☎ 54 43 30 83; www.snd.sk; Hviezdoslavovo námestie 1), the city's premier opera and ballet venue, completed in 1886, and the newly renovated **Carlton Hotel** (☎ 59 39 00 00; Hviezdoslavovo námestie 3). Unfortunately the only way to see the lush interior of the theatre is to attend a performance. At the western end is **Rybné námestie** (Fish Square), all that remains of the city's old fish market – yet another victim of the New Bridge.

South of the square on Mostová is the beautiful, neobaroque **Reduta Palace** (♡ only for Slovak Philharmonic shows; see p343), completed in 1914 as a dance hall.

West of Mostová is the rewarding **Slovak National Gallery** (Map pp336-7; ☎ 54 43 20 81; Rázusovo nábrežie 2; adult/child 80/40Sk; ♡ 10am-5.30pm Tue-Sun). This is Slovakia's biggest combined gallery and museum collection, with a good Gothic and baroque section and a wonderful display of 20th-century Slovak design and art. It's about the most you'll pay for a museum or gallery in Slovakia, but it's the best place to sample both historical and contemporary works from Slovak artists.

East of Mostová is the **Slovak National Museum** (Map pp336-7; ☎ 59 34 91 41; Vajanského nábrežie 2; adult/child 20/10Sk; ♡ 9am-5pm Tue-Sun), featuring unimaginative exhibits on archaeology, natural history and geology.

Námestie SNP & Around
Map pp336–7

The central feature of the vast námestie SNP is a bronze monument – dubbed by locals the 'Angry Family' – to the antifascist uprising for which the square is named. In November 1989 huge crowds assembled here in the days leading up to the fall of Communism, and it was also here that Slovak nationalists gathered before the Velvet Divorce from the Czech Republic.

Westward on Hurbanovo námestie, across from the Michael Tower, is the city's finest baroque church, the **Church of the Holy Trinity** (kostol Trinitárov; admission free; ♡ 7am-7pm), worth a look for the trompe l'oeil dome painted on the ceiling. Two blocks

northeast of námestie SNP is the city's only remaining **synagogue** (Heydukova 11-13; ♡ closed to the public) looking quite forlorn.

East of námestie SNP is Kamenné námestie, a major shopping district (as evidenced by the gigantic Tesco department store) and tram junction. The blocks of Štúrova just south of the square contain many fine revivalist style buildings dating from the end of the 19th century. Just east of Štúrova is the striking **St Elizabeth Church** or **Blue Church** (kostol Stv Alžbety/kostol Modrý; Bezručova 2; admission free; ♡ 7am-7pm). This church is dedicated to Bratislava's only home-grown saint who was born in Bratislava Castle in 1207. It's a cool shade of light blue and purely Art Nouveau in design. On Saturday it acts as a wedding machine.

Slavín Hill
Map pp336–7

On Slavín Hill, northwest of the old town, is a cemetery and garden with fine views over the city. Towering over it is the **Slavín War Memorial**, an enormous pillar erected in 1960 in memory of the 6000 Soviet soldiers who died pushing the Nazis out of western Slovakia.

To get here, take trolleybus No 208 west from Hodžovo námestie to the end of the line on Šulekova (20 minutes), and climb for 1km up Timravina and Mišíkova. Alexander Dubček (see p24) lived in enforced isolation at Mišíkova 46 from 1968 until his 'resurrection' in 1989, and afterwards until his death in November 1992.

ACTIVITIES
Hiking
Looming above Bratislava is **Kamzík Hill** (440m), the final southern bump of the Lesser Carpathians. It rises 300m above the Danube and is covered with woods and trails.

For a good hike, take trolleybus No 203 from Hodžovo námestie through the vineyards of Vinohrady to the end of the line at Koliba (25 minutes). A trail climbs north past a memorial to the 1683 victory over the Turks at Vienna, to the summit where there's a 200m TV tower (complete with restaurant).

Swimming
Zlaté piesky (Golden Sands) is a lake resort 7km northeast of the old town where locals escape the summer heat. You can hire

rowing boats and sailboards in summer. Trams No 2 (from the main train station) and No 4 (from the city centre) terminate here (20 minutes). Lakes closer to town include **Kuchajda** (Map p332), near the Polus Center, and **Štrkovecké jazero** (Map p332), near Hotel Junior. It normally costs around 20/10Sk for adults/children per day, and the lakes are generally open 9am to sundown June to August.

BRATISLAVA FOR CHILDREN
Bratislava isn't overly populated with playgrounds and activities for children, but there are a couple of places to keep the little ones entertained. **Bibiana** (Map pp336-7; ☎ 54 43 13 08; Panská 41; admission free; ☺ 10am-6pm Tue-Sat, 10am-7pm Sun) calls itself an International House of Art for Children; it displays art pieces aimed directly at kids, and also runs fun drawing classes. The **Puppet Theatre** is another option – see p343 for more details.

If you're looking for a baby-sitter try **Nikea** (Map pp336-7; ☎ 54 64 32 32; Panenská 7; ☺ 8am-4.30pm Mon-Fri).

QUIRKY BRATISLAVA
It's not the castle, new bridge or old town that tops the list as the most-photographed attraction in Bratislava. What attracts tourists' lenses like a magnet are three life-size bronze statues – **The Peeper**, **The Frenchman** and **The Photographer**. The Frenchman looks suspiciously like Napoleon himself, and can be found leaning on a park bench on Hlavné námestie. The Photographer, on Laurinská, is the epitome of the paparazzi, waiting patiently and almost cunningly for that perfect shot. The favourite though is The Peeper, a helmeted man inconspicuously peering out from a street manhole on Panská. You'd think with all the tourists crowded around he'd be easy to spot, but he's almost lost his head twice to careless driving.

TOURS
BIS organises **walking tours** (300Sk; ☺ 2pm) of the historical centre as well as themed walks, such as Gothic Bratislava or **Bratislava's Musical Heritage** (up to 19 persons 1000Sk; call to arrange).

One-hour sightseeing trips (Map pp336-7; ☎ 52 93 22 26; Fajnorovo nábrežie; adult/child 80/45Sk; ☺ 2.30pm Wed, Thu & Fri, 3.30pm & 5.30pm Sat & Sun May–mid-Sep) on the Danube, leaving from

the hydrofoil terminal, are a unique and less-strenuous way to view the city, but not as intimate as a walking tour. Other Danube experiences include a **hydrofoil trip** (adult/child 370/270Sk; ☺ 12.30pm Sat May-Aug, 11.30am Sat Sep) to Gabčíkovo, Slovakia's controversial dam south of Bratislava (p54).

FESTIVALS & EVENTS
Bratislava has a constant flow of events throughout the year. Below is a list of the major ones:

Bienále ilustrácií Bratislava (BIB; ☎ 54 43 13 08; www.bibiana.sk) This well-known international children's book illustration fair takes place in late September and early October on odd-numbered years.

Bratislava Carnival (☎ 54 41 21 02) In February.

Bratislava Music Festival (Bratislavské hudobné slávnosti, or BHS; ☎ 54 43 45 46; www.hc.sk/bhs) Late September to mid-October, the town's largest musical event.

Cultural Summer Festival (Kultúrne leto; ☎ 54 41 30 63) Runs from June to September; chamber concerts, opera, drama, jazz, folk music, brass bands and films in locations around the old town.

SLEEPING
Bratislava has its fair share of hotels, *pensions* and hostels, although it has yet to be graced by a five-star hotel (the Carlton, with four, is as close as it gets). There are not a lot of options in the very heart of the old town; most places are either on its borders or 10 to 15 minutes away by public transport. Reservations are recommended year-round, even

---

GAY & LESBIAN BRATISLAVA
Bratislava has the biggest gay and lesbian scene in Slovakia, but that's not saying much. A good organisation to quiz on the current scene is **Ganymedes** (Map p332; ☎ 50 22 87 04; www.ganymedes.info; Istropolis, Trnavské mýto 1), although it's best to check its website rather than popping along to the office as it's often vacant. The lesbian-specific group **Museion** (Saratovská 3) is another source of information.

Two well-established clubs around town are the slightly divey **Spider Club** (Map pp336-7; ☎ 0903 758 096; Jedlíkova 9) and the larger **Apollon Club** (Map pp336-7; ☎ 5567 Panenská 24) which stays open to 5am on weekends.

at top-end hotels, and, as you'd expect in a capital city, prices are higher compared to the rest of the country.

BIS can arrange accommodation (50Sk reservation fee; no phone reservations) as can the Internet café **Impetus** (Map pp336-7; ☎ 54 43 25 58; Nákupné Centrum, Michalská 2; reservation fee is cost of local phone call), which is tailored to budget accommodation.

Budget

In July and August it's fairly easy to sleep cheaply in Bratislava, though don't expect to be too near the city centre. The rest of the year, cheap accommodation is very hard to find; your best bet is to check with BIS or Impetus.

HOSTELS

The following student hostels only open from July to August and all have shared facilities.

Zvárač (Map p332; ☎ 49 24 66 00; ubyt@cert.vuz.sk; Pionierska 17; s/d from 600/850Sk; P) This student hostel has extremely clean rooms, kitchens for use, very friendly service and quiet surroundings. Take tram No 3 from the train station or bus No 50 from the bus station.

Bernolák (Map p332; ☎ 52 45 02 13; Bernolákova 1; s/d/tr 400/400/600Sk) About 15 minutes' walk from the train station, bus station and the old town, Bernolák is a good budget choice. Rooms are basic and clean, and – lo and behold – there's a laundry! A load will set you back 140Sk.

Mladá Garda (Map p332; ☎ 44 25 31 36; Račianska 103; s/d/tr 200/400/600Sk) Mladá Garda is about the cheapest option in town, and only a few blocks north of Zvárač (same transport connections). Rooms are clean but can be a little noisy due to the close proximity of train tracks.

PRIVATE ROOMS

BIS has a list of private rooms starting from 350Sk per person. Annoyingly, private rooms are more expensive off-season as student hostels aren't available.

CAMPING

Intercamp Zlaté piesky (☎ 44 25 73 73; www.inter camp.sk; Senecká cesta 2; tent/person/car/bungalow 60/70/80/890Sk; ☼ May–mid-Oct) Not only is Intercamp the closest camping ground to Bratislava, it also has the advantage of being a hop, skip and a jump away from Zlaté piesky lake. Its bungalows sleep up to three.

Mid-Range

Breakfast is generally included in the price in hotels and *pensions*, but make sure you double-check before you sign on the dotted line.

HOTELS – CENTRAL   Map pp336–7

Hotel Perugia (☎ 54 43 18 18; www.perugia.sk; Zelená 5; s/d 4280/5080Sk; P ⊠ ⌘) Small, stylish, incredibly central with high service standards, the Perugia is a cut above most accommodation options in central Bratislava.

Hotel Devín (☎ 54 43 36 40; Riečna 4; s/d 5500/6500Sk; P ⊠ ⌘) This austere hotel is one of the city's oldest. Rooms are not as modern as at Hotel Danube but have a more individual feel to them.

Hotel Danube (☎ 59 34 08 33; Rybné námestie 1; s/d €150/170; P ⊠ ⌘ ⌘) The Danube is a luxurious hotel that caters to business clients, with all the amenities you'd expect.

Hotel Tatra (☎ 59 27 21 11; www.hoteltatra.sk; námestie 1.mája 5; s/d 2920/3980Sk; P ⌘) The Tatra is a smart business hotel with modern but soulless rooms and a small fitness centre.

Botel Gracia (☎ 54 43 21 32; www.botel-gracia.sk; Rázusovo nárežie; s/d 2030/2760Sk; P) Want to spend a night on the Danube? Here's your chance – this moored boat has comfy but not particularly modern rooms that have a distinct slant to them.

HOTELS – SUBURBS   Map p332

Hotel Spirit (☎ 54 77 75 61; www.hotelspirit.sk; Vanéurova 1; s/d 990/1430Sk; ⌨) The interior of this avant-garde hotel is as bizarre as its exterior – all angles and colour. It's highly appealing though, and very handy to the train station (head for the last platform, not the main exit, and it's on the other side of the train track. Rooms are rather Spartan.

Hotel No 16 (☎ 54 41 16 72; hotelno16@internet.sk; Partizánska 16/A; s/d €95/125; P ⊠ ⌘) Located in a well-to-do neighbourhood below the castle, No 16 is a lovely old house furnished with antiques and finery, and has a cosy, intimate feel.

Hotel-Penzión Arcus (☎ 55 57 25 22; www.hotel arcus.sk; Moskovská 5; s/d 1600/2200Sk; P ⊠) This friendly, quiet hotel is only 15 minutes' walk from the old town. It's a popular place so book ahead as far as possible.

Trams No 8 from the train station and No 9 from the old town pass just south of the following hotels.

Hotel Echo (☎ 55 56 91 70; ptksr@internet.sk; Prešovská 39; s/d 1400/1740Sk; P ⚡) Situated on a quiet, leafy street, Echo is a small, welcoming hotel with bright, comfy rooms.

Hotel Nivy (☎ 55 41 03 90; www.hotelnivy.sk; Líščie Nivy 3; r 1400Sk; P ⚡) Rooms within this colourful tower block are bright and large – the only drawback is the stupidly expensive parking at 20Sk per hour.

PENSIONS   **Map pp336–7**

Caribic's Penzión (☎ 54 41 83 34; caribics@stonline.sk; Žižkova 1/A; s/d 990/1980Sk) Newly refurbished Caribic's has small but modern rooms 10 minutes' walk west of the old town.

Gremium Penzión (☎ 54 13 10 26; www.gremium.sk; Gorkého 11; s/d 920/1650Sk; P) With its prime location, fine rooms and busy bar, you'll have to book ahead to get one of the few rooms at Gremium.

Chez David Penzión (☎ 54 41 38 24; Zámocká 13; s/d 2177/3777Sk; P ⚡) This bright, modern guesthouse, in the old Jewish ghetto directly below the castle, has eight rooms and one apartment, all slightly overpriced. There's a fine restaurant on site.

Top End

HOTELS – CENTRAL   **Map pp336–7**

Carlton Hotel (☎ 59 39 00 00; Hviezdoslavovo námestie 3; r from €210; P ✖ ⚡) With plush, newly refurbished rooms, a prime location near the national theatre and plenty of character, this is easily the top dog in town. There's also a fitness centre, sauna, rooms with wheelchair access and bicycles available for guests.

Hotel Forum (☎ 59 34 81 11; www.forumba.sk; Hodžovo námestie 2; s/d €160/180; P ✖ ⚡ ⚡) What the Forum lacks in class it makes up in amenities, which include a full-blown wellness centre, a plethora of business facilities and wheelchair-access rooms.

EATING

Bratislava has come along in leaps and bounds in the restaurant department over the past few years. No longer is Slovakian cuisine the only option in town – trendy establishments have popped up offering international dishes alongside *bryndzové halušky* (small potato dumplings topped with sheep's cheese and fried bacon bits)

and *gulášová* (a traditional goulash). Prices are high for Slovakia, but compared to Western Europe they're pleasingly low. The best restaurants and cafés are concentrated in the old town.

Cafés

London Café (Map pp336–7; ☎ 54 43 11 85; Panská 17; light lunches 70-100Sk) Quiches, salads and English papers are all the rage at this, the British Council's café.

Kaffee Mayer (Map pp336–7; ☎ 54 41 17 41; Hlavné námestie 4; coffee around 40Sk) This Viennese-style and classy café has excellent, but pricey, coffee, cakes and light meals.

Quick Eats

Bagetka (Map pp336–7; Zelená 8; baguettes 40-60Sk; ⏰ 8.30am-9pm Mon-Sat, 2-9pm Sun) Tucked away down a narrow alley connecting Zelená and Michalská, this small baguette shop offers great sandwiches.

Café Laguna (Map pp336–7; Laurinská 7; ice cream from 6Sk) Maybe it's the location, maybe it's the ice cream, but whatever the reason there's always a queue of locals and tourists waiting patiently for their *zmrzlina*.

Restaurants

Prašná Bašta (Map pp336–7; ☎ 54 43 49 57; Zámočnícka 11; mains 100-200Sk) Popular with everyone in town, Prašná Bašta has an excellent Slovakian menu and appealing settings; choose from its quiet garden or cellar-like interior.

Hradná Vináreň (Map pp336–7; ☎ 59 34 13 58; námestie A. Dubčeka 1; mains around 200Sk) Located within the castle grounds, this quality wine tavern is the perfect spot for a romantic dinner, with candle-lit tables on the patio overlooking the old town.

Modrá Hviezda (Map pp336–7; ☎ 54 43 27 47; Beblavého 14; mains 120-200Sk) This atmospheric little eatery features Slovak and Hungarian dishes. The décor is almost medieval and there's a small patio with partial views of the city.

Tokyo Sushi Bar (Map pp336–7; ☎ 54 43 49 82; Strakova; sushi sets from 200Sk) For arguably the best Japanese in Bratislava head here. Its back courtyard is perfect on warm, summer evenings.

Lúčnica (Map pp336–7; Štúrova 6; mains 100-150Sk) What Lúčnica lacks in a quality menu it makes up with oodles of atmosphere. With walls adorned in farming implements and traditional music blearing out of the stereo, its like the Velvet Revolution, or the Communist era, never happened.

Domenico (Map pp336-7; ☎ 54 64 01 67; námestie Ľ. Štúra 4; mains 130-180Sk) Café by day, restaurant by night, Domenico serves up hearty Slovakian fare amid a mixture of simple furniture and antique pieces.

Pizza House (Map pp336-7; ☎ 54 43 18 40; Hviezdoslavovo námestie 15; pizzas 100-150Sk) Pizza house makes some of the best pizza in town.

Self-catering

There's a massive supermaket in the basement of the Tesco department store on Kamenné námestie. A small, indoor fruit-and-vegetable market can be found on Klobučnícká.

Vegetarian

Many restaurants have finally cottoned on to the concept of vegetarianism and added a number of meatless dishes to the menu, but it's still hard to find a veg-only establishment, even in the capital. **Divesta** (Map pp336-7; ☎ 54 43 36 58; Laurinská 8; meals from 60Sk; ⏰ 11am-3pm Mon-Fri) is one exception; its small, tasty selection is totally and utterly devoid of meat.

DRINKING

Bratislava's bar scene is not massive but it'll keep you entertained for a few nights. Michalská and Ventúrska have the largest concentration of bars but they all look, and feel, like cloned copies of each other.

Buddha Bar (Map pp336-7; ☎ 55 57 21 24; Medená 16) One of the best options in town, this small, cellar bar has quality DJs spinning smooth tunes (mainly jazz orientated), great juices and a very relaxed air.

Kut (Map pp336-7; Zámočnícka 11) Kut is another bar with good music (anything from drum 'n' bass to Slovak cabaret) and a chilled-out atmosphere. The bar staff may be a little drunk, but that only adds to the fun.

4 Izby (Map pp336-7; Heydukova 19) This dark, but by no means dingy, café/bar has an odd selection of comfy couches and chairs, an alternative feel and modern tunes.

Verne (Map pp336-7; ☎ 54 43 05 14; Hviezdoslavovo námestie 18) Verne has a definite bohemian feel, pavement seating and, once again, mismatched furniture.

Café Antik (Map pp336-7; ☎ 54 43 02 60; Rybárska brána 2; coffee around 30Sk) Antik has a distinctly relaxed atmosphere, with lots of deep reds and subdued light. If you're not into coffee, there's a superb range of spirits available, or you can change some money!

For fine cocktails, try either **Greenwich** (Map pp336-7; ☎ 54 43 18 52; Zelená 10) or **People's Lounge** (Map pp336-7; ☎ 54 64 07 77; Gorkého 1), both of which are highly stylish but have a slight air of snobbery about them.

If there are tourists in town, you're sure to meet them at **The Dubliner** (Map pp336-7; ☎ 54 41 07 06; Sedlárska 6), a massive Irish pub with an open fire and good Guinness, or next door at Spanish-themed **El Diablo** (Map pp336-7; ☎ 0903 771 778).

Other recommendations:

Azyl (Map pp336-7; Žďovská) Lots of wrought iron, views of the Cathedral and chilled tunes; a break from the bustling old town.

U Certa (Map pp336-7; Beblavého) Close to Azyl, in both atmosphere and location.

ENTERTAINMENT

Most entertainment options are either within the confines of the old town or skirting its borders. Here you'll find top opera, ballet and theatre, along with some very funky clubs. See p334 for entertainment publications.

Cinema

Films (100Sk) are generally shown in the original language with Slovak subtitles:

Kino Mladosť (Map pp336-7; ☎ 54 43 50 03; Hviezdoslavovo námestie 17)

Kino Tatra (Map pp336-7; ☎ 52 96 89 94; námestie 1.mája 5)

Film clubs are very popular in Bratislava; prices are low (membership costs 50Sk, admission around 20Sk) and films are generally international classics:

FK Múzeum (Map pp336-7; Hlavné námestie 1)

FK Nostalgia (Map pp336-7; ☎ 52 96 17 13; Starohorská 2)

Clubs

Entry into clubs ranges from zip to upwards of 100Sk.

Spojka (Map pp336-7; ☎ 52 73 33 76; Prešernova 4) Spojka's DJs spin some of the more progressive dance music around, which ranges from trance to drum 'n' bass.

Hlbočina (Map pp336-7; Kapucínska) Hlbočina is another club with top dance music; the ground floor is for chilling and the basement for shaking your groove thang.

Terminal (Map pp336-7; Špitálska 4) This cavernous place is one of the bigger clubs in town and plays mainstream dance music.

Sport

As in the UK it's safe enough to go along to a local football match, but you just need to be a little more alert to what's going on around you. To catch Slovakia's high flyers, SK Slovan, in action head to their home **football stadium** (☎ 44 37 30 83; Junácka 2).

Bratislava's ice hockey team **HC Slovan** (☎ 44 45 65 00; Odbojárov 3) plays at a stadium northeast of the old town.

Theatre, Opera & Classical Music

Opera and ballet are presented at the **Slovak National Theatre** (Slovenské národné divadlo; Map pp336-7; ☎ 54 43 30 83; www.snd.sk; Hviezdoslavovo námestie 1). Tickets are sold at the 'Pokladňa-Kassa' office (☒ 8am-5.30pm Mon-Fri, 9am-1pm Sat; Jesenského). An hour before the performance, ticket sales are at the theatre itself, but they're usually sold out (*vypredané*).

The **Slovak Philharmonic** (Map pp336-7; ☎ 54 43 33 51; cnr Palackého & Mostová) is based in the neorococo Reduta Palace, across the park from the national theatre. The **ticket office** (☒ 1-7pm Mon-Tue & Thu-Fri, 8am-2pm Wed) is inside the building.

Nová scéna (Map pp336-7; ☎ 52 92 11 39; Kollárovo námestie 20) presents operettas, musicals and drama (the latter in Slovak, so check first). The **ticket office** (☒ 12.30-7pm Mon-Fri) also opens an hour before the performance, but the tickets are usually sold out by then.

The fun **State Puppet Theatre** (Štátne Bábkové divadlo; Map p332; ☎ 52 63 47 40; Dunajská 36) puts on puppet shows for kids, usually at 9am or 10am and sometimes again at 1pm or 2pm.

SHOPPING

Bratislava is not a major shopping city. For folk handicrafts head to **Uluv** (Map pp336-7; ☎ 52 92 38 02; námestie SNP 12) or **Folk Folk** (Map pp336-7; ☎ 54 43 42 92; Obchodná 10), and for souvenirs to **Bratislava Shop** (Map pp336-7; ☎ 55 41 04 01; námestie SNP 13).

The **Polus City Centre** (Map p332; ☎ 49 10 20 31; Vajnorská), northeast of the city, and **Aupark** (Map p332; ☎ 68 26 61 11; Einsteinova), south across the Danube, are both large shopping complexes.

GETTING THERE & AWAY
Air

For details on flights within Slovakia, and to and from the Czech Republic, see p454.

Bus

At Bratislava's **main bus station** (☎ 02-55 56 73 49 for Slovenská autobusová doprava (SAD)/Eurolines information; Mlynské nivy), east of the city centre, you can usually buy your ticket from the driver if the bus is not full, but check first at the information counter. Advance tickets for the buses marked 'R' on the posted timetable may be purchased from the AMS counter.

Seven to 10 buses a day connect Bratislava to Vienna (Sudtirolerplatz, 480Sk, 1½ hours). Other international buses from Bratislava go to Budapest (four hours, daily), Frankfurt (2100Sk, 11½ hours, Tuesday, Thursday, Sunday) and Kraków (eight hours, weekly). Tickets may be purchased with crowns for most destinations within Eastern Europe (and Vienna) at the international ticket window in the bus station or at the adjacent Eurolines office for Eurolines destinations (generally cities in Western Europe).

National departures include three buses a day to Komárno (128Sk, 1¾ hours), six to Žilina (260Sk, 3½ hours), one to Dolný Kubín (344Sk, 5½ hours), 20 to Banská Bystrica (260Sk, 3½ hours), 14 to Poprad (428Sk, 5½–seven hours), five to Prešov (536Sk, seven to nine hours), eight to Košice (512Sk, 6½ to 7½ hours) and seven to Bardejov (560Sk, eight to ten hours). Journey durations vary depending on how many times the bus stops and which route it takes.

Car & Motorcycle

For information on local car-hire firms, see p344. **Avis** (☎ 53 41 61 11; www.avis.sk) is in the Hotel Forum and at the airport. **Hertz** (☎ 43 29 14 82) also has a desk at the airport.

Two 24-hour border crossings to Austria are at Petržalka and Jarovce.

Train

All express trains to Prague (700Sk, 4½ hours) pass through Brno (250Sk, 1½ hours). Express services to Košice (590Sk, five hours) are rare but there are plenty of regional trains (476Sk, six hours). Both stop at Poprad (384Sk, 4¾ hours) and Žilina (242Sk, 2¾ hours).

International services from Bratislava include six a day to Budapest (520Sk, three hours), two to Warsaw (1400Sk, 7¾ hours) and one to Moscow (2100Sk, 33 hours). Seven trains daily make the trip between Vienna (Südbahnhof) and Bratislava's main train station (376Sk, 1¼ hours). International train tickets can be purchased at the station.

Walking into Hungary or Austria

If you don't want to bother getting an international train ticket, take a local train or bus to Komárno and walk across the bridge to Komárom in Hungary.

The Austrian border is about 4km beyond Nový most along Viedenská cesta. Take bus No 81 from Hodžovo námestie southbound across the bridge and get off at the next stop after high-rise Hotel Incheba. Walk 2km to the border and clear customs.

GETTING AROUND
To/From the Airport

Bratislava's airport (Letisko MR Štefánika) is 7km northeast of the city centre. Bus No 61 runs from the train station (16Sk, 20 minutes), or get there by taxi (approximately 300Sk).

Car & Motorcycle

Headaches for drivers include pedestrian areas around the old town, numerous (and poorly marked) one-way streets, limited parking and sharp-eyed traffic police. Parking in the city centre is fairly restricted, so consider paying around 50Sk an hour at a private car park.

Public Transport

Bratislava's extensive **public transport** (Dopravný podnik Bratislava, or DPB; ☎ 59 50 59 50; www.dpb.sk - Slovak only) is based on a tram network complemented by bus and trolleybus. A ticket costing 14/16/20Sk remains valid for 10/30/60 minutes after validation, and you can transfer between bus and tram as many times as you like. Bags larger than 30 x 40 x 60cm need a half-fare ticket. Tourist tickets (*turistické cestovné lístky*), which are valid for 1/2/3/7 days and cost 80/150/185/275Sk, are good value.

Orange automats at main tram and bus stops sell tickets – validate the ticket in the little red machine on the bus or tram when you board. You can also buy tickets at DPB offices at the train and bus stations, in the underground passageway below **Hodžovo námestie** (⊙ 6am-7pm Mon-Fri) and on **Obchodná** (⊙ 9.30am-5.30pm Mon-Fri) near the Hotel Forum.

Trams and buses run from 5am to 11.30pm. **Night service buses** (linky nočnej dopravy; 20Sk) run through the small hours; schedules are posted at main stops.

Be aware that people are extremely polite on public transport in Bratislava – expect to give up your seat for the elderly or parents with children.

Taxi

If you require a taxi call **ABC Taxi** (☎ 16 100). Metered fares cost 13Sk per kilometre if ordered in advance, and 23Sk per kilometre when hailed from the street.

AROUND BRATISLAVA

DEVÍN CASTLE

About 9km west of Bratislava is one of Slovakia's most important historical monuments and one of the more impressive sights on the Slovakian stretch of the Danube, **Devín Castle** (☎ 65 73 01 05; Múránska; adult/child 40/10Sk; ⊙ 10am-5pm Tue-Fri, 10am-6pm Sat & Sun Apr-Oct). The castle's first walled buildings date from Roman times but it gained major status, and major fortifications, during the reign of Prince Rastislav of The Great Moravian Empire in the 9th century. With the fall of the Moravian Empire the Hungarians soon took it over and made it the main military bulwark in the area. It passed from one family to another in the ensuing centuries, before becoming uninhabitable in the 18th century; Napoleon's army basically finished the job by blowing it up in 1809.

In the first half of the 19th century Devín became a symbol of national identity and Slovak nationalist Ľudovít Štúr encouraged the designation of Devín as a 'national cultural monument'.

Inside the castle you'll find foundations dating from Roman times, plus a 15th-century guardhouse, 16th-century gate and

NEIL WILSON

New Bridge (Nový most) over the Danube River, Bratislava

NEIL WILSON

Neobaroque Slovak National Theatre (p338), Bratislava

Plague column (p368) in the main square (námestie sv Trojice), Banská Štiavnica

RICHARD NEBESKÝ

MARTIN MOOS

Well-lit Trenčín Castle (p359), Trenčín

Cable car (p396) ascending Lomnický štít (2634m), High Tatras

MARTIN MOOS

MARTIN MOOS

Hiking (p389) signpost at sunset in the High Tatras

A well-restored old building in the walled old town of Levoča (p411)

DAVID GREEDY

reconstructed foundations of a 9th-century church.

Just across the castle moat are the remains of a 16th-century palace, with an exhibit of artefacts on the lower level. At the western end of the complex is a restored 13th-century citadel. Don't miss the grand view across and down the Danube from the fortifications.

On weekdays and summer weekends, bus No 29 departs Bratislava about every half-hour from the stand beneath the New Bridge; the very last stop is at the castle's car park (16Sk, 20 minutes).

A better option is the highly recommended **Bratislava–Devín Castle ferry** (Map pp336-7; ☎ 52 93 22 26; Fajnorovo nábrežie; adult/child return 120/80Sk; ☷ 11am & 4pm Tue-Fri, 10am & 2.30pm Sat & Sun May–mid-Sep). It departs from the hydrofoil terminal in Bratislava.

DANUBIANA MUSEUM

Slovakia's flagship **modern art museum** (☎ 0903 605 505; Vodné dielo, Čunovo; adult/child 60/30Sk; ☷ 10am-8pm May-Sep, 10am-6pm Oct-Apr), about 20km south of Bratislava, was opened in 2000 and occupies an impressive position on a spit of land jutting into the Danube. The red, blue and silver construction houses some of the more cutting-edge art in Slovakia, which constantly changes. It's surrounded by a landscaped park, used as exhibition space itself, and has a great little outdoor café. If you're into modern art in any way, shape or form, this is definitely a place for you.

To get there take bus No 91 (20Sk, 40 minutes) from under the new bridge to the end stop, then follow the signs to the museum (about 3km).

West Slovakia

CONTENTS

It's a mighty pity that most visitors to Slovakia only catch a glimpse of the country's western expanse from the window of a speeding car, bus or train rushing between Bratislava and the high reaches of the Tatras. Unfortunately for them they miss out on the Slovak nation's oldest recorded settlements, theraputic and rejuvenating spas, romantic and ruined castles, wine valleys and Hungarian culture with a Slovak twist.

West Slovakia contains much of the country's lowlands, in the form of the vast Danubian plain and the valley of the Váh. Geographically, the region won't hold your attention for long, but there are a few small ranges where walkers can find solitude. The Lesser Carpathians, for instance, with its vineyards, wine trails and gently undulating hills, is a good choice for stretching the legs. Its flat southern region, bordered by Hungary and the not-so-blue Danube, is an area where you'll often be greeted with *Jó napot* rather than the obligatory *Dobrý deň*.

The regions towns, many of which are featured in the earliest Slovak chronicles, are a mix of old and new. Here you'll find architectural gems sidling up to communist-era monstrosities; Nitra and Trnava are perfect examples of this. The area's castles, striking reminders of West Slovakia's strategical importance, can be found on high, lonely ridges or dominating towns and are either derelict and eerie or painstakingly renovated.

Much of the area is within easy striking distance of Bratislava – perfect for a day trip or an overnight stay.

HIGHLIGHTS

- Step back into the Middle Ages in the handsome, walled old town of **Trnava** (p354)

- Indulge yourself with a mud bath and massage at the low-key spa town of **Piešťany** (p357)

- Enjoy some of the region's most evocative religious architecture in **Nitra** (p348), a former princely seat and bishopric

- Roam **Červený Kameň Castle** (p354) before sitting down to a picnic in its wooded surroundings

- Experience 'Medieval Days' in **Trenčín Castle** (p359) which, strangely enough, is held at night

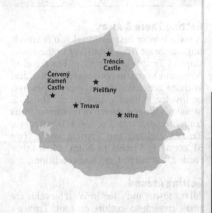

WEST SLOVAKIA

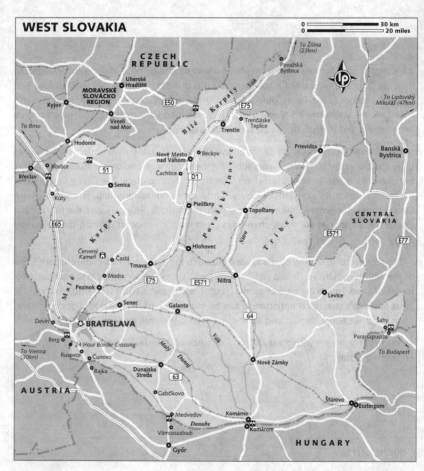

WEST SLOVAKIA

0 _____ 30 km
0 _____ 20 miles

CZECH REPUBLIC

To Žilina (23km)

Považská Bystrica

Uherské Hradiště

MORAVSKÉ SLOVÁCKO REGION

Kyjov

To Liptovský Mikuláš (47km)

E50

Veselí nad Mor

Trenčianske Teplice

To Brno

Hodonín

Trenčín

Prievidza

Banská Bystrica

Nové Mesto nad Váhom

Beckov

Košice

51

Čachtice

D1

Břeclav

Senica

Piešťany

Topoľčany

CENTRAL SLOVAKIA

Kúty

E65

E571

E77

Červený Kameň

Častá

Hlohovec

Trnava

Nitra

E75

E571

Modra

Pezinok

Levice

Senec

Galanta

Šahy

BRATISLAVA

64

Devín

Parassapuszta

Berg

24 Hour Border Crossing

To Vienna (30km)

Rusovce

Čunovo

To Budapest

Rajka

Nové Zámky

Dunajská Streda

63

AUSTRIA

Gabčíkovo

Štúrovo

Esztergom

Medveďov

Komárno

Danube

Vámosszabadi

Komárom

HUNGARY

Győr

Getting There & Away

A train is your best option if you're travelling northeast from Bratislava to the townships of Trnava and Trenčín. For travel to Nitra and Komárno, buses are a better deal as trains are either slower, more expensive, or involve tedious connections. The E75, Slovakia's longest stretch of motorway, runs from Bratislava to Považská Bystrica via Trnava, Piešťany and Trenčín, while Hwy 51 connects Trnava to Nitra. Most other roads are small but in good condition.

Getting Around

All the towns and cities in West Slovakia are small enough to explore on foot. Trnava's main shopping street is pedestrianised.

NITRA

☎ 037 / pop 87,300

Nitra, sprawling beneath a castle in a bend of the Nitra river 80km east of Bratislava, is the oldest documented settlement in Slovakia and the largest city in West Slovakia. It's a quiet town that's neatly split between the Upper Town, with the lion's share of architectural delights, the castle and empty cobble-stoned streets, and the Lower Town, where the modern town has developed.

History

The first Christian church in the Czech and Slovak Republics was founded here by an atheistic, but crafty, prince named Pribina in 833. After Pribina's patch was absorbed into the Great Moravian Empire in 833, Nitra was made a princely seat and bishopric. The first church is gone, but the clerical grip has persisted. In 1302 the Nitra bishops assumed feudal control of the region, strangling its development for almost five centuries.

In the 16th century the Turks pounded the town and nearly wrecked it in the 17th. During the 19th century industrialisation set in, and Nitra is now the republic's fourth largest city after Bratislava, Košice and Prešov. Recently, most of Nitra's money has been pumped into the sprawling Agricultural University and the surrounding Agrokomplex, a series of convention centres which is the largest in Slovakia. The town's historical sites, it seems, are only getting marginal attention; many are falling into disrepair.

Orientation

Beneath the castle is the former clerical enclave called the Upper Town (Horné Mesto). Southward are the remnants of the Lower Town (Dolné Mesto), centred on the grandiose Svätoplukovo námestie. The Lower Town's axes – Štefánikova and Štúrova – cross beside the big district market. The bus and train stations are 500m southwest of the Lower Town centre.

Information

I Net (☎ 0905 309 879; Farská 46; ◷ 9am-10pm Mon-Thu, 9am-11pm Fri, 10am-11pm Sat, noon-8pm Sun) Connect for one hour for 50Sk.

Main Post Office (Svätoplukovo námestie)

NISYS (☎ 741 09 06; info@nitra.sk; Štefánikova 1; ◷ 8am-6pm Mon-Fri, 9am-6pm Sat, 8am-noon Sun Jul & Aug, 8am-6pm Mon-Fri, 8am-noon Sat Sep-Jun) Helpful office offering the usual information services.

Všeobecná Úverová Banka (VÚB; Štefánikova 44) Has an exchange office and ATM.

Tesco department store (Štefánikova 48) Also has an exchange office and ATM.

Sights & Activities
UPPER TOWN

At the top of Farská, in the 19th-century District Hall (Župný dom), recast in 1908 in handsome Art Nouveau style, is the worthwhile **Nitra State Gallery** (Nitrianska štátna galéria; ☎ 772 17 54; Župné námestie 3; adult/child 20/10Sk; ◷ 10am-5pm Tue-Sun). Exhibits feature charcoal and watercolour graphic art by

local artist Stano Dusík, plus some modern oil works by lesser Slovak luminaries.

Through an arch to the gallery's right you enter the Upper Town, the old clerical district, now a historical reserve. The road bears right past the 17th-century **Franciscan Church** (Františkánsky kostol) and former monastery into **Pribinovo námestie**, a sloping square with a small garden, its baroque and neo-Renaissance façades glowering at a modern **statue** of Prince Pribina.

Across the whole south side stretches the 18th-century **Great Seminary** (Veľký seminár; ☎ 772 17 43; visits by appointment only), once again in use as a seminary. Its See Library, opened in 1877, holds one of the more impressive collections in Slovakia. Opposite is the **Lesser Seminary** (Malý seminár). The Atlas statue that supports the corner of the **Kluch Palace** (Kluchov palác), an 1820 canons' residence, appears on the labels of the local beer, Corgon. Atlas' toes are polished where local seminary students touch them for good luck. Unfortunately the Palace is in need of some serious TLC.

From here a path and steps climb northwest to the castle. Outside the castle's single gate are a splendid, baroque Marian plague column, a statue of SS Cyril and Methodius, and a good view northeast to Žibrica Hill.

NITRA CASTLE

The town's **castle** (☎ 772 17 24; admission free; ◷ 9am-noon & 2-4pm) is not actually much to look at but three small but beautiful churches, collectively known as **St Emeram Cathedral** (Katedrálny Biskupský Chram sv Emerama), make the climb up to its baroque fortifications worthwhile. The oldest is a tiny, 11th-century Romanesque rotunda, to the right of the anteroom (though it's not always open). Some sources say parts of Prince Pribina's original church were incorporated into the rotunda.

At the rear of the anteroom and up the stairs is the **Lower Church** (Dolný kostol; 1642) a dark, vaguely lopsided room with a remarkable marble relief of Christ being taken down from the cross. Up more stairs is the **Upper Church** (Horný kostol), completed in 1355 but dripping now with baroque gilt and red marble, a massive organ gallery, and frescoes and paintings everywhere.

NITRA

0 — 300 m
0 — 0.2 miles

| | | |
| A | B | C |

INFORMATION
I Net (Internet café)...........................1 B5
NISYS.......................................(see 16)
Tesco Department Store................2 B5
Všeobecná úverová banka............3 B5

SIGHTS & ACTIVITIES (pp349–51)
Agricultural University....................4 C5
Agricultural University....................5 C6
Agrokomplex Exhibition Hall......6 D6
Bishop's Palace.............................7 B3
Church of St Vincent De Paul....8 B5
Former Synagogue.........................9 B5
Franciscan Church........................10 B4
Great Seminary............................11 B4
Kluch Palace.................................12 B4
Lesser Seminary...........................13 B4
Municipal Theatre........................14 B4
Nitra Castle..................................15 B4
Nitra Museum..............................16 B4
Nitra State Gallery.......................17 B4
Piarist Church..............................18 B5
Pribinovo Námestie & Statue
  of Prince Pribina.......................19 B4
St Emeram Cathedral...................20 B3

SLEEPING   (p351)
Agroinštitút.................................21 D6
Hotel Olympia.............................22 D4
Hotel Zlatý Kľúáik.......................23 C2
Hotel Zobor................................24 B4

EATING   (p351)
Čínska..25 B4
Covered Market..........................26 B5
Furmanská vináreň......................27 B5
Gastro 2000...............................28 B5
Piano Café..................................29 B5

DRINKING   (p351)
Irish Times Pub...........................30 B4

TRANSPORT   (p352)
Bus No 10 to Hotel Zlatý Kľúáik..31 C4
Bus Station.................................32 A6

To Zobor
Hill (3km);
Žibrica (5km)

Orechová

Srma

Svätoplukova

Moušová

Pod

Zlatým brehom

23

Kamenná

Pánská

dolina

Jazerná

Dolnozoborská

Dobšinského

Jelenecká

Chrenovská

Nitra

Parkové nábrežie

Mestský
Park

Podzámska

7 20

15

Steps

13 19 12

17 10 11

Podzámska

Upper Town
(Horné Mesto)

Vŕkárska

Kráľa

Schurmannova

Darúrová

Lomnická

Lomnická

Lomnická

22

Mostná

Kmeťova

Svätoplukovo
námestie   14

30

25 16

24

31

Ľudovíta Okánika

Nábrežie mládeže

To Bratislava
(86km)

Kráľa

Vodná

Párovská

Paláňok

Radlinského

Lower Town
(Dolné Mesto)

8
9

27

Fr. Mojtu

Stančeková

Andreja Hlinku

Pištická

29 28

18

1@

3

Fr. Mojtu

Hviezdna

Štúrova

Vajanského

Cintorínska

Damborského

Štefánikova

Štúrova

2

26

4

P

Štúrova

Výstavná

Hollého

Mestský
cintorín

Coborho

Štefánikova

Chalupkova

Nitra

Nábrežie mládeže

5

21

Akademická

32

Staničná

Družstevná

Spítálska

Hodžova

Mojzeova

Nitra
Train
Station

To Komárno (69km)

To Bratislava

West of the cathedral you might get a peek into the courtyard of the 18th-century **Bishop's Palace**.

LOWER TOWN

Little is left of the original Lower Town (or Old Town) because of Turkish attacks, aristocratic rebellions against Hungary, a 1793 fire and post-Communist redevelopment. The huge, modernist **Municipal Theatre** and the 1882 Municipal Hall (Mestský dom), on Svätoplukovo námestie, merely emphasise their charmless surroundings. The latter is home to the **Nitra Museum** (☎ 741 97 71; Štefánikova 1; adult/child 10/5Sk; ☾ 8am-5pm Tue-Fri, 10am-5pm Sat & Sun), displaying an odd mix of Yugoslav folk paintings and local archaeological finds.

The neighbourhood is dominated by the gloomy, baroque **Piarist Church** (kostol Piaristov; Piaristická 8) and monastery on Piaristická. More beguiling are two little churches on lower Farská – the tall, neo-Romanesque **Church of St Vincent de Paul** (kostol sv Vincenta Pavlánskeho) with its former convent, hospital and school, and the tiny baroque **Church of St Michael** (kostol sv Michala; Na Vŕšku), originally a parish church. Around the corner on Pri synagoge is a heavy, distinctly Byzantine, **former synagogue** which often hosts classical concerts in summer.

WALKS

North of the city, **Zobor Hill** (588m) and **Žibrica** (617m) beyond it, the last vestiges of the Tribeč range, are part of a regional nature reserve and good for walks and huge views. Bits of old walls around the Zobor summit are remnants of ancient fortifications. To get there, take bus No 10 from just off Kmeťkova to the end of the line at Zobor.

Festivals & Events

Leto Nitra (Summer Nitra; kultura@msunitra.sk), which runs from June to September, is the town's premier cultural event and includes folk, classical and church music, exhibitions and films. The **Agrokomplex** (www.agrokomplex.sk) hosts a bunch of exhibitions throughout the year, the biggest of which is its international trade fair at the end of August.

Tours

NISYS runs **sightseeing tours** (400-500Sk; 1½ hrs) of the Upper and Lower Town, plus excursions into the surrounding area.

Sleeping

Nitra has no private rooms, but NISYS has a comprehensive list of hotels, *pensions*, and in summer, university dorms which go for around 150Sk-300Sk.

Hotel Zlatý kľúčik (☎ 655 02 89; www.zlatyklucik.sk; Svatourbanská 27; s/d 2300/4100Sk; P ✗ ✗) This is the top hotel and offers excellent views out over the ancient town. The fine restaurant attached has its own aquarium. Take bus No 10 from just off Kmeťkova to the residential neighbourhood below Zobor Hill.

Agroinštitút (☎ 653 33 61; recepia@agroinstitut.sk; Akademická 4; s/d 650/1550Sk; P ✗) The largest hotel in Nitra, Agroinštitút is a well-priced option opposite the Agrokomplex and within walking distance of the town centre.

Hotel Olympia (☎ 653 67 27; olympia@hotelolympia .sk; Andreja Hlinku 57; s/d 900/1120Sk; P) This cheap option doesn't look like much from the outside, but the rooms are comfortable and accommodating. Take bus No 12, 13, or 23 east on Štúrova.

Hotel Zobor (☎ 652 53 81; Štefánikova 5; s/d 800/1200Sk; P) Hotel Zobor is about as central as you'll get; the rooms are clean but nothing special.

Eating & Drinking

Piano Café (☎ 772 16 51; Farská 46; mains 80-100Sk) A classy spot for coffee, beer or a meal, Piano is located in a quiet courtyard. Come on a Friday or Saturday night for live piano music.

Izba starej matere (☎ 652 60 16; Radlinského 8; mains 80-100Sk) Izba has a friendly atmosphere, a menu stacked with Slovak specialties and a small patio.

Furmanská vináreň (☎ 652 82 60; Pri synagoge 6; mains around 60Sk) This low-key wine cellar serves good Slovak meals and is best enjoyed in winter.

Čínska (☎ 652 66 89; Kupecká 2; mains 80-120Sk) If you're tired of Slovak fare come here for some Chinese. Its midday menu is in popular demand.

Gastro 2000 (Štefánikova 33; pizzas & baguettes 30-60Sk) The name may not be very appealing, but the cheap, filling baguettes and pizzas at Gastro 2000 are.

If you're self-catering, load up on groceries at the supermarket in the Tesco department store or, better still, head to the big covered market on Štúrova.

For beer, try the **Irish Times Pub** (☎ 741 34 27; Kupecká 12).

Entertainment

The monthly magazine *Nitra* (8Sk) is a helpful guide to what's on in town even though it's in Slovak.

Getting There & Around

Buses to Nitra depart from Bratislava's main station at least every half hour (106Sk, 1½ hours). Avoid getting to Nitra by train, which could involve multiple transfers and take up to three hours. Three buses a day depart for Komárno (90Sk, 1¾ hours) and frequent buses head to Banská Bystrica (152Sk, two hours) and Trnava (67Sk, one hour).

Nitra has a good local bus network serving the outer suburbs while the Upper and Lower Towns are easily managed on foot.

KOMÁRNO

☎ 035 / pop 37,400

This Danube border town, is a convenient crossing point between Slovakia and Hungary. Frequent trains (with cheap domestic fares) run between these twin cities and onwards to Bratislava and Budapest, and it costs nothing to walk across the 1892 bridge linking Slovakia with Hungary.

Komárno feels more Hungarian than Slovakian, which isn't surprising; two-thirds of residents are Hungarian and all street signs in Komárno are bilingual in Slovak and Hungarian. It also serves as the cultural and political centre of southern Slovakia's large Hungarian community.

Though Komárno is pleasant enough, it certainly doesn't merit a special trip – except for the last weekend of April and the first week of May for the Komárno Days festival, with its many competitions, folk dances and songs. Expect to have a problem finding accommodation during this time.

Orientation

The train and bus stations are 15 minutes on foot north of the town centre, 20 minutes from the international border crossing. Slovak and Hungarian customs are together on a peninsula in the middle of the river.

Information

The **AiCES information office** (☎ 773 00 63; www.komarno.sk; Župná 5; ☼ 7.30am-3.30pm Mon-Fri) is on the town's main street. Internet access is available at **AutoCont** (☎ 773 14 32; Eötvösa 10; per hr 40Sk; ☼ 8am-10pm).

There are a number of ATMs scattered around town, including one at **Všeobecná Úverová Banka** (VÚB; ☎ 790 45 11; Tržničné námestie 3) which also has an exchange office.

Sights

Komárno's most interesting museum is the **Zichy Palace múzeum** (☎ 773 00 55; námestie gen Klapku 9; adult/child 20/10Sk; ☼ 10am-5pm Tue-Sat), in a small passage off the Župná. It's actually two museums – one devoted to local boys composer Ferenc Lehár and novelist Jókai Mór, and the second to the town's history. Photographs of 19th- and 20th-century Komárno are by far the most interesting display.

If you continue through the passage off Župná you'll come to one of the more bizarre squares in Slovakia, the **Europe Place** (Nádvorí Európy). Completed in 2000, the square's buildings have been completely redesigned to capture various architectural styles across Europe, ranging from Icelandic to Greek themes. It's very colourful and eye-catching, but a little bit on the strange side.

Two other museums worth a peek are the **Danube Museum** (Podunajské múzeum; ☎ 773 14 76; Palatínova 13; adult/child 20/10Sk; ☼ 9am-5pm Tue-Sat), with a historical and archaeological collection, and the beautifully restored **Roman Bastion** (Római Lapidárium; ☎ 773 14 76; Okružná cesta; adult/child 20/10Sk; ☼ 10am-5pm Tue-Sun) housing a small collection of Roman artefacts.

Festivals & Events

Komárno Days, on the last weekend of April and the first week of May, is as much a celebration of Hungarian culture as Slovakian culture; food and music from both countries can be sampled here.

Sleeping

Ring Bar Penzión (☎ 771 31 58; Letná 4; s/d 300/500Sk) This simple *pension* is nicely central, and rooms come with shared facilities.

Hotel Panorama (☎ 771 31 52; Športová; r 950Sk) A 15-minute walk east of town, Panorama has basic but comfortable en suite rooms. It also manages the adjacent **camping ground** (person/tent/car 60/60/60Sk), which is quite flat and bare.

Hotel Európa (☎ 773 13 49; www.hoteleuropa.sk; námestie Štefánika 1; s/d 990/1140Sk; P) This unmissable purple-and-white block has slightly overpriced big, clean rooms.

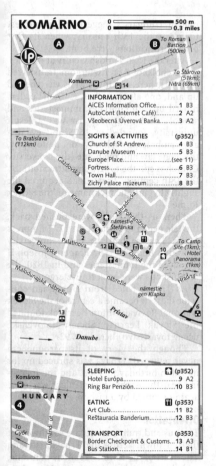

KOMÁRNO

0 ——— 500 m
0 ——— 0.3 miles

To Roman
Bastion
(500m)

To Štúrovo
(51km);
Nitra (69km)

INFORMATION
AiCES Information Office............1 B3
AutoCont (Internet Café)..........2 A2
Všeobecná Úverová Banka........3 A2

SIGHTS & ACTIVITIES (p352)
Church of St Andrew.................4 B3
Danube Museum 5 B3
Europe Place.........................(see 11)
Fortress................................6 B3
Town Hall..............................7 B3
Zichy Palace múzeum................8 B3

SLEEPING (p352)
Hotel Európa..........................9 A2
Ring Bar Penzión....................10 B3

EATING (p353)
Art Club...............................11 B2
Reštauracia Banderium............12 B3

TRANSPORT (p353)
Border Checkpoint & Customs...13 A3
Bus Station...........................14 B1

Eating

The best place to go is **Reštauracia Banderium** (☎ 773 19 30; námestie Štefánika; mains 130-250Sk) with a fine range of Slovak and Hungarian cuisine. For a bite to eat, or a quiet drink, try **Art Club** (Nádvorí Európy; baguettes 40-50Sk), an inviting pavilion serving filling baguettes.

Getting There & Away

Three buses (128Sk, 1¾ hours) and eight local trains (114Sk, 2¼ hours) a day run between Bratislava and Komárno. Three buses per day run between Nitra and Komárno (90Sk, 1¾ hours).

A bus to the Komárom train station, across the river in Hungary, leaves the Komárno train station three times a day.

LESSER CARPATHIANS

Stretching for 100km northeast from Bratislava are the undulating Lesser Carpathian (Malé Karpaty) mountains. Though not particularly dramatic, they are pleasant for walks and hikes. It's also one of Slovakia's biggest wine growing areas, with the vineyards extending right down into Bratislava's Vinohrady district. The map *Malokarpatská viná cesta* (1:75,000), available at AiCES in Modra, lists local wineries and castles, and shows colour-coded walking trails.

Modra

☎ 033 / pop 3000
Modra is the town where the Slovak nationalist Ľudovít Štúr (1815–56) spent his later years. It produces some of Slovakia's best red and white wines (as well as celebrated ceramics). The town is a popular stop on summer wine-tasting tours, and there are several *vináreň* (wine bars) where you can sample the goods. It's centred around Štúrova, the main street that runs past the bus stop before changing its name to Dukelská.

INFORMATION & SIGHTS

The **Small Carpathian tourist information office** (☎ 647 43 02; tik@post.sk; Štúrova 84; 9.30am-4.30pm Mon-Fri) sells maps and can help with accommodation queries. Nearby, **Slovenská sporiteľňa** (Štúrova 65) has an ATM.

The only notable sight is the **Ľudovíta Štúra Muzeum** (Štúrova 50; adult/child 20/10Sk; 9am-4pm Tue-Fri, 9am-3pm Sat) in the former town hall. Often it appears to be closed; ring the buzzer to enter and see Štúr's writing desk plus a small display of medieval Modra relics.

SLEEPING & EATING

Modra is better visited as a day trip, but if you're stuck overnight try **Penzión Club MKM** (☎ 647 53 13; Šturórova 25; r from 1500Sk; P) which has very nice en suite rooms and a good restaurant.

Modranský dvor (☎ 0905 605 208; Štúrova 46; mains 100-150Sk) is another place to sample local food and wines.

GETTING THERE & AWAY

Buses leave for Modra several times every hour from Bratislava's main station (36Sk,

WEST SLOVAKIA

one hour). To/from Trnava there are frequent bus connections on weekdays, but only a handful on weekends (50Sk, one hour). The best option for travellers coming from the Czech Republic over the Lesser Carpathians is to catch a bus from Hodonín to Trnava (1½ hrs, six daily) and then change for Modra.

Červený Kameň

Surrounded by woodlands about 5km northeast of Modra looms the castle of **Červený Kameň** (☎ 649 51 32; adult/child 130/70Sk; ☒ 9am-5pm Mon-Fri, 9am-6pm Sat & Sun May-Aug, 9am-4pm Mar-Apr & Sep-Oct, 9.30am-3.30pm Nov-Feb). Originally built in the 1230s by Queen Constance, wife of Czech King Přemysl Otakar I, it was acquired by a German merchant family, the Fuggers, in the 15th century and converted into a kind of fortified warehouse. In the late 16th century the Pálffy family made it into a deluxe chateau, and went on remodelling it until they fled Czechoslovakia in 1945.

Several reconstructed rooms now house a museum of European Renaissance, baroque and empire furniture, and an exhibit of weapons and armour. In order to see it you're obliged to join a group tour (English text provided). There's a restaurant outside the chateau gate, and a buffet inside.

If you're eager to hike, a road climbs from Modra for about 7km northwest to Piesok, a complex of private bungalows with a restaurant and a mountain hotel called Chata Zochova. From there, a trail meanders about 6km down to Červený Kameň.

Otherwise, most Trnava-bound buses stop at Častá village (get off at the 'Zakladina' stop), and Červený Kameň is 1km west on a green-marked trail or the local road.

TRNAVA

☎ 033 / pop 70,300

Trnava is Slovakia's oldest town, the first to get a royal charter as a free borough (from Hungarian King Béla IV in 1238). Though badly marred by modern development, its handsome fortified old town, a legacy of almost three centuries as Hungary's religious centre, merits a day trip from Bratislava, perhaps even an overnight stop.

History

Lying on the Prague–Budapest and Vienna–Kraków trade routes, Trnava was already one of Hungary's biggest and wealthiest towns by the 13th century, when its first brick fortifications were built.

After the 1526 Turkish victory at Mohács, the archbishops of Esztergom transferred their seat here, the town walls were beefed up and, one after another, Catholic orders moved in with churches, monasteries and schools. Crowning the list was a Jesuit university, founded in 1635 and eventually embracing schools of philosophy, theology, law and medicine (the University Church is still the town's star attraction). By the 18th century, Trnava had acquired the slightly hyperbolic nickname of 'the Slovak Rome'.

Then, as the Turks were pushed back, the tale began to unravel. In 1777 Empress Maria Theresa had the entire university moved to Buda. In 1782 Emperor Joseph II dissolved the monasteries and in 1820, the archbishops went back to Esztergom.

As Trnava faded from Hungarian consciousness, it became a centre of the Slovak National Revival; Anton Bernolák founded the Slovak Learned Society (Slovenské učené tovarišstvo) here in 1792.

Though the glory of its baroque era never returned, Trnava was spruced up for its 750th birthday in 1988, and the following year the Archbishop's Palace was once again occupied by a bishop.

Orientation

The bus and train stations are southwest of the old town, across the Trnavka stream. The heart of the town is Trojičné námestie, and the main shopping street, Hlavná, is pedestrianised.

Information

EMERGENCY

City Police (☎ 551 15 55; Trhová 3)
Hospital (☎ 553 61 03; Andreja Žarnova 11)

INTERNET ACCESS

Heso Com (Hviezdoslavova 13; ☒ 10am-midnight) Access for 30Sk per hour.

MONEY

Všeobecná Úverová Banka (VÚB; ☎ 556 98 11; Hlavná 31) Currency exchange and ATM.

POST

Main Post Office (Trojičné námestie 4)

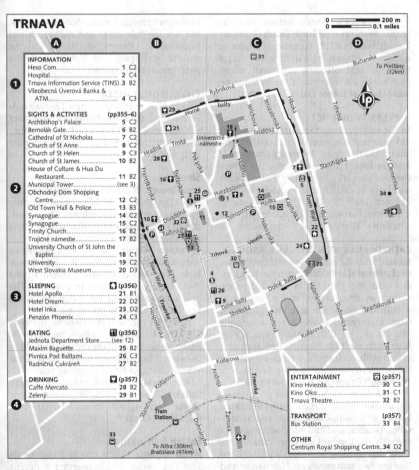

TRNAVA

INFORMATION
Heso Com	1	C2
Hospital	2	C4
Trnava Information Service (TINS)	3	B2
Všeobecná Úverová Banka & ATM	4	C3

SIGHTS & ACTIVITIES (pp355–6)
Archbishop's Palace	5	C2
Bernolák Gate	6	B2
Cathedral of St Nicholas	7	C2
Church of St Anne	8	C2
Church of St Helen	9	C3
Church of St James	10	B2
House of Culture & Hua Du Restaurant	11	B2
Municipal Tower	(see 3)	
Obchodný Dom Shopping Centre	12	C2
Old Town Hall & Police	13	B3
Synagogue	14	C2
Synagogue	15	C2
Trinity Church	16	B2
Trojičné námestie	17	B2
University Church of St John the Baptist	18	C1
University	19	C2
West Slovakia Museum	20	D3

SLEEPING (p356)
Hotel Apollo	21	B1
Hotel Dream	22	D2
Hotel Inka	23	D2
Penzión Phoenix	24	C3

EATING (p356)
Jednota Department Store	(see 12)	
Maxim Baguette	25	B2
Pivnica Pod Baštami	26	C3
Radničná Cukráreň	27	B2

DRINKING (p357)
Caffe Mercato	28	B2
Zelený	29	B1

ENTERTAINMENT (p357)
Kino Hviezda	30	C3
Kino Oko	31	C1
Trnava Theatre	32	B2

TRANSPORT (p357)
Bus Station	33	B4

OTHER
Centrum Royal Shopping Centre	34	D2

0 — 200 m
0 — 0.1 miles

To Piešťany (32km)

To Nitra (30km); Bratislava (41km)

TOURIST INFORMATION

Trnava Information Service (TINS; ☎ 551 10 22; www.trnava.sk; Trojičné námestie 1; ⏱ 8am-6pm Mon-Sat, 2-6pm Sun May-Sep, 8am-6pm Mon-Sat Oct-Apr) Located in the Municipal Tower.

Sights
AROUND TROJIČNÉ NÁMESTIE

Restored, 13th-century, brick town walls stretch almost completely around the historical centre. In the west wall is the **Bernolák Gate** (Bernolákova brána), the only surviving tower gate.

Through the gate and past the Franciscans' 1640 **Church of St James** (kostol sv Jakuba; ☎ 551 12 11; Františkánska; adult/child 20/10Sk; ⏱ 1-4pm Mon & Fri, 9-11am & 1-4pm Tue-Thu, 9-11am Sat) is the main

square, Trojičné námestie. It's dominated by a Renaissance **Municipal Tower** (Mestská veža; Trojičné námestie 1; adult/child 20/10Sk; ⏱ 10am-6.30pm Jun-Sep), built in 1574 but with a baroque top, which provides views of the city. The 17th-century **Trinity Column** in the square, removed by the Communists in 1948, was replaced in 1989 by popular demand.

The town's best and worst architecture is around the square. Among the best are Slovakia's first stone-built theatre, the 1831 **Trnava Theatre** (Trnavské divadlo), and the 1793 **Old Town Hall** just south on Hlavná. Among the worst are the domineering modern blocks of the **House of Culture** (dom kultúry) and the massive **Obchodný dom** shopping centre.

WEST SLOVAKIA

North of the square on Štefánikova is the Jesuits' twin-towered **Trinity Church** (Jezuitský kostol), built in 1729; its exuberant, baroque interior is outshone by a striking side chapel with stuccoed columns and tiled ceiling. East on Hviezdoslavova is the baroque **Ursuline Church of St Anne** (kostol sv Anny).

UNIVERSITY DISTRICT
In the baroque neighbourhood around the old university is one of Slovakia's finest churches, the huge **University Church of St John the Baptist** (Univerzitný kostol sv Jána Krstiteľa; Univerzitné námestie), designed by Pietro Spezzo and built by Italian and Viennese artisans between 1629–37. Though severe outside, it's all lush baroque and rococo inside, with a beautiful altar reaching to the ceiling.

CATHEDRAL OF ST NICHOLAS & AROUND
Named after the patron saint of merchants, the **Cathedral of St Nicholas** (dóm sv Mikuláša; námestie Mikuláša) was founded as a Gothic parish church in about 1380, and promoted to a cathedral when the archbishops arrived from Esztergom. It was given a baroque face-lift in the 17th century, and a new interior in the 18th century. Beside it, decorated with ecclesiastical coats-of-arms, is the old clerical homestead, the Renaissance **Archbishop's Palace** (Arcibiskupský palác).

South from St Nicholas is picturesque Kapitulská ulica. Lined with burghers' houses with Gothic basements and Renaissance façades, and full of shady trees, it's arguably the loveliest street in Trnava.

All that remains of Trnava's Jewish heritage are two **synagogues** on Halenárska and Havlíka; the former is used as a **modern art gallery** (☎ 551 46 57; adult/child 10/5Sk; ☽ 9am-noon & 1-5pm Mon-Fri, 1-6pm Sat & Sun) and has a small but impressive collection of Jewish artefacts, the latter for pigeon nests.

WEST SLOVAKIA MUSEUM
South from Kapitulská is the handsome former Clarist convent, dating from 1239. After Emperor Joseph II abolished the monasteries it was used as a veterans' home and a mental hospital until the 1950s. American pilots were apparently hidden here during WWII. Now it houses the excellent **West Slovakia Museum** (Západoslovenské múzeum; ☎ 551 29 13; Múzejné námestie 3; adult/child 40/20Sk; ☽ 8am-5pm Tue-Fri, 11am-5pm Sat & Sun). Some of it is fairly

incomprehensible for non-Slovak speakers, but not the folk dress and crafts, exhibits of Slovakian Olympic medallists, and the antique menorahs and Torahs from the local Jewish community.

CHURCH OF ST HELEN
Finally, be sure to wander past Trnava's oldest building, the lonely **Church of St Helen** (kostol sv Helena; Hlavná), built in the early 14th century and, except for a 19th-century steeple, pure early Gothic.

Sleeping
Hotel Dream (☎ 592 41 11; www.hoteldream.sk; Kapitulská 12; r 2200Sk; ℗ ☒ ☻) Almost opposite Pheonix is this upmarket hotel, which, with stylish rooms and a fine cellar restaurant, is probably the best in town.

Penzión Phoenix (☎ 534 36 91; commercial@nextra.sk; Kapitulská 16; r 1500Sk; ℗) This lovely little *pension* has superb, modern rooms that are almost too big to be practical. The only drawback is the three flights of stairs you have to climb to the rooms.

Hotel Inka (☎ 590 51 11; V. Clementisa 13; s/d 600/1200Sk; ℗) Hotel Inka is a basic but perfectly adequate hotel east of the centre. It's the first of two red-brown tower blocks south of the yellow Centrum Royal shopping centre.

Hotel Apollo (☎ 551 19 40; hotel.apollo@stonline.sk; Štefánikova 23; s/d 1800/2300Sk; ℗) Another fine choice is the Apollo. It's on a busier street than Hotel Dream.

Eating & Drinking
Maxim Baguette (Trojičné námestie 3; baguettes 30-50Sk) You could cobble together a decent breakfast or lunch at this cheap and cheerful sandwich shop.

Pivnica pod baštami (☎ 551 40 49; Hlavná 45; mains 120-150Sk) This upmarket beer hall has filling Slovak dishes and a value-for-money all day menu for 100Sk.

Phoenix (☎ 534 36 91; Kapitulská 16; mains 150-200Sk) At the *pension* of the same name is this quality restaurant serving Slovak and international dishes. There's also a large garden to take advantage of.

Radničná Cukráreň (cnr Radlinského & Hlavná; ice cream 6Sk) Don't go past this popular cake shop for ice cream, coffee and cake.

Self-caterers can stock up at the supermarket in the Jednota department store just southeast of the main square.

Caffe Mercato (Štefánikova 35) is a great spot for the whole family; it's situated in a quiet courtyard and there's a small playground for kids. **Zelený** (Štefánikova 24) is not suited to families; this tree-shaded courtyard boozer is quite picturesque but frequented by students and old drunkards, which gives you an indication of the price of its beer.

Entertainment

There are cultural – especially musical – programmes and exhibitions during the summer, particularly at the **Trnava Theatre** (☎ 551 13 53; Trojičné námestie 2); TINS has more comprehensive information.

The most central cinema is **Kino Hviezda** (☎ 551 10 42; Paulínska 1).

Getting There & Away

Trains leave Bratislava hourly for Trnava (express trains 72Sk, 40 minutes; regional trains 56Sk, one hour). There are buses from Bratislava's main terminal to Travna (67Sk, 50 minutes), Trenčín (106Sk, 1½ hours, six daily) and Nitra (67Sk, one hour, frequent services).

PIEŠŤANY

☎ 033 / pop 30,600

Piešťany, on the banks of the Váh river, is the Slovak Republic's best-known spa resort. Its warm springs and sulphuric mud have been documented since the 12th century and prescribed for aching joints since the 16th century.

The spa pulls in plenty of hard currency for Slovakia, and the international clientele has driven up prices for almost everything – except in winter, when the spa is nearly empty. Like most spa towns, Piešťany is relaxing but fairly boring.

Orientation

Shops and tourist hotels are all on or near Winterova. The top-end spas are on Kúpeľný ostrov (Bath Island), reached by the Colonnade Bridge (Kolonádový most) with the spa's symbol, a statue of a patient breaking his crutches in half. The train and bus stations sit side by side 2km northwest of the town centre.

Information

The helpful **AiCES office** (☎ 774 33 55; Nálepkova 2; ☼ 9am-5.30pm Mon-Fri, 8am-noon Sat) has maps, accommodation listings and international newspapers. For information on spa treatments head to **Kúpele Piešťany** (☎ 775 21 98; www.spa-piestany.sk; Winterova 29; ☼ 7.30am-3.30pm Mon-Fri), the headquarters of Slovthermae, the Slovak spa agency.

Sights & Activities

Winterova is a bland row of hotels and cafés, though it boasts a few modest Art Nouveau buildings. Of the spa facilities on Kúpeľný ostrov Art Nouveau, **Thermia Palace** is top of the line and worth a look inside. East of here are the neoclassical **Napoleon Baths** (Napoleónske kúpele; 1821) and to the north, three giant, modern Balnea spas stand in a line.

Warm **Eva Pool** (Kúpalisko Eva; per day 50Sk; ☼ 9am-5.30pm May-Sep) is a perfect place to soothe away any aches and pains. For something more active, the AiCES office rents bikes for 100Sk per day.

To the south of the town centre the Váh is dammed, forming a sizable lake. Between the months of June and October, it's possible to enjoy an hour-long **cruise** (☎ 0905 250 164; 120Sk; ☼ 9am-5pm) on the lake; boats leave from just south of Colonnade Bridge.

Spa Treatments

The sanatoria here are fit for a Thomas Mann novel, treating a variety of ailments – including 'chronic rheumatism, diseases of the nerves, and post-traumatic lesions of the bones, joints and organs' – with therapeutic mud, mineral waters and exercise regimes.

Check in for a day or a lifetime, and expect to pay around 500Sk for treatments; massages cost from 300Sk.

Festivals & Events

The town hosts a modest **music festival** from mid-June to mid-August, and a boot-scootin' **country music festival** at the end of August.

Sleeping

Kúpele Piešťany has a list of hotels that have package deals which include accommodation and treatments.

There are two camping grounds south of town on the lake – **Lodencia** (☎ 762 60 93; belecsak@py.internet.sk; ☼ Apr-Oct), 2km down the west side of the river (from Nitrianska take bus No 10), and **Sĺňava II** (☎ 762 35 63;

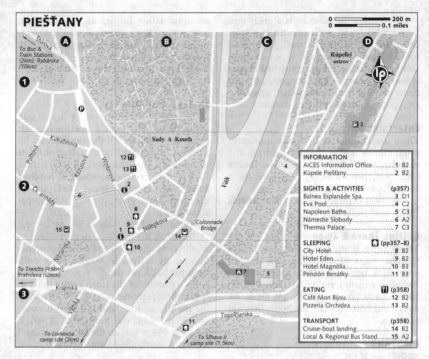

PIEŠTANY

0 — 200 m
0 — 0.1 miles

Kúpeľný ostrov

To Bus &
Train Stations
(2km); Rybárska
(10km)

Sady A Kmeth

Štúrova

Kukučínova

Winterova

Potrová

Rázusová

Čs. armády

Váh

Nálepkova

Colonnade
Bridge

Nitrianska

Krajinská

To Trenčín (45km);
Bratislava (69km)

Topolčianska

To Lodenica
camp site (2km)

To Sĺňava II
camp site (1.5km)

INFORMATION	
AiCES Information Office............1	B2
Kúpele Piešťany............2	B2
SIGHTS & ACTIVITIES	**(p357)**
Balnea Esplanáde Spa............3	D1
Eva Pool............4	C2
Napoleon Baths............5	C3
Námestie Slobody............6	A2
Thermia Palace............7	C3
SLEEPING	**(pp357–8)**
City Hotel............8	B2
Hotel Eden............9	B2
Hotel Magnólia............10	B3
Penzión Benátky............11	B3
EATING	**(p358)**
Café Mon Bijou............12	B2
Pizzeria Orchidea............13	B2
TRANSPORT	**(p358)**
Cruise-boat landing............14	B2
Local & Regional Bus Stand............15	A2

mid-May–mid-Sep), 1.5km down the east side (no public transport). Both cost per person/ car/tent/bungalow 85/85/150/550Sk.

Hotel Eden (☎ 772 47 09; hoteleden@stonline.sk; Winterova 60; s/d 1300/1800Sk; P) Eden is a fine choice right on pedestrianised Winterova.

Penzión Benátky (☎ 772 11 89; Topolčianska 1; r 890Sk; P) This attractive, riverside *pension* is another good option just outside the centre.

Other central options include the intimate **City Hotel** (☎ 772 54 54; www.hotelcity.sk; Winterova 35; s/d 1300/2000Sk; P ⊠) and the high-rise **Hotel Magnólia** (☎ 762 56 51; www.hotelmagnolia.sk; Nálepkova 1; 1740/2280Sk; P ⊠).

Eating

Winterova and its side streets abound in cafés, restaurants and ice-cream stalls. Two that stand out are **Pizzeria Orchidea** (☎ 772 88 68; Beethovenova 20; pizzas 120Sk) and **Café Mon Bijou** (Beethovenova 16; coffee around 30Sk); the former has top pizzas and covered outdoor seating and the latter excellent coffee, a quiet terrace and 1920s décor.

If you're into fresh fish then try **Rybárska** (☎ 0905 420 550; Bašovce; mains around 200-300Sk),

a small restaurant with its own breeding pond 10km north of Piešťany. The whole idea is to catch your own dinner, so the freshness of the fish is definitely not in doubt. You'll need your own transport to get out to the restaurant.

Getting There & Around

There are hourly trains from Bratislava that call at Piešťany every day (116Sk, one hour); over 20 buses make the same trip (106Sk, 1½ hours).

Almost every local bus runs between the train and bus stations and the town centre; get off at the Nitrianska stop.

ČACHTICE CASTLE

The fame of this castle, one of several 13th-century Hungarian strongholds between Piešťany and Trenčín, springs from its history. In the 17th century a mad Hungarian countess named Alžbeta Nádasdy-Báthory (known as Bloody Liz to her mates) tortured and murdered over 600 peasant women here and in another castle, Beckov, across the Váh. When her grisly doings

WEST SLOVAKIA

were finally found out she was imprisoned in Čachtice for the rest of her life.

Since a fire in 1708, there isn't much left of the castle, but it has great views (the surrounding area is a regional nature reserve) and an eerie, lonely atmosphere. There are no roads to the hilltop ruins, just a few scraggy trails.

There are no hotels here, and only a very basic *piváreň* (small beer hall) beside the Višňové train stop.

To get there from either Piešťany or Trenčín, change trains at Nové Mesto nad Váhom. From there it's a picturesque, 15-minute train ride to the whistlestop of Višňové (11Sk, six daily) and a 25-minute scramble up the hill to the ruins.

By car, Čachtice village is 7km southwest of Nové Mesto nad Váhom; Višňové and the castle are 5km from there on a side road heading west from the village.

TRENČÍN
☎ 032 / pop 57,900

For centuries, where the Váh river valley begins to narrow between the White Carpathians (Bilé Karpaty) and the Strážov hills, Trenčín Castle has guarded the southwestern gateway to Slovakia. Laugaricio, a Roman military post – Eastern Europe's northernmost Roman camp – was established here in the 2nd century AD. A rock inscription at Trenčín, dated AD 179, mentions the Roman 2nd Legion and its victory over the Germanic Kvad tribes.

The mighty castle that now towers above town was first mentioned in 1069 in a Viennese chronicle. In the 13th century the castle's master Matúš Čák held sway over much of Slovakia, and in 1412 Trenčín obtained the rights of a free royal city. The present castle dates from that period, and although both castle and town were destroyed by fire in 1790, much has been restored.

Modern Trenčín is an important centre of the Slovak textile industry and a bustling little community. The town's main sights – the castle and central square – can be covered in an afternoon. In summer it's worth spending the night for the Medieval Days performance at the castle.

Orientation
From the adjacent bus and train stations, walk west through the City Park and follow

the Tatra Passage under the highway to Mierové námestie, the town's long, main square.

Information
The **AiCES office** (☎ 743 35 05; www.trencin.sk; Štúrovo námestie 10; ⌚ 8.30am-6pm Mon-Fri, 8.30am-1pm Sat mid-Apr–mid-Oct, 8am-5pm Mon-Fri mid-Oct–mid-Apr) has accommodation and festival information. The **Map Shop** (Hviedoslávova 13; ⌚ 9am-5pm Mon-Fri) has a large selection of hiking maps and travel books.

There are a number of banks around town with ATMs, including **Všeobecná Úverová Banka** (VÚB; ☎ 741 71 11; Mierové námestie 37), on the main square. The **main post office** (☎ 748 42 01; Mierové námestie 21) is also to be found on the square. **I Café** (Palackého 17; ⌚ 10am-10pm) has Internet access for 50Sk per hour.

Sights
TRENČÍN CASTLE
The lofty **Trenčín Castle** (☎ 743 56 57; Matúšova 19; adult/child 80/40Sk; ⌚ 9am-5.30pm May-Aug, 9am-4.30pm Sep, 9am-3.30pm Oct-Apr) provides amazing views over the town and the Váh plain, though the main attraction is the castle itself. Its present layout dates more or less from the 15th century.

The so-called Well of Love on the first terrace is a fantastic construction 70m deep. Above is the castle's great central tower, with 300-degree views of the area. At night the castle is illuminated with green and purple lights. Nightly in summer between 9pm and 11pm there is a fantastic show called **Medieval Days** (adult/child 80/40Sk), which includes sword fighting and ghost stories and plenty of fun.

MIEROVÉ NÁMESTIE & AROUND
This pleasant square lined with Renaissance burghers' houses is dominated at the west end by the old town's only remaining **gate tower** (Mestská brána; 1534) as well as the **Piarist Church** (Piaristický kostol), built in baroque style in 1657.

In the centre of the square is a **plague column** (morový stĺp) that dates from 1712. At the square's eastern end is **Trenčín Museum** (☎ 743 47 16; Mierové námestie 46; adult/child 20/10Sk; ⌚ 9am-4pm Tue-Sun). It's filled with rather lacklustre natural history displays and the occasional art exhibition.

North of the gate tower is the former **synagogue** (☎ 743 47 16; Štúrovo námestie), now

TRENČÍN

0 ————— 200 m
0 ————— 0.1 miles

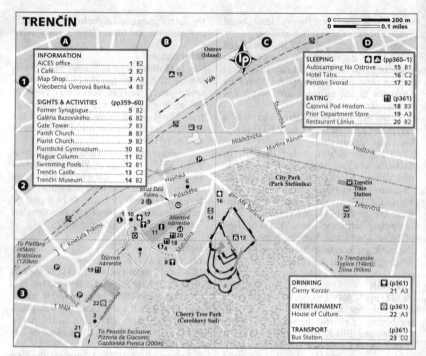

INFORMATION
AICES office..............................1 B2
I Café.....................................2 B2
Map Shop................................3 A3
Všeobecná Úverová Banka........4 B3

SIGHTS & ACTIVITIES   (pp359–60)
Former Synagogue....................5 B2
Galéria Bazovského...................6 B2
Gate Tower.............................7 B3
Parish Church..........................8 B3
Piarist Church..........................9 B2
Piaristické Gymnazium.............10 B2
Plague Column........................11 B2
Swimming Pools......................12 B1
Trenčín Castle.........................13 C2
Trenčín Museum......................14 B2

SLEEPING   (pp360–1)
Autocamping Na Ostrove 15 B1
Hotel Tatra.............................16 C2
Penzión Svorad.......................17 B2

EATING   (p361)
Čajovná Pod Hradom................18 B3
Prior Department Store.............19 A3
Restaurant Lánius....................20 B2

DRINKING   (p361)
Cierny Korzár..........................21 A3

ENTERTAINMENT   (p361)
House of Culture......................22 B3

TRANSPORT   (p361)
Bus Station.............................23 D2

---

restored and sporadically used for exhibitions. Around on Palackého is the lavishly renovated **grammar school** established by the Piarists for the instruction of local youth. Further east along Palackého is Trenčín's premier exhibition space, the **Galéria Bazovského** (☎ 743 68 58; Palackého 27; adult/child 20/10Sk; ☼ 9am-5pm Tue-Sun). Housed in a beautifully restored 19th-century palace, the gallery hosts a permanent display of works by Trenčín-born painter Miloš Bazovský (1899–1968) alongside work by local artists.

South from the tower a 16th-century covered **wooden staircase** (Kryté schody) climbs to a bright-yellow 14th-century **Parish Church** (Farský kostol), which has a simple outline bearing Gothic, Renaissance and baroque traces. The small cemetery chapel beside it is probably the only purely Gothic building in town. From here you can ascend to the castle gate.

OTHER ATTRACTIONS

South beneath the castle walls, on a footpath off Hviezdoslávova, is the forested **Cherry Tree Park** (Čerešňový sad). North of the city centre are summer and winter **swimming pools** (Mládežnícka; adult/child 50/20Sk; ☼ 9am-9.30pm Jun-Aug, 10am-5.30pm Sep-May).

Festivals & Events

Trenčín hosts Slovakia's largest musical event, **Pohoda** (www.pohodafestival.sk), for one weekend in mid-July. The festival attracts some of the top bands and DJs from around the world.

Sleeping

Hotel Tatra (☎ 650 61 11; www.hotel-tatra.sk; gen MR Štefánika 2; s/d 3490/4490Sk; Ⓟ ☒) This is easily the top hotel in town; rooms are plush and the whole place has a grandiose look about it.

The AiCES office has a list of about 20 *pensions* in town (around 1000Sk per double) and can make calls for you.

Penzión Exclusive (☎ 650 18 10; www.penzion exclusive.sk; Braneckého 14; s/d 990/1300Sk) Exclusive has spacious, modern rooms, all newly refurbished. It's above a busy mall and has a terrace for guests.

Penzión Svorad (☎ 743 03 22; www.svorad -trencin.sk; Palackého 4; s/d 450/800Sk; P ⊠) Svorad is a basic, clean and friendly *pension* in the grammar school building. Be aware that it's non-smoking throughout and rooms come with shower only.

Autocamping Na Ostrove (☎ 753 40 13; auto camping.yn@mail.pvt.sk; Na Ostrove; person/tent/car 85/ 120/85Sk, cabins 130-200Sk; ☉ May–mid-Sep) Situated on a small island in the middle of the Váh, this camping ground has shaded camp sites and wood cabins that sleep between two and five persons.

Eating & Drinking

Restaurant Lánius (☎ 744 19 78; Mierové námestie 20; mains 120-180Sk) This semi-upmarket beer hall has English-language menus and Slovak dishes. Its open fire is well used in winter, and its terrace full in summer.

In the same mall as Penzión Exclusive are two great little eateries, **Pizzeria da Giacomo** (☎ 658 32 26; J Braneckého 14; pizzas 100-130Sk), which has the best pizzas in town, and **Gazdovská Pivnica** (☎ 0905 928 639; J Braneckého 14; mains 60-80Sk), a cellar-like place with simple but filling meals.

Čajovná pod hradom (☎ 744 02 18; Mierové námestie 6; teas from 20Sk) For tea in a smoke-free environment head to this little place, upstairs in an arcade off the main square.

There's a Delvita supermarket in the Prior Department Store on Vajanského.

The main square has plenty of bars and cafés, but if you want to escape the crowds try **Čierny Korzár** (☎ 652 95 11; J Braneckého 6), a relaxing local pub that also serves fine food.

Entertainment

Kino Metro (☎ 743 44 15; Mierové námestie 4) is the most central cinema in town, and special events are sometimes held in the House of Culture (dom kultúry); check with the information centre for details.

Getting There & Away

All express trains on the main line from Bratislava to Košice (via Žilina, 162Sk, 1½ hours) stop at Trenčín. About six buses a day go to Bratislava (142Sk, 2½ hours), Piešťany (53Sk, 50 minutes), Trnava (106Sk, 1½ hours) and Žilina (106Sk, 1½ hours); eight buses a day go to Nitra (116Sk, two hours).

TRENČIÁSKE TEPLICE

☎ 032 / pop 5000

This sedate spa in the Teplička valley, 14km northeast of Trenčín, is worth a visit for good hikes in the surrounding hills and to enjoy the spa's treatments. It's also worth popping into at the end of June when the town hosts Art Film, Slovakia's premiere independent film festival (see www.artfilm.sk for details and interviews).

Orientation, Information & Sights

The train station is near the post office on Šrobárova, which runs north and parallel to the main road, Kupelná.

There's no information office in town, so you're best to head to the AiCES office in Trenčín, which sells the local hiking map *Trenčín-Trenčianske Teplice* (1:10,000; 100Sk). The travel agency **CK Pressburg** (☎ 655 12 50; Hotel Slovakia, TG Masaryka 3) can supply you with a map of the town.

The only building with a hint of character is the opulent 1888 Turkish-style **bath house** (hammam), on Kupelná opposite the Pax sanatorium. There are many attractive parks, and from mid-June to mid-August a varied musical programme is presented.

Sleeping & Eating

The inexpensive **Penzión Natalia** (☎ 655 28 58; Bagarova 26; s/d 300/500Sk) is up the steep road just before the Hotel Adria, and has Spartan rooms.

Hotel Slovakia (☎ 655 61 11; www.hotelslovakia.sk; TG Masaryka 3; s/d 890/1200Sk; P) is a five-storey monster, but the rooms are quiet and comfortable. The attractive **Hotel Adria** (☎ 655 34 72; Hurbanova 21; s/d 1150/1600Sk; P) has better rooms. It also hires out mountain bikes (300Sk per day).

Hotel Adria has a good **restaurant** (mains 100-200Sk) and bar. Better value is the **Art Film Restaurant** (TG Masaryka; mains 70-130Sk), which has meals named after film stars. While on the film theme, Trenčíaske Teplice hosts a small international film festival in mid-June.

You can buy circular spa wafers (and see them being made) at **Kúpeľné oblátky** (Kupelná 3; wafers 5-10Sk).

Getting There & Around

Trenčíaske Teplice is served by train from Trenčín, but the bus is quicker, cheaper and far more frequent (16Sk, 25 minutes).

Central Slovakia

CONTENTS

The main attractions of Central Slovakia are its landscapes. This is the most mountainous part of a republic famed for its mountains – here you'll find the western edge of the High Tatras, the smaller but no less impressive Low Tatras, and the very accessible Malá and Veľká Fatras. The ranges are perforated by limestone caves, blanketed with forest (with over 50% coverage, Central Slovakia is the most heavily wooded part of either republic) and carved with deep valleys, the most magical of which are the Vratná Valley in the Malá Fatra and the Demänova Valley in the Low Tatras.

But nature is not the only drawcard. Central Slovakia is steeped in history, and it's as easy as pie to get up close and personal to reminders of times past. Banská Štiavnica and, to a lesser extent, Banská Bystrica, contain wonderful examples of centuries-old architecture – leftovers from the heady days mining brought to the towns. It's not all about riches though; the folk-villages of Čičmany and Vlkolínec are pristine examples of peasant culture, art and architecture, which are enjoying something of a revival throughout the country.

And of the multitude of castles scattered the length and breadth of Slovakia, two of the best are here: Orava, impossibly perched on a high, rocky outcrop; and Bojnice, more fairy-talelike than Walt Disney could ever have imagined.

HIGHLIGHTS

- Discover the **Low Tatras** (p382), **Western Tatras** (p381) and the **Fatras** (p370) on foot, bicycle or skis
- Wonder at the highly decorated houses of **Čičmany** (p376)
- Climb to dizzying heights at **Orava Castle** (p380)
- Explore the architecturally striking former mining town of **Banská Štiavnica** (p368)
- Follow the crowd to **Bojnice** (p376), the most visited chateau in Slovakia

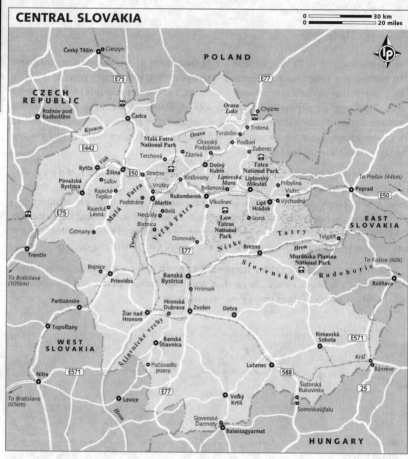

CENTRAL SLOVAKIA

Getting There & Away

Slovakia's main train line, connecting Bratislava and Košice, cuts across the top third of Central Slovakia, allowing fast connections to Žilina and Martin. For the region's more central towns and cities, it's best to take to the bus. If you have time though, the train journey from Košice to Banská Bystrica, along the southern border of the Low Tatras, is one of the most rewarding in the country.

Getting Around

Much of Central Slovakia is hilly and often mountainous. Therefore the bus may be your only option for transport to the region's more inviting areas. Roads are generally good but

you'll encounter some steep gradients and quite a few windy sections.

BANSKÁ BYSTRICA

☎ 048 / pop 83,000

Banská Bystrica, set in a valley where three major mountain ranges – the Nízke Tatry, Veľká Fatra and Slovenské rudohorie – intersect, is the region's administrative capital. It's a bustling, active city with a small but handsome old town centre that includes the remnants of a 15th-century citadel.

History

First Slavs, then German colonists, settled in the valley in the 13th century to extract and refine silver ore, and later copper, from the area's rich veins (*banská* means 'mining'). The town grew fat until the mines became worked out in the 17th century, then almost faded away completely until a post-WWII industrial boom.

A traditionally bolshie town and interwar communist hotbed, Banská Bystrica is best known to Slovaks as the cradle of the Slovak National Uprising (Slovenské národné povstanie, or SNP) against the Nazis and their Slovak puppet state. From here on 29 August 1944, resistance radio announced the start of the uprising.

Although the Slovak fascists did give way, two months later the German army marched in and crushed the revolt. German reprisals for the uprising included the torture and murder of some 900 Slovak men, women and children, along with some Russian and French partisans and several members of an Anglo-American military mission, at Nemecká, 20km east up the Hron Valley.

Orientation
Banská Bystrica's main square is námestie SNP, which gently runs into the town's main shopping street, Dolná. The bus and train stations are about 1km east of here, across a large, open, unnamed park. A regional train station, Banská Bystrica mesto, is across the river from the centre.

Information
BOOKSHOPS
Interpress Slovakia (Dolná 152/19) Wide range of international newspapers and magazines.
VKÚ Mapy-Knihy (námestie Štefana Moyzesa 13) Excellent selection of maps.

EMERGENCY
Police station (9 mája)
Polyclinic (☎ 413 52 41; Horná 60)

INTERNET ACCESS
Level 12 (☎ 0905 241 142; námestie SNP 25) Access for 50Sk per hour.
La Crêperie (námestie SNP 4) Also access for 50Sk; in a fine café.

MONEY
ATMs can be found outside the AiCES office and at the bus station.
Všeobecná úverová banka (VÚB; ☎ 450 11 11; námestie Slobody 1) Exchange desk.

POST
Main Post Office (☎ 415 47 80; Horná 1)

TOURIST INFORMATION
AiCES Information Centre (☎ 415 50 85; kis@pkobb.sk; námestie Štefana Moyzesa 26; ◷ 8am-7pm Mon-Fri, 9am-1pm Sat mid-May–mid-Sep, 9am-5pm Mon-Fri mid-Sep–mid-May)

TRAVEL AGENCIES
Satur (☎ 414 36 16; námestie Slobody 4)

Sights
NÁMESTIE SNP
This square lined with brightly painted burghers' houses was once the main market. Among its finest buildings are the **Benický House** on the north side, graced with frescoes and a Venetian-style loggia (covered area); the **town hall**; and **Thurzo House**, opposite at No 4, with sgraffito tracework and round upper windows. Thurzo House is now home to the **Central Slovakia Museum** (Stredoslovenské múzeum; ☎ 412 58 97; adult/child 20/10Sk; ◷ 9am-noon, 1-7pm Mon-Fri, 9am-noon, 1-4pm Sun) which has ethnographic displays, including some delicate bronze armlets and cloak pins.

The 16th-century **Clock Tower** (adult/child 20/10Sk; ◷ 10am-7pm mid-May–mid-Sep) at the east end offers fine views of the square. Nearby is the Jesuits' 17th-century **St Francis Xavier Cathedral** (katedrálny chrám sv Františka Xavierského).

OLD CITADEL
The sand-coloured buildings northeast of námestie SNP are the remains of the original citadel, a knot of Gothic and Renaissance churches and nobles' and merchants' houses that were surrounded at the end of the 15th century with heavy stone walls. You enter the central square, námestie Štefana Moyzesa, past a gate tower and the 16th-century former town hall, which now houses the **State Gallery** (☎ 412 41 67; námestie Štefana Moyzesa 25; adult/child 20/10Sk; ◷ 11am-6pm Tue-Sun Jul-Aug, 10am-5pm Mon-Fri, 10am-4pm Sat & Sun Sep-Jun). It's mainly set up to host changing exhibitions of 20th-century Slovak artists.

Banská Bystrica's showpiece and oldest building is the 13th-century Romanesque (later Gothicised) parish **Church of Our Lady** (kostol Panny Márie Nanebevzatej). Inside, a side chapel dedicated around 1500 to St

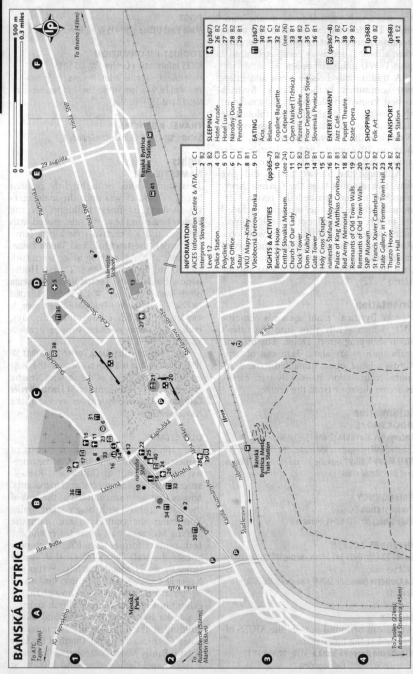

BANSKÁ BYSTRICA

To ATC
Tajov (7km)

To Brezno (43km)

To Zvolen (22km);
Banská Štiavnica (45km)

To Ružomberok (53km);
Martin (63km)

Barbara, patron saint of miners, boasts a fantastic Gothic carved altar by the master craftsman, Pavol of Levoča. The baroque interior renovation followed a severe town fire in 1761.

Behind the church is the Gothic **Holy Cross Chapel** (kostol Povýšenia sv Kríža), a small **palace** built for the Hungarian King Matthias Corvinus, plus three bastions, a peaceful cemetery and bits of the original citadel walls.

SNP MUSEUM
The oddly-shaped SNP Museum (☎ 412 32 59; Kapitulská 23; adult/child 25/10Sk; ☼ 9am-6pm Tue-Sun May-Sep, 9am-4pm Tue-Sun Oct-Apr), devoted to the national uprising, presents a serious subject in over-hyped Soviet style. A booklet with English translations of the captions helps with the otherwise unenlightening displays of posters, uniforms, weapons and occasionally gripping photos.

North and south of the SNP Museum are remnants of 16th-century walls erected against the Turks.

Tours
One-hour walking tours of the city (500Sk per person) are organised by AiCES.

Festivals & Events
Banská Bystrica hosts a few international music gatherings, ranging from the **Choral Singing Festival** at the end of April to the **Dixieland Festival** in September and October. The town's big shindig though is its **Cultural Summer**, which runs through July and August.

Sleeping
AiCES has student dorms (in July and August only), private rooms and hotels on its books, and can make reservations (25Sk fee).

ATC Tajov (☎ 419 73 20; Tajov; person/tent/car 85/120/85Sk; ☼ year-round) This is the nearest camp site, 7km west of town. It has a lovely rural setting.

Penzión Kúria (☎ 412 32 55; www.kuria.sk; Bakossova 4; s/d 700/1100Sk; P) It's a good idea to book Kúria in advance as its rustic feel, low price and central location are popular with tourists.

Hotel Arcade (☎ 430 21 11; www.arcade.sk; námestie SNP 5; s/d 1990/2430Sk; P) Arcade tops the list of high-end options in town, with large, attractive rooms, friendly staff and free parking.

Hotel Lux (☎ 414 41 41; lux@hotellux.sk; námestie Slobody 2; r from 1500Sk; P) The rooms at this massive tower-block of a hotel aren't particularly modern, but they're spacious, clean and come with balcony.

Národný dom (☎ 412 37 37; narodnydom@slovanet.sk; Národná 11; s/d 1450/1990Sk; P) The rooms at this central hotel are recently renovated and cheaper outside summer.

Eating
Námestie SNP has several attractive pavement cafés to choose from, and a number of decent restaurants.

Copaline Baguette (námestie SNP 8; baguettes from 50Sk) This simple place has fresh sandwiches, sweets and savouries.

Pizzeria Copaline (☎ 412 59 17; námestie SNP 12; pizzas & pastas from 60Sk) Copaline comes locally recommended and has large, filling pizzas and so-so pastas.

Ácia (Dolná 36; mains 100-150Sk) A bustling, vibrant restaurant with a large patio and a menu packed with local and national specialities.

Slovenská pivnica (☎ 415 50 36; Lazovná 18; mains 70-100SK; ☼ noon-8pm Mon-Fri) North off the square, this rustic restaurant gets high marks for Slovak specialities at low prices and a wide selection of beers.

The pancakes at the **Hotel Lux restaurant** are reputedly the best in the region; this may not be the case, but they're definitely mouth-watering. Otherwise try **La Crêperie** (námestie SNP 4; crêpes 50Sk), which has wonderful crêpes, an open terrace and toys for the kids to bust.

Belamo (Horná 3; breads & cakes from 10Sk; ☼ 7am-6pm Mon-Fri, 8am-noon Sat) This extremely popular bakery has delicious freshly baked bread and cakes.

For self-caterers, there's a small daily food market in námestie Štefana Moyzesa. Alternatively, try the supermarket in the Prior Department Store.

Drinking & Entertainment
Rock up to the **Jazz Café** (☎ 0905 421 317; Dolná 20) for a quiet pint, or a loud one on Wednesdays when there's live music.

The **State Opera** (☎ 412 44 18; Národná 11) has regular performances from September to June, as does the town's **Puppet Theatre** (Bábkové divadlo; ☎ 415 30 23; www.bdnr.sk; Skuteckého 14) – for both kids and adults. The puppet theatre also runs a summer programme for kids (also in English; 35Sk); activities include puppet making and performances.

Shopping

Folk Art (☎ 0903 397 7675; námestie SNP 7) has traditional handicrafts – clothes, wool rugs, wood, ceramics, embroidery – with an up-market slant.

Getting There & Away

Buses run between Banská Bystrica and Bratislava (260Sk, 3½–4½ hours), normally via Nitra (152Sk, two hours), every one to 1½ hours. Only one direct train a day makes the same journey (264Sk, four hours); usually there's a change at Zvolen or Vrútky. There are some beautiful local lines west to Martin (76Sk, one hour); and east up the Hron Valley towards Košice (264Sk, three hours 50 minutes).

BANSKÁ ŠTIAVNICA

☎ 045 / pop 10,900

Banská Štiavnica began as a medieval mining centre, exploiting some of Europe's richest gold and silver mines. Already a showcase town in the 13th century, in its 18th-century heyday it became Hungary's second largest town.

But then the mines began to dry up, and the town slipped out of the mainstream; today it's less than half its former size. Having missed the 19th-century boom that turned Banská Bystrica into a city, it's now an extraordinary mirror of earlier times, with a picturesque old centre full of Gothic and Renaissance houses, churches and two castles set beautifully in steep, wooded hills.

In 1972 the town was added to the Unesco World Heritage List. For the moment, slow restoration projects are not keeping up with the disintegration of many of the historical buildings, but Banská Štiavnica still makes an excellent day trip or overnight stay from Banská Bystrica.

Orientation

From the train and bus stations it's a 2km climb uphill through the factories and housing blocks of the new town to námestie sv Trojice in the old town. Only local buses and tour coaches stop in the old centre, at námestie Radničné. The hilly, snaky layout of the town can make this a confusing place to find your way around.

Information

The **AiCES office** (☎ 691 18 59; tikbs@banskastiavnica .sk; námestie sv Trojice 3; 8am-5.30pm May-Sep, 8am-4pm Mon-Fri, 8am-2pm Sat Oct-Apr) also doubles as an Internet café. **VÚB** (☎ 692 11 07; námestie Radničné 15) has an ATM and the **post office** (Kammershofská 30) is down the hill towards the bus station.

Sights

Unless otherwise stated, all museums and galleries open from 9am to 5pm Tuesday to Sunday, and cost 30/10Sk for adults/children. Museum tours leave on the hour and the last tour generally leaves an hour before closing.

NÁMESTIE SV TROJICE & NÁMESTIE RADNIČNÉ

Námestie sv Trojice (Holy Trinity), the old town's main square, sports a grand **plague column** and is flanked with the old palaces of German and Hungarian merchants and mine owners. Behind the bold sgraffito at No 8 is the **Jozefa Kollára Gallery** (☎ 691 34 31). The one-hour tour takes you through exhibits of Gothic to modern art, with the emphasis on local Slovak painter, Jozef Kollár. Several rooms have valuable Renaissance wood-cut ceilings and another room has a rich stucco decoration. Next door at No 6 is a **Mineral Museum** (☎ 691 25 44), with over 400 minerals from around the world and a historical mine mock-up.

At the bottom of the square, opposite the pastel-yellow **Fritz House** with its mining motifs, the Gothic parish **Church of St Catherine** (kostol sv Kateríny) still has some original murals and statues among the baroque furnishings. A little further west is the town hall, with a backwards clock, and across námestie Radničné a richly decorated 18th-century **Evangelical Church** (Evanjelický kostol).

From here you can explore the town's back alleys, lined with old miners' houses.

OLD CASTLE

Uphill from the town hall is Banská Štiavnica's ancient heart, the **Old Castle** (☎ 691 31 13; Starý zámocka; adult/child 60/30Sk). Between 1546 and 1559 an older Romanesque

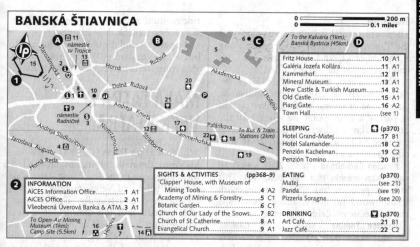

BANSKÁ ŠTIAVNICA

Fritz House...............................10 A1
Galéria Jozefa Kollára................11 A1
Kammerhof...............................12 B1
Mineral Museum........................13 A1
New Castle & Turkish Museum.....14 B2
Old Castle................................15 A1
Piarg Gate................................16 A2
Town Hall...........................(see 1)

SLEEPING   (p370)
Hotel Grand-Matej.....................17 B1
Hotel Salamander......................18 C2
Penzión Kachelman....................19 C2
Penzión Tomino........................20 B1

EATING   (p370)
Matej................................(see 21)
Panda...............................(see 19)
Pizzeria Soragna...................(see 20)

DRINKING   (p370)
Art Café.................................21 B1
Jazz Café...............................22 C2

INFORMATION
AiCES Information Office...............1 A1
AiCES Office..............................2 A1
Všeobecná Úverová Banka & ATM..3 A1

SIGHTS & ACTIVITIES   (pp368-9)
'Clapper' House, with Museum of
  Mining Tools...........................4 A2
Academy of Mining & Forestry........5 C1
Botanic Garden...........................6 C1
Church of Our Lady of the Snows....7 B2
Church of St Catherine..................8 A1
Evangelical Church.......................9 A1

church was walled in to protect the municipal riches from Turks, who never took the town. Still undergoing renovation, it houses a lapidarium, exhibits of baroque sculpture and, surprisingly enough, a mining exhibition.

NEW CASTLE & AROUND
Five years after the Old Castle was finished, the burghers evidently decided they needed another one. The strikingly simple **New Castle** (☎ 691 15 43; Novo zámocká; adult/child 50/20Sk), a whitewashed block with four corner towers, now houses a 'Museum of the History of the Struggle against the Turks on the Territory of Slovakia' and offers fine views over the town.

On the way up Andreja Sládkovičova, you pass a **'clapper' house** (klopačka), once apparently a kind of town alarm clock used for the miners' shifts, with a tiny **museum** (☎ 692 06 92) of mining tools and a very pleasant teahouse. Near the 18th-century **Piarg Gate** (Piargska brána), a gate for the once-bigger town, and the **Church of Our Lady of the Snows** (kostol Panny Márie Snežnej), is a footpath to the New Castle.

OTHER ATTRACTIONS
Europe's first mining academy was founded in Banská Štiavnica in the 1760s. Behind its grand complex above Akademická, now the Slovak Academy of Mining & Forestry, is a large public **botanic garden** (admission free; ☺ 9am-6pm).

Kammerhof (☎ 694 94 18; Kammerhofská 2) is another museum devoted to mining, this time dealing with its history. The working models of mining machines are its most intriguing displays.

The red-and-white hilltop church, visible from everywhere, is the topmost in a set of stations of the cross (in the form of baroque chapels with carved biblical scenes) that make up the **Calvary** (Kalvária; 1751). The wooded summit of the hill, about 1km northeast from the old town, offers great vistas.

If you still haven't had your fill of mining, there's a good open-air **Mining Museum** (Banské múzeum v prírode; ☎ 691 29 71; JK Hella 12; adult/child 60/30Sk) at a former mining camp 1.25km south of the city centre. There's machinery, workshops, a wooden miners' church and trips down the mine.

Tours
For 500Sk the AiCES office will arrange a guided tour of the town centre.

Festivals & Events
The annual three-day festival of **Salamander** starts on the Friday evening closest to 12 September. The origins of the festival go back to the 19th century when students at the mining academy held their various ceremonies (with some of the traditions going back centuries). This is one of Slovakia's best local festivals and is worth a weekend stay: many of the townspeople dress up in miners' clothing, and perform songs and dances.

Sleeping

There are several private rooms (look for the 'Zimmer frei' signs) and pensions along Kammerhofská and Sládokovicová. Ask about others at the AiCES office.

There's a basic **camp site** (☎ 0904 668 340; tent 200Sk; ☷ mid-Jun–mid-Sep) beside Počúvadlianske jazero, one of several artificial lakes created as part of a water-pumping scheme for the mines, 5.5km southwest of the old town on the road to Levice. In summer, up to four buses daily pass by the lake.

Penzión Kachelman (☎ 692 23 19; www.kachel man.sk; Kammerhofská 18; r from 600Sk; ℗) This homely *pension* has quaint rooms with stylish wood furniture, and a sauna, spa and barbecue available to guests.

Penzión Tomino (☎ 692 13 07; t.tokar@bb .telecom.sk; Akademická 9; s/d 550/700Sk) Rooms here don't have as much character as Kachelman's but they're still quite good value.

Hotel Grand-Matej (☎ 692 12 32; www.grand matel.sk; Kammerhofská 8; s/d 890/1500Sk; ℗) Grand-Matej has an air of sophistication about it and is one of the best options in town. There are also bicycles for rent at 300Sk a day.

Hotel Salamander (☎ 691 39 92; www.hotel salamander.sk; Palárikova 1; r from 1130Sk; ℗) This is an attractive old house with cosy, old-fashioned rooms.

Eating & Drinking

Matej (☎ 691 20 51; Akademická 4; mains 100-150Sk) Matej is the best option for Slovakian food in town and has a green, shaded terrace.

Pizzeria Soragna (☎ 691 20 01; Akademická 9; pizzas 80-120Sk) Next to Penzión Tomino is this excellent pizzeria; its large terrace is often packed in summer.

Panda (Kammerhofská 18; mains 100-150Sk) Another fine choice for Slovakian food, Panda has a refreshingly rural feel and a lovely courtyard.

For a coffee or something a bit stronger, pull up a pew in the **Art Café's** (Akademická 4) simple garden or at the welcoming **Jazz Café** (Kammerhofská 12).

Getting There & Away

Banská Štiavnica is not the easiest place to get to without your own transport. Only one bus daily departs from Bratislava (224Sk, 3½ hours) or Banská Bystrica (67Sk, 1¼ hours), at 1pm and 11am respectively. The fine train ride requires a change at Zvolen and Hronská Dubrava (82Sk, 1½–2 hours).

To park around the old town you need to buy a parking card (40Sk per hour), available from some hotels, shops or AiCES.

MALÁ FATRA & VEĽKÁ FATRA

While the High Tatras (see p387) are Slovakia's most dramatic mountains, the modest, forested ranges to the southwest – the Malá (Lesser) Fatra and Veľká (Greater) Fatra – are the most user-friendly. They're accessible by road, trail and chairlift for anyone with an urge to walk, ski or bicycle through its many valleys. Cheap *chaty* (mountain chalets) scattered throughout make long-distance walking a pleasure.

The Malá Fatra are the more popular of the two mountain groups; despite their name, they rise higher than the Veľká Fatra. The Váh river slices the Malá Fatra into two parts – the rounded Lúčanská Fatra west of Martin and the craggy Krivánska Fatra to the northeast. Most of the Krivánská Fatra is now the Lesser Fatra National Park (Národný park Malá Fatra), centred on the beautiful Vratná Valley (Vratná dolina).

The historic town of Martin in the broad Turiec Valley (Turčianska kotlina) and Žilina to the north are both convenient starting points for exploring.

MARTIN

☎ 043 / pop 60,100

This small town on the banks of the Turiec river is significant in Slovak history, for it was here that the Martin Memorandum was penned (see below). You could spend a day exploring its impressive ethnographic museum and two reasonable art galleries, and sampling the tasty local beer.

History

In 1861 Turčiansky Svätý Martin, a minor town in the broad Turiec Valley separating the Malá and Veľká Fatra ranges, was pushed into the history books when a meeting of intellectuals here issued the so-called Martin Memorandum, urging the establishment of a Slovak (and Slovak-language) district within Hungary.

This drew only silence from the authorities of the time. However, two years later a private cultural and educational foundation called Matica slovenská (the kernel of Slovakia) was founded. This foundation promoted Slovak-language schools, museums, musical societies, publishing etc. During subsequent years of Hungarian cultural domination, Martin became the epicentre of simmering Slovak aspirations. On 30 October 1918 the Martin Declaration, in which the Slovaks formally opted to federate with the Czechs, was issued here. Though Bratislava became the capital of Slovakia, the town of Martin remained its sentimental centre. Today the town is still known for its strong nationalist slant.

Orientation

Long-distance trains stop at the Vrútky station, in a modern industrial suburb to the north; from there bus Nos 10 and 12 go the 8km south to námestie SNP, the centre of what remains of 'old' Martin. The train station in the centre of town is used for regional connections.

The long-distance bus station is three blocks west of námestie SNP. The easiest place to catch local buses is by the open-air market south of námestie SNP.

Information

The helpful **AiCES office** (☎ 423 87 76; tik@martin.sk; Divadelné námestie 1; 9am-5pm Mon-Fri) is situated on the second floor of a funky

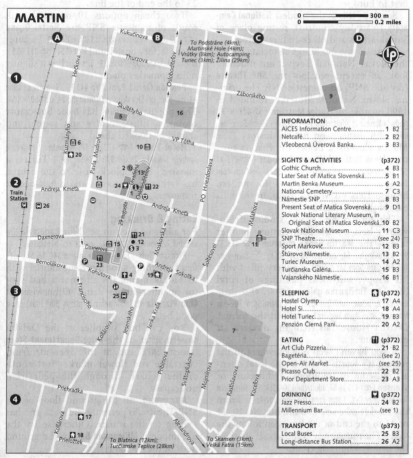

MARTIN

INFORMATION	
AiCES Information Centre	1 B2
Netcafé	2 B2
Všeobecná Úverová Banka	3 B3

SIGHTS & ACTIVITIES	(p372)
Gothic Church	4 B3
Later Seat of Matica Slovenská	5 B1
Martin Benka Museum	6 A2
National Cemetery	7 C3
Námestie SNP	8 B3
Present Seat of Matica Slovenská	9 D1
Slovak National Literary Museum, in Original Seat of Matica Slovenská	10 B2
Slovak National Museum	11 C3
SNP Theatre	(see 24)
Sport Markovič	12 B3
Štúrovo Námestie	13 B2
Turiec Museum	14 A2
Turčianska Galéria	15 B3
Vajanského Námestie	16 B1

SLEEPING	(p372)
Hostel Olymp	17 A4
Hotel Si	18 A4
Hotel Turiec	19 B3
Penzión Čierna Pani	20 A2

EATING	(p372)
Art Club Pizzeria	21 B2
Bagetéria	(see 2)
Open-Air Market	(see 25)
Picasso Club	22 B2
Prior Department Store	23 A3

DRINKING	(p372)
Jazz Presso	24 B2
Millennium Bar	(see 1)

TRANSPORT	(p373)
Local Buses	25 B3
Long-distance Bus Station	26 A2

glass-walled construction; it has loads of information on the surrounding area, including hiking and cycling maps. Internet access is available at **Netcafé** (Divadelná 7; 30Sk per hr; [clock] 10am-10pm).

There are plenty of ATMs scattered around námestie SNP. The main post office is on Pavla Mudroňa.

Sights

Martin's most worthwhile stop is the **Slovak National Museum** ([phone] 413 10 11; Maláhora 2; adult/child 50/25Sk; [clock] 9am-5.30pm Tue-Sun), to the east of the main square. Inside you'll find a thought-provoking photo exhibition on Roma life and an exhaustive collection of Slovak folk items, regarded as one of the best in Europe.

South of this is the modest **National Cemetery** (Národný cintorín), resting place of Slovak artists and other cultural heroes.

None of the buildings associated with the Slovak National Revival are much to look at, except possibly the **SNP Theatre** (divadlo SNP) on námestie SNP. The original Slovak National Museum, founded in 1906, is now the **Turiec Museum** ([phone] 423 06 39; Andreja Kmeťa 2; adult/child 20/10Sk; [clock] 10am-5pm Tue-Fri), with displays on natural history. The Matica slovenská began in what is now the **Slovak National Literary Museum** ([phone] 413 41 52; Osloboditeľov 11; adult/child 10/5Sk; [clock] 8am-4pm Tue-Sun), but is now housed in modern headquarters on Mudronňova, in the hills east of the city centre.

The former home and studio of Slovakia's best known 20th-century painter is now the **Martin Benka múzeum** ([phone] 413 31 90; Kuzmányho 34; adult/child 30/10Sk; [clock] 8am-4pm Tue-Fri, 9am-5pm Sat & Sun), a gallery filled with his happy, soft-focus paintings of rural life. The **Turčianska galéria** ([phone] 422 47 38; Daxnernova 2; adult/child 20/10Sk; [clock] 10am-5pm Tue-Sat May-Oct, 8am-4pm Tue-Fri Nov-Apr), in the former District House, has changing modern art exhibitions.

If you haven't seen one elsewhere in the region, it's worth a visit to the local open-air museum of traditional architecture or **skansen** ([phone] 413 26 86; adult/child 50/25Sk; [clock] 9am-5pm Tue-Sun May-Oct, 10am-2pm Tue-Sun Nov-Apr). From the market take southbound bus No 10, 11 or 41 to the end of the line then follow the signs. The museum is in the woods south of the Ľadoveň housing estate.

Activities

The Turiec valley and surrounding hills are not only good for hiking, they're also well set up for cycling. The **Turiec Bicycle Group** ([phone] 423 78 02; www.tbsjus.sk; Kukčínova 1) produces a handy map of bike trails in the surrounding area; check out its superb website for more information. For bike rental try **Sport Markovič** ([phone] 422 30 00; Osloboditeľov 6; [clock] 9am-5pm Mon-Fri, 9am-noon Sat; 300/1100Sk per day/week).

Sleeping

Autocamping Turiec ([phone] 428 42 15; www.autocampingturiec.sk; Kolónia Hviezda 92; person/tent/car 100/100/50Sk) is 1km west of the highway at Vrútky; from the market take northbound bus No 23 to the end of the line.

Two cheap options 10 minutes' walk south of námestie SNP are **Hostel Olymp** ([phone] 423 82 75; Kollárova 49; s/d 330/660Sk; [P]), a bare-bones factory hostel; and **Hotel Si** ([phone] 413 46 59; Prieložtek 1; s/d 300/500Sk; [P]), which is a slightly more upmarket place.

Penzión Čierna Pani ([phone] 413 15 23; www.penzion-cierna-pani.sk - Slovak only; Kuzmányho 24; s/d 600/900Sk) This popular *pension* has basic but comfy rooms, a fitness centre and sauna, and should be booked ahead.

Hotel Turiec ([phone] 422 10 17; www.hotel-turiec.sk; Andreja Sokolíka 2; s/d 970/2000Sk; [P]) Turiec, a massive yellow block close to the centre, has rather bland rooms and a half-decent restaurant.

Eating & Drinking

For a bite on the run head for **Bagetéria** (Divadelná 7; baguettes 30-50Sk), next to Netcafé.

Picasso Club (Osloboditeľov; mains 140-180Sk) offers something a lot more substantial with its Slovak menu; it's also not a bad spot for an after-dinner drink. Otherwise **Art Club Pizzeria** (Osloboditeľov 8; pizzas 80-120Sk) is a good bet.

You can buy supplies at the Delvita supermarket in the **Prior Department Store** (námestie SNP). and at the open-air fruit, vegetable and flower market just south of the square, through the pedestrian underpass.

Jazz presso, on the ground floor of the SNP Theatre, is perfectly laid-back and has seating on the square. Otherwise try the ultramodern **Millennium Bar** on the ground floor of the AiCES office.

Getting There & Away

A few express trains from Bratislava pass through Martin (286Sk, four hours), but generally you need to change at Vrútky, 7km north of the town. Local trains go south to Banská Bystrica (76Sk, 1½ hours). There are six daily direct bus connections from Bratislava (272Sk, 4½–5 hours), and 10 to Žilina (44Sk, 30 minutes).

LÚČANSKÁ FATRA

The western, non-national park half of the Malá Fatra range gets its name from its dominant peak, Veľká lúka (1476m).

Podstráne & Martinské Hole

Podstráne is a complex of ski chalets and holiday homes west of Martin, from which a year-round chairlift (lánovka) climbs to the Martinské hole (Martin Pinnacles) ski area on the slopes of Veľká luka. Or you can walk it, a half-day climb up the snaky yellow-marked trail.

Podstráne's A-frame **Horský Hotel** (☎ 042 34 67; www.hotelmartinskehole.sk; s/d 500/1000Sk; P 🛌), 300m beyond the bus stop, is open all year. Beyond it is the flash **Hotel Grandis** (☎ 422 00 15; www.grandis.sk; s/d 2400/3600Sk; P), easily the best hotel around. Martin's AiCES office has a list of some 17 chaty in the area.

To get to Podstráne, take northbound bus Nos 40 or 41 from the centre of Martin, about 4km to the end of the line. The chairlift is 800m from the bus.

Strečno & Starý Castles

In summer there are fine hikes from Martinské hole on the red-marked trail along the Lúčanská Fatra ridge. About 11km north on this trail, guarding the entrance to the Váh gorge, is **Strečno Castle** (☎ 041-569 74 00; adult/child 60/30Sk; ⏰ 9am-5.15pm May-Sep, 9am-4.15pm Sat & Sun Oct), built by the 14th-century warlord Matúš Čák (see p359). If that's too strenuous you can also hike up to the castle from the car park on the Žilina-Martin road, or from the Strečno train station across the river.

Nearby is a bright, white memorial to French partisans who died in the Slovak National Uprising. East via a bridge over the Váh, 2.5km away on another ridge, are the brooding 13th-century ruins of **Starý Castle** (admission free; ⏰ 24 hrs), accessible only on foot.

VEĽKÁ FATRA

Numerous marked trails drop from the Veľká Fatra (a 403 sq km national protected area) ridge line into the river valley south of Martin. Camp sites and chaty make for some fairly straightforward overnight trips (Martin AiCES office has lists for both); two better known ones are noted here. If you're planning any walking in the area, be sure to buy the detailed hiking and cycling VKÚ map No 121 (1:50,000; 80Sk).

Because the Veľká Fatra is relatively free of ski resorts and ski development, cross-country skiing is a bigger attraction in the winter than downhill pistes. Many popular tracks join up the small villages on the lower slopes. Of the nine small ski resorts within the confines of the Veľká Fatra, Záhradište is the biggest with 12 runs.

From Necpaly village, southeast of Martin, it's 13km east up the valley of the Necpalsoka to a primitive year-round chata on the peak of Borišov (1510m). An option is to return down the valley of the Belianska to Belá village. Both villages are linked by bus to Martin.

Long and short loop-trails start at the picturesque village of Blatnica, further south in the valley of the Turiec. A fine, long day or overnight trip follows the Gaderská to a chata at the foot of the 1574m Krížna peak, with an option to return down the valley of the Blatnicka past a 13th-century castle. The ridges between these two valleys contain several nature reserves. Another chata is near Blatnica.

ŽILINA

☎ 041 / pop 85,400

Žilina grew around a fortress at the intersection of several important trade routes and a ford on the Váh river, on the site of a 6th-century Slav settlement. An influential compendium of principles on civic rights and obligations, written here in 1370, might be the oldest existing text in the Slovak language.

Žilina was occupied by the Hussites from 1429–34 and, after being ravaged by the Thirty Years' War, faded away until the railway brought industrialisation in the late 19th century. Today it's one of Slovakia's most important transport junctions.

For tourists it serves mainly as a base for exploring the Malá Fatra, but it's also

ŽILINA

SIGHTS & ACTIVITIES	(pp374–5)
Burian Tower	4 C2
Church of St Barbara	5 B1
Church of the Holy Trinity	6 C2
Municipal Theatre	7 C2
Považská Galéria	8 C2
St Paul's Church	9 B2

SLEEPING	(p375)
Hotel Astoria	10 C1
Hotel Grand	11 B2
Hotel Slovakia	12 B3
Penzión Majovej	13 D1

EATING	(p375)
Bagetéria	14 C2
China Reštaurácia	15 C2
Emóica Galéria	(see 8)
Gazdovský	16 B2
Open-Air Market	17 B2
Tesco Department Store	18 C1
Záhrandá	19 C2

TRANSPORT	(p375)
Bus Station & WC	20 D1

INFORMATION	
AiCES Information Centre	1 C2
CK Selinan	(see 1)
Internet Café	2 C2
Všeobecná Úverová Banka & ATM	3 C2

an upbeat place with an attractive town square crowded with pastel-tinted Renaissance and baroque façades and an old castle on its outskirts.

Orientation

From the train and bus stations, the pedestrianised shopping street of Národná leads into the old market square, Hlinkovo námestie. Marble stairs and narrow Farská climb from here into the pedestrianised old town, centred on Mariánské námestie.

Information

The travel agent **CK Selinan** (☎ 562 14 78; Burianova medzierka 4; ☽ 8am-6pm Mon-Fri, 9am-noon Sat Jun-Aug, 8am-4.30pm Mon-Fri Sep-May) is part of the AiCES office network, and can provide ample information about Žilina and the Malá Fatra, including hiking maps. Log on at the small **Internet café** (Bottova 16; 50Sk per hr; ☽ 10am-midnight) just south of the main square.

VÚB (☎ 724 51 68; Na bráne 1), along with a couple of banks scattered around the centre, has an ATM. The main **post office** (Hviezdoslava)

is opposite the bus station. The train station has a **left luggage office** (☽ 24 hr).

Sights
OLD TOWN

The attractive Old Town square of Mariánské námestie is completely surrounded by arcaded burghers' houses, which are intruded upon by the Jesuits' 1743 baroque **St Paul's Church** (kostol sv Pavla). The fountain and several open-air cafés make this a fine place to pause over coffee and cake.

Once lined with stylish baroque houses, the lanes called Horný val (Upper Wall) and Dolný val (Lower Wall) ran round the inside of the original town walls. Where the eastern walls once stood, the old parish **Church of the Holy Trinity** (kostol Najsvätejšie Trojice) and a Renaissance belfry, the **Burian Tower** (Burianova veža; 1530; closed to the public), now loom over Hlinkovo námestie from atop an overweight marble staircase erected (along with the matching Municipal Theatre) in 1943.

Považská galéria (☎ 562 69 31; Štefánikova 2; adult/child 10/5Sk; ☽ 9am-5pm Tue-Fri, 10am-5pm Sat & Sun), on the southern side of the wide and open Hlinkovo námestie, displays thought-provoking contemporary art.

ST STEPHEN CHURCH

Don't miss this gem. The **St Stephen Church** (☎ 0903 116 624; ☼ for services only 7pm Fri, 8.30am & 10am Sun, otherwise call for appointment) is Žilina's oldest building and one of the earliest Romanesque churches in Slovakia. The most ancient bits, and some frescoes rediscovered in the 1950s, date from around 1250. It's 1.25km from the city centre, southwest down Hálkova and across the railway.

BUDATÍN CASTLE

North across the Váh, above its confluence with the Kysuca, **Budatín Castle** (Budatín zámok; ☎ 562 00 33; Topoľová 1; adult/child 30/15Sk; ☼ 8am-4pm Tue-Sun (also Mon Jun & Jul)) dates from at least the 13th century, when its Romanesque central tower was built. The Renaissance chateau was part of a face-lift in 1551, with fortifications added in the 17th century. The whole thing was restored in the 1920s but is now looking the worse for wear.

It houses the regional Považské múzeum, with an unusual tinkers' trade exhibition featuring *art naïf* figures of metal and wire, as well as displays on period furniture, church art and early history. Take bus No 21 or 22 from the train station; otherwise it's a 20-minute walk from Hviezdoslavova.

Sleeping

Penzión Majovej (☎ 562 41 52; Jána Milca 3; s/d 700/1300Sk; P) This place has quiet, clean rooms, a relaxed atmosphere and friendly staff.

Hotel Grand (☎ 564 32 65; www.hotelgrand.sk; Sládkovičova 1; s/d 1290/1890Sk; P) This attractive little hotel has a great location just off the main square.

Hotel Astoria (☎ 562 47 11; www.astoria-zilina.sk; Národná 1; s/d 1300/2300Sk; P) Astoria, Žilina's classiest hotel, has plush en suite rooms near the train station.

Hotel Slovakia (☎ 512 41 11; hotelslovakiamanager@bb.telecom.sk; Štúrovo námestie 2; s/d 1000/2000Sk; P ⓢ) This Communist-era hotel has a range of rooms in various states of refurbishment, plus a recently renovated pool.

Eating

Bagetéria (Hlinkovo námestie 5; baguettes 30-50Sk) If you're looking for a cheap bite to eat

on the run, Bagetéria will fulfil all your requirements.

Záhrandá (Bottova 8; mains 80-110Sk) This simple and reliable restaurant has hefty portions of the Slovak variety and covered outdoor seating.

Gazdovský (☎ 564 36 62; Horný val 37; mains 80-130Sk) For fine dining and Slovak cuisine head to this basement restaurant in a quiet corner of the old town.

China reštaurácia (☎ 562 66 74; Štúrova 5; mains 100-200Sk) Need a change from Slovakian? China does decent impersonations of Chinese cuisine.

Emócia Galéria (Štefánikova 2; coffee 30Sk) Emócia is a great cocktail of contemporary art, coffee, beer and a chilled atmosphere.

Self-caterers can try the **Tesco Department Store** (Hlinkovo námestie) or the small open-air **market** (Horný val).

Getting There & Away

Žilina is on the main railway line from Bratislava to Košice via Trenčín and Poprad, and is served by fairly frequent express trains. Express trains from Žilina go to Trenčín (104Sk, one hour), to Bratislava (242Sk, 2¾ hours), to Poprad (180Sk, two hours) and to Košice (286Sk, three hours).

Buses are quicker and more useful for regional destinations.

AROUND ŽILINA
Súľov Highlands

The Súľov Highlands (Súľovské Vrchy), southwest of Žilina (although the road leads out from Žilina in a northwesterly direction to circumvent the Súľovské Vrchy mountain range), offer some modest hiking and several crumbling castles. A good base for walks is the small village of **Súľov**, where you'll find a pub, a food store, and a very basic but pretty **camp site** (person/tent/car 10/20/50Sk; ☼ Jul & Aug).

Chata Kinex (☎ 557 41 13; per person 190Sk; ☼ May-Oct), 5km west of Súľov, is one place to get away from it all and has a small restaurant.

From here you have instant access to the weird rock formations of **Súľovské scaly**, and it's a short but steep trail to their high point, Brada (816m). Within a half-day's striking range in this protected region are the ruins of two castles, Súľovský hrad and Hričon hrad. VKÚ map No 157 (1:50,000; 80Sk) is the perfect hiking companion for the highlands.

GETTING THERE & AWAY

To get to Súľov from Žilina, take one of the hourly buses to Bytča (23Sk, 20 minutes), from where there are four buses daily (16Sk, 25 minutes).

Rajecká Lesná

This tiny village would be unremarkable save for the **Slovenský betlehem** (admission free; 9am-6pm), a 10m-long tableau of the Nativity, interwoven with tiny animated figures illustrating Slovak rural life. All the wooden figures were created by local wood carver Jozef Pekara who began this project in the early 1980s. The tableau is next to the church – follow signs from the bus stop. Čičmany and Prievidza-bound buses stop here.

Čičmany

Nestling in the snug Rajčanka Valley south of Žilina is the village of Čičmany, famed for a 200-year-old custom of painting its wooden cottages in patterns based on traditional embroidery motifs. It's a definite highlight of the region, and a striking example of Slovakian folk art.

A branch of the regional **Považské múzeum** (adult/child 15/10SK; 8am-6pm Tue-Sun), in one of the decorated houses, features old furnishings and another local speciality, embroidered snow-white folk dresses, along with a low-pressure pitch to buy the local handiwork. Across the road is a reconstructed two-family house (included in the entry fee).

If you feel like spending a night in one of the decorated cottages, **Penzión Katka** (549 21 32; penzionkatka@stonline.sk; s/d 290/580Sk), near the museum, is a perfect choice. It's nothing fancy, but you'll be made to feel right at home and the meals available are 100% home-made.

GETTING THERE & AWAY

Four daily buses from Žilina stop at Čičmany (44Sk, one hour) on their way to either Bojnice or Prievidza.

BOJNICE

046

This small town, 60km south of Žilina, has one big drawcard – its chateau. The grandeur of its fairy-tale appearance is easily matched by its rich interior; for more detailed information see p71.

Orientation & Information

The nearest train and bus stations are 2.5km east of Bojnice in the town of Prievidza. Local buses from Prievidza stop at the town's main square, Hurbanovo námestie, just below the castle.

The **AiCES office** (540 32 51; tik.bojnice@stonline.sk; Hurbanovo námestie; 9am-6pm Mon-Thu, 9am-7pm Fri & Sat, 10am-4pm Sun) is about 200m east of the castle. There are a couple of ATMs on the main square, and a **post office** on Sládkovičova.

Sleeping & Eating

Camping Bojnice (541 38 45; person/tent/car/bungalow 140/100/100/1080Sk; mid-May–mid-Sep) About 2km west of Bojnice on the road to Nitrianske rudno is this green, shady camp site. A small buffet and snack bar are on site.

Hotel pod zámkom (518 51 00; recephotel@stonline.sk; Hurbanovo námestie 2; s/d 1380/1850Sk; P) is nearest to the castle and has fine, if a little bland, rooms. If that's full try **Hotel Lipa** (543 03 08; Sládkovičova 20; s/d 750/900Sk; P).

There are a couple of eateries on Hurbanovo námestie, the best of which is **Pálfyho Pizzeria** (543 18 88; Hurbanovo námestie; pizzas 100-130Sk), with large pizzas and views of the castle.

Getting There & Away

There are three daily buses from Žilina (91Sk, two hours) and one from Bratislava (344Sk, 3¾ hours). Nearby Prievidza has more connections, from where local bus No 3 takes you to the castle.

The only place of interest you can get to easily by train from Prievidza is Nitra (88Sk, 2½ hours).

MALÁ FATRA NATIONAL PARK

041

The Krivánska Fatra – the eastern half of the Malá Fatra range, named after its tallest peak, Veľký Kriváň (1709m) – lies within the Malá Fatra National Park (Národný park Malá Fatra). It contains some of the most accessible high-altitude walking in Slovakia and the focus of this region is the beautiful Vratná dolina (Vratná Valley).

Terchová

Terchová, which stands at the entrance to the Vratná Valley to the north, was the birthplace of one of Slovakia's favourite folk heroes, Juraj Jánošík, in 1688. It's the best place to gather information and maps on the park.

The **Terchová information office** (☎ 599 31 00; www.terchovaregion.sk; Cyrila a Metoda 96; ☺ 8am-6pm Mon-Fri, 9am-5pm Sat & Sun), 200m west of the bus stop, has hiking and cycling maps, accommodation lists (including *pensions* and private rooms for around 280Sk per person), souvenirs, and Internet access for 100Sk per hour. Next door is an ATM.

Above the village of Terchová is an immense aluminium statue of Juraj Jánošík (see the boxed text below), and west of the village bus stop next to the town hall (Obecný úrad) is a little **museum** (Expozícia Jánošík; adult/child 12/6Sk; ☺ 9am-6pm Mon-Sun) devoted to him.

Nižné Kamence camping (☎ 569 52 33; www .camp-kamence.szm.sk; person/tent/car/bungalow 65/65/ 60/200Sk), 3.5km west of Terchová, is small and squeezed between the road and the Varinka river. Newly built **Hotel Gavurky** (☎ 500 35 02; www.hotelgavurky.sk; s/d 830/1100Sk; P), 500m east of Terchová, has very modern, clean rooms while **Hotel Diery** (☎ 569 53 22; diery@za.psg.sk; s/d 650/880Sk; P) a further 500m east, is not as new but has decent rooms with balcony. Both have restaurants and bars.

Across the narrow Varinka stream from the information office is **Starinkova včeláreň** (☎ 599 31 30; A Hliku 246; mains 100-130Sk), a cosy restaurant/tea shop with a small but inviting grill-menu. There's a big terrace, views of Malá Fatra and local honey for sale.

FESTIVALS & EVENTS
Jánošik Days, an international folk festival held at the beginning of August, features musical acts from Slovakia and around the world.

Vratná Valley
In 1987 the central area of the Krivánská Fatra became the 198 sq km Malá Fatra National Park, largely to protect the Vratná Valley, a thickly forested cul-de-sac that many say is Slovakia's most beautiful valley. It certainly has dramatic scenery, bracing hikes and plenty of summer accommodation along the trails.

Naturally it's overrun with visitors in the high summer and winter seasons, but there are enough trails to lose the crowds and it can be almost empty in May or September. You can visit it on a long day trip from Žilina, but longer stays are more rewarding.

ORIENTATION & INFORMATION
The valley turn-off is at Terchová, 25km east of Žilina, although the real gateway is a slot through pinnacled limestone crags called Tiesňavy. About 2.5km south from Terchová the road branches – left to the hamlet of Štefanová and right to the head of the valley at Chata Vrátna.

About 1km up the Štefanová road is a turn-off to the **Mountain Rescue Service** (Horská služba; ☎ 569 52 32), the best source of valley weather and trail information, and to the Hotel Boboty.

SLOVAKIA'S ROBIN HOOD

There are many Robin Hood characters in the annals of Slovakian history, but Juraj Jánošík is far and away the most famous.

Jánošík, the focus of untold folk songs and stories, is a mixture of fact and fiction. Born into a peasant family in 1688 in Terchová, he joined up with Ferenc Rákóczi II in 1703 to fight the Habsburgs. When the rebellion was crushed in 1711, he headed for Kežmarok. While away his mother died and his father was beaten to death by their landlord for taking time off to bury her. Jánošík then took to the hills and spent the next two years robbing from the rich and giving to the poor, although some say he didn't make much of a distinction about who he stole from.

In 1713 he was captured in a local pub; legend has it that the landlord betrayed him and as he went to escape he slipped on some peas an old lady had thrown on the floor. He was sentenced to an excruciating death – hung on a hook by the ribs in Liptovský Mikuláš. Even the location of his execution is in dispute; some say it was the town's main square, others 1.5km west near the prison where he was tortured or about 2km east of the square in what is now a residential area.

If you want to know more about the man, just ask any Slovakian; they'll surely be able to spin a few yarns about his superhuman feats.

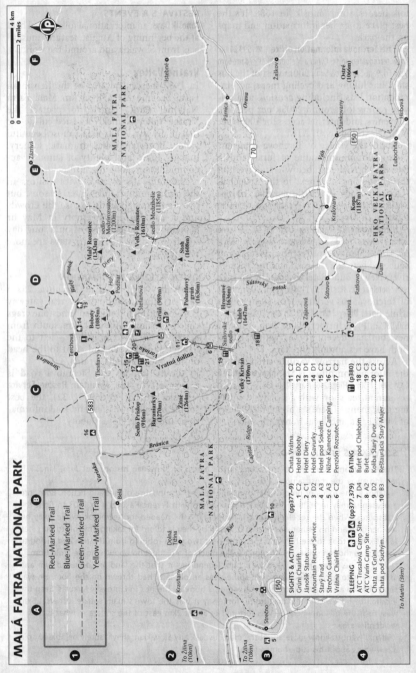

MALÁ FATRA NATIONAL PARK

0   2 miles
0   4 km

— Red-Marked Trail
— Blue-Marked Trail
- - - Green-Marked Trail
······ Yellow-Marked Trail

SIGHTS & ACTIVITIES   (pp377-9)
Grúň Chairlift........................**1** C2
Jánošík Statue.......................**2** C1
Mountain Rescue Service.........**3** D2
Starý hrad...............................**4** A3
Strečno Castle........................**5** A3
Vrátna Chairlift......................**6** C2

Chata Vrátna..........................**11** C2
Hotel Boboty..........................**12** D2
Hotel Diery............................**13** D1
Hotel Gavurky........................**14** D1
Hotel pod Sokolím..................**15** C1
Nižné Kamence Camping.........**16** C1
Penzión Rozsutec....................**17** C2

SLEEPING   🏕 🛏   (pp377,379)
ATC Trusalová Camp Site.........**7** D4
ATC Varín Camp Site...............**8** A2
Chata na Grúni.......................**9** D2
Chata pod Suchým..................**10** B3

🍴 (p380)
EATING
Bufet pod Chlebom.................**18** C3
Bufet......................................**19** C3
Koliba Starý Dvor....................**20** D2
Reštaurácia Starý Majer...........**21** C2

On the Chata Vrátna road, it's 1.5km from the fork to a bus stop and a side road by the Reštaurácia Starý Majer, and 2.5km more to Chata Vrátna and the chairlift to Veľký Kriváň. For online information on the valley check out www.vratna.sk.

SKIING
The Vrátna valley is one of the more popular winter destinations in Slovakia. The ski centre encompasses a total of 11 ski tows, two chairlifts and almost 13km of prepared pistes. The ski season here lasts around four months thanks to the production of artificial snow; a one day/one week pass costs 680/3100Sk for adults, 470/1990Sk for children.

HIKING IN THE KRIVÁNSKÁ FATRA
From near Chata Vrátna a year-round chairlift goes to **Snilovské sedlo** (Snilov Saddle), between Veľký Kriváň and the 1647m Chleb (120/160Sk one-way/return; purists can walk this in two hours), from where it's about a half-hour climb to either summit. From the top of the chairlift you could walk west then north down a side ridge to Reštaurácia Starý Majer (and buses back to Žilina), which is a five-hour loop.

For those with more time there are fine, uncrowded hikes all along the 43km **Hlávný hrebeň** (Capital Ridge) trail that stretches the length of the range. In fact you could do it all, from Strečno in the west to Zázrivá village in the east, in three days – the first night could be at Chata pod Suchým, the second at Chata Vrátna or Chata na Grúni in the valley (via the chairlift), and the third in a private room or *chata* at Zázrivá.

From Snilovské sedlo it's three or four hours down the southern side of the range. At Bufet pod Chlebom, on the south face of Chleb, a trail branches left (as you face south) via waterfalls to Šútovo village (and a train or bus west to Martin), while another branches right to **Zajacová** (695m) with a trail on to Trusalová camp site, 2km from the road to Martin.

One of the most beautiful, and most demanding, hikes is the trail from **Štefanová** (at about 620m) east to sedlo Medziholie, and then up over **Veľký Rozsutec** (1610m; some steep sections with ladders and chains). An easier trail leads east to sedlo Medzirozsutec, then down through Horné Diery to Podžiar, and back to Štefanová. (Note: the trail is closed from 1 October to 30 June.)

For anything more than a day hike, check with Mountain Rescue on weather and trail conditions and *chata* availability. Carry your own water and some food, even if you have a firm *chata* booking with meals, and don't go anywhere without the VKÚ *Malá Fatra* map (No 110; 1:50,000; 80Sk).

SLEEPING
There's a wide selection of accommodation to choose from around the valley.

Budget
Near Šútovo, about 12km east of Martin and 2km off the highway, is the quiet, tree-shaded **ATC Trusalová camp site** (☎ 429 26 36; person/tent/car/bungalow 95/70/75/230Sk; ☼ May–mid-Sep). On the opposite side of the mountains is the good **ATC Varín camp site** (☎ 041-562 14 78; person/tent/car/bungalow 95/100/85/750Sk; ☼ May–mid-Oct; ☎), 15km east of Žilina on the Terchová road.

There are a few *chaty* within the boundaries of the park. A recommended stop on the Capital Ridge trail is the 40-bed **Chata pod Suchým** (☎ 569 73 94; s/d 200/400Sk) at the western end of the park.

Mid-range
A quiet place in the valley away from the road is **Chata na Grúni** (☎ 569 53 24; s/d 350/700Sk), a 45-minute walk northeast from Chata Vrátna on a yellow-marked trail, and near the top of a year-round chairlift from the Štefanová road. **Chata Vrátna** (☎ 569 57 39; chata_vratna@vratna.sk; s/d 500/1000Sk; ℗) is a quaint, rustic mountain chalet that has basic but cosy rooms and a great restaurant. Summer walk-in prospects are good, but call ahead if possible.

Just before Reštaurácia Starý Majer is a turn-off to a couple of accommodation options, including **Penzión Rozsutec** (☎ 569 53 06; s/d 600/1000Sk; ℗), with panoramic views of the valley, and **Hotel pod Sokolím** (☎ 507 31 66; hotelpodsokolim@reservation.sk; s/d 800/1200Sk; ℗).

Hotel Boboty (☎ 569 52 27; hotel_bobty@vratna.sk; s/d 750/1500Sk; ℗ ☒ ☎) Up the hill behind the Mountain Rescue office, this hotel is well set up for both the summer and winter seasons, with a pool and a sauna, but the rooms are a bit cramped.

EATING

Outside the hotels and bigger *chaty*, there's not a lot of choice for eating out in the valley.

The touristy **Reštaurácia Starý Majer** (☎ 569 54 19; mains 100-150Sk) and the simpler **Koliba Starý Dvor** (mains 80-150Sk), at the bus stop 2.5km north of Chata Vrátna, are both solid bets. Some of the smaller *chaty* do meals by arrangement.

There is an overpriced *bufet* at the top of the Vrátná chairlift and **Bufet Pod Chlebom**, in a former chalet just over the saddle, though the latter keeps unpredictable hours.

You can buy groceries at the minimarket near the turn-off to the valley in Terchová.

GETTING THERE & AROUND

Plenty of buses serve Terchová from Žilina (36Sk, 45 minutes), particularly during the working week. Every two hours (five a day in July and August) they continue to Chata Vrátna (48Sk, one hour), with a detour to Štefanová.

Požičovňa bicyklov (☎ 0907 614 097; Cyrila a Metoda 96; ☉ 9am-5pm Mon-Fri, 9am-noon Sat), in Terchová, hires out mountain bikes for 250Sk per day.

ORAVA VALLEY

☎ 043

The Orava river rises in Poland, twists down through the highlands west of the High Tatras and eventually flows into the Váh east of Martin.

Hardship and isolation have given the Orava Valley a personality of its own. It suffered an iron feudal grip, Habsburg punishment for Protestant sympathies, crop failure and forced relocation in the early 18th century, and the flooding of the upper valley (and five villages) by the Orava Dam in 1954. Unregulated postwar industrialisation has also blighted great stretches of the valley.

But the villages between Oravský Podzámok and Nižná are scenic and relatively unspoilt, with ranks of brightly painted traditional log house-barns, some with carved fronts and colourful gardens. Other highlights include one of Slovakia's most photogenic castles, a first-rate *skansen*, and a hikers' back door into the High Tatras via the Orava's tributary valleys.

Getting There & Around

Transport is tedious unless you have a car. Trains trundle up and down the valley every hour or two, along with plenty of buses, but bus travel up the side valleys can be slow. About 6km north of Trstená on Hwy 59 is a border crossing to Chyzne in Poland, on the road to Kraków.

Five daily buses run from Dolný Kubín to Podbiel (36Sk, 35 minutes), but only three a day from there to Zuberec and the trailhead at Chata Zverovka (16Sk, 25 minutes).

DOLNÝ KUBÍN

There's not a lot to see here, but this small, peaceful town isn't a bad spot for a bite to eat, or to pick up accommodation info and hiking maps for the surrounding area.

On Radlinského, about 700m south of the bus and train stations, is VÚB's ATM. A hundred metres further south and close to the old centre, námestie Hviezdoslavova, is the **AiCES office** and travel agency **Slovako-tour** (☎ 865 40 56; Gäceľská 1; ☉ 9am-5pm Mon-Fri, 9am-noon Sat).

Bright **Penzión Marina** (☎ 586 43 51; www .marina.sk; námestie Hviezdoslavova 36; s/d 1000/1400Sk; P) has lovely, modern rooms, a friendly atmosphere and an excellent restaurant on the main square.

ORAVA CASTLE

For a full description of the castle, see p75.

The rooms at **Hotel Oravan** (☎ 589 31 15; r from 800Sk; P), on the main road below the castle, are value for money. **Restaurant Toliar** (☎ 589 31 24; mains 100-150Sk), at the foot of the castle, has chatty staff, a small patio and solid Slovakian fare.

Oravský Podzámok is 10km upstream of Dolný Kubín, by train (11Sk, ½ hour). The castle is just west of the train station, across the river.

ORAVA LAKE

Slovaks come up the valley to relax around a 35 sq km reservoir, Orava Lake (Vodná nádrž Orava). You can camp and swim here, or take a boat out to one of the few survivors of predamming times: the parish church of Slanica, now stranded on an island (Slanický ostrov) in the lake.

Near Orava Dam, a few kilometres south of Námestovo village, are two camp

ORAVA VALLEY

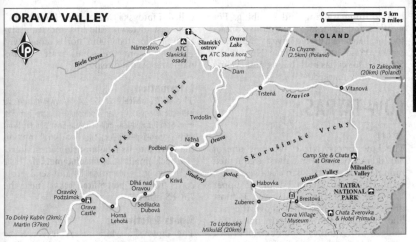

sites right on the lake's shoreline; **Stará hora** (☎ 552 22 23; www.campstarahora.host.sk/; person/tent/car/bungalow 70/50/50/360Sk; ☼ Jun-Sep) with a restaurant, shop and bungalows sleeping up to 12; and **ATC Slanická osada** (☎ 552 27 77; person/tent/car 60/50/60Sk; ☼ Jun-Sep), where you can hire water bikes for 100Sk per hour.

ZUBEREC & AROUND

The village of Zuberec, 13km up the Studený valley from Podbiel, is a pretty little gateway to the Western Tatras with its fair share of traditional architecture. Its **AiCES office** (☎ 539 51 97; www.zuberec.sk; Zuberec 289; ☼ 8am-6pm Mon-Fri, 8-11am & 2-5pm Sat & Sun Jun-Aug, 8am-4pm Mon-Fri Sep-May) can provide you with hiking maps and books, accommodation listings and public transport details. **Biela Hviezda** (☎ 539 52 94; Zuberec 449; ☼ 9am-5pm Mon-Fri, 9am-1pm Sat), a well-stocked sports store, rents mountain bikes for a song at 100Sk per day.

The big man-made attraction in the area is the **Orava Village Museum** (múzeum Oravskej dediny; ☎ 539 51 49; adult/child 40/30Sk; ☼ 8am-5pm). This is certainly one of Slovakia's best collections of old rural buildings, and its 50 or so structures offer a good window on the past. The oldest and most impressive is an early 15th-century wooden church from the village of Zabrež. You can walk round the place by yourself, though with a guide you'll see more interiors and their original furnishings.

Habovka, just north of Zuberec, and Zuberec itself, have plenty of private rooms. **Hotel Primula** (☎ 539 51 79; r 950Sk; Ⓟ) and

Chata Zverovka (☎ 539 51 06; www.chatazverovka.sk; r 600Sk; Ⓟ) are a few kilometres beyond the museum.

WESTERN TATRAS

One way to escape the eager crowds in the High Tatras is to explore the western end of the range, called the Western Tatras (Západné Tatry). However, you'll find the transport thin, facilities limited and the trails demanding.

One possible trailhead is at Chata Zverovka, from where a good day's walk is to make for Roháčska plesá (1719m), a small plateau hiding three alpine lakes and a picturesque waterfall.

Another route is up the valley of the Oravica river, which leaves the Orava at Tvrdošín. From Trstená (which you can get to by bus or train) it's about 15km, with a turn-off at Vitanová, to the trailhead at Oravice, where there's a *chata* and a very popular camp site, **ATC Oravice** (☎ 539 41 14; atczboja@za.psg.sk; person/tent/car/bungalow 50/80/80/400Sk). Buses make the run from Trstená (36Sk, 40 minutes) about half a dozen times a day. An alternative would be to walk or cycle the 8km green-marked trail from the Orava Village Museum, up the Blatná Valley and down the Mihulčie Valley.

Trails from these points quickly get up into some the highest mountains in central Europe (see p389), so they are no picnic. You should not attempt any long-distance treks here unless you have experience with high-altitude walking and climbing. For weather and mountain conditions contact the local **Mountain Rescue Service** (☎ 539 52 18; Zveroka; ☺ 8am-3pm); VKÚ map No 112 (1: 50,000; 100Sk) has both hiking and cycling trails clearly marked.

LOW TATRAS

☎ 044

The Low Tatras (Nízke Tatry) is one of Slovakia's favourite and most frequented mountain areas. The 80km east–west ridge, framed between the valleys of the upper Váh and the smaller Hron river, is most dramatic where it pushes above the tree line, though the lower eastern half is the wildest, with significant numbers of brown bear, wildcat and other wildlife.

Since 1978 most of this area has been part of the 810 sq km Low Tatras National Park (Národný park Nízke Tatry), but recreation and tourism development continues in the western half. Excellent hiking trails crisscross the range, though with fewer *chaty* than in the Malá Fatra.

Of the many deep lateral valleys, the most popular and most developed is the Demänova Valley (Demänskóva dolina), running south from the town of Liptovský Mikuláš to Jasná – Slovakia's best known ski resort – below the peak of Chopok (2024m). In summer the summit ridge between Chabenec (1955m) and Ďumbier (2043m), which is the highest peak in the range, is easily accessible by chairlift from both Jasná in the Demänova Valley and its southern counterpart, Bystrá dolina. There is more tourist development at Donovaly, at the western end of the range.

LIPTOVSKÝ MIKULÁŠ

pop 33,000

Liptovský Mikuláš' main claim to historical fame is as the place where Juraj Jánošík, the 'Slovak Robin Hood' (see the boxed text p377), was executed.

There's not a lot to see in the town, but it does make a useful base for visiting the Low Tatras and the surrounding area.

Orientation

The mighty Váh doesn't look so mighty here, pooling into a 24 sq km reservoir called Liptovská Mara, the 'Liptov Sea', just west of town. The bus and train stations are located 500m north along MM Hodžova from the small main square, námestie Osloboditeľov.

Information

The **AiCES office** (☎ 552 24 18; www.lmikulas.sk; námestie Mieru 1; ☺ 8am-7pm Mon-Fri, 8am-2pm Sat, noon-6pm Sun mid-Jun–mid-Sep, 9am-6pm Mon-Fri, 8am-noon Sat mid-Sep–mid-Jun) has loads of info on the town and its neighbouring attractions.

Check emails at **Z@vináč Internet Café** (Pišúta 19; 50Sk per hr; ☺ 10am-midnight) and send postcards from the **post office** (Hodžova), near the AiCES office.

Sights & Activities

The Liptovská Mara reservoir serves as the town's aquatic playground. It's ranked among the country's largest lakes so you'll find a plethora of boats, windsurfers and swimmers all jostling for position throughout the summer months. If you're looking to get out on the water, or just want a dip, head to the **ATC Liptovský Trnovec** (p383), where there's boat hire and a popular beach.

The leading poet of Slovak Romanticism is honoured at the **Janko Kráľ Museum** (☎ 552 25 54; námestie Osloboditeľov 30; adult/child 30/15Sk; ☺ 9am-4pm Tue-Fri, 10am-5pm Sat, also 10am-5pm Sun Jul & Aug), which also houses the quaint exhibits of 19th- and 20th-century town life and a gruesome reconstruction of the **torture chamber** (adult/child 10/5Sk) where Juraj Jánošik was 'interrogated'.

The **Petr Michal Bohúň Gallery** (☎ 552 27 58; Tranovského 3; adult/child 50/30Sk; ☺ 10am-5pm Tue-Sun) houses the second-largest art collection in the country (after the National Gallery in Bratislava). The exhibits range from Gothic and baroque to 19th and 20th century art. Just off the main square is the town's **synagogue** (Hollého 14; adult/child 20/10Sk; ☺ 11am-4pm Tue-Sat), now housing Jewish artefacts.

In the 17th century a huge wooden **Protestant church** (☎ 559 26 22; admission 20Sk; ☺ 9am-5pm Jun-Sep, 9am-3pm Oct-May) was built in Palúdzka without the use of metal nails; later, an onion-domed belfry was added. In 1980 it was moved to the village of Svätý Kríž, 8km southwest of Liptovský Mikuláš, to save it from being drowned by the

LIPTOVSKÝ MIKULÁŠ

INFORMATION	
AiCES Information Centre	1 D1
Z@vináč Internet Café	2 D2

SIGHTS & ACTIVITIES	(pp382–3)
Janko Kráľ Museum	3 D2
Jánošík's Dungeon	4 A2
Liptour	5 D1
Námestie Osloboditeľov	6 D2
St Nicholas Church	7 D2
Synagogue	8 D2
Town Hall	9 D1

SLEEPING	(p383)
Kriváň	10 D1

EATING	(p383)
Alcatraz	11 D2
Hypernova Supermarket	12 C2
Liptovska Izba	13 D2

Liptovská Mara reservoir. Frequent buses run to the village from the main bus station Monday to Friday (13Sk, 15 minutes). The church is hidden among trees, 750m south of the village and west of the road.

Half-way between town and the Liptovský Trnovec camp site is Slovakia's first aqua park, **Tatralandia** (☎ 547 45 36; adult/child 190/130Sk; ⊗ 9am-9pm May-Sep, 1-9pm Oct-Apr). Kids will love the many pools, slides and theme days. Parents, however, may prefer the **thermal pools** (☎ 439 26 51; adult/child 100/50Sk; ⊗ 10am-9pm) at Bešeňová, 18km west of Liptovský Mikuláš.

Festivals & Events

The most prestigious folk festival in Slovakia is held in the small village of **Východná**, 22km east of Liptovský Mikuláš, at the end of June or the beginning of July. People travel not only from all over Slovakia, but from all over Europe to attend this showcase of folk music and dance. The only accommodation in the small village is a makeshift camp site which springs up just for the festival – otherwise you'll have to make Liptovský Mikuláš, or even Poprad, your base.

Sleeping & Eating

ATC Liptovský Trnovec (☎ 559 84 58; www.atc trnovec.sk; Liptovský Trnovec; person/tent/car/bungalow 110/65/70/800Sk; ⊗ May-Sep) On the north side of the lake 6km from Liptovský Mikuláš is this family-oriented camp site.

Kriváň (☎ 852 24 14; Štúrova 5; s/d 300/600Sk) This central hotel has sparse but decent rooms with shared facilities, and, unfortunately, unfriendly staff.

Hotel Steve (☎ 552 89 99; www.hotel.stevelm.sk; 1. maja 699; r from 1200Sk; ℗) Another central choice is Steve, with plush rooms compared to Kriváň and free parking.

Liptovska izba (☎ 551 48 53; námestie Osloboditeľov 21; mains 100-150Sk) is a fine Slovak restaurant, all timber and tradition, offering hearty meals. **Alcatraz** (☎ 551 45 65; Belopotockého 2; mains 120-220Sk), however, is top dog in town with an international menu, comfy couches and an open fire in winter.

The massive **Hypernova supermarket** (⊗ 7am-9pm) is on Garbiarska.

Getting There & Away

Liptovský Mikuláš is on the main railway line between Bratislava (330Sk, four hours) and Košice (264Sk, two hours) and is served by fast trains every hour or two. Poprad (82Sk) and Žilina (116Sk) are both about an hour away. Bus connections are tedious unless you're heading to Starý Smokovec (81Sk, 1½ hours, six buses daily). Two buses a day connect with Dolný Kubin (53Sk, 50 minutes).

AROUND LIPTOVSKÝ MIKULÁŠ
Pribylina

About 21km northeast of Liptovský Mikuláš, just past Pribylina village, is another good *skansen*, called the **Museum of Liptov Village**

(☎ 529 31 63; adult/child 50/25Sk; ⊙ 9am-6.30pm Jul-Aug, 9am-4.30pm mid-May–Jun & Sep-Oct, 9am-3.30pm Nov–mid-May). Most of the buildings are from the Liptovská Mara area and were relocated here just before the dam was completed and the valley flooded. Apart from a good collection of local wooden houses (some full of period furniture, tools and clothing), there is also a wooden church and a fire station, as well as a small chateau. Four buses a day make the trip from Liptovský Mikuláš (44Sk, 45 minutes).

Važec Cave

This recently opened **cave** (☎ 529 41 71; adult/child 50/30Sk; ⊙ 9am-4pm Tue-Sun May-Nov, 10am-3pm Tue-Sun Feb-May) in the tiny village of Važec, 28km east of Liptovský Mikuláš, is famous for what it stored for thousands of years – fossilised cave bear bones from the Ice Age. Tours leave every hour, on the hour, and up to seven buses (44Sk, one hour) travel between Liptovský Mikuláš and Važec daily.

Vlkolínec

In 1993 this small folk village, about 27km west of Liptovský Mikuláš, entered the books of Unesco. All the fuss was over its 45 remarkably well-preserved log houses, which are highly uniform and typical for the mountainous region. The oldest dates from the 15th century. You can poke around one of the houses which has been turned into a **museum** (☎ 432 10 23; adult/child 25/10Sk; ⊙ 9am-3pm).

DEMÄNOVA VALLEY

Slovaks know the village of Jasná at the head of the Demänova Valley (Demänovská dolina) as the republic's best ski resort, and from January through April it overflows with people clunking around in ski and snow boots. In the summer it reveals itself as a pretty, forested valley under relentless development but featuring Slovakia's most accessible limestone caves, and with easy access by foot or chairlift to windswept walks along the crest of the Low Tatras.

Orientation

The valley begins near the village of Pavčina Lehota, 7km south of Liptovský Mikuláš. At the head of the valley is a diffuse collection of chalets, hotels and chairlifts called Jasná (1200m), a further 8km south.

Information

The **Slovakotour agency** (☎ 554 90 26; www.slovaktour.sk - Slovak only; ⊙ 7.30am-7pm Jun-Sep, 8am-6pm Oct-May) is near the Pavčina Lehota turn-off. It can help with accommodation, national park information, hiking maps and currency exchange, and can arrange an assortment of outdoor activities. In Jasná, there's another **agency** (☎ 559 16 79; ⊙ 7.30am-7pm Jun-Sep, 8am-6pm Oct-May), a post office, and an ATM.

The park's **Mountain Rescue Service** (☎ 559 16 78) is the place to go for trail and weather information if you're planning overnight walks in the mountains. Plenty of online information can be found at www.jasna.sk.

Sights & Activities

CAVES

Two limestone caves in the lower valley are part of Slovakia's biggest continuous cave system. About 2km of passages in the **Demänova Freedom Cave** (Demänovská jaskyňa Slobody; ☎ 559 16 73; adult/child 120/60Sk; ⊙ year round) are open to visitors, while the smaller **Demänova Ice Cave** (Demänovská ľadová jaskyňa; ☎ 554 81 70; adult/child 110/50Sk; ⊙ mid-May–Sep) has ice formations at the lowest level. Both caves are a 15-minute hike from the road.

Daily cave tours leave every hour on the hour between 9am and 4pm June to August; other months, tours begin at 9.30am, 11am, 12.30pm and 2pm. Take an extra layer against the subterranean chill.

HIKING & CYCLING

Better than going below ground is rising above it, on fine ridge walks with long views across the Low Tatras and north as far as the High Tatras on a clear day.

From the bus terminus at Jasná it's a 20-minute walk up (south) to the Koliesko Restaurant. From there a **summer chairlift** makes a 20-minute ascent (100Sk; ⊙ 8.30am-5pm; change halfway at Luková) almost to the top of **Chopok** (2024m).

Visiting Chopok is feasible even for families and couch-potatoes, and there are small buffets at the Luková and Chopok terminals. Take extra layers even in summer. The crowds are thick at Chopok, but just walk 200m in any direction to lose most of them. Check the last return time if you don't want to walk back down.

From Chopok a trail returns via Luková to Jasná. Alternatively, you can continue

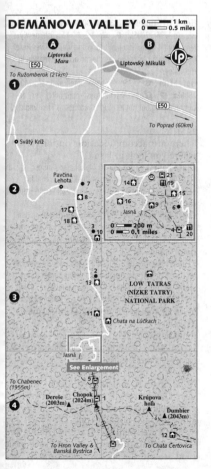

DEMÄNOVA VALLEY

SIGHTS & ACTIVITIES	(pp384–6)
Chopok Chairlift Station	**1** A4
Demänova Freedom Cave	**2** A3
Demänova Ice Cave	**3** A2
Koliesko Chairlift Station	**4** B2
Luková Chairlift Station	**5** A4
Mountain Rescue Service (Horská služba)	**6** B2
Slovakotour Agency	**7** A2

SLEEPING	(p386)
Bystrina Hotel & Camp Site	**8** A2
Chata Björnson	**9** A2
Chata Kamenná	**10** A2
Chata Lúčky	**11** A3
Chata Štefánika	**12** B4
Hotel Fim	**13** A3
Hotel Grand	**14** B2
Hotel Junior	**15** B2
Hotel Liptov	**16** B2
Hotel Tri Studničky	**17** A2
Penzión Limba	**18** A2

EATING	(p386)
Bistro Jasná	**19** B2
Chopok Bufet	(see 1)
Koliesko Restaurant	**20** B2
Luková Bufet	(see 5)

TRANSPORT	(p386)
Bus Terminus	**21** B2

another three or four days of walking (with no *chaty*, so you'll need a tent) down to a small hotel at Telgárt, from where you can take a bus or the beautiful train ride west down the Hron Valley to Banská Bystrica.

The best map for Chopok and surrounding area, with marked hiking and cycling routes, is VKÚs *Nízke Tatry* map No 1 (1:25,000; 100Sk). *The Low Tatras* book (240Sk), part of the Knapsacked Walking series, has detailed descriptions of 50 hiking trails in English and is a worthwhile investment if you're spending some time here.

A number of places in the valley, including **Crystal Ski** (☎ 559 14 60; www.crystalski.sk; Hotel Grand complex; ⏲ 9.15am-4.15pm), **SB Šport** (☎ 0907 458 957; Hotel Bystrina; ⏲ 8am-8pm May-Sep), Tri Studničky Hotel and Penzión Limba, rent **mountain bikes** for around 220/300Sk per half-day/full day. Crystal can also arrange a multitude of summer outdoor activities, including rafting, paragliding, horse riding and rock climbing.

down the far side into the less-developed Bystrá Valley by chairlift, or walk 1½ hours down to the road, where there are several hotels and the occasional bus out, via Brezno, to Banská Bystrica.

A rocky trail teeters along the crest, west for 35 minutes to **Dereše** (2003m), for 3½ to four hours to **Chabenec** (1955m), or for two or three days down to the tourist village of Donovaly (with camp site and *chaty*) on the Banská Bystrica–Ružomberok road.

This trail also takes you east to **Ďumbier** (2043m) in two hours, and to another north–south road at sedlo Čertovica in six hours, with two *chaty* en route. The wildest and least developed part of the range is east of Čertovica; a ridge-crest trail offers

SKIING

Jasná is the best downhill skiing area in the Czech and Slovak Republics. It is possible to ski both the northern (Jasná) and the southern (Chopok Juh) sides of Chopok mountain. There is a good range of runs to satisfy skiers of all levels. The Jasná runs are north-facing and thus tend to have a prolonged season beyond mid-December to March, especially if it is a long, harsh winter.

The rental ski/snowboard equipment is of a reasonable standard and priced at around 300/400Sk per day. During peak season, lift passes are 440/290Sk per day for adults/children, 2500/1650Sk per week.

Sleeping & Eating

The odds of finding a room without a booking are pretty good in summer but nil in winter. Prices noted are for the summer season (May–December); rates can be 50% higher over winter, and around 20% higher during July and August. Most hotels, and some *chaty*, have decent, and handy, restaurants or snack bars.

To book ahead, talk to Slovakotour (see p384) who can also help with private accommodation in the valley, at around 300Sk per person. **Liptour** (☎ 551 41 41; www .liptour.sk; Námestie mieru 1, Liptovský Mikuláš) in Liptovský Mikuláš; and **CA Limba** (☎ 02-54 41 86 01; www.limba.sk; Michalská 3, Bratislava) in Bratislava can also book a wide range of accommodation in the Low Tatras.

LOWER VALLEY

The valley road is dotted with hotels and *chaty*.

Bystrina Hotel (☎ 554 81 63; hotelbystrina@ stonline.sk; s/d 400/800Sk; camp site per person/tent/car 75/65/40Sk; P) Plain rooms and a summer camp site surrounded by trees.

Chata Kamenná (☎ 557 06 28; www.kamenna chatavj.sk; s/d 300/600Sk; P) Rustic feel, basic rooms, at the Ice Caves.

Chata Lúčky (☎ 559 16 83; www.chatalucky.cjb.net; s/d 315/630Sk; P) Below the bus terminus; simple, clean rooms.

Penzión Limba (☎ 554 82 05; limba@liptour.sk; s/d 500/1000Sk; P) Cosy rooms, apartments also available. Office for Liptour.

Hotel Tri Studničky (☎ 547 80 00; www.tristudnicky .sk; s/d 1725/2200Sk; P Ⓡ ✕ ⚅) Stylish, newly renovated 4+ star hotel, all stone and wood. Gives Hotel Grand a run for its money as the top accommodation in the valley.

Hotel Fim (☎ 547 99 99; www.hotelfim.sk; s/d 1400/ 1800Sk; P Ⓡ ✕ ⚅) Purpose-built hotel, very accommodating but not as much character as Tri Studničky.

JASNÁ

There are accommodation options everywhere you look in Jasná.

Chata Koliesko (☎ 559 16 74; koliesko@lm.psg.sk; s/d 500/1000Sk; P) At the foot of the Koliesko chairlift, a pleasant, rustic spot with great rooms, excellent restaurant and friendly staff.

Chata Björnson (☎ 559 16 77; www.chatabjornson .sk - Slovak & German only; s/d 250/500Sk; P) A good walk-in bet in summer, with rooms with shared facilities.

Hotel Grand (☎ 559 914 41; hotelgrand@jasna.sk; s/d 2150/2980Sk; P Ⓡ ✕ ⚅) Grand daddy of the valley, massive four-star place providing everything you need.

Hotel Junior (☎ 559 15 71; www.juniorjasna.sk; s/d 680/1060Sk; P Ⓡ) Giant alpine-style hotel with so-so rooms. Just downhill is Bistro Jasná, a fast-food style restaurant.

Hotel Liptov (☎ 559 15 06; hotelliptov@skijasna.sk; s/d 720/1440Sk; P) Huge hotel, with option of cheaper rooms with shared facilities.

More Spartan chalets – eg Chata Štefánika near Ďumbier peak and Chata Čertovica, a day's walk east at sedlo Čertovica – are dotted along the high-country trails.

There are small *bufets* at the Luková and Chopok chairlift terminals, which sell basic food around the 60Sk to 100Sk mark.

Getting There & Away

Almost hourly buses run between Liptovský Mikuláš and Jasná (23Sk, 40 minutes).

High Tatras

HIGH TATRAS

For the majority of foreign tourists, the High Tatra mountains are Slovakia's biggest attraction – and with a splendidly jagged and snow-patched central massif rising abruptly out of a green plain, it's easy to see why.

There are actually three ranges – the High Tatras (Vysoké Tatry), the Western Tatras (Západné Tatry) and the smaller Belá Tatras (Belianské Tatry) – but the High Tatras, the highest mountains in the Czech and Slovak Republics, and indeed in the entire Carpathian chain, take centre stage in every sense.

Naturally, the mountains are a magnet for fresh-air enthusiasts from all over Europe. They're heavily developed, with hundreds of kilometres of trails to keep you entertained for years, and in high summer and winter they're densely crowded – some five million people a year come to walk, climb, cycle or ski. You'll need to climb further than in Slovakia's other mountains to have some of it to yourself, but a bit of sweat never hurt anyone and the rewards are breathtaking.

For minimal crowds and decent weather, the best times to visit the High Tatras are late spring or early autumn, with August and September best for high-altitude walking.

HIGHLIGHTS

- Catch the **cable car** from Tatranská Lomnica up to the lake, **Skalnaté pleso**, and then continue on up to the towering 2634m summit of **Lomnický štít** (p396)

- Take to the **Tatranská magistrála trail** (p394), an alpine walkway hugging the mountain's steep slopes

- Discover the trails of **Belianské Tatry** and the folk cottages of **Ždiar** in the High Tatras forgotten eastern corner (p398)

- Ride the **funicular railway** from **Starý Smokovec** to Hrebienok (1280m) before exploring trails to the east or west (p395)

- And when you're exhausted, grab a sauna and massage at Starý Smokovec's Grand Hotel (p395)

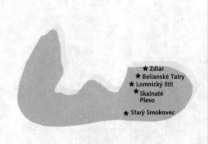

★ Zdiar
★ Belianské Tatry
★ Lomnický štít
★ Skalnaté Pleso
★ Starý Smokovec

TELEPHONE CODE: 052

HIGH TATRAS

Orientation

For all their majesty, the High Tatras are surprisingly compact – about 25km from west to east. They form part of the 795-sq-km Tatra National Park (Tatranský národný park), Czechoslovakia's first national park, founded in 1949. They're geologically young, with sharp, frost-shattered summits and broad valleys carved by glaciers. Three dozen valleys contain over 100 *plesy*, or tarns (small glacial lakes), and dense pine forest skirts the range below 1600m. At 2654m, Gerlachovský štít is the highest of some 25 peaks over 2500m, with the 2634m Lomnický štít in second place.

The main east–west regional highway (E50) passes through Poprad, the park's administrative centre, and the main gateway to the Tatras. An upper road following the base of the mountains links all the village resorts; Starý Smokovec, at 990m, is the biggest resort, with the most facilities and connections. To the west is the tacky Štrbské pleso (1350m), and to the east the more peaceful Tatranská Lomnica (850m). Poprad is linked to all the resorts by road and a convenient *električka* (electric train; see p392).

Information

For anything more than a day hike, you'll need a decent map (see Books & Maps below). The main artery of the trail network is the 65km, red-marked Tatranská magistrála, which runs along the southern flank of the High Tatras, and is accessible via dozens of branch trails.

A few of the popular walks are noted under each of the resorts – Štrbské Pleso, Starý Smokovec and Tatranská Lomnica. But with a map and advice from the park's **Mountain Rescue Service** (Horská služba; ☎ 442 28 20; ths@tanap.sk), those with experience and gear can invent their own walks. Don't overlook further treks in the Polish Tatras – you can spot Polish walkers on this side of the border by their ready greetings of a smile and quiet *cześć* (hello). Note that it is technically illegal for visitors to walk across the Slovak–Polish border in the mountains – if caught doing so you could be fined.

BOOKS & MAPS

The best hiking map is the VKÚ 1:25,000 map (No 2; 100Sk) although, due to its size, it can be a bit awkward to manoeuvre. You

---

BETTER TO BE SAFE THAN SORRY

Around 15 to 20 people die every year in the High Tatras, due mainly to extremely capricious weather conditions – it can change from warm brilliant sunshine to snow, rain, hail or wind within a few minutes. Check the weather forecast at the Mountain Rescue Service before setting out, especially for overnight trips, and take local advice seriously: they know the mountains best and it's their time, money and effort that's going to be expended getting you back safe and sound. It's a good idea to carry your own water and some food, even if you have a *chata* (mountain hut) booking with meals, because you'll burn up a lot of energy and be needing snacks along the way.

Essential equipment for walking in the park include:

- waterproof raincoat and overtrousers
- warm clothing – the summits can be very cold (occasionally snowy), even in summer
- hiking boots
- food and drink
- first-aid kit
- sunscreen and sunglasses
- sunhat and warm hat
- whistle for emergencies – six blasts is an internationally recognised distress call

Keep the park regulations in mind: stay on the trails, don't pick the flowers, take your rubbish with you and don't cut wood or build open fires. Stay off the ridge tops if they're in cloud. You'll need a guide to do ascents of the very highest peaks, with the exception of Lomnický štít, which is accessible by cable car (see p396).

There's snow by November (on some of the highest passes as early as September) and avalanches are a danger from November to June when the higher trails will be closed – ask someone to translate the notices at the head of the trails for you.

Note that some of the higher trails involve steep scrambling and climbing in exposed situations with the aid of chains and metal rungs – not recommended unless you have a head for heights.

HIGH TATRAS (VYSOKÉ TATRY)

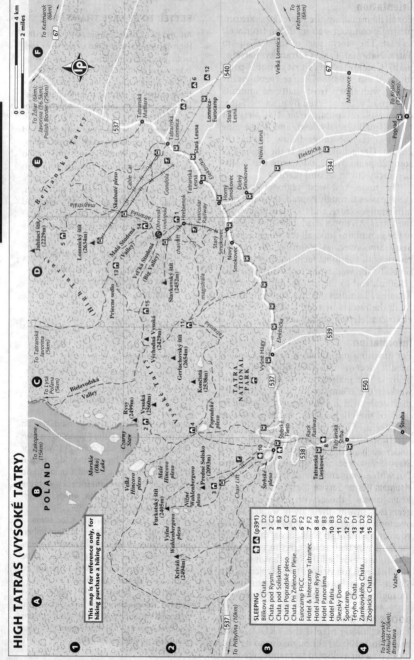

This map is for reference only, for hiking purchase a hiking map

might be better off with the 1:50,000 scale map (No 113; 100Sk).

A selection of guidebooks (some in English) and information booklets of varying usefulness are available from kiosks, travel agencies and top-end hotels. With 45 detailed hikes explained in English, *The High Tatras* (240Sk), part of the Knapsacked series, is one of the best.

TOURIST INFORMATION

There are information offices in all the major settlements (see the individual entries).

For weather and trail updates, call or email the park's **Mountain Rescue Service** (Horská služba; ☎ 442 28 20; ths@tanap.sk) or check out the Tatra National Park's website www.tanap.sk.

For general information accommodation, transport and services in the region, try www.tatry.net.

Sleeping

Frequent, cheap transport means you can stay almost anywhere, but Starý Smokovec and Tatranská Lomnica are the most convenient and attractive centres. Summer accommodation can be tight, although you can always find something modest on the spot through the various information offices. No wild camping is permitted within the Tatra National Park; *chaty* (mountain chalets) are your only sleeping option along the park's trails. The nearest camping grounds to the park are a couple of kilometres from Tatranská Lomnica (near the Tatranská Lomnica–Eurocamp train station on the line to Studený potok; see p397).

Rates given here are for the high winter and summer season. In spring and autumn prices dip by about 20%.

CHATY

The *chaty* in the Tatras run the gamut from plain alpine hostels – at around 250Sk to 350Sk per bed plus 150Sk per meal – to more luxurious *horské hotely* (mountain hotels) at 500Sk per bed and up. Many are accessible only on foot.

Chaty are open year-round unless noted, and should be booked in advance (although if you just arrive and there are no beds, they'll often let you crash on the floor for a small charge). PIA in Poprad, and Satur and the Mountain Guide Office in Smokovce can book accommodation at most of them.

The following are the main *chaty* on the upper trails, from west to east:

Chata pod Soliskom (☎ 0905 652 036; 1840m) Small (16 beds) mountain chalet and rescue post above Štrbské Pleso. No restaurant.

Chata Popradské pleso (☎ 449 21 77; popradskepleso@horskyhotel.sk; 500m) Large, hotel like *chata* with restaurant.

Chata pod Rysmi (☎ 0903 181 051; 2250m) Highest of them all, open June through October. (NB this *chata* was destroyed by an avalanche in February 2001; construction of a replacement in a safer location is underway although there is no word as to when it will re-open.)

Sliezský dom (☎ 442 52 61; 1670m) Mountain hotel with restaurant and cafeteria.

Zbojnícka chata (☎ 0903 638 000; 1960m) Dorm accommodation and restaurant.

Téryho chata (☎ 442 52 45; 2015m) Dorm accommodation and restaurant.

Zamkovského chata (☎ 442 26 36; zamka@nextra.sk; 1475m) Dorm accommodation and restaurant.

Bilíkova chata (☎ 442 24 39; 1220m) Wooden chalet with double rooms, restaurant and mountain service.

Chata pri Zelenom plese (☎ 446 74 20; 1540m) Dorm accommodation and restaurant.

Getting There & Away

BUS

Only one bus a day from Bratislava at 6am heads for Starý Smokovec (428Sk, six hours) via Nitra and Banská Bystrica.

From Starý Smokovec there are five buses a day to Lysá Poľana (53Sk, one hour), six to Levoča (53Sk, one hour), one to Bardejov (152Sk, three hours, noon), two to Žilina (188Sk, 2¾ to 3½ hours) and one to Trenčín (296Sk, five hours, 1.10pm).

There are seven daily connections to Poprad from Prague (8½ to 10½ hours) and four from Brno (7½ hours).

TRAIN

To reach the High Tatras, take any of the express trains running between Bratislava and Košice, and change at Poprad. Alternatively, get off the express at Tatranská Štrba, a station on the main line from Bratislava to Košice, and take the rack-railway (*ozubnicová železnica*) up to Štrbské Pleso.

The booking offices in Starý Smokovec and Tatranská Lomnica train stations can reserve sleepers and couchettes from Poprad to Prague, Karlovy Vary, Brno and Bratislava at an extra cost of 140Sk in 2nd class. Tatranská Lomnica's station has a **left-luggage** counter and an exchange office.

BORDER CROSSINGS

For anyone interested in walking or driving between Slovakia and Poland, there's a highway border crossing at Lysá Poľana near Tatranská Javorina, 30km from Tatranská Lomnica via Ždiar by bus. Here you'll find an ATM and an exchange office. The Slovak bus between the border and Starý Smokovec is occasionally crowded and the bus stop is just 100m from the border (bus times posted). On the Polish side, buses can be full with people on excursions between Morskie Oko Lake and Zakopane.

A bus direct from Poprad to Zakopane, Poland, leaves on Thursday and Saturday at 6am (2½ hours). You can also ask Satur about excursion buses to Zakopane and Kraków.

Getting Around

BUS

Local buses run between the Tatra resorts every 10 to 20 minutes, and are faster than the train, though with fewer stops. Schedules are posted at the main bus stops. Places renting mountain bikes are mentioned throughout the chapter.

TRAIN

Frequent electric trains (električka) run from Poprad to Starý Smokovec (16Sk, 30 minutes) and Štrbské Pleso (26Sk, one hour) every hour, as do trains from Starý Smokovec to Tatranská Lomnica (11Sk, 15 minutes). These trains are slow but make frequent stops along their routes; when there isn't a ticket window or machine at the station, after boarding go immediately to the conductor to buy a ticket. A three-/seven-day ticket giving unlimited travel on the električka costs 119/229Sk.

A rack-railway connects Tatranská Štrba (on the main Žilina–Poprad road and railway line) with Štrbské Pleso (28Sk, 15 minutes).

POPRAD

☎ 052 / pop 56,200

Despite a bit of Spiš architecture and a cheerful main square, Poprad is not a place to go out of your way for. However, it's a handy gateway to the High Tatras, a source of provisions at ordinary Slovak prices, and a possible base for visiting the Spiš region and the Slovenský raj (see p408).

Orientation

From the train and bus stations (and the električka terminal above the train station) it's a five-minute walk to the main square, námestie svätého Egídia, lined with shops and eateries. Poprad-Tatry airport, the highest in Europe, is about 5km west of town.

Information

The **Poprad Information Agency** (PIA; ☎ 772 17 00; www.poprad.sk; námestie svätého Egídia 114; 🕑 8am-6pm Mon-Fri, 9am-noon Sat Jul-Aug, 8.30am-5pm Mon-Fri, 9am-noon Sat Sep-Jun), on the main square, is the place for information of all kinds, including a very good accommodation service. Internet access is available at **Sinet** (námestie svätého Egídia 28; 40Sk per hr; 🕑 9am-9pm Mon-Sat, 1-9pm Sun).

Ľudová banka (námestie svätého Egídia 124) has an exchange counter and an ATM. The **post office** (Mnoheľova 11) has a line of telephones guarding its entrance.

Sights

In the middle of námestie svätého Egídia are the Gothic **Church of St Egidius**, sporting Spiš-style 'gablets'; the 19th-century **Evangelical Church** (both churches adult/child 20/10Sk; 🕑 8am-3.30pm Tue-Sun); and the **Bell Tower** (adult/child 5Sk/free; 🕑 8am-noon, 1-4.30pm Tue-Sun), which has views over the town towards the magnificent High Tatras. Natural history, town history and ethnography feature at the **Tatra Museum** (Podtatranské múzeum; ☎ 772 1924; Vajanského 4; adult/child 20/10Sk; 🕑 8am-3.30pm Tue-Sun).

SPIŠSKÁ SOBOTA

If you're coming from the Spiš region, this village (now a Poprad suburb) will be of little interest; otherwise the Germanic, broad-gabled wooden houses with heavy, front eaves and decorative carving may come as a surprise. The name comes from the Saturday (sobota) market once held here.

Colourful Renaissance merchants' and artisans' houses line the leafy central square, Sobotské námestie. In the late-Gothic interior of the **parish church** is an altar made by Master Pavol of Levoča in 1516. A little **museum** (adult/child 20/10Sk; 🕑 9am-4pm Mon-Sat) on the square features archaeology and church art.

Spišská Sobota is a 30-minute walk from námestie svätého Egídia, northeast on Štefánikova and north on Kežmarská, or you can take bus No 2 or 3.

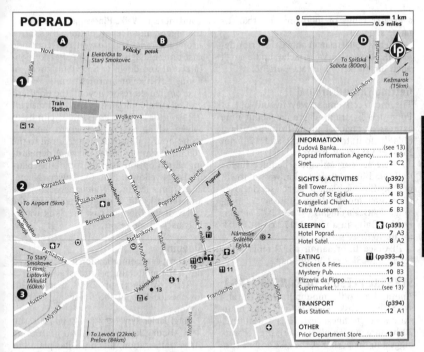

POPRAD

Sleeping

Although Poprad is about 10km from the mountains, it's worth visiting the PIA if you haven't prebooked your accommodation; it's probably the region's best accommodation office. Apart from hotel and *pension* listings, it also has private rooms going for around 250 to 300Sk per person.

Hotel Poprad (☎ 787 08 11; www.hotel-poprad.sk; Partizánska 677/18; s/d 1520/2900Sk; **P**) This colossal hotel is the best option in town, with modern rooms and views of the High Tatras.

Hotel Satel (☎ 716 11 11; www.satel-slovakia.sk; Mnoheľova 825; s/d 1600/2300Sk; **P**) Satel is another multistorey hotel with mountain views, and is more geared towards the business traveller.

Easily the best place to stay though is Spišská Sobota. Some of the striking houses lining the square have been lovingly restored and brought back to life as superb *pensions*. The only drawback is the dire lack of nightlife. All the following make fine choices:

Apropo (☎ 776 90 23; ppas@stonline.sk; Sobotské námestie 1743/38; s/d 450/900Sk) Large, sunny rooms, some with views of the Tatras.

Atrium (☎ 776 95 22; www.penzion-atrium.sk; Sobotské námestie 25; s/d 700/900Sk) Large, comfy rooms with simple furniture.

Dagmar (☎ 776 95 22; www.penzion-atrium.sk; Sobotské námestie 1731/8; s/d 700/900Sk) Dependence of Atrium, with similar rooms.

Fortuna (☎ 776 96 02; www.penzionfortuna.sk; Sobotské námestie 1768/43; r 1600Sk) More a hotel than a *pension*, with fine rooms, if a little overpriced.

Sabato (☎ 776 95 80; www.sabato.sk; Sobotské námestie 1730/6; r from €45) Three immaculate rooms, furnished with antiques.

SV Juraja (☎ 776 95 58; www.penzion-sv-juraj.sk; Sobotské námestie 29; s/d 700/900Sk) Modern, stylish rooms, some with antique furniture.

Eating

The main square is lined with eateries, including relaxed **Pizzeria da Pippo** (námestie svätého Egídia 2; pizzas 100-120Sk), with large pizzas. **Mystery Pub** (☎ 772 29 52; námestie svätého Egídia 3643; mains 100-130Sk), in the middle of the square, is a medieval-themed restaurant with a terrace on the first floor and Slovakian cuisine.

For cheap eats, try **Chicken & Fries** (1 mája 1; pizza, baguettes & langos around 30Sk), which has a greater range of food on offer than its name suggests.

There's a **supermarket** above the Prior department store on Vajanského, and a small open-air market on Joliota Curieho.

Getting There & Around

The most convenient way in and out of Poprad is by train. There are about nine express or regional trains from Bratislava (384Sk, four to 4¾ hours) and 17 from Košice (138Sk, 1¼ hours).

There are currently no scheduled flights to Poprad-Tatry airport, 5km west of town, but Sky Europe plans to start a service over the winter months from Bratislava. Hour-long, **sightseeing flights** (☎ 0905 154 275) from Poprad-Tatry in a Cessna 172 cost 4700Sk for up to three people.

PIA (see Information p392) rents bikes for 150/200Sk per half/full day.

ŠTRBSKÉ PLESO & TATRANSKÁ ŠTRBA

About 5km up the mountain from Tatranská Štrba, Štrbské Pleso is the Tatras' main ski resort. Its finest feature is a beautiful, 20-hectare, alpine *pleso* (lake), the second-biggest in the park. But the lake and its surroundings have been defaced by billboards and giant hotels, so the best thing to do here is skip the place completely and get up onto the Tatranská magistrála trail.

Orientation & Information

The red-marked Tatranská magistrála winds around the southern end of the lake here. To pick it up in the easterly direction, walk north from the station and after 500m bear right towards the Helios sanatorium; the trail is on the left, just past a small stream.

A branch of the **Tatry Information Office** (Tatranská informačná kancelária; ☎ 449 23 91; 8am-4pm Mon-Fri) is next to the Toliar department store (Obchodný dom Toliar); both are opposite the train station. There's also an ATM next to Hotel Panoráma.

Walks from Štrbské Pleso

The High Tatras map (p390) has these and other popular walks (mentioned throughout the chapter) marked on it.

A relatively easy (and crowded) walk is up the magistrála to **Popradské pleso** (1494m), which will take one to 1½ hours. A more demanding blue trail climbs be-

yond here to **Velké Hincovo pleso** (1946m), the biggest and deepest of the park's tarns. From Popradské pleso you can continue east on the magistrála to the Sliezsky dom (a *chata*) and down to Starý Smokovec, in a long day-hike or overnight trip.

From the ski resort beyond the northern end of Štrbské pleso, a year-round **chair lift** (one way/return in high season 130/190Sk) climbs to **Solisko**, which has a *chata*. From there it's a one-hour walk north on a red trail to the 2093m summit of **Predné Solisko**. A demanding all-day option from the top of the chairlift is via yellow trail to the Lower (Nížné) and Upper (Vyšné) Wahlenbergovo tarns and **Furkotský štít** (2405m), then down the valley of the Mlynica past the Skok waterfalls back to the resort.

Sleeping

For cheaper accommodation it's best to head down the mountain to Tatranská Štrba.

Refer to the High Tatras map (p390) for the location of the following sleeping options.

Hotel Junior Rysy (☎ 4484 845; s/d 750/1100Sk; P) About 2km north of the Tatranská Štrba train station, this hotel has plain but comfy rooms and a decent restaurant.

You really have to wonder what kind of drugs the architects were on while designing some of the hotels in Slovakia. Two prime examples are:

Hotel Patria (☎ 449 25 91; patria@tatry.net; s/d 1645/2230Sk; P) A little off centre – literally. Its leaning A-frame structure and outdated interior are quite a sight. Its rooms, however, are modern and of a good size.

Hotel Panoráma (☎ 49 21 11; hotel@hotelpanorama .sk; s/d 1100/2000Sk; P) Near the Štrbské Pleso train station, this 11-storey upside-down pyramid has great views, basic rooms and is simply weird.

SMOKOVCE RESORTS

Smokovce is the collective name for Old (Starý), New (Nový), Upper (Horný) and Lower (Dolný) Smokovec – all close to one another but separated by dense woods.

Information

The main **AiCES Tatry office** (☎ 442 34 40; zcrvt@sinet.sk; Dom služieb shopping centre, Starý Smoko-vec; 8am-8pm Mon-Fri, 8am-1pm Sat) has plenty of information on the region. Helpful **Satur**

(☎ 442 24 97; Starý Smokovec; ⌚ 8am-4pm Mon-Fri) can provide accommodation advice.

For information on weather and trail conditions, more accommodation options and almost every mountain activity under the sun, go to the **Mountain Guide Office** (☎ 442 20 66; Starý Smokovec 22; ⌚ 10am-6pm Mon-Fri, noon-6pm Sat & Sun Jun-Sep, 10am-6pm Mon-Fri Oct-May). Prices vary – the general rule is the more people in your group, the less it will cost. For one person, guided hikes start at 3000Sk, mountain bike tours at 2000Sk and rock climbing excursions at 2500Sk.

Všeobecná úverová banka (VÚB; ☎ 442 25 94), in the commercial centre above the bus station in Starý Smokovec, changes travellers cheques and has an ATM.

Walks from Starý Smokovec

A good half-day trip is up the **funicular railway** (one way/return 90/130Sk in summer, 70/110Sk rest of the year; ⌚ 7.30am-7pm) to **Hrebienok** (1280m), west on the magistrála to the Sliezsky dom, and down a yellow-marked trail back to Starý Smokovec.

If you're fit, a recommended option from Hrebienok is the green path past the Bilíkova chata to Obrovsky vodopad (waterfalls) on the **Studený potok** river. From there it's a four- to five-hour climb on a blue trail up the valley of the **Veľká Studená** to a (prebooked) hot meal and warm bed at the Zbojnícka chata. An extra day allows for an ascent of **Východná Vysoká** (2429m), offering the park's best look at Gerlachovský štít up close without a guide.

From Hrebienok you could instead take the red trail to Zamkovského chata (past more waterfalls) and head up a green trail into the valley of the **Malá Studená**. Four hours will see you at the **Téryho chata**, which is beside a lake at about 2010m. A return option is via Priecne sedlo to Zbojnícka chata.

A demanding, two-day trek from Hrebienok goes up the valley of the Veľká Studená to Zbojnícka chata, over a 2373m pass and down the long Bielovodská valley to Tatranská Javorina near the Polish border, where there are buses back to Starý Smokovec.

Sleeping

STARÝ SMOKOVEC
Grand Hotel (☎ 442 21 54; www.grandhotel.sk; s/d 1790/3050Sk; P ✕ ☎) Taking centre stage in Starý Smokovec is the majestic Grand

Hotel, with an elegant interior, plush rooms and a very, very soothing sauna.

Hotel Smokovec (☎ 442 51 91; www.hotelsmokovec.sk; Starý Smokovec 25; r from 1190Sk; P ☎) Immediately northwest of the Starý Smokovec train station, this pleasant hotel has a sauna and fitness centre.

HORNÝ SMOKOVEC
Hotel Panda (☎ 442 26 14; panda@tatry.net; s/d 1000/2000Sk; P) Modern Panda is quite reasonable for the price (includes half-board), and some rooms come with balcony.

Hotel Junior (☎ 442 26 61; s/d 300/400Sk; P) This is about the cheapest place you'll find in the area, and is open all year. Its rooms are simple but if you're just looking for a place to sleep, they're quite fine.

Hotel Bellevue (☎ 442 29 41; bellevue@pp.psg.sk; s/d 2400/2960Sk; P ☎) Just behind Šport and surrounded by trees is this mid-range hotel, with good-sized rooms.

Hotel Šport (☎ 442 23 61; s/d 390/680Sk; P) Plain rooms with shared facilities can be found at the friendly but run-down Hotel Šport.

NOVÝ SMOKOVEC
Penzión Vesna (☎ 442 27 74; vesna@slovanet.sk; Nový Smokovec 69; s/d 700/1400Sk; P) This friendly, family-run *pension*, behind the large sanatorium southwest of Nový Smokovec train station, is a great deal for the area. Rooms are comfy and the whole place has a warm, homey feel.

Villa Dr Szontagh (☎ 442 20 61; szontagh@isternet.sk; s/d 1500/1700Sk; P) Named after the physician who founded Nový Smokovec, this is a fine old wooden house with a Victorian feel.

Hotel Park (☎ 442 23 42; www.hotel-park.sk; Nový Smokovec 42; s/d 820/1640Sk; P) Built in 1970, Hotel Park doesn't look like it's had a facelift since. But the rooms aren't too bad and the price is quite reasonable.

Eating & Drinking

All the hotels have their own restaurants; the dining room at **Villa Dr Szontagh** (mains 120-200Sk) is a more upmarket dinner spot while the restaurant at **Hotel Grand** (dinner about 500Sk) is top rate.

Bistro-Fast Food Tatra (mains 50-100Sk; ⌚ 10am-7pm) Just northwest of the bus station at Starý Smokovec, this bistro is a fine place for a quick bite to eat.

SMOKOVCE RESORTS

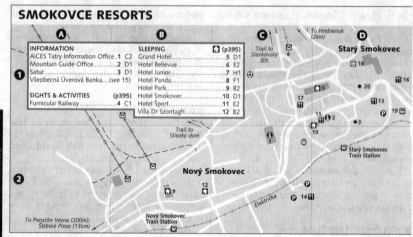

INFORMATION		SLEEPING	🏠 (p395)
AiCES Tatry Information Office..**1**	C2	Grand Hotel.......................**5**	D1
Mountain Guide Office...........**2**	D1	Hotel Bellevue.....................**6**	E2
Satur.....................................**3**	D1	Hotel Junior.......................**7**	H1
Všeobecná Úverová Banka....(see 15)		Hotel Panda.......................**8**	F1
		Hotel Park........................**9**	B2
SIGHTS & ACTIVITIES	(p395)	Hotel Smokovec...................**10**	D1
Funicular Railway...................**4**	C1	Hotel Šport.......................**11**	E2
		Villa Dr Szontagh.................**12**	B2

Restaurant Koliba (☎ 442 22 04; mains around 100-150Sk) This quaint restaurant, just southwest of the Starý Smokovec train station, serves typical Slovak food.

Tatrasport (☎ 442 52 41; mains around 150Sk) This friendly restaurant is another good option for Slovak cuisine.

Taverna Reštaurácia (mains 80-150Sk) East of the Grand Hotel, this good taverna is relatively cheap and has an open, sunny terrace.

There's a convenient supermarket between the Mountain Guide Office and Hotel Smokovec.

Tatry Pub, next to the Bistro-Fast Food Tatra, is worth stopping in for a pint or two, or an Irish coffee.

Entertainment

The Grand Hotel has **Cristal disco bar** (🕙 Wed-Sun), and there's a Laser disco at **Café Albas** (🕙 daily), behind the town hall.

Getting Around

You can rent a **mountain bike** for around 400Sk per day from a number of places, including **Tatrasport** (☎ 442 52 41; 🕙 9am-5pm Mon-Fri, 9am-1pm Sat) and **Hotel Park** (☎ 442 23 42; Nový Smokovec 42).

TATRANSKÁ LOMNICA

This is the quietest of the Tatra resorts, dotted with old trade-union hostels. Apart from its relaxed atmosphere, the only real attraction is the cable car up to Lomnický štít.

Information

The **AiCES Tatry office** (☎ 446 81 18; tik.tatry@sinet.sk; 🕙 8am-6pm Mon-Fri, 8am-1pm Sat & Sun) is on the main street diagonally opposite Penzión Encian. Next door is a well-stocked **bookshop** (🕙 9am-5pm Mon-Fri, 9am-noon Sat) where you can buy hiking maps and guidebooks.

Sights & Activities

A highlight of any visit is the **cable-car** journey from Tatranská Lomnica up to the lake (and winter ski area) called **Skalnaté pleso** (1751m), especially the second, white-knuckle ride to the 2634m summit of **Lomnický štít**, with views right across the Tatras' jagged crest.

When it's fine everybody else wants to do it too, so the queues tend to be huge. Each day's tickets to **Skalnaté** (adult/child one way 220/150Sk, return 350/220Sk in high season; 🕙 8.30am-7pm Jul & Aug, 8.30am-5pm Sep-Jun) usually sell out by early morning, and there are no advance bookings. The cable-car for **Lomnický štít** (adult/child return 420/250Sk; 🕙 8.50am-5.50pm Jul & Aug, 8.50am-3.50pm Sep-Jun) leaves from Skalnaté.

One way to beat the queues is to walk up to Skalnaté (2½ hours). There is also an ordinary **chairlift** (adult/child one way 150/90Sk; 🕙 8.30am-5.30pm Jul & Aug, 8.30am-4.30pm Sep-Jun) from Skalnaté to **Lomnické sedlo**, a 2190m saddle below the summit. The narrow summit ridge (site of a meteorology research station) will be crowded. Pack warm clothing – it's very cold, even in midsummer.

The **Tatra National Park Museum** (múzeum Tatranského národného parku; ☎ 446 79 51; adult/child

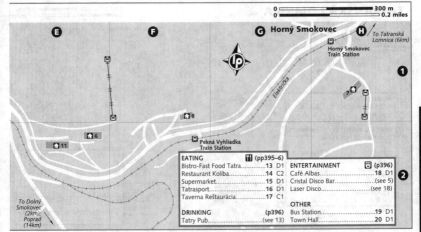

Horný Smokovec

Horný Smokovec
Train Station

To Tatranská
Lomnica (6km)

Pekná Vyhliadka
Train Station

To Dolný
Smokovec
(2km),
Poprad
(14km)

EATING	(pp395–6)		ENTERTAINMENT	(p396)
Bistro-Fast Food Tatra..............13	D1		Café Albas...............................18	D1
Restaurant Koliba..................14	C2		Cristal Disco Bar.................(see 5)	
Supermarket..........................15	D1		Laser Disco Bar................(see 18)	
Tatrasport.............................16	D1			
Taverna Reštaurácia...............17	C1		OTHER	
			Bus Station...............................19	D1
DRINKING	(p396)		Town Hall................................20	D1
Tatry Pub.............................(see 13)				

HIGH TATRAS

30/10Sk; ☺ 8am-noon & 1-5pm Mon-Fri, 8am-3pm Sat & Sun) is filled with unexciting displays on flora, fauna and regional ethnography and will kill an hour or two on a wet day.

WALKS FROM TATRANSKÁ LOMNICA

An easy (and popular), all-day loop starts with an early cable-car ascent to **Skalnaté pleso**. From here the red-marked magistrála trail offers grand views on its way to **Hrebienok**, where you can catch the funicular railway down to Starý Smokovec and the električka back to Tatranská Lomnica. An alternative is to descend to Tatranská Lomnica on a blue trail from the valley of the **Veľká Studená** (see Walks from Starý Smokovec p395)

Sleeping

BUDGET

See the High Tatras map (p390) for the location of the following camping grounds.

Eurocamp FICC (☎ 446 77 41; www.eurocamp-ficc.sk; per person/tent/car/bungalow 120/90/90/920Sk; ☺ year-round; ☒) The largest camping ground in the area, Eurocamp is a five-minute walk northeast from the Lomnica-Eurocamp train station. It's not as laid-back as the other two camping grounds, but its facilities are far superior, including above-average bunga-lows, restaurants (the good folkloric Koliba Restaurant), bars, shops, supermarket, swim-ming pool, tennis, sauna, disco, hot water and row upon row of parked caravans.

Športcamp (☎ 446 72 88; per person/tent/car 90/90/90Sk; ☺ Jun-Sep) A further eight-minute walk south past Eurocamp FICC is this less expensive, but also less interesting, camp-ing ground.

Hotel & Intercamp Tatranec (☎ 446 70 92; www .tanap.sk/tatranec.html; per person/tent/car/bungalow 100/ 80/90/1600Sk; ☺ camping Jun-Sep; ℗) Tatranec is approximately a 15-minute walk north of the Lomnica-Eurocamp train station, and has A-frame style bungalows open year-round.

MID-RANGE

Penzión Encian (☎ 446 75 20; pension-encian@sinet.sk; s/d 600/1200Sk; ℗) The best value in town is this *pension* with bright rooms and wel-coming staff.

Vila Park (☎ 478 09 11; www.vilapark.sk; s/d 1400/ 1960Sk; ℗) New Vila Park is a stylish *pension* with modern rooms, some of which have balconies and views of the mountains.

Hotel Wili (☎ 446 77 61; wili@tatry.sk; s/d 1150/ 1800Sk; ℗) This comfortable hotel has pleas-ant rooms with slightly dated furniture and is tucked away in a quiet part of the town.

Hotel Odborár (☎ 446 73 51; marketingodr@sorea .sk; s/d 800/1600Sk; ℗ ☒) Odborár is a huge orange recreational sanatorium, northeast of the train station, with plain rooms and a 25m pool.

TOP END

Grandhotel Praha (☎ 446 79 41; www.grandhotel praha.sk; s/d 2400/3400Sk; ℗ ☒) Built in 1905, this opulent hotel is one of Slovakia's most romantic hotels, and is hidden in the forest up the hill beside the cable car terminal.

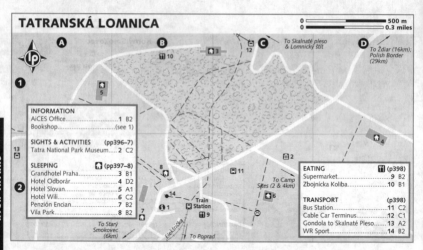

TATRANSKÁ LOMNICA

0 _____ 500 m
0 _____ 0.3 miles

To Skalnaté pleso & Lomnický štít

To Ždiar (16km); Polish Border (29km)

INFORMATION
AiCES Office..............................1 B2
Bookshop...........................(see 1)

SIGHTS & ACTIVITIES (pp396–7)
Tatra National Park Museum.....2 C2

SLEEPING (pp397–8)
Grandhotel Praha......................3 B1
Hotel Odborár...........................4 D2
Hotel Slovan.............................5 A1
Hotel Wili.................................6 C2
Penzión Encian........................7 B2
Vila Park..................................8 B2

EATING (p398)
Supermarket............................9 B2
Zbojnícka Koliba....................10 B1

TRANSPORT (p398)
Bus Station............................11 C2
Cable Car Terminus................12 C1
Gondola to Skalnaté Pleso.... 13 A2
WR Sport...............................14 B2

To Camp Sites (2 & 4km)

Train Station

To Starý Smokovec (6km)

To Poprad

Električka

Hotel Slovan (☎ 446 78 51; www.hotel-slovan.sk; s/d 1950/2400Sk; P ⬛) The simple rooms at this squat hotel are a tad overpriced, but it does have a soothing pool, extremely friendly staff and a fine restaurant.

Eating

Zbojnícka Koliba (mains 80-150Sk) For some true Slovak entertainment try this restaurant with its typical Tatra food and Roma band, which plays at your table. It is just off the road that leads to the Grandhotel Praha.

There are not a lot of options outside the hotel restaurants. Of them, the restaurant at **Penzión Encian** (mains 100-150Sk) is better than average, while the **Koliba** (mains 80-120Sk) at Eurocamp FICC offers reasonably priced, spit-roasted chicken and plenty of beer.

There's a supermarket just east of the train station.

Getting There & Around

In addition to the električka, you can catch a regular train from here to Kežmarok (17Sk, 30 minutes); change at Studený Potok.

WR Sport (☎ 0905 156 428; per half/full day 200/400Sk; ☽ 10am-6pm) rents out mountain bikes.

BELIANSKÉ TATRY

This small (64 sq km), eastern arm of the Tatras has until recently been off-limits, to protect its ecosystem (or old state secrets?), but trails are slowly being opened to the public. Limestone prevails here, and there is a large cave system at Tatranská Kotlina.

Tatranská Kotlina

Over 1km of **caves** (Belianské jaskyňa; ☎ 446 73 75; adult/child 100/50Sk; ☽ year-round) are open to the public, with hourly tours from 9am to 4pm Tuesday to Sunday, from mid-May to August, and every 1½ hours from 9.30am to 2pm the rest of the year.

Ždiar

Little Ždiar is the only substantial settlement predating the Tatra resorts, though its picturesque, timbered and decorated cottages, and a tradition of bright costumes and ceremonies, are being rapidly eroded by tourism. Several sections of the village are now historical reservations, and one house has been done up as the **Ždiar House Museum** (☎ 449 81 42; adult/child 20/10Sk; ☽ 9am-4pm Mon-Fri, 9am-noon Sat & Sun May-Sep, 9am-3pm Mon-Fri Oct-Apr). At the east end of the village there is the glittering **Galéria Jana Zoričáka** (☎ 449 81 81; admission free; ☽ 9am-3pm Mon-Fri), filled with contemporary glass pieces.

You can eat at the museum and stay overnight at the alpine-styled **Penzión Ždiar** (☎ 449 81 38; soltys1@nextra.sk; Ždiar 460; s/d 500/750Sk; P).

Getting There & Away

There are six buses daily travelling between Poprad and Ždiar via Starý Smokovec and Tatranská Lomnica (48Sk, one hour). Five of the buses continue on to the Polish border.

East Slovakia

East Slovakia is the country's remotest and poorest region, but if you have a taste for traditional architecture and stunning scenery, folk festivals and historical sites, or simply wish for a quiet, rural atmosphere, then it's the most appealing area to visit.

Its isolation has for centuries preserved many old ways, as well as protecting a rich architectural heritage. The small, quaint towns of Bardejov and Levoča still contain medieval centres hardly altered over the centuries, while the region's far reaches hide a plethora of striking Rusin wooden churches – a poignant reminder that religion is still the heart of some communities. Other man-made highlights include the lonely hilltop Spiš castle and neighbouring Spišská Kapitula, a 13th-century walled settlement and traditional religious stronghold.

Not everything is about history though. Košice, the country's second-largest city, is a grand mix of old and new, with a lively bar and café scene and a towering Gothic Cathedral, Europe's most easterly. And pockets of some of the country's best scenery can be found within the regional border: Pieniny National Park in the north is known for the dramatic Dunajec gorge and peaceful rafting trips; and south of this lie the popular hiking trails, deep ravines and waterfalls of the Slovenský raj (Slovak Paradise) and the caves of Slovenský kras (Slovak Karst). To the east is Poloniny National Park, a wild, untouched extension of the Eastern Carpathians.

Allow plenty of time to soak up the unique atmosphere of this intriguing region.

HIGHLIGHTS

- Take in the museums, churches, bars and cafés of **Košice** (p402)
- Shoot the rapids at **Dunajec gorge** (p417) in traditional wooden rafts called *plte*
- Hike one of a dozen pristine trails in the **Slovak Paradise National Park** (p408)
- Tour the arresting **wooden churches** (p425) scattered across the region
- Admire the well-preserved architecture of **Bardejov** (p423) and **Levoča** (p411)

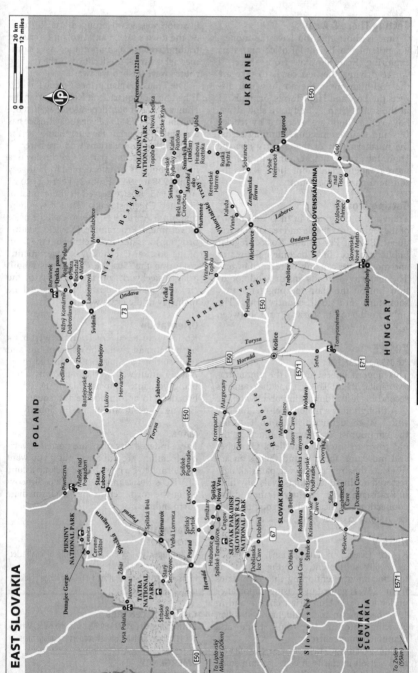

EAST SLOVAKIA

Getting There & Away

If time is short and you have the money, it's possible to fly into Košice and start exploring East Slovakia from there. If you're driving, the best roads to take are the E50 highway in the north, which dissects the Low and High Tatras, or the E571 in the south. Be prepared for a slow drive, however, as both are overused by trucks. Bus and train connections running across the northern part of the country (via the High Tatras) are quicker, and, in general, more frequent than connections across the southern part of the country.

Getting Around

Train and bus services in the western part of the region are reliable and reasonably frequent. East of Prešov and Košice, regular public transport links become quite scarce and most places can only be reached by bus. The majority of roads are in good condition, but off the main thoroughfares, they soon turn into small, country lanes. The only stretch of motorway runs between Košice and Prešov.

KOŠICE

☎ 055 / pop 236,100

This modern, upbeat town is the administrative capital of East Slovakia, and the country's second-biggest and most important city.

Although now a major steel-making city with vast residential districts built during the communist era, there is much in the old town to interest travellers. Churches and museums abound, and there's an active state theatre – plus a vast, painstakingly restored main square that rivals anything in Bratislava. With extensive train and bus connections, Košice is also a good base for excursions to other East Slovak towns.

History

Košice (Kassa in Hungarian) began life as a Slav settlement, and the first written document mentioning the town dates from 1230. It gained increasing importance under the early Hungarian empire and in 1342 became an independent royal town, growing into an important trade and manufacturing centre.

The invading Turks forced the city to fortify itself in the 16th century, and some of the fortifications still stand today. The invasion was a two pronged attack – one, on the town's safety, and two, on its crucial trading routes. Its importance as a commercial centre soon declined as the trading routes were pushed westward.

The Transylvanian prince Ferenc Rákóczi II had his headquarters at Košice during the Hungarian War of Independence against the Habsburgs (1703–11). Even today Košice has a strong Hungarian flavour, thanks to the 20,000 ethnic Hungarians who live here.

The town became part of Czechoslovakia in 1918 but was again occupied by Hungary from 1938 to 1945. From 21 February to 21 April 1945, Košice served as the capital of liberated Czechoslovakia. Thus it was here that, on 5 April 1945, the so-called Košice Government Programme (Košický vládny program) was declared, setting out the form of the postwar Czechoslovak government.

During the '50s the Communists built a large steelworks on the outskirts of the city, and the steel industry has remained the mainstay of the city's wealth.

Orientation

Košice is clustered largely on the west bank of the Hornád river. The adjacent bus and train stations are just east of the old town. A five-minute walk west along Mlynská will bring you into Hlavná (Main St), which broadens to accommodate the squares of Hlavné námestie and námestie Slobody.

MAPS

Large indexed city maps are posted at various locations around town, but if you want something to carry with you, pick up a copy of VKÚ's *Košice* map (1:15,000; 68Sk) covering the town centre and its immediate surroundings.

Information

BOOKSHOPS

AF Kníhupectvo (☎ 623 26 77; Mlynská 6) Small selection of fiction in English.
Marsab (☎ 625 75 97; Hlavná 41) Good range of hiking maps and town plans.

CULTURAL CENTRES

British Council (☎ 729 99 72; Barkóciho palác, Mäsiarska 11) Library with British newspapers and magazines.

EMERGENCY

Police (☎ 622 42 89; Pribinova 6)

KOŠICE

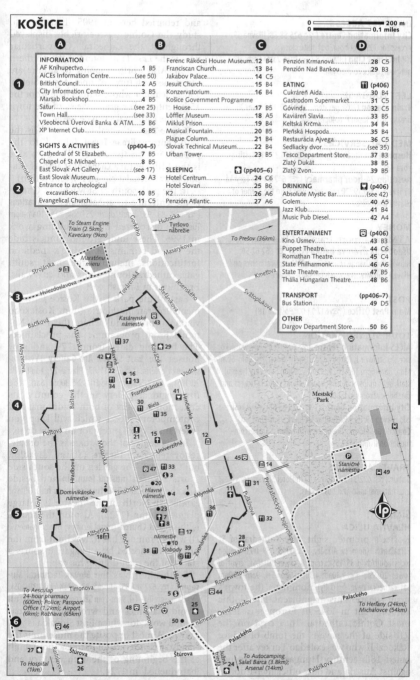

0		200 m
0		0.1 miles

INFORMATION
AF Knihupectvo	**1** B5
AiCEs Information Centre	(see 50)
British Council	**2** A5
City Information Centre	**3** B5
Marsab Bookshop	**4** B5
Satur	(see 25)
Town Hall	(see 33)
Všeobecná Úverová Banka & ATM	**5** B6
XP Internet Club	**6** B5

SIGHTS & ACTIVITIES (pp404–5)
Cathedral of St Elizabeth	**7** B5
Chapel of St Michael	**8** B5
East Slovak Art Gallery	(see 17)
East Slovak Museum	**9** A3
Entrance to archeological excavations	**10** B5
Evangelical Church	**11** C5
Ferenc Rákóczi House Museum	**12** B4
Franciscan Church	**13** B4
Jakabov Palace	**14** C5
Jesuit Church	**15** B4
Konzervatorium	**16** B4
Košice Government Programme House	**17** B5
Löffler Museum	**18** A5
Mikluš Prison	**19** B4
Musical Fountain	**20** B5
Plague Column	**21** B5
Slovak Technical Museum	**22** B4
Urban Tower	**23** B5

SLEEPING (pp405–6)
Hotel Centrum	**24** C6
Hotel Slovan	**25** B6
K2	**26** A6
Penzión Atlantic	**27** A6
Penzión Krmanová	**28** C5
Penzión Nad Bankou	**29** B3

EATING (p406)
Cukráreň Aida	**30** B4
Gastrodom Supermarket	**31** C5
Góvinda	**32** C5
Kaviáreň Slavia	**33** B5
Keltská Krčma	**34** B4
Pleňská Hospoda	**35** B4
Restaurácia Ajvega	**36** C5
Sedliacky dvor	(see 35)
Tesco Department Store	**37** B4
Zlatý Dukát	**38** B5
Zlatý Zvon	**39** B5

DRINKING (p406)
Absolute Mystic Bar	(see 42)
Golem	**40** A5
Jazz Klub	**41** B4
Music Pub Diesel	**42** A4

ENTERTAINMENT (p406)
Kino Úsmev	**43** B3
Puppet Theatre	**44** C6
Romathan Theatre	**45** C4
State Philharmonic	**46** A6
State Theatre	**47** B5
Thália Hungarian Theatre	**48** B6

TRANSPORT (pp406–7)
Bus Station	**49** D5

OTHER
Dargov Department Store	**50** B6

EAST SLOVAKIA

INTERNET ACCESS
City Information Centre (☎ 625 88 88; Hlavná 59)
Access for 30Sk per hour, but quite slow.
XP Internet Club (Hlavná 5; ☷ 8am-2am) Costs 50Sk
per hour, quick connection.

LEFT LUGGAGE
Train Station (20Sk per item; ☷ 3.30-12.30am, 30min
breaks at 12.30pm & 6.40pm)

MEDICAL SERVICES
Hospital (Fakultná nemocnica; ☎ 615 31 11; Rastisla-
vova 43)
Aesculap 24-hour pharmacy (☎ 642 94 91; Toryská
1) Take bus No 19 (10 minutes) west from the corner of
Hlavná and Štúrova.

MONEY
ATMs at airport, train and bus stations.
Všeobecná úverová banka (VÚB; ☎ 662 62 50;
Hlavná 8) Exchange counter and ATM; several banks on
Hlavná and Mlynská also have same services.

POST
Main Post Office (☎ 617 11 00; Poštová 18)

TOURIST INFORMATION
AiCES information centre (☎ 623 09 09; www.micko
sice.sk; Štúrova 1, Dargov department store; ☷ 9am-6pm
Mon, 8am-6pm Tue-Fri, 9.30am-2.30pm Sat) Very helpful
staff, sells maps and guidebooks, books concert tickets and
can book accommodation.
City Information Centre (☎ 625 88 88; www.kosice
.sk; Hlavná 59; ☷ 9am-6pm Mon-Fri, 9am-1pm Sat)
Council-run information office with cultural and accommodation listings.

TRAVEL AGENCIES
Satur (☎ 622 31 22; Hlavná 1) In Hotel Slovan, sells
international train and bus tickets.

Sights
HLAVNÁ ULICA
Košice's premier sight, the **Cathedral of St
Elizabeth** (dom sv Alžběty; ☎ 0908 667 093; guided
tours adult/child 35/15Sk; crypt & tower 30/10Sk, crypt or
tower 20/5Sk; ☷ 9.30am-4.30pm Mon-Fri, 9am-1.30pm
Sat; cathedral nave ☷ daily), dominates the town's
main square. This magnificent, late-Gothic
edifice, built in 1345, is Europe's eastern-
most Gothic cathedral. In a **crypt** on the
left side of the nave is the tomb of Prince
Rákóczi II who was exiled to Turkey after the
failed 18th-century Hungarian insurgency
against Austria and only officially pardoned

and reburied here in 1905. Take time to
study the Gothic frescoes richly displayed
throughout the cathedral. Of particular
note is the *Last Trial*, found at the northern
portal. Also worth stopping to admire are
the stone sculptures of one Master Štefan,
a local sculptor whose statues date from the
15th century. For grand views of the town
climb the cathedral's ornate **tower**.

Beside the cathedral to the north is the
14th-century **Urban Tower** (closed to the
public) and on the cathedral's south side
is the 14th-century **Chapel of St Michael** (ka-
plinka sv Michala; closed for renovation).

In the park south of St Michael's Chapel
is the entrance to **archaeological excavations**
(☎ 622 83 93; adult/child 25/15Sk; ☷ 10am-6pm
Tue-Sun), discovered during building work
in 1996. These underground tunnels hide
the buried remains of Košice's medieval
fortifications, including the moat, south
gate, cathedral foundations and city walls.
Brochures in English cost 10Sk.

East of the park is the Košice Government Programme House (dom Košického
vládného programu) where the 1945 National Front programme was proclaimed.
The building dates from 1779 and now
houses the **East Slovak Art Gallery** (Východo-
slovenská galéria; ☎ 622 11 87; Hlavná 27; adult/child
20/10Sk; ☷ 1-5.30pm Tue-Fri, 2-5.30pm Sat), the
first regional gallery in the country. Its
collection is a mix of both traditional and
contemporary pieces which will keep you
entertained quite nicely for an hour or so.

In the centre of the square is the ornate,
renovated **State Theatre** (Štátne divadlo),
built in 1899. The garden on the south side
sports a kitsch **musical fountain** and beside
it is the rococo 1780 **former town hall** (Hlavné
námestie 59). North of the theatre is a large
plague column (1723). Also on the square
is the **Jesuit Church** (kostol jezuitov; Hlavné námestie
71) which, rumour has it, was built from the
proceeds collected by a beggar; it sports a
statue of the man doffing his cap.

Further north is the **Slovak Technical Museum** (☎ 622 40 35; Hlavná 88; adult/child 30/10Sk;
☷ 8am-5pm Tue-Fri, 9am-2pm Sat, noon-5pm Sun), full
of old machines and wrought-iron ornamental work, for which East Slovakia is well
known. Almost opposite the museum is the
Franciscan Church (kostol Františkánov), built
at the beginning of the 15th century and
'baroquefied' in 1724.

AROUND HLAVNÁ ULICA

North of Hlavná is the **East Slovak Museum** (Východoslovenské múzeum; ☎ 622 30 61; Hviezdoslavova 3; adult/child 30/10Sk; ☼ 9am-5pm Tue-Sat, 9am-1pm Sun) which is dedicated to archaeology and prehistory. A highlight is the stunning Košice Gold Treasure (Košický zlatý poklad), with 2920 gold coins minted in Kremnica that were stashed in the wall of a house called the Spiš Chamber at Hlavná 74, and discovered in 1935. And if you've yet to see a traditional wooden church from East Slovakia, one has been reconstructed for your pleasure at the back of the museum.

East of Hlavná on Hrnčiarska is **Ferenc Rákóczi House Museum** (Hrnčiarska 7; adult/child 30/10Sk; ☼ 9am-5pm Tue-Sat, 9am-1pm Sun), housed in the Executioner's Bastion (Katova bašta) which was once part of Košice's 15th-century fortifications. There are exhibits of weapons and medieval miscellany but most impressive is the replica of Ferenc Rákóczi II's house, with some of his personal effects. Nearby is **Mikluš Prison** (Miklušova väznica; Pri Miklušovej väznici 10; adult/child 30/10Sk), a connected pair of 16th-century houses that once served as a prison equipped with medieval torture chambers and claustrophobic cells. It's open the same hours as the Ferenc Rákóczi House Museum, where you buy tickets.

South of the prison and museum is the **Evangelical Church** (Evanjelický kostol) and the fairytale-like **Jakabov Palace** (closed to the public), where President Beneš lived in early 1945.

Löffler Museum (☎ 622 30 73; Alžbetina 20; adult/child 20/10Sk; ☼ 10am-6pm Tue-Sat, 1-5pm Sun) shows off the Löffler family's collection of early 20th-century portraits and sculptures, plus some good works by contemporary Slovak artists.

Košice for Children

Košice's **Puppet Theatre** (Bábkové divadlo; ☎ 622 04 55; Rooseweltova 38) holds performances throughout the year for both children and adults. During the summer, kids can enjoy a **Steam Engine Train ride** (☎ 622 59 25; adult/child 10/5Sk; ☼ Sat & Sun only May-Aug), north of the centre. Take bus No 15 from outside the East Slovak Museum to the end stop.

In the small village of Kavečany, 9km north of Košice, there's more fun for the whole family. You'll find an adrenaline-pumping **Bob Sled ride** (☎ 633 49 01; 1 ride adult/child 30/20Sk, 6 rides 150/100Sk; ☼ 9am-7pm May-Oct), alongside the city **Zoo** (☎ 633 81 04; adult/child 30/10Sk; ☼ 9am-7pm May-Oct). To get there, hop on bus No 29 from near the East Slovak Museum to the final stop.

Tours

The AiCES office can arrange city tours in a number of languages, including English, German, French and Spanish (around 450Sk per hour).

Festivals & Events

The annual **East Slovak Folk Festival** takes place up and down Hlavná in mid-June. On the first Sunday in October, runners from many countries participate in an International Marathon **Race for Peace**, held here since 1924. During the first week of May, the city lets its hair down for **Košice Days**, a celebration which involves much singing and dancing.

Sleeping

BUDGET

K2 (☎ 625 59 48; Štúrova 32; s/d 300/600Sk; P) K2 is an attractive sports complex with cheerful rooms with shared facilities, a restaurant and bar, and sauna and fitness centre. It's an easy walk southwest from town but is often filled with groups.

Autocamping Salaš Barca (☎ 623 33 97; Alejová 24; person/tent/car/bungalow 70/60/80/500Sk; ☼ year round) This basic camp site, south of the city, is the only option around for campers. To get there from the train station, take tram No 3 south along Južná trieda (20 minutes) to the Juh SAD stop (about 200m before an overpass), then head right (west) on Alejová (the Rožňava Hwy) for about 500m.

Both tourist offices have a list of hostels open during summer priced at around 300Sk per person.

MID-RANGE

Penzión Krmanová (☎ 623 05 65; krmanova@elvs.sk; Krmanová 14; s/d 1350/1840Sk) This excellent central option has large, modern rooms and friendly staff. During the week it is often full so book ahead.

Penzión Nad Bankou (☎ 683 82 21; Kováčska 63, s/d 900/1400Sk; P) Bankou is centrally located above a bank, and has simple, clean rooms.

Penzión Atlantic (☎ 622 65 01; Rázousova 1; r from 900Sk; P) This small *pension* looks grubby from the outside, but its rooms are big, bright and reasonably modern.

Hotel Centrum (☎ 6783101; www.hotel-centrum.sk; Južná trieda 2a; r from 990Sk; P) Three-star Centrum has both renovated and nonrenovated rooms, but there's not much difference between them except the price.

TOP END

Hotel Slovan (☎ 622 73 78; www.hotelslovan.sk; Hlavná 1; s/d 2690/3390Sk; P) Slovan caters more for business clientele, with pricier rooms and plenty of conference space.

Eating

CAFÉS

The Art Nouveau **Kaviáreň Slávia** (Hlavná 63; coffee 30Sk) is a good upmarket place for coffee and cakes; the less pretentious **Cukráreň Aida** (cnr Hlavná & Biela; ice cream 6Sk) has a good selection of cakes and the best ice cream in town.

RESTAURANTS

Sedliacky dvor (☎ 622 04 02; Biela 3; mains 100-150Sk) This small restaurant has a rural décor and excellent Slovakian specialities at reasonable prices.

Pleňská Hospoda (☎ 622 04 02; Biela 5; mains 100-150Sk) Next door is another superb place, this time concentrating on Czech cuisine, although it's normally packed with locals more interested in the range of Czech beer.

Reštaurácia Ajvega (Orlia 10; mains around 100Sk) This inexpensive, vegetarian restaurant has English-language menus, tasty meals and friendly staff.

Zlatý Zvon (☎ 622 56 89; Zvonárska; pizzas 100-150Sk) This is a fine pizza joint, with small but very good pizzas situated on a quiet, cobblestoned street.

Góvinda (☎ 620 04 28; Puškinova 8; mains 80-120Sk ⏰ noon-7pm Mon-Sat) Run by Hare Krishnas, Góvinda offers divine vegetarian Indian food, extremely friendly staff and a quiet courtyard.

Keltská Krčma (Hlavná 8; mains under 100Sk) Inexpensive Keltská, with its open courtyard and sunny tables, is a popular place to eat or drink.

SELF-CATERING

There are supermarkets at the **Tesco department store** (Hlavná) and at **Gastrodom** (Mlynská) and there's a small **produce market** (Dominikánske námestie).

Drinking

Golem (☎ 728 91 01; Dominikánske námestie) If you get the chance, call in at Golem and have a pint. This small pub/restaurant is one of the few microbreweries in the country and it makes some damn fine beer; be sure to try both the dark and light versions.

There are a few popular places for a drink and a chance to shake that boodie:

Absolute Mystic Bar (Hlavná 92) A cellar-like place with one crazy door.

Jazz klub (Kováčská 39) Heaving club with an outdoor bar upstairs and dance floor downstairs.

Music Pub Diesel (Hlavná 92) A pseudo Irish pub with Guinness on tap and a disco on Thursday nights.

Entertainment

Pick up a copy of the free monthly publication *Kam do mesta*, which has comprehensive entertainment listings and is relatively easy to decipher.

CINEMAS

For cinema in the city centre, head to **Kino Úsmev** (☎ 622 12 22; Kasárenské námestie 1; tickets around 90Sk).

CLASSICAL MUSIC & THEATRE

The **State Theatre** (☎ 622 13 31; Hlavné námestie 58) holds regular performances, as does the **Thália Hungarian Theatre** (☎ 623 36 43; Timonova 3) and also the **State Philharmonic** (☎ 622 45 14; Moyzesova).

Romathan (☎ 622 49 80; Štefánikova 4) The country's only Romany theatre is well worth attending. Its Roma drama and concerts are a mix of song, dance and exuberance.

You can buy theatre tickets from the box office at the AiCES office.

CLUBS

Arsenal (Haniska pri Košiciach; ⏰ Fri & Sat) One of the largest and more mainstream clubs in Košice is 14km south of the city centre. Otherwise, try your luck at the bars mentioned in the Drinking section.

Getting There & Away

The AiCES office can provide a transport booklet with air, train, bus and tram timetables for Košice and its surrounding area.

AIR

Sky Europe (☎ 02-48 50 48 50; www.skyeurope.com) has daily flights to/from Bratislava (one

hour); **Slovak Airlines** (☎ 683 22 31; www.slovak
airlines.sk; airport office) flies only on Saturday.
ČSA (☎ 678 24 90; Hotel Centrum, Južná trieda 2a)
has three daily flights to and from Prague.
Prices for these flights fluctuate and depend
on availability.

BUS

There are frequent departures for Prešov
(44Sk, 40 minutes), Bardejov (91Sk, 1¾
hours), Levoča (116Sk, two hours), and
Spišské Podhradie (106Sk, 1¾ hours). Eight
buses daily run from Bratislava to Košice
(512Sk, 6½-7½ hours).

Three buses daily head for Uzhgorod,
Ukraine (140Sk, 4½ hours) at noon, 2.30pm
and 3.30pm. For buses to Poland, there is
a bus to Nowy Targ (175Sk, four hours) at
5.45am every Thursday and Saturday, and
to Krosno (170Sk) every Wednesday, Friday and Saturday at 6am.

Buses to Miskolc, Hungary (110Sk, two
hours), leave at 5.40pm Monday to Thursday, 6.30am and 3pm Friday and 6.30am
Saturday.

CAR

Hertz (☎ 729 28 42) and **Avis** (☎ 632 58 63) have
set-ups at the airport.

TRAIN

A daily sleeper train departs Košice each
morning for Kiev (Kyiv) in the Ukraine
(1600Sk, 22½ hours). Three daily trains
make the journey from Košice to Kraków,
Poland (920Sk, 6½ hours), while five trains
a day run from Košice to Miskolc, Hungary
(320Sk, two hours), via Hidasnémeti. Three
of these continue on to Budapest (890Sk,
four hours). This is an easy way to cross the
border as no reservations are required.

Overnight trains with sleepers and couchettes are also available between Košice and
Prague (1200Sk, 11 hours) and Brno (830Sk,
nine hours). Frequent daytime express
trains connect Košice to Prague (via Banská
Bystrica or Žilina, nine hours).

Express services from Košice to Bratislava (560Sk, five hours) via Poprad, Žilina
and Trenčín are rare, but there are plenty of
regional trains (476Sk, six hours).

Getting Around

Bus No 23 runs from the airport to the centre of town up to seven times daily.

Košice is served by both bus and tram;
tickets for one trip cost 12Sk and are available from tobacconists and newspaper
stands. For a taxi, call Elán on ☎ 674 74 74.

AROUND KOŠICE

The one claim to fame of **Herľany** is that it
has Slovakia's only **geyser** (gejzír), which,
from a depth of 400m below the surface,
erupts 15m to 20m in the air every 32 to 34
hours. Check with AiCES in Košice to find
out when it will next spout.

There are frequent bus connections
from Košice on weekdays, but fewer on
weekends, when only two buses depart, at
8am and 2.50pm (36Sk, 45 minutes).

SPIŠ REGION

The Spiš region to the northwest of East
Slovakia contains one of the country's most
appealing pockets of traditional culture, as
well as some outstanding escapes into
nature – most notably hiking in the vast
Slovenský raj (Slovak Paradise) national
park and river trips through the Dunajec
gorge. The region's finest architectural
landmarks are Levoča's old town, the stoic
ruins of Spiš Castle (Spišský hrad), and the
monastery at Červený Kláštor.

The towns in this area were already
part of a sturdy, independent-minded region by the late 12th century. From then
until the 15th century it was colonised by
Saxon settlers, first coaxed in by offers of
tax breaks from the Hungarian King Béla
III. It was these so-called Spiš Saxons who
formed their own union, a defensive alliance of several towns, in 1412. The old
royal towns of Levoča and Kežmarok
were the region's two most important
until the 20th century; today they're simply quiet, photogenic reminders of a more
glorious past.

SPIŠSKÁ NOVÁ VES

☎ 053 / pop 39,200

This old Saxon town on the Hornád river
is little more than a convenient jumping-off
point for access to the nearby Slovak Paradise National Park (p408). Self-catering
travellers should stock up on food here, as
there are few markets within the national
park's boundaries.

Orientation

The bus station is 200m southwest of the Spišská Nová Ves train station. To reach the centre from the train station, walk south on Odborárov and turn left on Dulianska. The AiCES office and Radničné námestie (the main square), which is bordered by Letná and Zimná, are about 300m further on.

Information

AiCES information centre (☎ 442 82 92; brantner@spisnet.sk; Letná 49; ☻ 8am-4pm Mon-Fri) Helpful, knowledgeable staff can assist with accommodation and have lots of national park information, including hiking maps.

Banks A couple of banks are on the main square with ATMs and exchange desks. There's also an ATM at the train station.

Internet Klub (☎ 441 44 02; Letná 27) Has Internet access for 48Sk per hour.

Left-luggage office (train station; ☻ 5.30am-7.30pm)

Sights

The long main square, Radničné námestie, is lined with Renaissance houses with mostly baroque or neoclassical façades. Here you'll find the town's one museum, the **Museum of the Spiš Region** (☎ 442 37 57; Letná 50; adult/child 30/10Sk; ☻ 8am-noon, 12.30-4.30pm Mon-Fri, 9am-1pm Sat, 1-5pm Sun). The building was once the administrative headquarters for the union of towns in this region in the 18th and 19th centuries; its stucco rococo façade dates from 1763–65.

Attached to the 14th-century **Gothic Parish Church** (Farský kostol) is an 86m tower, the highest church tower in Slovakia, added in the 19th century. Inside the church are Stations of the Cross carved by Master Pavol of Levoča in around 1520.

Sleeping & Eating

Metropol Hotel (☎ 442 22 41; www.hotel-metropol.sk; Štefánikovo námestie 2; s/d 1500/1650Sk; **P**) If you need to stay, try the conspicuous, green, 10-storey Metropol just west of the main square; it's quite fancy for the area.

Nostalgia (Letná 49; mains 140-200Sk) Near AiCES is a very popular restaurant with a menu ranging from Mexican to pasta dishes. Its walls are covered in memorabilia from the '50s, and there's a small playground for kids.

Opposite the bus station you'll find a massive supermarket.

Getting There & Away

Buses may take longer than the train to/from Levoča (16Sk, 20 minutes), but they're the only easy way to the Slovenský raj trailheads like Čingov (8Sk, 15 minutes, nine buses from Monday to Friday, one each on Saturday and Sunday) and Dedinky (60Sk, 1½ hours, three buses Monday to Friday), as well as to Spišský Štvrtok (16Sk, 15 minutes, frequent daily services).

Spišská Nová Ves lies on a main line served by regular daily express trains between Žilina (198Sk, 2¼ hours) and Košice (104Sk, one hour), with a stop at Poprad, as well as connections all day from Levoča (17Sk, 15 minutes).

SLOVENSKÝ RAJ

Slovak Paradise National Park (Národní park Slovenský raj, or NPSR; www.slovenskyraj.sk) boasts some of the finest scenery in East Slovakia. It is 90% covered in dense pine and deciduous forest, has several rare species found only within its borders including 17 butterfly types and 20 wildflower varieties, and is inhabited by eagles, lynxes, bears and wolves. Its peaks and gorges, waterfalls and rapids, and wide network of well-marked trails make it an extremely popular area for outdoor enthusiasts – mostly Slovak and Polish families in pursuit of peace and barbecues. Ideal for summer walking and winter cross-country skiing, the Slovenský raj is perhaps at its most beautiful in winter under a blanket of snow.

Orientation

The park lies west of Spišská Nová Ves, at the eastern end of the Low Tatras. The closest convenient bases with accommodation are Čingov, in the northeast of the park and only a short bus ride from Spišská Nová Ves, and the more picturesque Dedinky in the south of the park, approachable by bus from Rožňava or Spišská Nová Ves.

From these towns you can do day or overnight loop hikes, or an overnight hike between them.

Information

For those planning a hike or a bike, the best sources of trail and weather information, and help in booking a *chata* along the way, are the park's **Mountain Rescue Service** (Horská služba) stations. The **main office** (☎ 449 11 82; ☻ 8am-6pm) is at Čingov, and there's another

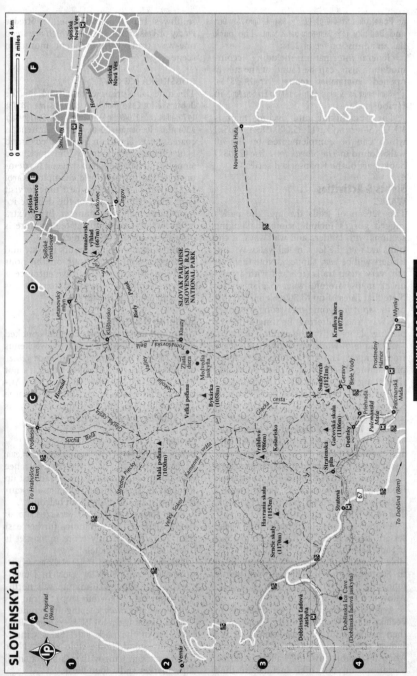

at **Podelcok** (☎ 449 03 39; 🕑 8am-4.30pm May-Oct) and **Dedinky** (🕑 9am-8pm Sat & Sun). The park has an admission fee of 20Sk.

General information, including accommodation lists, can be found at the newly opened **information centre** (☎ 429 98 54; 🕑 8am-6pm Jul & Aug, 8am-4pm Mon-Fri Sep-Jun) in Hrabušice.

The best hiking and cycling map is VKÚ's *Slovenský raj* (1:25,000, No 4, 150Sk) which can be complemented by the 40 walks found in *The Slovak Paradise* (240Sk) book, part of the Knapsacked series.

Sights & Activities
WALKS

The 326km of trails through the park's rugged gorges include some challenging sections with ladders and walkways. If the trails are wet, the logs, metal walkways and ladders will be very slippery. Note that certain very steep trails (marked with arrows on all maps) are one way, so plan ahead. Note that fines of up to 5000Sk are payable on the spot for going the wrong way on a one way track, littering, lighting a fire, or picking plants within the park.

A couple of worthwhile loop trails leave from Čingov. The first, which takes about nine hours, heads west to **Biely Potok** and then along the **Sokolia valley** to a photogenic lake at Klauzy via **Kysel rácestie** (735m). At Klauzy a trail heads back to Biely Potok. A second loop also heads west, but to ever-popular **Tomášovský Lookout** (Tomášovský výhlad; 667m) and on to **Letanovský mlyn** and the **Hornád river**. From here, head west again along the Hornád to **Kláštorská roklina**, then south up to **Kláštorisko** chata and a ruined Carthusian monastery. From here it's possible to take a trail east to Biely Potok. The walk takes about six hours.

Another popular loop trail leaves **Podlesok** and heads south up the dramatic gorge of **Suchá Belá**. At the top of the gorge it's possible to head east and wind your way down to **Kláštorisko** and the **Hornád river**, before following the river west back to Podlesok. Allow at least six hours.

A good all-day walk from **Podlesok** to **Dedinky** starts with the Suchá Belá gorge, then heads south via **Malá Poľana** and **Pod Suchým vrchom** to **Geravy** (1027m), from where it's a short downhill walk to Dedinky. Variations on this hike include heading

southwest from Podlesok to either **Stredné Piecky** or **Veľký Sokol**, both of which are steep one-way trails with excellent mountain scenery.

DOBŠINSKÁ ICE CAVE

This unusual World-Heritage listed site, the **Dobšinská Ice Cave** (Dobšinská ľadová jaskyňa; ☎ 788 14 70; adult/child 120/60Sk; 🕑 9am-4pm Tue-Sun Jun-Aug, 9.30am-2pm Tue-Sun May & Sep), west of Stratená, is coated in ice. The ice in the so-called Grand Hall (Veľká sieň) is up to 20m thick, and smooth and flat enough to skate on (as demonstrated by former world champion Karol Divín in the 1950s). The best time to visit is in May, before many of the delicate ice formations melt over summer. Bring extra layers because the ambient temperature is only a few degrees above freezing.

Tours leave every 1½ hours in May and September, and every hour on the hour from June to August. The cave entrance is a steep, 20-minute hike south from the bus stop and adjacent restaurant.

Sleeping & Eating

Chaty and most hotels are normally booked out in July and August and on weekends from May to September – advance reservations are crucial. At other times it's not hard to find a bed or two. In a pinch try Autocamp Podlesok (see opposite), as it's large and rarely 100% full. Freelance camping is not allowed anywhere within the park.

ČINGOV

Hotel Flora (☎ 449 11 29; flora_cingov@hotmail.com; s/d 700/1000Sk; Ⓟ 🐾) Near the park entrance (five minutes past Salaš Čingov and east up through the trees), Hotel Flora has a restaurant and spacious rooms with balcony.

Hotel Čingov (☎ 443 36 63; www.hotelcingov.sk; s/d 655/1310Sk; Ⓟ) Five minutes further east than Flora and slightly more upmarket is this clean, modern hotel.

Autocamping Tatran (☎ 429 71 05; person/tent/ car/bungalow/chaty 60/50/40/720/1950Sk) In Ďurkovec (on a hill about a 20-minute walk northwest from the Čingov bus stop), Tatran has bungalows and *chaty* sleeping up to nine.

Salaš Čingov (mains 100-150Sk; 🕑 10am-7.30pm) Just east of the park gate, Salaš Čingov serves up good, home-style meals. Near the car park at Čingov there's also a small supermarket and a food kiosk.

PODLESOK

Autocamp Podlesok (☎ 429 91 65; slovrajbela@ stonline.sk; person/tent/car/bungalow 50/50/50/750Sk) The year-round Autocamp has comfy bungalows, plenty of tent space and a couple of eateries, and is a stone's throw from the park. Buses don't run to the camp; the nearest you'll get is Hrabušice, from where it's a 2km walk.

KLÁŠTORISKO

The lone **restaurant** (☎ 449 33 07) here also rents out *chaty* year-round for 250Sk per person. If you'd like to stay in midsummer, call ahead to check availability.

DEDINKY

Penzión Pastierňa (☎ 058-798 11 75; s/d 300/600Sk; P) In the village itself and near the advancing pine trees is this excellent, five-room *pension*. The restaurant here is very good.

Hotel Priehrada (☎ 058-798 12 12; dedinky@ stonline.sk; s/d 400/800Sk; P) Right on the lake at Dedinky is Hotel Priehrada, with simple rooms and a small **camping ground** (person/tent/ car 40/40/20Sk in Jul & Aug, free rest of year).

STRATENÁ

Penzión Stratenka (☎ 058-798 11 32; r up to 3 people 890Sk; P ⛽) On the main road 300m west of the bus stop is this well-kept *pension* with a restaurant.

Getting There & Away

From Spišská Nová Ves (p408), there are frequent buses to Čingov and Dedinky. There's also a regular bus service from Rožňava to the Dobšinská Ice Cave via Dobšiná (28Sk, 30 minutes).

The daily Horehoronec fast train from Banská Bystrica to Košice stops at Dedinky (148Sk, 2¼ hours) and the ice cave (138Sk, two hours), before continuing to Košice. There are also frequent local trains on the main Žilina–Košice line from Margecany to Mlynky, Dedinky, Stratená and Dobšinská Ďadová Jaskyňa.

Getting Around

Hotel Flora rents out mountain bikes for 50/250Sk per hour/day, as does the **camping ground** (☎ 0905 539 695) at Dedinky.

SPIŠSKÝ ŠTVRTOK

This village, on the Poprad–Levoča road 12km west of Levoča, is marked by a wooden

church spire. The main attraction in the originally **Gothic church** (☎ 459 84 00; admission free; ☽ daily) is a 1493 side chapel built by local noble Štefan Zápoľský in the manner of French palace chapels of the time. The church was altered in baroque style in the 17th and 18th centuries. If the church is closed just knock or hang on the door bell until someone comes to fetch you.

Frequent buses make the 30-minute trip to Spišský Štvrtok from Poprad, Spišská Nová Ves or Levoča.

LEVOČA

☎ 053 / pop 14,400

Levoča rivals Bardejov as the region's most historically impressive town, full of fine, predominantly Renaissance buildings. It also has an almost complete set of original fortifications. Levoča is an easy stop on the way from Poprad to Košice.

History

In common with other Spiš towns, Levoča (Leutschau in German) was settled and enriched by a wave of Saxon artisans beginning in the 12th century. By 1271 it was the Spiš administrative seat.

It broke away from the union of Saxon Spiš towns in 1323 to become a free royal town, prospering from trade in gold and woodcarving. Much of its present Renaissance personality comes from a building boom after a huge fire in the 16th century.

In the 17th century Levoča's fortunes collapsed after an anti-Habsburg uprising. Its isolation was accentuated when it was bypassed by the railway in the 19th century (it's now at the end of a branch line).

A Slovak army garrison from Levoča joined in the Slovak National Uprising in 1944. The town was occupied by German troops until its liberation by the Soviets in February 1945.

Orientation

The bus and train stations are 1km south of the town centre, down the road beside the Hotel Faix. Note that most buses also stop at námestie Štefana Kluberta, a few blocks east of the main square, námestie Majstra Pavla.

Information

Kultúrno-informačné centrum (KIC; ☎ 451 37 63; www.levoca.sk; námestie Majstra Pavla 58; ☽ 9am-5pm

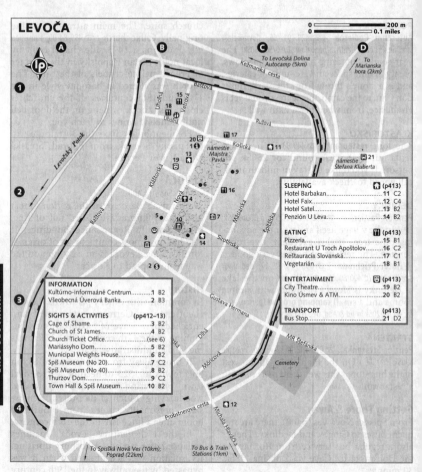

LEVOČA

0 — 200 m
0 — 0.1 miles

To Levočská Dolina
Autocamp (5km)
Kežmarská cesta

To Marianska hora (2km)

To Spišská Nová Ves (10km); Poprad (22km)

To Bus & Train Stations (1km)

INFORMATION

| Kultúrno-informaáné Centrum | 1 | B2 |
| Všeobecná Úverová Banka | 2 | B3 |

SIGHTS & ACTIVITIES (pp412–13)

Cage of Shame	3	B2
Church of St James	4	B2
Church Ticket Office	(see 6)
Mariássyho Dom	5	B2
Municipal Weights House	6	B2
Spiš Museum (No 20)	7	C2
Spiš Museum (No 40)	8	B2
Thurzov Dom	9	C2
Town Hall & Spiš Museum	10	B2

SLEEPING (p413)

Hotel Barbakan	11	C2
Hotel Faix	12	C4
Hotel Satel	13	B2
Penzión U Leva	14	B2

EATING (p413)

Pizzeria	15	B1
Restaurant U Troch Apoštolov	16	C2
Reštauracia Slovanská	17	C1
Vegetarián	18	B1

ENTERTAINMENT (p413)

| City Theatre | 19 | B2 |
| Kino Úsmev & ATM | 20 | B2 |

TRANSPORT (p413)

| Bus Stop | 21 | D2 |

Mon-Sat, 10am-2pm Sun) provides town and regional information, as well as accommodation assistance.

The KIC office has a currency exchange desk, as does **Všeobecná úverová banka** (VÚB; ☎ 451 43 17; námestie Majstra Pavla 28) which also has an ATM. There are a couple of public telephones outside the **post office** (námestie Majstra Pavla 42).

Sights

Levoča's main square is crammed with fine Renaissance buildings, though the jewel of the town is Gothic – the **Church of St James** (kostol sv Jakuba; ☎ 451 23 47; námestie Majstra Pavla 25; adult/child 50/30Sk; ☉ 11am-5.15pm Mon, 9am-5.15pm Tue-Sat, 1-5.15pm Sun), dating from around 1400. It's Slovakia's second-largest Gothic church and basically a museum of medieval religious art.

An extraordinary piece of craftsmanship is the 19m-high and 6m-wide wooden altar, the world's largest. It was carved by the renowned Master Pavol of Levoča, after whom the town square is named, between 1507 and 1518. The church frescoes, which adorn its walls and ceiling, match its architectural style; Gothic. They are some of the finest in the country and are a superb compliment to Master Pavel's altar. Tickets are available opposite the church in the former **Municipal Weights House** (budova mestských váh).

The originally Gothic **town hall** (radnica; ☎ 451 24 49; námestie Majstra Pavla 2; adult/child 20/10Sk;

(⏰ 9am-5pm Tue-Sun) and tower got a Renaissance face-lift in 1551; the town hall is now one of Levoča's most beautiful buildings. Inside is the first (and best) of three Spiš Museum (Spišské múzeum) branches, with folk dresses and town artefacts displayed in stunning wood-panelled chambers. South of the town hall is the **Cage of Shame** (Klietka hanby), originally a place of public humiliation for criminals.

In the second branch of the **Spiš Museum** (☎ 451 34 96; námestie Majstra Pavla 40; adult/child 20/10Sk; ⏰ 9am-5pm Tue-Sun) are religious and secular artworks, ceramics in regional styles, and some handsome wood-beamed rooms with hints of Renaissance frescoes. Across the square is the third and final **Spiš Museum branch** (☎ 451 34 96; námestie Majstra Pavla 20; adult/child 20/10Sk; ⏰ 9am-5pm Tue-Sun), devoted to the town's famous son, Master Pavol.

The houses on the square were the homes of rich artisans and traders. Finest is the **Thurzov dom** (1532), at No 7, with its characteristic Spiš Renaissance attic. Another well-preserved beauty is **Mariássyho dom** at No 43, noted for its interior. Others to look at close by are **Spillenbergov dom**, at No 45, **Krupekov dom**, at No 44, and **Hainov dom** at No 41.

Festivals & Events

On the first weekend in July each year, a **Marian Pilgrimage** (Marian púť) is held in a church on top of Marianska hora (hill), about 2km north of town. This is one of the most popular religious pilgrimages in Slovakia, with up to a quarter of a million pilgrims converging on the place. Masses are given hourly from 6pm on Saturday, but the one to wait for is at 10am on Sunday.

On selected days between June and October the town puts on **Master Pavel Days**, which are a celebration of the man and his works through traditional song and dance. Contact KIC for more information on both.

Sleeping

Penzión U Leva (☎ 450 23 11; www.uleva.szm.sk; námestie Majstra Pavla 24; s/d 1300/2300Sk; P) Super spacious, super clean, super modern – U Leva is one of the better places to stay in town. The only problem is the two flights of stairs you must climb to the rooms.

Hotel Barbakan (☎ 451 43 10; www.barbakan.sk; Košická 15; s/d 1150/1450Sk; P) Barbakan offers large, clean rooms decorated in dark wood and '70s furniture (but not on purpose).

Levočská Dolina Autocamp (☎ 451 27 05; person/tent/car/bungalow 60/60/80/250Sk) Five kilometres north of námestie Štefana Kluberta, on the road to Závada, is this welcoming camp site with a rural setting and a restaurant.

Hotel Satel (☎ 451 29 43; www.satel-slovakia.sk; námestie Majstra Pavla 55; s/d 1850/2400Sk; P) Top of the line is this four-star hotel, with stylish, modern rooms with everything you need.

Hotel Faix (☎ 451 11 11; Probstnerova cesta 22; s/d from 200/400Sk; P) This simple hotel, not far from the train station, has basic, clean rooms, mostly with shared facilities.

Eating

Good places for inexpensive Slovak cuisine are **Reštaurácia Slovenská** (☎ 451 23 39; námestie Majstra Pavla 62; mains 80-120Sk) and **Restaurant U troch apoštolov** (☎ 451 43 52; námestie Majstra Pavla 11; mains 100-150Sk).

The popular **Vegetarián** (Uholná 3; mains 60-100Sk; ⏰ 10am-3.15pm Mon-Fri) has tasty home-made vegetarian dishes, while the inviting **Pizzeria** (Vetrová 4; pizzas 80-120Sk), just off the main square, turns out a fine pizza.

Entertainment

There's not much going on after dark in town. **City Theatre** (mestské divadlo; námestie Majstra Pavla 55; ☎ 451 25 22) puts on drama (mostly in Slovak) plus the occasional musical. **Kino Úsmev** (☎ 451 22 08; námestie Majstra Pavla 58) is the place to catch a film.

Getting There & Away

Levoča is connected by 11 daily local trains to Spišská Nová Ves (17Sk, 15 minutes), which is 13km south on the main line from Bratislava to Prague and Košice. Bus travel is more practical as there are frequent daily services to Poprad (36Sk, 30 minutes) and Spišské Podhradie (20Sk, 15 minutes) and five daily to Košice (116Sk, two hours).

SPIŠSKÉ PODHRADIE & AROUND

Spišské Podhradie is 15km east of Levoča in the centre of East Slovakia. In the 12th century a settlement appeared below the neighbouring castle, developing into an artisans' town in the 13th century. The town itself is very dull, but the adjacent Spiš Castle (Spišský hrad) and Spišská Kapitula are a must-see.

EAST SLOVAKIA

Arrive early and give yourself at least 4½ hours (including walking time) to see both the castle and Spišská Kapitula.

Orientation & Information

Most long-distance buses stop in the main square, Marianské námestie, where you'll find a post office and an ATM. The train station is 1.5km northeast of town, nearer to the castle. There's an information desk and currency exchange in the courtyard of the castle.

You can leave your bags at the left-luggage office in the Spišské Podhradie train station (ask the stationmaster very, very nicely).

Spiš Castle

See p75 for a full description of the **castle** (☉ 8.30am-6pm). The castle is directly above the Spišské Podhradie train station; turn left into the car park and follow the yellow markers around 1.5km north up a steep hill. By car, the easiest approach is via the main highway from the east (Prešov) side of the castle. There are no buses to the castle.

Spišská Kapitula

If you're arriving by bus from Levoča, ask the driver to drop you at Spišská Kapitula, on a ridge 1km west of Spišské Podhradie. This 13th-century ecclesiastical settlement is completely encircled by a 16th-century wall, and the single street running between the two medieval gates is lined with picturesque Gothic houses. Until their eviction in 1948, the residents here were nearly all clergy. In fact, as the name hints, this was once the Spiš region's religious capital – from the 13th century an abbot resided here, and after 1776 it became the seat of a bishop.

At the upper end of the main street is the magnificent **Cathedral of St Martin** (adult/child 30/20Sk; ☉ 9am-noon, 1-4.30pm Mon-Sat, 10am-noon & 1-4.30pm Sun), originally built in 1273, with twin Romanesque towers and a Gothic sanctuary. Inside are three sumptuous folding Gothic altars (1499), a 1317 Gothic fresco of the coronation of King Karol Róbert and, near the door, a well-worn Romanesque white lion.

Sleeping & Eating

Kolping House (☎ 450 21 11; www.hotelkolping.sk; Spišská Kapitula 15; s/d 980/1460Sk; [P]) Near the cathedral is this fantastic place housed in the renovated Spišská chapter (a building formerly used to house members of the clergy). The plush rooms are decked out in antique furniture, and there's a great restaurant, beer hall and wine bar attached.

Penzión Podzámok (☎ 454 17 55; www.penzion podzamok.sk; Podzámková 28; s/d from 350/500Sk; [P]) If Kolping House is full, try this friendly *pension* in Spišské Podhradie, which also has a decent restaurant and views of the castle. Staff can also arrange horse riding trips. To get there, turn left after the bridge just south of Marianské námestie.

Getting There & Away

A secondary railway line connects Spišské Podhradie to Spišské Vlachy station (11Sk, 15 minutes) on the main line from Poprad to Košice. Departures are scheduled to connect with the Košice trains.

Buses from Levoča (20Sk, 15 minutes), Spišská Nová Ves (36Sk, 30 minutes) and Poprad (53Sk, 50 minutes) are quite frequent.

KEŽMAROK

☎ 052 / pop 17,400

Colonised by Germans in the 13th century and granted free royal town status in 1380, Kežmarok was the second most important Spiš town after Levoča from medieval times until the 19th century.

These days it's a quiet, fairly unremarkable town with a well-preserved old centre, a solid castle and one of the Spiš region's finest wooden churches. Kežmarok makes an easy day trip from Poprad and the High Tatra resorts.

Orientation

The bus and train stations are located northwest of the town centre. From the conspicuous New Evangelical Church, the town's axis runs north along Hviezdoslavova and pedestrianised Hlavné námestie and Hradné námestie to the castle.

Information

The **AiCES information centre** (☎ 452 40 47; www.kezmarok.net; Hlavné námestie 46; ☉ 8.30am-5pm Mon-Fri, 9am-2pm Sat & Sun Jun-Sep, closed Sun Oct-May) has plenty of information about the town and can help arrange day trips to the High Tatras. There's a small **Internet Café** (Hlavné námestie 62; 30Sk per hr; ☉ 10am-9pm) on the main

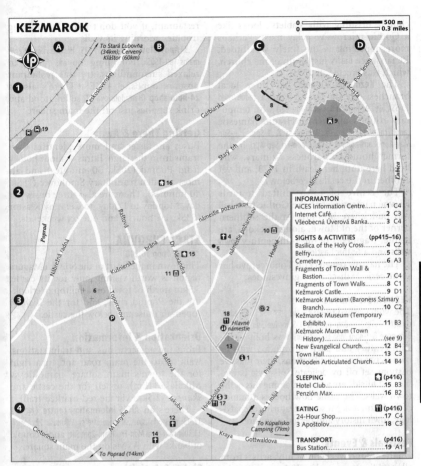

KEŽMAROK

To Stará Ľubovňa
(34km); Červený
Kláštor (60km)

INFORMATION
AiCES Information Centre............**1** C4
Internet Café.................................**2** C3
Všeobecná Úverová Banka..........**3** C4

SIGHTS & ACTIVITIES (pp415–16)
Basilica of the Holy Cross............**4** C2
Belfry...**5** C3
Cemetery......................................**6** A3
Fragments of Town Wall &
  Bastion....................................**7** C4
Fragments of Town Walls.............**8** C1
Kežmarok Castle..........................**9** D1
Kežmarok Museum (Baroness Szimary
  Branch)...................................**10** C2
Kežmarok Museum (Temporary
  Exhibits)..................................**11** B3
Kežmarok Museum (Town
  History)...............................(see 9)
New Evangelical Church.............**12** B4
Town Hall...................................**13** C3
Wooden Articulated Church.......**14** B4

SLEEPING (p416)
Hotel Club..................................**15** B3
Penzión Max..............................**16** B2

EATING (p416)
24-Hour Shop............................**17** C4
3 Apoštolov...............................**18** C3

TRANSPORT (p416)
Bus Station................................**19** A1

square. **Všeobecná úverová banka** (VÚB; ☎ 452 48 00; Hviezdoslavova 5) has an ATM.

Sights
The building you may remember the longest has little to do with ancient Kežmarok; it's the massive pea-green and red **New Evangelical Church** (Nový Evanjelický kostel; Mučeníkov; admission 30Sk; ⏰ 9am-noon & 2-5pm May-Oct, 10am-noon & 2-4pm Tue & Fri Nov-Apr), a pseudo-Moorish fortress of a church that was built at the turn of the 20th century with a semidetached 65m tower. Inside is the mausoleum of Imre Thököly, a contemporary of Rákóczi who was born in Kežmarok and, like him, fought against the Habsburg takeover of Hungary; he also died in exile in Turkey.

Far more dignified is the Protestant **Wooden Articulated Church** (Drevený artikulárny kostol; ☎ 452 22 42; admission 30Sk; ⏰ 9am-noon & 2-5pm May-Oct, 10am-noon & 2-4pm Tue & Fri Nov-Apr) next door. This squat and lopsided church contains a vast, beautiful, cross-shaped interior of carved and painted wood. Astonishingly, it was built in 1717 without a single metal nail (see photo p327). Inside it's one of Slovakia's loveliest churches.

On the site of the German settlers' original church is the late-15th-century **Basilica of the Holy Cross** (Bazilika Svätého Krížu; ☎ 452 22 20; Námestie požiarnikov; admission 10Sk; ⏰ 9am-5pm Mon-Fri Jun-Sep). Its wooden altars are said to have been carved by students of Master Pavol of Levoča. The tall tower of the church, bristling with 'gablets', looks like a Gothic microwave relay mast. Perhaps more appealing is the finely sgraffitoed, Renaissance **belfry** just south of the church, which was erected in 1591.

The **Kežmarok Museum** has three local branches: one on Dr Alexandra (adult/child 10/5Sk; 9am-noon & 1-4pm Tue-Sat) with temporary exhibits; another on Hradné námestie (adult/child 30/15Sk; 9am-noon & 1-5pm Tue-Sun May-Aug, 8am-noon & 1-4pm Mon-Fri Sep-Apr) in the former home of Baroness Szimary, who lived here until her death in 1973; and yet another in the castle (see below).

The centre of town shifted towards Hlavné námestie when the Gothic **town hall** was built there in 1461. At the southern corner of the old town, along Priekopa, are further fragments of the 14th-century **town walls** and a **Gothic bastion**.

The narrow **cemetery** on Toporcerova has some eerie 18th-century gravestones.

KEŽMAROK CASTLE

The whitewashed town **castle** (452 26 18; adult/child 60/20Sk; 8am-noon & 1-5pm Tue-Sun May-Sep, 8am-noon & 1-4pm Mon-Fri Oct-Apr) was built in the 15th century and later surrounded with its own Renaissance fortifications, their massive bastions set off by delicate Spiš-style battlements. Outside are a few remaining bits of the town walls. The castle now houses a branch of the Kežmarok Museum, featuring archaeology, town history and period furniture.

Festivals & Events

On the second weekend of July, artists from all over Europe travel to Kežmarok for the biggest **Craft Fair** in Slovakia. There's oodles of fine craft work, live music, food, drink and general merriment.

Sleeping & Eating

Penzión Max (452 63 24; duchon@sinet.sk; Starý trh 9; r from 1200Sk;) With extremely large, comfortable rooms and friendly, helpful owners, Max is the best place to stay in town.

Kúpalisko Camping (452 34 79; person/tent/car 70/70/70Sk; Jun-Aug) Located in the small village of Vrbov, 7km south of Kežmarok, this informal camp site moonlights as a thermal spa (adult/child 90/60Sk).

Hotel Club (452 40 51; hotelclub@sinet.sk; Dr Alexandra 24; s/d 1160/1670Sk;) This fine hotel has above-average rooms and a good restaurant, if you don't mind the hunting trophies adorning its walls.

3 Apoštolov (452 57 25; Hlavné námestie 9; mains 100-150Sk) For filling Slovak cuisine in relaxed surroundings, try this restaurant upstairs opposite AiCES. There's also a **24-hour shop** (Hviezdolavova 17) selling food and drink supplies just off the main square.

Getting There & Away

Buses are faster and more plentiful than trains from the High Tatras – about hourly from Poprad (20Sk, 30 minutes) and almost as often from Starý Smokovec (28Sk, 40 minutes). There are also three buses per day, Monday to Friday, to Červený Kláštor (53Sk, 1½ hours), and one on weekends.

STARÁ ĽUBOVŇA

052 / pop 16,200

This town in the heart of the Spišská Magura region is worth visiting only for its castle, 3.5km north of town on a hilltop overlooking the Poprad river, and for the *skansen* (open-air museum) below the castle.

Orientation & Information

From the adjacent bus and train stations, walk up to the main road and turn right for the town's main square, námestie sv Mikuláša (1km), or left for the castle and *skansen* (2.5km via the red-marked trail).

There's an **AiCES information centre** (432 17 13; mesto@sl.sinet.sk; námestie sv Mikuláša 12; 9-11.30am & 1-5pm Mon-Fri, 10am-2pm Sat) and a couple of banks with ATMs on the main square.

Sights & Activities

Ľubovňa Castle (432 20 30; adult/child 50/20Sk, 70/35Sk for castle & skansen; 9am-6pm May-Sep, 10am-3pm Mon-Sat Oct-Apr), thought to date from the 14th century and now a mix of Gothic, baroque and Renaissance styles, was the site of battles between Poles and both Hungarians and Austrians. It's half in ruins but still makes an interesting tour, and has a good view across the valley to the Magura mountains from its Gothic tower, taking in the Roma shanty town on the edge of Stará Ľubovňa. There are exhibits on the history of the castle, weapons and period furniture.

At the base of the castle is the **skansen**, a rather inorganic arrangement of traditional wooden houses, and a **church** (adult/child 30/15Sk; 9am-6pm May-Sep, 10am-3pm Oct). It is a blend of the styles typical of the Spišská Magura region – Slovak, Polish, Rusin and German. The domestic icons are clearly Russian Orthodox in flavour.

Sleeping & Eating

There really is no point staying here but if you're stuck, **Penzión Peters** (☎ 432 48 91; below the castle; s/d 200/400Sk; **P**) has basic rooms and a restaurant. **Reštaurácia U grófky Isabelly** (☎ 432 35 40; below castle; mains 100-150Sk) is a better bet for something to eat.

Getting There & Away

Buses are quick and frequent to most destinations, including Červený Kláštor (36Sk, 45 minutes), Bardejov (71Sk, 1¼ hours) and Kežmarok (44Sk, 45 minutes). There are eight trains a day between Stará Ľubovňa, Kežmarok (32Sk, 50 minutes) and Plaveč (21Sk, 20 minutes), where you change trains if you're bound for Poland.

Getting Around

Up to eight town buses travel to and from the castle and the train and bus stations Monday to Friday, but services are rare on weekends.

ČERVENÝ KLÁŠTOR

☎ 052

The main attraction in Červený Kláštor, on the banks of the Dunajec river in the region known as Zamaguria (beyond the Magura mountains), is a chance to float down the Dunajec gorge on a raft. You needn't even go into town, since everything worth seeing is on the eastern outskirts, right where the buses from Stará Ľubovňa stop.

Information on the area is available at a small **Information Centre** (☎ 482 21 22; www.pieniny.sk; ◷ 9am-5pm May-Oct) about 2km west of the Carthusian monastery.

Sights & Activities

DUNAJEC GORGE

Pieniny National Park (21 sq km), created in 1967, combines with a similar park in Poland to protect the 9km Dunajec river gorge between Červený Kláštor and Szczawnica, Poland. The river here forms the international boundary between the two countries.

Pieniny means 'foam' – caused not by pollution, but by the river rushing over its limestone bed. Towering over the river are tree-clad, 500m-tall cliffs, at their most impressive when shrouded in mist (which they often are).

Most visitors come here to raft the Dunajec river (adult/child 250/100Sk, canoe trips 300Sk; ◷ mid-Apr-Oct) but that's not the only attraction; it's worth coming just to hike or cycle through the gorge on the Slovak side (no such trail exists on the Polish side). In midsummer a 20Sk 'trail fee' is charged to enter the national park.

Rafting trips depart from two locations at Červený Kláštor: opposite the monastery and at another landing 2km upriver (west of the village). All raft trips end at the Polish border, where there's a foot-only crossing, open all year during the day. A raft will set out only when 12 passengers gather, and when business is slow you may have to wait around. The rafts (called *plte*) are long and uncomfortably narrow yet more stable than they first appear.

EAST SLOVAKIA

RAFTING IN POLAND

The Dunajec river divides Slovakia and Poland, though once on the river it's something like an international free-for-all, with rafts from both countries competing for customers.

At the moment the Poles are winning the contest – they have better guides, are better organised, and offer much longer trips, including a two-day, 50km voyage from Katy to Krościenko.

Depending on your stamina and visa status, it may be worthwhile crossing over into Poland to do your rafting from there. There's a pedestrian-only border crossing (to the Polish town of Szczawnica) at the **Lesnica raft landing** (◷ 9am-9pm Apr-Sep, 9am-5pm Oct-Mar). Visas are not issued here, so check with the closest Polish embassy to arrange a visa if you require one.

From Szczawnica there are frequent daily buses to Nowy Targ (38km), from where there are six daily buses to the main Polish rafting centre at Katy (31km). By car, you can cross the Slovak–Polish border at Lysá nad Dunajcom (6km west of Červený Kláštor) or Mníšek nad Popradom (46km east of Červený Kláštor).

The 9km journey beneath the towering walls of the gorge takes one to 1½ hours. The river is quite calm except for a few shallow rapids – great fun, but not for adrenaline junkies.

From the downriver terminus near Lesnica, you can hike the 8km back to the monastery, take a taxi (around 300Sk) or rent a bicycle (60Sk per hour) and pedal back along the river.

CARTHUSIAN MONASTERY & CHURCH

While waiting for your raft trip, or the bus, visit the once-powerful, 14th-century **Carthusian Monastery & Church** (☎ 482 29 55; adult/child 40/20Sk; ⏰ 9am-5pm May-Oct), which is at the gorge's mouth. Inside is a museum with folk crafts and some superb, 16th-century frescoes.

Festivals & Events

The annual **Zamaguria Folk Festival** (Zamagurský folklórny festival) in the middle of June is held mainly in a camping ground near a monastery (see below). Each September the **International Pieniny Canoe Slalom** (medzinárodný pieninský slalom) is held on the river here.

Sleeping & Eating

In July and August, hotels – and even camp sites – fill quickly on weekends, when you may have to fall back on a private room in the area. A perfect contact for private rooms is **CK Pieniny Klub** (☎ 439 73 03; www.sl.sinet.sk/pieniny), based in Lesnica, which can arrange a room for around 230Sk per person. Also note that it's nearly impossible to find accommodation outside the rafting season (April to October); your best chance is Pieniny chata, which opens earlier and closes later than the competition.

Hotel Pldnik (☎ 482 25 25; pltnik@szm.sk; s/d 300/600Sk; Ⓟ) An above average hotel with a restaurant, summer garden and, for some reason, a small football field. It's often booked out in summer.

Hotel Dunajec (☎ 439 71 05; s/d 600/1200Sk; person/tent/car/bungalow 50/50/50/440Sk) One kilometre up the road to Veľký Lipník from the monastery is Hotel Dunajec, with a rather ordinary camp site and a restaurant packed with busloads of tourists in summer. It also rents out mountain bikes for 350Sk per day.

Pieniny chata (☎ 439 75 30; s/d 240/480Sk) Near Lesnica is this inexpensive *chata* with basic rooms and a half-decent restaurant.

There are several *pensions* in Červený Kláštor and just across a small stream from the monastery is a quiet **camping ground** (person/tent/car 30/40/50Sk; ⏰ mid-Jun–mid-Sep).

Getting There & Away

Direct buses go frequently to Červený Kláštor from Poprad (81Sk, two hours) and, via Stará Ľubovňa, to Košice (152Sk, 3½ hours). Only one bus per day, Monday to Friday, runs to Lesnica from Stará Ľubovňa via Veľký Lipník (36Sk, 50 minutes).

SLOVAK KARST

☎ 058

The Slovak Karst (Slovenský kras) is a region of limestone canyons and caves at the eastern end of the Slovak Ore Mountains (Slovenské rudohorie), a major range that reaches to the border with Hungary. Its most spectacular landscapes are within the 440 sq km Slovak Karst Protected Landscape Region (Chránená krajinná oblast Slovenský kras), promoted to a Unesco World Heritage site in 1995.

The region's highlights include Domica Cave (Domica jaskyňa), said to be one of the biggest caves in the world; Zádielska canyon near the Hungarian border; and the dramatic Krásna Hôrka Castle. The region's most interesting festival, Gombasek's **Hungarian Folk Festival**, takes place in late July.

Public transportation is poor throughout the region, making it nearly impossible to see more than one cave in a day, usually by bus from Rožňava.

ROŽŇAVA

pop 19,300

A good base for exploring the Slovak Karst, Rožňava is an otherwise drab, former mining town with a big Hungarian-speaking minority. It was the region's main gold-, silver- and iron-mining centre until the 17th century when manufacturing took over as the town's main industry.

Orientation & Information

The train station is 2.5km south of námestie Baníkov, the town centre, and connected by an irregular bus service (none on weekends). The bus station is one block southeast of the centre, on Zeleného stromu.

The **AiCES information centre** (☎ 732 81 01; www.roznava.sk; námestie Baníkov 32; ☺ 8am-6pm Mon-Fri, 8am-4pm Sat, noon-4pm Sun Jun-Sep, 8am-4pm Mon-Fri, 9am-2pm Sat Oct-May) books private rooms and has plenty of information about the caves and public transport.

The **main post office** (Čučmianska) is just north of námestie Baníkov.

Sights
Námestie Baníkov's baroque buildings include the former **town hall**, and the 1654 **tower** (adult/child 30/15Sk; ☺ 10-11.30am & 1-5.30pm Mon-Fri, 10am-3.30pm Sat, noon-3.30pm Sun) standing in the middle of the square. At the northwest end of the square is the **Bishops' Cathedral**, with a Renaissance altar depicting miners at work.

Sleeping & Eating
The tourist office books private rooms for around 300Sk per person.

Hotel Čierny orol (☎ 32 81 86; námestie Baníkov 17; s/d from 500/1000Sk; Ⓟ) The best place in town has large, modern rooms and an excellent restaurant (mains around 100Sk).

Atrium (☎ 0907 589 901; Čučmianska 30; mains around 100Sk) North of the post office, the Atrium has good Slovak dishes and a lovely courtyard.

Getting There & Away
Rožňava is on the railway line between Košice (104Sk, one hour) and Zvolen (198Sk, 2½ hours), with four fast trains a day and more frequent local services to Košice (88Sk, 1¾ hours).

There are hourly buses to Krásna Hôrka Castle (9Sk, 10 minutes) and up to three a day to Dedinky (48Sk, one hour).

AROUND ROŽŇAVA
Krásna Hôrka Castle & Krásnohorské Podhradie
Krásna Hôrka Castle (☎ 732 47 69; adult/child 70/40Sk; ☺ 8am-4.30pm Tue-Sun May-Oct, 9.30am-2pm Tue-Sun Nov-Apr), on a hill above the village of Krásnohorské Podhradie, was built as a feudal residence in 1320. In the 16th century it was bought by the Andrássy family, renovated in Renaissance style and further fortified against the Turks. The building

burned down in 1817, but in the early part of the 20th century the last of the line, Count Dionysius Andrássy, restored it and turned it into a family museum.

The old village of Krásnohorské Podhradie below the castle has little to offer that isn't Andrássy-related. The **Andrássy Gallery** (☎ 732 42 38; Lipová; adult/child 5/3Sk; ☺ 9am-5pm Tue-Fri, 9am-2pm Sun) has a collection of 20 paintings, including Andrássy family portraits. The stunning **Art Nouveau Mausoleum** (☎ 732 20 34; adult/child 20/10Sk; ☺ 8am-4.30pm Tue-Sun May-Oct, 9.30am-2pm Tue-Sun Nov-Apr) of Dionysius Andrássy and his wife, Františka, is out on the road towards Košice, surrounded by a pleasant park. The sumptuous interior includes samples of marble from all over the world.

The green, shady **ATC Krásna Hôrka camping ground** (☎ 732 54 57; person/tent/car 130/40/100Sk) is just beyond the village on the way to the castle.

Krásnohorské Podhradie is about 8km east of Rožňava, with buses serving it almost hourly. Many (up to 11 daily) continue to Košice, 1¼ hours away. The train station is about 1km south of the town at Lípovník. The castle, visible from everywhere, is a 3km walk east of the village.

Betliar
The attraction of this town, 4km north of Rožňava, is a grand **chateau** (☎ 798 31 18; adult/child 70/40Sk; ☺ 8am-4.30pm Tue-Sun May-Oct, 9.30am-2pm Tue-Sun Nov-Apr), built in the 18th century for the Andrássy family. It's stuffed with their belongings and furnishings, relics collected in Africa and Asia, and a library of 20,000 books.

There are hourly buses through here from Rožňava (8Sk, 10 minutes). At least half a dozen trains stop daily at the station (11Sk), south of the village.

CAVES OF THE SLOVAK KARST
The whole of the Slovak Karst region contains 47 known caves (jaskyňa), but only a few are open to the public. Four of the major ones are described here. A fifth – Krásnohorská Cave – is soon to be opened; it contains the tallest stalagmite in the world (32.6m). Contact the AiCES office in Rožňava for more details. Unfortunately, public transport in the district is a bit sparse, especially on weekends.

Ochtinská Cave (Ochtinská Aragonitová Jaskyňa; ☎ 488 10 51; adult/child 90/50Sk; ☼ tours hourly 9am-4pm Tue-Sun Jun-Aug, half-hourly 9.30am-2pm Tue-Sun Apr-May & Sep-Oct), about 22km west of Rožňava, is one of the more striking caves – though one corner shows the effects of vandalism by a squad of drunken soldiers. Delicate aragonites, which are basically 'inside-out stalactites', are made up of thin limestone tubes that water passes through leaving deposits at the growing end. They twist in all directions, some resembling flowers.

Hotel Hrádok (☎ 486 01 10; r from 700Sk; P ⊠ ⊇), close to the cave entrance and surrounded by woods, is value for money. Its rooms are large and comfy, and each has a balcony. There's also a restaurant here.

From Tuesday to Friday, five buses run between Rožňava and the cave, and drop to two on weekends (28Sk).

Gombasecká Cave (Gombasecká Jaskyňa; ☎ 788 20 20; adult/child 60/50Sk; ☼ tours hourly 9am-4pm Tue-Sun Jun-Aug, half-hourly 9.30am-2pm Tue-Sun Apr-May & Sep-Oct), with its white and red-brown walls, and stalagmites and stalactites of all shapes and sizes, is perhaps the most accessible cave, only 15 minutes by bus from Rožňava (13Sk, eight Tuesday-Friday only).

Domica Cave (Domica Jaskyňa; ☎ 788 20 10; adult/child 80/40Sk, with boat trip 110/60Sk; ☼ tours 9am, 10.30am, 12.30am, 2pm, 3pm, 4pm Tue-Sun Jun-Aug, half-hourly 9.30am-2pm Tue-Sun Feb-May & Sep-Dec) is the biggest, best-known and most beautiful cave, full of colour and with some stalactites as thick as tree trunks. Almost 2km of the 5km length of the so-called Gothic House (Gotický dôm) is accessible by boat along the underground river Styx.

This cave is part of a 22km cave system, most of which is in Hungary (where it's called Baradla). There is talk of future tours taking in the Hungarian caves too, but talk has been going on for some time.

Domica is 28km south of Rožňava, via Plešivec. Buses depart up to 10 times a day from Tuesday to Friday (36Sk, 45 minutes) and three times on weekends. You can hike to Domica from Gombasek (15km) on a yellow and then a red trail via Silica.

The small and less-visited **Jasov Cave** (Jasovská Jaskyňa; ☎ 055-466 41 65; adult/child 60/30Sk; ☼ tours hourly 9am-4pm Tue-Sun Jun-Aug, half-hourly 9.30am-2pm Tue-Sun Apr-May & Sep-Oct) has been open to visitors since 1846, but it bears some graffiti apparently left by Hussites in

the 15th century. Over 2km long, about a quarter of its extent is open for tours.

The only place to stay is **Autokemping Jasov** (☎ 055-466 42 42; person/tent/car/bungalow 50/50/20/550Sk), on the north side of Jasov past a closed chateau. It has a rundown but altogether pleasant atmosphere, and a simple **restaurant**.

This cave is just south of Jasov, which means a 40km trip east of Rožňava to Moldava nad Bodvou, then 10km north. It's reached fairly easily by train from Rožňava, with a change at Moldava nad Bodvou (44Sk, 45 minutes); six trains a day go from Moldava to Jasov (17Sk, 20 minutes).

ZÁDIELSKA CANYON

Over 2km long, hemmed in by 250m cliffs, and at its narrowest just 10m wide, Zádielska Canyon (Zádielska tiesňava) has been carved by the little Blatnica stream (*potok*) from the limestone tablelands at the eastern edge of the Slovak Karst. The canyon itself was declared a nature reserve in 1986.

From the village of Zádiel it's an easy but dramatic 2km walk up through the wooded canyon on a red-marked trail. At the top you can backtrack or, if you take a trail along the rim of the canyon east and south to Turnianske Podhradie, it's just over a 4km walk back to the Košice road.

Rožňava–Košice buses (36Sk, 30 minutes) and local trains (32Sk, 30 minutes) stop at Dvorníky, from where it's 1km north to Zádiel.

ŠARIŠ REGION

PREŠOV

☎ 051 / pop 92,800

Prešov (Eperjes in Hungarian, Preschau in German) is a sprawling industrial centre. Many of the historical buildings on the main square have been renovated (most were heavily damaged during WWII) and although it's an attractive place, there's not much to see.

History

Archaeologists say there was a Slav settlement based in Prešov by the end of the 8th century. Hungarian colonists arrived in the 11th century, followed by German settlers in the 13th. Prešov received a royal charter in 1374 and, like Bardejov to the north and

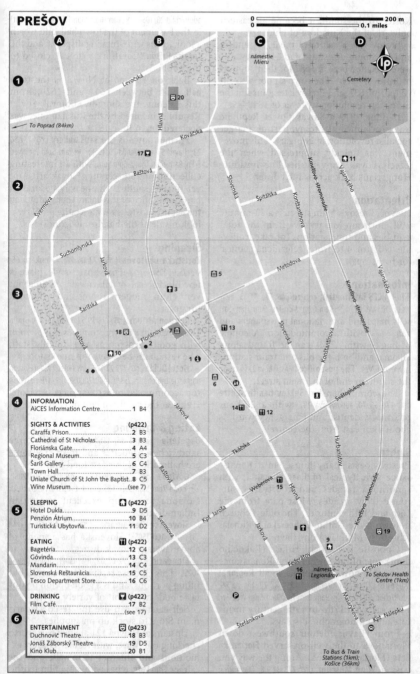

PREŠOV

0 _____ 200 m
0 _____ 0.1 miles

To Poprad (84km)

EAST SLOVAKIA

To Sekcov Health Centre (1km)

To Bus & Train Stations (1km); Košice (36km)

Košice to the south, it became an eastern bulwark of the Kingdom of Hungary.

Prešov was a centre of the 17th-century anti-Habsburg uprisings, and 24 Protestants were executed here in 1687 for their support of Imre Thököly. The town's poor also revolted, in 1831, and Prešov later joined in the European revolutionary fever of 1848–49.

In June 1919 a Slovak Soviet Republic was proclaimed at Prešov, part of a larger socialist revolution in Hungary. This movement was quickly suppressed when the Czechoslovak army pushed the invading Hungarians back across the border.

Orientation

Hlavná, Prešov's main street, is a 20-minute walk north up Masarykova from the adjacent bus and train stations (or take trolleybus No 1 or 4 to/from 'železničná stanica' for two stops).

Information

The **AiCES information centre** (☎ 773 11 13; pis@pis.sk; Hlavná 67; ☺ 9am-6pm Mon-Fri, 9am-1pm Sat) sells maps and international newspapers and can assist with accommodation. A couple of banks with ATMs can be found along Hlavná, and both the bus and train stations have ATMs. The **post office** (Masarykova 2) is near the southern end of the main street.

The comprehensive **Sekčov health centre** (☎ 770 56 70; Jurkovičova 19), with a 24-hour pharmacy, dentist and emergency ward, is about 1km east from the centre.

Sights

Prešov boasts many houses in a Renaissance style typical of East Slovakia, with sgraffitoed façades and courtyards surrounded by arcades. Most date from the 16th and 17th centuries. The oldest church in town is the Gothic **Cathedral of St Nicholas** (chrám sv Mikuláše) on Hlavná.

Opposite is Rákóchi House (Rákóciho dom), one of the town's finest Renaissance houses. It now contains a small **Regional Museum** (Okresné múzeum; ☎ 759 82 20; Hlavná 86; adult/child 30/10Sk; ☺ 9am-6pm Tue, 9am-5pm Wed-Fri, 1-6pm Sun), with 17th- to 19th-century furniture and ethnographic displays.

From Hlavná, detour southwest down Floriánova to the well-preserved **Floriánska Gate** (Floriánska brána). Along the way you pass a **Wine Museum** (☎ 773 31 08; Floriánova;

adult/child 20/10Sk; ☺ 8am-6pm Mon-Fri, 8am-noon Sat) in the basement of the town hall, and worth a look for its wine-making displays; and the **Caraffa Prison** (Caraffova väznica), closed to the public.

Back on Hlavná at No 73 is the **town hall**, built between 1511 and 1520; from this balcony, the short-lived Slovak Soviet Republic, inspired by the Russian one, was declared on 16 June 1919.

Further down is the **Šariš Gallery** (☎ 772 54 23; Hlavná 51; adult/child 20/10Sk; ☺ 9am-5pm Tue, Wed & Fri, 8am-6pm Thu, 2-6pm Sun), with an interesting collection of 20th-century Slovak art. And yet further south is the heavily decorated, baroque edifice of the **Uniate Church of St John the Baptist** (kostol sv Jána Krstiteľa). Have a look inside at the handsome iconostasis.

Sleeping

Turistická ubytovňa (☎ 772 06 28; Vajanského 65; s/d 250/500Sk; ℗) This hostel-style place a few blocks east of Hlavná has simple but very clean, modern rooms and a kitchen for guests.

Penzión Átrium (☎ 773 39 52, Floriánova 4; r from 1100Sk) Another central choice is this *pension* with good-sized rooms and friendly staff. The restaurant here gets top marks too.

Hotel Dukla (☎ 772 27 41; www.hotelduklapresov.sk; námestie Legionárov 2; s/d 1400/2000Sk; ℗) Prešov's top accommodation is the spruced-up Hotel Dukla at the southern end of Hlavná.

Eating & Drinking

Bagetéria (Hlavná 36; sandwiches 40-60Sk) Large sandwiches, baguettes and fresh croissants are hallmarks of this fast food joint.

Góvinda (☎ 772 28 19; Hlavná 70; mains 80-120Sk; ☺ noon-7pm Mon-Sat) Like its twin in Košice, Góvinda serves up excellent vegetarian Indian dishes.

Slovenská Reštaurácia (☎ 772 48 27; Hlavná 13; mains 100-150Sk) Slovenská has a menu of above-average Slovak dishes.

Mandarin (☎ 772 07 02; Hlavná 41; mains around 100Sk) This Chinese restaurant has small but filling portions, and is a good option if your taste buds need a bit of variety.

Self-caterers can use the Tesco Department Store to stock up on supplies.

Upstairs at Hlavná 121 are two bars worth checking out: **Wave**, with regular DJs, art exhibitions and Internet terminals; and the calmer **Film Café**, a bar with a big film fetish.

Entertainment

Jonáš Záborský Theatre (☎ 772 46 22; Námestie Legionárov 6) has occasional music and drama performances. Also check the **Duchnovič Theatre** (☎ 772 32 61; Jarková 77) for plays, often in Rusin language. For films, try **Kino Klub** (☎ 771 31 03) in the dom kultúrý.

Getting There & Away

Prešov is 36km north of Košice (38Sk, 30 minutes), on the Kraków–Budapest train line (the daily express between the two stops here). There are also daily local trains to Košice (38Sk, 45 minutes) and Bardejov (50Sk, 1¼ hours). Buses with a dozen or more departures a day are to and from Košice (44Sk, 35 minutes), Bardejov (53Sk, 50 minutes), Svidník (71Sk, 1½ hours), Levoča (81Sk, 1½ hours), Poprad (116Sk, 1¾ hours) and Stará Ľubovňa (81Sk, 1¾ hours).

BARDEJOV

☎ 054 / pop 33,200

Bardejov, in the foothills of the Lower Beskydy mountains, is one of the major towns of the Šariš region. Its small, preserved old town can be seen in an afternoon, but stay a day to visit the superb *skansen* in nearby Bardejovské Kúpele (p425).

History

Bardejov received municipal privileges in 1320 and it became a free royal town in 1376. Trade between Poland and Russia passed through the town and in the 15th century the Bardejov merchants grew rich, mainly through the production of cloth and fabrics.

The Thirty Years' War stopped the town's development in its tracks, but saved its fine Renaissance and Gothic centre from being renovated away. This town centre, a total of 84 buildings, was painstakingly restored between 1970 and 1990 at a cost of almost US$9 million. The result is a contribution to Europe's architectural heritage that earned Bardejov a gold medal in 1986 and Unesco World Heritage status in 2000.

Orientation & Information

The bus and train station is a five-minute walk northeast from Radničné námestie, the town's main square.

The helpful **AiCES information centre** (☎ 488 26 73; www.bardejov.sk; Radničné námestie 21; 9am-6pm Mon-Fri, 10am-noon, 1.30-4pm Sat, 10am-noon Sun mid-Jun–mid-Sep, 9am-4.30pm Mon-Fri mid-Sep–mid-Jun) can assist with guides, accommodation and currency exchange.

For Internet access, head to the small **Internet café** (☎ 0904 852 803; Radničné námestie 12; 35Sk per hr) on the main square. The train station has a **left-luggage office** (6am-7pm Mon-Fri, 7am-6pm Sat & Sun).

Všeobecná úverová banka (VÚB; ☎ 472 26 71; Kellerova 1) has an ATM, and the main **post office** (Dlhý rad 14) is just outside the city walls.

Sights

On the walk from the station to the main square you pass through the restored **Upper Gate** (Dolná brána). Other remnants of the town's original defences include the **Powder Gate** (Prašná brána) to the south and the chunky, 14th-century **bastion** on Dlhý rad to the northwest, now occupied by a bar.

At the northern end of cobbled Radničné námestie is the 15th-century **Basilica of St Egídius** (Bazilika sv Egídia; adult/child 25/10Sk, tower 40/20Sk; 10am-4.30pm Mon-Fri, 10am-2.30pm Sat, 11.30am-2pm Sun), with one of central Europe's most splendid Gothic interiors, full of paintings, carved wood and stone, and 11 altars. Note the beautifully carved main column.

The former **town hall** (☎ 474 60 38; Radničné námestie 48; adult/child 35/10Sk; 8.30am-noon & 12.30-5pm), in the middle of the main square, was built in 1509 and is a unique piece of early Renaissance architecture; the bay staircase, the carved stone portals and the wooden inlay ceiling in the Meeting Room are all worth a look. The town hall also has a historical exhibition on the Šariš region, with paintings, coins, weapons and handwritten books.

More impressive as collections go is the **Šariš Icon Museum** (☎ 472 20 09; Radničné námestie 27; adult/child 35/10Sk; 8.30am-noon & 12.30-5pm). Highlights include the church icons and models of wooden churches and a 17th-century painting of the Last Judgement with gruesome depictions of Hell.

Across the street is another branch of the Šariš Museum, the not-so-enthralling **Nature Museum of Northeastern Slovakia** (☎ 472 26 30; Rhoduho 4; adult/child 35/10Sk; 8.30am-noon, 12.30-5pm). A third branch of the **Šariš Museum** (☎ 472 49 66; Radničné námestie 13; adult/child 35/10Sk; 8.30am-noon & 12.30-5pm) has temporary exhibits.

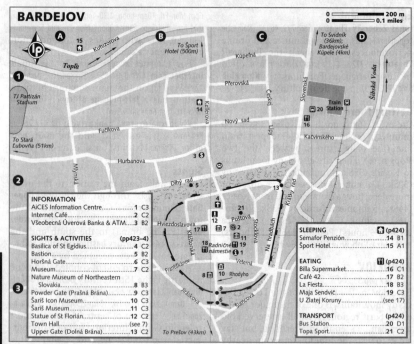

BARDEJOV

0 — 200 m
0 — 0.1 miles

To Svidník (36km); Bardejovské Kúpele (4km)

To Šport Hotel (500m)

TJ Partizán Stadium

To Stará Ľubovňa (51km)

To Prešov (43km)

INFORMATION
AiCES Information Centre.................. 1 C3
Internet Café.................................. 2 C2
Všeobecná Úverová Banka & ATM....3 B2

SIGHTS & ACTIVITIES (pp423–4)
Basilica of St Egídius....................... 4 C2
Bastion... 5 B2
Horšná Gate.................................. 6 C3
Museum.. 7 C2
Nature Museum of Northeastern
  Slovakia..................................... 8 B3
Powder Gate (Prašná Brána)............ 9 C3
Šariš Icon Museum....................... 10 C3
Šariš Museum.............................. 11 C3
Statue of St Florián...................... 12 C2
Town Hall................................(see 7)
Upper Gate (Dolná Brána)............ 13 C2

SLEEPING (p424)
Semafor Penzión.......................... 14 B1
Šport Hotel................................. 15 A1

EATING (p424)
Billa Supermarket......................... 16 C1
Café 42....................................... 17 B2
La Fiesta..................................... 18 B3
Maja Sendvič.............................. 19 C3
U Zlatej Koruny.......................(see 17)

TRANSPORT (p424)
Bus Station................................. 20 D1
Topa Sport................................. 21 C2

Two of the best Renaissance and baroque houses on the square are the municipal building at No 16 and a former inn at No 42. The 18th-century **Great Synagogue** (Mlynská) is boarded up and sadly falling to pieces.

Festivals & Events
The town hosts several festivals; one of the liveliest is **Jarmork** (The Market) around the end of August, when Radničné námestie turns into one big marketplace.

Sleeping & Eating
There aren't a lot of options in town.

Semafor Penzión (☎ 0905 830 984; semafor@ stonline.sk; Kellerova 13; s/d 700/900Sk; P) Easily the best option is this superb *pension* with bright, large, modern rooms, a kitchen for guests and unbelievably helpful owners.

Šport Hotel (☎ 472 49 49; Kutuzovova 34; r from 500Sk; P) In a two-storey block overlooking the Topľa River, Šport Hotel has basic rooms.

La Fiesta (☎ 474 25 84; Radničné námestie 31; pizzas around 100Sk) A cellar-like place with large

pizzas, a lively atmosphere and a cheap midday menu (70Sk).

U zlatej koruny (☎ 472 53 10; Radničné námestie 41; mains 100-150Sk) Upstairs, this restaurant serves good, if typical, Slovak meals.

Maja sendvič (Radničné námestie 15; sandwiches 30-50Sk) is the place to go for a quick bite on the run; and **Café 42** (Hviezdoslavova; coffee 30Sk) is a fine spot to rest those weary feet.

There's a handy **Billa supermarket** (Slovenská) within spitting distance from the bus and train stations.

Getting There & Around
Local trains run between Bardejov and Prešov (50Sk, 1¼ hours) but if you're coming from Košice, buses are faster (53Sk, one hour). If you want to go to the High Tatras, look for a bus to Poprad (128Sk, 2½ hours); there is one bus daily direct to Starý Smokovec (152Sk, three hours), three to Bratislava (572Sk, eight-10 hours) and six to Žilina (308Sk, 4½-six hours).

Topa Sport (☎ 474 42 82; Poštová 1; 9am-5pm Mon-Fri, 9am-noon Sat) rents bicycles for 30/ 100Sk per hour/day.

BARDEJOVSKÉ KÚPELE

Just 4km north of Bardejov is Bardejovské Kúpele, a pleasant little spa town where diseases of the alimentary and respiratory tracts are treated. It was founded in the 13th century but only developed as a spa in the 1920s. Because of a big fire early in the 20th century, there's not much history to look at – a deficiency amply filled by Slovakia's best *skansen*, set in the spa's foothills. A good time to visit is mid-July for the annual two-day Rusin–Šariš Folk Festival.

Orientation & Information

The bus station is at the spa's southeast end; turn left onto the main road and go straight ahead for the Hotel Minerál (300m) and *skansen* (800m).

There's no tourist office here, but the AiCES in Bardejov can supply you with a free map.

Sights

Even if you haven't booked a spa cure, you're welcome to partake of the drinking cure. Crowds of locals constantly pace up and down the 1972 **colonnade** (⊙ 6-8am, 10.30am-1pm & 4.30-6.30pm), where an unending supply of hot, sulphurous mineral water streams from eight different springs.

Near the colonnade is a superb **skansen** (adult/child 35/10Sk; ⊙ 8.30am-5pm), with 24 full-scale buildings ranging from old barns and smithy workshops to rustic houses and wooden churches, all brought here from villages across Slovakia. The *skansen*'s layout has a snug village feel, and there are

---

WOODEN CHURCHES OF EAST SLOVAKIA

East Slovakia has its own typical wooden churches, the product of overlapping Slovak, Polish and Ukrainian cultures. Most of the churches are Greek Catholic or Uniate, with some Russian Orthodox; there are very few Roman Catholic ones.

Most churches that are still standing were built in the 18th century, though the earliest dates from around 1500. Their simple, yet somehow sublime, outward appearance belie their rich, colourful interiors packed to overflowing with religious images. Though they are protected national monuments, many are still used for services; the feeling you get on entering these works of art is not one of viewing a tourist attraction, but rather one of witnessing real human devotion to God, and to the churches themselves.

All have some elements in common, such as shingled roofs, but they differ in size and shape, and whether they have onion-domed towers (from one to three) or plain, simple towers. The typical Rusin church is built in or near a village, in a dominant position but away from other structures. The most common wood used in their construction is spruce, but oak and beech are also used. The most important feature of all churches is the iconostasis, which separates the sanctuary and altar from the nave. Icons on this may include the Last Supper, the Madonna and Child, the Last Judgement, and often the saint to whom the church is dedicated.

The Eastern Borderlands (p426) has the largest concentration of such churches in Slovakia, but you can also find examples in the *skansens* at Svidník, Humenné and Bardejovské Kúpele, and the East Slovak Museum in Košice.

The following churches around Bardejov are relatively easy to reach:

■ **Jedlinka** This small three-tower Greek-Catholic church (1763) with a baroque interior was built in honour of the Mother Mary, of whom there is a highly prized icon. It's 14km north of Bardejov, and frequent buses between Svidník and Bardejov stop here.

■ **Lukov – Venecia** The Orthodox church of SS Cosmas & Damian (1708–09) here has a very fine iconostasis made in two different eras: the lower part was made in 1736 by the Bardejov artist Andrej Gajecký; the top part is from the second half of the 18th century. It's 14km west of Bardejov; several buses pass through the village daily.

■ **Hervartov** The Roman Catholic Church of St Francis of Assisi at Hervartov is the oldest wooden church in Slovakia. The interior of the nave is from 1665, and is richly decorated with frescoes. It's 9km southwest of Bardejov; at least three buses daily travel between the town and Bardejov.

plenty of nice touches, like beehives made of straw, and frilled domes on the church.

If you're after a treatment or simply a massage, head to the **Spa House** (☎ 477 44 70; www.kupele-bj.sk), just north of the colonnade. Prices range from 50Sk to 1500Sk, but most treatments are close to the 200Sk mark.

Sleeping

Almost all of the hotels are reserved for patients undergoing medical treatment. The only option is **Hotel Minerál** (☎ 472 41 22; hotel.mi neral.bardejov@satel-slovakia.sk; s/d 880/1200Sk; **P**) with large, but not particularly modern rooms.

Getting There & Away

There's no train station here, but Barde-jovské Kúpele is connected hourly to Bardejov by city bus Nos 1, 2, 7, 8, 10 and 12. The last bus back is at around 7.30pm. Otherwise it's an easy 3km walk north from Bardejov, with the last 1.5km meandering through wooded countryside.

EASTERN BORDERLANDS

It's hard to imagine that this little visited cor-ner of Slovakia is part of the same country as bustling Bratislava and the tourist-swamped High Tatras. Life here is generally quiet and rural and the connection to neighbouring Ukraine can be seen everywhere – many vil-lage name-signs use the Cyrillic alphabet and the region is home to a large Rusin minority (see boxed text opposite).

Must-sees in the Eastern Borderlands in-clude striking wooden churches which dot the countryside and a real surprise find, the Andy Warhol museum in Medzilaborce.

MICHALOVCE

☎ 056 / pop 39,900

There's little reason to stop here except to change buses or stay the night en route to Humenné, Medzilaborce or the Vihorlatské Highlands.

From the bus station, cross the road and turn left onto the main drag, námestie Osvoboditeľov. The **AiCES information centre** (☎ 642 35 55; námestie Osvoboditeľov 77; ◷ 8am-6pm Mon-Fri, 8am-noon Sat), 300m ahead, is pretty hopeless. The train station is 1km southwest of the centre; follow Stanična to Humenská and turn right, then go left on Štefánikova.

If you have a couple of hours between buses, the renovated main street, complete with musical fountain, is quite pleasant to stroll down, or check out the **Zemplínske múzeum** (☎ 644 10 93; Kostolné námestie 1; adult/child 40/10Sk; ◷ 9am-noon & 1-4pm Tue-Fri), in the chateau behind the bus station, which has exhibits on regional history and folklore.

Four-star **Hotel Jalta** (☎ 642 60 86; www.jalta.sk; námestie Osvoboditeľov 70; s/d 1400/2200Sk; **P**) is the best place to stay in town, with very spacious, modern rooms and a decent restaurant.

Getting There & Away

There are plenty of buses from Košice (81Sk, 1½ hours) and almost hourly serv-ices to Sobrance (28Sk, 30 minutes). There's a regular train service to Humenné (44Sk, 30 minutes) but only one, at 1.57pm, con-tinues directly onto Medzilaborce (76Sk, two hours).

VIHORLATSKÉ HIGHLANDS & AROUND

The **Vihorlatské Highlands** (Vihorlatské vrchy), east of Michalovce, have some scenic areas for walking, particularly around the popular lake of Morské oko. There is also a major, though not very interesting, resort at the ar-tificial lake of Zemplínska šírava, south of the highlands. If you do plan to avail your-self of the lake's facilities, skip around its northern edge to one of the smaller villages such as Kaluža or Klokočov. Here you'll find camping grounds, the best beaches and the possibility of boat hire.

Bordering both Poland and Ukraine is the 29,805-hectare **Poloniny National Park**, a wild area 90% forested with beech and fir-oak trees and home to the likes of wolves, lynxes and wild cats. Its network of walking and cycling tracks are perfect for escaping the crowds.

Plonked between the Vihorlatské High-lands and Poloniny National Park is the nondescript town of **Snina**, which has an excellent **AiCES information centre** (☎ 768 57 35; unitur@stonline.sk; Strojárska 102; ◷ 8am-5pm Mon-Fri, 8am-4pm Sat & Sun Jun-Sep, closed Sun Oct-May) towards its eastern end. The office can help with accommodation, transport, informa-tion on walks and wooden churches, and arranges bike tours throughout the sur-rounding area (there are plans to rent out bikes for 100Sk per day, but nothing had been confirmed at the time of writing).

RUTHENIA AND THE RUSINS

The Rusins (Rusíni) are an eastern Slavic people who over many centuries have developed a distinct culture and dialect, as well as their own brand of Orthodox Christianity. No-one knows their true origins, but for centuries they were an isolated group of farmers and woodcutters. Shifting borders saw their homeland fall variously within Lithuania, Poland and the Austro-Hungarian Empire, though they never acquired a self-governing territory of their own.

When Czechoslovakia was founded after WWI, a large part of Hungarian Ruthenia called Podkarpatská Rus (Sub-Carpathian Ruthenia) was included in the new state. It achieved a brief period of semiautonomy in 1938 but was quickly taken over by Hungary in 1939. The Czechoslovak state ceded part of Ruthenia to Stalin's Russia in 1945, leaving a minority of Rusins in Slovakia.

Today most of historical Ruthenia falls within Ukraine, with its 'capital' at Uzhgorod. Slovakia has no official centre of Rusin culture, although Prešov and Svidník could feasibly take the title. Prešov is home to the Rusin-slanted Duchnovič Theatre (the 7th World Congress of Rusin Culture was recently held here) and the Rusin newspaper *Nardony Novynky*. Svidník is physically closer to the Ukraine and boasts a *skansen* of Rusin architecture, a museum of Ukraine-Rusin culture and hosts the Rusin-Ukrainian Cultural Festival every June.

According to the 2001 census, only 24,000 Slovaks called themselves Rusin, though there are thought to be many more. Another one million live in the Ukraine, and there are 60,000 in Poland. Over the last 10 years there has been a low-key campaign for greater Ruthenian autonomy within the Ukraine, and even calls for outright independence.

Sights & Activities
WOODEN CHURCHES

Near the Ukrainian border are some beautiful examples of traditional Rusin architecture, striking wooden churches. The churches are best explored by car as transport is rather thin on the ground.

About 16km northeast of Sobrance, on a hill below the tiny village of **Inovce**, is a three-domed church (1840). Halfway through the village of **Ruská Bystra** is another church in fairly good repair. To reach the church at **Hrabová Roztoka**, head 2km off the main road to Šmigovec and turn left (the road is poorly signposted).

The church at **Kalná Roztoka**, 14km east of Snina, is one of the few plastered wooden churches in Slovakia. One of the most impressive churches in the area, 35km east of Snina in the village of **Uličske Krivé**, is quite large, as wooden churches go, and has a highly decorated baroque interior.

Generally churches are locked and only open for services. Outside service times, inquire at the village pub; someone will know who has the key. The cost is usually a small donation to the church (around 20Sk), and a beer for the person who helped you.

HIKING

A vigorous two to three hour walk in the Highlands starts from Remetské Hámre and climbs to lake Morské oko. From Morské oko you can continue north to Sninský kameň (1005m), where you climb a series of ladders to gain fine views from the summit. From there you can continue three hours to Snina and catch a train to Humenné, Michalovce or Košice. The map to have is VKÚ's 1:50,000 *Vihorlatské vrchy* (No 126, 90Sk), with clearly marked walking trails.

A popular day walk within the national park begins at the village of Nová Sedlica and makes a beeline for the highest point in the park, Kremenec (1221m), which marks the converging borders of Slovakia, Poland and Ukraine. The trail then follows a ridge west along the Polish border, taking in the highpoints of Kamenná (1200m) and Dzurkpwiec Durkovec (1189m) before dropping down to the Ruské pass (795m). From here it's possible to cross into Poland (summer-only border crossing; there's also another at Balinca) to a small camping ground and *chata*; otherwise, head south to the village of Topoľa and catch a bus to Snina (28Sk, last bus at 5.52pm Monday to Friday). Don't go anywhere without the VKÚ map *Bukovské Vrchy* (1:50,000, No 118, 90Sk).

Sleeping

If you're bound for the lake of Zemplínska šírava, try **Hotel Poštár** (☎ 056-649 23 50; r 1200Sk; Ⓟ) in Kaluža.

About 3km southeast of Snina in the local summer playground of Sninské Rybniky you'll find a small **camping ground** (☎ 057-768 2285; person/tent/car 20/20/20Sk; ☼ Jun-Aug) and the accommodating **Hotel Kamei** (☎ 057-768 21 87; www.kamei.sk; r from 1100Sk; P).

In Stačkín is the **Hotel Armales** (☎ 057-767 42 47; armales-hotel@armales.sk; s/d 500/1000Sk; P), a modern hotel with comfortable rooms.

Getting There & Away

Buses run frequently from Michalovce to Vinné (9Sk, 15 minutes) and there are almost hourly services to Sobrance (28Sk, 30 minutes). From Sobrance there is only one bus Monday to Saturday to Snina (via Ubĺa, 71Sk, 1½ hours), and two running in the opposite direction. Remetské Hámre can be reached from Sobrance seven times from Monday to Friday (20Sk, 24 minutes). Regular buses connect Humenné with Snina (28Sk, 40 minutes), and there are five buses Monday to Friday from Snina to Nová Sedlica (81Sk, two hours).

Trains run all day between Snina and Humenné (28Sk, 40 minutes), and between Michalovce and Humenné (28Sk, 30 minutes).

HUMENNÉ

☎ 057 / pop 35,200

This peaceful town on the Laborec river has a French-style baroque chateau which began as a Gothic castle, and which now houses a **Museum of Local History** (Vlastivedné múzeum; ☎ 775 22 40; adult/child per exhibition 35/10Sk; museum & skansen 85/50Sk; ☼ 9am-6pm Mon-Fri, 2-6pm Sat & Sun May-Oct), with exhibits on archaeology, local history and feudal housing.

Considerably more interesting is a **skansen** (adult/child 30/15Sk; ☼ 9am-6pm) of about 10 Rusin wooden houses from around the region, dating from the 19th and early 20th centuries. Pride of place goes to a wooden church built in 1754.

The adjacent bus and train stations are 500m due west of the vast, pedestrianised main square, námestie Slobody (really a 600m-long avenue). Turn right onto Staničná and walk below the overpass; the *skansen* and museum are at the square's northern end (turn left), and the Hotel Chemes towards its southern end.

Hotel Chemes (☎ 776 26 09; hotelchemes@ stonline.sk; námestie Slobody 51; s/d from 950/1140Sk;

P) is the best place in town, and has a fine restaurant. Colourful **Yes** (☎ 0903 655 770; námestie Slobody; mains 100-150Sk), midway between Chemes and the museum, is a great place to stop for a bite to eat, and specialises in meat dishes cooked on an open grill.

Getting There & Away

Humenné is 50 minutes from Michalovce, on the same rail spur as Medzilaborce. Trains to and from Košice, Prešov and Bardejov require at least one change. Buses are better for other destinations; there are up to four a day from Svidník (91Sk, two hours), seven from Prešov (91Sk, 1½ hours) and three from Košice (116Sk, two hours).

MEDZILABORCE

☎ 057 / pop 6700

This plain town in the Lower Beskydy, in the far northeast corner of Slovakia, has exactly one strange claim to fame: the **Andy Warhol Family Museum of Modern Art** (☎ 748 0072; adult/child 100/50Sk, tours 200Sk; ☼ 9am-4.30pm Tue-Fri, 10am-3.30pm Sat, 12.30-5pm Sun May-Sep, variable times Oct-Apr).

Though the artist Andy Warhol (1928–87) was born in the USA (in Pittsburgh, as Andrej Varchola), his parents came from the village of Miková, 8km northwest of Medzilaborce. They emigrated to the USA early in the 20th century, as had many other Rusins since the 19th century. Warhol never acknowledged his roots, even though he could speak Rusin. He used to joke, 'I came from nowhere'. The museum was founded after his death by his US and Slovak relatives, especially his brother John.

The museum on Andyho Warhola, the town's main street, is in a crumbling concrete building below the Russian Orthodox church; from the train station turn left on to Andyho Warhola and keep going straight for 800m – look for the Campbell's soup cans framing the door. Inside are family memorabilia and many Warhol originals, including *Red Lenin*, *Campbell Soup II*, *Hammer & Sickle* and *Mao Tse Tung*. There are also paintings by his nephew James Warhol and older brother Paul Warhola. Paul, a chicken farmer living near Pittsburgh, took up painting at the age of 61; his *Heinz Ketchup Bottle* painting sold for $US10,000.

Sleeping & Eating

Opposite the museum is the comfortable **Penzión Andy** (☎ 732 16 40; dpd@he.sknet.sk; Andy Warhola 121; r up to 3 people 1500Sk; **P**), with large apartments and a decent restaurant adorned with Warhol prints.

Getting There & Away

Medzilaborce is up a rail spur from Humenné (50Sk, 1¼ hours, up to six daily). Coming from Prešov, you need to change trains at Strážske. Almost all buses from Prešov (from 106Sk, two to four hours) and Košice (from 150Sk, 2½ to four hours) require a change at Humenné.

SVIDNÍK

☎ 054 / pop 12,400

This bland town is saved only by its excellent *skansen* and a chance to get up close and personal with Rusin culture at its Rusin museum.

Svidník evolved from Vyšný and Nižný (Upper and Lower) Svidník, both of which were destroyed in heavy fighting between German and Soviet forces in November 1944. The Germans knew that if the Soviets breached German defences around the Dukla Pass they could easily advance across the plains to the south, so some of the most ferocious fighting of WWII took place here.

Orientation & Information

There is no train station. The bus station is 500m east of town, just off Centrálna.

The **City Information Centre** (☎ 752 04 61; Sovietskych hrdinov 38; ☽ 9am-4.30pm Mon-Fri) sells maps but is otherwise unhelpful. **Všeobecná úverová banka** (VÚB; ☎ 752 22 59; Centrálna) has an exchange desk, and an ATM.

Sights

The **skansen** (☎ 752 29 52; Festivalová; adult/child 60/30Sk, guided tour extra 100Sk; ☽ 8.30am-6pm Tue-Fri, 10am-6pm Sat & Sun May–mid-Oct) of Rusin culture is a fine collection of traditional architecture and furnishings, and has old houses, barns, a school, fire station, mill and wooden church built in 1776.

The **Museum of Ukraine-Rusin Culture** (☎ 752 22 71; Centrálna 258; adult/child 60/30Sk; ☽ 8.30am-4pm Tue-Fri, 10am-4pm Sat & Sun) offers a good look at traditional Rusin culture and history. Unfortunately, everything is labelled in Slovak and Rusin only; the best bits are the folk dresses and painted Easter eggs.

A five-minute walk brings you to the **Dezider Milly Gallery** (☎ 752 16 84; Partizánska; adult/child 30/10Sk; ☽ 8.30am-4pm Mon-Fri, 10am-4pm Sat & Sun), with its excellent collection of icons from the 16th to 19th centuries, plus paintings by contemporary Rusin artists.

Opposite the *skansen*, on the other side of Bardejovská, stands a 37m-tall **Monument to the Soviet Army** (Pamätník Sovietskej armády) and a common grave for 9000 Soviet soldiers. Closer to the town centre is a **Military Museum** (Vojenské múzeum; ☎ 752 13 97; Bardejovská; adult/child 20/8Sk; ☽ 8am-4pm Tue-Fri, 8.30am-5pm Sat & Sun Jul-Aug, 8am-4pm Tue-Fri,

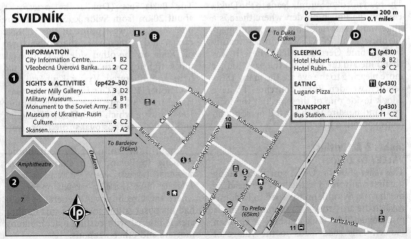

SVIDNÍK

| 0 | 200 m |
| 0 | 0.1 miles |

INFORMATION
City Information Centre............1 B2
Všeobecná Úverová Banka.......2 C2

SIGHTS & ACTIVITIES (pp429–30)
Dezider Milly Gallery.................3 D2
Military Museum.......................4 B1
Monument to the Soviet Army...5 B1
Museum of Ukrainian-Rusin
  Culture...................................6 C2
Skansen...................................7 A2

SLEEPING (p430)
Hotel Hubert.............................8 B2
Hotel Rubin..............................9 C2

EATING (p430)
Lugano Pizza..........................10 C1

TRANSPORT (p430)
Bus Station.............................11 C2

To Dukla (20km)
To Bardejov (36km)
To Prešov (65km)
Amphitheatre

9.45am–2pm Sat & Sun Sep–Jun), which includes photographs and maps of the Dukla battle. Outside, like a military *skansen*, is a collection of tanks, armoured vehicles and a US-made Dakota transport aircraft with Soviet markings.

Festivals & Events

Each year in late June Svidník hosts the **Rusin-Ukrainian Cultural Festival** (Slav-nosti kultúry Rusínov-Ukrajincov Slovenska), with music and dance troupes not only from Slovakia but from the Ukraine, Germany, Scandinavia and elsewhere.

Sleeping & Eating

Hotel Rubín (☎ 752 42 10; Centrálna; s/d 400/800Sk; P) The modern Hotel Rubin is most appealing with plain but comfortable rooms.

Hotel Hubert (☎ 752 32 33; Sovietskych hrdinov 221; s/d 600/1200Sk) Slightly further afield is Hotel Hubert, with the look and feel of an old hunting lodge.

Eating options are grim – both hotels have decent restaurants, or you can dine on pizza and calzone at **Lugano Pizza** (☎ 752 39 90; Sovietskych hrdinov 467; pizzas 80–120Sk).

Getting There & Away

There are regular bus connections to and from Bardejov (48Sk, one hour), Prešov (81Sk, 1½ hours), Košice (116Sk, two hours) and Dukla (28Sk, 40 minutes).

AROUND SVIDNÍK

The road north of Svidník leads to the Dukla Pass on the Polish border, where there is a huge war memorial. This area is an open-air museum of WWII weaponry – mainly Soviet, some German – left where it was abandoned in the battle for the pass. Rather more pleasing to the eye are the many 18th-century, wooden Rusin churches. To have a look inside one of these, ask at the local pub (and be sure to shout the person who helps you out a beer).

Sights & Activities

VALLEY OF DEATH

The **Valley of Death** (Údolí smrti) lies along the first major road to the left after heading north from Svidník on the road to Ladomi-rová; at the crossroads is a monument made of a Soviet T-34 tank crushing a German Panzer. This road leads to the village of **Dobroslava** and its wooden, three-domed church. Along the road are preserved Soviet tanks, seemingly frozen in the act of advancing across the fields. There are two daily buses to Dobroslava from Svidník (13Sk, 15 minutes, none on Sunday).

WOODEN CHURCHES

Head back to the main road and turn left towards **Ladomirová**, the first village northeast of Svidník; it has a handsome, onion-domed church built in 1742. Take the southeast turn-off at Krajná Poľana to reach a second church at **Bodružal** and, on a brief detour almost to the Polish border, the three-domed church at **Príkra**, built in 1777. A few kilometres south of Bodružal is a photogenic three-domed church at **Miroľa**.

Back on the Svidník–Dukla road, in **Nižný Komárnik**, is one of the region's more striking wooden churches, with bright-yellow doors, bits of stained glass and unusually broad towers.

The last village with a church before the Dukla Pass is **Vyšný Komárnik**. A few hundred metres before the Vyšný Komárnik turn-off, on the left (west) side of the highway, is a marker for a 30-minute loop trail past foxholes and anti-aircraft guns.

Buses run to the wooden churches along the main Svidník–Dukla road at regular intervals, but to reach the others you'll need a car.

DUKLA PASS

The **Dukla Pass** (Dukliansky priesmyk), about 20km from Svidník (35 minutes by bus), is the lowest point in the Laborec range, and named after the Polish town of Dukla on the other side. Czechoslovak units fighting with the Soviets crossed here and liberated Vyšný Komárnik on 6 October 1944. The battle for the pass lasted from 8 September to 27 November 1944, during which 85,000 Soviet soldiers and 6500 Czechoslovaks died or were wounded.

About 1km from the 24-hour border crossing to Poland is a 49m stone **war memorial** (admission free; ⏱ 8.30am–5pm Tue–Fri, 9.30am–6pm Sat & Sun mid-Apr–mid-Oct), on the spot where the Czechoslovak General Svoboda had his observation post. The surrounding area is littered with rusting machine guns, mortars and other weapons.

Directory

CONTENTS

ACCOMMODATION

Accommodation options run the gamut from camp sites to hotels at all price levels. You're unlikely ever to get caught out without a place to stay. Most towns have at least one hotel, and even in the smallest village you can usually find someone to rent you a room in their home.

The listings in the sleeping sections of this guidebook come in three broad categories of budget, mid-range and top-end, with the entries listed in order of the author's preference. The general price range split starts at up to 400Kč/600Sk per double for budget options, anything between 400Kč/600Sk and 1500Kč/2000Sk per double for mid-range, and anything above that for top end. As expected, the capitals are more expensive. Bratislava's split is up to 900Sk for budget accommodation and 3000Sk for mid-range. Top dog Prague is in a league of its own, with 'budget' meaning anything from 600Kč to 1300Kč per double, and mid-range places up to 4500Kč. Accommodation in West Bohemian spa towns such as Karlovy Vary and Mariánské Lázně is often 'Prague priced' as well.

Unless otherwise noted, we quote high-season rates. High season varies, but is usually April or May to September or October, plus the Easter and Christmas–New Year holidays. Some places drop their rates in the off season. Major ski areas like the Krkonoše and Tatras mountains have a winter price peak from January to about April that exceeds the summer one, with especially steep hikes at Christmas/New Year, and low-season prices in spring and autumn.

Some hotels are quoting in euros (in anticipation of their inclusion in the EU) and if they do so we've done the same.

Two services you generally have to fork out extra for (more often in Slovakia) are parking and breakfast. Parking can be anything from 100Kč/100Sk per day to 450Kč/300Sk, and breakfast around the 80Kč/100Sk mark.

Note that a new accommodation tax has been introduced in Slovakia; it is usually included in the rate but check beforehand. It's a minimal fee of anything between 10Sk and 15Sk per day, including the day you leave.

Local tourist offices are generally of great help in finding accommodation. Čedok or Satur travel agency offices can also be of assistance, but they often only have hotels on offer. Failing this, stroll around the backstreets and look for signs advertising 'Zimmer frei' (German for 'room available'). If this doesn't work, go into a pub and say 'Hledám levný hotel/Hladám lacný hotel' (I'm looking for a cheap hotel) – and/or dobrý (good), čistý/čistá (clean), blízký (nearby).

Before setting out, try the following websites:

www.travelguide.cz; www.travelguide.sk Comprehensive online accommodation listings, with booking facilities.

www.interhome.cz Specialises in holiday houses and apartments.

www.camp.cz Excellent for Czech camp sites.
www.czechhotels.cz; www.hotel.cz Concentrate on hotels in the Czech Republic.
www.ubytujsa.sk Covers the whole accommodation spectrum in Slovakia; often has online discounts.
www.limba.sk Slovak travel agent; cottages, hotels and *pension* listings.

Apartments

If you're planning on spending a while in Prague, it's worth considering renting an apartment or studio. The *Prague Post*'s classified section is a good source of information; the websites www.happyhouserentals.com and www.praguehome.com are also helpful. Apartments with kitchens start at around 13,000Kč per month. See the Prague chapter for more details (p125).

Camping

Most camp sites have pitches for both tents and caravans. Some also have unheated huts or bungalows, which can be good budget options if you have your own transport. The general rule of thumb is that most camp sites only open over the summer months.

Camp sites vary greatly across both countries; many are quite basic and don't offer much greenery, but they differ widely in attitude and amenities. Typical prices include a per-person rate (generally from around 50Kč/80Sk to 120Kč/100Sk, with discounts for kids) plus charges per tent (50Kč/60Sk to 100Kč/100Sk), car or van (70Kč/80Sk to 90Kč/100Sk), and electrical hook-up. Huts or bungalows, if any, are usually 120Kč/150Sk to 260Kč/250Sk per bed. Most camp sites have showers, and many have communal kitchens and at least a snack bar.

Hostels

A hostel can be anything from a bunk bed in a gymnasium to a double room with shower, the common factor being that filling the other beds is up to the management, not you. While a few operate year-round, most are sports clubs and student dormitories that offer beds to travellers only in the summer; look for the Czech *ubytovna* and Slovak *ubytovná* (accommodation), which often refers to such places. Some of these *(turistická ubytovna* or *ubytovná)* make private rooms available to travellers at hostel prices. In general, rooms are quite Spartan but clean and accommodating.

The number of hostel beds jumps from late June to August when school is out. We have tried to indicate the year-round ones. Typical per-bed prices are from around 150Kč/200Sk to 350Kč/300Sk, and reach up to 400Kč/600Sk in Prague and Bratislava. Only a few have places to eat on the premises. Most do not have curfews.

PRACTICALITIES

- Flick through the English-language weeklies the *Prague Post* and the *Slovak Spectator* for current affairs and up-to-date listings.

- Couch potatoes can enjoy state-run channels ČT 1 and ČT 2, and privately-run channels Nova and Prima in the Czech Republic. The Slovakian equivalents are STV 1 and STV 2, and Markíza and JOJ. Generally programmes are dubbed rather than subtitled.

- Electric outlets in both republics have the two small round holes common throughout central Europe (220V AC, 50Hz). North American (110V) appliances will need a transformer.

- If you have a weak bladder, always carry around small change (anything from 2 to 5Kč/Sk) for public toilets. Hygiene can vary from spotless to downright disgusting, and some public-toilet attendants can be stingy with toilet paper. Men's are marked *muži or páni*, women's *ženy* or *dámy*.

- Česky Krumlov, Brno and Prague have self-service laundrettes; outside that you're left to your own devices or the extremely slow traditional laundry (*prádelna* in Czech, *čistiareň* or *práčovňa* in Slovak).

- The metric system is used throughout the republics; a comma is used at the decimal place and full stops at the thousands, millions etc; a dash comes after prices rounded to the nearest crown.

Hotels

A hotel can be anything from simple worker's accommodation with shared facilities to a five-star bonanza with all the works. Generally speaking though, most hotels fall roughly between the two (there are no five-star hotels in Slovakia as yet).

In the high season in major tourist centres (eg Prague, the West Bohemian spa towns, and the Krkonoše and Tatras resort areas), you cannot be sure of finding space in a top-end hotel without booking ahead at least a few weeks. Otherwise, if your standards are flexible, you won't need reservations.

Single occupancy of a double room is normally more than half the cost of full occupancy, and some places insist you pay the full double rate. Some refurbished hotels have 'minisuites', with two or three rooms (each with its own lock) sharing a toilet and shower – a compromise between cheap communal facilities and pricey en suite ones. Many hotels also have more expensive *apartmá* (meaning suites, not apartments).

Nearly all hotels at mid-range and above have a restaurant and usually a snack bar, night bar and/or café.

Mountain Chalets

An additional option in the Krkonoše, Tatras and other mountain areas is the *bouda* or *chalupa* (in Czech) or *chata* (in Slovak) – some call themselves *horský hotel* (mountain hotel).

These are mountain chalets or high-altitude lodges, often open year-round, located at intervals along mountain trails or at the top of cable-car or funicular lines. Some are small and spartan, while others are essentially full-scale hotels. Some can be booked through agencies in nearby towns, while others are first come, first served. All have dining facilities of some description. Prices are quite reasonable at around 200Kč/250Sk to 300Kč/500Sk per person, and clean air and splendid views are thrown in for free.

Pensions

Pension or *penzión* used to mean a boarding house: a home or apartment block, family-run and fitted out with locking doors, wash basins, extra toilets and sometimes a café or snack bar. Nowadays the word has been coopted by some hotels that want to sound homy. Real *pensions* do exist and they are a

> ### 'HOTEL GARNI'
> You may see this in some hotel names. It means they're not equipped with a full restaurant and can only offer a simple breakfast – a 'B&B hotel'.

nice compromise between the comforts of a hotel and the personal touches of a private home. But they're not all cheap (generally between 600Kč/600Sk and 1500Kč/1200Sk per double outside the capitals), and they're often out on the fringes of a town or city.

Private Rooms

Renting rooms in private homes is a booming sector in both republics, particularly in the more popular tourist destinations. In Prague, for instance, touts swarm around the main train stations, most of them honest amateurs with good deals to offer – but check the map and the transport, as some places are way out in the suburbs. Quality can range from the ridiculous to the sublime.

These days, many private rooms are listed by the local tourist office. If not, you can normally scout around any neighbourhood that takes your fancy; look for *'Zimmer frei'* signs. In very small towns and villages with no hotels or only a deluxe one, this may be the only option available.

Rooms generally go for around 200Kč/250Sk to 350Kč/400Sk per person; add another 30% for Prague prices. Many people offer discounts for longer stays, but put their prices up for Easter, Christmas and some European holidays.

BUSINESS HOURS

Most shops open from 9am to 5pm or 6pm Monday to Friday, and till noon or 1pm on Saturday. Some big department stores and shopping complexes close late on Friday, and trade on Saturday afternoon and Sunday.

Restaurant and café hours are fluid, but most places operate from at least 11am to 11pm daily, although some close on Monday. In smaller towns it can be difficult to find something to eat after 9.30pm.

As a general rule, bars and pubs open from around noon to 1am, but often open later on Friday and Saturday and close early on Sunday. You'll find many clubs outside Prague and Bratislava only open on weekends.

DIRECTORY

Banking hours vary, but the useful banks are open 9am to 5pm weekdays. Many exchange offices are open daily from 9am until 11pm or later, and there are some 24-hour places.

Government office hours, including post offices, are weekdays from 8.30am to 5pm.

Note that many places, including some tourist offices, take a lunch break between noon and 1pm.

CHILDREN

Czechs and Slovaks are generally family oriented, and children are made welcome at tourist attractions, theatres and restaurants. While the attitude towards children is welcoming, breast feeding and nappy changing in public is pushing the limit. More often than not, children under six gain free entry into sights and travel free on public transport; children between six and 14 receive a 50% discount. There are plenty of activities for children in both republics including ever-popular puppet theatres (*Loutkové divadla* in Czech, *Bábkové divadlá* in Slovak). Unfortunately, many theatre performances, pantomimes and films are only in Czech or Slovak.

Most restaurants do not specifically cater to children, and you'll rarely find one with a kid's playground and high chairs. Some restaurants list a children's menu (*dětský jídelníček* in Czech; *detský jedálny lístok* in Slovak), but even if they don't they can usually provide smaller portions for a lower price. Everything you find in western countries, such as disposable nappies and baby food, is widely available throughout the larger towns. Daycare centres are practically nonexistent, but some of the top-end hotels have baby-sitting services. Generally speaking, only the top-end hotels can provide cots and other child-oriented equipment. International and more reliable car-rental agencies hire out child safety seats.

At present, there are no organisations specifically catering to children's travel needs in either republic. Many travel agents, however, cater to school children; for a comprehensive list log on to the Czech or Slovak Association of Travel Agents websites (www.ackcr.cz, www.sack.sk). Otherwise the best idea is to ask the local tourist office for advice on activities that'll keep children entertained for a while.

A useful source of information is Lonely Planet's *Travel with Children* by Cathy Lanigan.

Czech Republic

Some of the country's many museums, theatres, parks and lakes are ideal for children. In Prague try the Toy Museum, the National Technical Museum, the Military Museum or the Transport Museum.

Prague's Petřín Hill is a large park where parents can take a break from sightseeing with their children. Two outstanding theatres for kids in Prague are Divadlo Minor and the marionette theatre Divadlo Špejbla a Hurvínka. See the Prague chapter (p124) for more details.

At present, the Czech Tourist Authority is pushing what they call the Fairytale Project, which is a movement to promote family activities and attractions throughout the regions of the Czech Republic. The Czech Tourist Authority is planning to include something on their website at www.czechtourism.com in the future.

Slovakia

Many parks have playgrounds and during summer some lakes have boat rental facilities. Slovaks also take their children to the folk festivals where there is plenty of music, dancing and food – even children dress up in costumes and perform dances.

Great entertainment for children around the country includes the annual Ghost Festival at Bojnice Chateau (p71), Bibiana, an art house for children in Bratislava (p339), and the zoo, bob sled and steam railway in Košice (p405).

CLIMATE CHARTS

The damp continental climate of most of the Czech Republic is characterised by warm, showery summers and cold, snowy winters. Spring and autumn feature generally changeable conditions. Slovakia is characterised by cold, harsh winters and temperate – if wet – summers. Although the Czech Republic enjoys marginally milder weather than Slovakia, variations between them are small compared with those between low and high elevations.

The following climate charts show average temperatures and rainfall in the larger cities, but these can vary wildly from year

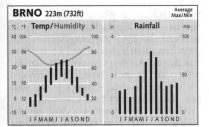

BRNO 223m (732ft)

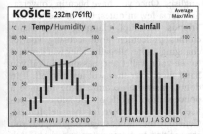

KOŠICE 232m (761ft)

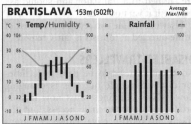

BRATISLAVA 153m (502ft)

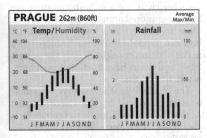

PRAGUE 262m (860ft)

to year. For instance, in the summer of 2002, both countries experienced some of the heaviest rainfall since records began (Prague's dramatic floods were a result of this) and in 2003, temperatures soared to uncomfortable levels.

See p9 for more information on seasons.

COURSES

If you're interested in learning a few tongue-twisters in Czech or Slovak, a language course is the way to go. Only the larger centres have language schools; some of the better establishments are listed below:

Prague

Charles University in Prague (UJOP; ☎ 224 990 417; www.ujop.cz; Vratislavova 10, Prague 2) Runs a four-week Czech language course for foreigners in August (€910) and intensive courses lasting from six weeks (€520) to 10 months (€3050).

City of Prague Language School (☎ 222 232 235; www.sjs.cz; Školská 15, Prague 1) Has a range of courses, including a four-month course for 4000Kč.

Bratislava

Institute for Language and Academic Preparation for Foreign Students (ÚJOP; Map p332; ☎ 55 57 74 88; www.uniba.sk/ujop; Šoltésovej 41) One of the larger institutions in Bratislava; three-week summer courses cost €450.

Berlitz (Map pp336-7; ☎ 54 41 24 80; www.berlitz.sk; Na vŕšku 6) Tailor-made courses for individuals.

CUSTOMS

You can import personal effects and up to 6000Kč/Sk worth of gifts and other 'non-commercial' goods tax and duty-free. If you're over 18, you can bring in 2L of wine, 1L of spirits and 200 cigarettes (or equivalent other tobacco products). Pets can be brought into the republics with a rabies vaccination certificate and an examination certificate made out within three days of departure.

You cannot export genuine antiques. If you have any doubt about what you're taking out, talk to curatorial staff at the National Museum (in Prague or Bratislava) or the Museum of Decorative Arts in Prague, or go to the **customs post office** (Prague Pošta celnice; Sokolovska 22, Prague 8; Bratislava Poštovní colnica; Tomášikova 54). Anything that looks like an antique will need a certificate declaring that it is not an 'article of national cultural heritage'; the antique dealer should be able to help.

In the Czech Republic you can import or export unlimited amounts of Czech and foreign currency, but amounts exceeding 350,000Kč must be declared. Slovakia allows the import or export of up to 150,000Sk of local or foreign currency.

DANGERS & ANNOYANCES
Extra Charges

One Prague-specific aggravation that just won't go away is extra restaurant bill items.

Magically appearing from nowhere, they can range from a cover charge to bread you've not even ordered, let alone touched (bread is generally not included in cover charges in the republics). The best course of action is not to get mad, but just act like it's an honest mistake; you'll have more luck having the item taken off the bill.

Lost or Stolen Belongings

It's usually helpful to go to your embassy in Prague or Bratislava first. It ought to furnish you with a letter to the police, preferably in Czech or Slovak, requesting a police report (without which you cannot collect on insurance, for example). But since reports in foreign languages don't always go down well with insurance claims officials back home, try to get the embassy to provide their own report in English.

For a police report, go to the main police station in the town where you've had trouble. If your passport has been stolen, this must be reported to your embassy, which can help arrange a replacement. Prague, Bratislava and the regional capitals have special police and passport offices for foreigners, where you can apply for a replacement visa if necessary.

Theft

Tourism and heady commercialism have spawned an upsurge in petty (and not-so-petty) crime in Prague and to some extent in Bratislava. For tourists, the biggest problem is pickpockets, and naturally enough, the prime trouble spots are where tourists gather in crowds. There's no point in being paranoid, but it makes sense to carry valuables well out of reach and to be alert in crowds.

Classic Prague scams involve someone asking directions and thrusting a map under your nose, or a woman with baby hassling

---

WHICH NUMBER?

You're walking down the street in Slovakia, looking for your hotel, and lo and behold, every house you come across has two numbers, one in black and one in red. Which is correct? Well, both actually, but the one you're looking for is in black, which is the actual address number. Red indicates the house registration number.

---

you for money – anything to attract your attention – while accomplices delve into your bags and pockets. If anything like this happens, immediately check your bags and look around you. Another favourite situation for pickpocket gangs is boarding a crowded tram or metro train – again, watch your bags if anyone seems to be crowding you.

Another ploy involves a 'lost tourist' asking for directions (usually in halting English). Once you have been in conversation for a few minutes, two of the tourist's 'friends' interrupt, claiming to be plain-clothes policemen and accusing you of changing money illegally. They will demand to see your wallet and passport, but if you hand them over they will just run off. If in doubt, insist on accompanying them to a police station. While on the subject of police, they're not known for their helpfulness. Generally they don't speak English, but you are entitled to a translator and should ask for one if it isn't offered.

Elsewhere in the two republics, the risk of crime directed at tourists is fairly remote.

DISABLED TRAVELLERS

No attention used to be paid to facilities for disabled people but this is changing slowly. New buildings must now include provision for wheelchair access, but the law is not retrospective. However, ramps for wheelchair users in both countries are becoming more common, especially at the more expensive hotels, major street crossings and in public buildings. Transport is a major problem though, as only the newest buses and trams have anything resembling wheelchair access.

The handy *Wheeling the Czech Republic* booklet, produced by the Czech Tourist Authority in association with **Centrum Paraple** (☎ 274 771 478; paraple@paraple.cz; Ovčárská 471; 108 00 Prague 10), a centre for the paralysed, is worth getting hold of. It has information on arriving in the Czech Republic and lists wheelchair-friendly hotels and tourist attractions across the country.

In Prague several bus routes and metro stations are wheelchair accessible; a list is available from Prague public transport (DP) information offices and on their website www.dp-praha.cz. Czech Railways (ČD) claims that any of the larger stations in the Czech Republic has ramps and lifts for wheelchairs onto the train but the harsh reality is that the service is poor.

The **Prague Wheelchair Users Organisation** (Pražská organizace vozíčkářů; ☎ 224 827 210; pov@gts.cz; Benediktská 688/6 Prague 1) is a good source of information and publishes a handy guide and CD-ROM called *Accessible Prague*. The **Association of Disabled People** (Sdružení zdravotně postižených v; ☎ 224 816 997; Karlínské náměstí 12, Karlín, Prague 8) is another. The vision-impaired are represented by the **Union of the Blind and Weak Sighted** (Sjednocená organizace nevidomých a slabozrakých v ČR; ☎ 224 816 775; sons@braillnet.cz; Krakovská 21, Prague 2).

Unfortunately Slovakia is quite a bit behind its neighbour. Organisations in Slovakia include the **Slovak Union for the Disabled** (Slovenský zväz telesne postihnutých; ☎ 02-50 22 87 08; Trnavské mýto 1, Bratislava), but little English is spoken here. Most top-end hotels have wheelchair ramps and Slovakia's trains often have a wheelchair access carriage; it's just a pity that the train stations aren't as user-friendly.

DISCOUNT CARDS
Hostel Card
Hostels in the Czech and Slovak Republics do not require a Hostelling International (HI) or affiliate card. That said, the HI card entitles you to 20% to 30% discounts at some hostels and junior hotels. Apply for your HI card at home.

Seniors Cards
While senior residents of the Czech and Slovak Republics get many concessions, such as on museum admission and public transport, there are no formal discounts for senior travellers.

The Rail Europe Senior (RES) Card gives you about 30% off international journeys, and domestic journeys connecting with an international service. To be eligible for this card, you must have a senior citizens' railcard from your own country, the availability of which depends on the country you're in.

Student & Youth Cards
ISIC and Euro26 cards will get you discounts at some hotels and most museums, galleries and theatres. You may even get a discount on air, bus and train tickets. It's possible to buy a Euro26 card in both countries.

EMBASSIES & CONSULATES
It's important to realise what your own embassy – the embassy of the country of which you are a citizen – can and can't do to help you if you get into trouble. Generally speaking, it won't be much help in emergencies if the trouble you're in is remotely your own fault. Remember that you are bound by the laws of the country you are in. Your embassy will not be sympathetic if you end up in jail after committing a crime locally, even if such actions are legal in your own country.

In genuine emergencies you might get some assistance, but only if other channels have been exhausted. For example, if you need to get home urgently, a free ticket home is exceedingly unlikely – the embassy would expect you to have insurance. If you have all your money and documents stolen, it might assist with getting a new passport, but a loan for onward travel is out of the question.

Czech Republic
CZECH EMBASSIES & CONSULATES
The Ministry of Foreign Affairs website www.mfa.cz contains a full list of embassies and consulates around the world:

Australia Canberra (☎ 02-6290 1386; www.mfa.cz /canberra; 8 Culgoa Circuit, O'Malley, Canberra, ACT 2606); Sydney (☎ 02-9371 0860; www.mfa.cz/sydney; 169 Military Rd, Dover Heights, Sydney, NSW 2030)

Austria Vienna (☎ 01-894 21 25/6; www.mfa.cz/vienna; Penzingerstrasse 11-13, 1140 Vienna)

Canada Ottawa (☎ 613-562 3875; www.mfa.cz/ottawa; 251 Cooper Street, Ottawa, Ontario, K2P 0G2)

France Paris (☎ 01-727 6130; www.mfa.cz/paris; 75 Bd Haussmann, Paris 75008)

Germany Berlin (☎ 030-226 380; www.mfa.cz/berlin; Wilhelmstrasse 44, 10117 Berlin); Bonn (☎ 0228-919 70; www.mfa.cz/bonn; Ferdinandstrasse 27, 53127 Bonn)

Hungary Budapest (☎ 01-351 0539; www.mfa.cz /budapest; Rózsa utca 61, Budapest VI. 1064)

Ireland Dublin (☎ 01-668 1135; www.mfa.cz/dublin; 57 Northumberland Road, Ballsbridge, Dublin 4)

Italy Rome (☎ 06-324 4459; www.mfa.cz/rome; Via dei Gracchi 322, 00192 Rome)

Japan Tokyo (☎ 03-340 08122-3; www.mfa.cz/tokyo; 16-14, Hiroo 2-chome, Shibuya-ku, Tokyo 150-0012)

Netherlands Den Haag (☎ 070-346 97 12; www.mfa.cz /hague; Paleisstraat 4, 2514 JA Den Haag)

New Zealand Auckland (☎ 09-353 9766; Auckland@ honorary.mzv.cz; Bank of New Zealand Tower, 125 Queen Street, PO Box 3798, Auckland)

Poland Warsaw (☎ 022-628 7221; www.mfa.cz/warsaw; Koszykowa 18, 00-555 Warsaw)

Slovakia Bratislava (☎ 02-59 20 33 05; www.mfa.cz
/bratislava; Hviezdoslavovo námestie 8, 810 00 Bratislava 1)
UK London (☎ 020-7243 1115; www.mfa.cz/london; 26
Kensington Palace Gardens, London W8 4QY)
USA Washington (Embassy; ☎ 202-274 9100; www.mfa.cz
/washington; 3900 Spring of Freedom St NW, Washington,
DC 20008); Los Angeles (Consulate; ☎ 310-473 0889; www
.mfa.cz/losangeles; 10990 Wilshire Blvd, Suite 1100, Los
Angeles, CA 90024); New York (Consulate; ☎ 212-717
5643; www.mfa.cz/newyork; 1109-1111 Madison Ave, New
York, NY 10028)

EMBASSIES & CONSULATES IN THE CZECH REPUBLIC

Most consulates are open for visa-related
business weekdays until noon or 1pm and
are in Malá Strana:

Australia (☎ 296 578 350; Klimentská 10, Prague 1)
This is an honorary consul but Australians can get emer-
gency help at the UK embassy; the nearest Australian
embassies are in Warsaw and Vienna.
Austria (☎ 257 090 511; www.austria.cz; Viktora Huga
10, Prague 5)
Canada (☎ 272 101 800; www.canada.cz; Muchova 6,
Prague 6)
France (☎ 251 171 711; www.france.cz; Velkopoevorské
námestie 2, Prague 1)
Germany (☎ 257 113 111; zreg@prag.auswaertiges
-amt.de; Vlašská 19, Prague 1)
Hungary (☎ 233 324 454; huembprg@vol.cz;
Českomalínská 20, Prague 6)
Ireland (☎ 257 530 061; irishembassy@iol.cz; Tržiště
13, Prague 1)
Japan (☎ 257 533 546; bunka.jp@volny.cz; Malá Strana,
Maltézské námestie 6, Prague 1)
Netherlands (☎ 224 312 190; nlgovpra@ti.cz;
Gotthardská 6/27, Prague 6)
New Zealand (☎ 222 514 672; egermayer@nzconsul.cz;
Dykova 19, Prague 10)
Poland (☎ 257 530 388; ambrpczechy@mbox.vol.cz;
Valdštejnska 8, Prague 1)
South Africa (☎ 267 311 114; saprague@terminal.cz;
Ruská 65, Prague 10)
UK (☎ 257 402 111; www.britain.cz; Thunovská 14,
Prague 1)
Ukraine (☎ 233 342 000; www.ukraine.cz; Charlese de
Gaulla 29, Prague 6)
USA (☎ 257 530 663; www.usembassy.cz; Tržiště 15,
Prague 1)

Slovakia
SLOVAK EMBASSIES & CONSULATES

For a comprehensive embassy list, check
out the Ministry of Foreign Affairs website
(www.foreign.gov.sk):

Australia (☎ 02-6290 1516; www.slovakemb-aust.org;
47 Culgoa Circuit, O'Malley, Canberra, ACT 2606)
Austria (☎ 01-318 905 5200; zuwien@aon.at;
Armbrustergasse 24, A-1190 Vienna)
Canada (☎ 613-749 4442; www.slovakembassy.com; 50
Rideau Terrace, Ottawa, KIM 2A1)
Czech Republic (☎ 233 113 051; skembassy@pha.inec
net.cz; Pod Hradbami 1, 160 00 Prague 6)
France (☎ 01-4414 5600; zuparis@wanadoo.fr; 125, Rue
du Ranelagh, 750 16 Paris)
Germany (☎ 030-889 26 20; www.botschaft-slowakei
.de; Pariser Strasse 44, 107 07 Berlin)
Hungary (☎ 01-460 9010; slovakem@matavnet.hu;
Stefania ut 22-24, 1143 Budapest XIV)
Ireland (☎ 01-660 0012; slovak@iol.ie; 20 Clyde Road,
Ballsbridge, Dublin 4)
Italy (☎ 06-367 151; amb.slovac@virgilio.it; Via dei Colli
della Farnesina 144, 00194 Rome)
Japan (☎ 03-3400 8122; embassy@slovak-embassy.jp;
150-8691, 2-16-14, Hiroo, Shibuya-ku, Tokyo)
Netherlands (☎ 070-416 7777; embslow@bart.nl;
Parkweg 1, 2585 JG Den Haag)
Poland (☎ 022-525 8110; www.ambasada-slowacji.pdi
.pl; Litevska 6, 00-581 Warsaw)
UK (☎ 020-7313 6470; www.slovakembassy.co.uk;
25 Kensington Palace Gardens, London W8 4QY)
Ukraine (☎ 044-212 0310; slovak@i.kiev.ua; Jaroslavov
val 34, 010 34 Kiev)
USA (☎ 202-237 1054; www.slovakembassy-us.org;
3523 International Court, NW, Washington DC 20008)

EMBASSIES & CONSULATES IN SLOVAKIA

For consular services, Australians and New
Zealanders should apply to their embassies
in Prague or Vienna. The following embassies can be found in Bratislava:

Austria (☎ 02-59 30 15 00; www.embassyaustria.sk;
Ventúrska 10)
Canada (☎ 02-59 20 40 31; Mostová 2)
France (☎ 02-59 34 71 11; www.france.sk; Hlavné nám 7)
Germany (☎ 02-59 20 44 00; www.germanembassy.sk;
Hviezdoslavovo nám 10)
Hungary (☎ 02-59 20 52 00; www.hungemb.sk;
Sedlárska 3)
Ireland (☎ 02-54 43 57 15; bratislava@iveagh.irlgov.ie;
Carlton Savoy Building, Mostová 2)
Japan (☎ 02-59 80 01 00; taishikan7@jpembassy.sk;
Hlavné námestie 2)
Netherlands (☎ 02-52 62 50 91; Fraňa Kráľa 5)
Poland (☎ 02-54 43 27 44; weh@polamb.sk; Zelená 6)
UK (☎ 02-59 98 20 00; www.britishembassy.sk; Panská 16)
Ukraine (☎ 02-59 20 28 10; www.ukrembassy.sk;
Radvanská 35)
USA (☎ 02-54 43 33 38; www.usis.sk; Hviezdoslavovo
nám 5)

FESTIVALS & EVENTS
Czech Republic
The vast array of festivals and celebrations in the Czech Republic is quite impressive, and ranges from international jazz festivals to village folk fairs. Events run throughout the year, so you should be lucky enough to find something going on no matter when you visit. The website www.czecot.com lists a zillion happenings right across the spectrum; it's often only in Czech but it's not too hard to interpret.

For folk festivals, the **Folklore Association of the Czech Republic** (www.fos.cz) is a good starting point. Its website lists many happenings throughout the country. The Moravské Slovácko region (p317), in South Moravia, is a hot spot for such events.

The following events are either 'significant days' *(významné dny)* or cultural events that happen yearly. Local festivals and events are listed under their relevant destinations:

January
Tři králové (Three Kings Day; 6 January) Formal end of the Christmas season, sometimes with carols, bell-ringing and gifts to the poor.
Anniversary of Jan Palach's Death (19 January) In memory of the Charles University student who in 1969 burned himself to death in protest against the Soviet occupation.

March
Birthday of Tomáš Garrigue Masaryk (7 March) Commemorates Czechoslovakia's first president and national father-figure.

April
Velikonoce (Easter Monday) Traditionally an old pagan springtime ritual called *pomlázka* where Czech men of all ages wander through their village swatting their favourite women (or any women they can find) on the legs with decorated willow switches. This is supposed to bring rejuvenation, though now it's often taken a bit too far.
Pálení čarodějnic (Burning of the Witches; 30 April) Essentially the Czech version of *Walpurgisnacht*, a pre-Christian festival for warding off evil influence, especially witches. Bonfires are lit all over the country, old brooms are put to the torch and people party on through the night.

May
České povstání (Czech Uprising; 5 May) Anniversary of the 1945 anti-Nazi revolt preceding the arrival of the Soviet army.

November
Start of the Velvet Revolution (17 November) Anniversary of the beating of nonviolent student demonstrators by security police in Prague, triggering the fall of the Communist government.

December
Čert a Mikuláš (Devil & St Nicholas; 5 December) The Devil and St Nicholas (dressed-up parents, uncles or neighbours) tour the homes of children to find out if they have been good or bad, and leave gifts – usually fruit, nuts and chocolate, or coal and potatoes. The Devil wears a mask, horns on his head, an old black fur coat and, preferably, a tail. St Nicholas dresses a bit like the Pope, with a tall white hat decorated with a cross, a long white coat and a staff.
Vánoce (Christmas) Celebrations begin on Christmas Eve, also called *Štědrý večer* (Generous Evening), the big day for family meals and gift-giving. Most people wait until the morning of this day to put up their Christmas tree, which is usually a spruce. The traditional Christmas Eve dinner starts with carp soup, followed by either carp fried with breadcrumbs and potato salad or *kapr na černo* (carp with black sauce). Dessert is usually *vánočka*, a light fruitcake. After dinner everyone attacks the presents under the tree.

Slovakia
Slovakia is even more folk-oriented than its larger neighbour, reflected in its festivals. The general impetus is towards folk music and dance, with a spattering of folk art markets and festivals thrown in. The most famous and well attended is the Východná Folk Festival (p383), in late June/early July in Central Slovakia, an event which attracts performers from all over Europe. The Slovak Tourist Board's website (www.slovakiatourism.sk) has a comprehensive list of cultural and sporting events held throughout the year.

The following is a list of events or 'significant days' which are celebrated annually throughout the country; local festivals and events are listed in the destination chapters:

February
Fašiangy (Shrovetide Carnival; 2 February) A religious festival preceding Lent, during which masks and costumes are worn in some villages.

April
Veľkánoc (Easter Monday) Similar to the Czech Republic rituals, but this time with water. Men try to throw water on their chosen women, or any woman within striking distance. For some reason the women are supposed to respond peaceably with refreshments and gifts of eggs,

hand-painted or otherwise decorated. Quite often the women take revenge by dousing the men in cold water the following day.

Deň nespravodlivo stíhaných (13 April) Day for victims of persecution.

May
Výročie úmrtia Milana Rastislava Štefánika (4 May) Anniversary of the death of MR Štefánik in 1919. Štefánik was the Slovak co-founder of the first Czechoslovakia.
Deň víťazstva nad fašizmom (8 May) A celebration of the defeat of Fascism in 1945.

August
Deň Matice Slovenskej (4 August) Anniversary of the founding of the Slovak Matice (an important cultural institution set up to teach the Slovak language) in 1867.

October
Deň obetí Dukly (6 October) Anniversary of the battle of Dukla Pass in 1944.

November
Deň boja proti totalitě (Day of the fight against totalitarianism; 17 November) Anniversary of the start of the Velvet Revolution (see p26).

December
Sv Mikuláš (St Nicholas' Day; 5 December) See Czech Republic Festivals & Events earlier.
Vianoce (Christmas) See Czech Republic Festivals & Events earlier.

FOOD

A full rundown on local cuisine, drinks, dos and don'ts and when and where to eat can be found in the Food & Drink chapter (p61). Eating entries in the larger centres have been broken down into the following categories: Cafés, Restaurants, Quick Eats (sandwich and baguette shops, ice-cream parlours and the like) and Self-Catering (supermarkets and small convenience stores). Prague, as always, is an exception to the rule; listings are categorised into budget (mains around 90Kč), mid-range (mains averaging 150-200Kč) and top end (anything over 300Kč) under various district headings. In all circumstances, listings are placed in order of the author's preference.

GAY & LESBIAN TRAVELLERS
Czech Republic

Homosexuality is legal in the Czech Republic (the age of consent is 15), but Czechs on the whole are not accustomed to seeing gays showing affection to each other in public; it's best to be discreet. Prague, of course, is more tolerant than anywhere in either republic (see p126 for Gay & Lesbian Prague).

Gay Iniciativa (☎ 224 223 811; gay.iniciativa.cz - Czech only; Senovážné náměstí 2, 110 00 Prague 1) is the national organisation for gay and lesbians; it offers information on events, venues and resources.

The bimonthly gay magazine *Amigo* (www .amigo.cz) is a combination of personal ads and a guide to gay and lesbian Prague. Useful online websites include www.gay.cz and prague.gayguide.net.

Slovakia

Homosexuality has been legal since the 1960s (age of consent is 16). Gay-bashing is very rare and there is a lot of tolerance towards homosexuals. However, there is no official government organisation or financial support for privately-run ones. Slovakia is still quite a conservative country and the local populace is not accustomed to public displays of gay affection; it's best to be discreet.

The largest gay and lesbian organisations are **Ganymedes** (☎ 50 22 87 04; www.ganymedes.info; Istropolis, Trnavské mýto 1) and the lesbian-oriented **Museion** (vamo@ba.psg.sk; Saratovská 3; PO Box 121), both located in Bratislava. Helpful websites listing gay bars, hotels and cruising areas countrywide include www.gay.sk and www .gayinfo.sk.

HOLIDAYS

The following are public holidays in the Czech and Slovak Republics, when banks, offices and department stores and many shops close. Some restaurants, museums and tourist attractions stay open, but public transport is greatly reduced.

School holidays fall in the months of July and August, over the Christmas period and during Easter. Like elsewhere, families take advantage of these times so expect accommodation and transport facilities to be severely strained.

Czech Republic
Nový rok (New Year's Day) 1 January.
Also **Den obnovy samostatného éeského státu** (anniversary of the founding of the Czech Republic).
Pondělí velikonoční (Easter Monday) March or April
Svátek práce (Labour Day) 1 May

Den osvobození (Liberation Day) 8 May
Den Cyrila a Metoděje (SS Cyril & Methodius Day) 5 July
Den Jana Husa (Jan Hus Day) 6 July
Den éeské státnosti (Czech Statehood Day) 28 September
Den vzniku Československa (Independence Day) 28 October
Den boje za svobodu a demokracii (Freedom & Democracy Day) 17 November
Vánoce (Christmas) 24-26 December

Slovakia

Nový rok (New Year's Day) 1 January.
Also **Deň vzniku Slovenskej republiky** (anniversary of the founding of the Slovak Republic).
Tri králové (Three Kings Day) 6 January
Veľké Nocy (Easter Friday & Monday) March or April
Sviatok práce (Labour Day) 1 May
Deň ví ťazstva nad fašizmom (Victory Day) 8 May
Sv Cyril a Metod (SS Cyril & Methodius Day) 5 July
Slovenské národné povstanie (Slovak National Uprising) 29 August
Deň Ústavy Slovenskej republiky (Constitution Day) 1 September
Sedembolestná Panna Maria (St Mary's Day) 15 September
Sviatok Všetkých svätých (All Saints Day) 1 November
Vianoce (Christmas) 24-26 December

INSURANCE

A travel insurance policy to cover theft, loss and medical problems is worth organising for your trip. There is a wide variety of policies available, so check the small print.

Some policies specifically exclude 'dangerous activities' (eg motorcycling, rock climbing, canoeing and even hiking). If you're planning on doing any of these activities, be sure to choose a policy that covers you.

You may prefer a policy that pays doctors or hospitals directly rather than you having to pay on the spot and claim later. If you have to claim later make sure you keep all documentation. Some policies ask you to call back (reverse charges) to a centre in your home country where an immediate assessment of your problem is made.

Check that the policy covers ambulances or an emergency flight home.

For health insurance see insurance (p462). For information on car rental insurance matters, see the Transport chapter (p457).

INTERNET ACCESS

Like almost every country in Europe, the republics are quite Internet savvy, so Internet

---

THE CZECH CALENDAR

While most Western European languages name the months of the year according to their old Latin names, Czech – in common with some other Slavic languages like Ukrainian, Slovene and Serbo-Croat – uses far more poetic names taken from nature. Even Czechs are uncertain of the derivations of some of these names – the list below is the best we could manage.

- **leden** January; from *led* (ice), the month of frost and ice
- **únor** February; from *nořít* (to sink), possibly to do with the breaking and sinking of ice on the rivers
- **březen** March; from *bříza* (birch tree), the month of birches
- **duben** April; from *dub* (oak tree), the month of budding oaks
- **květen** May; from *květ* (flower), the month of blooming flowers
- **červen** June; from *červ* (worm), the month when worms (which were once used to make a red dye) were collected; the word *červen* also means 'red'
- **červenec** July; as for June
- **srpen** August; from *srp* (sickle), the month of harvest
- **září** September; either from *za říje* (before the rutting season; see *říjen* below), or from *zářít* (to shine, glow), a reference to sunny autumn evenings
- **říjen** October; from *říje* (the rut), the month when rutting deer are heard roaring in the woods and hills
- **listopad** November; from *list* (leaf) and *pád* (fall), the month of falling leaves
- **prosinec** December; from an old Czech word meaning 'grey'

addicts shouldn't have too many problems getting connected. For websites about the Czech and Slovak Republics see p10.

Internet Cafés

You'll find plenty of Internet cafés in the major cities, a couple in the smaller cities and at least one in most towns. Villages can sometimes prove to be a problem but often the local tourist office doubles as an Internet café. Places are listed throughout this book.

Connection speeds and number of terminals vary from one café to the next; some places are lightning quick and have more terminals than they'll ever need, others are so slow it might be faster to send correspondence via snail mail. As with connection speeds, prices vary greatly. In bigger cities it's best to hunt around as prices can be as low as 20Kč/20Sk per hour and as high as 75Kč/120Sk. In smaller centres expect to pay from around 30Kč/30Sk to 60Kč/50Sk.

Free Web-based email services include **Yahoo** (www.yahoo.com), **MSN Hotmail** (www.hotmail.com) and **ekno** (www.ekno.lonelyplanet.com).

Plugging In

If you've brought your notebook or palmtop computer with you, remember that the power supply voltage in the Czech and Slovak Republics may be different from that at home, risking damage to your equipment. Invest in a universal AC adaptor for your appliance, which will enable you to plug it in anywhere without frying the innards. You'll also need a European plug adaptor; often it's easiest to buy these before you leave home.

Also, your PC-card modem may or may not work once you leave your home country – and you won't know for sure until you try. The safest option is to buy a reputable 'global' modem before you leave home, or buy a local PC-card modem if you're spending an extended time abroad.

Most newer, upper-end hotels will have Internet facilities for business customers, and rooms may have telephone jacks, usually USA standard (RJ-11). Adaptors for older jacks can be found in electronic supply shops. Internet cafés in the capitals will sometimes let you plug your laptop into their server.

When hooking up to a local ISP (Internet Service Provider), be sure that it has local rather than nationwide dial-up numbers;

you don't want to be wasting your money on expensive calls. This should be no problem in larger cities, but may cause some headaches in smaller towns. Major ISPs in the Czech Republic include **Czech On Line** (www.col.cz) and **Cesky Telecom** (www.telecom.cz), and in Slovakia **Slovak Telecom** (www.telecom.sk - Slovak only) and **Stonline** (www.stonline.sk - Slovak only).

International ISPs such as **AOL** (www.aol.com), **CompuServe** (www.compuserve.com) and **AT&T** (www.attbusiness.net) have dial-in nodes throughout the Czech and Slovak Republics; it's best to download a list of the dial-in numbers before you leave home.

LEGAL MATTERS

Penalties for possession of drugs are harsh and it's unlikely that your embassy can do much to help if you are caught. In the Czech Republic it was, until recently, legal to possess and use cannabis (though it was illegal to sell it). However, in 1999 it became illegal to possess 'more than a small amount' of drugs. Unfortunately the law does not define 'a small amount' or specify which drugs, giving the police a free hand to nick anyone in possession of any amount of any drug. Slovakia's situation is quite similar; you can be sentenced up to five years for possession of a small amount of marijuana. It's simply not worth the risk to import, export or possess any illegal substances.

If you find yourself under arrest in either republic for any reason whatsoever, you are entitled to call your embassy. Note that it is technically illegal not to carry some form of identification (normally your passport). If you can't prove your identity, police have the right to detain you for up to 48 hours.

Drink-driving is strictly illegal; both republics have a zero blood-alcohol limit for drivers. Traffic fines are generally paid on the spot (ask for a receipt); for more information on road rules see the Transport

---

JUST SO YOU KNOW:

- Voting Age: 18
- Drinking Age: 18
- Driving Age: 18
- Hetero Consenting Sex Age: 15 (gay/lesbian age of consent is 15 in the Czech Republic and 16 in Slovakia)

chapter (p457). The fine for littering can be as much as 1000Kč/Sk.

MAPS
Country Maps

Maps of the Czech and Slovak Republics are available in any good bookshop throughout the republics; outside the region it's best to try the German and Austrian publishers Freytag & Berndt. Freytag & Berndt maps are generally available in any good map shop around the world.

Some of the best Czech country maps are those by Kartografie Praha, particularly its series *Česká republika automapa* (1:500,000 to 1:750,000) and *Česká republika atlas* (1:150,000 to 1:700,000). Freytag & Berndt's good multilingual *Czech Republic Road Map* (1:500,000) has route distances, sights of interest, mountain-shading and other geographical info.

VKÚ (www.vku.sk), a Slovak publisher, produces the best maps of Slovakia by far. There is the *Automapa Slovenská republika* (1: 250,000 to 1:1,000,000) or the more detailed *Autoatlas Slovenská* (1:150,000 to 1:500,000). It also produces *Vreckový Autoatlas Česká & Slovenská republika* (1:1,000,000), a pocket atlas of both republics. Freytag & Berndt's *Slovakia Road Map* (1:250,000 or 1: 500,000) is another good choice, although some of the country's smaller villages are left off. The German publisher GeoCenter sells similar, high-quality maps, all readily available in Slovakia.

Regional & Street Maps

For hiking or cycling trips, it's best to buy a map. VKÚ covers both countries with very detailed maps, either at 1:50,000 or 1: 25,000, with hiking trail routes and, where appropriate, mountain bike paths, ski lifts and tracks clearly marked. Some editions come with a handy booklet (in Czech or Slovak – English and German editions are supposedly in the pipeline) with specific information on trails. VKÚ also produces excellent cycling maps (1:100,000). Freytag & Berndt publishes a series of 1:50,000 maps for the popular hiking and cycling areas in both republics.

VKÚ produces maps of cultural and touristy sights (1:100,000) for Slovakia, with an accompanying booklet in Slovak, English and German.

Most major tourist towns have several street maps from various publishers but only VKÚ covers most of the major and some minor Slovak towns (the majority of which have a scale of 1:10,000).

You can buy street maps and regional maps from tourist information offices, bookshops or travel agencies in most towns. Numerous versions are available for Prague and Bratislava.

MONEY

The Czech and Slovak Republics have separate currencies, the Czech crown (Kč) and the Slovak crown (Sk). US dollars and euros are the most sensible foreign currencies to pack. This book's inside cover has a handy exchange rate table, and the Getting Started chapter (p10) has a general rundown on costs. The euro will not be introduced until 2007 at the earliest.

The Koruna česká (Kč), or Czech crown, is divided into 100 haléřů, or heller (h). Notes come in 20Kč, 50Kč, 100Kč, 200Kč, 500Kč, 1000Kč and 5000Kč denominations. Coins are 1Kč, 2Kč, 5Kč, 10Kč, 20Kč and 50Kč, and 50h. Always have a few 2Kč and 5Kč coins for use in public toilets, telephones and ticket machines.

The Slovenská koruna (Sk), or Slovak crown, is divided into 100 halierú or heller (h). Notes come in 20Sk, 50Sk, 100Sk, 200Sk, 500Sk, 1000Sk and 5000Sk denominations. Coins are 1Sk, 2Sk, 5Sk and 10Sk, and 10h, 20h and 50h.

ATMs

Far and away the best way to carry money around is not to. ATMs *(bankomat)*, which accept debit and credit cards – Visa, Master-Card, Plus, Cirrus, Eurocard and EC – can be found everywhere in the Czech and Slovak Republics, even in smaller towns, and you generally get a good rate of exchange.

Credit Cards

Although not as widely spread as in many Western European countries, credit cards are becoming more and more acceptable in both republics. American Express, MasterCard and Visa are widely accepted at up-market and mid-range hotels, restaurants and tourist shops; Diners Club less so. Credit cards can often be used for cash advances in the major banks – Komerční Česká spořitelna,

Československá obchodní banka (ČSOB) and Živnostenská in the Czech Republic, Všeobecná úverová banka (VÚB), Slovenská sporiteíňa and TatraBanka in Slovakia – but charges by your bank at home will probably be higher than with a debit card.

International Transfers

If you're not an American Express or Thomas Cook customer, the fastest way to get emergency money from home is through **Western Union** (☎ 224 222 954; www.westernunion.com; Válavské náměstí 15, Prague 1), although you will only be paid in crowns. In Slovakia, Western Union transfers can be made through VÚB and TatraBanka branches. Post offices in both countries also handle international money transfers, but they generally take a week or longer to process the transaction.

Moneychangers

Private exchange offices are quite often conveniently located, but that's about as far as the convenience goes. Some have great rates of exchange but high commissions (up to 10% in Prague) or an 'undisclosed' handling fee, while others have zero commission but a dismal rate of exchange. Private currency exchanges in Bratislava, however, are an exception; some offer good rates for cash with zero commission. Before using them though, be sure to check all rates and fees twice.

Hotels typically charge 5% commission while travel agencies and post offices charge around 2%. Banks also take around 2% and generally have the best rate of exchange, but their opening hours are usually short and they are closed on weekends and holidays.

You'll have no problem exchanging US dollars, British pounds and euros, but it's harder to change Polish zlotys and Hungarian forints.

Travellers Cheques

American Express, Thomas Cook and Visa travellers cheques are accepted at most banks, and are relatively easy to replace if lost. Eurocheques are also widely accepted with a cheque guarantee card.

Major banks in the Czech Republic (see Credit Cards earlier) charge around 2% commission on travellers cheques, in Slovakia there is a standard 1% charge.

Both the American Express and Thomas Cook offices in Prague (p86) change their own and other companies' travellers cheques without charging commission. TatraBanka is the American Express representative in Slovakia.

POST
Postal Rates

The two republics' postal services, **Česká pošta** (www.cpost.cz) and **Slovenská pošta** (www.slposta.sk), are fairly efficient and not too expensive. In both republics it's safest to mail international parcels from main post offices in large cities. However, anything you can't afford to lose should go by registered mail or Express Mail Service (EMS).

Mail to Europe (automatically airmail) is 9Kč/16Sk for letters and postcards up to 20g; to anywhere else is 14Kč/21Sk. EMS is fast and secure and is available in both countries; prices start at 600Kč/600Sk for anything up to 500g. A 2kg parcel (by airmail) costs around 500Kč/650Sk to Europe, 685Kč/570Sk to the US, and around 1000Kč/1000Sk to Australasia. Only larger post offices will let you send parcels of books or printed matter up to 15kg.

If you are sending anything that looks like an antique you will probably be directed to the nearest customs clearance post office (*Pošta celnice/Poštovní colnica*).

Remember to always ask for a receipt (*potvrzení/potvrdenie*) when mailing anything larger than a letter by airmail or a more expensive mail service to ensure that it is actually sent via the correct service.

Sending & Receiving Mail

You can buy stamps in post offices and also from street vendors and newsagents. Letters go in the orange boxes outside post offices and around town.

Most larger post offices have a separate window for poste restante mail (*uložené zásilky/poste restante*), though the most reliable services are at the main post offices in Prague and Bratislava. You must present your passport to claim mail. Check under your given name too.

SOLO TRAVELLERS

There's no stigma attached to travelling solo in either country. Many hostels, *pensions* and hotels have a couple of single rooms available; they generally cost a little more than half the price of a double room.

A growing number of young people speak a smattering of English and are happy to give it a whirl, though outside the larger cities it can prove hard to meet locals. That's not to say that it won't happen, but you'll probably have to make the first move, so to speak.

Prague is easily the best city to meet other travellers and expats. The Bohemia Bagel (p133) is a well-known meeting point, as are the more popular Irish bars around town. Some hostels have their own bars so you may not even have to leave the building to start up a conversation. In Bratislava, The Dubliner (p342) is *the* place to meet fellow travellers and resident expats.

TELEPHONE

The telephone system in the Czech and Slovak Republics received a massive overhaul in 2002 to bring it in line with international standards, and many phone codes and numbers changed. Things have settled down quite nicely, and now competition is on the increase, bringing with it lower prices.

Czech Republic

The Czech Republic's country code is ☎ 420. Now all numbers consist of nine digits; you have to dial all nine for any call, local or long distance. For directory inquiries dial ☎ 1180, international directory inquiries call ☎ 1181.

INTERNATIONAL CALLS

To make direct-dial international calls from within the Czech Republic, dial ☎ 00, the country code and the phone number. Peak-rate calls from public phones using a phonecard are 17Kč a minute to New Zealand, and 10Kč to Australia, Canada, the USA and the UK. Trick Card (see later) calls to most places in the world cost 7.40Kč per minute.

MOBILE PHONES

The Czech Republic is no different to the rest of Europe – everyone seems to have a mobile phone. The country uses GSM 900, which is compatible with the rest of Europe and Australasia, but not with the North American GSM 1900 or the totally different system in Japan (though some North Americans have GSM 1900/900 phones that do work here).

Mobile phones are by far the most convenient way to stay in touch while travelling, but if you decide to use your GSM phone while on the road beware of expensive calls being routed internationally; first check with your provider at home about call charges. If you plan to spend some time here, consider purchasing a pay-as-you-go SIM card. The main players in the market are **EuroTel** (www .eurotel.cz), **T-Mobile** (www.t-mobile.cz – Czech only) and **Oskar** (www.oskarmobil.cz). Cards sell for anything between 300Kč and 2000Kč. Your mobile must be unlocked before these cards can be used; check with your home provider on your phone status before leaving home.

Many T-Mobile and EuroTel stores rent phones for up to one month; T-Mobile rents phones for a flat rate of 183Kč per day, EuroTel 680/1945Kč per week/month. A deposit of about 4000Kč is required. Renting or buying a new SIM card won't allow you to use your existing number.

PUBLIC PHONES & PHONECARDS

Blue coin telephones accept only 2Kč, 5Kč, 10Kč and 20Kč coins and can be used to make local, long-distance and international calls.

These, however, are slowly being replaced by card telephones, which take *telecard* (phonecards). Phonecards are the best option for local, long-distance and international calls. They are sold at post offices, newsagents, newsstands, petrol stations and supermarkets and come in 175Kč and 320Kč sizes. Trick Cards, a relatively new phonecard from Czech Telecom, allow you to make calls, send SMS and emails and log on to the Internet from selected pay phones. They come in amounts of 150/200/300Kč.

Slovakia

Slovakia's country code is ☎ 421. When dialling a long distance number within Slovakia you must also include the area code, for instance ☎ 02 for Bratislava, with the number. Local calls do not require the area code, you only need to dial the local seven (eight for Bratislava) digit number.

For all directory inquiries call ☎ 0800-123 456.

INTERNATIONAL CALLS

To make direct-dial international calls dial ☎ 00, the country code and the number. Phonecards are the simplest and cheapest way to make international calls; peak-rate calls to the UK cost 32Sk per minute, 96Sk to the USA or Australia and 160Sk to New Zealand or South Africa.

MOBILE PHONES

Like the Czech Republic, Slovakia uses GSM 900, and the same rules apply when using your phone. It's also possible to buy pay-as-you-go SIM cards. Slovakia's two local service providers, **Orange** (www.orange.sk) and **EuroTel**, have cards for sale, ranging from 400Sk to 1000Sk. Only EuroTel rents phones, and only from its Bratislava outlets; one-week/month rental costs 500/1500Sk, plus a 2000Sk deposit. You can't use your home number with either service.

PUBLIC PHONES & PHONECARDS

Coin-operated phones take 1Sk, 2Sk, 5Sk and 10Sk coins and can be used for local, long-distance and international calls.

Phonecards *(telefónna karta)* in Slovakia are a better bet for long-distance and international calls. The cards are sold in post offices, newsagents, petrol stations and InfoTel shops (Slovak Telecom's public arm) and come in denominations of

---

COUNTRY-DIRECT NUMBERS

Many countries have arrangements for direct-dial connections from the Czech Republic to a domestic operator for reverse-charge (collect), account and credit-card calls.

In the Czech Republic dial ☎ 00 420 then:

- Australia: ☎ 06101
- Canada: ☎ 00151
- France: ☎ 03301
- Germany: ☎ 04949
- Ireland: ☎ 35301
- Italy: ☎ 03900
- Netherlands: ☎ 03101
- UK:
    BT ☎ 04401
    C&W ☎ 04450
- USA:
    AT&T ☎ 00101
    MCI ☎ 00112
    Sprint ☎ 87187

100/140/180/350Sk for calls within Slovakia and 200/400/1000Sk for international calls. Card phones are becoming more common than their coin-operated counterpart.

TIME

Like the rest of Continental Europe, the Czech and Slovak Republics are both on Central European Time, ie GMT/UTC plus one hour (see the time-zone world map p467). Clocks are moved one hour forward to daylight-saving time (DST) on the last weekend in March and back again on the last weekend in October.

When it's noon in the republics' summer, it's 3am in San Francisco and Vancouver; 6am in New York; 11am in London; 8pm in Sydney; and 10pm in Wellington. When it's noon in Prague's winter, it's 10pm in Sydney and midnight in Wellington.

Czechs and Slovaks quote time on a 24-hour clock so there is no equivalent of 'am' and 'pm'. But they commonly add *ráno* (morning), *dopoledne/dopoludnia* (before noon), *odpoledne/popoludní* (afternoon) or *večer* (evening).

TOURIST INFORMATION
Local Tourist Offices
CZECH REPUBLIC

The **Czech Tourist Authority** (Česká centrála cestovního ruchu or ČCCR; head office ☎ 221 580 111; www .czechtourism.com; Vinohradská 46, PO Box 32, 120 41 Prague 2) handles tourist information about sights, museums, festivals etc for the entire Czech Republic. Their network of municipal information centres *(městské informační centrum* or *středisko)* covers all the major tourist areas throughout the Czech Republic and is easily the best source of information.

SLOVAKIA

There's a useful network of municipal information centres *(mestské informačné centrum)* in Slovakia; most of these are members of the **Association of Information Centres of Slovakia** (Asosiácia Informačných Centier Slovenska or AiCES; head office ☎ 044-551 45 41; www.infoslovak.sk; námestie mieru 1, 031 01 Liptovský Mikuláš). A few towns and cities also run their own information centres.

The **Slovak Tourist Board** (Slovenská agentúra pre cestovný ruch; ☎ 048-413 614 648; www.slovakia tourism.sk; námestie L.Stura 1, PO Box 35, 974 05 Banská Bystrica) is mainly concerned with producing promotional materials.

Tourist Offices Abroad

If you're close to any of the following tourist offices, it's worthwhile stopping by for general information on sights, accommodation and transport.

CZECH TOURIST AUTHORITY

Austria Vienna (☎ 01-533 21 93; tourinfo-wien@visit-czechia.at; Herrengasse 17, 1010 Vienna)
Canada Toronto (☎ 416-363 9928; ctacanada@iprimus.ca; Czech Airlines Office, Suite 1510, Simpson Tower, 401 Bay St, Toronto, Ontario M5H2YA)
France Paris (☎ 01 53 73 00 32; crparis@attglobal.net; Rue Bonaparte 18, Paris)
Germany (www.czech-tourist.de) Berlin (☎ 030-204 47 70; Karl Liebknecht Strasse 34, 10 178 Berlin); Munich (☎ 089-548 85 91; Karlsplatz 3, 80335 Munich)
Hungary Budapest (☎ 01-374 1070; andras.sziranyi@fischer.hu; Teréz krt. 25, 1067 Budapest)
Japan Kagoshima (☎ 0995-58 4868; www.czta.org; Czech Village, 876-15 Fumoto, Mizobe-cho, Aira-gun, Kagoshima-ken); Tokyo (☎ 03-5402 4425; 2-10-12 Higashi-Shinbashi, Minato-ku, Tokyo)
Netherlands Amsterdam (☎ 020-575 30 14; www.tsjechie.nl; Strawinskylaan 517, 1077 XX Amsterdam)
Switzerland Zürich (☎ 01-287 33 44; travel@cedok.ch; Am Schanzengraben, 11, CH – 8002 Zürich)
UK London (☎ 020-7631 0427; info@visitczechia.org.uk; Morley House, 320 Regent Street, London W1B 3BG)
USA New York (☎ 212-288 0830; travelczech@pop.net; 1109 Madison Ave, New York, NY 10028)

SLOVAK TOURIST BOARD

Austria (☎ 01-513 95 69; sacr-wien@aon.at; Slowakische Zentrale für Tourismus Parkring 12, 1010 Vienna)
Czech Republic (☎ 224 946 082; sacrpraha@seznam.cz; Purkynova 4 110 00 Prague 1)
Netherlands (☎ 020-575 2181; info@slowaaks-verkeersbureau.nl; WTC Amsterdam, Strawinskylaan 623, 1077 XX Amsterdam)
Poland (☎ 022-827 00 09; sacr@poczta.onet.pl; ul. Krakowskie Przedmiescie 13 pok.17, 00-071 Warszawa)

VISAS

Both the Czech Republic and Slovakia join the EU in 2004 (with the possible introduction of the euro in 2007) so the following information may not be completely accurate; check with your closest embassy for up-to-date regulations.

Czech Republic

Without a visa, nationals of the UK can visit the Czech Republic for up to 180 days; citizens of all other EU countries, New Zealand and the USA can visit for up to 90 days. Australians, Canadians and South Africans must obtain a 90-day tourist visa (even if in transit; around $US50) from an embassy outside the Czech Republic; visas are not issued at airports or border crossings. Once issued, they must be used within six months. Everything you need to know about applying for a visa can be found on the Ministry of Foreign Affairs' website (www.mfa.cz).

Within three days of arrival in the Czech Republic all foreign visitors are expected to register at the local police station. If you're staying in ordinary tourist accommodation, this will be done for you automatically; otherwise it's up to you.

Immigration officials can ask you to prove that you have at least $US30 a day (or a valid credit card) for the duration of your stay.

Slovakia

Nationals of most EU countries, Australia, Canada and New Zealand do not need a visa for tourist visits of up to 90 days. UK citizens can stay up to 180 days without a visa; US, Italian and South African citizens only 30 days.

If you need a visa ($US35) apply for it in advance of your trip – you won't be able to get one at the border or at airports.

All visitors are expected to register at the district foreigners' police office within three working days, but this is not necessary if you're staying in tourist accommodation. Technically, visitors must have the equivalent of US$50 for each day they plan to spend in the country and have medical insurance.

Visa Renewals & Extensions

The quickest, most hassle-free way to renew your visa is to take a day trip across the border, or visit a Czech or Slovak embassy in one of the neighbouring countries.

Within the republics visa extensions are supposedly available from Foreigners' Police & Passport Offices (*Úřadovna cizinecká policiea pasové služby/Úřadovňa cudzineckej polície a pasovej služby*) in the larger cities, but it's hard to get an official word on this. Reports from travellers state that such extensions do not exist and the only option is to leave and re-enter the country. The best thing to do is check with your local foreigners' police office but don't leave it till the last minute – these places keep short hours (normally 7.30am to 11.30am and 12.30pm to 3pm Monday to Friday) and have long queues.

Offices include:

Prague (☎ 974 820 238; Olšanská 2, Prague 3)
Brno (☎ 974 620 255; Kopečná 3)
Bratislava (☎ 0961-01 11 11; Sasinkova 23)
Košice (☎ 642 68 78; Tr. SNP 35)

WOMEN TRAVELLERS

To many Westerners the Czech and Slovak Republics seem to be picking up, sexually speaking, where they left off in 1948. Some newsstands stock dozens of porno titles; even mainstream advertising has no qualms about using the occasional naked breast to sell products.

The darker side is that sexual violence has been on the rise since 1989, at least in Prague. Attacks on local women have happened in all parts of Prague, but, statistically speaking, women are far safer in the Czech and Slovak Republics than in the West. The most dangerous area for women at night is the park in front of Prague's main train station.

Czech and Slovak women have made progress towards equality in the workplace, and state financial support for maternity leave is good (six months on 90% of salary), but at home most are still expected to look after the kids and do all of the housework.

Women (especially solo travellers) may find the atmosphere in many nontouristy pubs a bit uncomfortable, as they tend to be exclusively male territory. *Kavárny/kavárné* (coffee shops) often dispense beer and wine too, and are more congenial; *vinárny/vinárně* (wine bars) are another good place for drinks and a meal.

There are very few services for women such as helplines and refuge or rape crisis centres; one good contact throughout the Czech Republic is **Bílý kruh** (White Circle; head office ☎ 257 317 110; www.bkb.cz - Czech only; Duskova 20, 150 00 Prague 5). In Slovakia contact the **Alliance of Women** (☎ 0903 519 55).

WORK
Czech Republic

Prague is the centre for job opportunities for foreigners. English teaching is by far the biggest employer and work is not that hard to find as long as you have a TEFL (Teaching English as a Foreign Language) certificate. Computing, finance, real estate, management firms and the arts are also possibilities. The classified ads in the *Prague Post* (www.praguepost.com) and *Prague Business Journal* (www.pbj.cz) are good starting points; *JobMaster* (www.job master.cz), a weekly publication, sometimes has jobs advertised in English.

Normally your employer will organise a work visa for you. If you need to arrange a visa yourself, you must apply for one at a Czech embassy or consulate outside the Czech Republic. For more information go to the Travel and Living Abroad section of the Ministry of Foreign Affair's website (www.mfa.cz); with the Czech Republic joining the EU in 2004, these regulations could easily change.

Trustworthy language schools in Prague include:

Berlitz (☎ 222 125 555; praha@berlitz.cz; Hybernská 24, Prague 1)
London School of Modern Languages (☎ 222 515 018, 222 253 437; www.lsml.cz; Londýnská 8, Prague 2)
Státní jazyková škola (☎ 222 232 235; www.sjs.cz; Školská 15, Prague 1)

If you're up for volunteer work over summer, **KMC** (Young Travellers Club; ☎ 222 220 347; www.kmc.cz; Karolíny Světlé 30, 110 00 Prague 1) is a helpful organisation to contact.

Slovakia

The chances of finding work in Slovakia are far lower. There are not many opportunities for non-Slovak speakers unless you are working for a foreign company – in which case it is much easier to find the job from home.

EU citizens can apply for a work permit from within Slovakia; all other nations must have a work permit in their passport before arriving in the country. Once again, this may all change with Slovakia's inclusion into the EU in 2004, so check with your nearest Slovak embassy.

Your best bet is to find a job teaching English, but there are not that many schools in Slovakia. Reputable schools include The British Council (p333) and Berlitz (p435). The Slovak Spectator's *Career and Employment Guide* has a lot of useful information on subjects such as visas, work conditions, firms and studying in Slovakia. Its website (www.slovakspectator.sk) has a classified section advertising jobs.

Transport

CONTENTS

GETTING THERE & AWAY

Being landlocked countries in the heart of Europe, the Czech and Slovak Republics don't prove too hard to get to; transport options available to the average traveller are quite good. Regular and no-frills airlines connect Prague and Bratislava with other capitals across Europe; the extensive train network of Continental Europe crosses the republic's borders some 30 times; and by road, visitors can enter the Czech Republic at almost 70 points and Slovakia at about 30 (not counting crossings between the republics). You can even arrive in Bratislava by passenger boat from Vienna and Budapest.

This section only deals with travel to the republics; travel between the republics is dealt with in Getting Around, p454.

ENTERING THE COUNTRY

Your passport must be valid for at least nine/six months after your intended departure date when you enter the Czech/Slovak Republics.

AIR

International flights all arrive at the two capitals, Prague and Bratislava, except for flights between Vienna and Košice and

---

> **THINGS CHANGE**
>
> The information in this chapter is particularly vulnerable to change. Check directly with the airline or a travel agent to make sure you understand how a fare (and ticket you may buy) works and be aware of the security requirements for international travel. Shop carefully. The details given in this chapter should be regarded as pointers and are not a substitute for your own careful, up-to-date research.

between Moscow and Karlovy Vary (and inter-republic ones). The airports of Brno-Turany and Ostrava-Mosnov in the Czech Republic and Tatry-Poprad (the highest in Europe) in Slovakia are normally only used for charter flights.

Prague has been a popular destination for quite some time, so you'll find plenty of international connections. Bratislava is slowly coming of age and with its first no-frills airline, Sky Europe, recently getting off the ground, flying to Slovakia has become an affordable and easy option.

The high season for air travel to the Czech and Slovak Republics is roughly May to September, plus the Easter and Christmas–New Year holidays.

Airports & Airlines

Prague's **Ruzyně Airport** (code PRG; ☎ 220 113 314; www.csl.cz; Nove Letiste 160 08, Prague 6, Ruzyně) receives over 38,000 scheduled international flights a year, so there's a multitude of airlines arriving and departing from its runways. The main culprits include:

Aeroflot (☎ 224 819 689; www.aeroflot.com; Truhlářská 5)

Air Canada (☎ 224 810 181; www.aircanada.ca; Kozí 3)

Air France (☎ 221 662 662; www.airfrance.com; Ruzyně Airport)

American Airlines (☎ 224 234 985; www.americanairlines.com; Železná 14)

Austrian Airlines (☎ 220 116 272; www.aua.com; Ruzyně Airport)

British Airways (☎ 222 114 444; www.britishairways.com; Ruzyně Airport)

ČSA (České aerolinie; ☎ 220 104 310; www.csa.cz; V Celnici 5) The Czech Republic's national airline.

Delta Airlines (☎ 224 946 733; www.delta.com; Narodni 32)

Easy Jet (☎ 296 333 333; www.easyjet.com)

German Wings (☎ 0800 142 287; www.german wings.com)

Lufthansa (☎ 224 228 849; www.lufthansa.com; Na Příkopě 24)

KLM (☎ 220 114 148; www.klm.com; Ruzyně Airport)

In Bratislava the **MR Štefánika Airport** (code BTS; ☎ 02-48 57 33 53; www.airportbratislava.sk; Ivanská cesta) receives international flights from the following operators:

Aeroflot (☎ 02-43 33 75 81; www.aeroflot.com; MR Štefánika Airport)

Air Slovakia (☎ 02-43 42 76 68; www.airslovakia.sk; MR Štefánika Airport)

ČSA (České aerolinie; ☎ 02-52 96 10 42; Sturova 13)

Sky Europe (☎ 02-48 50 11 11; www.skyeurope.com; Ivanská cesta 26, 820 01 Bratislava 21)

Slovak Airlines (☎ 02-48 57 51 70; www.slovakairlines .sk; MR Štefánika Airport)

Another feasible option is to fly to Vienna's **Schwechat Airport** (code VIE; ☎ 0043-1-70 070; www.viennaairport.com), which is only 65km from Bratislava. Sky Europe has regular flights to Schwechat, with bus connection to central Bratislava.

Tickets

Buying tickets in the Czech and Slovak Republics won't save you much money, so if you're going only there, take advantage of the lower cost of a return (round-trip) ticket bought at home. No-frills airlines (German Wings, EasyJet and Sky Europe) may have cheap one-way tickets available, but if you leave booking flights to the last minute, you'll probably have to pay an over-inflated price.

Except during fare wars, airlines themselves don't usually offer the cheapest tickets. For these you must shop around the travel agencies, look for adverts in major newspapers' travel sections, and watch for special offers. A good travel agent can be worth its weight in gold; agents have the low-down on special deals, ways to avoid long stopovers and plenty of other useful advice.

Perhaps a more convenient option is booking over the Internet. Along with booking directly with airlines, there is a plethora of web-based companies selling flights, and you can sometimes come up with bargain fares. With any luck, you'll find something that takes your fancy with the following websites:

Airbrokers (www.airbrokers.com) US company specialising in cheap tickets.

Cheap Flights (www.cheapflight.com or www.cheap flights.co.uk) Very informative site with specials, airline information and flight searches mainly from the USA and UK.

Cheapest Flights (www.cheapestflights.co.uk) Cheap worldwide flights from the UK; get in early for the bargains.

Expedia (www.expedia.co.uk) UK-based company listing major airlines; the earlier you book the better.

Flight Centre (www.flightcentre.co.uk) Respected operator handling direct flights, with sites for Australia, New Zealand, the UK, the USA and Canada.

Hotwire (www.hotwire.com) Bookings from the US only, some cheap last-minute deals.

Last Minute (www.lastminute.com) One of the better sites for last-minute deals, including hotels.

Price Line (www.priceline.com) Name-your-own-price US site.

Orbitz (www.orbitz.com) Cheap deals when flying from the US.

STA Travel (www.statravel.com) Prominent in international student travel but you don't necessarily have to be a student; website linked to worldwide STA sites.

Travel (www.travel.com.au or www.travel.co.nz) Reputable online flight bookers from Australia and New Zealand.

Travelocity (www.travelocity.com) US site that allows you to search fares (in US$) to/from practically anywhere.

DEPARTURE TAX

Flying internationally to or from either republic, the departure tax (which applies to flights between the two republics as well) is 468Kč from Prague and 490Sk from Bratislava, but this is more often than not included in the price of any ticket bought from a travel agency.

From Australasia

Check the travel agencies' ads in the Yellow Pages, and the Saturday travel sections of the *Sydney Morning Herald*, the *Age* in Melbourne and the *New Zealand Herald*.

Fares to Europe are normally about $A2000 and you'll have to transit through London, Frankfurt, Paris or other large European airports to reach Prague, Bratislava or Vienna.

STA Travel (NZ ☎ 0800 874 773; www.statravel.co.nz; Australia ☎ 1300 360 960; www.statravel.com.au) and **Flight Centre** (NZ ☎ 0800 243 544; www.flightcentre.co.nz; Australia ☎ 131 600; www.flightcentre.com.au) are good starting points. Both have offices throughout Australasia.

From Continental Europe

From most Continental cities, routes to and from Prague are sewn up between the main airline from the home country and ČSA. Usually fares are agreed between the two airlines on a route, and revenue divided, so there is no real competition and fares are high. German Wings is about the only cheap alternative, flying from Stuttgart and Cologne/Bonn.

There are regular flights to Prague from many European cities, but the majority arrive from Amsterdam, Frankfurt, Munich, Paris, Vienna and Zurich. Look to pay around €300 for a return flight, but they can go for as low as €150.

Bratislava receives scheduled flights from Berlin, Munich, Moscow and Zurich, with prices again around the €300 mark. It's also possible to fly to Košice (code KCS; www.airportkosice.sk) from Vienna once a day Monday to Friday with **Tyrolean Airways** (www.tyrolean.at). Once again, it may prove cheaper to fly to Vienna's Schwechat Airport and then take a bus to Bratislava.

The following travel agents can be recommended:

NETHERLANDS
Airfair (☎ 020 620 5121; www.airfair.nl)
NBBS Reizen (☎ 0900 10 20 300; www.mytravel.nl)

GERMANY
STA Travel (☎ 01805 456 422; www.statravel.de)
Just Travel (☎ 089 747 3330; www.justtravel.de)

FRANCE
OTU Voyages (☎ 0820 817 817; www.otu.fr)
Voyageurs du Monde (☎ 01 42 86 16 00; www.vdm.com)
Nouvelles Frontières (☎ 0825 000 747; www.nouvelles-frontieres.fr)

ITALY
CTS Viaggi (☎ 06 462 0431)
Passagi (☎ 06 474 0923)
Viaggi Wasteels (☎ 06 446 6679)

From the UK

Discount air travel is big business in London. In addition to the travel sections of the major Sunday papers, check the Travel classifieds in London's weekly *Time Out* and *TNT* entertainment magazines. Outside London it's not so easy to find flights to the republics, however EasyJet flies to Prague direct from Newcastle, East Midlands and Bristol.

The cheapest flights are often offered by obscure bucket shops that don't even appear in the telephone book. Many are honest and solvent, but be careful as some may take your money and disappear, only to reopen elsewhere under a new name.

Some of the more reliable agents in London include:
Bridge the World (☎ 0870 444 7474; www.b-t-w.co.uk)
Flightbookers (☎ 0870 010 7000; www.ebookers.com)
Flight Centre (☎ 0870 890 8099; www.flightcentre.co.uk)
STA Travel (☎ 0870 160 0599, www.statravel.co.uk) Popular travel agency for students or travellers under 26 years.
Trailfinders (☎ 020-7938 3939; www.trailfinders.co.uk)

Return flights from the UK can be as low as £100, but are generally around £200 to £250.

Some travellers have noted that flights from London to Prague are often full to overflowing, and there have been occasions of flights being overbooked. If you don't want to risk having to wait for a later plane, it's advisable to turn up early.

From the USA & Canada

Discount travel agents in the USA are known as consolidators (although you won't see a sign on the door saying Consolidator). San Francisco is the ticket consolidator capital of America, although some good deals can be found in Los Angeles, New York and other big cities.

ČSA has daily direct flights to Prague from New York, and from Montreal and Toronto twice a week. Flights generally cost about US$800 to US$1000 but you may pick something up for US$500. The cheapest way is probably to fly to London and buy an onward ticket there.

There are no direct flights into Bratislava from North America. Austrian Airlines, however, has frequent direct flights to Vienna from New York and Washington DC, and the occasional direct flight from Montreal and Toronto.

Recommended travel agents include:
STA Travel (☎ 800 781 4040; www.statravel.com) Has offices throughout the USA.

Travel Avenue (☎ 1-800 333 3335; www.travelavenue .com) Well-established travel agent, based in Chicago.
Travel CUTS (☎ 800 667 2887; www.travelcuts.com) Canada's national student travel agency.

LAND
Border Crossings

As long as all your paperwork is in order, you should have no problems crossing into the Czech or Slovak Republics. You may encounter delays travelling to or from Poland or the Ukraine, but that's about it. See also customs (p435) and visa (p447) requirements.

Both of the country maps (p78 and p328) show major, 24-hour international border crossings for cars, buses and motorcycles. Be aware that some crossings are only for citizens of the Czech or Slovak Republics and the neighbouring country. Any comprehensive country map has a complete list of border crossings and their opening times. See p454 for information on crossing between the two republics.

BICYCLE & WALKING

There are a number of border crossings that are limited to pedestrians and cyclists in both countries. Others are limited to people on foot, bicycle or moped. Some open only during the summer months, while others are open year-round; most are mentioned in the destination chapters.

Crossing from Slovakia to the Ukraine by foot is a definite no-no, and by bicycle it's frowned upon.

Bus

Travelling by bus may not be the most comfortable way to cross Europe, but it is the cheapest. It's easiest to book with **Eurolines** (www.eurolines.com), a consortium of coach companies with offices all over Europe. Coaches are air-conditioned, as fast as the train, and they stop frequently for food and facilities. Services to Prague are comprehensive – there are direct buses from London, Amsterdam, Paris, Munich, Berlin and dozens of other major European cities. Bratislava is connected to London, Brussels, Paris, Munich, Zurich and a number of other destinations. For Slovakia, it is also worth considering buses to Vienna, then a connection to Bratislava (see p343).

Eurolines coaches from London to Prague (22 hours, £62 return) and Bratislava (24 hours, £82 return) are cheaper if booked 15 days in advance; book at any National Express office. All fares are 10% to 15% cheaper if you book from within the Czech and Slovak Republics.

For quick trips around Europe, both Eurolines and **Busabout** (☎ 020-7950 1661; www .busabout.com), a London based firm, have bus passes. The Eurolines Pass covers 31 major European tourist cities (including Prague and Bratislava) over 15/30/60 days from June to mid-September for £174/259/299, mid-September to May £135/189/239.

Busabout offers two passes for travelling around 50 European cities, including Prague, Terezín and Český Krumlov. Its Flexi Pass allows so many days travel over a set period; seven days travel within one month costs £219, 12 days in two months £349. The Consecutive Pass is similar to the Eurolines Pass; 14/21/30 days travel costs £219/289/359. And like the Eurolines Pass, it's cheaper outside the summer months.

Kingscourt Express (☎ 020-8673 7500; www.kce .cz) and **Capital Express** (☎ 020-7243 0488; www .capitalexpress.cz), two Czech companies, connect London with Prague and Brno for a little less than Eurolines.

Youth and senior discounts are available on almost all fares and passes.

Car & Motorcycle

For more about driving between and within the two republics, including Czech-Slovak border crossings, road rules and fuel, see p454 and pp456–7.

The Czech Republic recognises British and EU driving licenses; all other nationalities require an International Driving Permit. All foreign national driving licenses with photo ID are valid in Slovakia but it's a good idea to have an International Driving Permit too. Drivers must also have their passport, vehicle registration papers and the 'green card' that shows they carry at least third-party liability insurance (see your domestic insurer about this). Without proof of insurance you'll be forced to take out insurance at the border, for around US$160 a month for a car or US$55 a month for a motorcycle. Insurance is not available at all border crossings. If the car isn't yours, avoid potential headaches by carrying a notarised letter from the owner saying you're allowed to drive it.

In your car you will need to carry a first-aid kit and a red-and-white warning triangle. You must display a nationality sticker on the rear.

Hitching

Hitching is never entirely safe anywhere in the world, and we don't recommend it. Travellers who decide to hitch should understand that they are taking a small but potentially serious risk. Those who choose to hitch will be safer if they travel in pairs, and let someone know where they are planning to go.

If you are still set on hitching across Europe, a worthwhile website to check is www.hitchhikers.org. It provides information on drivers looking for passengers for trips across the continent. Most drivers ask a minimal fee from those catching a lift.

Train

The train network of Europe is a massive spider web of rail tracks stretching right across the continent. It's a popular and comfortable form of transport that at times, particularly over the summer, can get rather crowded. It's not a bad idea at this time to book at least a few weeks ahead to save yourself any headaches. Fares quoted here are based on advertised average rates at the time of writing.

The Czech and Slovak Republics are well connected to the rest of the European train network. The capitals of Prague and Bratislava (via Vienna) can be reached from most major European cities on a daily basis. Most long distance trains have both 1st- and 2nd-class carriages, plus a sleeper wagon which is more expensive but by far the most comfortable way to travel if you're making an overnight journey. It's advisable to reserve a sleeper any time, year-round.

In the UK, buy your tickets through **Rail Europe** (☎ 08705-848 848; www.raileurope.co.uk). The cheapest and most direct 2nd-class, return ticket from London to Prague is via Paris and Frankfurt (£274, 20 to 25 hours). Tickets are good for two months and you can break your journey anywhere en route. Other 2nd-class return fares to Prague include those from Paris (€280, 15½ hours), Amsterdam (€300, 13½ hours) and Vienna (€70, 4½ hours). For Bratislava, it's best to head for Vienna from London (£272, 19½ hours), from where frequent trains (€16 return, one hour) make the journey to Slovakia's capital.

Prices for international trains are cheaper if you book in Prague or Bratislava. Some sample 2nd-class, international train fares from Prague are: Budapest (1350Kč, nine hours), Kraków (900Kč, 10 hours), Vienna (930Kč, six hours), Warsaw (1200Kč, 12 hours) and Berlin (1440Kč, 5½ hours).

There's no need to book domestic rail travel before you get there.

RAIL PASSES

If you plan to travel widely in Europe, the following special tickets and rail passes may be better value for getting in and out of the Czech and Slovak Republics, but not within them. Some of these may have different names in different countries. You can purchase rail passes from travel agents at home or in Europe, or from the companies supplying them.

InterRail Pass

Only available to anyone who has lived in Europe for at least six months, this pass gives travellers unlimited, 2nd-class travel for up to one month on most of the state railways of Western and central Europe (except in their own country). The 'Zone D' pass for travel in the Czech and Slovak Republics, Hungary, Poland and Croatia costs £219 for 22 days (£149 for those under 26). If you want to go out of this zone into another then a two-zone pass, valid for a month, is £275/195.

European East Pass

The European East Pass is only available in the USA and provides unlimited travel in the Czech and Slovak Republics, Austria, Hungary and Poland for any five days within a month. Tickets for 1st-/2nd-class travel cost US$225/158. Extra days cost US$25/18.

INTERNATIONAL TRAIN DEPARTURES

Within the Czech and Slovak Republics, you can front up to the window for international tickets (*mezinárodní jízdenky* or *medzinárodný lístok*) in a big-city train station, but it's easier to make international bookings (and get any discounts you're entitled to) through a reliable travel agency. Some are identified under individual towns. There's often a ČD (České dráhy or Czech Railways) agency in bigger stations. The youth-oriented GTS international or CKM office in some major cities and the local Čedok or Satur office may not be the cheapest but are usually competent.

Warning

The overnight international trains to/from the Czech Republic have become notorious for bold thefts from sleeping passengers, so keep a grip on your bags.

RIVER

Hydrofoils ply the Danube between Bratislava and Vienna, Austria (one way/return €21/32, 1¾ hours), once a day, Wednesday to Sunday from April to October, every day from June to August. It's also possible to hydrofoil it from Bratislava to Budapest, Hungary (€59/84, four hours), once daily between April and October, twice daily in August. Tickets can be bought at the **hydrofoil terminal** (Fajnorovo nábrežie 2, Bratislava).

GETTING AROUND

Whether your choice of transportation is train, plane, automobile, or pedal power, the Czech and Slovak Republics are not hard to get around. Both have good railway networks; in fact the Czech Republic has one of the most dense networks in Europe. Slovakia's is less extensive due to its mountainous landscape. The bus network in the republics is excellent. Trains are comfortable but slower and more expensive than buses. The general rule of thumb is if you're travelling between larger cities take a train, otherwise catch a bus.

Roads are in good condition, and there are over 1000km of European-style motorways. Most main thoroughfares, however, pass through small villages, making the going slow but scenic.

An excellent source of online transport information, including public city transport, for the Czech Republic is the website www.idos.cz. The Slovakian equivalent is www.cp.sk.

Bus and train connections given here are direct services only, unless otherwise stated. Prices are for one-way journeys and for 2nd-class seats on trains.

See the Directory p441 for information about travel insurance.

Border Crossings between the Republics

The Czech-Slovak border functions like any other border in Europe and there are currently 15 official border crossings. Czechs and Slovaks flash their documents to the guards and barely stop when crossing the border, but foreign drivers are more thoroughly checked. The most well-used border crossing is on the E65 Highway at Kúty, between Brno and Bratislava. Note, however, that this is the only crossing which cannot be used by foot passengers.

AIR

Air travel in the republics is quite limited. There are seven main airports: Prague Ruzyně (PRG), Brno-Turany (BRQ), Ostrava (OSR) and Karlovy Vary (KLV) in the Czech Republic; Bratislava MR Štefánika (BTS), Košice (KSC) and Poprad-Tatry (TAT) in Slovakia.

ČSA is the national carrier of the Czech Republic and a major carrier in Slovakia. Slovak carriers are Sky Europe, Air Slovakia and Slovak Airlines. For airline contact details, see p449.

Domestic Flights

ČSA flies twice a week between Prague and Brno (one hour) and up to three times daily

AIR FARES		
Prices are for return flights booked three weeks in advance:		
From	**To**	**Cost**
Prague	Bratislava	3000Kč/3500Sk
Prague	Košice	3000Kč/4000Sk
Prague	Brno	2500Kč
Prague	Ostrava	5000Kč
Bratislava	Košice	2000Sk

between Prague and Ostrava (one hour). Within Slovakia, Sky Europe flies up to three times daily between Bratislava and Košice (one hour). Slovak Airlines only flies from Bratislava to Košice on a Saturday.

Inter-Republic Flights

From Prague, ČSA has up to four flights a day to Bratislava (one hour) and Košice (1½ hours). Sky Europe flies between Bratislava and Prague five times a week.

BICYCLE

For general information on cycling in the Czech and Slovak Republics, see p58, and for maps, see p443.

Hire

The Czech and Slovak Republics are slowly cottoning on to the fact that a buck can be made from renting bikes. Many of the bigger cities have a bike-rental place or two (Bratislava has none but this could easily change), as do the popular tourist spots and mountainous regions (Krkonoše in the Czech Republic, High Tatras and the Fatras in Slovakia). Outside these areas, your best bet is to try upmarket hotels. Bike rental places are mentioned throughout the destination chapters.

Purchase

If you're planning to spend some time cycling around the republics and you can't be bothered dragging your bike with you, buying one there is a feasible option. A new mountain bike costs from 10,000Kč/13,000Sk to 15,000Kč/19,000Sk and almost every town has a bike shop. This also means that it's easy to get spare parts. Second-hand bikes are not so popular in either republic, but they are available. Expect to pay at least 1500Kč/2000Sk for something half decent; anything less than that and you're probably putting your life at risk.

BOAT

On the whole, most Czech and Slovak rivers are too shallow for passenger transport. In the Czech Republic in summer, boats go along the Vltava between Prague and Štěchovice, and on the Labe between Děčín and Hřensko. During summer in Slovakia there are occasional trips along the Danube between Bratislava and Gabčíkovo (p339).

BUS

Buses in both republics are cheap, fast, and popular. Bus stations are normally within walking distance of town centres, and often adjacent to the train station. During the week there are generally frequent services, but this peters out to either only a handful on weekends, or none at all. Long-distance coach connections tend to be faster, more frequent and cheaper than train connections, and remote locations require fewer transfers.

ČSAD (Česká automobilová doprava or Czech Bus Transport; stv@csad.cz) is the state bus company in the Czech Republic, and **SAD** (Slovenská autobusová doprava; ☎ 02-5556 7349) operates in Slovakia. The Czech Republic has at least two private lines too, with prices a shade less than ČSAD's. From Prague, **Čebus** (☎ 542 211 956; www.cebus.cz) and **Český národní expres** (CNE; ☎ 312 285 550; www.cne.cz) go to Brno. CNE also serves Klado from Prague.

Buses between the Republics

Your coach may not stop at the border checkpoint between the two republics, but you'll avoid hassles later (mainly over how long you've been in the country) if you insist on stopping for an entry stamp in your passport.

Costs

Bus travel in both republics is cheap. Fares are calculated, surprisingly enough, by the kilometre; a 100km journey costs around 100Kč/120Sk. One-way fares and times:

Destination	Cost	Duration
Bratislava–Košice	512Sk	6½–7½hr
Bratislava–Poprad	428Sk	5½–7hr
Brno–Bratislava	200Kč	2hr
Košice–Brno	610Sk	9–11hr
Košice–Prague	812Sk	10½–12hr
Prague–Bratislava	300Kč	4¾hr
Prague–Brno	150Kč	2½hr
Prague–Hradec Králové	72Kč	1½hr

Reservations

Travel agencies don't book internal coaches, though some may have timetable information. Short-haul tickets are sold on the bus, long-distance tickets usually at the station. If you're travelling on a weekend on one of the more popular routes, it's not a bad idea to book ahead. You can hand the clerk a

TRANSPORT

BUS TIMETABLE SYMBOLS

✕	workdays (normally Mon to Fri)
S	Saturdays if not a state holiday
†	holidays
N	holiday just before a workday
b	✕ & Saturdays
a	Saturdays and holidays only
P	workday following a holiday only
V	workday before weekends & holidays
c	schooldays only
r	not on 24 December
x	stops on request
MHD	stop situated in an urban mass transit area
⌐	bus takes another route
l	bus doesn't stop here

---

scrap of paper with your destination, departure time (24-hour clock) and date (month in Roman numerals) and get the nearest thing on offer, which is a lot more fun than wrestling with the timetables.

Big stations like Florenc in Prague have charts with all the route numbers for each major destination and all the departure times for each route number, plus timetables for every route. To figure out when the next bus leaves, you'll probably have to look at more than one timetable. They'll drive you cross-eyed, peppered with symbols showing the days buses do and don't run. See the boxed text above for an explanation of the most common symbols, but be ready for local variations.

CAR & MOTORCYCLE

The Czech and Slovak Republics are covered by a network of generally good roads, though they often follow old routes through villages and small towns, with sudden sharp bends and reduced speed limits. There are over 1000km of European-style motorways, the main ones being the D1 or E50/E65 between Prague, Brno and Olomouc, the D2 or E65 between Brno and Bratislava, the D5 or E50 linking Prague and Plzeň and the D1 or E75 between Bratislava and Považská Bystrica.

The major motorways have a toll charge (800/200/100Kč for one year/one month/10 days in the Czech Republic, 600/100Sk for one year/15 days in Slovakia) which is payable at most border crossings, some petrol stations and at the automobile organisations in both countries. Fines of up to 5000Kč/Sk are payable if you're caught without a sticker.

Motorways and city centres have heavy traffic, while country roads tend to have light traffic. Excessive speed and passing on blind corners are the main problems in both countries, so it's best to drive defensively.

The Czech Republic has two automobile associations: the **Ústřední AutoMotoKlub** (ÚAMK; ☎ 1230; www.uamk.cz) and **Autoklub Bohemia Assistance** (ABA; ☎ 1240; www.aba.cz). Slovakia's automobile association is the **Autoklub Slovakia Assistance** (ASA; ☎ 18 124; www.autoklub.sk).

Bringing Your Own Vehicle

There are no major hassles bringing your own vehicle into either republic. Cars with foreign license plates are prime target for thieves (as in any country) but the number of car thefts in the republics is no higher than in Western Europe. See p452 for information on the documents required to take your car into the republics.

Fuel

Petrol or gasoline (benzín) is not hard to find. Diesel (nafta), leaded petrol (special is 91 octane, super is 96 octane), and unleaded petrol (natural is 95 octane, super is 98 octane) are available at all stations. Prices are well below Western European prices with unleaded petrol costing about 30Kč/35Sk per litre. LPG (autoplyn) is available in every major town, but at very few outlets and rarely at petrol stations. You're not allowed to take more than 10L of fuel in or out of the country in a spare container.

Hire

Normally you have to be 21 years of age to hire a car, sometimes 25. Apart from that, renting a car is relatively easy. A major domestic car-rental agency is **CS Czechocar** (☎ 261 222 079; www.czechocar.cz), with offices in many big cities of the Czech Republic. In Slovakia, **Advantage Car Rental** (☎ 02-6241 0510; www.acr.sk), based in Bratislava, is a reliable domestic firm. Rates start at around 1600Kč/1500Sk per day with unlimited mileage for the smallest vehicle and discounts are available for long-term rentals.

Other local car-rental agencies include:
Abacar Auto Praha (☎ 266 310 041; www.abacar.cz)
Eurocar (☎ 259 632 117; www.eurocar.sk)
Vecar (☎ 224 314 361; www.vecar.cz)

Holiday Autos (www.holidayautos.com), a car-rental agency with offices throughout Europe, often has cheap deals. It's possible to arrange a pick-up within the Czech and Slovak Republics or in your home country. If you decide on the latter option, be sure to check that there are no hefty charges for taking the rental car into either republic. Major international rental companies **Hertz** (www.hertz.cz; www.hertz.sk) and **Avis** (www.avis.com; www.avis.sk) are represented in both countries.

Insurance

Third-party insurance is required in either country. If you arrive at the border in an uninsured car, you'll have to pay for insurance on the spot (see p452). If you're hiring a car, be sure to check your liability in case of an accident. Rather than risk paying out thousands of dollars if you do have an accident, you can take out your own comprehensive insurance on the car, or (the usual option) pay an additional daily amount to the rental company for an 'insurance excess reduction' policy.

In the case of an accident the police should be contacted immediately if repairs are required or if there is an injury. It's essential to get a police report if you plan to make an insurance claim.

Parking

Most city centres have restricted parking within marked zones at parking meters, and parking rules are similar to those in the rest of Europe. They are controlled either by parking meters or parking cards, which can be bought in kiosks, shops or hotels. Carry plenty of small change as most parking meters don't take bank notes. In larger cities, street parking is at a premium and finding a space can prove impossible, so it's often better to head for the nearest car park.

Road Rules

Road rules in both republics are basically the same as the rest of continental Europe; drive on the right-hand side of the road, always wear a seatbelt, children under 12 must ride in the back, mobile telephones can only be used with a hands-free set and pedestrians have the right of way at zebra crossings (although this is hardly ever obeyed). In the Czech Republic vehicles

must have their headlights turned on 24 hours a day from November to March. Don't drink and drive: regulations stipulate zero blood alcohol, and penalties are severe. The legal driving age is 18.

The speed limit within built-up areas is 50/60km/h in the Czech/Slovak republics. On major roads the limit is 90km/h, and on motorways 130km/h for both countries. The official speed limit at the country's many railway crossings is 30km/h, but you're better off stopping and looking, since many well-used crossings have no barriers and some don't even have flashing lights.

Riders of motorcycles greater than 50cc must wear helmets and goggles, and their passengers must wear helmets. The motorcycle's headlight must be on at all times (on low beam). The maximum speed for motorcycles, even on major highways, is 90km/h.

Fines for speeding and minor offences are between 200Kč/Sk and 2000Kč/Sk, levied on the spot. Fines for foreigners are sometimes inflated; if you don't get a docket or receipt (*paragon* or *doklad*), you may be getting overcharged – so politely insist on a receipt. If that does not work try to bargain the fine down.

Pay particular attention to trams: it's best to give them the right-of-way in every situation as you'll come off second best if one happens to bump into you.

Road Signs

Standard European signs are in common use throughout both republics. Some that may be unfamiliar to Britons and non-European visitors are:
Blue disk with red border and crossed red slashes No stopping.
Blue disk with red border and red slash No parking.
Red disk with horizontal white line No entry.
White disk with red border No vehicles allowed.
White triangle (point down) with red border Give way to crossing or merging traffic.
Yellow diamond on white background You have the right of way; a black slash through it means you don't have the right of way.

In cities and towns, keep a sharp eye out for *pěší zóna* signs, indicating pedestrian-only areas, many of which look just like normal streets.

TRANSPORT

HITCHING

As stated earlier, hitching is never entirely safe anywhere in the world, and we don't recommend it. Travellers who decide to hitch should understand that they are taking a small but potentially serious risk. Those who choose to hitch will be safer if they travel in pairs, and let someone know where they are planning to go.

That said, many Czechs and Slovaks, women included, do hitch and do pick up hitchhikers, especially from one small village to the next. It can be an easy and friendly way to get around.

LOCAL TRANSPORT

Public transport in towns and cities normally consists of a comprehensive bus network, which is sometimes complemented by trams and trolley-buses (electric buses). They're well used by locals, so you'll often find more services in the morning and early evening.

Bus, Tram & Trolley-Bus

On the whole, services are frequent and reliable. Typical hours of operation are 5am to 11pm or midnight. Prague, Brno and Bratislava also have limited night bus services.

Depending on the town, a ride is just 5Kč/8Sk to 12Kč/12Sk, with big discounts for kids aged from 10 to 16 years and for parents accompanying very young children. Children aged under 10 and the elderly ride free.

Tickets are sold individually or in discounted books at public transport offices, newsstands, tobacco kiosks, and from machines at major stops. In smaller towns it's often possible to purchase a ticket from the driver. In most places a single ticket is valid for all forms of transport. In Prague, Brno and Bratislava you can also buy multiday and monthly passes for unlimited travel.

You validate your ticket by punching it in a little machine on board (or in Prague's metro station lobbies). It's an honour system, but inspectors pop up fairly often and are keen to levy instant fines on anyone without a valid ticket.

Metro

Prague is the only city with a metro, and that consists of three lines. For more information, see p149.

Taxi

Most towns have at least a few taxis for hire. Prague, however, is plagued with crooked taxi-drivers (for some of the problems involved in hiring taxis there, and ways to cope with them, see p151), but taxi-drivers in Brno, Bratislava and smaller towns are more courteous and will generally treat you fairly. It's normally cheaper to call a taxi than hail one on the street.

TRAIN

ČD (České dráhy or Czech Railways; www.cd.cz) is the state rail company in the Czech Republic and its Slovakian equivalent is **ŽSR** (Železnica Slovenskej republiky or Railways of the Slovak Republic; www.zsr.sk). Their combined network is among Europe's densest and most major cities are linked by several trains a day.

Classes

The fastest trains are SC (SuperCity), EC/IC (EuroCity/InterCity), and express (rychlík/rýchlik), which are shown in shaded columns and bold print in timetables (on the two railways maps in this book all are grouped together as Express Trains). They're often reservation-only, marked with an R in a box; an un-boxed R means reservations are recommended. 'Fast trains' (spěšný vlak/spešný vlak) make more stops but cost a bit less; times are printed in bold on timetables. Slowest of all are the local trains (osobní vlak/osobný vlak).

Most trains have both 1st- and 2nd-class carriages, along with a smoking section, although some local trains may do away with 1st-class. Only SC, IC, EC and express trains have a dining car (restaurační vůz/reštauráčnij vozeň).

If you wish to transport your car, it is possible but only on the route between Prague and Poprad. Canoes can be transported in special carriages, and bicycles are transported in the normal cargo carriages.

Costs

Travel is cheap by Western standards. Foreign and local passengers pay the same fare, and kids receive discounts: children under six ride free, between six and 15 travel for half price. Like buses, train fares are calculated by the kilometre; a 100km journey costs 120Kč/120Sk. First class is about 50% more. Taking the train is more expensive

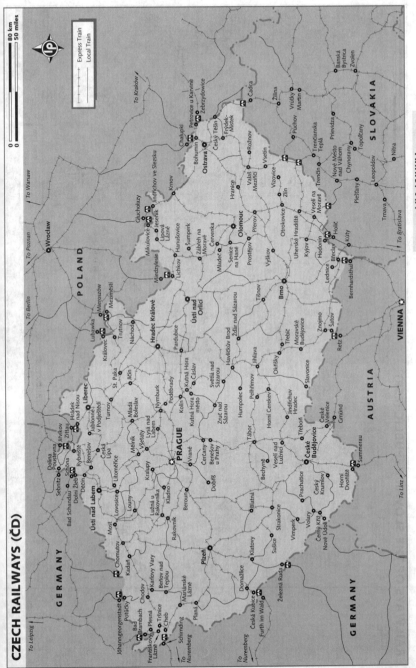

CZECH RAILWAYS (ČD)

TRANSPORT

RAILWAYS OF THE SLOVAK REPUBLIC (ŽSR)

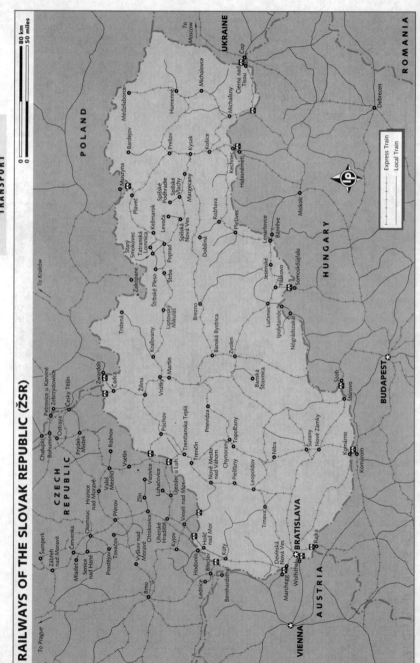

than taking the bus, but the occasional short hop can be cheaper by train. The following are 2nd-class one-way fares and times on express services between some major towns:

Destination	Cost	Duration
Bratislava–Košice	590Sk	5hr
Bratislava–Poprad	384Sk	4¾hr
Brno–Bratislava	200Kč	1½hr
Prague–Bratislava	570Kč	4½hr
Prague–Brno	140Kč	3hr
Prague–Hradec Králové	140Kč,	1½hr

Reservations

You can buy an unreserved ticket (*jízdenka/lístok*) right up to departure time, or make a reservation (*místenka/miestenka*) up to an hour beforehand. You can get a seat (*místo/miesto*), and on longer routes a couchette (*lehátkový vůz/ležadlo* – narrower than a sleeper and only a blanket is supplied) or sleeper (*lůžko/spací vozeň* – more like a bed with sheets included). On fast trains, if ordinary (*jednoduchý*) places are sold out, 1st-class (*prvotřídní/prvotriedny*) ones will probably be available.

Sleepers and couchettes should be booked at least one day before departure; on the same day they can only be purchased from the conductor, when available. Most travel agencies won't make domestic train reservations. However, Czech Railways has its own travel agency, the ČD, that has offices around the country.

If you're buying your own ticket, it's easiest to write down your destination, departure time (24-hour clock) and date (month in Roman numerals) for the clerk. If you don't specify anything else, you'll probably get a one-way, 2nd-class ticket on a local train. 'Return' is *zpáteční/spiatočný*. See the boxed text below for some useful symbols found on timetables.

Train Passes

Before purchasing either of the following passes, check to see if they are going

---

TRAIN TIMETABLE SYMBOLS

🏠 after the name of the station = tickets issued on train only

✗ in the train column = dining car included

🛏 in the train column = train includes sleeping cars or couchettes

R in the train column = for indicated cars, reservation is possible

R̄ in the train column = train with obligatory seat reservation

🛏 in the train column = train carries only sleeping cars and couchettes

♿ in the train column = there is a coach for wheelchairs

x in front of time descriptions = request train to stop only

🚲 the notes have information on transport of bicycles

↙ train travels on another line

| train doesn't stop at this station

① Mon ② Tue ③ Wed ④ Thu ⑤ Fri ⑥ Sat ⑦ Sun

✗ workdays only (normally Mon-Fri)

† holidays (except 24 Dec, 1 & 8 May, 5 Jul) and 2 Jan only

---

to save you money; it's probably cheaper to buy local tickets for travelling around either republic.

EURODOMINO PASS

If you don't plan to be on the move all that much, this pass allows a few days per month of unrestricted 2nd-class train travel within a particular country. In the Czech Republic, for example, any three/eight days in a designated month is £32/70, in Slovakia £27/51.

KILOMETRICKA BANKA PASS

This pass allows 2000km of 2nd-class travel in the Czech Republic over a period of six months and costs 1350Kč. It's only valid on trains after 10am. In Slovakia, the same pass again allows 2000km of travel, but this time in both 1st- and 2nd-class (1990Sk). The only catch is each journey must be a minimum of 100km.

TRANSPORT

Health

Travel health depends on your predeparture preparations, your daily health care while travelling and how you handle any medical problem that does develop. Healthwise, the Czech and Slovak Republics are not going to worry you, and the worst you'll get is a stomach upset or dehydration from too much beer the night before.

BEFORE YOU GO

Prevention is the key to staying healthy while abroad. A little planning before departure, particularly for pre-existing illnesses will save trouble later: see your dentist before a long trip; carry a spare pair of contact lenses and glasses, and take your optical prescription with you. Bring medications in

---

GOVERNMENT WEBSITES

It's usually a good idea to consult your government's travel health website before departure, if one is available:

Australia www.dfat.gov.au/travel/
Canada www.travelhealth.gc.ca
United Kingdom www.doh.gov.uk/traveladvice/
United States www.cdc.gov/travel/

---

their original, clearly labelled, containers. A signed and dated letter from your physician describing your medical conditions and medications, including generic names, is also a good idea. If carrying syringes or needles, be sure to have a physician's letter documenting their medical necessity.

INSURANCE

For EU citizens, an E111 form available from health centres (or post offices in the UK) covers you for most medical care. E111 will not cover you for nonemergencies or emergency repatriation home. Citizens from other countries should find out if there is a reciprocal arrangement for free medical care between their country and the republics. If you do need health insurance, make sure you get a policy that covers you for the worst possible scenario, such as an accident requiring an emergency flight home. Find out in advance if your insurance plan will make payments directly to providers or reimburse you later for overseas health expenditures.

RECOMMENDED VACCINATIONS

The World Health Organisation (WHO) recommends that travellers should be covered for diphtheria, tetanus, measles, mumps, rubella and polio, as well as hepatitis B, regardless of their destination. Since most vaccines don't produce immunity until at least two weeks after they're given, visit a physician at least six weeks before departure.

ONLINE RESOURCES

The WHO's publication *International Travel and Health* is revised annually and is available online at www.who.int/ith/. Other useful websites include:
www.ageconcern.org.uk Travel advice for the elderly.
www.fitfortravel.scot.nhs.uk General travel advice for the layperson.
www.mariestopes.org.uk Information on women's health and contraception.
www.mdtravelhealth.com Travel health recommendations for every country; updated daily.

FURTHER READING

Health Advice for Travellers (currently called the 'T6' leaflet) is a leaflet that is updated annually by the Department of Health in the UK and is available free in UK post offices. It contains some general information, legally required and recommended vaccines for different countries, reciprocal health agreements and an E111 application form.

Lonely Planet's *Travel with Children* includes advice on travel health for young children. Other recommended references include *Traveller's Health* by Dr Richard Dawood and *The Traveller's Good Health Guide* by Ted Lankester.

IN TRANSIT

Deep vein thrombosis (DVT) is a blood clot that may form in the legs during plane flights, chiefly because of prolonged immobility. The longer the flight, the greater the risk. The chief symptom of DVT is swelling or pain of the foot, ankle, or calf, usually but not always on just one side. When a blood clot travels to the lungs, it may cause chest pain and breathing difficulties. Travellers with any of these symptoms should immediately seek medical attention.

To prevent the development of DVT on long flights you should walk about the cabin, contract the leg muscles while sitting, drink plenty of fluids and avoid alcohol and tobacco.

IN THE CZECH & SLOVAK REPUBLICS

AVAILABILITY & COST OF HEALTH CARE

Medical care in Prague, Brno and Bratislava is generally quite good and the chances of finding an English-speaking doctor are high (few doctors outside major cities speak English though). Every sizable town has a *polyklinika*, though few have seen many foreigners. Medical training, equipment and standards of hygiene (and funds for training doctors) are not what most Westerners expect, though they are adequate for routine, walk-in problems. Embassies, consulates and four- and five-star hotels can usually recommend doctors or clinics.

In some cases, medical supplies required in hospital may need to be bought from a pharmacy and nursing care may be limited.

Everybody pays for prescribed medications, though prices are low. Almost every town has a state-run pharmacy. It's a good place to buy aspirin and vitamin C, though not to fill most Western prescriptions.

INFECTIOUS DISEASES
Rabies

Spread through bites or licks on broken skin from an infected animal, rabies is always fatal. Animal handlers should be vaccinated, as should those travelling to remote areas where a reliable source of postbite vaccine is not available within 24 hours. Three injections are needed over a month. If you have not been vaccinated, you will need a course of five injections starting 24 hours, or as soon as possible, after the injury. If you have been vaccinated, you will need fewer injections and have more time to seek medical help.

Tick-borne encephalitis

This serious infection of the brain is spread by tick bites. Vaccination is advised for those travelling in risk areas who are unable to avoid tick bites (such as campers, forestry workers and ramblers). Two doses of vaccine will give a year's protection, three doses up to three years' protection. Short-lasting vaccines are available in the Czech and Slovak Republics.

Typhoid & Hepatitis A

Both typhoid & hepatitis A are spread through contaminated food (particularly shellfish) and water. Typhoid can cause septicaemia; hepatitis A causes liver inflammation and jaundice. Neither is usually fatal but recovery can be prolonged. Typhoid vaccine (typhim Vi, typherix) will give protection for three years. In some countries, the oral vaccine Vivotif is also available. Hepatitis A vaccine (Avaxim, VAQTA, Havrix) is given as an injection; a single dose will give protection for up to a year, a booster after a year gives ten years' protection. Hepatitis A and typhoid vaccines can also be given as a single-dose vaccine, hepatyrix or viatim.

TRAVELLER'S DIARRHOEA

To prevent diarrhoea, avoid tap water unless it has been boiled, filtered or chemically disinfected (with iodine tablets) and steer clear of ice. Eat only fresh fruits or vegetables if cooked or peeled; be wary of dairy products that might contain unpasteurised milk. Eat food which is hot through and avoid buffet style meals. If a restaurant is full of locals the food is probably safe.

If you develop diarrhoea, be sure to drink plenty of fluids, preferably an oral rehydration solution eg dioralyte. A few loose stools don't require treatment but if you have more than four or five stools a day, you should start taking an antibiotic (usually a quinolone drug) and an antidiarrhoeal agent (such as loperamide). If diarrhoea is bloody, persists for more than 72 hours or is accompanied by fever, shaking, chills or severe abdominal pain you should seek medical attention.

ENVIRONMENTAL HAZARDS
Heatstroke
Heat exhaustion occurs following excessive fluid loss with inadequate replacement of fluids and salt. Symptoms include headache, dizziness and tiredness. Dehydration is already happening by the time you feel thirsty – aim to drink sufficient water to produce pale, diluted urine. To treat heat exhaustion, replace fluids with water and/or fruit juice and cool the body with cold water and fans. Treat salt loss with salty fluids such as soup or Bovril, or add a little table salt to foods.

Heatstroke is much more serious, resulting in irrational and hyperactive behaviour and eventually loss of consciousness and death. Rapid cooling by spraying the body with water and fanning is ideal. Emergency fluid and electrolyte replacement by intravenous drip is recommended.

Hypothermia
Proper preparation will reduce the risks of getting hypothermia. Even on a hot day in the mountains, the weather can change rapidly. Carry waterproof garments, warm layers and inform others of your route.

Acute hypothermia follows a sudden drop of body temperature over a short time. Chronic hypothermia is caused by a gradual loss of temperature over hours.

Hypothermia starts with shivering, loss of judgment and clumsiness. If not rewarmed, the sufferer deteriorates into apathy, confusion and coma. Prevent further heat loss by seeking shelter, warm dry clothing, hot sweet drinks and shared body warmth.

Frostbite is caused by freezing with subsequent damage to the body's extremities. It is affected by wind chill, temperature and length of exposure. Frostbite starts as frostnip (white numb areas of skin) from which complete recovery is expected with rewarming. As frostbite develops the skin blisters and then becomes black. The loss of damaged tissue eventually occurs. Adequate clothing, staying dry, keeping well hydrated and ensuring adequate calorie intake best prevent frostbite. Treatment involves rapid rewarming, avoiding refreezing, and rubbing the affected areas.

Insect Bites & Stings
Ticks, which are common in forests, scrublands and long grass, can carry encephalitis (see Infectious Diseases p463). Wearing long trousers tucked into boots or socks and using insect repellent is the best prevention against tick bites. If you find that one has burrowed into your skin, don't pull it off, as that can leave the head in place and increase the risk of infection. Coax it out with Vaseline, oil or alcohol, and try not to touch it even then.

Mosquitoes are found in most parts of Europe. They may not carry malaria but can cause irritation and infected bites. Use a DEET-based insect repellent.

Bees and wasps cause real problems only to those with a severe allergy (anaphylaxis). If you have a severe allergy to bee or wasp stings carry an 'epipen' or similar adrenaline injection.

Sandflies are found around the Mediterranean beaches. They usually cause only a nasty itchy bite but can carry a rare skin disorder called cutaneous leishmaniasis.

Bed bugs lead to very itchy lumpy bites. Spraying the mattress with crawling insect killer after changing bedding will get rid of them.

Scabies are tiny mites which live in the skin, particularly between the fingers. They cause an intensely itchy rash. Scabies are easily treated with lotion from a pharmacy; other members of the household also need treatment to avoid spreading scabies between asymptomatic carriers.

Snake Bites
The only poisonous snake in either republic is the *zmije* (viper) for which an antivenin is

HEALTH SPAS

Across the length and breadth of the two republics are hundreds of mineral springs whose waters, taken externally or internally, are said to be excellent for all sorts of ailments. The waters often taste quite odd (ranging from rotten eggs to rust) due to their mineral content, but it's easy to convince yourself that they are doing you a power of good.

Locals and foreigners – mostly elderly – take the cure at dozens of spas. Although many spa towns make fine trips, the spas themselves are for medical treatment and generally not geared for drop-in visits, but it is possible to undergo the odd treatment.

Some better-known spa towns and their specialities are:

■ **Bardejovské Kúpele** (p425) in East Slovakia; stomach, gall bladder and respiratory diseases; ☎ 054-477 44 70 or visit www.kupele-bj.sk.

■ **Františkovy Lázně** (p184) in West Bohemia; cardiac disease, rheumatism, gynaecological disorders; ☎ 354 201 104 or see www.franzensbad.cz.

■ **Jeseník** in North Moravia; allergies, respiratory and thyroid diseases; ☎ 645 491 111 or check out www.priessnitz.cz.

■ **Karlovy Vary** (p193) in West Bohemia; diseases of the liver, gall bladder, stomach and intestines, metabolic disorders; ☎ 353 224 097 or see www.karlovyvary.cz.

■ **Luhačovice** (p323) in South Moravia; respiratory and nervous diseases, stomach disorders; ☎ 577 197 421 or visit www.mesto.luhacovice.cz.

■ **Mariánské Lázně** (p189) in West Bohemia; diseases of the kidney, urinary tract and skin, as well as metabolic and respiratory disorders; ☎ 354 622 474 or email infocentrum@marianske lazne.cz.

■ **Piešťany** (p357) in West Slovakia; rheumatism, nervous diseases; ☎ 033-775 24 58 or check out www.spa-piestany.sk.

■ **Poděbrady** in Central Bohemia; heart disease; ☎ 324 615 720 or email knihovna@hsp.anet.cz.

■ **Teplice** in North Bohemia; motor, nervous and vascular disorders; ☎ 417 577 738 or email teptour@teptour.cz.

■ **Trenčiáske Teplice** (p361) in West Slovakia; rheumatism, motor conditions, respiratory diseases; ☎ 032-655 22 88 or see www.slktn.sk.

Of these, the most venerable, famous and attractive (and heavily touristed) towns are Karlovy Vary and Mariánské Lázně.

A spa course, typically lasting about three weeks, must be booked well in advance directly through the spa resort. Room, board and treatment start at about €100 per person per day in summer, less in winter, still less for companions not taking treatment.

widely available. It is unlikely to be deadly unless you are allergic to the venom. It's recognisable by a wavy black line that stretches the length of its grey back. Avoid getting bitten by wearing boots, socks and long trousers while hiking and do not stick your hand into holes or cracks. Half of those bitten by venomous snakes are not actually injected with poison (envenomed). If bitten, do not panic. Immobilise the bitten limb with a splint (eg a stick) and apply a bandage over the site with firm pressure, similar to a bandage over a sprain. Do not apply a tourniquet, or cut or suck the bite. Get the victim to medical help as soon as possible so that antivenin can be given if necessary.

Water

Tap water may not be safe to drink so it may be best to use bottled water or boil water for 10 minutes, use water purification tablets or a filter. Don't drink water from rivers or lakes as it may contain bacteria or viruses that can cause diarrhoea or vomiting.

TRAVELLING WITH CHILDREN

All travellers with children should know how to treat minor ailments and when to seek medical treatment. Make sure the children are up to date with routine vaccinations, and discuss possible travel vaccines well before departure as some vaccines are not suitable for children under a year.

Remember to avoid contaminated food and water. If your child is vomiting or has diarrhoea, then lost fluid and salts must be replaced. It may be helpful to take rehydration powders for reconstituting with boiled water.

Children should be encouraged to avoid and mistrust any dogs or other mammals because of the risk of rabies and other diseases. Any bite, scratch or lick from a warm blooded, furry animal should immediately be thoroughly cleaned. If there is any possibility that the animal is infected with rabies, immediate medical assistance should be sought.

WOMEN'S HEALTH

Emotional stress, exhaustion and travelling through different time zones can all contribute to an upset in the menstrual pattern. If using oral contraceptives, some antibiotics, diarrhoea and vomiting can stop the pill from working and lead to the risk of pregnancy – take condoms with you just in case. Time zones, gastrointestinal upsets and antibiotics do not affect injectable contraception.

Travelling during pregnancy is usually possible but there are important things to consider. Always seek a medical check-up before planning your trip. The most risky times for travel are during the first 12 weeks of pregnancy and after 30 weeks.

SEXUAL HEALTH

Emergency contraception is most effective if taken up to 24 hours after unprotected sex. The International Planned Parent Federation (www.ippf.org) can advise about the availability of contraception in different countries. If emergency contraception is needed in the Czech and Slovak Republics, head to the nearest hospital or health-care centre.

Condoms are readily available throughout both republics. When buying condoms, look for a European CE mark, which means they have been rigorously tested, and then keep them in a cool dry place or they may crack and perish.

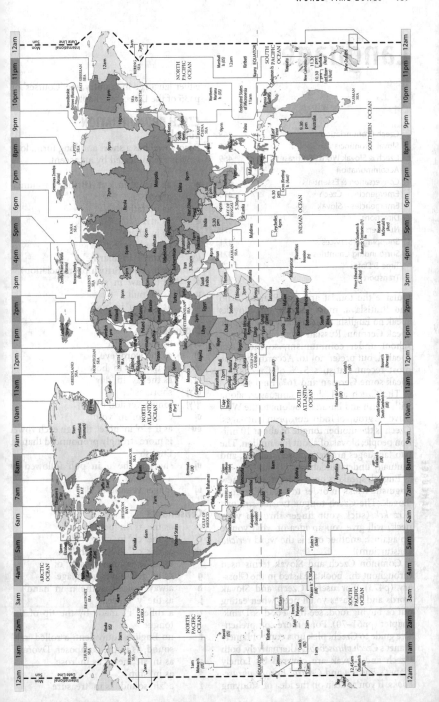

468

Language

Outside the tourist areas of Prague, Brno and Bratislava, most Czechs and Slovaks speak no English, though many older people speak German. Russian was compulsory in school under communism, so most can speak it, but prefer not to. According to the most recent statistics 51% of Czechs can speak some German and 16% English.

The Czech and Slovak languages, along with Polish and Lusatian, belong to the West Slavonic group of Indo-European languages. Czech is the mother tongue of about 10 million people; Slovak of about five million. The two languages are very closely related, and mutually understandable.

English speakers need to learn some new linguistic tricks in order to speak Czech or Slovak. The Czech tongue-twister *strč prst zkrz krk* (stick your finger through your neck) will give you an idea of what you're up against; another one is the word *řeřicha* (nasturtium).

Common Czech and Slovak terms used throughout this book are listed in the Glossary (p473). For useful Czech and Slovak words and phrases you'll need when eating out or buying food, see the 'Food & Drink' chapter (pp61–70). For a more comprehensive guide to Czech, pick up a copy of Lonely Planet's *Czech phrasebook*. Alternatively, both Czech and Slovak are covered by Lonely Planet's *Eastern* and *Central Europe phrasebooks*. If you're keen on the idea of studying either language in-country, see 'Courses' on p435 of the Directory chapter.

CZECH PRONUNCIATION
Vowels
Each vowel has a short and long form; long vowels are indicated by an accent.

a	as the 'u' in 'cut' (British pronunciation)
á	as in 'father'
e	as in 'bet'
é	as in 'there'
i/y	as the 'i' in 'bit'
í/ý	as the 'i' in 'marine'
o	as in 'pot' (British pronunciation)
ó	as the 'aw' in 'saw'
u	as in 'pull'
ú/ů	as the 'oo' in 'zoo'

Diphthongs
aj	as the 'i' in 'ice'
áj	as the word 'eye'
au	as the 'ow' in 'how'
ej	as the 'ay' in 'day'
ij/yj	short; as 'iy'
íj/ýj	longer version of ij/yj
oj	as the 'oi' in 'void'
ou	as the 'o' in 'note', though each vowel is more strongly pronounced than in English
uj	short; as the 'u' in 'pull' followed by a 'y' sound
ůj	longer version of uj

Consonants
c	as the 'ts' in 'pets'
č	as the 'ch' in 'chew'
ch	as the 'ch' in Scottish *loch*
f	as in 'fever', never as in 'of'
g	as in 'get', never as in 'age'
h	always voiced, as the 'h' in 'hand'
j	as the 'y' in 'year'
r	a rolled 'r', made by the tip of the tongue
ř	no English equivalent; a rolled 'rzh' sound, as in the composer, Dvořák
s	as in 'sit', never as in 'rose'
š	as in 'ship'
ž	a 'zh' sound, as in 'treasure'

The letters **ď**, **ň** and **ť** are very soft palatal sounds, produced by a momentary contact between the tongue and the roof of the mouth, as if a 'y' is added; eg the 'ny' in 'canyon'. The same sound occurs with **d**, **n** and **t** followed by **i**, **í** or **ě**.

All other consonants are similar to their English counterparts, though **k**, **p** and **t** are unaspirated, ie pronounced with no puff of breath after them.

SLOVAK PRONUNCIATION
Vowels
Vowels may be short – **a**, **ä**, **e**, **i**, **y**, **o**, **u** – or long – **á**, **é**, **í**, **ý**, **ó**, **ú**. They're much the same as in Czech except for **ä**, which is like the 'a' in 'act'.

Diphthongs
The combinations **ia**, **ie** and **iu** are best pronounced by running the vowel sounds together as one syllable. The **ô** sound is like linking the 'u' in 'pull' and the 'o' in 'pot' to make one syllable. Other diphthongs are pronounced as in Czech.

Consonants
Slovak consonants are similar to those in Czech. The letters **l**, **d**, **n** and **t** become soft palatal sounds when followed by **e** or **i**, and also when accompanied by the palatal marker – thus, **ľ**, **ď**, **ň**, **ť**.

The following consonants are not found in the English alphabet:

ľ	as the 'li' in 'million'
ď	as the 'dy' in 'wood yard'
ň	as the 'ny' in 'canyon'
ť	as the 'tu' in 'tudor' (British pronunciation)
dz	as 'th' in that
dž	as the 'j' in 'jet'

Word Stress
In Czech and Slovak the first syllable of a word is usually stressed.

CZECH & SLOVAK WORDS & PHRASES
While many words in Czech and Slovak are spelt and pronounced the same way, in the following list of words and phrases we've included both languages; the Czech is listed first, the Slovak second. Elsewhere in this book, words separated by a slash are Czech/Slovak translations respectively; where only

one word is given, it's the same in both languages.

ACCOMMODATION
Do you have any rooms available?
Máte volné pokoje?   *Máte voľnú izbu?*
How much is it per night?
Kolik stojí jedna noc?   *Koľko stojí na noc?*

I'd like ...
Přál/a bych si ... (m/f)   *Chcel/a by som ... (m/f)*
We'd like ...
Přáli by jsme si ...   *Chceli by som ...*
  a single room
  jednolůžkový pokoj   *jednoposteľovú izbu*
  a room with a bathroom
  pokoj s koupelnou   *izbu s kúpeľňou*
  a double room
  dvoulůžkový pokoj   *dvojposteľú izbu*

accommodation	*ubytování*	*ubytovanie*
bed	*postel*	*posteľ*
cheap hotel	*laciný hotel*	*lacný hotel*
good hotel	*dobrý hotel*	*dobrý hotel*
nearby hotel	*blízky hotel*	*blízky hotel*

bathroom	*koupelna*	*kúpeľňa*
blanket	*pokrývka*	*deka*
cold water	*studená voda*	*studená voda*
hot water	*horká voda*	*horúca voda*
key	*klíč*	*kľúč*
room number	*číslo pokoje*	*číslo izby*
shower	*sprcha*	*sprcha*
soap	*mýdlo*	*mydlo*
toilet paper	*toaletní papír*	*toaletný papier*
towel	*ručník*	*uterák*
window	*okno*	*okno*

clean/dirty	*čistý/špinavý*	*čistý/špinavý*
light/dark	*tmavý/světlý*	*tmavý/svetlý*
quiet/noisy	*tichý/hlučný*	*tichý/hlučný*
cheap/expensive	*levný/drahý*	*lacný/drahý*

CONVERSATION & ESSENTIALS
Good Day. (polite)
Dobrý den.   *Dobrý deň.*
Goodbye. (polite)
Na shledanou.   *Do videnia.*
(na-skhle-da-nou)
Hello/Goodbye. (informal)
Ahoj or Čau. (ciao)   *Ahoj or Čau. (ciao)*
Yes.
Ano/Jo.   *Áno/Hej.*
No.
Ne.   *Nie.*

LANGUAGE

EMERGENCIES – CZECH

Help!	Pomoc!
I'm ill.	Jsem nemocný/á. (m/f)
I'm lost.	Zabloudil/a jsem. (m/f)
Go away!	Běžte pryč!
dentist	zubní lékař/zubař
hospital	nemocnice
Call ...!	Zavolejte ...!
a doctor	doktora
an ambulance	sanitku
the police	policii

EMERGENCIES – SLOVAK

Help!	Pomoc!
I'm ill.	Som chorý/a. (m/f)
I'm lost.	Nevyznám sa tu.
Go away!	Chod/Chodte preč! (sg/pl)
dentist	zubný lekár/zubár
hospital	nemocnica
Call ...!	Zavolajte ...!
a doctor	lekára
an ambulance	záchranku
the police	políciu

Excuse me.
S dovolením. / Prepáčte mi.

Could you help me please?
Prosím, můžete mi pomoci? / Môžete mi prosím pomôcť?

May I? (Do you mind?)
Dovolte mi? / Dovolíte?

Sorry. (excuse me, forgive me)
Promiňte. / Prepáčte.

Please.
Prosím. / Prosím.

Thank you (very much).
(Mockrát) děkuji. / Ďakujem (pekne).

That's fine. (You're welcome)
Není zač. / Nie je za čo.

Good morning.
Dobré jitro/ráno. / Dobré jitro/ráno.

Good afternoon.
Dobré odpoledne. / Dobrý deň.

Good evening.
Dobrý večer. / Dobrý večer.

Good night.
Dobrou noc. / Dobrú noc.

How are you?
Jak se máte? / Ako sa máte?

Fine, thanks.
Děkuji, dobře. / Ďakujem, dobre.

May I take your photo?
Můžu si vás vyfotit? / Možem si vás odfotit?

Do you speak English?
Mluvíte anglicky? / Hovoríte anglicky?

Does anyone here speak English?
Mluví někdo anglicky? / Hovorí niekto anglicky?

I speak a little ...
Mluvím trochu ... / Hovorím trochu ...

I don't speak ...
Nemluvím ... / Nehovorím ...

I understand.
Rozumím. / Rozumiem.

I don't understand.
Nerozumím. / Nerozumiem.

Could you write that down, please?
Můžete mi to napsat, prosím? / Mohli by ste mi to napísať, prosím?

Could you speak slower please?
Můžete mluvit pomaleji? / Hovorte pomalšie prosím?

Can I have my change back, please?
Můžete mi vrátit drobné, prosím? / Můžete mi vrátit drobné, prosím?

I wish to contact my embassy/consulate.
Přeju si mluvit s mým velvyslanectvím/konzulátem. / Chcel by som hovoriť s mojím veľvyslanectvom/konzulátom.

DIRECTIONS

Go straight ahead.	Jděte přímo.	Choďte rovno.
Turn left.	Zatočte vlevo.	Zatočte vľavo.
Turn right.	Zatočte vpravo.	Zatočte vpravo.
behind	za	za
in front of	před	pred
far	daleko	ďaleko
near	blízko	blízko
opposite	naproti	naproti

NUMBERS

0	nula	nula
1	jeden	jeden
2	dva	dva
3	tři	tri
4	čtyři	štyri
5	pět	päť
6	šest	šesť
7	sedm	sedem
8	osm	osem
9	devět	deväť
10	deset	desať
11	jedenáct	jedenásť
12	dvanáct	dvanásť
13	třináct	trinásť
14	čtrnáct	štrnásť

SIGNS – CZECH	
Vchod	Entrance
Východ	Exit
Informace	Information
Otevřeno	Open
Zavřeno	Closed
Zakázáno	Prohibited
Policie	Police Station
Telefon	Telephone
Záchody/WC/Toalety	Toilets
Muži/Páni	Men
Ženy/Dámy	Women

SIGNS – SLOVAK	
Vchod	Entrance
Východ	Exit
Informácie	Information
Otvorené	Open
Zatvorené	Closed
Zakázané	Prohibited
Polícia	Police Station
Telefón	Telephone
Záchody/WC/Toalety	Toilets
Muži	Men
Ženy	Women

15	patnáct	pätnásť
16	šestnáct	šestnásť
17	sedmnáct	sedemnásť
18	osmnáct	osemnásť
19	devatenáct	devätnásť
20	dvacet	dvadsať
21	dvacet jedna	dvadsaťjeden
22	dvacet dva	dvadsaťdva
30	třicet	tridsať
40	čtyřicet	štyridsať
50	padesát	päťdesiat
60	šedesát	šesťdesiat
70	sedmdesát	sedemdesiat
80	osmdesát	osemdesiat
90	devadesát	deväťdesiat
100	sto	sto
200	dvě stě	dvesto
300	tři sta	tristo
400	čtyři sta	štyristo
500	pět set	päťsto
600	šest set	šesto
700	sedm set	sedemsto
800	osm set	osemsto
900	devět set	deväťsto
1000	tisíc	tisíc
one million	jeden milión	jeden milión

It's quite common for Czechs to say the numbers 21 to 99 in reverse, for example, *dvacet jedna* (21) becomes *jedna dvacet*.

SHOPPING & SERVICES
I'm looking for ...
Hledám ...   Hľadám ...
Where is ...?
Kde je ...?   Kde je ...?
  the police station
policejní stanice   policajná stanica
  the toilet
záchod   záchod

art gallery	umělecká galérie	umelecká galéria
bank	banka	banka
building	budova	budova
city centre	centrum	centrum
embassy	velvyslanectví	velvyslanectvo
information	informační	informačné
centre	centrum	centrum
laundry	čistírna/prádelna	práčovňa
main square	hlavní náměstí	hlavné námestie
market	tržiště/trh	tržnica/trhovisko/trh
museum	muzeum	múzeum
monument	památník/pomník	pamätník
old city/town	staré město	staré mesto
post office	pošta	pošta
ruin	zřícenina	zrúcanina
stadium	stadión	štadión
statue	socha	socha
synagogue	synagóga	synagóga
telephone centre	telefonní ústředna	telefónna ústredňa
theatre	divadlo	divadlo
village	vesnice/obec/	dedina/obec
	dědina	

SURROUNDING COUNTRIES
Austria	Rakousko	Rakúsko
Germany	Německo	Nemecko
Hungary	Maďarsko	Maďarsko
Poland	Polsko	Poľsko
Ukraine	Ukrajina	Ukrajina

TIME & DATES
When?	Kdy?	Kedy?
What time is it?	Kolik je hodin?	Koľko je hodín?
in the morning	ráno	doobeda
in the afternoon	odpoledne	poobede
in the evening	večer	večer
today	dnes	dnes
now	teď	teraz
yesterday	včera	včera

tomorrow	zítra	zajtra
day (days)	den (dny)	deň (dni)
night	noc	noc
week	týden	týždeň
month	měsíc	mesiac

Monday	pondělí	pondelok
Tuesday	úterý	útorok
Wednesday	středa	streda
Thursday	čtvrtek	štvrtok
Friday	pátek	piatok
Saturday	sobota	sobota
Sunday	neděle	nedeľa

January	leden	január
February	únor	február
March	březen	marec
April	duben	apríl
May	květen	máj
June	červen	jún
July	červenec	júl
August	srpen	august
September	září	september
October	říjen	október
November	listopad	november
December	prosinec	december

summer	léto	leto
autumn	podzim	jeseň
winter	zima	zima
spring	jaro	jar

year	rok	rok
century	století	staročie
millennium	milénium or tisíciletí	tisícročie

beginning of ...	začátek ...	začiatok ...
first half of ...	první polovina ...	prvá polovica ...
middle of ...	polovina ...	stred ...
second half of ...	druhá polovina ...	druhá polovica ...
end of ...	konec ...	koniec ...
around ...	kolem ...	okolo ...

TRANSPORT

What time does the train/bus leave?
V kolik hodin odjíždí vlak/autobus?
Kedy odchádza vlak/autobus?

What time does the train/bus arrive?
V kolik hodin přijíždí vlak/autobus?
Kedy prichádza vlak/autobus?

Which platform?
Které nástupiště?
Ktoré nástupište?

Excuse me, where is the ticket office?
Prosím, kde je pokladna?
Prosím, kde je pokladna?

I want to go to ...
Chci jet do ...
Chcem ísť do ...

I'd like ...
Rád/a bych ... (m/f)   *Chce/la by som ... (m/f)*

a one way ticket
jednosměrnou jízdenku   jednosmerný lístok

a return ticket
zpáteční jízdenku   spiatočný lístok

two tickets
dvě jízdenky   dva lístky

a student's fare
studentskou jízdenku   študentský lístok

1st class
první třídu   prvá trieda

2nd class
druhou třídu   druhá trieda

train station
železniční nádraží/ČD   železničná stanica/ŽSR

dining car
restaurační vůz   reštauračný vozeň

express
rychlík   rýchlik (expresný vlak)

local
osobní   osobný vlak

sleeping car
lůžkový/lehátkový vůz   lôžkový vozeň

Also available from Lonely Planet:
Czech phrasebook, Central Europe phrasebook

Glossary

You may encounter the following terms and abbreviations in your travels throughout the two republics. Where relevant, the Czech/Slovak terms are separated by a slash (/). See also the Language (p468) and Food & Drink (p61) chapters.

A
atd – etc

B
bankomat – ATM
Becherovka – potent herb liqueur
benzín – petrol/gasoline
bez poplatku – free of charge
bouda (s), **boudy** (pl) – mountain hut or huts
boží muka/božie muky – wayside column or shrine

C
čajovna – tearoom
ČD – Czech Railways
Čedok – Czech travel agency
celnice/colnica – customs
čeština – the Czech language
chalupa/chata (s), **chaty** (pl) – mountain hut
CHKO (chráněná krajinná oblast/chránená krajinná oblasť) – Protected Landscape Region
chrám/dóm – cathedral
cintorín – cemetery (Slovak)
čistírna/čistiareň – drycleaners
cizinci/cudzinci – foreigners
ČSA – Czech Airlines
ČSAD – Czech Bus Lines
ČTK – Czech Press Agency
cukrárna/cukráreň – cake shop

D
dámy – sign on women's toilet
dolina – valley, dale
dům kultury/dom kultúry – house of culture, for concerts and music practice
dům umění/dom umenia – house of art, for exhibitions and workshops

H
h. (hod) – hours
hlavní nádraží/hlavná stanica – main train station
hora – mountain
hospoda or **hostinec** – pub

hrad – castle
hřbitov – cemetery (Czech)
HZDS (Hnutie za demokratické slovensko) – Movement for Democratic Slovakia

I
impuls (s), **impulsů** (pl) – `beep' or time interval used for determining telephone charges

J
jeskyně/jaskyňa – cave
jezero/jazero – lake
jídelní lístek/jedálny lístok – menu
jízdenka – ticket
JZD – state farm (during communist rule)

K
kaple/kaplinka – chapel
kavárna/kaviareň – café
Kč (koruna česká) – Czech crown
KDH (Kresťansko demokratické hnutie) – Christian Democratic Movement
kino – cinema
knihkupectví/kníhkupectvo – book shop
koloniál – mixed goods shop
kostel/kostol – church
koupaliště/kúpalisko – swimming pool
kreditní karta – credit card
KSČM (Komunistická strana Čech a Moravy) – Czech & Moravian Communist Party

L
lekárna/lekáreň – pharmacy
les – forest
lístek/lístok – ticket

M
maso uzeniny/mäso – meat, smoked meat and sausages
město/mesto – town
místenka/miestenka – reservation
mlékárna/mliekáreň – dairy
most – bridge
muži – sign on men's toilet

N
n.l (př.n.l)/n.l (pr.n.l) – AD (BC)
nábřeží (nabř)/nábrežie (nábr) – embankment
nádraží/stanica – station
nafta – diesel fuel

náměstí/námestie (nám) – square
natural – unleaded petrol/gasoline
nemocnice/nemocnica – hospital

O
ODS (Občanská demokratická strana) – Civic Democratic Party
OF (Občanské fórum) – Civic Forum
OSN – UN
ostrov – island
otevřeno/otvorené – open
ovoce & zelenina – fruit & vegetables, greengrocer

P
páni – sign on men's toilet
paragon – receipt or docket
parkoviště/parkovisto – car park
pekárna/pekáreň – bakery
penzión – homy hotel
pěší zóna – pedestrian zone
pivnice/piváreň – (small) beer hall
pivo – beer
pivovar – brewery
platební karta – ATM cash card
pleso – mountain lake, tarn (Slovak)
počítač – computer
pokladna – cash desk
po-pa/po-pi – Monday to Friday
potok – stream
potraviny – grocery or food shop
prádelna/práčovňa – laundry
přestup/prestúp – transfer or connection

R
radnice – town hall
řeka/rieka – river
rokle – gorge
Roma – a tribe of people that migrated to Europe from India in the 10th century
rybník – fish pond

S
SAD – Slovak Bus Lines
sady – park
samoobsluha – self-service supermarket
samoobslužná prádelna – self-service laundry
Satur – Slovak travel agency
SDĽ (Strana demokratické ľavice) – Democratic Left Party
sedlo – saddle (in mountains)
sem – pull (sign on door)
sgraffito – mural technique in which the top layer of plaster is scraped away or incised to reveal the layer underneath
Sk (Slovenská koruna) – Slovak crown

skansen – open-air museum of traditional architecture
slovenčina – the Slovak language
SNP (Slovenské národné povstanie) – Slovak National Uprising
so-ne – Saturday and Sunday
svatý/svätÿ (sv) – saint

T
tam – push (sign on door)
taximetr – taxi meter
tel. č – telephone number
telecard or **telefonní karta/telefónna karta** – telephone card
toalet – toilet
toaletní papír – toilet paper
tramvaj – tram
třída/trieda – avenue

U
ubytovna/ubytovňa – dormitory accommodation
účet volaného – a collect or reverse-charges call
údolí/údolie – valley
ulice – street
uložené zásilky/poste restante – poste restante
úschovna/úschovňa – left-luggage office

V
V. Brit. – UK
vesnice/dedina – village
věž/veža – tower
vinárna/vináreň – wine bar
vlak – train
vrchy – hills
vstup – entrance
vstup zakázán – no entry
výstup – exit

W
WC – toilet

Z
záchod – toilet
zadáno – reserved
zahrada – gardens, park
zakázán – prohibited
zámek/zámok – castle
zastávka – bus, tram or train stop
zavřeno/zatvorené – closed
zelenina – see ovoce
železniční zastávka/železničná stanica – railway stop
ženy – sign on women's toilet
Zimmer frei – room free (for rent)
ŽSR (Železnica Slovenskej republiky) – Railways of the Slovak Republic

Behind the Scenes

THIS BOOK

The 1st edition of Lonely Planet's *Czech & Slovak Republics* was written by John King and Richard Nebeský. John King, Scott McNeely and Richard Nebeský updated the 2nd edition. Neil Wilson and Richard Nebeský updated the 3rd edition. This 4th edition was updated by Neal Bedford, Jane Rawson and Matt Warren.

THANKS FROM THE AUTHORS

Neal Bedford Firstly, thanks to Tim Ryder for involving me in this book, and for his undeniable help with my plethora of questions. Big thanks go to my co-authors, Jane and Matt – my eyes and ears in the Czech Republic – for their invaluable insights, supportive emails and all-out camaraderie.

Katarína Horská, from the Slovak Tourist Board, stands head-and-shoulders above a crowd of people who helped out in Slovakia. Andrea Zsigová and Anton Bača, also from the Slovak Tourist Board, added the icing on the cake to queries, as did Ladislav Korán, whose knowledge of Košice goes unmatched. And how could I forget the Košice posse – Marek, Sylvia and Vlado? Thanks for all the insider tips and superb welcome; I owe you more than a haka!

In Bratislava, special thanks to Adriana for great conversation and nightlife knowledge, and Dagmar, for her excellent restaurant and bar suggestions.

Veronika Procházková, of the Czech Tourist Authority, cannot be thanked enough for her ability to answer all my questions without losing her patience. Thanks also goes to Barbora Bílíková for providing contacts.

Last but by no means least, thanks to Marty and Anne for their lowdown on Bratislava and to Kathryn Greene, for her take on Bratislava and for stealing my change for the train-station toilet.

Jane Rawson Firstly, and most importantly, vast quantities of thanks – thanks dressed in Speedos, socks and sandals, and listening to České covers of Sheena Easton on Radio Impuls – to my co-authors, Neal and Matt. Youse blokes are legends. Back at HQ, thanks to Tim Ryder and David Else, and to previous authors Neil and Richard for such great research. Thanks to Daisy for being so astronomical and to mum and dad for all the moral, financial and technical support. In Praha, thanks to Steph for getting the ball rolling, to the OHC crew – Blade, Wok, Sarah, Jen, Lisa, James, Jason, Jamie, Markéta, Scott and especially Bennem Bennetem – for persistently standing between me and my computer waving *pivo*, to Andrea for apartment help, to Ben and Simon for warping space and time, to Mali for telling me what to do, to the Havlickova family, and to fantastic tour guide, volcanian and future sheep farmer Dr Honza Dral.

Matt Warren Big thanks go to Sammi for huge hospitality and considerable constitution – here's to Alien versus Predator! – Bill and Rebecca for their flying frolics, Jana for an intro to Moravian life and all those at the Czech tourist offices for keeping my headaches to a minimum.

THE LONELY PLANET STORY

The story begins with a classic travel adventure: Tony and Maureen Wheeler's 1972 journey across Europe and Asia to Australia. There was no useful information about the overland trail then, so Tony and Maureen published the first Lonely Planet guidebook to meet a growing need.

From a kitchen table, Lonely Planet has grown to become the largest independent travel publisher in the world, with offices in Melbourne (Australia), Oakland (USA), London (UK) and Paris (France).

Today Lonely Planet guidebooks cover the globe. There is an ever-growing list of books and information in a variety of media. Some things haven't changed. The main aim is still to make it possible for adventurous travellers to get out there – to explore and better understand the world.

At Lonely Planet we believe travellers can make a positive contribution to the countries they visit – if they respect their host communities and spend their money wisely.

CREDITS

Series Publishing Manager Virginia Maxwell oversaw the redevelopment of the country guides series with help from Maria Donohoe. Regional Publishing Manager Katrina Browning steered the development of this title. The series was designed by James Hardy, with mapping development by Paul Piaia. The series development team included Shahara Ahmed, Susie Ashworth, Gerilyn Attebery, Jenny Blake, Anna Bolger, Verity Campbell, Erin Corrigan, Nadine Fogale, Dave McClymont, Leonie Mugavin, Rachel Peart, Lynne Preston and Howard Ralley.

Tim Ryder and Judith Bamber were the commissioning editors for this project. Eoin Dunlevy was the project manager. Editing was coordinated by Charlotte Keown with assistance from David Andrew, Susie Ashworth, Andrea Baster, Peter Cruttenden, Stefanie Di Trocchio, Jocelyn Harewood, Tegan Murray, Danielle North, Fionnuala Twomey and Helen Yeates. Cartography was coordinated by Jolyon Philcox with assistance from Csanad Csutoros, Tony Fankhauser, Jack Gavran, Chris Lee Ack, Kim McDonald, Anthony Phelan, Jacqui Saunders, Julie Sheridan, Amanda Sierp and Natasha Velleley. The layout team consisted of Margie Jung and David Kemp, with assistance from Steven Cann and Sally Darmody. Cover design and artwork was done by Brendan Dempsey.

Thanks also to Melanie Dankel, Bruce Evans, Mark Griffiths, Quentin Frayne, Michelle Glynn, Jane Hart, Martin Heng, Michelle Lewis, Adriana Mammarella, Kate McDonald, Darren O'Connell and LPI.

Last but not least, děkuji to the authors – thanks for all your hard work and patience along the way.

THANKS FROM LONELY PLANET

Many thanks to the travellers who used the last edition and wrote to us with helpful hints, useful advice and interesting anecdotes:

A Nick Adlam, Keiko Akiyama, Carole Amaio, Bashar Amso, Gus Andres, Josee Archambault, Georgianne Arnold, Brian & Mary Ashmore, Sini Asikainen, Becky Askew **B** Ivan Babiuk, Kate Bamberg, Warren Baxter, Fero Bedner, Matt Beks, Tony Bellette, Maria & Tony Benfield, Dennison Bertram, Alisa Bieber, Brenda Bierman, Gerry Bierman, Esther Blodau-Konick, Lorraine Boardman, Luis Jorda Bordehore, Stephen Boswell, Richard Bradley, Jo Breen, Carol Brown, Carol & Gail Brown, Anne Burgess **C** Will Carr, Fred Carreon, Steven Carrick, Buzz Cavalier, Matt Chaffe, Greg Chandler, Mary Ann Chegezy, Vincent Choo, Erica Clarke, Rob Coley, Martha W Connor, Jerry Cooke, Brad Crews, Bryan Cumner, Jen Currin, David Cushman **D** Sigal Dabach, Gillian M Davis, Jaap de Boer, Mary De Ruyter, David DeFranza,

Philippe Dennler, Luc Desy, Marian Dinga, Floris Dirks, Elizabeth Dobie-Sarsam, James Done, C A Donkin, Ryan Dougherty, Ravit & Sagi Dror, Christine Durrant, Michael Durrant **E** Corne Els, Martin Eyberger **F** Mario Falzon, Mark Farber, Hugh Ferrar, Vicky Fifis, Kristine Flora, Kamil Fogel, Helen Frakes, Trudy Fraser, Nicola Freeman, Tini Frey, Charlotte Froomberg, Ludek Frybort, Geer Furtjes **G** Alberto Giannetto, Kenneth Morton Gill, Bruce Gilsen, Paul W Gioffi, Ruth Glenwright, Larry Goga, Irene Gomez, Adrian Greenwood, Robin Grimmond, Dagmara Gumkowska **H** Alan Hakim, Leah Hamilton, Vanessa Haye, Irene Herrera, John Hickman, Carolyn Hill, Marrianne Hoeyland, Catherine Holland, Aryeh Houminer, Petr Hruska, Silvia Hruskova, Jan Hruza, Laura Hughes, Martyn Hughes, Eva Hunt, Mark Huntsman **I** Bruce & Kay Ikawa, Christine Ingemorsen **J** Tom Jacoby, Lieke Jansen, Greta Janzow, Rok Jarc, Garland W Jaskiewicz, Ida Johansson, John Johnson, Oliver Johnston, Margaret Jones, Thomas Neumark Jones, Lee Joyner, Maritta Jumppanen **K** Paul Kail, Adam Karlin, Andrew Keeley, John Keep, Cate Khursandi, Adam Kightley, Kerry King, David Klur, Timo Knaebe, Warren Knock, Juraj Kosticky, Eva Kouw, Donna Krupa, Georgina Kwei **L** S W Lam, Ed Lambert, Diane & Ben Lapinski, David Leadbeater, Geraldine Leadbeater, David & Caroline Lee, Rod Lee, Ruth Gretechen Leon, Juha Levo, Zhixin Li, Adam Lloyd, Rachael Lummis, Alicia López-Miedes, Don Lowman, Uli Ludikowski, Risto Luukkanen, Nick Lux **M** Deirdre MacBean, Bruce MacDonald, Andrea MacLeod, Dee Mahan, Judy Maherney, Carmen Major, Stephane Makk, Mitja Majerle, Massimo Malavasi John Malcolm, Olivier Mauron, Darren McAven, Ian McLoughlin, Sally McKenzie, Matiss Melecis, Majda Mesic, John Metcalf, Vicky

SEND US YOUR FEEDBACK

We love to hear from travellers – your comments keep us on our toes and help make our books better. Our well-travelled team reads every word on what you loved or loathed about this book. Although we cannot reply individually to postal submissions, we always guarantee that your feedback goes straight to the appropriate authors, in time for the next edition. Each person who sends us information is thanked in the next edition – and the most useful submissions are rewarded with a free book.

To send us your updates – and find out about LP events, newsletters and travel news – visit our award-winning website: **www.lonelyplanet.com**.

Note: We may edit, reproduce and incorporate your comments in Lonely Planet products such as guidebooks, websites and digital products, so let us know if you don't want your comments reproduced or your name acknowledged. For a copy of our privacy policy visit www.lonelyplanet.com/privacy.

Michels, Lee Gerard Molloy, David Morris, George Mosley, Linda Mottram, Brian Moulton, Moira Mount, Phil Mowatt **N** Petra Naavalinna, Martin Navratil, Jan Nesnidal, Glynis Norris, Jamie Norris **O** Jacqui O'Connell, Paul Obrecht, Zhenia Olson, Carlos Ortiz, Paul Osborne **P** Rolf Palmberg, Kate Partridge, Jerry Peek, Miguel A Pérez-Torres, Sam Perry, Judy & Andrew Piel, Stacey Piesner, Michel Pinton, Marcia Popper, Amanda Potter, Robert Prochazka **R** Philippa Rawling, Deborah L Refalo, Val Renegar, Catherine Rentz, Christina Rick, Ronald Jan Rieger, Barbara D Ripel, Luchy Roa, Sylvia Roberge, Wayne Roelke, Vicki Roubicek, Jaroslaw Rudnik, Ian Rutt **S** Petra Safarova, Claudio Sandroni, Frank Schaer, Jeffrey Schoeman, Larry Schwarz, Robin Seager, Paul Sebastian, Synnøve Seglem, Janne Seletto, Tal Shany, Kathy Shearer, Lori Shortreed, Jean D Sinclair, Jone Solvik, Raewyn Somerville, Agnes Stassen, David Staunton Lambert, Lyn Steele, Julie Stenberg, Martin Stich, Samo Stritof **T** Terence Tam, Sarah Taylor, Reynald Thierrin, Sandra Marguerat Thierrin, Peter Thompson, Roger & Chris Thornback, Patricia A Tillman, Josh Titley, Katka Trnkova **U** Boaz Ur, Judy Urquhart, Carolyn Urquhart-Barham **V** Sergio Valdes, Caroliena van den Bos, Marian van der Maat, Wilbert van Haneghem, Marije van Kempen, Stefan Vranka **W** Benedict Wabunoha, Stuart Waddington, Michelle Warburton, Carol Waser, Danielle Weber, Tom Wellings, Fiona Wilson, Amber Wood, Giles Woodruff **Y** Niki and Shlomo Yom Tov, Andrew Young, MG Young **Z** Will Zucker

ACKNOWLEDGMENTS

Many thanks to the following for the use of their content:

Mountain High Maps® © 1993 Digital Wisdom, Inc.

Index

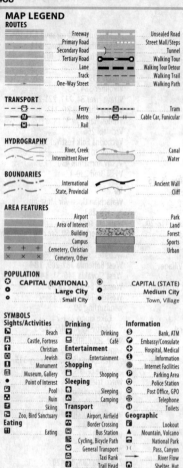

MAP LEGEND

ROUTES

Freeway	Unsealed Road
Primary Road	Street Mall/Steps
Secondary Road	Tunnel
Tertiary Road	Walking Tour
Lane	Walking Tour Detour
Track	Walking Trail
One-Way Street	Walking Path

TRANSPORT

Ferry	Tram
Metro	Cable Car, Funicular
Rail	

HYDROGRAPHY

River, Creek	Canal
Intermittent River	Water

BOUNDARIES

International	Ancient Wall
State, Provincial	Cliff

AREA FEATURES

Airport	Park
Area of Interest	Land
Building	Forest
Campus	Sports
Cemetery, Christian	Urban
Cemetery, Other	

POPULATION

○ CAPITAL (NATIONAL)	◉ CAPITAL (STATE)
● Large City	◉ Medium City
● Small City	○ Town, Village

SYMBOLS

Sights/Activities
- Beach
- Castle, Fortress
- Christian
- Jewish
- Monument
- Museum, Gallery
- Point of Interest
- Pool
- Ruin
- Skiing
- Zoo, Bird Sanctuary

Eating
- Eating

Drinking
- Drinking
- Café

Entertainment
- Entertainment

Shopping
- Shopping

Sleeping
- Sleeping
- Camping

Transport
- Airport, Airfield
- Border Crossing
- Bus Station
- Cycling, Bicycle Path
- General Transport
- Taxi Rank
- Trail Head

Information
- Bank, ATM
- Embassy/Consulate
- Hospital, Medical
- Information
- Internet Facilities
- Parking Area
- Police Station
- Post Office, GPO
- Telephone
- Toilets

Geographic
- Lookout
- Mountain, Volcano
- National Park
- Pass, Canyon
- River Flow
- Shelter, Hut
- Waterfall

LONELY PLANET OFFICES

Australia
Head Office
Locked Bag 1, Footscray, Victoria 3011
☎ 03 8379 8000, fax 03 8379 8111
talk2us@lonelyplanet.com.au

USA
150 Linden St, Oakland, CA 94607
☎ 510 893 8555, toll free 800 275 8555
fax 510 893 8572, info@lonelyplanet.com

UK
72–82 Rosebery Ave,
Clerkenwell, London EC1R 4RW
☎ 020 7841 9000, fax 020 7841 9001
go@lonelyplanet.co.uk

France
1 rue du Dahomey, 75011 Paris
☎ 01 55 25 33 00, fax 01 55 25 33 01
bip@lonelyplanet.fr, www.lonelyplanet.fr

Published by Lonely Planet Publications Pty Ltd
ABN 36 005 607 983

© Lonely Planet 2004

© photographers as indicated 2004

Cover photographs by Lonely Planet Images: Bojnice Chateau, reconstructed in the early 20th century, Richard Nebeský (front); sunlight streams through the window into Hostinec Pub, Prague, Richard Nebeský (back). Many of the images in this guide are available for licensing from Lonely Planet Images: www.lonelyplanetimages.com.

Printed through SNP SPrint Singapore Pte Ltd at
KHL Printing Co Sdn Bhd Malaysia